EQUITY, TRUSTS AND SPECIFIC RELIEF

along with a chapter on
FIDUCIARY RELATIONSHIPS

EQUITY, TRUSTS AND SPECIFIC RELIEF

along with a chapter on

FIDUCIARY RELATIONSHIPS

by

B.M. GANDHI

B.A., LL.B. (Bom), LL.M. (Guj)

Author : 'Law of Torts', 'Interpretation of Statutes', 'Indian Penal Code' and 'Hindu Law'

Revising author : 'Landmarks in Indian Legal and Constitutional History'

EBC

Lucknow | Delhi | Prayagraj | Guwahati
Bengaluru | Ahmedabad | Nagpur

EBC

Website: www.ebc.co.in, E-mail: sales@ebc-india.com,
Webstore: www.ebcwebstore.com

Lucknow (H.O.): 34, Lalbagh, Lucknow-226 001
Phones: +91–522–4033600 (30 lines), Fax: +91–522–4033633

Delhi: 1267, Kashmere Gate, Old Hindu College Building, Delhi-110 006
Phones: +91–11–23917616, +91–9313080904, Fax: +91–11–23921656

Bengaluru: 25/1, Anand Nivas, 3rd Cross, 6th Main, Gandhinagar,
Bengaluru-560 009, Phone: +91–80–41225368

Prayagraj: Manav Law House, Law Publishers & Booksellers, Near Prithvi Garden,
Opp. Dr. Chandra's Eye Clinic, Elgin Road, Civil Lines, Prayagraj-211 001
Phones: +91–532–2400877, 2422023, Fax: +91–532–2623584

Ahmedabad: Satyamev Complex-1, Ground Floor, Shop No. 7
Opp. High Court Gate No. 2 (Golden Jubilee Gate)
Sarkhej — Gandhinagar Highway Road, Sola, Ahmedabad-380 060
Phones: +91–9228012539, +91–7567903245

Nagpur: F-9, Girish Heights, Near LIC Square, Kamptee Road, Nagpur-440 001
Phones: +91–712–6607650, +91–7028924969

Guwahati: Advika, Unit No. 205, 2nd Floor, M.G. Road, Pan Bazar, Guwahati-781 001
Phone: +91–8736091956

www.scconline.com/blog
www.facebook.com/easternbookcompany
www.twitter.com/ebcindia
www.ebcexplorer.com

First Edition, 1983
Second Edition, 1993
Third Edition, 2001
Fourth Edition, 2007

Reprinted, 2010
Reprinted, 2011
Reprinted, 2015
Reprinted, 2016
Reprinted, 2017
Reprinted, 2018
Reprinted, 2019
Reprinted, 2021
Reprinted, 2022

Reprinted, 2023

9789394364714

Published by Eastern Book Company, 34, Lalbagh, Lucknow–226 001 under licence from EBC Publishing (P) Ltd., Lucknow
Printed and Produced by Media Network, A-388, Sarita Vihar, New Delhi–110 076

PREFACE TO THE FOURTH EDITION

The fourth edition of this popular book comes in the hands of its readers with additional authoritative case-law useful for practitioners and students too.

To bring the book in line with revised law curriculum a new Chapter XXI: ''Fiduciary Relationships'' has been added, discussing what is fiduciary relationship, how it comes into existence along with a list of cases, wherein it springs up.

New and recent cases, discussing the general parens patriae jurisdiction of courts over religious and charitable trusts [*Executive Officer, Ardhanareshwar Temple* v. *Sathyamurthy*, (1999) 3 SCC 115]; guidelines when one trustee may act for all [*J.P. Shrivastava & Sons (P) Ltd.* v. *Gwalior Sugar Co. Ltd.*, (2005) 1 SCC 172] what type of questions might arise in cases for specific performance [*Rajeshwari* v. *Puran Indoria*, (2005) 7 SCC 60] and benefit gained by unjust encrichment (from fiduciary relationship) must be restored back to the trust—S.P. Gaekwad's case, (2005) 11 SCC 314 have been included.

It is the author's sincere effort to keep the readers abreast of recent position of law in this area.

I am thankful to the Eastern Book Company, the publishers Malik Brothers and the ever enthusiastic staff of the publishers for their meticulous assiduousness and judicial accuracy in bringing out this mini volume on Equity, Trusts and Specific Relief.

—BHANU PRASAD M. GANDHI

PREFACE TO THE FIRST EDITION

Principles of equity are the very essence and kernel of a legal system. It is these principles that reduce the brittleness and rigidity of law. Legal principles when they can no longer serve the purpose and fulfil their station require to be amended or replaced either by interpretation or by amendment and enactment because anything static must droop and die and law is no exception. It is the art of interpretation tempered with equitable principles that is put to work in removing the gangrenes of injustice in a system. Principles of equity are thus an instrument of this nature but the instrument has to be kept constantly sharpened to meet novel situations or else it also becomes blunt with the passage of time: time being the greatest killer—कालाय तस्मै नम: It was for this reason that in England the House of Lords very recently refused to follow some of its own decisions where they were productive of injustice; moreover it is unwise to perpetuate a mistake. In India this feeling found its exposure from Justice Bhagwati of the Supreme Court in *Minerva Mills case*, (1980) 3 SCC 625, 681. (*See* Chapter 1, p. 35 *infra*).

In the words of John G. Fleming a book should be "more function-oriented than many of its competitors, more concerned with the effect and operation of legal rules, with their aims and reason, than with mechanistic problems of internal consistency of decisions within the framework of any given system. . . ."

Keeping this in view this book is an attempt to state the principles of equity in a lucid and pointed way and to introduce the topics in a systematic and somewhat elaborate manner without tending to depart from the central idea.

The book is divided into four parts and twenty-five chapters, each chapter having its own synopsis. Part I deals with the nature of Equity, its history, courts and important maxims in action, Part II with specific equities, equitable doctrines and equitable rights—the area wherein these principles were introduced and tested, Part III with principles of trusts with special reference to Indian Trusts Act, 1882 and Part IV with principles of specific performance and other equitable remedies with special reference to the Specific Relief Act, 1963 in India.

To make this book more useful many points that escaped discussion in certain books have been considered and discussed with reference to prevailing situation in society. Amendments wherever necessary have been pointed out. Elaborate subject index and table of cases add to the utility of the book.

I shall feel amply rewarded if the style and presentation of the subject meet the requirements of the readers.

I do claim to be original in all that I have written. I have depended on several authorities which are mentioned in the Bibliography and I am indebted to them.

I am thankful to the Eastern Book Company, the publishers, and the everready Mr. Surendra Malik and his editorial staff for their constant vigilance and enthusiasm in bringing out this edition.

In the end I am no less obliged to my friends, Professor G.M. Patel and Librarian Shri Surendra Desai, both of Bhagat and Sonavala Law College, Nadiad and Mr. Kanchanlal Patel, Librarian of N.S. Patel Law College, Modasa. I thank them all.

—BHANU PRASAD M. GANDHI

CONTENTS

PART II

SPECIFIC EQUITIES, EQUITABLE DOCTRINES AND EQUITABLE RIGHTS

PART III

TRUSTS

PART III-A

FIDUCIARY RELATIONSHIPS

TABLE OF CASES

PART I
EQUITY

Chapter I

Equity—Its Nature, History and Courts

"No, we ought to think of the relation between common law and equity not as that between two conflicting systems, but as that between Code and Supplement, that between text and gloss. And we should further remember this, that equity was not a self-sufficient system—It was hardly a system at all—But rather a collection of additional rules. Common Law was, we may say, a complete system—If the equitable jurisdiction of the Chancery had been destroyed, there still would have been law for every case, somewhat rude law it may be, and law imperfectly adapted to the needs of our time, but still law for every case. On the other hand if the Common Law had been abolished equity must have disappeared also, for at every point is presupposed a great body of common law."

—Maitland: *Lectures on Equity*, p. 153, 1969 Edn.

SYNOPSIS

1. HISTORICAL BACKGROUND

England was conquered by the Normans in the year 1066. The period preceding this date is called that of Anglo-Saxon law of which little is known. There was no common law for the whole of England at any time before the Norman conquest.

With the Norman conquest, the period of tribal rule came to an end and feudalism was installed. It prepared and paved the way for the development of the Common Law.

The creation of Common Law (*Comune Ley*) was to be the exclusive work of the Royal Courts of Justice, usually called the courts of the Westminster, after the name of the place where they sat from the thirteenth century.[1] Common Law

1. R. David and Brierley: *Major Legal Systems in the World Today*, p. 258.

is that part of the law of England which before the Judicature Acts, 1873-75 was adjudicated by the Common Law courts (especially the former Courts of Queen's Bench, Common Pleas and Exchequer at Westminster), as opposed to equity, or that part of the law which was administered by the Court of Chancery at Lincoln's Inn.[2]

Blackstone defines Common Law as the municipal law of England or the rule of civil conduct prescribed to the inhabitants of the kingdom.[3] It is "experience expressed in law"[4]. It is composed of established customs, established rules and maxims such as "the King can do no wrong"[5].

In the earlier times the Common Law courts provided no remedy in many cases where one was required. Hence the custom grew of applying for redress to the King in Parliament or to the King in Council, who referred the matter to the Chancellor. In later times petitions were presented to the Chancellor directly. The Chancellor being an ecclesiastic, and keeper of the King's conscience, did not feel bound to follow the rules of Common Law, but gave such relief as he thought the petitioner or plaintiff entitled to "in equity and good conscience"[6]. Equity thus represents the conscience of law, and a moral correction of law in order to accord more with justice.

It is with this "equity" and its principles that we are concerned with in this book.

2. WHAT IS EQUITY

In its primary sense equity is fairness, or that rule of conduct which in the opinion of a person or class ought to be followed by all other persons.[7] According to Osborne[8] it is primarily fairness or natural justice.[9] In the classic words of Sir Henry Maine it is a "fresh body of rules by the side of the original law, founded on distinct principles and claiming to supersede the law by virtue of a superior sanctity inherent in those principles".

"In progressing societies social necessities and social opinions are always more or less in advance of law. The gulf that is thus created between the social opinions and the existing law is bridged by three instrumentalities, namely, (*i*) Legal Fictions, (*ii*) Equity, and (*iii*) Legislation. When law becomes fixed, legal fictions liberalise it, when legal fictions also become outdated, equity softens the rigour of law, till finally a point is reached when expansion of equity ceases."

Derived from the Roman term "aequitas" (aequus-equal) equity means equalization or leveling down any arbitrary preferences or denial of justice. It is a means to reach as near as possible to natural or ideal justice, but one cannot

---

2. Jowitt: *Dictionary of English Law*, p. 426
3. Blackstone: *Commentaries on English Law*, 4th Edn. of Chase's Edn., p. 29.
4. Mukherji: *New Jurisprudence,* p. 124.
5. Blackstone: *Commentaries on English Law*, 4th Edn. of Chase's Edn., p. 29.
6. Jowitt: *Dictionary of English Law*, p. 724.
7. *Ibid.*
8. Osborne: *Dictionary of English Law*, p. 124.
9. Walker D.M.: *The Oxford Companion to Law*, 1980 Edn., p. 424.

forget that equity is not natural justice. It differs from it. Thus equity means to do unto all men as we would they should do unto us. "Equity is no part of the law, but a moral virtue, which qualifies, moderates and reforms the rigour, hardness and edge of the law, and is a universal truth; it does also assist the law where it is defective and weak in the constitution (which is the life of law) and defends the law from crafty evasions, delusions and new subtleties, invented and contrived to evade and delude the Common Law, whereby such, as have undoubted right, are made remediless; and this is the office of equity, to support and protect the Common Law from shifts and crafty contrivances against the justice of the law. Equity therefore does not destroy the law nor create it, but assists it.[10] "This new body of rules (or 'equity') is distinguishable from the general body of law, not because it seeks to achieve a different end (for both aim at justice), nor because it relates necessarily to a different subject-matter, but merely because it appears at a later stage of legal development."[11]

In *DDA* v. *Skipper Construction Co. (P) Ltd.*[12], the Supreme Court observed that the jurisdiction and power of Supreme Court to make orders *to do complete justice* is exercised to meet the situations which cannot be effectively dealt with under the existing law. This was a case of fraud committed by public servants. Referring to the case of *A.G. for India* v. *Amratlal Prajivandas*[13], the Court observed: "After all, all these illegally acquired properties are earned and acquired in ways illegal and corrupt at the cost of the people and the State. The State is deprived of its legitimate revenue to that extent. These properties must justly go back where they belong, i.e., to the State. What we are saying is nothing new or heretical." Approving the observations in *Reid case*[14], the Supreme Court said that absence of provision in law for relief cannot deter the Supreme Court from doing justice between the parties. Doing justice between the parties is a compulsion of judicial conscience on the part of the Supreme Court as a Court of Equity. The fiduciary relationship may not exist as in the present case nor it is a case of a holder of public office, yet if it is found that someone has acquired properties by defrauding the people and if it found that the persons defrauded should be restored to the position in which they would have been but for the said fraud, the court can make all necessary orders. This is what equity means and in India the courts are not only courts of law but also Courts of Equity.[15]

In the area of service law too, for doing complete justice to the parties, the court acts as a Court of Equity. In *Chenga Reddy case*[16] the Court observed that

---

10. *Dudley* v. *Dudley*, (1705) Prec Ch 241, *per* Sir Nathan Wright, L.K.
11. *Snell's Principles of Equity*, 27th Edn., p. 6.
12. (1996) 4 SCC 622: AIR 1996 SC 2005.
13. (1994) 5 SCC 54.
14. *A.G. for Hong Kong* v. *Reid*, (1993) 3 WLR 1143: (1994) 1 All ER 1.
15. (1996) 4 SCC 622, *supra*.
16. *C. Chenga Reddy* v. *State of A.P.*, (1996) 10 SCC 193: 1996 SCC (Cri) 1205: 1996 Cri LJ 3461.

a Court of Equity must so act within the permissible limits so as to prevent injustice. "Equity is not past the age of child-bearing" and an effort to do justice between the parties is a compulsion of judicial conscience. Courts can and should strive to evolve an appropriate remedy in the facts and circumstances of a given case, so as to further the cause of justice, within the available range and forge new tools for the said purpose, if necessary to chisel hard edges of the law.

However, the power to make orders *to do complete justice*[17] should be left undefined so that it may be flexible enough to be exercised depending upon needs of the particular case. The power has to be used with circumspection.[18]

3. EQUITY AND EQUITABLE: MEANING

Equity

The word equity is used in two senses[19]—one, in a broad popular sense and second, in a narrow technical sense.

In its *popular broad sense* it resembles natural justice or morality. However it is not coextensive with the principles of natural justice in so far as many matters of natural justice are left to the dictates of public opinion or to the conscience of each individual instead of being subject to legal sanctions.

In its *technical narrow sense* it may be said to be "a portion of natural justice which, though of such a nature as properly to admit of being judicially enforced, was, for certain circumstances omitted to be enforced by the Common Law courts—an omission which was supplied by the Court of Chancery".

The broad and popular sense is thus very near to principles of natural justice or morality; the narrow and technical sense is concerned with only a part of the principles of natural justice which the Common Law courts failed to enforce.

Besides these two main senses, the word equity can be viewed from different angles, *e.g.*, in its *primary* sense, it is fairness or justice according to natural law or right; *philosophically* it means to do unto all men as we wish they should do unto us; in a *moral* sense, construing the positive laws not according to their strict letter but in a reasonable and benignant spirit is equity. In this last sense it *corrects mere law, where the mere law fails on account of its universality*. In the *sense of fairness* it is frequently opposed to law and legality, because that which is fair does not always constitute a legal claim or defence. Equity in the *Roman sense*, the details of which we shall see later on, is a body of moral principles introduced in the Roman law by Praetor by the side of civil law (*jus civile*). In the *English sense* it is a system of rules originating in the English Chancery Courts and comprising a settled and formal body of legal and procedural rules and doctrines that supplement, aid and override common and

---

17. See *Delhi Administration* v. *Nand Lal Pant,* (1997) 11 SCC 488: AIR 1997 SC 3068.
18. (1996) 4 SCC 622, *supra*.
19. *Snell's Principles of Equity*, 27th Edn., p. 13.

statute law and is designed to protect rights and enforce duties fixed by substantive law.

Adumbrating the situation one may say that in its basic meaning equity is evenness, fairness, justice and is used as a synonym for natural justice. In a secondary meaning it can be contrasted with strict rules of law (*aequitas* as against *strictum jus* or *rigour juris*): in this sense it is the application to particular circumstance of the standard of what seems naturally just and right, as contrasted with the application to those circumstances of a rule of law, which may not provide for such circumstances or provide what seems unreasonable or unfair... . In a third sense equity is the body of principles and rules developed since mediaeval times and applied by the Chancellors of England and the Courts of Chancery... .[20]

Equitable

In the sense of fairness equity is frequently opposed to law and legality, because that which is fair does not always constitute a legal claim or defence. Hence when a legal rule or remedy is capable of two interpretations or applications, one literal or restrictive and the other liberal (*i.e.*, calculated to make the rule or remedy operate fairly, and to extend its benefit to as many cases as possible), the latter is called an *equitable construction* or application. It is in this sense that the right of stoppage in transit and the old section of ejectment are said to be *equitable remedies*; and the *jurisdiction* of Common Law courts to set aside judgments obtained by default and confession was called an equitable one. And when a statute contains a provision which applies literally to only a particular class of cases but it is clear from the nature of the provision that if another class of cases had been present to the framer's mind, it would have been extended to them; they are said to be *within the equity of the statute*, the reason being that the law-makers could not possibly set down all cases in express terms. Thus an old statute literally applying only to executors was held *to extend by equity* to administrators.[21]

In other words equitable is what is fair, reasonable and right and also what was recognised, regulated and enforced by the Courts of Equity or Chancery in accordance with the principles of equity as developed and understood by those courts with differed in many respects from what was recognised, regulated and enforced by courts of Common Law.[22]

4. NEED FOR EQUITY

Laws are not rules of thumb for the mechanical regulation of society.[23] Every human law contains an aspiration towards ideal justice or an approximation to ideal justice. This presupposes the law to be sufficient unto

20. Walker D.M.: *The Oxford Companion to Law*, 1980 Edn., pp. 424, 425.
21. Jowitt: *Dictionary of English Law*, p. 724.
22. Walker D.M.: *The Oxford Companion to Law*, 1980 Edn., p. 423.
23. Allen: *Law in the Making*, citing Carlyle, p. 383.

itself. But it is not so and hence the need for supplementary or residuary jurisdiction.

As cited by Allen,[24] speaking about the aspirations of law and need for equity, Plato said that "... the best thing of all is not that the law should rule, but that a man should rule, supposing him to have wisdom and royal power". This is "because the law cannot comprehend exactly what is noblest or most just, or what is best, for all. The differences of men and actions and the endless irregular movements of human beings do not admit of any universal and simple rule. No art can lay down rule which will last for ever". But this is exactly what law seeks to accomplish; like an "obstinate and ignorant tyrant" it does not yield to circumstances, does not allow anything to be done contrary to his appointment or any question to be asked—not even in sudden changes of circumstances, when something happens to be better than what he commanded for someone. This rigidity and stiffness of law is sought to be softened by using the natural sense of justice.

If truth lies at the bottom of a well, so does justice, and it will be found only by those who know how to swim, not by those who throw themselves in at a venture.

Nevertheless the natural sense of justice—or what has been called "*vulgaris aequitas*", is not a meaningless term. All law must postulate some kind of common denominator of just instinct of the community. There is no meaning in any legal system unless this foundation exists. Incalculable though the variations of subjective opinion may be, it needs no subtle dialectic to demonstrate that there is in man at least an elementary perception of justice as a form of the right and the good, which no law, save under an irresponsible tyrant, dare flagrantly transgress.

It is upon some such primary sense of justice that a great deal of early law—not merely what we have come to recognise as equity in a special sense—is founded.

Putting it in a different way, law aims at establishing generalization, uniformity and universality. By *uniformity* we mean that the essential meaning and intention of a rule must be uniform. There can be no exception to it. To the quality of *universality* there may be apparent exceptions but no generalization can be completely general, as no straight line can be perfectly straight. Law and Justice exist for the regulation of rights and duties and the incompleteness of the generalisation which is certain to make itself felt at some point or the other, may produce results which are antithetic to the very purpose of generalization. In many legal systems, therefore, a discretionary or moderating influence has been superadded to the rigour of formulated law. It has assumed different names at different times. When a rule works hardship in a particular case, it is not only permissible but it is necessary to ask, "Is it not a bad rule?" Not infrequently it is proved to be so, and in the light of the "glaring case" it stands self-condemned. A change must then be made. And it is by this somewhat painful process of trial

24. Allen: *Law in the Making,* citing Carlyle, p. 383, pp. 387, 388.

and error that a great many necessary reforms in all legal systems have been effected, formerly by fiction when legislation was less sensitive to social needs than it is today; in modern times by legislation.[25]

5. DESCRIPTIONS OF EQUITY

Per Sir Nathan Wright, L.K.,[26] equity is no part of law, but a moral virtue, which qualifies, moderates and reforms the rigour, hardness and edge of the law, and is a universal truth, it does also assist the law where it is defective and weak in the constitution (which is the life of law) and defends the law from crafty evasions, delusions and new subtleties, invented and contrived to evade and delude the common law, whereby such as have undoubted right are made remediless; and this is the office of equity, to support and protect the common law from shifts and crafty contrivances against the justice of the law. *Equity therefore does not destroy the law, nor create it, but assists it.*

Aristotle speaks about equity in more general and idealistic terms as: "It is equity to pardon human failings and to look to the lawgiver and not to the law; to the spirit and not the letter; to the intention and not to the action; to the whole and not to the part; to the character of the actor in the long run and not in the present moment; to remember good rather than evil, and good that one has received rather than good that one has done; to bear being injured; to wish to settle a matter by words rather than by deeds; lastly to prefer arbitration to judgment, for the arbitrator sees what is equitable, but the judge only the law and for this an arbitrator was first appointed, in order that the equity might flourish." Above all the inelegances of positive law, he says, "the one-remains, the many (laws) change and pass".[27]

As observed by Underhill: "Equity was originally the result of common sense against the pedantry of law and trammels of the feudal system; it became a highly artificial and refined body of legal principles and it is at the present day an amendment and modification of the Common Law." Per Wooddenson: "Equity was a judicial interpretation of laws, which presupposing the legislator to have extended what was just and right, pursued and effectuated that intention."

6. DEFINITIONS OF EQUITY

Plato expressed that "equity is a necessary element supplementary to the imperfect generalization of legal rules".

Aristotle described equity as eternal and immutable and reiterated that "the equitable is just and better than one kind of justice—not better than absolute justice, but better than the error that arises from the absoluteness of the statement;...it is a correction of legal justice".

---

25. Allen: *Law in the Making*, Chapter V.
26. *Dudley* v. *Dudley*, (1705) Prec Ch 241, 244.
27. Cited in Allen: *Law in the Making*, p. 391.

Blackstone defines equity as the soul and spirit of all law. Positive law is construed and natural law is made by it. In this, equity is synonymous with justice, in that it is the true and sound interpretation of the rule.

West, J., describing equity as "an intellectual energy", expressed that "it moulds its deductions from one set of data as the common law to another into continued adaptation to the growing need of society".[28]

According to Snell, equity is "a portion of natural justice which, although of a nature suitable for judicial enforcement, was for historical reasons not enforced by the Common Law courts, an omission which was supplied by the Court of Chancery".

Story defines it as "that portion of remedial justice which was exclusively administered by a court of equity as contradistinguished from that portion of remedial justice which was exclusively administered by a court of Common Law".

Maitland says that "we ought not to think of Common Law and Equity as of two rival systems" but, "we ought to think of Equity as supplementary law, a sort of appendix added to our code, or a sort of gloss written round our code... which used to be administered by the High Court of Justice as part of the code".

Thus equity is an original attempt to solve the riddles of law, where difficult and complex problems confront a legal system. The general nature that lurks through all the above definitions is that it is founded in natural justice, honesty and right. It is the true and sound interpretation of a rule. We may also say that it existed alongside the original civil law, not to supersede or destroy the law but to assist it. It is the inherent capacity of law to adjust itself and override its hardships and formalities which it acquires in course of time.

7. SUBJECT-MATTER OF EQUITY

Pointing to the field of equity and its subject-matter Snell explains that "although in many cases equity intervened to put right an injustice, it must not be thought that every injustice was the subject of an equitable intervention. In truth, there was no certainty when equity would come into play". He gives two instances for this purpose: Firstly, wherein land devised to the heir was not liable to contract debts of the ancestor where debt was incurred for purchasing that very land and secondly, wherein a father was not allowed to succeed as heir to the real estate of his son. These were subsequently remedied but this proves the above proposition that every injustice was not the subject-matter of equity and it is not possible to define equity solely in terms of natural justice. Thus any definition of equity must take into account not the substance or principle but the form and history of equity because "*equity is a historical accident*".[29]

28. *Kahandas Narandas, In re*, (1880) 5 Bom 154, 172.
29. *Snell's Principles of Equity*, 27th Edn., pp. 6-7.

Morals and ethics though not enforceable as a part of the principles of equity, do play an important role in the procedural matters and decisions of the courts.[30]

8. EQUITY UNDER THE ROMAN LEGAL SYSTEM

Romans had also evolved an equity jurisprudence. The kings in Rome were the absolute monarchs and held all the reins of religious and temporal powers. There were also forms of action like those under the English Common Law. In course of time the law they administered became hard, formal and arbitrary and many wrongs remained without remedy.

In 366 BC the first praetor was appointed who administered law on behalf of the King and had complete powers to change and modify the law in order to do justice in particular cases. He thus created new rules known as *edictum novum*; consequently, a body of moral principles was introduced to the Roman Law which existed by the side of the original civil law (called *jus civile*).

9. HISTORY OF EQUITY IN ENGLAND

(A) Origin of Common Law

Prior to the Norman conquest in the eleventh century certain customs and usages had become common to almost the whole of England and now and then some of them were also recognised in their 'dooms' issued by kings, with the advent of the Normans they swelled in number in an unwritten form. The kings' judges in the course of hearing a case tried to find out these common customs and based their decisions thereon. The view of one judge was then adopted by another, because that course saved the judges the trouble of ascertaining such customs and usages again and again and in this way grew the precedents and the doctrine of *stare decisis*. In course of time these customs were applied by judges as having the force of law, and thus developed a body of rules which, as Professor Munro says, "had really never been ordained by any monarch or enacted by any legislative body, but which merely represented the crystallization of usages and customs, and these gradually came to be known as the Common Law".[31]

By the time of Edward I, Common Law had taken definite shape. It was administered by King's Justice on circuit and the three Common Law courts, namely, King's Bench, Common Pleas and Exchequer. King's Courts administered equity also but at that time they did not regard themselves as administering a new body of law.[32] They were trying to give relief in hard cases. As noted by Allen[33] and others, Norman and English kings were fountains of justice and the defenders of the poor and defenceless. They themselves

30. *Snell's Principles of Equity*, 27th Edn., pp. 6-7.
31. Munro: *Government of Europe*, 3rd Edn., (1938), p. 298, cited by H.P. Dubey: *A Short History of the Judicial Systems of India*, (1968), p. 407.
32. Maitland: *Lectures on Equity*, p. 5.
33. Allen: *Law in the Making*, Chapter V.

dispensed justice under a prerogative of mercy and equity was an essential part of their regal office.

Of the three courts of Common Law, the Exchequer was not only a court of law but was also an administrative department, its secretarial section being called a Chancery. The head of this section was called a Chancellor, whose business was to collect State revenue and to decide disputes concerning the same. The Court of the Exchequer department met thrice a year on the occasion of the three great feasts of the temple. The Chancellor has been described by Maitland as the "King's prime minister".[34]

If a person wanted to start an action at Common Law, he had to obtain a writ on payment of prescribed fees from the Chancery section. The Chancellor issued such writs. It should be noted that in the 13th Century the available writs covered a very narrow ground. An injured party could only sue at Common Law if his complaint came within the scope of an existing writ or form of action. Many genuine cases remained unredressed and the plaintiff was without a remedy because his cause of action did not fit into any of the existing forms of action. This position has been expressed as the "dancing of the Common Law round the recognised forms of action". As noted by Snell, a plaintiff was often unable to obtain a remedy in the Common Law courts, even when they should have had one for him. The dictum therefore was that "where there is no writ, there is no remedy". Even when the claim came within the scope of an existing writ, it may have been that due to the power and influence of the defendant, he could intimidate the jury and defy even the court, and the plaintiff could not get justice before a Common Law court. In those rough days of the 13th Century, it was the King and the King alone in his council who had wide discretionary powers to do justice among his subjects. The plaintiff therefore had to petition to the King in council praying for a remedy. The Chancellor looked after this aspect and issued new writs. By 1348, the King completely assigned his equity jurisdiction to the Chancellor. This formed a custom and the same was confirmed and recognised by Edward III in 1349 by an order. But the Chancellor's discretion to issue writs was fettered by precedents and provisions of the Oxford, 1258[35] and the Statute of Westminster II, 1258 (called *in consimili casu*). In the 14th century these petitions were addressed directly to him. By the end of the 15th century, the Chancellor heard the petitions and decided them independently without the aid of the council. He made decrees in his own name. This position continued up to 1474. As pointed out by Potter,[36] it is well to remember that the origin of the Common Law courts is to be found in the need to administer the law, while the Chancellor inherited a jurisdiction to do justice where the law gave none. This came to be recognised by the judges themselves. So a Chancellor said: "If a man had nothing in writing and the

34. Hanbury: *Modern Equity*, Chapter I.

35. A plan of reform containing the first constitutional provisions in English history. *See* Walker: Oxford Companion to Law, p. 911.

36. *Butterworth's Dictionary*, Vol. 2, (1969), p. 173.

debtor was dead he would have no remedy at Common Law, and yet here by this court of conscience he will have a remedy."

Thus came into being the equitable jurisdiction of the Chancery.

(B) Deficiencies of Common Law

The special deficiencies or imperfections of medieval Common Law were as to the law itself, that its rules were too strict and that it did not cover the whole field of obligations; as to its administration, that it had no effectual means of extracting the truth from the parties, that its judgments were not capable of being adopted to meet special circumstances; and that they were often unenforceable through the opposition of the defendant, or were turned into a means of oppression.[37]

There were thus three types of major deficiencies:

(*i*) incomplete or no remedies in many cases;

(*ii*) inadequate relief; and

(*iii*) incomplete and defective procedures.

As noted by Pomeroy, (*i*) rigidity of judicial precedents, (*ii*) adherence to feudalistic institutions and technicalities of forms, (*iii*) antipathy towards Roman Law, and (*iv*) the defective and rigid procedure, were the outstanding defects of the Common Law.

Besides this, influence of the defendant enabled him to be get rid of the law.

(C) The Chancellor

In medieval times, the Chancellor was the most important and the most powerful personage in the country next to the King himself. He has been described as 'the King's prime minister', 'the King's secretary of State for all departments' and 'the keeper of the King's conscience'. The Chancery issued royal writs which began an action at law. The Chancellor kept the King's seal and all the writings which were to be in the King's name were done under his supervision. As noted by Snell[38] his jurisdiction was undefined, his powers were wide and vague and co-extensive with the authority that evoked them. He exercised those powers on the ground of conscience which in theory was based on universal and natural justice. As the personal representative of the King he acted entirely to the dictates of his conscience and proceeded by the rules of equity unhampered by any judicial precedent, which gave rise in due course to the well-known legal term, "*rules of equity, justice and good conscience*", which moderated the rigour of the Common Law, considering the intention rather than the words of law.[39]

As said before, due to strict compliance with formalist procedures which were archaic and typically English, the Common Law had become stiff and

---

37. *Butterworth's Dictionary*, Vol. 2, (1969), p. 173.
38. *Snell's Principles of Equity*, 27th Edn., p. 8.
39. H.P. Dubey: *A Short History of the Judicial Systems of India*, (1968), p. 410.

rigorous and litigants could not get justice at its hands. They had therefore no alternative but to appeal to the King "for the love of God and in the way of charity". In course of time the King in 1348 completely assigned his equity jurisdiction to the Chancellor. Chancellors were mostly drawn from ecclesiastics and up to the time that they were so drawn equity principles were not systematised and there was nothing like precedents. These Chancellors did not keep proper records and the rules which guided their conscience and good sense of justice and equity were drawn either from the Common Law, or from the Roman Law or from their individual notions of right and wrong.

This state of affairs provoked John Selden to remark that: "Equity is a roguish thing. For law we have a measure...equity is according to the conscience of him that is Chancellor, and as that is longer or narrower, so is equity. 'Tis all one as if they should make the standard for the measure a Chancellor's foot."[40]

Development of Chancellor's Intervention.—During the wars of Roses[41] (1453-1485) the Chancellor became more and more autonomous deciding in the name of the King and his council upon a delegated authority. Due to procedural difficulties and judicial traditionalism of Common Law, the Chancellor's intervention was more and more required. During the 16th century Sir Thomas Moore (1530-32) was appointed the first lawyer-Chancellor. The Tudor absolutism in this century was based on an extensive use of the royal prerogative. The notorious Star Chamber being a formidable threat to the liberty of the subjects, the Chancellor's equitable jurisdiction was considerably broadened.[42] At the close of the 16th century the increasing popularity of the Chancellor, who by exercise of his unrestrained power made additions or corrections to the 'legal' principles applied by the royal courts, brought him into open conflict.

A decree was obtained before Chief Justice Cock by means of gross fraud. Lord Ellesmere, the Chancellor, therefore gave a permanent injunction against it so that the decree could not be enforced. Cock, C.J., questioned the very validity of such an injunction and declared that anybody obtaining injunctions in this way so as to challenge a decree of the Common Law courts would henceforth be punished. At last in 1616 King James I has to step in and with the help of Bacon, the attorney-general, gave a judgment in favour of the Chancery.[43]

Though the procedure of the Chancery was favoured by the King and was preferred by the people, disputes such as the above were simmering under the surface on account of which litigants had to suffer. A tacit and common understanding was therefore established between the two courts that though the Chancery Court and the Chancellor would remain, they would attempt no new encroachment at the expense of the Common Law courts. Moreover it was to adjudicate according to its precedents and the King would not in future create any new court like the chancery by using his prerogative. (In 1850, a

---

40. *Table Talk of John Selden*, p. 43, cited in Hanbury: *Modern Equity*, p. 5.
41. David & Brierley: *Major Legal Systems in the World Today*, p. 273.
42. *Ibid.*, p. 275.
43. Hanbury: *Modern Equity*, p. 11.

commission was appointed to investigate and suggest ways and means to demarcate the lines of powers for both the courts.)

As noted by Potter,[44] with the fall of Wolsey the old and vague equitable jurisdiction passed into the hands of lawyer-Chancellors. But they were bred in the stern school of precedents... . They would not be satisfied with 'so indefinite a thing as a man's conscience for guide'. In the course of another century, therefore, two forces of conscience and practice came together[45] in the *Earl of Oxford case*[46]. As Lord Ellesmere said in that case, "the office of the Chancellor is to correct men's consciences for frauds, breach of trusts, wrongs and oppressions, of what nature so ever they be, and to soften and modify the extremity of the law which is called *summum jus*".[47]

From the period of Wolsey to that of Nottingham these principles were consolidated and systematised and in the 16th and 17th centuries this was considered to be the practice of the court. Due to precedents, the discretion of a Chancery Court judge slowly decreased but in cases not covered by the precedents, it remained. In Lord Eldon's period equity ceased to expand. It had turned almost as hidebound by precedent as the Common Law[48]—a *rigour aequitas* had developed. So much so that in 1878, Judge Jessel, M.R., remarked[49] that "this court is not, as I have often said, a court of conscience, but a court of law".[50]

Thus, a history of the Chancellors of England has been the history of equity.

(D) Practice, Procedure and Process of Equity Courts

By filing a bill of complaint in the Court of Chancery the proceedings started. The bill was in the plaintiff's own simple language. It was addressed to the Chancellor. Bona fides of the complaint were to be guaranteed by some persons who were to satisfy the defendant's damages if the petitioner did not succeed. After receiving the complaint, the chancery issued a writ of *subpoena* (summons) calling the defendant to appear personally and to present his reply. If he disregarded the summons and/or remained absent he was imprisoned. If he was unable to appear the court granted a commission to take his answer. At first he was examined viva voce and upon oath. So were the plaintiff and other witnesses. By the middle of the 15th century this used to be in writing. The answer from the defendant, as has been noted by Lord Macclesfield, served two purposes; it supplied the plaintiff with the evidence and the plaintiff could request for discovery of facts and materials for his advantage. A judgment was then given. It would be interesting to note here that the Chancellaria kept no written record of their judgments. The first reports available from the chancery

44. Potter: *Outlines of English Legal History*, p. 251.
45. Potter: *Outlines of English Legal History*, p. 252.
46. (1615) 12 Ch Rep 1.
47. *Ibid.*
48. Potter: *Outlines of English Legal History*, p. 253.
49. *National Funds Assurance Co., Re*, (1878) 10 Ch D 118.
50. *Snell's Principle of Equity*, 27th Edn., p. 11.

are from 1535. Thus in later times the bill of complaint was indorsed with a note of the decision and the decrees enrolled.

It should be noted here that the procedure of the chancery was secret, written and inquisitorial while that of Common Law courts was oral and public. In the Common Law courts there were prescribed forms while in the chancery even an oral complaint (in the beginning) was received. The Chancellor was concerned with the substance and not the form.

The decisions and decrees of Chancery Courts were not directly enforceable. Their effectiveness was however assured by the possibility of imprisoning the contravening party or by sequestration of his property, that is to say, its judgments were enforced by a process of contempt against the defendant's person—equity acted *in personam.*

(E) Classification of Equity Jurisdiction

Up to the middle of the 14th century, as seen before, the Common Law courts reigned supreme. In 1349 the Chancellor was empowered to give justice on behalf of the King, and this slowly increased his powers, which culminated into a separate and independent Chancery Court in 1474. A number of subjects fell into the Chancellor's hands. In cases where the Common Law court could not recongise expected rights and therefore could give *no relief*, the Chancellor came to the help of the petitioners. Also in cases where the Common Law afforded *no adequate relief* at least without great delay and circuitry, and in cases where the Common Law courts had *no proper procedure* either to compel the presence of a witness and defendant or to compel the production of a document, the chancery court came forward to the rescue of the petitioner by granting him adequate relief by arrest of the witness and sequestration of the defendant's property in suitable cases.

The jurisdiction of an Equity Court has been classified by Story[51] as exclusive, concurrent and auxiliary. Prior to Judicature Acts the main work of equity could be classified as follows:

1. *Exclusive Jurisdiction*: *New Rights.*—Cases wherein according to conscience there should be a right, but the Common Law courts failed to recognise one or grant relief, were fitting subjects for exclusive equity jurisdiction. Rights of persons claiming under uses and trusts, rights of a married woman in relation to property for her separate use, mortgages, right of redemption of a mortgage, penalties and forfeitures and administration of assets of a testator and intestate were the subjects wherein equity courts recognized the equitable right or interest and granted relief. Over these matters equity had an exclusive jurisdiction and hence the nomenclature "exclusive jurisdiction". These were the matters which the Common Law courts could have dealt with, but did not.

2. *Concurrent Jurisdiction*: *New Remedies.*—Cases wherein the plaintiff at his option could proceed either at the Common Law courts or at the chancery courts and wherein the relief granted to the plaintiff was almost the same but the

51. *Story on Equity*, 3rd Edn., p. 39 cited by *Snell's Principles of Equity*, p. 13.

method and manner in which it was granted by the Common Law courts was not so effective and sweeping as that of the chancery courts were, where equity developed a wide range of remedies for enforcement of Common Law rights which were available in addition to the remedies provided by it. These remedies were not wholly unknown to the Common Law, but it failed to develop them. In cases of actual or express fraud, accident, mistake, partnership, recovery of specific chattels, specific performance of contracts, set-off, partition and dower, it was the novelty and effectiveness of the procedure employed by the chancery court that attracted the petitioners. The remedies successfully tried and effectively employed may be stated as delivery of chattels, specific performance of contracts for sale and purchase of land, injunctions and rectification of instruments. We may thus say that equity jurisdiction in such cases was based on inadequacy of legal remedies employed by the Common Law. In other words an equitable remedy was available only when a legal one could lie.[52]

3. *Auxiliary Jurisdiction: New Procedure.*—Cases wherein the plaintiff sought the help of equity courts to render a relief granted by the Common Law courts more effective became the subject of its auxiliary jurisdiction. Such relief from the Equity Courts could be obtained, as Ashburner points out, either before adjudication in the Common Law courts (thereby maintaining status quo), or even after the decision in the suit was reached. Its main purpose was to prevent transgression of rights of the parties to a suit. The remedies granted under this kind of jurisdiction rested mainly on legal principles; equity intervening merely to supply the defects of the legal process. As pointed out by Ashburner[53] the guiding principle in such cases was prevention of multiplicity of suits or prevention of an irreparable injury. Under this heading fell the following matters: Prevention of waste of property and nuisance, prevention of the breach of patent right or a copyright, injunction in cases of breach of executed contracts and discovery, perpetuation of testimony and examination of witnesses.

Thus, where a contract was broken and the person guilty of its breach held the document production of which was necessary to assess the damage, discovery of the same was ordered by the Chancery Courts. In case of apprehension of danger of losing testimony before it could be produced at the proper time, the court ordered its preservation and perpetuation and in case of old and infirm witnesses and in case of a single valuable witness, equity courts took proper steps to ensure their examination in time. Since the chancery courts aided the Common Law courts its jurisdiction has been named as the auxiliary jurisdiction.

This shows that the procedure in the Common Law courts was defective in so far as it could not compel or even allow a defendant to give evidence and in limiting the inquiry to the parties to the action, however great an interest other persons might have in the result of the action.[54]

---

52. *Colls* v. *Home and Colonial Stores Ltd.*, 1904 AC 179.
53. Ashburner: *Principles of Equity*, 2nd Edn.
54. *Snell's Principles of Equity*, p. 14.

This threefold division of the subject was rendered obsolete by the Judicature Acts which removed the necessity for one court to supplement the jurisdiction of another.[55]

(F) Basis of Authority of Equity

As could be observed before, the emergence of equity was due to the incompleteness of the Common Law. The Common Law had become rigid, inflexible and hard in all respects. It had no remedy for genuine grievances, its procedure was faulty and powerless and its judgments were often unenforceable or were turned into a means for oppression. It could do no justice. The aggrieved party, as an alternative, prayed to the King for relief which he gave. In course of time the King delegated his authority or the "prerogative" to the Chancellor who gave relief where needed. Out of this delegation the Chancellor worked wonders. "The royal jurisdiction was converted from a fact to a constitutional fiction."[56]

Equity was a matter of grace, to be prayed and obtained from the Chancellor, and not a matter of right. Moreover equity represented the conscience of law and it acted upon the conscience of the litigants too. As said by Lord Chancellor Hatton: "The Holy conscience of the Queen for the matter of equity is, by Her Majesty's goodness, in some sort committed to me, but the law is the inheritance of every man." Thus the King's prerogative to do mercy and justice could be prayed for and obtained as a matter of grace, which worked on the conscience of the subjects, through the Chancellor.

Snell here has rightly expressed that "what had begun as an irregular process of petitioning the Crown in extraordinary circumstances had become a regular system of courts with a recognised jurisdiction".[57]

Hanbury[58] puts this position very succinctly thus: "Developed systems of law have often been assisted by the introduction of a discretionary power to do justice in particular cases, where the strict rules of law cause hardship. In Roman Law Praetor performed this function." In England this was supplied by the exercise by the Chancellor of the residual discretionary power of the King to do justice among his subjects, where for one reason or another justice could not be obtained in a Common Law court. *Principles of justice and the insistence upon acting according to conscience are the basis of equity jurisdiction.*

10. TRANSFORMATION OF EQUITY INTO A MODERN SYSTEM

To take a bird's eye view of the expansion of equitable jurisdiction, it can be said that in the reign of Edward III, 1349, the Chancellor was empowered to exercise the King's prerogative of mercy and grant relief in extraordinary cases. In 1474, he became an independent judge. On account of the popularity of uses, a "great field of substantive law" fell into the Chancellor's hands. Even the

---

55. *Ibid.* Also *see* Maitland: *Lectures on Equity*, p. 20.
56. Allen: *Law in the Making*, p. 399.
57. *Snell's Principles of Equity*, p. 10.
58. Hanbury: *Modern Equity*, (1969), p. 4.

Statute of Uses, 1535 failed to stop this abuse and hence the popular equitable jurisdiction broadened and expanded. In the 16th century due to cases of fraud, accident and breach of trust, this jurisdiction broadened still further and the rules of equity, justice and good conscience emerged.

Until 1529 AD Chancellors were drawn from ecclesiastics. Cardinal Wolsey (1515-1529) was one of them. Sir Thomas Moore (1530-1532) was the first lawyer-Chancellor. With Sir Christopher Halton (1587-1591) conscience became the conscience of the Queen. He was designated as the keeper of the Queen's conscience. Lord Ellesmere (1596-1617) instead of following "the inclination of the moment" began to consider the practice of the court and gave momentum to the process of precedents. It has, therefore, been correctly remarked that: "*To ecclesiastical Chancellors Equity owes its formation, to legal Chancellors it owes its transformation.*"

From the beginning of the Chancellorship of Lord Nottingham in 1673 and to the end of that of Lord Eldon in 1827 equity was transformed from a jurisdiction based upon the personal interference of the Chancellor into a system of established rules and principles.[59] Lord Nottingham (1637-1682), who is considered to be the father of equity, systematised the rules of equity and laid the foundations for an intelligent process. As remarked by Strahan, *"he turned equity from matter of chance into matter of principle*".

To him we owe the doctrine that there can be no "clog on the equity of redemption",[60] a classification of trusts[61] and the modern rule against perpetuities.[62] From the end of the 17th century, and throughout the 18th century, equity became the great force that moulded the progress of the law right up to the 19th century. It is during this period that the conflict between the Common Law court judges and a Chancellor came to the surface. It was a period of legislative stagnation. Equity had to struggle for its life with the Common Law in which the latter narrowly escaped death by a common tacit understanding with equity. In this period, as noted by Hanbury,[63] the modern law of trusts developed and was shaped to meet entirely new conditions of social life; equity took in hand the administration of the estates of deceased persons on which depended the doctrines of election, satisfaction, redemption, marshalling of assets and performance.[64] This period saw many great Chancellors, Talbot (1733-37), Hardwicke (1737-60), Camden (1766-71), Thurlow (1778-93), culminating in Lord Eldon (1801-1806, 1807-27), one of the greatest of equity lawyers. His decisions were thorough, painstaking, learned and clear. As Holdsworth said: "He had a thorough grasp of existing rules and principles; but he looks as anxiously into all facts and circumstances of each case... . But it is hardly surprising that the business of the court was scandalously in arrears." The pattern and principles of equity were now

59. Hanbury: *Modern Equity*, p. 11.
60. *Howard* v. *Harris*, (1683) 1 Vern 33.
61. *Cook* v. *Fountain*, (1676) 3 Swan 585.
62. *Duke of Norfolk case*, (1683) 2 Swan 454.
63. Hanbury: *Modern Equity*, p. 12.
64. *Ibid.*, pp. 462, 476, 486, 490, 558.

established. "Nothing would inflict on me greater pain in quitting this place," said Lord Eldon, "than the recollection that I had done anything to satisfy the reproach that the equity of this court varies like the Chancellor's foot."[65] In the 18th century equity was administered as a recognised part of the law of the land. Its reports were regularly published.

The 19th century was a period of enormous industrial, international and imperial expansion of Britain necessitating developments in equity to deal with a number of new problems, like administration of companies and partnerships; and the change in emphasis from landed wealth to stocks and shares. The business of the court had considerably increased and at the end of the third quarter of the century when the chancery courts were abolished, the two courts of Common Law and Chancery were "not rivals but partners in the work of administration of justice".[66] The time for fusion had come.

11. THREE BLOWS TO EQUITY COURTS

By the Common Law Procedure (Amendment) Act, 1854, the Common Law courts were given limited powers to grant injunctions, which increased their powers. They had powers already to grant damages, either instead of, or in addition to, an injunction for specific performance but at the same time some additional powers were given to the Common Law courts.

These piecemeal amendments, however, did not go to the root of the problem and the litigants were driven from one court to another. Justice became very dear and the hardships of the litigants could not be mitigated. The Judicature Acts, 1873 and 1875 (effective from 1-11-1875) were therefore passed and both the courts were merged into one Supreme Court of Judicature which administered both law and equity.

12. THE FUSION AND ITS EFFECTS

To remove the abuses of double administration of justice the Judicature Acts fused law and equity, thereby replacing the court of Chancery and the Common Law courts by the Supreme Court of Judicature. Snell notes that the fusion was not a fusion, or anything of the kind; it was vesting in one tribunal of the administration of law and equity in every cause, action or dispute which should come before it. It was a fusion of administration rather than of principles because the fusion did not necessitate a wholesale modification of the rules either of law or of equity.[67] In other words the principles either of law or of equity did not change but they were now administered by one court which consequently saved time, inconvenience and expense of the litigant public. As has been well said, the two streams have met and now run in the same channel; but their waters do not mix.[68] The streams, so to say, run side by side but do not

---

65. Holdsworth: *History of English Law*, pp. 468-69 cited in Hanbury: *Modern Equity*.
66. Holdsworth: *History of English Law*, pp. 468-69 cited in Hanbury: *Modern Equity*, p. 668.
67. *Snell's Principles of Equity*, p. 17.
68. Hanbury: *Modern Equity*, pp. 462, 476, 486, 490, 558.

mingle their water in so far as the distinction between legal and equitable claims, between legal and equitable remedies, has not been broken down.

The following are the divisions of the Supreme Court:[69]

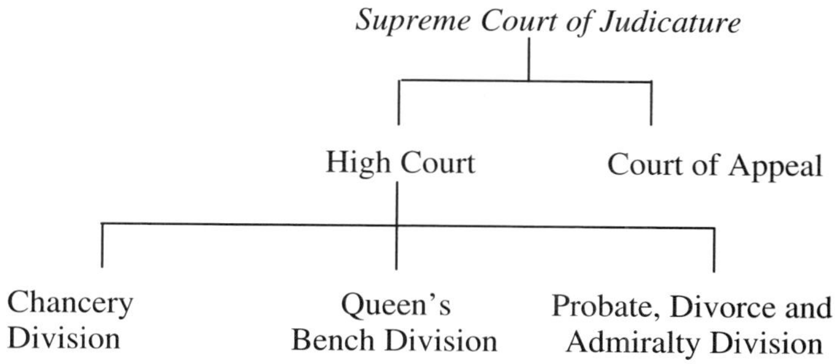

Effect of fusion

(1) A new and uniform procedure, assimilating the best rules of both the old systems, was established.

(2) Law and equity were administered concurrently but where the rules of Common Law and Equity were in conflict on a particular point, rules of equity prevailed—Section 25(11).

(3) The Judicature Acts [Section 25(11)] have neither made ineffective the principles of equity nor have they superseded the law, but they have sustained the existence of both. In effect they have brought about the fusion without affecting the substantive rights at law and in equity. This is supported by *Britain* v. *Rossiter*[70].

(4) They have done away with the auxiliary jurisdiction and converted the exclusive jurisdiction into a concurrent one, the simple reason as is apparent is, that now a court is capable of granting all the necessary reliefs, be legal or equitable or both. It is now a court of complete jurisdiction.[71]

(5) The distinction between legal and equitable remedies has not been broken down as could be seen from *Joseph* v. *Lyons*[72].

(6) The fact that certain rules (nine in all)[73] of equity contradicted rather than complemented the rules of law came to light; of course they were resolved.[74]

(7) In case of equitable lease,[75] variation of deed,[76] executors' liability for assets,[77] and contribution between sureties[78] the conflict was resolved by

69. By an order in Council in 1880.
70. (1879) 11 QB 123.
71. *Pugh* v. *Heath*, (1882) 7 AC 235.
72. (1884) 15 QBD 280.
73. See *Snell's Principles of Equity*, pp. 14-15.
74. *Ibid.*
75. *Walsh* v. *Lonsdale*, (1882) 21 Ch D 9.
76. *Berry* v. *Berry*, (1929) 2 KB 316.
77. *Job* v. *Job*, (1877) 6 Ch D 562.
78. *Lowe* v. *Dixon*, (1885) 16 QBD 455.

allowing rules of equity to prevail. Thus *Joseph case* and *Britain case* explain that there was no conflict, but the latter four cases expose the same.

(1) *Walsh* v. *Lonsdale*[79].—*L* agreed in writing but not by deed, to grant seven years' lease of a mill to *W*. Rent was payable quarterly in arrears but a year's rent was payable in advance if demanded. *W* entered into possession without any lease having been granted and paid his rent quarterly in arrears. Subsequently *L* demanded a year's rent in advance. *W* claimed an injunction and damages for illegal distress. His ground was that in law he was a tenant from year to year at a rent not payable in advance. Legal remedy by distress was therefore not open to *L*. The Court of Appeal decided however that *W* held on the same terms as if a lease had been granted, since the agreement was one of which the court would order specific performance. Jessel, M.R., said: "There is an agreement for a lease under which possession has been given. Now since the Judicature Act the possession is held under the agreement. There are not two estates, as there were formerly, an estate at Common Law by reason of the payment of rent from year to year and an estate in equity under the agreement. *There is only one court and the equity rules prevail in it.* The tenant holds under an agreement for a lease. He holds therefore under the same terms in equity as if a lease had been granted, it being a case in which both parties admit that relief is capable of being given by specific performance...that being a lessee in equity he cannot complain of the exercise of the right of distress merely because the actual parchment has not been signed and sealed."[80]

The principle in *Walsh* v. *Lonsdale*, however, does not apply to India (for details *see* under headline "15. Recognition of Equity under Indian Legal System").

(2) *Berry* v. *Berry*[81].—Under a deed of separation a husband covenanted to pay his wife a certain allowance. Afterwards the parties agreed in writing not under seal to reduce the allowance. An action brought by the wife to enforce the terms of the deed was dismissed on the ground that although at law a contract made by deed could be varied only by another deed, in equity, a simple contract varying the terms of a deed was a good defence to an action brought on the deed; and the equity rule now prevailed.

(3) *Job* v. *Job*[82].—An executor of a testator (watch repairer) handed over the stock-in-trade of the testator's shop to his son so that it could be sold. The son who was a jeweller and a watch repairer became insolvent and his receivers sold his property along with the testator's stock-in-trade. On the question whether the executor was liable it was held that, at law, an executor was liable for the loss of any assets of his testator when once they had come into his

---

79. (1882) 21 Ch D 9. Before Judicature Act, 1873, equity would intervene by granting an injunction to prevent a landlord evicting the tenant in breach of agreement. *Snell's Principles of Equity*, p. 16.
80. John Tilley: A *Case-book on Equity and Succession*, (1968), p. 13.
81. (1929) 2 KB 316. See also *ibid.*, p. 21 and *Snell's Principle of Equity*, p. 16
82. (1877) 6 Ch D 562. See also *ibid.*, p. 333 and p. 16 respectively.

hands.[83] In equity, however, the executor was not liable for such assets if they were accidentally lost without fault on his part. And since the Judicature Act the equitable rule is also the rule of law.

(4) *Lowe* v. *Dixon*[84].—*A*, *B* and *C* were sureties for the payment of £3000 and *A* became insolvent. The rule at law was that *B*'s and *C*'s liability to pay £1000 each remained. But in equity those who can pay their shares must also make good the shares of those who cannot and so *B* and *C* were liable for £1500 each. Here, therefore, the rule of equity prevails.

(5) *Britain* v. *Rossiter*[85].—The plaintiff agreed to serve for more than a year. This was not in writing as required by the Statute of Frauds. Thus before the Judicature Act the plaintiff had no remedy at law for want of writing. At equity also a contract of hire and service was not enforceable. But the plaintiff based his case on part performance. As the agreement had been partly performed it could not come within the Statute of Frauds and therefore he could sue for wrongful dismissal. But this argument was rejected and it was held that by virtue of the Judicature Act, the plaintiff did not acquire any right which he did not have prior to the Act of 1873. The true construction of the Judicature Acts is that they confer no new rights, they only confirm the rights which previously were to be found existing in the courts either of law or equity; if they did more they would alter the rights of parties, whereas in truth they only change the procedure... . The different divisions of the High Court may dispose of matters within the jurisdiction of the Chancery and the Common Law court; but they cannot proceed upon novel principles.

As said before, that the distinction between legal and equitable rights is not removed but still persists is apparent from the decision in *Joseph* v. *Lyons*, discussed below:

(6) *Joseph* v. *Lyons*[86].—*A* assigned to *B* "all his stock-in-trade to be acquired during the continuance of the security" as security for money lent. This method of transferring property not in existence or ownership or possession at the date of transfer was not allowed at law, but in equity assignment of after-acquired or future goods *was* possible if it was for value.[87] On the principle that equity looks on that as done which ought to be done, this was treated as a contract to assign when the property comes into existence and the assignment becomes perfect.[88] In this case *A* after acquiring the property pledged it with *C* who took it without notice of prior assignment. *B* sued *C* to recover the goods contending that his equitable right had become a legal one due to Judicature Acts and it was available as against purchasers without notice. This argument was negatived and rejected for it was not intended by the Legislature that legal

83. *Crosse* v. *Smith*, (1806) 7 East 246.
84. (1885) 16 QBD 455, *Snell's Principles of Equity*, p. 16.
85. (1879) 11 QB 123.
86. (1884) 15 QBD 280.
87. *Tailby* v. *Official Receiver*, (1888) 18 AC 523.
88. *Collayer* v. *Isaacs*, (1881) 19 Ch 342.

and equitable rights should be treated at a par and identical, but that the courts should administer both legal and equitable principles.

Thus at appropriate places rules of equity were allowed to prevail but the fusion did not change the nature of the substantive rights at law and in equity. In other words "it is only on matters of principle that the equity rule prevails, and not on matters of practice. Where there was a difference in the practice of the two courts before the Judicature Acts, the more convenient practice is now followed. . . . A legal estate is still a legal estate and an equitable interest is still an equitable interest. It is still of great practical importance whether a right is one which was formerly recognised at law or only in equity.[89] Thus a person who acquires a legal estate in property for value and without notice of another person's equitable interest therein, takes free from that equitable interest; but if he acquires merely an equitable interest, he will usually be subject to the prior equitable interest, in spite of the fact that he has no notice of its existence and that he gives value".[90] *Joseph* v. *Lyons* reiterates this principle.

13. ATTAINMENTS OF EQUITY

It has been the constant aim of a court of equity to do justice, by deciding upon and settling upon the rights and liabilities of all persons interested in the subject-matter of the suit to prevent future litigation. According to Maitland, *equity had come not to destroy the law but to fulfil it.* In order to understand this proposition the achievements of equity shall have to be viewed.

Equity, as has been said often, *is the conscience of law, it corrects law where necessary and softens its rigour.*[91] It did so by creating new rights, new remedies and new procedures.

New Rights.—The Common Law courts failed to enforce many rights which the equity courts enforced. If a right exists, there must be a chance to the public to exercise this right. In that period, to avoid and defeat the Common Law provisions people tried to abuse the 'use of land' by transferring land to somebody else's name. Equity legalised these matters and thus created new rights. *Equity in this sense, therefore, enforced that portion of natural justice which the Common Law courts failed to enforce.*

New Remedies.—To enforce a right under the Common Law, there were, as has been said, set forms of action or writs. If a plaintiff's case did not fit into those writs, he had no remedy. This position was clearly against the rules of natural justice. There should be not only a right to vindicate 'right' but also a remedy against those who hinder its enjoyment, *i.e.*, wherever there is right, there must be a remedy available for its breach. In this sense the equity courts developed new remedies of specific performance of contracts, of injunctions, of

---

89. For an interesting discussion about the traditional view (*Snell's Principles of Equity*, pp. 14-15) and the radical view about fusion, *see* Nathan: *Equity Through Cases*, 4th Edn., (1961), pp. 17 to 20.
90. *Snell's Principles of Equity*, p. 17.
91. *Babita Prasad* v. *State of Bihar*, 1993 Supp (3) SCC 268, 285: (1993) 25 ATC 598.

appointment of a receiver and for an order for account. While doing so it considered the conduct of the parties which entitled or disentitled them for these equitable remedies.

New Procedure.—Not only were new rights and new remedies not available at Common Law courts, but the procedure for enforcement of the existing rights was also quite unsatisfactory. A defendant could not be compelled to appear and give evidence in a court of Common Law; and even the parties who were interested in a suit could not be called. Besides this, no discovery of documents could be made. A defendant intimidated the jury and could disregard the summons of the court without any fear of punishment. But equity had the courage to come forward and afford such long-sought remedies as above.

14. NEED FOR A NEW EQUITY

In 1952 Lord Denning[92] wrote: "... I have considered the three ways of filling the gap which Maine suggested, fiction, equity and legislation. If they are exhausted where is a new means to be found? It is at this point that I begin to regret the fusion of law and equity. We have now to call upon natural justice. We have one system of courts and one system of law. We have a Lord Chancellor but we have no overriding equity. The courts of Chancery are no longer courts of Equity. They have no jurisdiction to mitigate harshness or to soften rigidity. They are as fixed and immutable as the courts of law ever were."

Quoting Sir William Holdsworth he explains that in early days the Common Law lawyers were concerned much with the dealings in land and devolution of estates. In those branches of law certainty is, quite rightly, of paramount importance. In this branch of the law words are the masters who must be obeyed. Our real property law was devoid of moral concepts as mathematics. Right and wrong did not enter into it, nor did the redress of grievances. In short they looked for certainty and gave justice a second place. The result was that in their hands the law of contract and torts tended to become as technical and rigid as the law of property. But the Judicature Acts had a beneficial effect and it was due to this that Lord Atkin in his classic judgment in *Donoghue* v. *Stevenson*[93], started with the Christian precept "thou shalt love thy neighbour as thyself", meaning thereby and laying down a rule that "in law you must not injure your neighbour". It is a matter of satisfaction that here the common man has a remedy. But new days bring new wrongs or wrongs of new kind, and the law must be developed so as to provide redress for them.

Explaining this, Lord Denning further writes: "The law, as I see it, has two great objects: to preserve order and to do justice; and the two do not always coincide. Those whose training lies towards order, put certainty before justice,

92. (1952) 5 Current Legal Problems 1, cited in *Lloyd's Jurisprudence*, p. 840.
93. 1932 AC 562, 580.

whereas those whose training lies towards the redress of grievances, put justice before certainty. The right solution lies in keeping the proper balance between the two." He was thus much concerned about the rigidity of equity and therefore expected "another Bentham to rise, to expose the fallacies and failings of the past and to point the way to a new age and a new Equity".

Lord Denning thus rejected the House of Lords as an instrument for producing what he calls the "new equity", as it was then bound by its own decisions. Although, since 1966 it has had the freedom to depart from previous decisions where these are thought to be wrong, it is a power used most sparingly. Nevertheless the House of Lords is a more creative body than it was twenty years ago. The creation of the Law Commission and the prospect of codification may be said to have changed Lord Denning's[1] perspective somewhat.[2]

15. RECOGNITION OF EQUITY UNDER INDIAN LEGAL SYSTEM[3]

Prior to the Anglo-Indian law, that is before 1600, Equity had its place in India in Hindu and Mohamedan law. Hindu legal system or Hindu jurisprudence is embeded in *Dharma* as propounded in The Vedas, Puranas, Smritis and other works on the topic. *Dharma* is an expression of the widest import; it cannot be defined but can be explained. It has wide variety of meanings: it is used to mean justice (*nyaya*), what is right in a given circumstance, moral, religious, pious or righteous conduct, being helpful to living beings, giving charity or alms, natural qualities or characteristics or properties of living beings and things, duty and usage or custom having the force of law and also a valid royal edict (*rajashasana*).[4] In short what sustains is *dharma* and Manu expresses the necessity of scrupulous practice of Dharma.[5] In Hindu law according to jurists like कौटिल्य (Kautilya) and याज्ञवल्क्य (Yagnavalkya) where there was a conflict between Dharma text and reason, the text had to give way and this was on principles of equity which they named as युक्तिविचार (Yukti Vichar).[6]

Yagnavalkya laid down:[7]

स्मृत्योर्विरोधे न्यायस्तु बलवान व्यवहारत: ।

Where there is a conflict between two Smritis the principles of equity as determined by popular usages (व्यवहार) shall prevail. This rule indicates, in the cases of conflict between two Smritis, the King was not given any power or

1. (1966) 3 All ER 77, a decision declared on July 29, 1966.
2. Based on *Lloyd's Jurisprudence*, (1972), pp. 840-841.
3. Based on M.C. Setalvad: *Common Law in India*, Chapter 1.
4. Rama Jois: *Legal & Constitutional History of India*, Vol. 1, Chap. 1, Concept of Dharma, p. 3
5. *Manusmriti*: VIII—15: Dharma protects those who protect it. Those who destroy Dharma get destroyed: Rama Jois, p. 8.
6. West & Majid: *Hindu Law*, p. 14; K.P. Jaiswal: *Manu & Yagna*, p. 80
7. *Yagnavalkya*, 2: 21.

discretion to make a choice but he was required to apply the law as approved by custom and usage by the people themselves.

धर्मश्च व्यवहारश्च चरित्रं राजशासनम्।
विवादार्थ चतुष्पाद पश्चिम: पूर्वबाधक: ।।

Out of these four, Dharmashastra, Economics, Practice or Custom and King's fiats, that which appears last, i.e., राजशासनम् (Rajshasanam) is the most authentic.[8] This is evident from Narad Smriti which explains the method of solving disputes regarding usufruct of the trees grown on a boundary.[9] The methods prescribed for settlement of boundary disputes were four: firstly, by arbitration, secondly, by the residents of the locality, thirdly, by the King on the basis of evidence and on the failure of all these methods, by the King according to his best judgment which is equivalent to decisions given according to Justice, Equity and Good Conscience. Moreover a judge should not rely merely on the text of the Shashtras, for it may work to the detriment of Dharma. Thus,

केवल शास्त्रमाश्रित्य न कर्तव्यो विनिर्णय: ।
युक्तिहीन विचारेषु धर्महानि: प्रजायते ।।

Under Muslim law Abu Hanifa expounded such principles known as *Istihsan* or juristic equity. This could be observed from the decisions of the courts.[10]

One has to note at the same time that under the British rule there never were in India any separate courts administering equity. The Supreme Court had both Common Law and Equity jurisdictions. As courts of equity they had power and authority to administer justice as nearly as may be according to the rules and procedure of the High Court of Chancery in Great Britain. In a sense these courts combining both common law and equity jurisdictions, brought about in advance the fusion of law and equity jurisdictions, which was effected in England by the Judicature Act of 1873. In England the Judicature Act did not fuse the two system of rules.[11] In India, however, law and equity were always treated as part of the same system. But the state of affairs before the Charter Act of 1833 was so sad and perplexing and "widely differing from each other but co-existing and co-equal" that it led to the enactment of the Charter Act of 1833. Slowly and silently the principles of English law came to be administered, particularly in the mofussils as "justice, equity and good conscience". In effect what was applied in India was the Common Law as liberalised by Equity. *In India Equity worked through and not in opposition to the Common Law.*[12]

---

8. Kautilya: *Arthashastra*, 1: 2.
9. Quoted by Rama Jois: *Legal and Constitutional History of India*, Vol. 1, Chap. 12, p. 205, Boundary Dispute, *Narad Smriti*, pp. 157-58, 13-14 (*Dharma Kosa*, p. 946).
10. *Hamirabibi* v. *Zubeida*, (1916) 43 IA 294.
11. Holdsworth: *Some Makers of English Law*, p. 208, cited in Setalvad: *Common Law in India*, pp. 58-59.
12. On this point *see* Rama Jois: *Legal and Constitutional History of India*, Vol. 2, Ch. 3, pp. 39, 41, 46.

Thus every court in India is a court of equity as well as of law. It possesses as inherent in its very constitution as such, powers as are necessary to do the right and to undo a wrong in administering justice.[13]

In absence of specific rules of law the court will follow the practice of the English equity courts with required modifications.[14] Such a practice however should be to give full, systematic and uniform effect to the principles of equity and good conscience.[15] Besides where the law exists, it is the law that must prevail and not equitable principles.[16] Section 151 of the Civil Procedure Code is designed to do real and substantial justice and to prevent failure of justice. This power is to be exercised by the court—*ex debito justitiae*—as of right and the court has no discretion to refuse.[17]

In this connection it has to be noted that under Article 372(1) of the Constitution of India the law that was in force in India immediately before the coming into effect of the Constitution, continues in force until it is amended, altered or replaced by a competent authority.

The principles of equity have found statutory recognition in India in:

(*a*) The Specific Relief Act, 1877

(*b*) The Indian Trusts Act, 1882

(*c*) The Indian Succession Act, 1925

(*d*) The Guardians and Wards Act, 1890

(*e*) The Indian Contract Act, 1872

(*f*) The Transfer of Property Act, 1882

(*g*) The Indian Divorce Act, 1869 (Section 7).

Macaulay who spoke in Parliament on Codification, reiterated this simple principle: "*Uniformity when you can have it; Diversity when you must have it, but in all cases Certainty*",[18] and accordingly the Codes and Acts were formed. In applying the principles of equity the Indian courts in their prolonged career of judicial legislation have shown remarkable discrimination.

In England an equitable right or estate is recognised as something different from a legal right or estate. The interest of a beneficiary in trust property is in England an equitable interest while the legal interest in the estate is in the trustee. Again in England if a person agrees to sell land he creates in the buyer an equitable interest in the land. These equitable interests were the creation of the Court of Chancery. The law in India never recognised any distinction between legal and equitable interests. As early as in 1872, the Privy Council

---

13. *Varden Seth Sam* v. *Lukhpathy*, 9 MIA 303; *Waghela* v. *Sk. Masluddin*, (1887) 14 IA 89. *Also see* Section 151 of CPC; *Watson* v. *Ramchand*, (1891) 18 Cal 10 and *Jogesh Chandra* v. *Annada*, 53 Cal 590.
14. *Manchersha* v. *Kamru Begam*, 5 Bom 109.
15. *Shapurji* v. *Dossabhai*, 30 Bom 359.
16. *Mohd. Ahmed* v. *Akhlagurlah*, 1950 RD 165(2).
17. *Hukumchand* v. *Kamalanand*, (1906) 33 Cal 931.
18. Cited by M.C. Setalvad: *Common Law in India*, p. 28.

said: "*The law of India, speaking broadly knows nothing of the distinction between legal and equitable property in the sense in which it was understood when equity was administered by the Court of Chancery in England.*"[19]

It is not surprising, therefore, that some of the peculiar equitable doctrines were not found acceptable by the Indian courts, they held that provisions in favour of children or other persons for their advancement were unknown among Indians. The general law of Succession in India, the Indian Succession Act, did not enact the rule of English law by which a child who received a benefit must account for it on a distribution when a father dies intestate. The rule has however been held to apply to persons subject to English law in India.[20]

As observed by the Supreme Court[21] the principle, i.e., the equity in *Walsh* v. *Lonsdale* does not apply to India.

A question whether an agreement to lease requires registration came up for discussion before court in *Trivenibhai* v. *Lilabai*[22]. This case was referred in the *State of Maharashtra* v. *Atur India (P) Ltd.* wherein a reference to Mulla's *Transfer of Property Act* (7th Edn.), p. 647 was given which specifies distinction between an agreement to lease and an agreement of lease. "An agreement to lease may effect an actual demise in which case it is a lease."

"On the other hand the agreement to lease may be a merely executory instrument binding the parties, the one to grant, and the other, to accept a lease in future."

As to such an executory agreement the law in England differs from that in India. An agreement to lease not creating a present demise is not a lease and requires neither writing nor registration.

As to an executory agreement to lease it was at one time supposed that an intending lessee, who had taken possession under an agreement to lease capable of specific performance, was in the same position as if the lease had been executed and registered. These cases have, however, been rendered obsolete by the decision of the Privy Council that the Equity in *Walsh* v. *Lonsdale*[23] does not apply in India.

The equity of part performance which in England mitigated the rigour of the Statute of Frauds by taking a parole contract out of it when it had been partly performed, seemed at one time to apply to India to the extent of taking away the application of the laws requiring registration and other formalities in such cases.[24] The doctrine has now been in a partial form incorporated into the statute governing transfer of property.[25]

---

19. *Ibid.*, p. 60, citing *Tagore* v. *Tagore*, 1872 IA Supp 47, 71; also Lord Davey in *Webb* v. *Macpherson*, (1903) 8 CWN 41 (PC).
20. *Kerwick* v. *Kerwick*, (1920) 47 IA 275.
21. *State of Maharashtra* v. *Atur India (P) Ltd.*, (1994) 2 SCC 497, 505 to 509.
22. AIR 1959 SC 620: 1959 Supp (2) SCR 107.
23. (1882) 21 Ch D 9.
24. *Mohomed Musa case*, (1914) 42 IA 1.
25. S. 53-A of Transfer of Property Act, 1882.

However, the statute law of India has incorporated in itself to a substantial extent equitable rules and doctrines. The Indian Trusts Act of 1882 embodies in a concise form the whole structure of trusts built up by the Equity Courts in England. The Act also deals with "certain obligations in the nature of trusts". These are attempts to enumerate broadly circumstances under which a person may be placed in the position of a trustee in reference to another. These "obligations in the nature of trusts" are no different from the implied and constructive trusts found in the decisions of the English equity courts.[26]

Another instance of an almost bodily transplantation of the doctrines of the English equity courts is to be found in the Specific Reliefs Act of 1877. It deals with cases in which a court will order restitution of specific property and order contracts to be specifically performed. It also enumerates the circumstances in which the courts will grant the relief of rectification and cancellation of instruments. The Act is in a sense a blend of common law and equity in as much as it also makes provision in a qualified manner for the writ of mandamus in certain cases. This statute powerfully illustrates how those who were charged with the task of drawing suitable codes for India discarded the distinction between law and equity in English jurisprudence, not hesitating to include in the Act dealing mainly with the equitable relief of specific enforcement, a remedy in the nature of the Crown writ of mandamus.[27]

Thus English law and its principles were almost directly introduced in the presidency towns of Calcutta, Madras and Bombay. In the greater part of the country it obtained its sway in the guise of the principles of "equity, justice and good conscience". A prolific source of incorporation of these principles into Indian jurisprudence were the decisions of the Indian courts. In the words of Sir Henry Maine the higher courts openly borrowed the English rules thinking and believing that they were taking them from some abstract body of legal principles which lay behind all law and the inferior judges, no doubt honestly, thinking in many cases that they were following the rule prescribed for them to decide "by equity and good conscience" wherever no native law or usage was discoverable. The process continues to this day.[28] In the case of *Indira Bai* the Supreme Court of India observed to this effect and said that *the courts in this country are primarily the courts of equity, justice and good conscience and they cannot permit the respondent to defeat the right of the appellant and invoke a right (in this case a right of pre-emption) which has been called a weak and inequitable right.*[29] Whatever the situation, the Supreme Court cannot permit injustice to perpetuate.[30]

In England great concern was projected by Lord Denning[31] in 1952, and fortunately in 1966 the House of Lords resolved that it had freedom to depart

26. M.C. Setalvad: *Common Law in India*, pp. 60-61.
27. *Ibid.*, pp. 61-62.
28. M.C. Setalvad: *Common Law in India*, pp. 61-62.
29. *Indira Bai* v. *Nand Kishore*, (1990) 4 SCC 668.
30. *Madan Pal Singh* v. *State of U.P.*, (2000) 1 SCC 683: 2000 SCC (L&S) 228.
31. (1952) 5 Current Legal Problems 1, cited in *Lloyd's Jurisprudence*, p. 840.

from previous decisions where they were thought to be wrong; though it is a power used most sparingly. The House of Lords has thus proved its creativeness. The Indian Supreme Court has not lagged behind and has expressed the same kind of concern in *Minerva Mills Ltd.*[32] in respect of *stare decisis*, Justice Bhagwati, delivering a separate opinion said:

> "Certainty and continuity are essential ingredients of the rule of law. Certainty in applicability of law would be considerably eroded and suffer a serious setback if the highest court in the land were readily to overrule the view expressed by it in earlier decisions even though that view has held the field for a number of years... and since the decision on many of such questions may depend upon choice between competing values, two views may be possible depending upon the value judgment or the choice of values made by the individual judge. Therefore if one view has been taken by the court after mature deliberation, the fact that another Bench is inclined to take another view would not justify the court in reconsidering the earlier decision and overruling it. It would create uncertainty, instability and confusion if the law propounded by this court on the faith of which numerous cases have been decided and many transactions have taken place is held to be not the correct law after a number of years. *But the doctrine of stare decisis should not be regarded as a rigid and inevitable doctrine which must be applied at the cost of justice. There may be cases where it may be necessary to rid the doctrine of its petrifying rigidity.*"

In *D.S. Nakara case*[33] wherein the *Minerva Mills Ltd. case*[34] and *Randhir Singh case*[35] were relied on the Supreme Court of India through Chandrachud, Tulzapurkar, D.A. Desai, O. Chinappa Reddy and Bahrul Islam, JJ., observed to the same effect in the following words:

> "*Every new norm of socio-economic justice, every new measure of social justice is commenced for the first time at some point of history. If at that time it is rejected as being without a precedent, the law as an instrument of social engineering would have long since been dead and no tears would have been shed. To be pragmatic is not to be unconstitutional.* In its onward march, law as an institution ushers in socio-economic justice. In fact, social security in old age commenced itself in earlier stages as a moral concept but in course of time it acquired legal connotation. The rules of natural justice owed their origin to ethical and moral code. Is there any doubt that they have become the integral and inseparable parts of rule of law of which any civilised society is proud? Can anyone be bold enough to assert that ethics and morality are outside the field of legal formulations? Socio-economic justice stems from the concept of social morality coupled with abhorrence for economic exploitation. And the advancing society

---

32. *Minerva Mills Ltd.* v. *Union of India*, (1980) 3 SCC 625, 681.
33. *D.S. Nakara* v. *Union of India*, (1983) 1 SCC 305.
34. (1980) 3 SCC 625: AIR 1980 SC 1789: (1981) 1 SCR 206.
35. *Randhir Singh* v. *Union of India*, (1982) 1 SCC 618: 1982 SCC (L&S) 119: (1982) 1 LLJ 344: 1982 Lab IC 806.

converts in course of time moral or ethical code into enforceable legal formulations. Overemphasis on precedent furnishes an insurmountable road-block to the onward march towards promised millennium. *An overdose of precedents is the bane of our system which is slowly getting stagnant, stratified and atrophied. Therefore the absence of a precedent on this point need not deter us at all. We are all the more happy for the chance of scribbling on a clean slate.*"[36]

The *aim and object of equity* is to promote honesty and not to frustrate the legitimate rights. Equity is always known to defend the law from crafty evasions and new subtleties invented to evade law. There is no equity in favour of the defaulting party which may justify interference by the courts in exercise of equitable jurisdiction under Article 226 of the Constitution. A court of equity while exercising equitable jurisdiction under that article so act as to prevent perpetration of a legal fraud as courts are obliged to do justice by promotion of good faith.[37]

16. EQUITY AND TAXATION LAWS[38]

Though equity and taxation laws are often strangers, attempt should be made that these do not remain so and if a construction results in equity rather than injustice, then such construction should be preferred to the literal construction.[39]

There is no equity or intendment in tax law, yet the same principle does not and shall not extend to a penal proceeding.[40]

In that famous passage marked by a happy turn of the phrase, Rowlatt J. said, "there is no equity about a tax. There is no presumption as to a tax. There is no equity about a tax in the sense that a provision by which a tax is imposed has to be construed strictly regardless of the hardship that such a construction may cause either to the treasury or to the tax payer. If the subject falls squarely, within the letter of law, he must be taxed, howsoever inequitable the consequences may appear to the judicial mind. If the revenue seeking to tax cannot bring the subject within the letter of the law, the subject's free no matter that such a construction may cause serious prejudice to the revenue. In other words though what is called equitable construction may be admissible in relation to other statutes or other provisions of a taxing statute, such construction is not admissible in the interpretation of charging or taxing provision of a taxing statute.[41] Equity cannot be relied on even by the revenue to tax an amount which is not taxable under the statute. Under Article 265 of the

---

36. *See* also *S.C. Varma* v. *Chancellor, Nagpur University*, (1990) 4 SCC 55; *Punjab Land Development & Reclamation Corpn. Ltd.* v. *Presiding Officer, Labour Court, Chandigarh*, (1990) 3 SCC 682 (Case of 17 appeals) (Paras 37, 53, 59).
37. *A.P. State Financial Corpn.* v. *Gar Re-Rolling Mills*, (1994) 2 SCC 647, 662: (1994) 80 Comp Cas 140: (1994) 13 CLA 335.
38. Taxmann's Law Dictionary, pp. 228-229.
39. *CIT* v. *J.H. Gotla*, (1985) 4 SCC 343: (1985) 156 ITR 323 (SC).
40. *T.R. Rajkumari* v. *ITO*, (1972) 83 ITR 189 (Mad).
41. *Murarilal Mahavir Prasad* v. *B.R. Wad*, (1976) 37 STC 77 (SC).

Constitution tax cannot be levied on the basis of equity. Just as reliance upon equity does not avail an assessee, so it does not avail the revenue.[42]

In a very recent case[43] the court discussed the *role of equity* in field of tort. In this case the building contractor constructed a building in violation of municipal regulations which resulted in demolition of top four floors. The allottee-owners of the demolished flats, having not been informed by the builder about the illegal construction and not given notice of caveat emptor, they suffered loss. On grounds of equity considerations the builder was held liable to pay damages, including the amount paid by the allottees.

In the tort liability arising out of contract, equity steps in and takes over and imposes liability upon the defendant for unquantified damages for the breach of duty owed by the defendant to the plaintiff. Equity steps in and relieves the hardships of the plaintiff in a common law action for damages suffered by the plaintiff on account of the negligence in the case of the duties or breach of the obligation undertaken or failure to truthfully inform the warranty of title and other allied circumstances.[44]

Principles of justice and conscience are the basis of equity jurisdiction, but it must not be thought that the contrast between law and equity is one between a system of strict rules and one of broad discretion. Equity has no monopoly of the pursuit of justice. Equitable principles are rather too often brandied about in common law. Just as the common law has escaped from its early formalism, so over the years equity has established strict rules for the application of its principles. Indeed, at one stage the rules became so fixed that a "*rigor aequitatis*" developed: equity itself displayed the very defect which it was designed to remedy. Today some aspects of equity are strict and technical, while others leave considerable discretion to the court.[45]

---

42. *Kapil Mohan* v. *CIT*, (1999) 1 SCC 430: (1999) 235 ITR 278 (Question in this case was levying income tax on the amount of annuity deposit. Court did not allow the same to be taxed.)
43. *Manju Bhatia* v. *New Delhi Municipal Council*, (1997) 6 SCC 370.
44. *Id.*, p. 377.
45. *Id.*, p. 373.

Chapter II

Equitable Rights and Interests: Nature and Classification

"We must be content to regard equitable interests as hybrids, midway between jura in rem *and* jura in personam. *They are not quite the former, because of the doctrine of bona fide purchaser and they are not quite the latter because of the doctrine of trust funds."*

—Hanbury: *Modern Equity*

"The true way to understand the nature and incidents of equitable ownership is to start with the notion not of real ownership, which is protected only in a court of equity, but of a contract with the legal owner which cannot be enforced at all or cannot be enforced completely except in a court of equity."

—Sir Frederick Pollock:
Principles of Contract, 9th Edn., p. 223.

SYNOPSIS

1. ORIGIN

Owing to defects in Common Law, Equity Courts came into existence and they gave birth to equitable remedies, equitable rights and equitable interests. There was a double system of administration of justice in England prior to the Judicature Acts, 1873-75. Legal rights and interests were those that were recognised and protected by the Common Law courts. Equitable rights and interests were those that found recognition and protection from the courts of equity.

2. EQUITABLE RIGHTS AND INTERESTS

Simple examples of equitable interest and equitable right can be cited as follows:

A mortgages his property with *B* for Rs 5000. It is agreed that *A* should pay back Rs 5000 plus interest to *B* within two years. If not, after two years *A* would lose all his legal interest in the property and *B* will be its legal owner. *A* fails to pay back the amount within two years. After two years therefore *A*'s legal interest in the property is forfeited at law and the property goes to *B*. This might be proper at one time but Equity on the principle of binding the conscience of a person and that "a mortgage cannot be a mortgage on one side only" did not allow this unjust and inequitable state of affairs to continue. It gave a remedy and consequently *A* could recover his property from *B* if he paid the amount with interest and expenses to *B*, even after the expiry of two years' period. Here *A*'s interest in the property under the forfeited mortgage is an equitable one. Thus interests recognised and enforced by the equity courts are *equitable* interests.

A husband had a right at common law in the property of his wife. Against this the wife had an *equitable right* against the husband for a reasonable provision for her and her children.

English law thus recognised two types of estates, legal and equitable. Law in India recognised no such distinctions.

Equitable construction is applicable only if the provision is ambiguous.[1] But equity cannot override written law or settled law, or clear statutory provisions.[2] An order in equity is equitable to all the parties concerned.[3] Considerations of equity are not applicable to statutorily prescribed period of limitation.[4] This is so because law prevails over equity.[5] Even mercy cannot subvert any legal right upheld by lower court.[6]

3. ESTATES AT LAW

An estate is the condition and circumstances in which an owner stands with reference to his property. A legal estate is a limitation of interests in reality. Thereby a party, at law, gets rights of ownership and profits. Equitable estate is an interest recognised by equity only. It arises when a right vested in one person by law, should in view of equity be, as a matter of conscience, vested in another. A trustee has a legal estate vested in him, while the beneficiary has an equitable estate granted to him. Similarly where there is a valid contract for sale of land, the vendor has the legal estate with him till a conveyance has been executed, while the purchaser immediately on the contract, gets an equitable estate in land.

Estates according to English law are of three broad kinds. These divisions are based on (*i*) quality (type) of interest and duration of estate, (*ii*) time of enjoyment, and (*iii*) number of connections of tenants. Each division has sub-divisions. In division one there are: (*a*) freeholds of inheritance, (*b*) freeholds not of inheritance, (*c*) estates less than freeholds, and (*d*) estates upon condition. In division two, there are (*a*) expectancies, (*b*) remainders, and (*c*) reversions. In the third division, there are (*a*) severalty, (*b*) joint tenancy, (*c*) coparcenary, (*d*) tenancy in common, and (*e*) entireties. These sub-divisions have sub-divisions too. As we are not concerned with the details thereof it would suffice here to say that the Law of Property Act, 1925 has cut down the list of legal estates to—

(*i*) fee-simple absolute in possession;

---

1. See *Siddappa Vasappa Kuri* v. *Special Land Acquisition Officer*, (2002) 1 SCC 142.
2. *P.M. Latha* v. *State of Kerala*, (2003) 3 SCC 541 (application of equity therefore not justified.) *E. Palanisamy* v. *Palanisamy*, (2003) 1 SCC 123 (clear statutory provisions).
3. *Union of India* v. *Modiluft Ltd.*, (2003) 6 SCC 65.
4. *India House* v. *Kishan N. Lalwani*, (2003) 9 SCC 393 (S. 12(2) and 29(2), Limitation Act).
5. *Laxminarayan R. Bhattad* v. *State of Maharashtra*, (2003) 5 SCC 413.
6. *K. Ganesh Shet* v. *A.K. Jayarama Sheka*, (2005) 1 SCC 493.

(*ii*) the term of years absolute; and

(*iii*) certain legal interests or charges.[7]

The first is the greatest estate granted to a man and his heirs. A legal estate is one that is valid against the whole world.

4. NATURE OF EQUITABLE RIGHTS AND INTERESTS

As Snell puts it, an infringement of a plaintiff's legal right entitled him to a general and unqualified judgment at law irrespective of the circumstances of the infringement and his own conduct. But in equity there was no right to relief and the plaintiff's conduct or other surrounding circumstances might lead equity to refuse any equitable remedy even though the plaintiff proved his case. Equity does not interfere with a man's legal rights unless it would be unconscionable on his part to take advantage of them. Equity acts on the conscience. The Judicature Acts, 1873-1875 fused the double systems of administration into one but the distinction between legal and equitable rights,[8] and between legal and equitable remedies continue. It is therefore very important from the practical point of view to know whether a right is one which had its origin and recognition at law or only in equity.

Whether jura in personam or in rem.—At their origin, equitable interests were *jura in personam* because their birth can be traced to the doctrine that equity acts on the conscience.[9] In course of time they were enforced not only against persons originally bound but also against their heirs or a donee or a purchaser with notice[10] and finally against all, except a bona fide purchaser for value, without notice. They were thus looked upon as rights *in rem* or proprietory rights; "what began as a mere personal equity has ended as a right of property".[11]

A *controversy*[12] exists on this point whether equitable rights are rights *in personam* or rights *in rem*. A lucid summary of the various conflicting views appears in Winfield.[13]

Legal rights as rights *in rem* are enforced against all but equitable rights will not be enforced against a purchaser without notice of them, and therefore they cannot be regarded as rights *in rem*.

On the point whether equitable rights are *jura in rem* or *jura in personam* there are two schools of thought—one in favour of *jura in personam* called the "personalists" and the other in favour of *jura in rem* called the "realists" by Dr Hanbury. Maitland citing a passage from Austin's *Jurisprudence* sharply

7. Walker D.M.: *The Oxford Companion to Law*, 1980 Edn., p. 432.
8. *Gentle* v. *Faulkner*, (1900) 2 QB 267.
9. *Joseph* v. *Lyons*, (1884) 15 QBD 280.
10. Maitland: *Lectures on Equity*, p. 112.
11. *Snell's Principles of Equity*, p. 22 citing *Sinclair* v. *Brougham*, 1914 AC 398.
12. H.C. Hanbury, (1929) 45 LQR 199.
13. Winfield: *Province of the Law of Tort*, (1931), pp. 108-112, cited in *Snell's Principles of Equity*.

remarks,[14] that Austin has failed to bring out the difference between *jura in rem* and *jura in personam* and it is "not merely nonsensical but mischievous". The point that Maitland has to push is that equitable estates and interests are not *jura in rem* but essentially *jura in personam*.

To a certain extent, contrary to the "realists" and contrary to Maitland's view is the view held by Megarry[15] which seems to be a very clear and concise exposition of the position as that expressed by Snell.[16] He says, "it is perhaps best to treat them as hybrids being neither entirely one nor entirely the other. They have never reached the status of rights *in rem*, yet the class of persons against whom they will be enforced is rather large for mere rights *in personam*". Maitland and Pollock belong to the "personalist" school and Professor Scott to the "realist" school. Dr Hanbury's view is a compromise between these two extremes. Thus we may consider equitable rights as hybrids occupying a middle position between *jura in rem* and *jura in personam* because they are clearly more than mere rights *in personam*.

5. CHARACTERISTICS

(1) *Recognition by Court of Chancery.*—An equitable interest is an interest recognised as such by the courts of Chancery. It affects the conscience of the legal owner. Thus, "where a right vested in one person by law, should in the view of equity be vested in another",[17] an equitable right arises. Equitable rights are therefore merely extensions and modifications of legal rights of property.[18]

(2) *Same Incidents as Corresponding Legal Estate.*—As pointed out by Snell, an equitable interest has generally been treated as having the same incidents as the corresponding legal estate.[19] This is based on the principle of the maxim that equity follows the law. In this respect it holds similarities with legal estate.

(3) *Not Superior to Legal Estate.*—Equitable estate is not superior to legal estate and (unlike legal estate), from equitable estate no other estate can be carved out.

(4) *Jura in Personam.*—Equitable interest is for the use of a person and therefore personal (*jura in personam*).

(5) *Competition between two Equitable Interests.*—Where there are two equitable estates and one is created in point of time prior to the other, they will be governed by the maxim, "where there are equal equities, the first in time shall prevail", or in other words, he who is earlier in time is stronger in law.

(6) *Equitable interest and legal interest.*—Where there are two equitable estates and out of them one has a legal estate also, the holder of a legal as well

---

14. Maitland: *Lectures on Equity*, (1969), pp. 106-107, citing Austin: *Jurisprudence*, p. 388.
15. Megarry & Wade: *Law of Real Property*, (1946), pp. 78-79.
16. *Snell's Principles of Equity*, 27th Edn., p. 23.
17. Strahen: *Digest of Equity*, p. 21.
18. *Supra* note 3.
19. *Snell's Principles of Equity*, 27th Edn., p. 23.

as an equitable estate shall be preferred on the principle "where there is equal equity, the law shall prevail". In other words, a legal estate is superior as between two persons having equitable estates because equity follows the law.

(7) *Different from Mere Equities.*—As an equitable interest is different and therefore can be distinguished from a legal interest, it can also be distinguished from mere equities. An equitable interest is an actual right in property e.g., an interest under trust.[20] Mere equities have a procedural flavour and mainly are rights to relief in respect of property e.g. a right to set aside a transaction for fraud,[21] or undue influence,[22] or to have a document rectified for mistake,[23] or by inserting a repairing covenant,[24] and even the right of a deserted wife to remain in occupation of the matrimonial house.[25]

(8) *Aim of Equity.*—Defects and deficiencies of the Common Law were the foundation-stones upon which the edifice of equity jurisdiction came to be erected, and the three main purposes for which these equitable rights and interests were created were, protection of confidences, promotion of fair dealings, and prevention of oppression.

6. POSITION IN INDIA

Law in India recognises no distinction between Law and Equity as understood in English law, but in view of the fact that most of the equitable principles have been incorporated in various enactments in India, one cannot appreciate those principles without referring to the English system of law and equity. Similarly, the definition of the interest of the beneficiary rests on the very premises and postulates no less than it provides for double ownership. Moreover, the rights and interests of the beneficiary, though laid down in the statute, retain almost all the characteristics, limitations and flavour of the legal and equitable estates. They therefore deserve, on their own merits, the nomenclature "hybrids under the Indian law".

A similar view of the position seems to have been expressed by Mr M.C. Setalvad:[26]

> " ... the statute law of India has incorporated in itself to a substantial extent equitable rules and doctrines. The Indian Trusts Act of 1882 embodies in a concise form the whole structure of trusts built up by the equity courts in England... . Another instance of an almost bodily transplantation of the doctrines of the English equity courts is to be found in the Specific Reliefs Act of 1877... . In the greater part of the country it obtained its sway in the guise of 'equity , justice and good conscience'... the process continues to this day."

20. *Banks* v. *Riplay*, 1940 Ch 719.
21. *Earnest* v. *Vivian*, 1863 Ch 513.
22. *Bainbridge* v. *Brown*, (1881) 18 Ch D 188.
23. *Garrard* v. *Franknell*, (1862) 30 Beav 445.
24. *Smith* v. *Jones*, (1954) 1 WLR 1089.
25. *Westminster Bank Ltd.* v. *Lee*, 1956 Ch 7.
26. Setalvad: *Common Law in India*, pp. 61-62.

It has therefore been aptly remarked in *Seedee Ali* v. *Raja Ajoodhya*[27], that in India, there is "but one kind of proprietory right , call it legal or equitable you choose, which is recognised by the court, it is an equity, not divisible into parts or aspects".

EQUITABLE JURISDICTION

As held in *Skipper Construction (P) Ltd. case*[28] the jurisdiction and power of Supreme Court is exercised to meet the situations which cannot be effectively dealt with under the existing law. However, the power should be left undefined so that it may be flexible enough to be exercised depending upon needs of the particular case. But it should be used with circumspection. If there is no provision in law, that will not deter the Supreme Court to proceed under Article 142 *to do complete justice* between the parties.

Equitable jurisdiction of Supreme Court under Article 136 is compared to that of High Court under Article 226 in *Samarendra Kishore case*[29] as under: while Supreme Court could interfere with punishment imposed in a departmental inquiry, there was no corresponding power or jurisdiction with the High Courts/Central Administrative Tribunal for exercising such power or jurisdiction. Further, jurisdiction of Central Administrative Tribunal is analogous to High Court under Article 226.

Scope and other principles of non-interference have been discussed by the Supreme Court in Sushanta Tagore and other cases.[30]

7. DIFFERENCE BETWEEN LEGAL AND EQUITABLE ESTATE

This difference may be succinctly stated as follows:

(*a*) Legal estate is always superior to equitable estate in a sense that the latter in itself requires something more to fructify itself into a legal estate.

(*b*) From an equitable estate no other estate can be created, but from a legal estate an equitable estate can be carved out.

(*c*) Moreover, legal estate is enjoyed against the whole world and it is governed by Common Law in so far as its creation and transfer are concerned. Legal estate is therefore known as *jura in rem* while an equitable estate, being for the use of a person, is known as *jura in personam*. Of course this point is controversial but a happy compromise can be struck as discussed in this chapter elsewhere.

---

27. (1867) 8 WR 399.

28. *DDA* v. *Skipper Construction Co. (P) Ltd.*, (1996) 4 SCC 622: AIR 1996 SC 2005. See also *Attorney General for India* v. *Amratlal Prajivandas*, (1994) 5 SCC 54; *Manju Bhatia* v. *New Delhi Municipal Council*, (1997) 6 SCC 370.

29. *State Bank of India* v. *Samarendra Kishore Endow*, (1994) 2 SCC 537, 543: 1994 SCC (L&S) 687: 1994 (27) ATC 149: (1994) 1 LLJ 872: (1994) 1 SLR 516.

30. *Sushanta Tagore* v. *Union of India*, (2005) 3 SCC 16, (Art. 136, Scope of interference and equity jurisdiction discussed); *Union of India* v. *V.B. Chandramohan*, (2005) 10 SCC 649 (Scope of interference under Art. 136, Constitution); *Chief Secy.* v. *Students of A.P.A.U.*, (2005) 12 SCC 448 (acid throwing on University Student—Decision., Non-interference by Supreme Court on humanitarian grounds.)

(*d*) In so far as conflict and competition between these two estates is concerned, it is the legal estate that succeeds because equity follows the law, and because one who has a legal estate as well as an equitable one has naturally a far superior claim than the one who has only an equitable estate. Where there is a competition between two equitable estates, the one created prior or first in point of time prevails. The question of priority depends upon certain rules and principles evolved by the courts of equity.

8. CLASSIFICATION OF EQUITABLE RIGHTS

Although fraud, accident and breach of confidence are considered as the basis of equity jurisdiction, this original or "primitive trio" is merely a convenient way to roughly express the foundations on which the structure stands. It does not connote the exact and exclusive jurisdiction but is a rough and ready estimate thereof. Story has classified these rights into three heads but the same may not be considered to be final, exhaustive and satisfactory:[31]

(A) Equities to protect confidences, i.e., trust.

(B) Equities to prevent oppression. This includes Penalties and Forfeitures, Mortgages and Liens, Married Women, Infants, Idiots and Lunatics.

(C) Equities to promote fair dealings. This includes Conversion, Election, Performances, Satisfaction and Ademption, Administration of Assets, Mistake, Misrepresentation, Fraud and Undue Influence, Accident and Set-off.

---

31. *Cf.* Story: *Equity Jurisprudence*, 3rd Edn., pp. 32, 38-39; Ashburner: *Principles of Equity*, 2nd Edn., p. 73.

Chapter III

Maxims of Equity

"स्वल्पाक्षरमसंदिग्धं
सारवद्विधतोमुखम् ।
अस्तोभमनवधं च
सूत्रं सूत्रविदो विदुः । ।"

A sutra is a pithy statement, being unambiguous, substantial, universal and logically sound—so say the pundits or (Sutravid).

Maxims are short, pithy formulations of broad and general principles of common sense and justice.

Walker D.M.: *The Oxford Companion to Law*, 1980 Edn., p. 818

"These are not to be taken as positive laws of equity which will be applied literally and relentlessly in their full width, but rather as trends or principles which can be discerned in many of the detailed rules which equity has established."

—Snell's Principles of Equity, p. 27

SYNOPSIS

Working Principles of Equity.—As seen before equity has a haphazard origin and is not a complete system. Its working principles are embodied in the so-called maxims of equity. These principles do not cover the whole of the ground of equity and tend to overlap. There can be no logical division of these maxims. Therefore, these maxims are short or concise technical sentences used as memorial rules (V.S. Apte: Sanskrit English Dictionary, p. 610, 1963 Edn.). They represent the nectar of the experience of judicial administration of five centuries by equity courts. They did not come into existence all of a sudden and at the very outset. They are the outcome of the zeal and sincerity of the Chancellors' conscience striving to do justice. As pointed out by Salmond: "Maxims are the proverbs of the law. They have the same merits and defects as other proverbs, being brief and pithy statements of partial truths. They express general principles without the necessary qualifications and exceptions, and they are therefore much too absolute to be taken as trustworthy guides to the law. Yet they are not without their uses. False and misleading when literally read, these established formulae provide useful means for the expression of leading doctrines of the law in a form which is at the same time brief and intelligible." According to Justice Stephen: "They are rather minims than maxims, for they give not a particularly great, but a particularly small amount of information. As often as not the exceptions and qualifications are more important than the so-called rules, which while they mostly serve as good indexes to the law, are mostly bad abstracts of it." There are twelve such maxims but the overlapping is so much so that "it would not be difficult to reduce them all under the first and the last".[1]

As observed in *Nirmal Sachdeo case*[2], the general principles upon which the court of chancery exercised its jurisdiction have been embodied as maxims of equity. They however, are not to be treated as positive laws to be applied literally and to their widest possible amplitude since equity does not demand that its suitors shall have to lay themselves blameless. It lends assistance to the cause of justice and avoids inequities. Ethics and good conduct sub-serve the need of justice and equitable maxims denote the same. The applicability of the equitable maxims is to be had only in the event of their being a reasonable amount of certainty about the unclean hands. The Supreme Court in *Nalakath Sainuddin case* has observed that the Transfer of Property Act embodies mostly principles of equity, justice and good conscience in view of codification in India. And these principles stand modified to the extent of provisions otherwise in Transfer of Property Act.[3]

1. *Snell's Principles of Equity*, 27th Edn., p. 27.
2. *Municipal Corpn. of Delhi* v. *Nirmal Sachdeva*, (2001) 10 SCC 364.
3. *Nalakath Sainuddin* v. *Koorikadan Sulaiman*, (2002) 6 SCC 1.

The maxims give a clue to just and reasonable interpretation. Equity, as observed by the Apex Court, is an integral part of Article 14. Interpretation of service law should be made in such a way that justice is done to the parties.[4]

One must, however, note that Tax and Equity are strangers. Equity cannot be relied on by the Revenue to tax an amount which is not taxable under the Statute. In short, tax cannot be levied on the basis of Equity.[5]

The Synopsis to this chapter lists the twelve maxims which have been individually discussed hereunder:

1. EQUITY WILL NOT SUFFER A WRONG TO BE WITHOUT A REMEDY

(*a*) *Meaning*.—Where there is a right, there is a remedy. This idea is expressed in the Latin maxim *ubi jus ibi remedium*. It means that no wrong should go unredressed if it is capable of being remedied by courts. This maxim indicates the width of the scope and the basis on which the structure of equity rests. Thus it is responsible for the entire equitable jurisdiction of the court of Chancery to prevent failure of justice. But the meaning of the maxim should not be understood to embrace every moral wrong. The maxim imports that where the common law confers a right, it gives also a remedy or right of action for interference with or infringement of that right.[6] The maxim therefore must be taken as referring to rights which are suitable for judicial enforcement but which were not enforced at common law owing to some technical defect. The following cases can best illustrate the maxim.

(*b*) *Application and Cases*.—In *Ashby* v. *White*[7], wherein a qualified voter was not allowed to vote and who therefore sued the returning officer, it was held that if the law gives a man a right, he must have "a means to vindicate and maintain it, and a remedy, if he is injured in the exercise of and enjoyment of it. It is, indeed, a vain thing to imagine a right without a remedy, for want of right and want of remedy are reciprocal". It was argued that the candidate for whom the plaintiff wanted to vote was elected and that there was no precedent for such an action; and if it was allowed, that would lead to multiplicity of proceedings but the same were rejected and Lord Holt observed that "*if man will multiply injuries, actions must be multiplied too, for every man that is injured ought to have his recompense*".[8]

As noted by Snell, it was on this maxim that the court of Chancery based its interference to enforce uses and trusts. Where *A* conveyed land to *B* for the use of and in trust for *C*, and *B* claimed to keep the benefit of the land to himself, *C* had no remedy at law. But this was an abuse of confidence, which was a wrong capable of redress in a Chancery Court.

---

4. *K.C. Joshi* v. *Union of India*, 1992 Supp (1) SCC 272; *Union of India* v. *Kishorilal Bablani*, (1999) 1 SCC 729 (service law); *Delhi Development Authority* v. *Ravindra Mohan Aggarwal*, (1999) 3 SCC 172 (providing plot against public interest by a public authority).
5. *Kapil Mohan* v. *CIT*, (1999) 1 SCC 430.
6. Walker D.M.: *The Oxford Companion to Law*, 1980 Edn., p. 1246,
7. *Smith's Leading Cases*, 13th Edn., p. 253.
8. *Ibid*.

In cases where some document was with the defendant and it was necessary for the plaintiff to obtain its discovery or production, a recourse to the Chancery Courts had to be made for the Common Law courts had no such power; consequently the wrongs at Common Law becoming "wrongs without remedies". This situation was remedied by equity courts. This jurisdiction was extended to appointment of a receiver by way of equitable execution,[9] and to action for ejectment too, excepting discovery in case of penalties and forfeitures, for equity is against these two. The Judicature Acts have now made the discovery automatic. Similarly a mortgager was allowed in equity to sue the mortgagee for land and for the rent thereof even though the latter was possessed of the legal estate. A trustee for the breach of a trust could be sued in equity because it was a wrong and no wrong should go unredressed. Where a defamatory matter is published or where a document is not produced or where there is a breach of right regarding water, light or air, there also the equity courts ordered either for arrest or granted an injunction as was suitable.

(*c*) *Limitations of the maxim.*—Equity courts supplemented the Common Law courts wherever they afforded no remedy at all or afforded incomplete remedy or had insufficient procedure to collect evidence. But to this there were certain limitations that:—

(*a*) the equity courts could not help where there was breach of a moral right only. Thus only the breaches of legal rights and equitable rights were capable of being redressed;

(*b*) the equity courts afforded no relief where the right and its remedy both were within the jurisdiction of the Common Law courts;

(*c*) the equity courts afforded no relief, where due to his own negligence a party either destroyed or allowed to be destroyed, the evidence in his own favour or waived his right to an equitable remedy.

(*d*) *Recognition in India.*—The Indian Trusts Act, Section 9 of the Civil Procedure Code and the Specific Relief Act in India have incorporated the above principles. The Civil Procedure Code entitles a civil court to entertain all kinds of suits unless they are prohibited. The Specific Relief Act provides for equitable remedies like specific performance of contracts, rectification of instruments, injunctions and declaratory suits.

It can be said that the writ provisions in the Constitution, the Administrative Law and the Public Interest Litigation devices have now extended the scope and effective working of this maxim.

2. EQUITY FOLLOWS THE LAW

(*a*) *Meaning.*—The maxim indicates the discipline which the Chancery Courts observed while administering justice according to conscience. As has

---

9. *Lloyds Bank Ltd.* v. *Medway U.N. Co.*, (1905) 2 KB 359, cited in *Snell's Principles of Equity*, p. 663.

been observed by Jekyll, M.R.[10]: "The discretion of the court is governed by the rules of law and equity, which are not to oppose, but each, in turn, to be subservient to the other; this discretion in some cases follows the law implicitly, in others assists it, and advances the remedy; in others again it relieves against the abuse or allays the rigour of it; but in no case does it contradict or *overturn* the grounds or principles thereof."[11] *Thus equity came not to destroy the law but to fulfil it, to supplement it, to explain it.* "Every jot and every title of the law was to be obeyed, but when all this had been done, something might yet be needful, something that equity would require"[12], and that was added by equity. Their goal was the same but by their nature and due to historical accident they chose different paths. Equity respected every word of law and every right at law but where the law was defective, in those instances, these Common Law rights were controlled by recognition of equitable rights and in other cases they were rendered more effective (than they were at Common Law) by throwing open equitable remedies to their holders. In the words of Story[13] "where a rule either of the common or statute law is direct and governs the case with all its circumstances, or the particular point, a court of equity is as much bound by it as a court of law and can as little justify a departure from it". It is only, as Snell puts it, when there is some important circumstance disregarded by the Common Law rules that equity interferes. Thus "*equity follows the law, but not slavishly, nor always*".[14]

(*b*) *Application and Cases.*—A case on the point is *Stickland* v. *Aldridge*[15]. As regards legal estates, rights and interests, equity was and is strictly bound by the rules of law and it has no discretion to deviate therefrom. At Common Law, where a person died intestate who owned an estate in fee-simple, leaving sons and daughters, the eldest son (according to the rules of primogeniture) was entitled to the whole of the land to the exclusion of his younger brothers and sisters. This was unfair, yet no relief was granted by Equity Courts. But in this case it was held that if the son had induced his father not to make a will by agreeing to divide the estate with his brothers and sisters, equity would have interfered and compelled him to carry out his promise, because it would have been against conscience to allow the son to keep the benefit of a legal estate which he obtained by reason of his promise. Equity recognised and respected legal rules but the circumstance of giving a promise by the son to the father had added an element of conscience to the rule which equity must consider, because it acts on the conscience of a person. It was held therefore that the son must take it as a trustee for himself and his brothers and sisters. Thus where a court of law missed an important point, equity corrected the law and followed it on the

---

10. *Lloyds Bank Ltd.* v. *Medway U.N. Co.*, (1905) 2 KB 359, cited in *Snell's Principles of Equity*, p. 663.
11. *Cowper* v. *Cowper*, (1734) 2 PWms 720: 24 ER 930. *See also* Story: *Equity Jurisprudence*, 3rd Edn., (1920), p. 34.
12. Maitland: *Lectures on Equity*, p. 17.
13. Story: *Equity Jurisprudence*, p. 34.
14. *Per* Cardozo, C.J. in *Graf* v. *Hope Bldg. Corpn.*, 254 NY 1, cited in *Snell's Principles of Equity*.
15. (1804) 9 Ves 516.

simple principle of conscience. Provisions of law cannot be allowed to be misused or abused or made an instrument of fraud or to perpetuate injustice by creating a breach of trust and a breach of contract.

Where the law was based on feudal tenure, equity refused to follow it. Equity thus rejected the technical doctrines of seisin and escheat and recognised a wide range of future interest in land. Such exceptions are not many and therefore the rule that equity follows the law.[16] As regards equitable estates and interests, equity though not strictly bound by the rules of law, has acted and still acts in analogy to those rules where analogy exists.[17] For example where *R* gives his property in trust to *M*, *H* being the beneficiary; *H*'s interest though equitable will be governed by a legal rule in the following situation and not by any equitable rule. If the trustee *M* by a mistake of fact pays somebody a particular amount from trust property, *H* can file an action and this he will have to do within a period of six years. *H*'s interest being equitable, equity cannot help him in this respect, because, provisions of law in this regard are very definite and specific. There being analogy[18] here rules of law will apply. Thus when deciding titles to equitable estates, regarding construing of covenants and in construing words of limitation equity follows the rules of law. All these go to lead to one explanation of the maxim that *equity though going far ahead of law, never goes in opposition to established principles, and in that sense it is controlled by law.*[19]

(*c*) *Limitations of the maxim.*—(*i*) Where a rule of law did not specifically and clearly apply, or (*ii*) where even by analogy the rule of law did not apply, equity formulated and applied its own rules, on the reason that injustice must be remedied.

(*d*) *Position in India.*—India has not recognised the well-known distinction between legal and equitable interests. Equity rules in India, therefore, cannot override the specific provisions of law. As for example, every suit in India has to be brought within the limitation period and no judge can create an exception to this or can prolong the time-limit or stop the rule from taking effect on principles of equity.[20] Similarly no court can confer rights which can be acquired only by registration of a document, on a party, without getting the document registered.

In *Appa Narsappa Magdum case*[21], it was contended that the provisions of Land Reform Acts being welfare legislation enacted for the benefits of tenants should be construed in a liberal manner. This was rejected by the Supreme Court of India holding that, the provisions of law regarding the period within which tenant must exercise right to purchase land of widow landlady being clear, relief cannot be granted on the basis of Equity. Equity must yield to law.[22]

---

16. *Snell's Principles of Equity*, p. 30
17. *Paget* v. *Gee*, (1753) Amb 198.
18. *Alderson* v. *Madison*, 8 AC 497. *See also* Law of Property Act, 1925.
19. *Ibid.*
20. *Yaswant* v. *Walcahnd*, AIR 1951 SC 16.
21. *Appa Narsappa Magdum* v. *Akubai Ganapati Nimbalkar*, (1999) 4 SCC 443.
22. *Shamsu Suhara Beevi* v. *G. Alex*, (2004) 8 SCC 569.

Where law is clear no equitable relief is warranted.[23] A decree holder, who has failed to furnish the requisite stamp papers, cannot stop the running of period of limitation because none can take advantage of his own wrong.[24]

3. HE WHO SEEKS EQUITY MUST DO EQUITY

(*a*) *Meaning.*—The maxim means that to obtain an equitable relief the plaintiff must himself be prepared to do "equity", that is, a plaintiff must recognise and submit to the right of his adversary, because, you must do unto your neighbour what you wish him to do unto you. There must be reciprocity. Scriptures of Islam also inform us to be conscientious:[25]

> "Woe to those who stint the measure:
>
> who when they take by measure from others, exact the full;
>
> But when they mete to them or weigh to them,
>
> minish... ."

If you want to exact the full measure, your must also be prepared to reciprocate. As said by Ashhurst, J., in *Deeks* v. *Strutt*[26], a court of law cannot impose terms on the party suing. If he is entitled to a decision, the law must take its own course; but the practice of the Chancery Court was different in that while giving equitable relief it imposed such terms on the applicant which are agreeable to the conscience, because equity acts on the conscience of the party. In fact, the maxim lays down a bare abstract principle. What those terms could be was left to the discretion of the court. Snell[27] therefore points out that: "This is a rule of 'unquestionable justice', which, however, 'decides nothing in itself', for you must first inquire what are the equities which the defendant must do, and what the plaintiff ought to have."

(*b*) *Application and Cases.*—This rule has many applications, *e.g.*:—

(*i*) Illegal loans

(*ii*) Doctrine of Election

(*iii*) Consolidation of mortgages

(*iv*) Notice to redeem mortgage

(*v*) Wife's equity to settlement

(*vi*) Equitable estoppel

(*vii*) Restitution of benefits on cancellation of transaction

---

23. See *W.B. SEB* v. *Patel Engineering Co. Ltd.*, (2001) 2 SCC 451. Relief on basis of equity on ground of mistake—when cannot be granted.); *E. Palanisamy* v. *Palanisamy*, (2003) 1 SCC 123 (In face of clear statutory provisions considerations of equity not applicable); *Karnataka Rare Earth* v. *Senior Geologist, Department of Mines and Geology*, (2004) 2 SCC 783 (persons active without lawful authority cannot be in a better position than a person acting with lawful authority.)
24. *Chiranji Lal (Dr)* v. *Hari Das*, (2005) 10 SCC 746.
25. Titus and Keeton: *The Range of Ethics*, 1972 Edn., p. 379.
26. (1794) 3 TR 690, 693: 101 ER 384.
27. *Snell's Principles of Equity*, p. 30.

(*viii*) Set-off (conflicting claims in one proceeding).

(*ix*) Waiver

(*i*) *Illegal Loans.*—In *Lodge* v. *National Union Investment Co. Ltd.*[28], the facts were as follows. One *B* borrowed money from *M* by mortgaging certain securities to him. *M* was an unregistered money-lender. Under the Money-lenders' Act, 1900, the contract was illegal and therefore void. *B* sued *M* for return of the securities. The court refused to make an order except upon the terms that B should repay the money which had been advanced to him. This decision was based on the principle of this maxim.

The criticism levelled against this case is that it does not lay down any wide general principle; and it has been distinguished on certain points which have been discussed hereunder.

If *B* had asked merely for a declaration that the mortgage was void, he could have obtained the relief without repayment of the amount, because that is not an equitable relief but a legal one, being available under the Act. Moreover *B* by suing *M* in detinue or trover could have also recovered the securities without repayment. Comparing this case with *Chapman case*[29] one can easily find out the difference between a legal and an equitable remedy. In both the cases the plaintiff had borrowed money from the defendants who were not registered under the Money-lenders' Act. In the case of Lodge, the plaintiff did ask for a declaration (legal relief) to the effect that the loan was void and could not be recovered. Chapman also demanded the same legal relief but the difference is that in the former case, Lodge besides declaration asked for return of securities which was an equitable relief, and this was refused, except on his fulfilling a condition attached by the court, which it was competent to impose. In *Lewis* v. *Plunkett*[30], it was also held that when a mortgagor is in possession of mortgaged property and the mortgagee's right is time-barred, the mortgagor can recover the title deeds from the mortgagee without repaying the loan. This is a new dimension added to the position as it stands at present which goes to support the pronouncement of the decision in *Kasumus' case*[31] that *Lodge case* does not lay down any wide and general principle.

(*ii*) *Doctrine of Election.*—Stating the gist of the doctrine succinctly it may be said that where a donor *A* gives his own property to *B* and in the same instrument purports to give *B*'s property to *C*, *B* will be put to an election, either to retain his own property and reject the benefit under the instrument or to accept the benefit granted to him by the donor, and allow the gift of his own property made by *A* to *C* to take effect. But in no case can *B* choose to keep the benefit granted to himself and at the same time retain his property referred to in the instrument. As Maitland puts it, "he who accepts a benefit under a deed or will or other instrument must adopt the whole content of that instrument, must

28. (1907) 1 Ch 300.
29. *Chapman* v. *Michaelson*, (1909) 1 Ch 238.
30. 1937 Ch 306.
31. 1956 AC 539.

conform to all its provisions and renounce all rights that are inconsistent with it". This position is expressed as "one cannot both approbate and reprobate;"[32] benefits and burdens go together; one cannot blow hot and cold in the same breath; and that one cannot have a cake and eat it too. As Snell puts it "equity fastens on the conscience of a person who is put to election and refuses to allow him to take the benefit of a disposition contained in the will, the validity of which is not in question, except on certain conditions."[33]

(*iii*) *Consolidation of mortgages.*—Where a person has become entitled to two mortgages from the same mortgagor, he may consolidate these mortgages and refuse to permit the mortgagee to exercise his equitable right to redeem one mortgage unless and until the other is redeemed, i.e., unless there is simultaneous redemption of all. This is called equity of consolidation. This is naturally on the principle that he who comes into equity must do equity. It is to be noted that if the mortgagor exercises his legal right to redeem within the time mentioned in the deed this doctrine does not apply but when this time has passed, only the equitable right to redeem remains to which this maxim will apply.[34] This right of consolidation now exists in England but after the enactment of the Law of Property Act, 1925, it can exist only by express reservation in one of the mortgage deeds.[35]

(*iv*) *Notice to redeem mortgage.*—Notice to a mortgagee to redeem one's mortgage is an equitable right of the mortgagor.

(*v*) *Wife's equity to a settlement.*—There was a time when in England at Common Law the wife could not hold independently any property. This was the effect of marriage. Legal existence of the wife so to say merged into that of her husband, the husband consequently becoming the absolute owner of her moneys, goods and chattles, things in action and estates.[36] But equity saw injustice in this situation and therefore departed from the Common Law principle in three cases—by recognising the wife's equity to a settlement, recognising the wife's right to a separate estate in certain circumstances, and by putting fetters on the wife's right to alienate that separate property or disabling her to anticipate future income called "the restraint on anticipation". When, therefore, a husband sought the aid of the Chancery Court to obtain possession of his wife's equitable property to which he was entitled in right of his wife, the courts refused to assist him unless he accepted the terms and conditions imposed by the equity courts in order to compel him to make a reasonable provision for her and her children. Thus in securing his equitable right the husband had to do equity. But now, as Snell notes, under the Law Reform (Married Women and Tortfeasors) Act, 1935, a married woman's property is no longer her "separate property" but is simply her "property"; and it belongs to her in all respects as if she were a *feme sole*, with the same rights of ownership and disposition,

---

32. *See* Maitland: *Lectures on Equity*, p. 287.
33. *Snell's Principles of Equity*, p. 484.
34. See *Jennings* v. *Jordon*, (1882) 6 AC 698. The doctrine was affirmed by the House of Lords in *Pledge* v. *White*, 1896 AC 187 on the principle of *stare decisis*.
35. *See* Section 93 of the Law of Property Act, 1925.
36. *See* for details *Snell's Principles of Equity*, pp. 513-514.

whether *inter vivos* or by will, as an unmarried woman or man.[37] This illustration has therefore become obsolete and of academic interest only.

(*vi*) *Equitable estoppel:*[38] *Meaning, Nature and Purpose.*—This concept at Common Law, which was confined in the beginning to various formal matters, was later on expanded by equity courts which covered in its sweep any representation of existing facts, whether by words or by conduct which was acted upon by a person before whom it was made and the maker of the representation was not allowed to go back upon it. Later on this doctrine of "equitable estoppel" was expressed in two forms called "promissory estoppel" and "proprietary estoppel".

Estoppel is a principle which precludes a party from alleging or proving in legal proceedings that a fact is otherwise than it has appeared to be from the circumstances. Apart from estoppel from record and estoppel by deed, a promissory estoppel arises where a party has expressly or impliedly, by conduct or by negligence, made a statement of fact, or so conducted himself, that another would reasonably understand that he might act in reliance thereon, and has so acted, that the party who made the representation is not allowed to allege that the fact is otherwise than he has represented it to be.[39] The doctrine has been known by various names: promissory estoppel, equitable estoppel, quasi-estoppel and new estoppel or estoppel *in pais* (by conduct).

It is a principle evolved by equity to avoid injustice and though commonly named as promissory estoppel, it is neither in the realm of contract nor in the realm of estoppel.[40] It has, as a matter of fact, transcended these limits and gained new dimensions in recent years. The full implications of this new kind of estoppel are yet to be spelled out. It is a principle that advances the cause of justice.[41]

It was Mr Justice Denning, in England, who first rescued the doctrine from obscurity in *Central London Property Trust Ltd.*[42] , and laid the foundation for its applicability in *Robertson* v. *Minister of Pensions*[43], reiterating and expanding the scope of its application even to the Crown in *Howell* v. *Falmouth Boat Construction Co.*[44], in the following words:—

(1) that the assurances intended to be acted upon and in fact acted upon were binding, and

(2) that where a government department wrongfully assumed authority to perform some legal act, the citizen is entitled to assume that it had that authority.

---

37. *Rees* v. *Huges*, 1946 KB 517 cited in *Snell's Principles of Equity*, p. 515.
38. B.M. Gandhi: "*The Proper Place for Promissory Estoppel*", (1986) 3 SCC (Jour) 45 to 54.
39. Bhagwati, J., in *Motilal Padampat Sugar Mills Co. Ltd.* v. *State of U.P.*, (1979) 2 SCC 409, 425; Walker: *The Oxford Companion to Law*, (1980), pp. 432-33; *Sardar Vallabhbhai Patel Memorial Society* v. *State*, (1983) 2 GLR 1329: AIR 1984 NOC 16 (Guj).
40. *Motilal Padampat Sugar Mills Co. Ltd.* v. *State of U.P.*, (1979) 2 SCC 409, 422.
41. Hedge J., in *Turner Morrison & Co. Ltd.* v. *Hungerford Investment Trust Ltd.*, (1972) 1 SCC 857.
42. *Central London Property Trust Ltd.* v. *High Trees House Ltd.*, (1956) 1 All ER 256; *Union of India* v. *Godfrey Philips India Ltd.*, (1985) 4 SCC 369 at 383.
43. LR (1949) 1 KB 227; *Express Newspapers (P) Ltd.* v. *Union of India,* (1986) 1 SCC 133 at 248.
44. LR 1951 AC 837; *Express Newspapers (P) Ltd.* v. *Union of India*, (1986) 1 SCC 133 at 249, *supra*.

Essentials & Basis

The essential factors[45] giving rise to an estoppel *in pais* are:

(*a*) a representation intended to induce a course of conduct on the part of the person to whom the representation was made;[46]

(*b*) resulting from the representation, an act by the person to whom it was made;[47]

(*c*) detriment to such person from the act.[48]

There must be a necessary factual foundation for the application of the doctrine. It depends upon the facts of each case whether there was a representation or not. The representation must be unambiguous and clear and there must be a nexus or a connection between the representation and action whereby the plaintiff alters his position. It should be noted that the doctrine is *limited* to public law area[49] and the petitioner praying for relief must have his hands clear and must prove that equity is in his favour.[50] *The doctrine has its basis in justice to an individual and though often described as a rule of evidence, more correctly it is a principle of law.*[51] Justice here prevails over truth.

Application in India

Originated in equity, first pressed into service by Calcutta High Court[52] in 1880 and thereafter by the Supreme Court[53] in 1951 and onwards till today the doctrine has been applied in various cases and fields, especially in the field of

---

45. *Greenwood* v. *Martin's Bank*, 1933 AC 51; *Territorial & Auxiliary Forces Assn.* v. *Nichols & Parker*, (1949) 1 KB 35, 49; *Municipal Corpn. of Bom.* v. *Secy. of State*, ILR (1905) 29 Bom 580 (the Government may be bound by a representation made by it). See *B.L. Sreedhar* v. *K.M. Munireddy*, (2003) 1 ILD 185 (SC).

46. *Evenden* v. *Guildford City Assn. Football Club Ltd.*, (1975) 3 All ER 269 quoted with approval in *Motilal Padampat Sugar Mills Co. Ltd.* v. *State of U.P.*, (1979) 2 SCC 409, 424; *Jatinder Kumar* v. *State of Punjab*, (1985) 1 SCC 122 (invitation to apply for service is not to hold out any promise to select or appoint); *S.N. Yadav* v. *Bihar State Electricity Board*, (1985) 3 SCC 38; *Bakul Cahsew Co.* v. *STO, Quilon*, (1986) 2 SCC 365; *Delhi Cloth & General Mills Co. Ltd.* v. *Rajasthan State Electricity Board*, (1986) 2 SCC 431.

47. *D.R. Kohli* v. *Atul Products Ltd.*, (1985) 2 SCC 77; *Union of India* v. *Godfrey Philips India Ltd.*, (1985) 4 SCC 369; *Express Newspapers (P) Ltd.* v. *Union of India*, (1986) 1 SCC 133; *Bakul Cashew Co.* v. *STO, Quilon*, supra; *Delhi Cloth & General Mills Co. Ltd.* v. *Rajasthan SEB*, supra.

48. *Motilal Padampat Sugar Mills Co. Ltd.* v. *State of U.P.*, (1979) 2 SCC 409, 452; *S.N. Yadav* v. *Bihar State Electricity Board*, supra; (1985) 4 SCC 369 and (1986) 1 SCC 133, supra; *Satish Sabharwal* v. *State of Maharashtra*, (1986) 2 SCC 362.

49. *Jasjeet Films (P) Ltd.* v. *DDA*, AIR 1980 Del 83:ILR (1979) 2 Del 742; *Union of India* v. *Anglo-Afghan Agencies*, AIR 1968 SC 718: (1968) 2 SCR 366; see also *Express Newspapers (P) Ltd.*, supra, p. 133, paras 178, 179.

50. *Ibid.*

51. *Express Newspapers (P) Ltd.* v. *Union of India*, (1986) 1 SCC 133. For meaning, nature and purpose of the doctrine *see also* the following cases: *R.K. Kwatra* v. *D.S.I.D.C.*, AIR 1992 Del 28 (doctrine used, both as a shield and a sword); *State of H.P.* v. *Ganesh Wood Products*, (1995) 6 SCC 363 (Govt. industry); *Amrit Banaspati Co. Ltd.* v. *State of Punjab*, (1992) 2 SCC 411: (1992) 59 ELT 13 (furnishes a cause of action to a citizen); *Kasinka Trading* v. *Union of India*, (1995) 1 SCC 274: AIR 1995 SC 874 (when the doctrine is not applicable to Government).

52. *Ganges Mfg. Co.* v. *Sourujmull*, ILR (1880) 5 Cal 669.

53. *Collector of Bombay* v. *Bombay Municipal Corpn.*, AIR 1951 SC 469: 1952 SCR 43: 54 Bom LR 122.

public law. The starting-point of such application may be considered to be the case of *Collector of Bombay* v. *Municipal Corpn., Bombay*[54], wherein the view was expressed by Chandra Shekhar Aiyar, J., that holding out of the promise by the Government was binding on the Government and that a court of equity must prevent the perpetration of a legal fraud. *Anglo-Afghan case*[55], a leading case on the point accepted this view in 1968. It was in this case that Shah, J., applying the principle against the Government exploded the doctrine of executive necessity as a defence. He observed:[56]

> "Under our jurisprudence the government is not exempt from liability to carry out the representation made by it as to its future conduct and it cannot on some undefined and undisclosed ground of necessity or expediency fail to carry out the promise solemnly made by it, nor claim to be the judge of its own obligation to the citizen on an ex parte appraisement of the circumstances in which the obligation has arisen."

Had this defence been allowed it would have been very easy for the executive to take away the constitutional rights of the people. In other words to allow such powers to the executive would be to strike at the very root of the rule of law. Justice to an individual has been the underlying principle of this doctrine and the *Aglo-Afghan case*[57] balances the administrative flexibility against justice to an individual.

Public bodies are as much bound by the principle as private individuals. In *Century Spinning & Manufacturing Co. Ltd.* v. *Ulhasnagar Municipal Council*[58], the principle was applied to a public body because the court ordinarily would not allow different standards of conduct for the people and the public bodies. Similarly in case of purely executive functions of the State,[59] in regard to schemes of administrative nature and administrative directions and orders[60] the doctrine has

---

54. *Collector of Bombay* v. *Bombay Municipal Corpn.*, AIR 1951 SC 469: 1952 SCR 43: 54 Bom LR 122. See *Food Corpn. of India* v. *Babulal Agrawal*, (2004) 2 SCC 712; *Bannari Amman Sugars Ltd.* v. *CTO*, (2005) 1 SCC 625 (party invoking this doctrine must lay down positive foundation with supportive material in the petition itself. Court should consider the result to be achieved and for public good, Keeping in mind the fundamental principles of equity tax matter); *State of Karnataka* v. *Sangappa Dyavappa Biradar*, (2005) 4 SCC 264; *Bangalore Development Authority* v. *R. Hanuamaiah*, (2005) 12 SCC 508 (Basis and essence of the doctrine restated); *Larsen and Toubro Ltd.* v. *Union of India*, (2005) 3 SCC 654 (case-law discussed); *Rom Industries Ltd.* v. *State of J&K*, (2005) 7 SCC 348 (Premature withdrawal of promissory estoppel.)
55. *Union of India* v. *Anglo-Afghan Agencies*, AIR 1968 SC 718: (1968) 2 SCR 366.
56. AIR 1968 SC 718, 728; *Union of India* v. *Anglo-Afghan Agencies*; see *Vasantkumar Radhakisan Vora* v. *Board of Trustees of the Port of Bombay*, (1991) 1 SCC 761.
57. *Union of India* v. *Anglo-Afghan Agencies*, AIR 1968 SC 718: (1968) 2 SCR 366.
58. *Century Spinning & Manufacturing Co. Ltd.* v. *Ulhasnagar Municipal Council*, (1970) 1 SCC 582; *Prakash Warehousing Co.* v. *Municipal Corpn. of Greater Bombay*, (1991) 2 SCC 304 (eviction from corporation premises).
59. *Bhim Singh* v. *State of Haryana*, (1981) 2 SCC 673.
60. AIR 1968 SC 718, supra; *Kothari Oil Products Co., Rajkot* v. *Govt. of Gujarat*, AIR 1982 Guj 107; *Amratlal Ramanlal* v. *State of Gujarat*, AIR 1972 Guj 260; *Sardar Vallabhbhai Patel Memorial Society* v. *State of Gujarat*, (1983) 2 GLR 1329; *Satish Sabharwal* v. *State of Maharashtra*, supra.

been applied. Even in case of Universities,[61] municipality,[62] a trust[63] and in cases where there is manifest injustice[64] the doctrine has been pressed into service. The decision in *Anglo-Afghan case*[65] thus came to be followed in many areas. The principle, however, found its powerful exponent in Bhagwati, J., in *Motilal Sugar*[66]. At this juncture it should be noted that the authority of the *Motilal Sugar*[67] was sought to be shaken by *Jit Ram case*[68] wherein it was observed that *Motilal decision*[69] was "not in accordance with the view consistently taken by the Supreme Court in some respects".[70] However the conflict was resolved by the Supreme Court in *Godfrey Philips*[71]. Regarding *Jit Ram*[72] which "takes a slightly different view and holds that the doctrine of promissory estoppel is not available against the exercise of executive functions of the State and the State cannot be prevented from exercising its functions under the law",[73] the Court said that considering both the decisions "we are clearly of the view that what has been laid down in *Motilal Sugar*[74] represents the correct law in regard to the doctrine of promissory estoppel and we express our disagreement with the observations in *Jit Ram case*[75] to the extent that they conflict with the statement of the law in *Motilal Sugar*[76] and introduce reservations cutting down the full width and amplitude of the propositions of law laid down in that case".[77] *Motilal Sugar*[78] thus overruled *Jit Ram*[79] and put the law of promissory estoppel on sound basis, establishing that the application of the principle is a necessary instrument in the hands of the court to control arbitrary exercise of discretion by government departments. This view was fully endorsed in a recent case of *Gujarat State Financial Corpn.* v. *Lotus Hotels (P) Ltd.*[80]. The Corporation first sanctioned a loan of Rs 29.93 lacs to Lotus Hotels for construction of a hotel by creating an equitable mortgage. The plaintiff relying thereon proceeded to act and execute the project, but subsequently the Corporation changed its mind and refused to disburse it. Relying upon the decision

61. *Sangeeta Srivastava* v. *Prof U.N. Singh*, AIR 1980 Del 27; *Hardwari Lal* v. *G.D. Tapase*, AIR 1982 P&H 439: ILR (1982) 1 P&H 223.
62. *Century Spg. & Mfg. Co. Ltd.* v. *Ulhasnagar Municipal Council*, (1970) 1 SCC 582.
63. *Atam Nagar Coop. House Building Society Ltd.* v. *State of Punjab*, AIR 1979 P&H 196.
64. *M. Ramanatha Pillai* v. *State of Kerala*, (1973) 2 SCC 650.
65. *Union of India* v. *Anglo-Afghan Agencies*, AIR 1968 SC 718: (1968) 2 SCR 366.
66. *Motilal Padampat Sugar Mills Co. Ltd.* v. *State of U.P.*, (1979) 2 SCC 409.
67. *Ibid.*
68. *Jit Ram Shiv Kumar* v. *State of Haryana*, (1981) 1 SCC 11, 37.
69. *Motilal Padampat Sugar Mills Co. Ltd.* v. *State of U.P.*, (1979) 2 SCC 409.
70. *Jit Ram Shiv Kumar* v. *State of Haryana*, (1981) 1 SCC 11, 37.
71. *Union of India* v. *Godfrey Philips India Ltd.*, (1985) 4 SCC 369.
72. *Jit Ram Shiv Kumar* v. *State of Haryana*, (1981) 1 SCC 11, 37.
73. *Union of India* v. *Godfrey Philips India Ltd.*, (1985) 4 SCC 369, at p. 387.
74. *Motilal Padampat Sugar Mills Co. Ltd.* v. *State of U.P.*, (1979) 2 SCC 409.
75. *Jit Ram Shiv Kumar* v. *State of Haryana*, (1981) 1 SCC 11, 37.
76. *Motilal Padampat Sugar Mills Co. Ltd.* v. *State of U.P.*, (1979) 2 SCC 409.
77. *Union of India* v. *Godfrey Philips India Ltd.*, (1985) 4 SCC 369.
78. *Motilal Padampat Sugar Mills Co. Ltd.* v. *State of U.P.*, (1979) 2 SCC 409.
79. *Jit Ram Shiv Kumar* v. *State of Haryana*, (1981) 1 SCC 11, 37.
80. (1983) 3 SCC 379.

in *Motilal Sugar*[81] the Supreme Court ruled that the Corporation was bound by its promise and must discharge its statutory duty; the decision in *Jit Ram*[82] could not save the Corporation. This is because "when the officer acts within the scope of his authority under a scheme and enters into an agreement and makes a representation and a person acting on that representation puts himself in a disadvantageous position, the Court is entitled to require the officer to act according to the scheme and the agreement or representation. The officer cannot arbitrarily act on his mere whim and ignore his promise on some undefined and undisclosed grounds of necessity or change the conditions to the prejudice of the person who had acted upon such representation and put himself in a disadvantageous position".[83] Similarly in *Tapti Oil Industries* v. *State of Maharashtra*[84], the State Government was compelled to provide incentives to an industrial concern and fulfil its promise; in *Kothari Oil Products*[85] it was made to act on its promise of granting sales tax free loan for five years to a firm and in *Sardar Vallabhbhai Patel Memorial Society*[86] it was estopped from going back upon its promise where the applicants had altered their position due to representation. Besides, in a number of cases[87] the principle has been affirmed and applied in areas of grant of largesse[88] and policy making.[89]

---

81. *Motilal Padampat Sugar Mills Co. Ltd.* v. *State of U.P.*, (1979) 2 SCC 409.
82. *Jit Ram Shiv Kumar* v. *State of Haryana*, (1981) 1 SCC 11, 37.
83. *Ibid.*
84. AIR 1984 Bom 161: (1984) 56 STC 193.
85. *Kothari Oil Products Co., Rajkot* v. *Govt. of Gujarat*, AIR 1982 Guj 107.
86. (1983) 2 GLR 1329.
87. *Century Spining & Manufacturing Co. Ltd.* v. *Ulhasnagar Municipal Council*, (1970) 1 SCC 582 (principle applied to public body); *Turner Morrison & Co. Ltd.* v. *Hungerford Investment Trust Ltd.*, (1972) 1 SCC 857 (principle affirmed); *Radhakrishna Agarwal* v. *State of Bihar*, (1977) 3 SCC 457 (lease for collection of Sal seeds—principle approved); *Kusheshwar Singh* v. *State of Bihar*, AIR 1974 Pat 267; *Khunnoo Lall and Sons* v. *Union of India*, AIR 1974 All 170; *Laghu Udyog Karmachari Co-operative Housing Society Ltd.* v. *State of M.P.*, AIR 1975 MP 93; *S.K.G. Sugar Ltd.* v. *State of Bihar*, AIR 1975 Pat 123; *M.P. Sugar Mills* v. *State of U.P.*, (1979) 2 SCC 409 (principle affirmed and explained. Exceptions carved out. Principle refined laying down that it is a weapon of offence too, i.e., can found a cause of action); *Kothari Oil Products Co., Rajkot* v. *Govt. of Gujarat*, AIR 1982 Guj 107 (State compelled to fulfil its promise of S.T. free loan); *Bhim Singh* v. *State of Haryana*, (1981) 2 SCC 673 (assurance by Govt. to its employees); *S.V. Patel Memorial Society* v. *State of Gujarat*, (1983) 2 GLR 1329 (principle applied to administrative orders of the Government); *Satish Sabharwal* v. *State of Maharashtra*, (1986) 2 SCC 362 (principle applied in land case, compensation & interest on investment granted); *Garments International (P) Ltd.* v. *Union of India*, AIR 1991 Kant 52 (principle applied in export assistance scheme announced by Central Government).
88. *Chowgule & Co. (P) Ltd.* v. *Union of India*, AIR 1972 Goa 33; *Amratlal Ramanlal* v. *State of Gujarat*, AIR 1972 Guj 260; *S.K.G. Sugar Ltd.* v. *State of Bihar*, AIR 1978 Pat 157; *K.C. Rout* v. *State of Orissa*, AIR 1979 Ori 120: ILR (1979) 1 Cut 412; *Hrudananda* v. *Revenue Divisional Commr., Cuttack*, AIR 1979 Ori 13.
89. *Abodha Kumar Mohapatra* v. *State of Orissa*, AIR 1969 Ori 80: ILR 1968 Cut 587; *State of Punjab* v. *Amrit Banaspati Co. Ltd.*, AIR 1977 P&H 268; *J.S. Vanaspati Ltd.* v. *Union of India*, AIR 1979 Del 122: ILR (1978) 2 Del 722; *Atam Nagar Coop. House Building Society Ltd.* v. *State of Punjab*, AIR 1979 P&H 196; *Bakul Cashew Co.* v. *STO*, (1986) 2 SCC 365; *D.C.M.* v. *Rajasthan SEB*, (1986) 2 SCC 431, *supra*.

Very recently the doctrine moved into the area of service jurisprudence. In *Surya Narain*[90], the question was about the absorption of trainee engineers and the State Electricity Board of Bihar failed to stand up to its representations to absorb them. The engineers had foregone opportunities to seek employments and in the process had become age-barred for any public employment. Reversing the High Court's judgment by applying the doctrine Misra, J., of the Supreme Court upheld the claim of State Electricity Board engineers and directed the Board to absorb them. In *Jatinder Kumar*[91], it was held that selection and recommendation of candidates by the Selection Board to the government by a notification issued, was only an invitation to the candidates to apply for selection for recruitment. It was not any promise held out that the selection would be made or the selected candidates would be appointed. This therefore did not create any right in the candidates and consequently the doctrine would not apply. Similarly the doctrine was not applied where the facts indicated that the Central Excise Department was inveigled into a trap by the respondent, the *Atul Products Ltd.*[92] and at the same time it did not do anything prejudicial to its interest relying upon the representation made on behalf of the department. After 1979, the year 1985 is memorable for two important decisions by the Supreme Court in this area: *Godfrey Philips*[93] and *Express Newspapers*[94].

In the first case the question was about charging excise duty on secondary or final packing. The Central Board of Excise and Customs, as a result of representations by cigarette manufacturers to exempt them from charge of excise duty on secondary packing, replied that no tax would be charged on secondary packing but subsequently on November 2, 1982 on reconsideration the secondary packing was sought to be charged to excise. The Court applied the principle of promissory estoppel and no excise was chargeable during May 24, 1976 and November 1, 1982 as the representation which was within the powers of the department to make and which was not contrary to law was binding on the government. This case bears great importance for it not only applied the doctrine but also reiterated that *besides a weapon of defence, it is a weapon of offence,* the law laid down in *Motilal Sugar case*[95] is the correct law and the decision in *Jit Ram case*[96] was overruled to the extent it conflicted with the statement of law in *Motilal Sugar*[97]. In the second case A.P. Sen, J., of the Supreme Court estopped the Governor of Delhi from acting arbitrarily and ruled that the successor government was clearly bound by the decision taken by the Minister particularly when it had been acted upon. In other words

90. *Surya Narain Yadav* v. *Bihar State Electricity Board*, (1985) 3 SCC 38; see also *C. Chenga Reddy* v. *State of A.P.*, (1996) 10 SCC 193: 1996 SCC (Cri) 1205: 1996 Cri LJ 3461.
91. *Jatinder Kumar* v. *State of Punjab*, (1985) 1 SCC 122.
92. *D.R. Kohli* v. *Atul Products Ltd.*, (1985) 2 SCC 77.
93. *Union of India* v. *Godfrey Philips India Ltd.*, (1985) 4 SCC 369.
94. *Express Newspapers (P) Ltd.* v. *Union of India*, (1986) 1 SCC 133.
95. *Motilal Padampat Sugar Mills Co. Ltd.* v. *State of U.P.*, (1979) 2 SCC 409.
96. *Jit Ram Shiv Kumar* v. *State of Haryana*, (1981) 1 SCC 11, 37.
97. *Motilal Padampat Sugar Mills Co. Ltd.* v. *State of U.P.*, (1979) 2 SCC 409.

the government was precluded by promissory estoppel from questioning the Minister for granting the approval as the Minister had acted within the scope of his authority in granting permission of the lessor to the lessee, the Express Newspapers to build. Here the principle was used to stop fraud on power. The principle has thus moved in a wide area in Administrative Law for doing justice to an individual and to control arbitrary action of the government.[1]

Limitations

Limitations of the doctrine, however, cannot be overlooked. The doctrine obviously (1) cannot apply against the State legislature[2]; and (2) to Acts of Parliament because they are no representations; [3] (3) no one can be compelled to act against the statute.[4] The government or public authority cannot be compelled to carry out a representation or promise[5] which is contrary to law or which was outside the authority or power of the officer of the government or of the public authority to make.[6] (4) Even where the liability or obligation is imposed by statute[7] or (5) where there is statutory prohibition[8] or (6) where there is no representation or promise made out by government the principle does not apply.[9] (7) In public law the most obvious limitation on the doctrine is that it cannot be evoked so as to give an overriding power which it does not possess. That is, no estoppel can legitimate action which is ultra vires.[10] (8) The doctrine does not operate at the level of government policy[11], however, it operates against public authority in minor matters of formality where no question of ultra vires arises.[12] Similarly (9) the advice given by a negligent officer cannot

---

1. *Arun Kumar*, (1988) 21 R (J&K) 491; *Suresh Pal* v. *State of Haryana*, (1987) 2 SCC 445 (education); *Delhi Cloth & General Mills* v. *Union of India*, (1988) 1 SCC 86 (Railway department); *R.K. Deka* v. *Union of India*, AIR 1992 Del 53; *Amrit Banaspati Co. Ltd.* v. *State of Punjab*, (1992) 2 SCC 411: (1992) 59 ELT 13 (representation when binding on Govt.); *N.A. Mohammed Kasim* v. *Sulochana*, 1995 Supp (3) SCC 128: AIR 1995 SC 1624 (applicable against private party); *C. Chenga Reddy* v. *State of A.P.*, (1996) 10 SCC 193: 1996 SCC (Cri) 1205: 1996 Cri LJ 3461 (in field of service law).
2. *M. Ramanatha Pillai* v. *State of Kerala*, (1973) 2 SCC 650; *Union of India* v. *Godfrey Philips India Ltd.*, (1985) 4 SCC 369.
3. *Godfrey Philips*, supra; *Jasjeet Films Pvt. Ltd.* v. *DDA*, AIR 1980 Del 83.
4. *Kedar Lal Verma* v. *Secy., Board of High School and Intermediate Education*, AIR 1980 All 32; *Paradise Printers* v. *Union Territory, Chandigarh*, (1988) 21 R (SC) 223.
5. *Vidyaranyanagar Petty Shop-Keepers' Assn.* v. *Corpn. of City of Bangalore*, (1986) 4 R (Ker) 13 (SP); *Vasantkumar Radhakisan Vohra* v. *Board of Trustees of the Port of Bombay*, (1991) 1 SCC 761.
6. (1985) 4 SCC 369, *supra*.
7. (1979) 2 SCC 409, supra; *Kedarlal*, supra; *CIT* v. *B.N. Bhattacharjee*, (1979) 4 SCC 121.
8. (1985) 4 SCC 369, *supra*.
9. *Jatinder Kumar* v. *State of Punjab*, (1985) 1 SCC 122; *Excise Commr.* v. *Ram Kumar*, (1976) 3 SCC 540.
10. *Express Newspapers (P) Ltd.* v. *Union of India*, (1986) 1 SCC 133; *Vasantkumar Vohra case*.
11. *LIC of India* v. *Bangalore LIC Employees' Housing Co-op. Society Ltd.*, (1988) 23 R (Karn) 113.
12. *Ibid*.

change the legal position and hence the doctrine has no application.[13] (10) Lastly, where there is fraud or collusion[14], (11) where the public interest suffers[15] and where (12) it would be inequitable[16] to endorse the doctrine[17], it will not be applied.

Conclusion

Estoppel is thus, a complex legal notion involving a combination of several essential elements[18], which have been enumerated ante.[19] Accordingly it matters not whether the transferor acted fraudulently or innocently in making the representation and that what is material is that he did make a representation and the transferee had acted upon it. Where the transferee knows as a fact that the transferor does not possess which he represents he has, he cannot be said to have acted on it when taking the transfer. The transfer fails.[20] Moreover estoppel is not a cause of action but it is only a rule of evidence, you cannot found an action upon estoppel.[21] It is *a rule of equity* flowing out of fairness striking on behaviour deficient in good faith.[22] Though it is *a branch of the law of evidence* it is also capable of being viewed as *a substantive rule of law* insofar as it helps to create or defeat rights, which would not exist, or be taken away, but for that doctrine. It may have the effect of creating substantive rights as against the

---

13. *Asstt. Custodian, Evacuee Property* v. *B.K. Agarwala*, (1975) 1 SCC 21; *see also* (1985) 4 SCC 369, *supra*.
14. *D.R. Kohli* v. *Atul Products Ltd.*, (1985) 2 SCC 77; *Haripada Das* v. *Utkal University*, AIR 1978 Ori 68; *Satish Kumar Rao* v. *Gorakhpur University*, AIR 1981 All 377.
15. (1979) 2 SCC 409, *supra*: *Kedarlal*, supra; *CIT* v. *B.N. Bhattacharjee*, supra; (1981) 1 SCC 11, *supra*; see also *Delhi Development Authority* v. *Ravindra Mohan Aggarwal*, (1999) 3 SCC 172 according to which estoppel does not operate where considerations of public interest are involved.
16. (1979) 2 SCC 409, *supra*.
17. *Asstt. Commr. of Commercial Taxes* v. *Dharnendra Trading Co.*, (1988) 3 SCC 570: (1988) 25 R (SC) 355. See also *State of M.P* v. *G.S. Dall & Flour Mills*, 1992 Supp (1) SCC 150: (1991) 187 ITR 487 (revocation of exemption); *Indian Aluminium Co. Ltd* v. *Karnataka Electricity Board*, (1992) 3 SCC 580, 607 (in area of statutory power); *Pine Chemicals Ltd.* v. *Assessing Authority*, (1992) 2 SCC 683, 703 (no right derived from Minister's speech); *Amrit Banaspati Co. Ltd.* v. *State of Punjab*, (1992) 2 SCC 411: AIR 1992 SC 1075; *Asstt. Excise Commissioner* v. *Issac Peter*, (1994) 4 SCC 104, 123: (1994) 1 KLT 698: (1994) KLJ 645; *Home Secy., U.T. of Chandigarh* v. *Darshjit Singh Grewal*, (1993) 4 SCC 25 (acts contrary to law or ultra vires the Govt. power); *Shabi Construction Co.* v. *City & Industrial Development Corpn.*, (1995) 4 SCC 301 (acts contrary to law); *Kumari Madhuri Patil* v. *Addl. Commr., Tribal Development*, (1994) 6 SCC 241, 257: 1994 SCC (L&S) 1349: (1994) 28 ATC 259: (1994) 5 SLR 206 (social status certificate obtained fraudulently); *S.V.R. Mudaliar* v. *Rajabu F. Buhari*, (1995) 4 SCC 15: AIR 1995 SC 1607 (persons playing foul with equity); *Ester Industries Ltd.* v. *U.P. SEB*, (1996) 11 SCC 199 (where there is a duly executed contract); *I.T.C. Bhadrachalam Paperboards* v. *Mandal Revenue Officer*, (1996) 6 SCC 634 (no estoppel against statute); *Union Territory, Chandigarh Admn.* v. *Managing Society, Goswami GDSDC*, (1996) 7 SCC 665: AIR 1996 SC 1759; *D.C.M. Ltd.* v. *Union of India*, (1996) 5 SCC 468 (doctrine not limited to its application only to defence but it can also find a cause of action).
18. *B.L. Sreedhar* v. *K.M. Munireddy*, (2003) 1 ILD 185 (SC).
19. Under Caption "*Essentials and basis.*"
20. *Jumma Masjid Mercara* v. *Kodimaniandra Deviah*, AIR 1962 SC 847.
21. Lindley L.J. *in Low* v. *Bouvenia*, (1831) 3 Ch 82, 101.
22. See *Indira Bai* v. *Nand Kishore*, (1990) 4 SCC 668.

person estopped. An estoppel which enables a party as against another party to claim a right or property which in fact he does not possess is described as *estoppel by negligence or by conduct* or *by representation* or *by holding out* ostensible authority. Estoppel, then, may itself be the *foundation of a right* as against the person estopped, and indeed, if it were not so, it is difficult to see what protection the principle of estoppel can afford to the person by whom it may be invoked or what disability it can create in the person against whom it operates in cases affecting rights. Where rights are involved estoppel may with equal justification be described both as a rule of evidence and as a rule creating or defeating rights.[23]

There is no estoppel in Income Tax.—Merely because the assessee wrongly included the income in its return for a particular year, it cannot confer jurisdiction on the department to tax that income in that year, even though legally such income did not pertain to that year.[24]

Estoppel is different from admission.—Admissions being declarations against an interest are good evidence but they are not conclusive and a party is always at liberty to withdraw admissions by proving that they are either mistaken or untrue. But estoppel creates an absolute bar.[25]

As held in *Banwari Amman Sugars Ltd.* v. *CTO* the party invoking this doctrine must lay down positive foundation therefore with supporting material in the petition itself. While applying the principle the court has to do equity and the fundamental principles of equity must for ever be present in the mind of the court.[26]

The soul and "basis of the doctrine is the interposition of equity" which "always true to form has stepped in to mitigate the rigours of strict law".[27] The Principle stands on honesty and good faith of public bodies. Also in *Express Newspapers*[28] (relying on Prof Smith and Prof Wade) A.P. Sen, J., observed that:

> "Estoppel is often described as a rule of evidence, but more correctly it is a principle of law. As a principle of law it applies only to representations about past or present facts. But there is also an equitable principle of "promissory estoppel" which can apply to public authorities."

---

23. *B.L. Sreedhar* v. *K.M. Munireddy*, (2003) 1 ILD 185 (SC).
24. *CIT* v. *Bharat General Reinsurance Co. Ltd.*, (1971) 81 ITR 303 (Del). See *Mycon Construction Ltd* v. *State of Karnataka*, (2003) 9 SCC 583: AIR 2002 SC 2089 (Inapplicability of equity to tax matters. Sales Tax Act, Karnataka.); *CST* v. *Shri Krishna Engineering Co.*, (2005) 2 SCC 692.
25. *Chhaganlal Keshavlal Mehta* v. *Patel Narandas Haribhai*, (1982) 1 SCC 223: (1982) 2 SCR 166.
26. (2005) 1 SCC 625: (2005) 139 STC 86: (2005) 1 KLT 601 (doctrine restated); *see* also *Food Corpn. of India* v. *Babulal Agrawal*, (2004) 2 SCC 712.
27. *Ibid.*, p. 630.
28. *Express Newspapers (P) Ltd.* v. *Union of India*, (1986) 1 SCC 133; *Union of India* v. *Godfrey Philips India Ltd.*, (1985) 4 SCC 369.

Furthermore in words of Hedge, J.:

> "The principle has gained new dimensions in recent years. A new class of estoppel, i.e., promissory estoppel has come to be recognised by the courts in this country... . The full implication of promissory estoppel is yet to be spelled out. The rule advances the cause of justice.[29] The Delhi High Court echoed this very idea in *Jasjeet*[30] and signalled that the equitable remedies must be adjusted according to circumstances and genuine public interest."

This doctrine which was born in equity, was married to contract in the field of consideration and which is now flirting with administrative law to have its due place is now *not only a weapon of defence but also a weapon of offence* and consequently the law laid down in *Low* v. *Bouverie*[31] that estoppel is not a cause of action is no longer applicable in India. The doctrine exists for controlling a legal fraud and that it can found a cause of action. This is the refinement of the doctrine.

However, its proper place is now well established in Administrative Law, it must be noted.[32]

(*vii*) *Restitution of benefits on cancellation of transaction.*—It is but proper justice to return the benefits of a contract which was voidable, and, equity enforced this principles in cases where it granted relief of recession of a contract. If *A* induces *B* by fraud to enter into a contract and when the same is set aside at the instance of *B*, *B* has to restore any benefit he may have received from *A* and to make compensation to *A* as the justice of the case may require. A party cannot be allowed to take advantage of his own wrong.[33]

So far as the infants' contracts are concerned, the position is peculiar. At Common Law all contracts, barring contracts of necessaries and contracts of beneficial services made by an infant were voidable at his option. This attitude of the Common Law landed the other party to such contracts into difficulties. Besides, a cloak of protection was thrown round the infants so that a contract could not be converted into a tort and vice versa. This position generated a number of cases of fraud by infants and equity had to intervene because infancy is no license to commit a fraud. Equity therefore obliged them to make restitution where the things procured by contract were in the infant's possession. But in cases of goods procured and consumed, moneys obtained and spent, what is to be done? In *Leslie* v. *Sheill*[34], the defendant by misrepresenting his age obtained money of which the lender claimed repayment. Lord Summer held that the action was not maintainable because the moment the identity of the goods in the infant's hands was lost, there was no means of tracing them and therefore

29. Hegde, J., in *Turner Morrison & Co. Ltd.* v. *Hungerford Investment Trust Ltd.*, (1972) 1 SCC 857.
30. AIR 1980 Del 83.
31. (1891) 3 Ch 82.
32. *See* Bhagwati. C.J., in *Union of India* v. *Godfrey Philips India Ltd.*, (1985) 4 SCC 369; *see* (1986) 3 SCC (Jour) 45.
33. *Priyanka Overseas (P) Ltd.* v. *Union of India*, 1991 Supp (1) SCC 102.
34. (1914) 3 KB 607.

restitution was made impossible. To force him to pay for such goods would amount to enforcing a contract which was quite improper. Therefore "restitution stopped where repayment began". This is, then, the limit of this doctrine that no compensation can be ordered where the contract is void.[35]

(viii) Set-off.—Where there have been mutual credits, mutual debts or other natural dealings between the debtor and any creditor, the sum due from one party is to be set-off against any sum due from the other party, and only the balance of the account is to be claimed or paid on either side respectively.[36]

Formerly the defence of cross-claim was not available at Common Law while according to natural equity cross-demands should compensate each other and the difference was the only sum due.[37] At Common Law each party was left to his own, to sue separately for their sums.[38]

Under Queen Anne's reign only mutually connected debts were allowed to be set-off at law. In 1705 set-off was allowed in bankruptcy cases and during the reign of George II the "statute of set-off" was passed but it did not apply to goods or specific things detained. But equity allowed the defendant to resist a claim on the ground of his countervailing claim. This was done on the grounds of justice and prevention of multiplicity of actions. For this purpose equity evolved a principle that the plaintiff would be allowed the remedies of investigation and enforcement of his right on the condition that he should be prepared to allow the defendant's claim together with his own. The court had jurisdiction to determine validity of equitable set-off and a claim for equitable set-off was not available as a matter of right, but it lay in discretion of court to entertain.[39]

Equity courts exercised this jurisdiction independently and even before the existence of the statutes of set-off and exercised it even beyond the law. There is now no difference between set-off at law and in equity.

The following are the salient features for a set-off claim:—

(1) that the claim should not be a time-barred one,

(2) that it should be of a liquidated sum,

(3) that the claim was to be enforceable by action,

(4) that the parties must be the same,

(5) that the claim should exist in the same right,

(6) that the assignee of the defendant may claim set-off, and

---

35. *Thurston* v. *Notingham P.B. Building Society*, (1902) 1 Ch 1.

36. *Snell's Principles of Equity*, p. 313. For details on set-off in bankruptcy see *Williams on Bankruptcy*, 18th Edn., 1968, p. 207 and *N.W. Bank Ltd.* v. *Halesowen Press Work and Assemblies Ltd.*, 1972 AC 785.

37. Bhagwati, J., in *Motilal Padampat Sugar Mills Co. Ltd.* v. *State of U.P.*, (1979) 2 SCC 409, 425; Walker: *The Oxford Companion to Law*, (1980), pp. 432-33; *Sardar Vallabhbhai Patel Memorial Society* v. *State*, (1983) 2 GLR 1329: AIR 1984 NOC 16 (Guj).

38. *Green* v. *Farmer*, 1 Burr 2220 *per* Lord Mansfield.

39. *Union of India* v. *Karam Chand Thapar & Bros. (Coal Sales) Ltd.*, (2004) 3 SCC 504.

(7) that a third party's equity must not be affected or prejudiced thereby and if the demand for set-off arose out of the same transaction even unascertained sums were allowed. Provided equitable grounds for protection of defendant's right existed, the Equity Courts went beyond the law and gave relief on the principle that he who seeks equity must do equity.

(8) The cross-demands must arise out of the same transaction or the demands must be so connected in their nature and circumstances that they can be looked upon as part of one transaction. In *Laximchand and Balchand case* the amount claimed by the State Government under a separate contract on the ground that the contractor had committed a breach of that contract could not be allowed to be adjusted against the decretal amount. This was so because there was no evidence bringing the Government's claim to adjustment within the operation of the doctrine as the amount sought to be adjusted had yet to be determined as a liability against the contractor[40] (*see* Order 21, Rules 18 and 2).

(*ix*) *Waiver.*—For its lotteries, the government appointed an organising agent under an agreement. The agent failed to deposit agency fee and prize money for several draws. State condoned his past lapses and defaults on condition of his good conduct. Due to further defaults state terminated his agency. The agent sued the state for damages under Contract Act, 1872. (Ss. 54, 63, 73). Held States Condonation would not amount to a perpetual waiver of agent's lapses and defaults. Agent has behaved against equitable principle, that "He who seeks Equity must do Equity." State-conduct does not amount to perpetual waiver.[41]

(*c*) *Limitations of the maxim.*—(*i*) In order that Equity courts can stretch their helping hands to a defendant by applying this maxim, the demand for an equitable relief must arise from a suit that is pending. That is to say, it should arise from the same transaction, or the same subject-matter. To cases wherein it arose from two different suits, the maxim will not apply.

(*ii*) This maxim is applicable to a party who seeks an equitable relief. Those who wish to prosecute and exercise their legal rights and ask for legal relief from a court of equity will not be allowed to avail the benefit of this maxim.

(*d*) *Recognition in India.*—(*i*) *Indian Contract Act*, Under Section 19-A of the Indian Contract Act contracts entered into under undue influence are voidable and therefore a party to a contract who has the option of getting the contract declared void will have to return the benefits so obtained to the party from whom he obtained it under such contract. This is but proper, because one

---

40. *Lakshmichand and Balchand* v. *State of A.P.*, (1987) 1 SCC 19, 21, 22: AIR 1987 SC 20.
41. *Krishna Bahadur* v. *Purna Theatre*, (2004) 8 SCC 229: AIR 2004 SC 4282. See also *Sikkim Subba Associates* v. *State of Sikkim*, (2001) 5 SCC 629 (Past defaults waived upon future good conduct. This does not amount to perpetual waiver. The maxim reiterated.)

cannot benefit twice.[42] One cannot opt out of the liabilities of a contract and at the same time retain the benefits which he obtained from such contract.[43]

In *Mohori Bibee* v. *Dharmodas Ghose*[44], as an infant's contract was void, no directions for repayment were made because as decided in *Tahal Singh* v. *Bisseswar Lal*[45], "it is not every case in which a man has benefited by the money of another, that an obligation to repay the money arises... . To raise an equity of that kind there must be an obligation express or implied to repay". Thus the maxim works here satisfactorily. In *Allcard* v. *Skinner*, Lindley, L.J., said: "The equitable doctrine of undue influence has grown out of and been developed by the necessity of grappling with insidious forms of spiritual tyranny and with the infinite varieties of fraud."

(*ii*) *Transfer of Property Act.*—Under the Transfer of Property Act, Section 35 embodies the principle of election which rests on the principle of "approbate and reprobate" as is known in Scotland[46], meaning thereby that a man shall not be allowed to approbate and reprobate. This principle in India rest on forfeiture while in England it rests on compensation. A party who elects against the document has to compensate the disappointed donee and the rest he can retain; while in India the refractory donee's interest is forfeited.

In *Devan case*[47], which was under Section 54 of the Transfer of Property Act, where land was purchased under genuine sale deeds by different persons from a common vendor, out of a large plot of land and where there were allegations of encroachment by one against the other, the Supreme Court directed that the shortfall of land was to be suffered by both the parties in equal proportions in order to safeguard their interests. And this was on equitable considerations arising under the maxim.

Section 51 of the Transfer of Property Act is also based on this maxim and enjoins that he who seeks equity must do equity. It explains the position of a person with a defective title who makes improvements on the land in his possession, believing that he is absolutely entitled to it. But when the rightful owner who has a better title, evicts such a person from the property, he will have to pay for the improvements as on the date of eviction[48] on the principle that he did not stop the person in possession from making improvements. Thus the owner is estopped by his conduct. It will be interesting to note here the difference between Section 115 of the Indian Evidence Act and Section 51 of the Transfer of Property Act. In the former it is based on the true owner's conduct, while the latter is based on the belief of the person making

42. *Subhas Chandra Das* v. *Ganga Prasad*, AIR 1967 SC 878; *Allcard* v. *Skinner*, (1887) 36 Ch D 145.
43. Sections 64 and 65, Indian Contract Act.
44. ILR (1903) 30 Cal 539 (PC).
45. (1875) 2 IA 131, 143.
46. *Snell's Principles of Equity*, 484; *Pitman* v. *Chum Ewing*, 1911 AC 217.
47. *G.N. Devan* v. *Habibunnissa*, 1987 Supp SCC 688.
48. *J. Narayan Rao* v. *Basavarayappa*, AIR 1956 SC 727.

improvements. Section 51 requires the true owner to do equity by paying for improvements.

For this section to apply the following conditions must be satisfied:[49]

(1) The person claiming compensation should not be a trespasser, but a transferee.

(2) He should believe in good faith that he was absolutely entitled to property either as a donee or as a purchaser.

(3) He should have made improvements.

(4) The person attempting to evict must have a better title.

(iii) Specific Relief Act and Indian Trusts Act.—The maxim is illustrated also in Sections 30 and 33 of the Specific Relief Act and Sections 62 and 86 of the Trusts Act.

Under Section 30 of the Specific Relief Act a court may require parties rescinding a contract to do equity by restoring, so far as may be, any benefit which he may have received from the other party, and to make any compensation to him which justice may require.[50] Under Section 33, a court has power to require benefit to be restored or compensation to be made when an instrument is cancelled or is successfully resisted as being void or voidable.

Moreover, it is perfectly open to a court in control of a suit for specific performance to extend the time for deposit. The specific performance, said the Supreme Court, is an equitable relief and he who seeks equity can be put on terms to ensure that equity is done to the opposite party even while granting the relief. The final end of law is justice, and so, the means to it too should be informed by equity. That is why he who seeks equity shall do equity. In this case the assignment of the mortgage is not a quietless discharge of the vendor's debt as implied in the agreement to sell but a disingenuous disguise to arm herself with a mortgage decree to swallow up the property in case the specific performance litigation misfires. To sterilise this decree is necessary equity to which the appellant must submit himself before she can enjoy the fruits of specific performance.[51]

In a recent case of *V.S. Palanichamy Chettiar Firm*, a decree to enforce a contract for sale was granted. The decree was confirmed by High Court without extending time limit for depositing the balance amount. No explanation was given by the decree-holder for omission to deposit the amount within time granted by the trial court. It was held that, equity required that the discretion of the court under Section 28, of the Specific Relief Act, 1963 to extend the time for payment should not be exercised in favour of the respondent decree-holder on the principle that "He who seeks equity must do equity".[52]

---

49. See *Ramsden* v. *Dyson*, (1866) LR 1 HL 129.

50. *Allcard* v. *Skinner*, (1887) 36 Ch 45; *Petherpermal* v. *Muniandi*, 35 Cal 551 (PC).

51. *K. Kalpana Saraswathi* v. *P.S.S. Soma Sundaram Chettiar*, (1980) 1 SCC 630 at p. 633; see also *V.S. Palanichamy Chettiar Firm* v. *C. Alagappan*, (1999) 4 SCC 702.

52. *V.S. Palanichamy Chettiar Firm* v. *C. Alagappan*, (1999) 4 SCC 702, 709-710, para 17.

Similarly, under Section 62 of the Indian Trusts Act, where a beneficiary seeks a declaration of trust or retransfer of trust property wrongfully bought by the trustee, the court will impose upon him an equitable condition to repay the trustee the purchase money with interest plus other legitimate expenses, if any. And Section 86 also imposes an equitable condition to repay to the transferor the consideration received by the transferee under a rescindable contract.

(*iv*) *Civil Procedure Code.*—In *Clerk* v. *Ruthnavaloo*[53], it was decided that equitable set-off can be pleaded in India. Conditions for a legal set-off are considered in Order 8, Rule 6 of the Civil Procedure Code.

4. HE WHO COMES INTO EQUITY MUST COME WITH CLEAN HANDS

(*a*) *Meaning.*—Equity, as it was based on good faith and conscience, demanded fairness, uprightness and good faith not only from the defendant but also from the plaintiff. It is therefore aptly said that "he that hath committed an inequity, shall not have equity". This very idea is expressed in this maxim but in a different terminology. It is well known that *ex turpi causa non oritur actio*, no cause of action arises from a base cause. As said in the previous maxim, he who seeks equity must do equity, that is, one must be prepared and willing to behave and to do what, according to the principles of morality, justice and reason, is fair and just. While applying this maxim the court believed that the behaviour of the plaintiff was not against conscience before he came to the court for its assistance. The previous maxim related to the plaintiff's *conduct inside the court and thereafter*. But this maxim goes a step ahead and expects the plaintiff's conduct above reproach, just and fair *before he comes to the court*. The conduct complained of must have an immediate and necessary connection to the equity sued for. It must be depravity in the legal as well as the moral sense and not a general *depravity*.[54] That is to say, he must be clear of any participation in fraud or similar inequitable conduct.[55] To impose injustice upon another and then to seek the court's assistance smacks like Satan preaching the Bible to his adversaries. It is therefore certain that one who has not acted equitably[56] is not entitled to it, and the doors of the equity courts will be shut against him in the sense that the court will refuse to interfere on his behalf to acknowledge his right or to grant him any relief.

(*b*) *Application and Cases.*—The maxim is very clear when it talks about equitable misconduct, for those who act within the limits of their legal rights are free from any blemish and this has been shown very strikingly by the cases of *Chasemore* v. *Richards*[57] and the *Gloucester* v. *Grammar School case*[58], which go to explain that a legal act does not become illegal merely because of the improper motives of its doer. The misconduct under this maxim is not

53. (1865) 2 Mad HCR 296.
54. *Moody* v. *Cox*, (1917) 2 Ch 71 cited in *Snell's Principles of Equity*.
55. *Abdul Kadar Alibhoy* v. *Mohomedally Hyderally*, 3 Bom LR 220.
56. *Baban* v. *Vishvanath*, AIR 1934 Pat 681; *Mahavir Prasad Jain* v. *Ganga Singh*, (1999) 8 SCC 274.
57. 7 HLC 349.
58. (1410) YB 11 Hen IV FO 47 PL 21.

necessarily that one which constitutes a basis of legal action or punishable as crime. The maxim as has been pronounced in *Mason* v. *Clarke*[59] is so good and active as it might have been in its inception, that even a reprehensible conduct in *a suit matter* is enough to invoke the assistance of the court in applying this maxim. This explains that to bar one's claim, the depravity must have an immediate and necessary relation to the equity sued for.[60]

An early illustration in this regard is the *Highwaymen case*[61]. Two robbers were partners in their own way. Due to a disagreement in shares one of them filed a bill against another for accounts of the profits of robbery. Courts of equity do grant such a relief in case of partnership but here was a case where the cause of action arose from an illegal engagement or occupation. The maxim is *ex turpi causa non oritur actio*, and according to that the Equity Court refused to help them. Not only this, but their solicitors also were taken into custody, fined £ 50 and imprisonment till payment and the counsel who signed the bill was made to pay the costs.

In the case of *Rasiklal Vaghajibhai Patel* v. *Ahmedabad Municipal Corpn.*[62], as the petitioner was guilty of suppression of a material fact of his second employer his Special Leave Petition was dismissed. The petitioner in this case was removed from service on ground of proved misconduct, getting employment in another service by stating in his application that he had voluntarily left the previous service because of transfer. Even though such conduct did not fall within the specified misconduct, the second employer removed him from service considering his act as a misconduct. The petitioner went to the Labour Court and High Court of Gujarat but failed. He therefore filed Special Leave Petition under Article 136, Constitution of India before the Supreme Court which also failed. It was expressly stated by the Court here that persons seeking relief must come before the Court with clean hands.[63]

Similarly, a person who uses the plaintiff's registered label with a view to represent his own wares and manufactures goods resembling those of others does a deliberate wrong. He therefore cannot be allowed to take out an injunction against others restraining them from imitating his label.[64]

Where a minor fraudulently concealing his age induced his trustees to commit a breach of trust and deliver a certain amount, he cannot get assistance from Equity Courts to recover that amount again from them. The basis of this decision was the infant's inequitable conduct.[65]

---

59. 1955 AC 778.
60. *Moody* v. *Cox*, (1917) 2 Ch 71.
61. 9 LQR 197.
62. *Rasiklal Vaghajibhai Patel* v. *Ahmedabad Municipal Corpn.*, (1985) 2 SCC 35.
63. See also *M. Mohmedali* v. *Chief Conservator of Forests, Trivandrum*, AIR 1990 NOC 145 (Ker). See also *Anil Bansal* v. *Ashok Kumar Bansal*, (2005) 9 SCC 368.
64. *Abdulkadar Alibhoy* v. *M.H.*, 3 BLR 220.
65. *Overton* v. *Banister*, (1844) 3 Hare 503.

The maxim is applicable to a plaintiff as well as a defendant.[66] It is applicable to cases of benami transactions. In such transactions property is conveyed in the name of a benamidar but the real person who purchases the property is another. Such transactions are concocted with a particular purpose of fraud and therefore when the purpose has been achieved, the real owner will not be allowed to recover the property.[67]

The working of the maxim could be seen while giving the reliefs of specific performance, injunction, rescission or cancellation. Persons invoking an equitable extraordinary jurisdiction under Article 226 should come with clean hands and should not conceal the material facts.[68] Clean hands is thus a pre-condition to invoke aid of equity.[69] Similarly one cannot abuse the process of Court and yet claim its protection. In the instant case, once the SLP was dismissed for abuse of the process of the Court. However, this fact was not disclosed and a second petition was made which was dismissed for want of clean hands.[70] But in *Ahmed Siddiqui case*[71] it has been held by the Supreme Court that appeal could not be dismissed only on ground that appellant had not approached the court with clean hands.[72]

Moreover it is not necessary that the defence of the plaintiff's unclean hands must proceed from the defendant. If the court is satisfied otherwise than through the defendant of the plaintiff's misconduct or depravity in relation to the claim litigated, it is bound to take notice of it and refuse its assistance to the plaintiff.[73]

(*c*) *Limitation of the maxim.*—While applying this maxim, as it is pointed out before, general or total conduct of the plaintiff is not to be considered. His general conduct may not be satisfactory or praiseworthy but if that has nothing to do with the matter of the suit or if that has no immediate and necessary connection with the equity sued for, the court should not take it into account. In the words of Brandies, J., in *Loughran* v. *Loughran*[74], "equity does not demand that its suitors shall have led blameless lives".

> "What bars a claim is not a general depravity but one which has an immediate and necessary relation to the equity sued for."[75]

(*d*) *Exceptions to the maxim.*—There are two exceptions to the maxim where the requirement of clean hands has been dispensed with:

---

66. *Eastern Mortgage and Agency Co. Ltd.* v. *Raboti Kumar*, 3 CLJ 260.
67. *Guddappa* v. *Balaj*, ILR 1941 Bom 575; *Pitt* v. *Pitt* cited by Wills, A.G.
68. *Ramjas Foundation* v. *Union of India*, 1993 Supp (2) SCC 20, 24: AIR 1993 SC 852.
69. *J.H. Patel* v. *Subhan Khan*, (1996) 5 SCC 312.
70. *S.B. Noronah* v. *Union of India*, (1994) 1 SCC 372.
71. *Ahmad Siddiqui* v. *Prem Nath Kapoor*, (1993) 4 SCC 406, 409: AIR 1993 SC 2525.
72. See also *Prakash Wati* v. *R.L. Kapur*, 1995 Supp (3) SCC 709; *Lalit Kumar Jain* v. *Jaipur Traders Corporation (P) Ltd.*, (2002) 5 SCC 383; *Karnataka Rare Earth* v. *Senior Geologist, Deptt. of Mines & Geology*, (2004) 2 SCC 783.
73. *Gedge* v. *R.E. Assurance Corpn.*, (1900) 2 QB 214.
74. (1934) 292 US 216, 229.
75. *Dering* v. *Earl of W.*, (1787) 1 Cox Eq 378; *Moody* v. *Cox*, (1917) 2 Ch 71 cited by *Snell's Principles of Equity*, p. 32. See also *Duchess of A.*, v. *Duke of A.*, 1967 Ch 302, 332.

(*i*) Where a transaction is against public policy and the plaintiff's hands are tainted, still, however, for the sake of the public, justice has to be given to uphold the policy or the moral values[76] and the parties thereto may be relieved.

(*ii*) Where a party with unclean hands repents for his conduct before his unjust plans are carried out, the court will not stick to the letter of the maxim and will extend its assistance for doing justice.[77]

(*e*) *Recognition in India.*—The principle established in *Overton* v. *Banister* discussed earlier that an infant's receipt for money though ineffectual to discharge a debt, albeit as he obtained the same by misrepresentation, he cannot set up a defence of the invalidity of the receipt given by him, has been incorporated in Section 23 of the Indian Trusts Act.

Similarly, a plaintiff's unfair conduct will disentitle him to an equitable relief of specific performance of the contract under Sections 17, 18 and 20 of the Specific Relief Act, 1963. Where the plaintiff is guilty of sharp practices, fraud and undue influence as detailed under Section 18 or where there is a contract to sell or let property by a plaintiff who has no title as specified under Section 17, specific performance will not be granted to the plaintiff. The jurisdiction to specific performance under Section 20 is discretionary and the court is not bound to grant such a relief merely because it is lawful to do so. The court's discretion is not arbitrary but sound and reasonable, guided by judicial principles and capable of correction, by a court of appeal.

The principle of coming with clean hands has been reiterated by the Allahabad High Court in *Suraj Kumari case*[78]. The Court observed that the High Court should take care of the situation that extraordinary jurisdiction under Article 226 should not be allowed to be misused and in cases where it comes to the conclusion that the petitioner has approached the Court with unclean hands, or has filed a writ petition stating facts, which are false, the petitioner must be visited with penal consequences.

On the same principle, injunctions are granted. But no injunction can be granted for continuance of a legal wrong, or continuance of fraud, invasion of copyright, and continuance of immoral or libellous acts. Reliefs of rescission and cancellation of instruments are also instances of equitable reliefs.

(*f*) *Distinction.*—There is a difference between the present maxim and the previous one in that:

(*i*) The previous maxim does not proceed on the assumption of *existence of any unconscionable conduct* of the plaintiff. Where both the parties have claims to equitable relief against each other, equity courts would grant relief to the plaintiff only on the condition that he should also recognise the defendant's equitable right to relief, instead of driving

76. See *Drury* v. *Hooke*, (1636) 2 Ch Cas 176.
77. (1755) 1 Amb 264.
78. *Suraj Kumari* v. *District Judge, Mirzapur*, AIR 1991 All 75.

him to file a separate suit for the same. That is, the plaintiff seeking equity must do it to the defendant. But where the defendant has no separate claim to relief and the plaintiff's conduct is unfair, this maxim of coming with clean hands would apply and that will disentitle the plaintiff to relief requested by him.

(*ii*) Both the maxims purport to regulate equitable relief and both seem at first sight to be expressing the same thing, but the present maxim is a condition precedent to seeking equitable relief while the preceding maxim exposes the condition subsequent to the relief sought.

(*iii*) The present maxim refers to the plaintiff's conduct before he approaches the court while the preceding maxim refers to the plaintiff's conduct as the court thinks it ought to be, after he comes to the court.

(*iv*) According to the present maxim, if the plaintiff's conduct is unfair and unconscionable, it would not entitle him to the relief sought, while according to the preceding maxim the plaintiff has to mould his behaviour according to the impositions by the court and thus to pay the price to the court in this form for enforcing his equitable claim.

(*v*) Consequently in the preceding maxim the plaintiff has an option or a choice before him either to submit to the conditions put by the court or to get out of the court, while in the present maxim his previous inequitable conduct has taken away and snatched that choice from him. His equitable right therefore can neither be recongised nor enforced.

(*vi*) The present maxim looks to the past, while the preceding one looks to the future.

5. DELAY DEFEATS EQUITIES

"Vigilantibus, non dormentibus, jura subvenient"

(Equity aids the vigilant and not the indolent)

(*a*) *Meaning.*—It is an undisputed axiom that eternal vigilance is the price of liberty. If one sleeps upon his rights, his rights will slip away from him and therefore this maxim has been expressed in a rather different form, shouting to the passive, otiose and the slothful that: "Equity aids the vigilant and not the indolent." Where an injured party has been slow to demand a remedy for a wrong which he has for a long time regarded with apparent indifference, the court will decline to give him that remedy on grounds[79] of public policy. In the famous words of Lord Camden, L.C., "a court of equity has always refused its aid to stale demands, where a party has slept upon his right and acquiesced for a great length of time. Nothing can call forth this court into activity, but conscience, good faith and reasonable diligence; where these are wanting, the

79. *Smith* v. *Clay*, (1767) 3 Bro CC 639.

court is passive, and does nothing." Delay which is sufficient to prevent a party from obtaining an equitable remedy is technically called "laches".[80] Thus legal claims are barred by statutes of limitation and equitable claims may be barred not only by limitation law but also by unreasonable delay, called laches.[81]

Therefore there should be some time-limit for prosecution of a claim in a court of justice because it is dangerous and impracticable to leave it to the sweet will of a person entitled to it. This idea has been accepted by every legal system and this maxim is an indicator for the time-limit though in a crude form.

This maxim applies only when a claim is made to equitable relief.[82]

(*b*) *Application.*—To cases which are governed by statutes of limitation[83] (in England) either expressly or by analogy the maxim will not apply. Such cases fall into three categories as noted by Snell:[84]

(*i*) firstly those equitable claims to which the statute applies expressly, and

(*ii*) secondly to which the statute applies by analogy.

(*iii*) In the third instance there are equitable claims to which the statute does not apply and hence they are covered by ordinary rules of laches. Dr Hanbury[85] puts the idea in this way: In cases of *purely equitable claims,* equity courts have a discretion either to grant or to refuse the equitable relief, unless the equitable claim is expressly covered by a statute. In case of legal claims or equitable claims closely analogus to legal claims the limitation period prescribed by the statute will be followed. But in cases of fraud of the defendant, where it could not be discovered by the plaintiff even up to and after the limitation period was over, equity resolved that time against the plaintiff will begin to run only on and from the date when the fraud was first discovered.

Doctrine of laches: Plaintiff's unreasonable delay is a weapon of defence by the defendant against the plaintiff. If the plaintiff is passive and apathetic to his rights for a considerably longer time than prescribed, his delay does not remain *a mere delay* but *a delay that has worked to his disadvantage*. Where a long time has elapsed, even beyond the statutes of limitation, and the plaintiff has never insisted upon his rights and therefore neither the statute applies nor can the analogy be invoked, one has to look to the delay and the surrounding circumstances which provide an explanation for the delay and a basis of interference for the court. If the inference that can be reasonably drawn is that the plaintiff agreed to abandon or release his rights or acted in a manner as to induce

80. *Snell's Principles of Equity*, p. 33.

81. *Union of India* v. *Kishorilal Bablani*, (1999) 1 SCC 729: AIR 1999 SC 917; *Municipal Council, Ahmednagar* v. *Shah Hyder Beig*, (2000) 2 SCC 48: AIR 2000 SC 671.

82. Lord Chelmsford in *Clarke and Chapman* v. *Hart*, (1858) 6 HL Cas 633.

83. Limitation Act, 1939.

84. *Snell's Principles of Equity*, p. 33.

85. *Modern Equity*, pp. 50-51.

other parties to alter their position[86] on the reasonable faith that he has done so, the matter is over, because, the plaintiff's claim will be treated as abandoned.[87] In such cases the lapse of time and delay are most material. But apart from such circumstances delay will be immaterial. But for deciding whether there is inexcusable delay or not there is no readymade rule or formula because so many facts have to be considered, *e.g.*, the nature of the claim, the character of the claimant (whether he is an individual or a corporation), and the subject-matter of litigation. Moreover, ignorance of the rights, undue influence and disability would form a satisfactory explanation for delay. It should be noted that laches is a personal disqualification and will not bind successors-in-title.[88]

(*c*) *Cases*.—In a *Bombay case*[89], the plaintiff allowed his land to be occupied by the defendant and this was acquiesced by him even beyond the period of limitation. On a suit by the plaintiff for possession of the land it was decided that as the period of limitation to recover possession had expired, no relief could be granted.

In the same way where *A* seeks to set aside a contract of purchase he must apply for relief within the limitation period. But where he makes unreasonable delay and during that time other parties have acquired rights or where the property in question has deteriorated in value or where conditions are changed, the court will refuse rescission.

Allcard v. *Skinner*[90]: When Miss Allcard was about 35 years of age she felt a desire to devote her life to good works. She became associated with the Sisters of the Poor and after a few years became a professed member of that Sisterhood and bound herself to observe the rules of poverty, chastity and obedience. The rule as to poverty required a member to surrender all her property either to her relatives, the poor or to the Sisterhood itself. The rules also provided that no sister should seek advice from anyone outside the order without the consent of the Lady Superior. Within a few days of becoming a member Miss Allcard made a will bequeathing all her property to Miss Skinner, Lady Superior, and in succeeding years made gifts to the value of about £ 7000 to the same person. When Miss Allcard left the Sisterhood about eight years later she immediately revoked her will but waited a further six years before commencing an action to recover what was left of the money given to Miss Skinner.

The questions of law which arose on these facts were: (*i*) whether the gift is vitiated by the circumstance that it was in favour of the religious superior by a person under her religious influence; (*ii*) what are the circumstances in which such a gift can be set aside.

---

86. *Allcard* v. *Skinner*, (1887) 36 Ch D 145.
87. *Lindsay Petroleum Co.* v. *Hurd*, (1874) LR 5 PC; *Black* v. *Gale*, (1886) 32 Ch D 571; cf. Hanbury: *Modern Equity*, 1969 Edn., p. 37; *Snell's Principles of Equity*, p. 35.
88. *Nwakobi* v. *Nzekwu*, 1964 WLR 1019.
89. *Chatrabhuj* v. *Mansukhram*, AIR 1925 Bom 183.
90. (1987) 36 Ch D 145 (Court of Appeal).

The trial court dismissed the action. Justices Colton, Lindley and Bowen, L., JJ., considered the appeal. All these three judges were of the opinion that at the time of the gift the relationship between the donor and the donee was such that in the absence of competent advice from others interested in the donee, the gift cannot stand. She was not a free agent in making a gift of her property. When she left the Sisterhood in 1879, she was entitled to set aside the transfer.

On the question, however, whether the plaintiff was entitled to set aside the transfer there was a difference of opinion between Colton, L.J., and Lindley. Justice Colton was of the opinion that in regard to the property which was still in the hands of the donee, the plaintiff could recover it. Justice Lindley was of the opinion that the plaintiff's inaction for six years after she left the Sisterhood indicated her intention to confirm the gift. Laches and acquiescence thus disentitled her from claiming back the property. Justice Bowen agreed with Justice Lindley.

It was held that if she had sued to recover the amount of her gifts which had not been expended on the fulfilment of the purposes of the Sisterhood at an earlier date she would have succeeded on the ground of undue influence, but it was her acquiescence that rendered her claim barred by laches.

In England, cases of equitable claims are now controlled by the Limitation Act, 1939. Before that the claims were controlled by the Real Property Limitation Act, 1833[91] and the Trustee Act, 1888[92]. Claims by a beneficiary to recover trust property or in respect of any breach of trust, claims to the personal estate of a deceased person, claims to redeem mortgaged land and claims to foreclose mortgages of real or personal property are now controlled by express application of the Limitation Act, 1939.[93]

As noted by Snell, the class of cases to which the statute is applied by analogy is extremely small and the court normally retains a discretion governed by the doctrine of laches, to refuse or to grant an equitable remedy in aid of a legal right even though the right is subject to an express statutory period which has not expired.[94]

In *Bablani case*[95], the maxim was applied to service law area. The respondent, in this case, successfully passed IAS and Allied Services Examination in 1974. Due to error in computation of vacancies by the department, he was placed in Class II post in 1976 instead of Class I post. The respondent represented in 1983. His representation was rejected in 1985. He therefore moved the court. Contention of the department was that it was not possible to reopen the issue after several years. The Tribunal in 1994 allowed respondent's application. Against this the Union of India came in appeal. It also granted benefit of Class I post to the respondent. Other persons claimed similar benefit.

---

91. Section 24.
92. Section 8.
93. Sections 19, 20, 12 and 4 respectively.
94. *Poole Corpn.* v. *Moody*, 1945 KB 250.
95. *Union of India* v. *Kishorilal Bablani*, (1999) 1 SCC 729; see also *DDA* v. *Ravindra Mohan Aggarwal*, (1999) 3 SCC 172 (a case of providing a plot, against public interest, to the aggrieved party after 14 years.)

Denying relief to other persons, the Supreme Court held that delay defeats equity, is a well known principle of jurisprudence. Delay of 15 and 20 years cannot be overlooked when an applicant before the court seeks equity. During all these years, the respondent had no legal right to any particular post. After more than 10 years, the process of selection and notification of vacancies cannot be and ought not to be reopened in the interest of proper functioning and morale of the concerned services. It would also jeopardise existing positions of a large member of members of that service.

The relief already granted to the respondent is therefore maintained, but it cannot be granted to anyone else.

(*d*) *Delay when fatal*: In the following three cases delay is fatal for a party desirous of enforcing his right:

(*i*) As a result of delay when the available evidence is lost or destroyed.

(*ii*) When the other party is induced to assume or draw an inference from one's conduct that one has waived his rights.[1]

(*iii*) Delay provides a ground to the other party and leads him to believe that one has agreed to abandon or release his rights.

(*e*) *Limitations or exceptions to the maxim.*—Delay is not fatal in the following circumstances and they form the exceptions to the maxim so that the maxim does not apply to them—

(*i*) where the law of limitation expressly applies,

(*ii*) where it applies by analogy, and

(*iii*) where the law of limitation does not apply but the cases are governed by ordinary rules of laches.

Similarly where the respondents have neither pleaded nor shown any prejudice caused to them by the alleged time-lag, where the Court has acted without jurisdiction and on the misconception of the question... it cannot be said that the petitioners are guilty of delay or laches in approaching the court for relief.[2] A claim cannot be rejected merely on ground of delay or laches.[3] Delay, it must be remembered, destroys the remedy but not the right,[4] however, in certain cases it defeats the right as well as the remedy.[5]

(*f*) *Laches and Acquiescence.*—Acquiescence is an assent to an infringement of rights, either express or implied from conduct, by which right to equitable relief is normally lost. One may acquiesce in that which does not meet his views but which he does not care to contest. It is different from agreement, concurrence or from coinciding. It takes place when a person with full

---

1. *Sahdeo Jha* v. *Union of India*, (1992) 2 SCC 190: 1992 SCC (L&S) 368: (1992) 20 ATC 207: (1992) 1 CLR 592 (appellants claim rejected due to laches. Service law).
2. *Thakuri Bai* v. *Laxmi Chand*, AIR 1990 Del 223.
3. *Mahadav Kalekar* v. *State Bank of Hyderabad*, (1990) 4 SCC 174.
4. *Gauri Shankar Gaur* v. *State of U. P.*, (1994) 1 SCC 92, 125: 1993 All LJ 1207.
5. *Ratan Chandra Sammanta* v. *Union of India*, 1993 Supp (4) SCC 67: 1994 SCC (L&S) 182.

knowledge of his own rights and of any acts which infringe them, has, either at the time or after infringement, by his conduct led the person responsible for the infringement to believe that he has waived or abandoned his rights. It is frequently associated with the word laches (i.e. slackness) in the phrase "laches and acquiescence".[6] As decided acquiescence sometimes denotes a conduct which is evidence of an intention by a party conducting himself to abandon an equitable right, sometimes it denotes a conduct from which another party would be justified in inferring such an intention.[7] As Snell puts it,[8] "acquiescence primarily means conduct from which it can be inferred that a party has waived his rights.[9] Thus an injunction to restrain the use of a house as a shop was refused on proof that the plaintiff had himself brought goods there; but acquiescence in a small breach will not bar proceedings to restrain a wider breach". A time-lag that can be explained does not spell laches. "Laches is such negligence or omission to assert a right as, taken in conjunction with the lapse of time, more or less great, and other circumstances causing prejudice to an adverse party, operates as a bar in a court of equity."[10] Laches is a passive state, while acquiescence connotes an active permission or connivance. Therefore such a permission by conduct amounts to an estoppel or a bar against oneself. As decided in *Hall* v. *Otter*[11], laches is a state wherein there is passivity or lethargy to take further steps. When you see a party occupying and using your property but no timely steps are taken to stop him from doing so, you will not be heard later on in a court of justice against the defendant's acts. Your conduct here results in acquiescence.[12] Therefore Snell explains that "lapse of time is an important factor in considering whether there has been acquiescence, but there may be acquiescence even without any delay. It is to be noted that laches may exist as a defence even in circumstances not amounting to acquiescence, *e.g.*, where the defendant's witnesses have died. The areas of acquiescence and laches thus overlap, yet neither is wholly included in the other".

(*g*) *Recognition in India.*—As declared by Suhrawardy, J., in *Jadunath case*[13], "The English doctrine of delay and laches showing negligence in seeking relief in a court of equity cannot be imported into the Indian law in view of Article 113 of the Limitation Act, which fixes a period of three years within which a suit for specific performance should be brought." The law of limitation may harshly affect a particular party, but it has to be applied with all its rigour when the statute so prescribes and the courts have no power to extend the period

---

6. Fernald J.C.: *Frunk and Wagnalls Standard Hand Book*, 1973, p. 31; Burke: *Jowitt's Dictionary of English Law*, Vol. 1, 1977 Edn., p. 31: cited in Gandhi: *Law of Tort*, 1987 Edn., p. 290.
7. *Krishan Dev* v. *Ram Piari*, AIR 1964 HP 34, 37; *Murarilal* v. *Balkisan*, AIR 1926 Nag 416; *Gur Pershad* v. *Asharfi Devi*, AIR 1956 Punj 143; *Kanhiya Shanker* v. *Mohabata Sedhu*, AIR 1960 Punj 494.
8. *Snell's Principles of Equity*, pp. 632-633.
9. *Duke of Leeds* v. *Earl of Amherst*, (1846) 2 PH 117.
10. Per Menon J., in *P.R. Raghavan Nair* v. *State*, AIR 1956 Trav. Co. 77 referring to Ferris: *Extraordinary Legal Remedies* quoted in: *Thakuri Bai* v. *Laxmi Chand*, AIR 1990 Del 223.
11. (1695) 3 Lev 411.
12. Ibid.; *Tannu Singh* v. *State of U.P.*, AIR 1992 NOC 9 (All) (meaning of laches explained).
13. *Jadunath* v. *Chandra Bhushan*, (1858) 6 HL Cas 633.

of limitation on equitable grounds. Thus equity cannot be the basis for extending the period of limitation.[14] However, a party should not be penalised for failing to adopt legal proceedings when the facts have been willfully concealed from him.[15]

The doctrine has therefore no general application to India but has only a limited scope. Where there is a long lapse of time in challenging the defendant's title the presumption would be that it had a lawful origin and the court would fill in the details obliterated by time. In case of costs, laches may be a ground for a refusal.

The Doctrine of Acquiescence that was first propounded in *Ramsden* v. *Dyson*[16] and reiterated in *Willmot* v. *Barber*[17] and *A.G. to Prince of Wales* v. *Collom*[18] and has been followed in India by the Privy Council in *Forbes* v. *Rall*[19] is known as Equitable Estoppel.[20] This doctrine aids a bona fide holder under a defective title. As explained before, acquiescence is a state of affairs where a person abstains from interfering while a violation of his legal rights is in progress. Lord Cranworth[21] has explained it thus: "If a stranger begins to build on my land supposing it to be his own, and I, perceiving his mistake, abstain from setting him right and leave him to persevere his error, a court of equity will not allow me afterwards to assert my title to the land on which he has expended money on the supposition that the land was his own." Thus this doctrine operates by way of estoppel against the true owner.

Section 51 of the Transfer of Property Act in India embodies this doctrine but with a difference. The difference between the doctrine as laid down in *Ramsden case* and that incorporated in the Transfer of Property Act can be summarised as follows:

(*i*) The former arises out of a presumption of a contract while the latter (Section 51, Transfer of Property Act) rests on the maxim "He who seeks equity must do equity".

(*ii*) The former principle is wider than the latter one.

(*iii*) Where the former is invoked there is no question of eviction at all and the estoppel party has not to pay compensation while the latter does not prevent eviction but puts the evictor on equitable terms as regards compensation with an option to sell his interest to the person sought to be evicted.

(*iv*) The former considers the conduct of the estopper—the plaintiff, while the latter looks to the conduct of the defendant—whether he has made

14. *P.K. Ramachandran* v. *State of Kerala*, (1997) 7 SCC 556.
15. *Pallav Sheth* v. *Custodian*, (2001) 7 SCC 549.
16. (1866) LR 1 HL 129.
17. (1880) 15 Ch D 96.
18. (1916) 2 KB 193.
19. AIR 1925 PC 146. This case does not exclude the wider principle laid down in *Ramsden case*.
20. *See* Section 51 of the Transfer of Property Act.
21. In *Ramsden case*.

improvements in the bona fide belief that he had an undisputed title to the property.

6. EQUALITY IS EQUITY

Acqualitas est quasi acquitas

(*a*) *Meaning.*—Plato defines equality as "a sort of justice" and further points out that "If you cannot find any other, equality is the proper basis".[22] This maxim is explained also as "equity delighteth in equality", which means that as far as possible equity would put the litigating parties on an equal level so far as their rights and responsibilities are concerned. The maxim expresses the object of both law and equity in order to effectuate a distribution of property and losses, proportionate to several claims and liabilities of the parties concerned. Equality therefore means proportionate equality. In interpreting the words and enforcing the rules of law, equity so acts that no party gets an undue advantage over the other or is put to unjustified loss. By its very nature common law courts zealously preferred and protected individual interests to common interests. But equity regarded and maintained the rights of all those who were connected by any common bond of interest and obligation. Benefits and burdens of common interests and obligations cannot be imposed upon and pressed against any one individual but should be spread equally over all, following the principle of equality contained in this maxim. In *Steel* v. *Dixon*[23], Justice Fry said: "When I say equality, I do not mean necessarily equality in its simplest form, but which has been sometimes called *proportionate equity*."

Where, therefore, interpretation of words caused inequality and hardship or unequal treatment, it was relieved by equity by construing the words equitably. As Snell puts it succinctly, "in absence of any sufficient reasons for any other basis of division, those who are entitled to property should have the certainty and fairness of equal decision; for equity did delight in equality".[24]

(*b*) *Application and Cases.*—Application of this maxim can be discerned from the following:

(*i*) Equity's dislike for joint tenancy and presumption of tenancy-in-common.

(*ii*) Equal distribution of joint funds and joint purchases.

(*iii*) Contribution between co-trustees, co-sureties, and co-contractors.

(*iv*) Rateable distribution of legacies.

(*v*) Power to appoint.

(*vi*) Marshalling of assets.

(*i*) *Equity's dislike for joint tenancy and presumption of tenancy-in-common.*—Just as one person can hold property, so two, three or several persons can hold it, and that is called co-ownership or ownership in community. Three

---

22. *Jones* v. *Maynard*, 1951 Ch 572; *Dickens, Re*, 1935 Ch 267
23. (1881) 17 Ch D 825.
24. *Petit* v. *Smith*, 1965 1 PWms 7, cited in *Snell's Principles of Equity*, p. 36.

types of such ownership are recognised under English law, (1) joint tenancy, (2) tenancy-in-common, and (3) coparcenary (arising out of custom).

When property is given to two or more persons without words of severance, *i.e.*, to *A* and *B*, or to *A* and *B* jointly, it is held concurrently with the other. Against strangers all such holders are regarded as one individual.

Common Law favoured this type of tenancy because of certain peculiar incidents that were attached to this system. As the title was vested ultimately in a single individual, it facilitated investigation and conveyance of title, it rendered easy the performance of feudal services like paying of rents, services at war times and working in Lord's fields, etc., and it prevented the burden on the land which would have increased otherwise.

The main incidents of joint tenancy can be laid down as (1) unity of possession, (2) unity of interests, (3) unity of time, and (4) unity of title. Every joint tenant is (*seisin per my et per tout*) 'possessed of the joint property by every part and by the whole', they have a single title and their possession is not advese *inter se*. The interest of each joint tenant originates from the same act, the estate of each begins at the same time and the extent and nature of interest of each joint tenant is the same as that of the other.

But the most damaging and notoriously inglorious incidence attached to this system was the principle of *jus accrescendi* or the right of survivorship resulting in the right of joint tenants to have their interests in the joint property increased by inheriting the interests of deceased joint tenants until the last survivor inherits the entire property. For example, where property is given to *A*, *B* and *C* jointly, and where *A* dies, his interest goes to *B* and *C*, and where *B* dies, his entire interest goes to *C*, who becomes the absolute owner. Thus common law and the feudal lords had to deal with only one person and one title.

Insofar as tenancy-in-common is concerned, there is no principle of survivorship; each tenant is an exclusive owner of his share; their shares also need not be equal and the only unity is the unity of possession; the rest of the unities being absent. In the foregoing example, therefore, when any tenant (*A* or *B* or *C*) dies, his interest will not increase his co-sharer's interest, but it would go to the heirs of the deceased.

In the former system one who lived longer became the absolute owner. This element of living longer is an element of chance, accident or risk. But equity was concerned with the present; and certainty and equality cannot be preserved and protected by the otherwise imperfect and speculative measure of chance introduced by the doctrine of *jus accrescendi*. Tenancy-in-common was devoid of such a fluctuating future element. In the former, therefore, what was branded as equality was merely an equality of chance. This attitude of the Common Law, though generated by history, was improper and productive of injustice and inequality. Equity therefore disliked joint tenancy and severed it on the slightest pretext by putting such construction on the words as to avoid the principle of survivorship. Thus tenancy in common in equity existed not only at Common Law but also in certain other cases where intention to create the same could be inferred or discerned. In the following instances it was held to exist.

(1) *Joint purchase in unequal shares.*—Where property is jointly purchased with co-purchasers, *A* and *B* providing money in *unequal shares* and *A* dies, *B* becomes entitled to the whole of the property at law. But in equity *B* was treated as holding *A*'s share in trust for *A*'s representative proportionately to the purchase money advanced. But we have to note that in case of *equa*l *advancement* of purchase money the principle of survivorship still holds the field[25] on the ground that the co-purchasers intended to benefit by the rule of survivorship. Here there is joint tenancy both at law and in equity.

(2) *Joint loan on mortgage.*—In case of loan on mortgage, advanced by *A* and *B* jointly to *C*, either in equal or in unequal shares, the surviving mortgagee is to hold the same in trust for the representative of the deceased mortgagee proportionately to the money advanced. Here also the presumption of joint tenancy at law was repelled.[26]

(3) *Purchase by partners.*—The principle of joint tenancy does not apply as between partners in a business and this is for the benefit of business so that the growth of commerce may be fostered. The Latin expression for this is *inter mercatores locum non habet pro beneficio commercili*[27], which explains that the right of survivorship has no place among merchants. As has been said before, on the slightest pretext in cases of joint tenancy at law and in equity, equity came forth to sever it and avoided the incident of survivorship.[28] This it did in various ways *e.g.*, in case of alienation by one of the joint tenants, in case of acquisition of a, greater interest by one co-tenant than that of the other, in case of partition and in case of an application to the court for an order for sale.[29] By the Law of Property Act, 1925 where a legal estate (not being settled land) is vested in joint tenants beneficially, any tenant may sever the joint tenancy in equity, either by giving a written notice to others or by doing some such acts or things as would have been effectual to sever it. But no severance of the legal joint tenancy in land is now possible after 1925.

(*ii*) *Equal distribution of joint funds or joint purchases.*—In *Gower* v. *Mainwarning*[30], where the trustees were to divide real and personal estate among the settlor's relations, where it was "most necessary", it was held by Lord Hardwicke that the trustees must distribute the same according to the rule, but as observed by Sir J. Jekyll in *Doyle* v. *A.G.*[31], where no intention of the settlor for distribution of the estate could be gathered from the instrument, the court "would prefer an equal division to any other mode of division".

Moreover where a husband and his wife operated a joint bank account, wherein they both paid their income and upon which they both drew, the court,

---

25. *Lake* v. *Craddock*, (1732) 3 PWms 158.
26. *Jackson* v. *Sibthorpe*, (1887) 34 Ch D 732.
27. *Buckley* v. *Barber*, (1851) 6 Exch 164.
28. *Brown* v. *Raindle*, (1796) 3 Ves 256.
29. *Williams* v. *Hensman*, (1861) 1 J&H 546; *Hawkesley* v. *May*, (1956) 1 QB 304, followed *Draper's Conveyance, In re*, (1969) 1 Ch 486: (1968) 84 LQR 462.
30. 28 ER 57.
31. 22 ER 67.

after there had been a divorce declined to dissect the account meticulously but divided the balance equally between them.[32] But between a husband and his wife when they are living together, their bank account is not subjected to this principle because then their rights in a joint bank account are not meant to be attended by legal consequences and each will be the sole beneficial owner of any property which he or she buys with money drawn from the joint bank account, subject to any contrary intention.[33] Between a man and his mistress also this principle has been rejected.

A very interesting example is cited by Snell[34] in connection with the copyright of Charles Dickens' work (*Life of Christ*) wherein this maxim is applied. In this case the author bequeathed the manuscript of a work to *A* and the copyright to *B*. The publication was possible only by using the manuscript. *Prima facie*, the proceeds of the sale of the copyright will be divided equally between *A* and *B*.

(*iii*) *Contribution between co-trustees, co-sureties and co-contractors.*[35]— Where a creditor has a simple claim against several debtors, he may realise his claim from any one of them. The debtor who was thus compelled to pay the whole of the claim had no remedy against the others at Common Law. This provided an undesired impetus to the creditor to select his own victim and upon motives of mere caprice and partialism to make a common or a joint burden a gross personal oppression. But equity, in order to set right the injustice and in order to treat all the debtors on the basis of equality, gave the debtor a right to contribution from the rest, thus pressing the burden equally on all. With co-sureties and co-contractors, the same rule is applied.

As cited by Story[36], this principle of Rhodian Jurisprudence was borrowed by the Romans, and the English borrowed from the Romans, its commonest example being contribution between co-sureties.

Some important points in this regard may be noted:

(1) In case of co-sureties where one of them became insolvent, according to Common Law their liabilities remained unaffected and the insolvent had nothing to pay, but equity abolished this position and decided that the remaining solvent sureties should pay proportionately.

(2) In other cases until the sureties paid more than their shares they could not take any action for contribution at Common Law but this position was also relieved by equity courts by allowing action even before payment (called *quia timet* action).

---

32. *Jones* v. *Maynard*, 1951 Ch 572; *Rimmer* v. *Rimmer*, (1953) 1 QB 63.
33. *Gage* v. *R.*, (1961) 1 QB 188; *Bishop, Re*, 1965 Ch 450. Doubted *Warm & Warm, In re*, (1969) 8 DLR (3d) 466.
34. *Snell's Principles of Equity*, p. 39, *Dickens, Re*, 1935 Ch 267 (Charles Dickens: *Life of Christ*).
35. *Lowe* v. *Dixon*, (1885) 16 QBD 455.
36. *Story on Equity*, 3rd Edn., p. 202.

(3) As decided in *Craythorne* v. *Swinburne*[37], right to contribution though not based on contract may be modified by a contract, as, where *A* and *B* were co-sureties, according to their agreement only in the event of *B* defaulting, *A* would be liable. In such a case, therefore, *A* could not call upon *B* to contribute.

(4) There is no right to contribution where the trustee who has made good the loss is also a beneficiary.[38]

In case of insolvency of a debtor, Common Law allowed priority to some creditors leaving others to their luck, unprotected. But equity ended this preferential treatment and brought all the creditors under a common list and on equal footing. Thus all were allowed to share the debtor's estate according to the amount of their credit, on a *pro rata* basis, because it was equity's cardinal principle that no wrong should remain unredressed and that equals should be treated equally.

(*iv*) *Rateable distribution of legacies.*—By the end of the 18th century suits for legacies came within the exclusive jurisdiction of the court of Chancery.

The principle is that while the testator bequeaths, he presumes that he has sufficient assets to answer all the legacies, but in cases where in fact it is not so, he is presumed to have meant that the deficiency must be borne by all the legatees *pari passu* or on an equal footing. In such cases, where a legatee whose legacy was liable to abate is paid in full, he must return the excess payment, for the benefit of all. This rule of abatement applies to the legatees of the same class.

(*v*) *Power to appoint.—Powers are of two types.*—(1) general power of appointment, and (2) special power of appointment. A power given by deed or will which empowers the donee of the power to appoint *any person* (*including himself*) to take an interest in property is a general power of appointment; and a power which empowers the donee to appoint *any member of a specified class of persons* to take an interest in property is a special power of appointment.

In cases where the donee of a power, in the nature of a trust fails to exercise his power, the court of equity on the principle of equality will carry the same into effect, so that it may not fail, and distribute the property equally among the persons concerned.

(*vi*) *Marshalling of assets.*—Insofar as marshalling is concerned, equity, on the principle of equal treatment to equals, so marshalled (or arranged) funds that no cause of injustice could arise.

Thus in *Well* v. *Smith*[39], it has been explained that "where there are two creditors of the same debtor, one creditor having a right to resort to two funds of the debtor for payment of his debt and the other, a right to resort to one fund

37. (1807) 14 Ves 160.
38. *Chillingworth* v. *Chambers*, (1896) 1 Ch 685 (Court of Appeal) (*Cracknell's Case Book*, C. No. 64, 1974 Edn.).
39. (1885) 30 Ch D 192.

only, the court will so 'marshal' or arrange the funds that both creditors are paid as far as possible". This arrangement has been made on the principle of *Aldrich* v. *Cooper*[40] which states that "it shall not depend upon the will of one creditor to disappoint another".[41]

(*c*) *Recognition in India.*—All these four doctrines resulting from the application of the maxim "equality is equity" have been recognised in India under various enactments:

(*i*) Indian Contract Act, Section 42, illustrates tenancy in common as regards devolution of liabilities.

(*ii*) Section 43 illustrates that one of a number of joint promisors who has performed the promise is entitled to compel the other promisors to contribute equally with himself.

(*iii*) Sections 69 and 70 illustrate the doctrine of marshalling.

(*iv*) Sections 146 and 147 explain that co-sureties are liable to contribute equally.

(*v*) Under the Transfer of Property Act, Section 56 illustrates the doctrine of marshalling.

(*vi*) Section 82 speaks about contribution to mortgage debt by co-mortgagors.

(*vii*) Section 330 of the Indian Succession Act incorporates and illustrates the principle of rateable distribution of assets explaining that the legacies abate rateably.

(*viii*) Under the Indian Trusts Act, Section 27, there is contribution also as between co-trustees.

(*ix*) Section 73 of the Civil Procedure Code.

(*x*) Section 45 of the Transfer of Property Act also illustrates the incorporation and application of this principle.

7. EQUITY LOOKS TO THE INTENT RATHER THAN THE FORM

(*a*) *Meaning.*—As is seen before, Common Law was very rigid and inflexible.[42] It could not respond favourably to the demands of time. In respect of acquisition and transfer of property, it regarded the form of a transaction to be more important than its substance. Moreover it expected the contracting parties to rigidly observe their agreements and to perform their stipulations to the very letter (*litera scripta*) of every promise or agreement.[43] Common Law thus was fond of mere technicalities. But, as expressed by Romily, M.R. in *Parkin case*[44], "courts of equity make a distinction in all cases between that which is matter of

---

40. (1803) 32 ER 4022.
41. *Lenoy* v. *Duke of Athole*, (1742) 2 ATK 446 per Lord Hardwicke.
42. *Paradine* v. *Jane*, (1647) Alyn 26; *Thiis* v. *Byres*, (1876) 1 QBD 244.
43. *Ibid.*
44. *Parkin* v. *Thorold*, (1852) 16 Beav 59, 66.

substance and that which is matter of form; and if they found that by insisting on the form, the substance will be defeated, they hold it to be inequitable to allow a person to insist on such form, and thereby defeat the substance". Equity thus looks to the spirit and not to the letter, it looks to the intention of parties and not to the words, and it looks to the realities rather than to mere appearances. Instead of swimming on the surface of mere form, it penetrates through the external form of a transaction to discern and decide the real intention of the parties, because the external form of a transaction cannot be allowed to conceal or throw a cloak on the real object, purpose and consequences of a transaction.

(*b*) *Application and Cases.*—In case of sale of land, if a party fails to complete it within the time fixed for it, he is at Common Law, in breach of the contract, but equity did not take this rigid attitude. It allowed a reasonable time to the party concerned to complete it.[45] Moreover, in case of construction and enforcement of an agreement equity did not give undue importance to its negative side but looked through the document to find out its real substance and intent.

Unlike Common Law, equity was not impressed by mere form and technicalities and avoided circuitry of action. Thus a transaction which could lawfully have been effected by two or more separate transactions was held by equity to be valid, though it was unauthorised.[46] The maxim therefore contains in itself the equitable rule of construction of documents.

The application and working of this maxim can well be examined from the following instances:

(*i*) Relief against penalties and forfeitures.

(*ii*) Relief in regard to precatory trusts.

(*iii*) Relief in regard to mortgages, the doctrine of equity of redemption and the doctrine of clogs on redemptions.

(*iv*) Attitude in regard to statute of frauds.

(*i*) *Relief against penalties and forfeitures.*—Common Law courts insisted on the rigid and *litera scripta* performance of all agreements and promises. In cases of contracts when there was a provision to forfeit a certain amount or to charge penalty in case of breach of contract, Common Law imposed these on the party in default. It may be that the actual damage sustained was less. This unjust situation was relieved by equity by interpreting the purpose and intent of the contract itself. The principal object of the contract lies in its performance and not in imposition of penalty. The damage sustained may be therefore compensated, imposition of penalty and forfeiture being subsidiary. This it did by applying the maxim.

(*ii*) *Precatory trusts.*—A trust is created when the author of the trust indicates with reasonable certainty by any words or acts (1) an intention on his part to create a trust thereby, (2) the purpose of the trust, (3) the beneficiary, and

---

45. *Parkin* v. *Thorold*, (1852) 16 Beav 59, 66.
46. *Collard's W.T.*, *Re*, 1961 Ch 293.

(4) the trust property. In case of precatory trusts, the author of the trust in raising the trust does not use express and unequivocal words but expresses his desire by such words as 'I hope', 'I request' or 'I recommend', giving thereby a latitude to the trustee so as to ignore the request of the author. All the certainties are present here except number one. The intention is there, but its expression is not proper and compulsive. Equity in such cases ignored the form and looked to the intention which can easily be found out by having a reference to other ingredients of the trust and the conduct of its author. The document as a whole was taken into consideration and not its part. The principles that govern such cases are expressed in *Knight* v. *Knight*[47] by Lord Langdale, M.R., as follows: "As a general rule it has been laid down that when property is given absolutely to any person and the same person is, by the giver who has power to command, recommended or entreated or wished to dispose of that property in favour of another, the recommendation, entreaty or wish shall be held to create a trust, first, if the words are so used that upon the whole they ought to be construed as imperative; secondly, if the subject of the recommendation or wish be certain; and thirdly, if the objects or persons intended to have the benefit of the recommendation or wish be also certain."

But this cruel kindness of the equity courts to construe and interpose a trust where in many cases none was intended was questioned in *Lombe* v. *Eames*[48], *R. Adams and Kensington Vestry*[49] and in *Re Atkinson*[50] by Sir William James, L.J., Lindley, L.J., and James, L.J., respectively. But it should not be taken that the doctrine is abolished; the liberty of "cruel kindness" is now used but not so liberally as before.[51]

(iii) Relief in regard to mortgages.—A mortgage is a conveyance of property whereby one person (mortgagor) secures to another (mortgagee) the payment of money whether already owing or advanced at the time or to be advanced (called mortgage debt). This he does by vesting in him some property or interest in property.

Being thus a security for a debt a mortgage differs from a sale. The mortgagor has a right to obtain his property back by payment of the debt and that is his *right of redemption.* The mortgagee has a right to repayment of his advance and in case of default by the mortgagor the mortgagee can exercise his right of recovery of his amount by foreclosure or by getting the property sold. The mortgagor's right of redemption is guarded by courts and this has been expressed in a well-known legal maxim, "once a mortgage, always a mortgage, and nothing but a mortgage". If the mortgagor cannot redeem his property within the time set in the mortgage deed (a contract), his legal right is gone but he can still have, in equity, his right to redeem the property on the principle of

47. (1840) 49 ER 58.
48. (1871) 6 Ch App 597.
49. (1884) 27 Ch D 394.
50. (1911) 80 LJ Ch 370.
51. *Comiskey* v. *Bowring*, 1905 AC 84.

this maxim. As expressed by Lord Davey in *Noakes & Co.* v. *Rice*[52], "a mortgage cannot be made irredeemable and a provision to that effect is void".

The extension of this principle of right to redeem has found further expression in the well-known doctrine of clog on redemption. A clog is a check, an impediment or an obstruction which makes the release of security impossible. It was therefore expressed by Lindley, M.R.[53], that any provision inserted in a mortgage deed preventing redemption is meant to be a clog or fetter on the equity of redemption, and is void. A leading case on this point is *Salt* v. *Marquess of Northampton*[54], wherein on the death of his son (mortgagor), the father was allowed to redeem the mortgage even though there was a deliberate contract by the son that the securities should belong absolutely to the mortgagee. Thus any craft, contrivance or design bypassing this right is void as it amounts to a clog.

(*iv*) *Attitude in regard to statute of frauds.*—The statute of frauds always insisted upon writing and signature of the party sought to be bound in regard to land transactions. At the same time equity courts saw that these very contrivance could not help any party to create or to cover a fraud. For this purpose it created two exceptions. Where a contract which though required to be in writing, was, due to the defendant's fraud, not reduced to writing, equity granted relief and the statute was not allowed to be pleaded as a defence against specific performance. Similarly contracts wherein equity usually granted specific performance but which were covered by the statute, were not allowed to remain unenforced because part performance of the contract by the plaintiff took it out of the statute.

In regard to covenants in respect of land positive covenants (to do something) never pass. They may be enforced between the contracting parties, but they are not ordinarily binding on subsequent transferees or assigns. Negative covenants restraining the use of one land for the benefit of another are binding even on subsequent transferees if they have notice of them. *Tulk* v. *Moxhay*[55] is a leading case on this point. Of course, the above principle has its own limitations; that it applies to negative covenants only and not to affirmative covenants. Also, where its application makes the transferee put his hand into his pocket, the principle does not apply. At the same time equity will look to the substance and intent of the covenant; thus, if it is in substance a negative covenant, the court will restrain its violation but if it is a positive one which actively enforces a party to spend, it will not enforce it.

With regard to contracts under seal at Common Law, presence of seal could not produce any effect in equity on the rights and duties of the parties concerned.

---

52. 1902 AC 24.
53. *Stanley* v. *Wilde*, (1899) 2 Ch 474.
54. 1892 AC 1. See also *Howard* v. *Harris*, (1683) 1 Vern 190; *Trimbak* v. *Sakharam*, 16 Bom 599; *Vernor* v. *Bethell*, (1672) 2 Eden 110, 113.
55. (1848) 11 B 571.

(*c*) *Recognition under Indian Law.*—The principle contained in the maxim has been recognised under Indian law in Sections 55 and 74, Indian Contract Act and Sections 114 and 114-A, Transfer of Property Act.

As provided by Section 55, if time is the essence of the contract, and it is not performed within the stipulated time, the contract or a part of it which is unperformed would be voidable at the instance of the promisee. If time is not of the essence of the contract, it will not become voidable but entitles the promisee to damages. Moreover, when performance is accepted at a time other than the stipulated one in the contract, the promisee is not entitled to damages.

Under Section 74 of the Indian Contract Act, only a reasonable compensation can be claimed by the party complaining of a breach of contract, in spite of their agreement to the contrary. Where no actual damage is proved to have been caused by the breach, there also this right of reasonable compensation is given.

As observed by Justice Sundara Aiyar in *Muthu Krishna case*[56]: "The doctrine... is confined to the carrying out of the primary contract and does not extend to a secondary or subsidiary contract, to come into operation if the primary contract is broken." Since the secondary contract is for securing the fulfilment of the primary one, "the courts both in England and in India do not feel bound to carry out such a secondary contract apart from its justice and reasonableness".[57] The test to be applied in such cases is to consider whether the amount represents a genuine and a reasonable pre-estimate of the probable damage. If it is so, it would be liquidated damages, but if not so, it would be a penalty.[58] Thus the section incorporates the principle of reasonableness of damages and looks to the primary intent of the parties rather than to the form.[59]

Forfeiture clauses in a lease are similarly disregarded in some cases where they are inserted only for securing or ensuring the prompt payment of the rent. These provisions, based on this maxim, are incorporated in Sections 114 and 114-A of the Transfer of Property Act.

It is within the competence of the parties to enter into any reasonable agreement regarding mortgage and its redemption right, but where their agreement makes it impossible or indefinite for the mortgagor to redeem his mortgaged property, equity will not allow such provisions to prevail and will give relief. Thus clogs on the right of redemption are not tolerated by Section 91 of the law of property.

8. EQUITY LOOKS ON THAT AS DONE WHICH OUGHT TO BE DONE

(*a*) *Meaning.*—As between two persons, where one of them has incurred an obligation and undertaken upon himself to do something for the other, the equity

56. *Muthu Krishna Iyer* v. *S. Pillay*, (1912) 36 Mad 229.
57. *Ibid.*
58. *Kemble* v. *Farren*, (1829) 130 LR 1234; c.f. *Dunlop Pneumatic Tyre Co. Ltd.* v. *New Garage & Motor Co. Ltd.*, 1915 AC 79.
59. *Wallingford* v. *Mutual Society*, (1850) 5 AC 685.

courts look on it as done and as producing the same results as if the obiligation or undertaking had been actually performed.[60] Equity treats a contract to do a thing as if the thing were already done, though only in favour of persons entitled to enforce the contract specifically and not in favour of volunteers.[61] In other words, as to the consequences and incidents of the subject matter of contract, it will be treated as if the final acts anticipated and contemplated by the parties have been carried out in the same manner as they *ought to have been* and not as they *might have been* carried out. Equity acts on the conscience of a person. What one has undertaken to do, binding his conscience, ought to be done and equity courts therefore look to the acts of the person bound by his conscience and interpret and construe them in such a way that they amount to what ought to be done.

(*b*) *Application and Cases.*—A person who enters into possession of land under a specifically enforceable agreement for a lease, is regarded in any court having jurisdiction to enforce it as being in the same position as between himself and the other party to the agreement as if the lease had actually been granted to him.[62] In the same way, *A* by his will leaves Rs 50,000 to *T* upon trust to purchase land for the use of *P*. *T* does not purchase land and *P* by the time dies, leaving all immovables to *X* and the rest of his property to *Y*. Who should get the amount of Rs 50,000, *X* or *Y*? *Y* says he is entitled to the money as it has remained so. *X* says he is entitled to the amount because it was earmarked for the purchase of land. Had *T* not omitted his duty of purchasing the land, the money would have been in the form of land. Equity in such cases would definitely regard the purchase of land which ought to have been made as made, and earmark and impress upon the fund the character and all the incidents of land. The money would thus go to *X* and not to *Y*, as they would be treated as land.

The working of this maxim can be seen in (*i*) the doctrine of conversion, (*ii*) executory contracts, and (*iii*) doctrine of part performance.

(*i*) *Doctrine of Conversion.*—The notional change in the nature of property whereby realty is considered to be personalty and personalty as realty, is known as the doctrine of conversion. The leading case on the point is *Lachmere* v. *Lady Lachmere*[63], wherein Jekyll, M.R., observed that "what ought to have been done shall be taken as done" is the rule in such cases, and "a rule so powerful it is as to alter the very nature of things; to make money land, and on the contrary, to turn land into money; thus money agreed to be laid out in land shall be taken as land and descend to the heir, and on the other hand, land agreed to be sold shall be considered as personal estate".

---

60. Story: *Equity Jurisprudence*, 3rd Edn., pp. 37-38 and Pomeroy: *Equity Jurisprudence*, Vol. II, 5th Edn., pp. 16-17.
61. *Snell's Principles of Equity*, p. 40.
62. *Walsh* v. *Lonsdale*, (1882) 21 Ch D 9; John Tilley: *Case Book of Equity & Succession*, 1968 Edn., p. 13.
63. (1735) Cas Temp Talb 80: (1735) 25 ER 673.

The facts of *Lachmere case* may be succinctly stated as follows. In 1719, Lord Lachmere upon his marriage covenanted to lay out £ 30,000 within one year of the marriage in the purchase of freehold land. The land was to be settled for the benefit of the husband and his wife for life, remainder to their sons in tail male, and remainder to the husband and his heirs. On the husband dying issueless and intestate, the question arose whether his heir (who was entitled only to real estate) could take the money. It was held that the freehold lands in fee-simple in possession purchased and contracted to be purchased by Lord Lachmere after the marriage were to be taken to have been purchased towards performance of the covenant, and their value deducted from £ 30,000. In short, the money should be taken as land, that is real estate. It therefore went to the heir and not to the personal representatives.[64]

By the Administration of Estates Act, 1925, in England, the two systems of intestate succession [whereby personal property devolved upon the nearest in relationship (next of kin) and real property (land) to the heir] are now no longer in force. All the property now vests in the administrator, who would distribute it according to new rules brought in line with modern needs. This doctrine of equitable conversion has therefore lost much of its importance and is no longer pressed into service for the purpose of altering the course of devolution of estate.

(ii) Executory Contracts.—(1) *Assignment of future property.* When an assignment of property was made for consideration equity treated it as a contract to assign. When the property came into existence in such a contract it was treated as a complete assignment. As expressed in *Collyer* v. *Issacs*[65], it was not possible at Common Law[66] to assign property to be acquired in future, because it had no existence. But in equity this could be done. When the property has come into existence, equity on the principle of the maxim fastened upon the property and the contract to assign[67] becomes a complete assignment.[68] As a leading case on this point, *Holroyd* v. *Marshall*[69] can be cited.

In this case, *A* transferred his machinery to one *P*, who should hold it in trust for *H*. Machinery which was the subject of transfer included the machinery in the mill and also the one that would be purchased and added thereto or substituted for the present one. New machinery was added thereafter. The point of dispute was whether *H* could claim it, or the execution creditor of *A* could claim it. It was held that *H*'s claim would prevail over that of the execution creditor, as *H* obtained an equitable title as soon as the new machinery was added to the old.

---

64. J.G. Ridall: *Cracknell's Law Students' Companion*, 1974 Edn., Case No. 176. To this effect see *Ackroyd* v. *Smithson*, (1780) 1 Bro CC 503; *Fletcher* v. *Ashburner*, (1779) 1 Bro CC 497; *Lawes* v. *Bennet*, (1785) 1 Cox Ch Cas 167.
65. (1881) 19 Ch D 342 *per* Jessel, M.R., *followed* in *Gaya Din* v. *Kashi Gir*, (1907) 29 All 163.
66. *Snell's Principles of Equity*, p. 81.
67. *Holroyd* v. *Marshall*, (1862) 10 HLC 191.
68. *Performing Right Society Ltd.* v. *London Theatre of Varieties Ltd.*, (1924) AC 1.
69. (1862) 10 HLC 191.

Thus future property may be transferred for consideration in equity.[70]

(2) *Agreement for a transfer.*—As seen before in the doctrine of conversion, equity changed the very nature of things; it turned money into land and land into money to give effect to the intention of the parties which ought to have been done. For example, where *A* validly agrees to sell his house to *B* for Rs 50,000 according to the doctrine of conversion for the purpose of devolution of property of *A*, the house would be treated as money and for the purpose of devolution of *B*'s fund of Rs 50,000 it would be treated as a house. Under English Common Law no legal right or interest was lost or obtained by mere agreement unless certain formalities were gone through. Under the circumstances, *A* was still the owner at Common Law and could convey the house to a third person free from any claim. At the most he could be made to pay damages for non-performance of the contract, but nothing further. Now let us look at *B*'s position at Common Law. *B* has acquired no interest or proprietory rights in the house. He cannot therefore take possessory action for its recovery. At the most he can recover damages from *A* for breach of the agreement. Thus it is very clear that unless and until a deed of conveyance is not executed between *A* and *B*, no legal estate is lost or obtained between the two. In other words an agreement for a transfer did not by itself create any legal title at Common Law. But equity could not tolerate this unjust position. It therefore conferred an equitable title upon the person having the agreement in his favour. This stand of equity is made clear in the well-known case of *Walsh* v. *Lonsdale*[71], wherein it was decided that an agreement for lease could be treated as a lease in equity. In order that the doctrine may operate with full force, the following conditions must be fulfilled:

(1) *A contract to transfer* a legal title must exist.

(2) It should be *capable of being proved*, either by some acts of part-performance or by writing.

(3) It should be *capable of specific performance.*

(4) The suit should be *filed within prescribed time.*

(5) The title so sought to be acquired must have *support at law.*

(6) *The relief* must be obtainable in the same court in which the legality of the act is questioned. (The principle contained in this case is not accepted in India, as Indian law does not recognise equitable estates.)

(*iii*) *Doctrine of Part Performance.*—The working of the maxim can also be seen in the doctrine of part-performance. We have seen earlier that the Statute of Frauds in England always insisted upon writing and the party's signature in so far as land transactions were concerned. But equity did not allow these provisions of the Statute of Frauds to be used as an instrument or an engine for generating or covering frauds. As observed by Lord Westbury:[72]

70. *Tailby* v. *Official Receiver*, (1888) 13 AC 523.
71. (1882) 21 Ch D 9.
72. *McCormick* v. *Grogan*, (1856) 6 HL Cas 633.

"The courts of equity had, from a very early period, decided that any Act of Parliament shall not be used as an instrument of fraud; and if in the machinery of perpetrating a fraud an Act of Parliament intervenes, the court of equity does not set aside the Act of Parliament but it fastens on the individual who gets a title under that Act, and imposes upon him a personal obligation because he applies the Act as an instrument for accomplishing a fraud." Viewing it from this angle the doctrine of part-performance was a very bold step by the Equity Courts. When agreements which could not be relied on in a court of law due to want of writing were brought before equity courts they were specifically enforced where sufficient evidence in regard to part-performance was satisfactorily adduced. Thus under the equitable doctrine of part-performance contracts pertaining to land were allowed to be formed by oral evidence where one of the parties did acts of part-performance. *Maddison* v. *Alderson*[73], is a leading case on the point. *A* agreed to remain in *B*'s service in consideration of an oral agreement whereby *B* was to leave *A*, by will, a life estate in certain land. The estate was bequeathed by will. The will failed for want of due attestation. The heir-at-law brought an action to recover the land. Can *A* raise the defence of part-performance? Relying on the dictum of *O'Reilly case*[74], it was held that *A* should fail because the act of part-performance must be referable to the contract, and the act should not precede the contract. Equity is very active in such cases. To lay down the difference between this doctrine and the principle enunciated in *Walsh* v. *Lonsdale*[75], it can be said that two main conditions for the enforcement of equity in *Walsh* v. *Lonsdale*[76] are a must: (1) evidence of a contract, and (2) suit for specific performance to be within time-limit. To invoke the equity in respect of specific performance on the basis of part-performance on the other hand, it is not necessary that the contract must be admissible in evidence and that it should be within the time-limit.

(*c*) *Limitations of the Maxim.*—As the maxim goes, "it looks on that as done which *ought to be done*", but it does not treat as done what might be done or what could have been done. It thus touches upon a very soft and sensitive chord of human conscience. Again, this maxim does not work in favour of every person. It can help those and only those who hold some equitable right or who have performed some act against those on whom the duty with reference to such right or performance has devolved. That is to say, equity treats a contract to do a thing as if the thing were already done, though only in favour of those entitled to enforce the contract specifically and not in favour of volunteers.[77]

In so far as applicability of the maxim to tax statutes is concerned it is not possible to look upon a thing as done which ought to have been done for which Legislature has separately featured differently in a fiscal statute.[78]

---

73. (1888) 8 AC 467.
74. *O'Reilly* v. *Thompson*, (1791) 30 ER 126.
75. (1882) 21 Ch D 9.
76. (1882) 21 Ch D 9.
77. *Snell's Principles of Equity*, p. 40; *Anstis, Re*, (1886) 31 Ch D 596.
78. *State of U.P.* v. *Kasturilal Harlal*, (1987) 67 STC 154.

(*d*) *Recognition in India.*—The principle contained in the maxim has been recognised in Indian law under the following enactments:

(1) Section 40 of the Transfer of Property Act.

(2) Section 12 of the Specific Relief Act.

(3) Section 53-A of the Transfer of Property Act.

(4) Section 91 of the Indian Trusts Act.

The English doctrine of conversion of realty into personality cannot be bodily lifted from its native English soil and transplanted into statute-bound Indian law. However, many of the doctrines of English equity have taken statutory form in India and have been incorporated in occasional provisions of various Indian statutes (such as Indian Trusts Act, the Specific Relief Act, the Transfer of Property Act, etc.) and where a question of interpretation of such equity-based statutory provisions arises, aid from the equity source can be justifiably sought.[79]

Where property is transferred absolutely with the direction that it should be enjoyed in a particular manner by the transferee, he is entitled to ignore the directions under Section 11 of the Transfer of Property Act. But where such directions are made in regard to a piece of immovable property for the purpose of securing the beneficial enjoyment of another piece of immovable property, they can be enforced. This special saving in case of a direction affecting another piece of property is developed in Section 40. Thus restrictive and negative covenants can be used by a third party against the transferee as laid down in Section 40.

The Illustration to Section 40 runs as follows: *A* contracts to sell Sultanpur to *B*. While the contract is still in force, he sells Sultanpur to *C*, who has notice of the contract. *B* may enforce the contract against *C* to the same extent as against *A*.

It should be remembered that under English law such contract passes the ownership of land from *A* to *B* in equity on the principle of this maxim. But under Indian law as contained in Section 54 of the Transfer of Property Act, a contract to purchase land does not pass any interest in the land at all and therefore such a contract does not come under the rule of perpetuities and as such would not be regarded as invalid.[80] On the contrary such a contract comes within para 2 of Section 40 and as such it is enforceable on the principle of the maxim.[81]

Section 12 of the Specific Relief Act relating to the specific performance of part of a contract also illustrates the application of the maxim.

Section 53-A of the Transfer of Property Act illustrates the doctrine of part-performance as based on this maxim. This doctrine was first recognised

79. *Bai Dosabai* v. *Mathurdas Govinddas*, (1980) 3 SCC 545.

80. *Munuswami Naidu* v. *S. Naidu*, 49 Mad 387; *Alud Ali* v. *Syed Ali*, 49 All 527.

81. *Ram Baran Prasad* v. *Ram Mohit Hazara*, (1967) 1 SCR 293: AIR 1967 SC 744; *Narandas Karasandas* v. *S.A. Kamtam*, (1977) 3 SCC 247: (1977) 2 SCR 341.

in *Mohd Musa case*[82] and was referred to in *Ariff case*[83]. It was decided later on, in *Pir Bux case*[84] that the English doctrine of part performance is not available in India by way of defence to an action of ejectment.[85] If conditions laid down in Section 53-A are not satisfied, the benefit of the section is not available. Thus, the equity recognised in this section is a passive one which is available to protect the transferee's possession. The equity recognised under English law is an active one capable of supporting a suit for specific performance or for injunction to restrain eviction. In short, the doctrine recognised in India can be used as a shield for protection but cannot be used as a sword to inflict injury.

Insofar as equitable assignments are concerned no equitable estate is recognised in India. A transfer of future property for consideration, however, operates as a contract to be performed in future. As soon as such property comes into existence, the contract may be specifically enforced.[86] In *Jugalkishore* v. *Raw Cotton Co.*[87], *X* transferred his book debts to *Y*. At the date of transfer *X* had sued for one such debt. A decree was passed by the court in favour of *X*. Though *Y* had not applied to the court to put his name on record in place of *X*, his claim that he could execute the decree was allowed by the Supreme Court on the ground that he was the real owner of the debt. The principle contained in *Walsh* v. *Lonsdale* is not applicable in India as decided by the Privy Council in *Currimbhoy & Co.* v. *Creet*[88]. Section 91 of the Indian Trusts Act dealing with property acquired with notice of existing contract is also illustrative of the application of this maxim. It explains that where a person acquires property with notice that another person has entered into an existing contract affecting that property, of which specific performance could be enforced, the former must hold the property for the benefit of the latter to the extent necessary to give effect to the contract.

9. EQUITY IMPUTES AN INTENTION TO FULFIL AN OBLIGATION

(*a*) *Meaning.*—Equity courts came into existence to do justice. They firmly believed that a person must be prepared to do what is right and fair. As the old saying goes, one must be just before one professes to be generous. It is on this accepted dictum that equity considered, estimated and construed acts of parties. Thus where a person is under an obligation to do a certain act, and he does some other act which is capable of being regarded as an act in fulfilment of his obligation, the latter will prima facie be so regarded for "it is right to put the most favourable construction on a man's acts, and to presume that he intends to be just before he affects to be generous".[89] Equity in such cases presumes and

---

82. 42 Cal 801 (PC).
83. 58 Cal 1235.
84. 51 Bom 650.
85. *Ramchandraiyya* v. *Satyanarayan*, AIR 1964 SC 876.
86. *Baldeo* v. *Miller*, 31 Cal 667.
87. AIR 1955 SC 376.
88. 60 Cal 980 (PC).
89. *Snell's Principles of Equity*, p. 40.

imputes an intention that the latter act was intended to be in performance of the former. In other words a person is presumed to do what he is bound to do.

In *Sowden* v. *Sowden*[90], a husband covenanted with the trustees of his marriage settlement to pay to them £ 50,000 to be laid out by them in purchase of land in a particular area *D*. He, in fact, never paid the sum, but after marriage purchased land at *D* in his own name, for £ 50,000. He died and could not bring the land into settlement. Equity courts construed that he purchased land to fulfil his obligation created by the covenant. On principle, the act done may not be exactly the same as agreed upon, but if it bears so much resemblance to it that it may fairly be taken to have been his design to satisfy the obligation, equity will impute to such an act an intention to fulfil one's obligation.

(*b*) *Application and Cases.*—The following doctrines and concepts rest on the application of this maxim:

(*i*) Doctrine of performance and satisfaction.

(*ii*) Ademption.

(*iii*) Doctrine of presumption of advancement.

(*iv*) Relief against defective execution of power of appointment.

(*i*) *Doctrine of performance and satisfaction.*—As explained before, *Sowden* v. *Sowden* and *Lachmere* v. *Lady Lachmere* are examples of performance. If a man has covenanted to purchase land and settle it on his wife and issue, and he fully carries it out, he has, of course, performed his covenant but the doctrine of performance in equity is connected with notional performance rather than actual. "The whole doctrine proceeds upon the ground that a person is presumed to do that which he is bound to do; and if he has done anything, that he has done it in pursuance of his obligation."[91]

As we shall see afterwards, the question of performance arises in these cases: one, where there is a statutory obligation or a covenant to purchase and settle lands and a purchase is in fact made, and second, where there is a covenant to leave personally to *A*, and property in fact comes to *A* under the covenantor's will or intestacy.[92]

Satisfaction is "the donation of a thing with the intention that it is to be taken either wholly or in part in extinguishment of some prior claim of donee".[93]

For example, where a donor who is already in obligation to the donee, effects a donation under circumstances which indicate an intention that this shall be taken in satisfaction of a prior obligation, equity in such cases applies the principle by construing his words in such a way as to extinguish the prior claim of the donee. Thus the doctrine of satisfaction is pressed into service in construing instruments. In *George Will Trusts case*[94], *G*, a farmer, in his will left

90. (1785) 1 Bro CC 582: 29 ER 1111.
91. *Per* Lord Brougham, L.C., in *Tubbs* v. *Broadwood*, (1831) 2 Russ & M 487; *Blandy* v. *Widemore*, 2 W&T 47.
92. *Snell's Principles of Equity*, p. 495.
93. *Per* Lord Romilly, M.R., in *Chichester* (*Lord*) v. *Coventry*, (1867) LR 2 HL 71.
94. (1948) 2 All ER 1004.

two-thirds of his residue to his son *E* and one-third to his son *R*. The will further provided that if *E* within one month of the testator's death notified the trustees of his wish to carry on the farm, the residue was to be valued and that one-third should constitute the share of *R* and two-thirds the share of *E*, and that *R* should allow his share to remain invested in the farm for three years. *G* later made a gift to *E* of the live and dead stock which was valued at £ 2060. After *G*'s death a summon was taken out to determine whether (under the rule against double portions) the gift to *E* was in satisfaction of the legacy. Held, the gift to *E*, which put him in immediate possession of his intended inheritance, was deemed to be in satisfaction of the legacy. In any case, the same was sufficiently *ejusdem generis* with the option conferred on *E* to carry on the farm to satisfy this requirement.

But as observed in *Talbot* v. *Shrewsbury*[95]: "If a debtor without taking notice of the debt, bequeaths a sum as great as or greater than the debt, to his creditor, this is to be deemed a satisfaction of the debt; but the legacy of less amount than the debt is not regarded as a satisfaction *pro tanto*, nor will a contingent legacy ever operate as a satisfaction."

Thus this maxim is helpful where the presumed intention of the testator is to be found out; where the intention is express the maxim has no application.[96]

(*ii*) *Ademption.*—Ademption is a transfer of property which is irrespective of the donor's wish, in law, operates as a complete or pro tanto (proportionately) substitution for a gift previously made by the will of the donor which is unrevoked at his death e.g., *X* by his will leaves his daughter *Y* one-third of his residuary estate. Thereafter on *Y*'s marriage *X* gives *Y* Rs 20,000. *X* dies. The will was neither revoked nor altered by him. Rs 20,000 is an ademption—complete or proportionately to the gift of one-third share of the residuary estate of *X*. The question of *Y*'s option in the case need not arise.

(*iii*) *Presumption of advancement.*—As the word "advancement" suggests it is the establishing of a beneficiary in an early period of life.[97] When a transfer or a purchase of property without consideration is made by a father or a person in *loco parentis*[98], to or in the name of a child, a presumption arises. And the presumption is that it was for the benefit of the child. Such presumption, which in law is known by the terminology of "advancement", is made in order to rebut an ordinary presumption of a "resulting trust", in favour of the father or the *loco parentis* who paid the consideration. As decided in *Tollet* v. *Tollet*[99] "it is the duty of every man to pay his debts and a husband or a father to provide for child".

95. (1714) 24 ER 177 *per* Sir John Trevor, M.R.
96. *Chancey case*, (1725) 24 ER 448.
97. *Snell's Principles of Equity*, pp. 262-271.
98. *Currant* v. *Jago*, 1 Coll 261.
99. (1728) 2 P Wms 494.

Advances for the purchase of a house or for a settlement on marriage are the ordinary instances. The doctrine applies to cases of parent and child[1], husband and wife[2], of mother and child[3] and even to illegitimate child[4], but not to a man and his mistress[5]. Thus, the presumption of advancement applies to all cases in which the person providing the purchase money is under an equitable obligation to support, or make provision for, the person to whom the property is conveyed, i.e., where the former is the husband or father of, or stands in *loco parentis* to, the latter.

This presumption can also be rebutted in certain appropriate cases.[6]

The power of advancement authorising a trustee to apply the income or capital of the trust for the beneficiary is contained in a settlement. The trustees so advancing must have a good cause and must see that its purpose is carried out.

Compared with the word "benefit", advancement is a word of limited connotation. The exercise of this power is however subject to certain limitations.

(*iv*) *Relief against defective execution of power of appointment.*—A power is an authority vested in a person to deal with or dispose of property not his own.[7] A power may be legal or equitable but after 1925 all powers of appointment are necessarily equitable. A mere power is discretionary, while a trust is imperative e.g. *A* holds Rs 50,000 upon trust to divide among a certain class of persons.

A has no option in this matter. He is bound to carry out the trust. On his failing to do so, the court will see that the property is duly divided.

But if *A* is given a mere power to appoint among a certain class, he is not bound to exercise them. If he fails to exercise the power either by design or by accident the members will have no claim to money and the amount will pass on to the persons entitled in default of appointment.[8]

In marginal cases where the distinction between a power and a trust is blurred, equity will not allow an injustice to the intended objects and will take upon itself the duties of the donee of the power.

Where the holder of a power of appointment fails to exercise it or exercises it in an unauthorised way, the objects of the power take nothing; of course there are some statutory relaxations in this regard. In case of total non-execution of a mere power, equity will not aid, but in three cases such relief is granted:

---

1. *Dyer* v. *Dyer*, (1788) 2 Cox 92.
2. *Moate* v. *Moate*, (1948) 2 All ER 486.
3. *Sayre* v. *Hughes*, (1868) LR 5 Eq 376.
4. *Beckford* v. *Beckford*, Lofft's R 490.
5. *Soar* v. *Foster*, (1858) 4 K&J 152.
6. *Snell's Principles of Equity*, pp. 262-271.
7. *Freme* v. *Clement*, (1881) 18 Ch D 499.
8. *McPhail* v. *Doulton*, 1971 AC 424; *Brown* v. *Higgs*, (1803) 8 Ves 581.

(1) *In case of favoured persons.*—Where the execution is defective by reason of some accident or mistake, equity will grant relief against such formal defects.[9] Such equitable relief would be available in respect of certain favoured persons who are regarded to have supplied good consideration. Thus a purchaser, i.e. a mortgagee, or a lessee, a creditor, a wife, a legitimate child and a charity are favoured persons, but a husband, an illegitimate child, a grandchild or remote relations, generally, or a volunteer are not favoured persons.

(2) *Where defects are not of the essence and substance of the power.*—Defects of form of power is excused or relieved.[10]

(3) *Where there is covenant.*—Where it has been provided by the donee that in (default of appointment) *A* shall not take less amount or some smaller amount, his hands are tied and he cannot appoint in a way which is prejudicial to *A*.

Thus "a defective execution will always be aided in equity under the circumstances mentioned, it being the duty of every man to pay his debts, and a husband or a father to provide for child".[11]

(*c*) *Recognition in India.*—Sections 177, 178 and 179 of the Indian Succession Act make a deliberate departure from the English doctrine of satisfaction. As the first section goes: "Where a debtor bequeaths a legacy to his creditor and it does not appear from the will that the legacy is meant as a satisfaction of the debt, the creditor shall be entitled to the legacy as well as the debt."

This departure is on grounds suggested by the Law Commissioners in their report that presumptions recognised in England are objectionable in themselves or specifically inapplicable to India.

Presumption against satisfaction as indicated in the section, it may be noted, is not displaced by a mere equality of the legacy and the debts. In one case[12] a testator, who had a sum of Rs 9000 as deposit from his brother, gave to his brother a legacy of Rs 9000 and it was held that the brother was entitled to both, the legacy and his deposit. But as decided in *Rajmanuar case*[13] where a will contained a clear indication that the legacy was meant as a satisfaction of the debt due to *X*, *X* could not claim both as the section explains.

One should note that there is a difference between performance and satisfaction and that is, that in the former the question is whether a notional act (rather than actual) or an identical act (to that which he contracted to do) has been performed; while in the latter the question is whether the thing done was intended as a substitute for the thing covenanted.

Section 92 of the Indian Trusts Act puts into practice the principle of this maxim. It explains that "where a person contracts to buy property to be held on

9. *Tollet* v. *Tollet*, (1728) 2 P Wms 494.
10. *Ibid.*
11. *Ibid.*
12. *Hasanali* v. *Popatal*, 37 Bom 211.
13. 25 Mad 361.

trust for certain beneficiaries and buys the property accordingly, he must hold the property for their benefit to the extent necessary to give effect to the contract". Equity thus imputes an intention to fulfil an obligation.

The doctrine of advancement does not apply in India. The reasons given in this regard are usages and practice prevailing among the Hindus and Mahomedans to purchase property and make grants in benami without any intention of vesting the property in the donee.[14]

(1) Law as to Benami Transaction in India

In one *Supreme Court case*[15] the question before the court was whether a transaction was *benami*. The facts may be summarised as under:

B acquired a house from *MB* and granted its patta (in 1940) to his brother (Plaintiff 1) and his nephew (Plaintiff 2) on passing BSc examination by Plaintiff 2. The defendant, another brother to *B*, lived in that house along with *B*. *B* had made several statements of his intention to make plaintiff 2 the absolute owner of the house. *B* died thereafter in September 1955. The plaintiffs filed a suit for recovery of possession of the house. The defendants pleaded that the house was theirs due to rights of survivorship and their joint purchase along with *B*. The plaintiffs were at the most holding property as benamidars, the defendants said. The trial court decreed the suit in favour of the plaintiffs. The High Court however decided that the house was purchased by *B* out of his own money in the names of the plaintiffs without any intention to confer any beneficial interest on them and that the house belonged to *B*, and on his death to his surviving brothers including the plaintiff, and the defendant succeeded to his estate which included the suit house in equal shares. In appeal to the Supreme Court it was held that under the English law, when real or personal property is purchased in the name of a stranger, a resulting trust will be presumed in favour of the person who is proved to have paid the purchase money in the character of the purchaser. It is however open to the transferee to rebut that presumption by showing that the intention of the person who contributed the purchase money was that the transferee should himself require the beneficial interest in the property. There is however an exception to the above rule of presumption made by the English law when the person who gets the legal title under the conveyance is either a child or the wife of the person who contributes the purchase money to his grandchild, whose father is dead. The rule applicable in such cases in known as the Doctrine of Advancement which requires the court to presume that the purchase is for the benefit of the person in whose favour the legal title is transferred even though the purchase money may have been contributed by the father or the husband or the grandfather, as the case may be, unless such presumption is rebutted by evidence showing that it was the intention of the person who paid the purchase money that the transferee should not become the real owner of the property in question. The doctrine of

14. Lord Atkin in *Kerwick* v. *Kerwick*, (1921) 47 IA 275; *Gopikrist* v. *Gangaprasad*, 6 MIA 53 and *Sayed Uzurali* v. *Musammat Altaf Fatima*, 13 MIA 232.
15. *Thakur Bhim Singh* v. *Thakur Kan Singh*, (1980) 3 SCC 72, 81-84.

advancement is not in vogue in India. The *counterpart* of the English law of resulting trust referred to above is the Indian law of benami transaction.

(2) Benami Transactions in India: Their rise and decline

(*a*) *Position up to 18-5-1988.*—(*i*) *General.*—Since the Equity courts came into existence to do justice they firmly believed that a person must be prepared to do what is right and fair and that one must be just before one professes to be generous. This it did by imputing an intention to fulfil an obligation.

On this principle benami transactions were statutorily recognised in India. As expressed by Sir George Farewell in 1915, such transactions were proper and "quite unobjectionable".[16] Hindus and Mahomedans used this device alike and made grants in benami without any intention of vesting the property in the donee.[17] Benami transactions had thus a very strong footing in the Indian Legal system and their judicial recognition came from very early time, the first case being *Calcutta case*[18] wherein a purchase in wife's name was held to be *Farzi* (fictitious). In this and other cases[19] it was held that the property vested in the person to whom the grant was made and not necessarily in the person whose name was made use of.

(*ii*) *What is Benami Transaction.*—As observed in *Pitchayya case*[20] "where a person acquires an interest in property with his funds in the name of another for his own benefit, the latter is called *benamidar*. A benamidar is not a trustee in the strict sense of term. He has the *ostensible title* to the property standing in his name, but the property does not vest in him, but is vested in the real owner. He is only a *name-lender* or *an alias* for the real owner. The cardinal distinction between a trustee known to English law and a benamidar lies in the fact that a trustee is the legal owner of the property standing in his name and the *cestui que trust* is only a beneficial owner, whereas in the case of benami transaction the real owner has got the legal title though the property is in the name of benamidar".

In other words, a benami purchase or conveyance leads to a resulting trust in India, just as a purchase or transfer under similar circumstances leads to a resulting trust in England.

The word benami means without name.

(*iii*) *Characteristics.*—(*a*) Use of an alias in respect of holding of property, and (*b*) concealment of the real owner's name are the two main characteristics of a benami transaction.

---

16. *Bilas Kunwar* v. *Desraj Ranjit*, (1915) ILR 37 All 557: AIR 1915 PC 96.
17. Lord Atkin in *Kerwick* v. *Kerwick*, (1921) 47 IA 275; *Gopikrist* v. *Gangaprasad*, 6 MIA 53 and *Syed Uzurali* v. *Musammat Altaf Fatima*, 13 MIA 232.
18. *SK. Bahadur Ali* v. *Sk. Dhomu*, 1 Cal Sud R Diw Rep 250 cited in Tyabji: *Muslim Law*, 1968, p. 396, fn 1: 57th Report L.C. of India, August 7, 1973, Chap. 1.
19. *Balanjyappa Chetty* v. *Arumugam Chetty*, (1864) 2 MHCR 26; *Bipin Bihari Chowdhary* v. *Ram Chunder Roy*, (1870) 14 WR 12; *Tagore* v. *Tagore*, (1872) IA Supp 47 (Tagore Case).
20. *Pitchayya* v. *Ratamma*, AIR 1929 Mad 268, 269.

The essential point is this that there is no intention to benefit the person in whose name the transaction stands, i.e., a benamidar. This benamidar as pointed out by the Privy Council[21] is simply an alias for that of the person beneficially interested. He has the ostensible title to the property standing in his name; but the beneficial ownership of the property does not vest in him, but in the real owner. The person in whose favour the transaction is effected is called the *benamidar* and the transaction is a *benami* transaction. The real owner in a benami transaction keeps in the background under a secret trust and allows the ostensible owner to appear as true owner. As between benamidar and the real owner the former is not the real owner, but the latter is the real owner. However, as between third parties and the benamidar, the benamidar is the real owner. The benamidar can pass a good title to *bona fide* transferee.[22]

All benami transfers are not necessarily fraudulent, though all fraudulent transfers are necessarily benami. Once it is proved that the consideration for a sale in favour of wife flowed from her husband, the sale is *benami* and the wife is merely benamidar.

(*iv*) *Essentials of a benami transaction.*—The following are the essentials of a benami transaction:

(*i*) Custody of the title deed.

(*ii*) Source from which the purchase money flows.[23]

(*iii*) The motive of the purchaser of property.

(*iv*) The possession of property.

(*v*) Relationship between the parties.[24]

(*v*) *Types of Benami Transactions in India.*—Two types of benami transactions are generally recognised in India:

(*a*) Where a person buys a property with his own money but in the name of another person without any intention to benefit such other person the transaction is called benami: *See* Section 82 of the Indian Trusts Act.[25] In such a case the transferee holds the property for the benefit of the person who has contributed the purchase money, and he is the real owner.

(*b*) In the second case, which is loosely termed as a benami transaction, a person who is the owner of the property executes a conveyance in the favour of another without the intention of transferring the title to the property thereunder. Here also the transferor continues to be the real

---

21. Note the wordings of S. 81 in this regard; *Petherpermal* v. *Muniandi*, 1908 ILR 35 Cal 551, 558, PC; *Gurunarain* v. *Sheolal*, AIR 1918 PC 140.

22. *See* S. 41, Transfer of Property Act.

23. *N. Johnstone* v. *Gopal Singh*, AIR 1931 Lah 419: 6 MIA 53; *Thakur Bhim Singh* v. *Thakur Kan Singh*, (1980) 3 SCC 72.

24. *Gopaadibai* v. *State of M.P.*, (1980) 2 SCC 327: AIR 1980 SC 1040; *Jaydayal Poddar* v. *Bibi Hazra*, (1974) 1 SCC 3: AIR 1974 SC 171; *Manmohan Das* v. *Ramdei*, AIR 1931 PC 175.

25. *See* Comment to S. 82 in Light of the Benami Transactions (Prohibition) Act, 1988.

owner: *See* Section 81, the Indian Trusts Act and the comment thereunder. The difference between cases under Sections 82 and 81 is this, that in the former there is an operative transfer, from the transferor to the transferee, though the transferee holds the property for the benefit of the person who has contributed the purchase money; in the latter case there is no operative transfer at all and the title rests with the transferor notwithstanding the execution of the conveyance. One common feature, however, in both these cases is that the real title is divorced from the ostensible title and they are vested in different persons.

(*vi*) *Principles for determination of Benami Transactions*.—These principles may be summed up as follows:

(*i*) The burden of showing that a transfer is a benami transaction lies on the person who asserts that it is such a transaction.[26] Mere suspicious character of the grantor is not enough.[27] The surrounding circumstances, the position of the parties, their relations to each other and their subsequent conduct are factors which go to decide the benami nature of a transaction.[28]

(*ii*) If it is proved that the purchase money came from a person other than the person in whose favour the property is transferred, the purchase is *prima facie* assumed to be for the benefit of the person who supplied the purchase money, unless there is evidence to the contrary.

(*iii*) The true character of the transaction is governed by the intention of the person who has contributed the purchase money.

(*iv*) The question whether a transaction is benami or not mainly depends upon the intention of the person who has contributed money as explained in Section 82 of the Trusts Act[29] and upon the intention of the person who has executed the conveyance as explained in Section 81 of the Trusts Act.

(*v*) A benami transaction is not necessarily a sham transaction, it may be a gift as has been recognised by the Privy Council in *Mohmad Sadik case*[30].

(*vii*) *Distinction between a sham transaction and a benami transaction*.—The distinction between these two types of transactions is that in a sham transaction the title does not pass and, as a matter of fact, is not intended to pass whereas in the benami transaction it does pass until it is questioned by the real owner.[31]

---

26. *Sitaram* v. *Ramrao*, AIR 1931 Nag 91: 130 IC 817.
27. (1962) BLJR 314 (SC); *Jagdamba Prasad Lala* v. *Badri Prasad Jhunjhunwala*, AIR 1937 Cal 203: 171 IC 522.
28. *Jaydalal Poddar* v. *Bibi Hazra*, (1974) 1 SCC 3 following *Manmohan Das case*, AIR 1931 PC 175: 134 IC 669.
29. This is explained in *Meenakshi Mills* v. *CIT*, AIR 1957 SC 49.
30. *Mohd. Sadik Ali Khan* v. *Fakr Jahan Begum*, AIR 1932 PC 13, 20: 59 IA 1.
31. *Rangappa* v. *Rangaswami*, AIR 1925 Mad 1005: 1925 MWN 232.

In the former there is no transfer at all while in fraudulent benami transaction there is a transfer. Consequently it is plain that the former is a nullity and therefore there is nothing to be set aside while in the latter the transaction is to be set aside.

A sham transaction being a pretence or a ruse has no legal existence at all and is therefore not intended to have any legal effect. On the other hand a benami transaction was legal up to 18-5-1991, after 18-5-1991 it is illegal.

In the former no money is given or taken by either the purchaser or the seller while in the latter the purchase money is paid by the real owner.

The important difference between the two is one of intention. This distinction between the two is discussed in *Meenakshi Mills* v. *CIT*[32].

(*viii*) *Causes of origin.*—A question may be posed as to why this practice of holding property in this way arose though it is risky to do so. To this question the, possible answer may be made, that to avoid the following greater risks the benami transactions were resorted to:

(*i*) To avoid certain political and social risks.

(*ii*) To avoid appreciable risk from one generation to another.

(*iii*) To avoid loss of property on hostile conquest or confiscation of property.

(*iv*) Besides this, love of secrecy is also a possible reason.

(*v*) Lastly as Pollock[33] says it is quite natural for ingenious persons to discover that the means of concealment which formerly were a shelter from the strong hands of princes and adventurers can be turned into peaceful times to the less ambitious but not less lucrative end of baffling the creditors.

(*vi*) Besides this, a benami transaction was resorted to with a view to avoid claims of other members of one's own family.

(*vii*) Sometimes to escape restrictions imposed upon by Government Servants' Conduct Rules, was a good device.

(*viii*) To this list one may add, as the report of the Commission says,[34] one more convincing reason— a desire to evade taxes like income tax, wealth tax etc.

(*b*) *Position from 19-5-1988.*—Experience has shown that such transactions sometimes become fraudulent and create legal and factual controversies[35] and consequently complexity and uncertainty in law is generated. On account of benami transactions not only an individual but the State is also a loser. This problem therefore caused great concern to the taxing authorities and

32. 1956 SCR 691.
33. Pollock: *Law of Fraud, Misrepresentation and Mistake,* 1894, pp. 83, 84.
34. Ch. 1.
35. Cf. observations of JJ. Patel and Wagle in *Hasman Gani Ahmed Sahib* v. *Vidyadhar Krishna Rao Mung*, Appeal No. 533 of 1968 decided on 17-1-1969.

consequently the Benami Transactions (Prohibition of the Right to Recover Property) Ordinance, 1988 was passed on May 19, 1988, to come into force at once. The Benami Transactions (Prohibitions) Act, 1988 has replaced the Ordinance.

(*i*) *Benami Transactions (Prohibition) Act, 1988.*—The Act received President's assent on 5-9-1988. It has 9 sections. It extends to the whole of India except the State of Jammu and Kashmir (Section 1). Sections 3, 5 and 8 came into force at once and the rest of the provisions were deemed to have come into force on 19-5-1988 (Section 1). Section 2 relates to definitions and Section 3 prohibits all types of benami transactions except purchases of property made in name of one's wife or unmarried daughter. Section 3(*i*) raises a presumption that unless the contrary is proved the property so purchased shall be presumed to have been purchased for the benefit of the wife or the unmarried daughter. Such presumption, which in law is known by the terminology of "advancement" is made in order to rebut an ordinary presumption of a "resulting trust" in favour of the person purchasing the property. Section 3(3) makes it an offence to enter into benami transaction and the offence would be punishable with imprisonment up to 3 years or fine or both. The offence is non-cognizable and bailable. Section 4 prohibits recovery of the property held benami and according to Section 5 benami properties are liable to acquisition by Government without payment of any amount. Section 7 repeals the following provisions:

(*a*) Sections 81, 82 and 94 of the Indian Trusts Act, 1882,

(*b*) Section 66 of the Civil Procedure Code, 1908, and

(*c*) Section 281-A of the Income Tax Act, 1961.

(*ii*) *Constitutional validity of the Act.*—The Benami Transactions (Prohibition) Act, 1988 cannot be treated as an enactment relating to transfer of property. The Act does not deal with land. The enactment is referable to Entry 10 of List III in Seventh Schedule to the Constitution. It can, in no sense, be related to the legislative head "Transfer of Property" in Entry 6 of List III. Any trenching upon Entry 18 in List II is only incidental, and it does not affect the validity of the Act or the competence of Parliament.[36] In *Velayudhan Ramkrishnan* v. *Rajeev*[37], it was held that the Benami Transactions (Prohibition of Right to Recover Property) Ordinance, 1988 is not violative of Article 19 of the Constitution.

(*iii*) *Scope of Section 4.*—Section 4 of the Act prohibits the filing of a suit by the real owner against the benamidar on the ground that the latter was holding the property benami. Similarly, a defence cannot be raised in a suit that the defendant was holding the property benami. However, a mere allegation that the property is held benami by the plaintiff will not attract the provisions of Section 4 of the Act. Defendant must lead proof to substantiate the plea.[38] A suit

---

36. *S. Mohammad Anwaruddin* v. *Sabina Sultana*, (1987) 179 ITR 442 (AP).
37. AIR 1989 Ker 12: (1988) 174 ITR 482.
38. *Kesho Ram* v. *Chetan Dass*, (1991) 192 ITR 446 (P&H).

for specific performance by a purchaser of land does not lie on the ground that the land was held benami.[39]

The court is bound to consider at every stage, to find out whether there is a defence of benami put forward before it. The court has necessarily to say to the persons who project such a plea that it will not be allowed. The court is duty-bound to be on the alert in the discharge of this statutory duty; to find out whether any benami defence has been put forward. If it notices one, it has firmly to disallow it.[40]

Section 4 of the Benami Transactions (Prohibition) Act prohibits the filing of the suit by the real owner against another on the ground that the latter was holding the property benami. Similarly, the defence cannot be raised in a suit that the defendant was holding the property benami. In the instant case, apart from the indirect assertion in the pleadings that the property in suit was purchased in the name of the plaintiff from the vendors benami, no proof was led to substantiate the pleas. Merely an allegation that the property is held benami by the plaintiff will not attract the provisions of Section 4 of the Benami Transactions (Prohibition) Act.[41]

(*iv*) *Retroactive operation of the Act.*—In its sweep Section 4 envisages past benami transactions also within its retroactivity. In this sense the Act is both a penal and a disqualifying statute. The expression "any property held benami" in Section 4 is not limited to any particular time, date or duration. All the real owners are equally affected by the disability provision irrespective of the time of creation of the right. A right is a legally protected interest. The real owner's right was hitherto protected and the Act has resulted in removal of that protection.[42]

When Section 4(2) nullifies the defences avialable to the real owner in recovering the benami property from the benamidar, the law must apply irrespective of the time of the benami transactions. The expressions "shall lie" in Section 4(1) and "shall be allowed" in Section 4(2) are prospective and shall apply to present (future stages) and future suits, claims or actions only.[43]

The Law Commission has also taken the view that the legislation replacing the Ordinance (2 of 1988) should be retroactive in operation and that no *locus*

---

39. *P. Ramchandra Rao* v. *G. Jangaiah,* (1989) 179 ITR 438 (AP).
40. *Velayudhan Ramakrishnan* v. *Rajeev*, AIR 1989 Ker 12: (1988) 174 ITR 482.
41. *Kesho Ram* v. *Chetan Dass*, (1991-1) 99 Punj LR 511.
42. *Mithilesh Kumari* v. *Prem Behari Khare*, (1989) 2 SCC 95: (1989) 177 ITR 97; *Prem Vati Bhandari* v. *Ved Parkash*, (1991) 191 ITR 47 (P&H); *Narinder Kumar Jain* v. *Munieubrat Dass*, (1989-2) 96 PLR 453: (1990) 181 ITR 305 (P&H); *Vishan Devi* v. *Sun Beam Rubber Mills*, (1991) 192 ITR 611 (P&H): (1991-2) C PLR 144; *S. Mohammad Anwaruddin* v. *Sabina Sultana*, (1989) 179 ITR 442 (AP); *Rajan Ammal* v. *P.K. Pillai*, AIR 1991 Mad 310; *Champa Devi* v. *Kaushalaya Devi*, (1991) 1 PLJR 38.
43. *Mithilesh Kumari* v. *Prem Bihari Khare*, (1989) 2 SCC 95: (1989) 177 ITR 97; *Prem Vati Bhandari* v. *Ved Prakash*, (1991) 191 ITR 47 (P&H); *Narinder Kumar Jain* v. *Munieubrat Dass*, (1989-2) 96 PLR 453: (1990) 181 ITR 305 (P&H); *Vishan Devi* v. *Sun Beam Rubber Mills*, (1991) 192 ITR 611 (P&H): (1991-2) 100 PLR 144; *S. Mohammad Anwaruddin* v. *Sabina Sultana*, (1989) 179 ITR 442 (AP); *Rajan Ammal* v. *P.K. Pillai*, AIR 1991 Mad 310; *Champa Devi* v. *Kaushalaya Devi*, (1991) 1 PLJR 38.

penitentia need be given to the persons who had entered in the benami transactions in the past.[44]

The Act, even though retroactive in operation cannot create a bar against the legal owner of the property to reinforce his right against the legal representatives of the benamidar in respect of property which ceased to be benami before the Act came into force as a consequence of execution of a relinquishment deed in favour of legal owner. The legal owner was, therefore, entitled to recover possession from the legal representatives of the benamidar.[45]

(*v*) *Pending suits.*—The word "suit" includes an appeal from the judgment in suit. The prohibition on pending suit, claim or action under Section 4(2) includes pending appeals against decree passed on such suit, claim or action. Section 4 of the Act is retroactive in nature and applies to pending suits and appeal arising out of such suits.[46] The deprivation of a defence is not confined to a suit hereafter to be filed; it extends to the projected areas of a claim, or an already initiated action. The Act takes in transactions entered into long ago and litigations instituted and already pending whatever be the age and stage of the legal proceedings.[47] Execution of decree for possession by the real owner is also barred.[48]

See also "Retrospective operation of the Act" *supra.*

(vi) Expressions "claim or action" and "shall lie" in Section 4(1): Meaning of.—The words 'claim or action' are general in nature and of wide import and are not to be given time-bound or stage-bound or forum-bound meaning. Coming to the expression "shall lie" it is not possible to annexe to it a stringent meaning so as to say it will apply only to proceedings of the nature of a suit, claim or action to enforce any right spoken to in Section 4(1) to be initiated after the provisions of the Act came into force, and not to proceedings initiated anterior to it, but which have not been put an end to once and for all in the eyes of the law. It will take in also a case where the suit, claim or action already laid is being prosecuted stage after stage until finally disposed of, as permitted by law and wherein no finality or conclusiveness has been reached. Until and unless a finality or conclusiveness therein is reached in the eyes of the law, the case will come within the expression "shall lie". Two of the ordinary dictionary meanings given to the expression "lie" are—'to press' and 'to have a position' the expression, in the context in which it appears and giving due significance to

---

44. *Mithilesh Kumari* v. *Prem Behari Khare*, (1989) 2 SCC 95: (1989) 177 ITR 97; *Prem Vati Bhandari* v. *Ved Parkash*, (1991) 191 ITR 47 (P&H); *Narinder Kumar Jain* v. *Munieubrat Dass*, (1989-2) 96 PLR 453: (1990) 181 ITR 305 (P&H); *Vishan Devi* v. *Sun Beam Rubber Mills*, (1991) 192 ITR 611 (P&H): (1991-2) 100 PLR 144; *S. Mohammad Anwaruddin* v. *Sabina Sultana*, (1989) 179 ITR 442 (AP); *Rajan Ammal* v. *P.K. Pillai*, AIR 1991 Mad 310; *Champa Devi* v. *Kaushalaya Devi*, (1991) 1 PLJR 38.
45. *Satyabhamabai Balaji Kitey* v. *Pandurang Marotrao Pawar*, (1990) 183 ITR 290: AIR 1990 Bom 134.
46. *Mithilesh Kumari* v. *Prem Bihari Khare*, (1989) 2 SCC 95: (1989) 177 ITR 97.
47. *Velayudhan Ramakrishnan* v. *Rajeev*, AIR 1989 Ker 12: (1988) 174 ITR 482 (Ker); *C.T. Mohanan* v. *C. Yesoda*, (1990) 185 ITR 31 (Ker).
48. *Urmila Bala Dasi* v. *Probodh Chandra Ghosh*, (1990) 184 ITR 604 (Cal): AIR 1989 Cal 283; *C. Narayanan* v. *Gangadharan*, AIR 1989 Ker 256.

the subjects and reasons behind the statute, in which it is found, must be given the meaning that the plea shall not be advanced, prosecuted, pressed forth or placed in any suit, claim or action whatever be the stage of the suit, claim or action.[49]

(*vii*) *Property purchased in the name of wife or unmarried daughter.*— Section 3 provides for a prohibition in relation to a benami transaction. Section 4, *inter alia*, prohibits a contention or a defence either by the plaintiff or the defendant based on any right in respect of any property held benami.[50]

It is true that sub-section (3) of Section 4 of the said Act does not bring within its fold the expressions provided for under sub-section (2) of Section 3 expressly, but as the law itself, which was enacted for the purpose of suppressing a mischief it will lead to an absurdity if such an exception is denied to a person in a suit where a past benami transaction is in question. Thus Sections 3 and 4 of the said Act will have to be read together and it must be held that Section 4 derives its colour from Section 3 in relation to such transactions which have been saved in a limited way by reason of sub-section (2) of Section 3 of the said Act. As Section 3 is prospective in nature, a transaction contemplated under sub-section (2) of Section 3 of the said Act, on its own force, shall exclude the applicability of Section 4 of the Act in relation to the transaction which had already taken place.[51]

It is now well-settled that in India, acquisition of a property by a husband in the name of his wife has become a common feature. However, such type of acquisition of property by the husband in the name of his wife could have been for the purpose of entering into a benami transaction or for the purpose of making a grant of such a property to his wife. It is now well-settled that if a person raises a plea that an apparent state of affairs is not the real state of affairs or the apparent owner is not the real owner, the onus of proof to prove the necessary ingredients of a benami transaction lies upon the person who sets up such a plea. However, in a case where a plea is raised that such an acquisition was made by the husband for the benefit of his wife, i.e., by way of gift or grant, the burden of proof shifts to the other side. Therefore, where a husband has purchased a property in the name of his wife and raised substantial structure thereupon, Parliament did not intend to bar a remedy or a defence.[52]

When a property is purchased by a person in the name of his wife, there is a rebuttable presumption that the property had been purchased for the benefit of the wife.[53]

(*viii*) In *Premvati Bhandari* v. *Ved Prakash*[54], the Punjab and Haryana High Court has taken the view that sub-section (2) of Section 3 of the Act, no doubt,

49. *Minor Habib Rahman* v. *Ramu Pandaram*, (1991) 1 Mad LJ 254.
50. *Najmam Bibi* v. *Jamila Khatoon*, (1991) 87 ITR 548 (Pat).
51. *Ibid.*
52. *Ibid.*
53. *Mithilesh Kumari* v. *Prem Behari Khare*, (1989) 2 SCC 95: (1989) 177 ITR 97; *Rajan Ammal* v. *P.K. Pillai*, AIR 1991 Mad 310.
54. (1991) 191 ITR 47 (P&H): (1991-1) 99 Punj LR 490.

creates an exception to the effect that property can be purchased by any person in the name of his wife or unmarried daughter but this does not mean that the rigour of Section 4(1) of the Act which bars the filing of a suit, claim or action to recover such a property is taken away. What is saved by sub-section (2) of Section 3 of the Act is that a person can buy the property benami in the name of his wife or unmarried daughter but he shall not be punishable under sub-section (3) of the Act, but this does not mean that the plaintiff retains the right to recover the property from the benami holder by filing a suit. A person can purchase the property under sub-section (2) of Section 3 of the Act benami in the name of his wife or unmarried daughter but the right of the real owner to recover the property from the benami holder has been eliminated by Section 4 of the Act. Earlier, there was a right to recover or resist the claim of the real owner against the benamidar but now that remedy stands barred and the right rendered unenforceable.[55]

Acquisition of property in the name of the wife of a coparcener by the joint family will constitute a benami transaction and will not be saved under Section 3(2) of the said Act.[56]

(*ix*) *Suit by third party*.—Under Section 4(1) the real owner cannot bring any suit, claim or action to enforce his right as the real owner on the plea that ostensible owner is a benamidar. Section 4(1) of the Act prohibits the right of the real owner to enforce the same through court against the benamidar and Section 4(2) destroys the right of defence of the owner to claim that he is real transferee when the benamidar brings a suit to enforce his right. Hence Section 4 takes into its ambit the right of a real owner vis-a-vis ostensible owner. The prohibition, under Section 4(1) and (2) does not prohibit the right of a third party to get such a declaration. Therefore, a third party has a right to get a declaration that the transferee was a benamidar.[57]

(*x*) *Nominal transactions*.—Generally benami transactions are cases where property is purchased by a person in the name of another after paying consideration by himself. In the case of nominal transactions, no title is passed and the title is never intended to be passed. In *Bathula Anasuya* v. *Bathula Rayudu*[58], the Andhra Pradesh High Court laid down that the Benami Transactions (Prohibition of the Right to Recover Property) Ordinance, 1988 (which has been replaced by Act 45 of 1988) does not affect nominal transactions. The court can examine the question on merits and find out whether the transaction in question is a nominal transaction or not.

The above view was taken on ground that Section 82 of the Indian Trusts Act, 1882 alone was repealed by the Ordinance keeping Section 81 of the said Act on the statute book. But the Act which replaces the Ordinance repeals Sections 81, 82 and 94 of the Indian Trusts Act, 1882. Therefore in view of the fact that Sections 81 and 82 of the Indian Trusts Act, 1881 were repealed by

55. *Premvati Bhandari* v. *Ved Prakash*, (1991) 191 ITR 47 (P&H): (1991-1) 99 Punj LR 490.
56. *Rameshwar Mistry* v. *Babulal Mistry*, AIR 1991 Pat 53.
57. *Gopal Bariha* v. *Satyanarayanan Das*, AIR 1991 Ori 131.
58. (1990) 182 ITR 45 (AP): AIR 1989 AP 290.

Section 7(1) of the Benami Prohibition Act sham and nominal transactions are also hit by the provisions of the Benami Transactions (Prohibition) Act, 1988.[59]

(*xi*) *Fraudulent transfer*.—The plaintiff, a financial company, filed a suit against Defendants 1 to 5. It was alleged that the Defendant 1 took some loan from the plaintiff and fraudulently diverted the loan amount to Defendants 2, 3 and 5 and acquired assets in their names. The defendants claimed that the suit was barred by Section 4 of the Act. It was laid down that exception provided in Section 6 saves actions covered by Section 53 of the T.P. Act as well as transfers for an illegal purpose. If it is ultimately found that Defendant 1 fraudulently diverted the amount of the loans raised by him from the plaintiff, in favour of the other defendants and out of such diverted funds immovable properties were purchased fraudulently by other defendants, then certainly the plaintiff is entitled to follow such properties in the hands of other defendants also.[60]

(*xii*) *Property*.—As per the definition, property would include any right or interest in such property and hence the right to purchase under hire-purchase agreement shall certainly come within the ambit of property.[61]

(*xiii*) *Amendment of plaint*.—In 1983 the plaintiff filed a suit for declaration of title and some other consequential reliefs. After commencement of the Act he filed an application praying for amendment of the plaint. As per the proposed amendment the case of the plaintiff was that his case was covered by Section 4(3)(*b*) of the Act. Before the commencement of the Act, there was no need for the plaintiff to specifically mention whether the benami transaction was of a category coming under Section 4(3)(*b*) of the Act. It was laid down that there was no inconsistency in the stand of the plaintiff. By the proposed amendment, the plaintiff pleads that this is a particular type of benami transaction which comes under Section 4(3)(*b*). It does not amount to a new case.[62]

(*xiv*) *Drawbacks of the Act*.—The Benami Transactions (Prohibition) Act, 1988 has however certain inherent drawbacks which are required to be remedied.

(*a*) The Act is silent on the legality or otherwise of the benami transactions entered into prior to 19-5-1988, i.e., before the operation of the new law.

(*b*) A male or female who purchases benami property for the benefit of his or her minor sons, minor grandsons and granddaughters or for her husband would be in hot water because Section 3(3) and (4) make it a non-cognizable and bailable offence to purchase property by a benami transaction. This provision is therefore quite impracticable and oppressive.

(*c*) By this Act a benamidar is not benefited at all since the property in question is normally retained by the real owner. It is possible on the part of a

---

59. *Kathoon Bivi Ammal* v. *S. Mohamad*, (1990) 2 Mad LJ 42.
60. *P.N.B. Finance Ltd.* v. *Shital Prasad Jain*, AIR 1991 Del 213: (1990) 185 ITR 298 (Del).
61. *R. Rajagopal Reddy* v. *Padmini Chandrasekaran*, (1990) 1 Mad LJ 234.
62. *A. Kodandachari* v. *Radhamma*, (1991) 167 ITR 616 (AP). See also *Tara Devi* v. *Kailash Chand Joshi*, (1989) 1 Raj LR 844.

real owner to create a lease deed or tenancy deed of the benami property and thus occupy the property in a practical sense. Consequently what is protected is the right of the real owner and not the right of a benamidar.

(*d*) Under this Act property can be held in a fictitious name and the Act would not apply to such a transaction.

(*e*) Section 4 of the Act prohibits the right to recover property held benami. This provision which is intended to deter the real owners behind the curtain, of the benami property, from recovering the property through court is and would be hardly effective and would be hardly resorted to by the real owners because political patronage and muscle power of the mafia gangs are speedy and more powerful instruments than the power of a court to regain the property. Justice is dear and the law's delays are now a regular feature of lawcourts. This is enough to undermine the confidence of people in justice given by a lawcourt after many years. Instances of such gangs forcing a tenant to vacate the premises and murdering him if he refuses to vacate are many. This is the product of our civilization. Somebody has rightly said that—society prepares the crime and the criminal commits it. One may say, therefore, that the present situation in society makes the provision merely a symbolic one, ineffective and redundant.

(*f*) From the wordings of the provisions it seems that the Act would not apply to holding of property in the name of a coparcener of a Hindu Undivided Family, and holding property as a trustee in any other fiduciary capacity for another's benefit.

(*g*) Similarly Section 53 of the Transfer of Property Act i.e. transfer for an illegal purpose, is not affected.

(*h*) A question may arise here, as to whether this Act affects property purchased by the real owner in joint names, i.e. by putting his name along with other names of close relatives like wife, minor son, etc. Whether this can be called a benami transaction? Unfortunately the Act is silent on this point too.

As the Report of the Law Commission[63] goes there were 3 alternatives available to check tax evasion, fraud, etc. The first alternative was that entering into a benami transaction should be made an offence. This is implemented by prohibiting all types of benami transactions and making it an offence to enter into any benami transaction. The second alternative was that a provision should be made to the effect that in a civil suit a right shall not be enforced against the benamidar or against a third person, by or on behalf of the person claming to be the real owner of the property on the ground of benami. A similar provision could be made to bar defences on the ground of benami. Section 4 of the Act does this. The third alternative was that the present presumption of resulting trust (Section 82 of the Trusts Act) may be displaced (as in England) by the presumption of advancement in cases where the person to whom the property is transferred is a near relative. This is done by Section 3(2) but the provision is half-heartedly made.

---

63. 57th Report of the L.C. of India, August 7, 1973, Ch. 6.

(*i*) The Act would create difficulties in regard to property transferred under the power of attorney (POA). In result the POA who is considered to be an owner of property for income tax purposes would not be able to enforce his rights in respect of the property against the real owner who may not fulfil his obligations and retain or pocket the money obtained by sale of such property.

(*j*) By Section 7 of the Act, Section 281-A of the Income Tax Act, 1961 has been repealed. According to the present position there are persons who have declared their benami transactions in the income tax department and pay taxes accordingly. These persons now, on and from 19-5-1988 cannot hold property in benami. They are liable to be punished under the present Act. It is not understandable at all, what benefit the government is going to get by disturbing the position of assesses in the income tax and wealth tax departments. This will increase litigation and the government revenue would be reduced as a result of injunctions granted in litigation against the government as is the case with customs department where duty unpaid due to injunctions obtained amounts to crores of rupees.

(*k*) The provision of Section 5 regarding acquisition of benami property without any payment is really harsh, unjust and oppressive to the extent of naming it as draconian. Due to this provision those who have declared their benami transactions in the past genuinely, would be under difficulties, so much so that they would not only be punished under Section 3 but their properties are liable to be acquired under Section 5 without any payment. This is nothing short of legal robbery and atrocity which generate the use of muscle power and reduce the faith of people in the administration of law and the rule of law.

Thus the Act creates more problems[64] than it solves.

10. WHERE THERE IS EQUAL EQUITY, THE LAW SHALL PREVAIL

11. WHERE THE EQUITIES ARE EQUAL, THE FIRST IN TIME SHALL PREVAIL

These two maxims relate to the question of priority and they have been separately dealt with therefore.[65]

12. EQUITY ACTS IN PERSONAM

(*a*) *Meaning.*—Courts of equity, described as courts of conscience, operate primarily *in personam* binding the conscience of a person and thus bringing an individual's conscience under its sway. Its decrees were regarded not merely as decisions concerning the rights and properties in dispute but as decrees, decisions, and directions, positive or negative, addressed to the individual party or parties. Thus on one side an individual's conscience was sought to be bound, and on the other, the Chancellor exercised his jurisdiction guided according to

64. Dhodi & Sarin: *Law of Fraud, Benami Transactions and Fraudulent Transfers in India*, 3rd Edn., 1989.

65. *See* Chapter IV, Priorities and Assignments.

his own conscience. This maxim being descriptive of the Equity Courts' procedure covers a large portion of its procedural and remedial action. So much so that "*in a sense it comprises the whole of the equity*".[66] The extent of its application initiated Mukherjea, J.[67] to remark that "the rule of acting *in personam* was really the weapon with which the early chancellors sought to establish their jurisdiction in opposition to that of the Common Law courts". But this very extent and exercise of jurisdiction impelled Lord Esher to remark in the last quarter of the nineteenth century in *Mocambic case*[68] that such an exercise of jurisdiction amounted to doing indirectly what the court dared not to have done directly. As this amounted to overriding the jurisdiction of foreign courts, the significance of the maxim is now decreasing. It can be explained better with regard to methods of enforcing judgments, and jurisdiction over property abroad.

(*b*) *Application and Cases.*—A judgment of the Common Law courts was enforced by one of the writs of execution as a result of which forcible possession of the goods or property of the defendant was obtained and given to the plaintiff. But equity did not follow this method. It issued orders against the defendant personally and made him act accordingly, failing which he was punished for disobedience by attachment of his property or committal for contempt. The decrees of Equity Courts thus addressed the defendant in terms of personal command and he either obeyed it willingly or was made to obey in spite of his dissent, either through sequestration of his property or imprisonment. This execution *in personam* was peculiar to equity courts.[69] When imprisonment became ineffective to compel obedience equity courts invented and applied a writ of sequestration whereunder property in dispute was taken possession of by sequestrates appointed for the purpose and that was retained until the defendant acted as ordered. This also did not prove to be as effective as was intended. These powers were supplemented by statute by making vesting orders and appointing a person to execute a transfer. Where this was ignored by the defendant equity nominated a person to do the act for him. Equity thus purged the corrupt conscience of the defendant to bring him round and to compel him to carry out its orders. Since the Judicature Acts the orders of the Chancery Division could be enforced by way of legal writs of execution. Thus conveyances, contracts and documents were executed, or negotiable instruments were indorsed and trust funds were administered by equity.[70] But as observed by Lord Campbell, no jurisdiction was conferred on equity courts by the mere fact that an equitable remedy was claimed.[71] Moreover Equity Courts in suitable cases restrained unconscientious proceedings initiated in the Common Law courts, issued injunctions against execution of a foreign

---

66. Hanbury: *Modern Equity*, 2nd Edn., p. 89.
67. *Moolji Jetha & Co.* v. *K.S. & W. Mills & Co.*, AIR 1950 FC 83.
68. *Companhia Mocambic* v. *British South Africa Co.*, (1892) 2 QB 358: 1893 AC 602.
69. *Lever Bros.* v. *Kneale*, (1937) 2 KB 84.
70. *United States of America* v. *Dollfus*, 1952 AC 582; *Sultan of Johore* v. *Abubakar Tunku*, 1952 AC 318.
71. *Duke of Brunswick* v. *King of Hanover*, (1848) 2 HLC 1.

judgment and stayed proceedings in a foreign court if the same matter was pending in England.[72]

As equity's jurisdiction is primarily over the defendant personally, it is immaterial whether the property in dispute is within the jurisdiction of the court or otherwise. It may be situated abroad or may not be within the reach of the court, but if the defendant was within its jurisdiction or was capable of being served with the proceedings outside the jurisdiction, equity courts made orders against him personally. Accordingly in exercise of its jurisdiction *in personam* a court of equity could compel the performance of contracts and trusts[73] relating to property not locally situated but situated outside its jurisdiction. *Penn* v. *Lord Baltimore*[74] and *Ewing* v. *Orr Ewing*[75] are the leading examples on the point.

In the first case specific performance of an agreement was sought. The agreement was entered into between two parties for settling the boundaries of land situated in America, then a British colony. The agreement which otherwise could not be enforced *in rem* was enforced by a process of contempt *in personam*, as the defendant was within the court's jurisdiction. Lord Harwicke, C., observed in this case that the conscience of the party was bound by an agreement and being within the jurisdiction of the court which acts *in personam* the court may properly decree it as an agreement.[76] The courts have always been accustomed to compel the performance of contracts and trusts as to subjects which were not either locally or *ratione domicilii* within their jurisdiction. They have done so as to land in Scotland, in Ireland, in the Colonies and in foreign countries.[77]

In *Ewing case*[78], the House of Lords held that where some of the executors and trustees of a will were in England, the English court had jurisdiction to administer the real and personal assets of a testator who died domiciled in Scotland, even though the greater part of the personality and all the realty were situated in Scotland. Eventually however an administrative action was started in Scotland and the House of Lords stayed the English administration on the ground of convenience.[79]

In other circumstances even a defendant may be restrained from taking proceedings in a foreign country.[80]

This maxim was applied and the jurisdiction was exercised by equity courts in the following matters affecting land outside England—

(*i*) for the redemption and foreclosure[81] of a mortgage of it,

---

72. *C.F. Ewing case and North Carolina Estate Co. Ltd., Re,* (1889) 5 TLR 328.
73. *Ewing* v. *Orr Ewing,* (1883) 9 AC 34.
74. (1750) 1 Res Sen 444: 27 ER 1132.
75. (1883) 9 AC 34.
76. *Penn* v. *Lord Baltimore,* (1750) 1 Ves Sen 444: 27 ER 1132.
77. *Ewing* v. *Orr Ewing,* (1883) 9 AC 34.
78. *Ibid.*
79. *Snell's Principles of Equity,* p. 42.
80. *North Carolina Estate Co. Ltd., Re,* (1889) 5 TLR 328.
81. *Paget* v. *Ede,* 43 LJ Ch 571.

(*ii*) for specific performance[82] of an agreement to create a mortgage of it, or

(*iii*) for sale[83], or

(*iv*) its rent[84], or

(*v*) for an account of the rents and profits of it, or

(*vi*) for the appointment of a receiver[85] thereof if necessary.

(*c*) *Limitations of the Maxim.*—The main principle underlying the application of the maxim is that the plaintiff must have an equitable right of remedy in his favour to enforce; if it is not, there the maxim cannot be availed of, the action in regard to it being "local" where the land or property is situate.[86] The Judicature Act, 1873 has not conferred any new jurisdiction on courts and therefore no action to obtain damages for trespass to land outside England or to recover a rent charged on such land can be brought in England.[87]

Thus where the remedy requested for is not equitable, where the decree granted could not be effectively executed, and when the dispute is not one of the conscience, equity courts would not act under this maxim.

(*d*) *Recognition and Application in India.*—According to opinions of many learned text writers[88] no such jurisdiction is recognised by Indian courts while according to some, the courts in India have but *limited powers* of making a decree *in personam*.[89] The opinions are thus divided. The Civil Procedure Code, Section 16 does not deal with this problem; it explains the division of jurisdiction of the municipal courts only.[90] Till now we have no such decisions bearing directly on this issue. Clause 12 of the Letters Patent Act is also not so clear about this.[91] But as noted by Mulla[92], the court of equity in England will entertain such suits if the contract is made in England and the defendant resides or carries on business in England though the land may be situated abroad. Similarly where lands abroad have been acquired by fraud of a party residing in England, a suit to set aside the transaction will be entertained by the court of equity in England.[93] It will also entertain a suit to enforce express trusts affecting land situate in a foreign country or for preservation or protection of the trust fund situate in a foreign country if the trustee resides in England, but has

---

82. *Smith, Lawrence* v. *Kitson, Re*, (1916) 2 Ch 206.
83. *Richard West & Ptns. Ltd.* v. *Dick*, (1969) 2 Ch 424.
84. *Ibid.*
85. *St. Pierre* v. *S.A. Stores Ltd.*, (1936) 1 KB 382.
86. *Hawthorne, Re*, (1883) 23 Ch D 743.
87. (1892) 2 QB 358, *supra*.
88. Collett (Specific Relief Act), Nelson (Indian Contract Act), Dr Banerjee (Specific Relief Act) and *Shree Nath* v. *Kally Das*, (1879) 5 Cal 82.
89. *Stokes Anglo Indian Codes*, Vol. I, p. 684; *Holker* v. *Dadabhai*, (1890) 14 Bom 353.
90. *Moolji Jetha & Co.* v. *K. S. & W. Mills & Co.*, AIR 1950 FC 83; *Krishnaji Gajanan, Re*, (1909) 33 Bom 373.
91. *Ibid.*
92. *Civil Procedure Code*, 13th Edn., 1965, pp. 133-36.
93. *Lord Cranstown* v. *Johnston*, (1796) 3 Ves 170.

no jurisdiction to interfere with administration of a trust which has to be conducted in a foreign territory.[94] It has also no jurisdiction to entertain suits for recovery[95], or for partition of land[96], or for damages for trespass to land.[97]

If neither the person of the defendant nor his personal property is within jurisdiction, the court will not entertain a suit for a relief respecting immovable property situate beyond its jurisdiction, for the court cannot in that event execute its decree either *in rem* or *in personam* and a court does not entertain a suit if it cannot enforce its decree in the suit.[98] Consequently, though courts in India have but limited powers of making a decree *in personam*, Equity may act *in personam* in India too. The proviso to Section 16 of the Civil Procedure Code is thus an application, though in a highly modified form, of the maxim "*equity acts in personam*".[99]

---

94. *Bilasrai Joharmul* v. *Shivanarayan S.*, 71 IA 47; *Nelson* v. *Bridport*, (1628) 8 Bear 547.
95. *Hawthrone*, *In re*, (1883) 23 Ch 748.
96. *Cartwright* v. *Pettus*, (1675) 2 Ch Ca 214.
97. *British South Africa Co.* v. *Companhia de Mocambique*, 1893 AC 602: (1892) 2 QB 358.
98. See *Trimbak* v. *Laxman*, (1896) 20 Bom 495 cited in Mulla: *Civil Procedure Code*.
99. Mulla: *Civil Procedure Code*, 13th Edn., 1965, pp. 133-136.

Chapter IV
Priorities and Assignments

"Equitable estate is not as strong as a legal estate. It is liable to be defeated by a claim of bona fide purchase for value without notice. It then meets its Waterloo. Such a purchaser is Equity's darling and in his presence the poor owner of his equitable estate is forgotten."

"It warns us... that legal estates and equitable estates are not rights of one and the same order; they belong to different orders; the one is a right in rem, the other, the outcome of an obligation, a trust, and of the rule that trusts can be enforced against those who when they obtain ownership know or ought to know of those trusts."

—Maitland: *Lectures on Equity,* p. 130

SYNOPSIS

A. PRIORITIES

Maxims number 10 and 11 which are not dealt with in the previous chapter are now discussed here. These two maxims, taken together, express the principle regarding priority. In this chapter we shall discuss the idea of priority; how it arises, how it works and the doctrine of notice connected therewith.

1. TWO MAXIMS

(1) Where the equities are equal, the first in time shall prevail.

(2) Where there is equal equity, the law shall prevail.

Questions of priority or precedence may arise where there are rival conveyances of land or assignments of beneficial interests in trust funds. Usually such questions arise in connection with mortgages.

2. PRIORITY: DEFINITION AND MEANING

By Priority we mean precedence, that which pre-exists, foregoes or is first in rank. As expressed in *Rice* v. *Rice*[1], priority is the right of a party to satisfy its own claim of interest first in comparison to others.

In the preceding chapter we have discussed the nature of an equitable interest and its distinction with a legal interest.

The first maxim lays down that "as between persons having only equitable interests, if their equities are *in all other respects equal*, priority of time gives the better equity; or *qui prior est tempore potior est jure*".[2] When all other tests give way and are not able to decide whose equitable interest came into being first, the test of time is the deciding factor. Let us take a concrete case.

A mortgages his property to *B*. He again mortgages it to *C*. The market price of the property is Rs 20,000. *A* has obtained Rs 15,000 from *B* and Rs10,000 from *C*. If *B* and *C* both desire to satisfy their claims from the property, at the same time, which is insufficient to satisfy both, the question arises as to whose claim should be satisfied first, or who should be paid first. This question is then the question of priority. The answer to simple question like this would also be simple if we press into service the first maxim which explains that if the interests of the contestants are in all other respects equal the first in time shall prevail.

It may be that both the mortgages are legal or both equitable, or the one legal and the other equitable, or vice versa. It may also be that the estate mortgaged is legal but the mortgages made are merely equitable; or that there are successive mortgages of an equitable interest. In such cases, the rules regarding precedence or priority, as discussed below, are to be applied to the facts of the case.

---

1. (1853) 2 Drew 73: (1854) 23 LJ 289.
2. Vice Chancellor Kindersley in *Rice* v. *Rice*, ibid.

3. CONDITIONS FOR GETTING PRIORITY

The first condition is (*i*) that prior existence in point of time is not the sole criterion to decide priority between two competing equities. Other factors, which are no less important than pre-existence, are also to be taken into account. Moreover, (*ii*) this rule applies only to those cases where the equities are equal; where they are unequal the rule cannot be enforced. In cases of unequal equities it is a foregone conclusion that one is stronger than the other.

The principle that follows from the above has, no doubt, certain exceptions which would be considered when both the maxims are taken up together. But one thing is obvious and certain, that a plaintiff claiming priority according to this principle will lose it on account of his misdemeanour, or where he is grossly negligent or commits a fraud. *Rice* v. *Rice*[3] is an apt example of this situation.

4. APPLICATION AND CASES

A vendor conveyed land to a purchaser without receiving the purchase money. The deed of conveyance contained a receipt for the money by the vendor, who delivered the title deeds to the purchaser. The purchaser created an equitable mortgage by deposit of title deeds with a mortgagee. He then absconded with the money advanced to him without paying the vendor or the mortgagee. A question arose as to which should take priority, the vendor's equitable lien for the unpaid purchase money or the equitable mortgage. Held, "as between persons having only equitable interests, if their equities are in all other respects equal, priority of time gives the better equity; or, *qui prior est tempore potior est jure*". Although the vendor's lien was prior in time, owing to the negligence of the vendor in giving a receipt when the money had not been paid, the equities were not equal. Therefore, the mortgagee's equitable interest took priority over the vendors.[4]

With this maxim is connected the doctrine of notice, which we shall shortly discuss.

In India, Section 48 of the Transfer of Property Act (priority of rights created by transfer) incorporates this principle. Section 78 of the same Act explains the first exception when a prior mortgage is postponed and Section 79 enumerates the second exception regarding a subsequent mortgage made with notice of a prior mortgage.

The other maxim is a different sort of measure which goes to explain as under. When both the contestants are equally entitled to obtain help from courts of equity (because their equities are equal), the party who has law in his favour will succeed. For example, *A* agrees with *B* to sell his property for Rs 5000. Thereafter in breach of the above agreement, *A* sells the property to *C* for Rs 6000 and making a document hands over the possession of the property to *C*. As a result of the agreement *B* did not get any legal interest in the property. He is therefore not entitled to take possession of the property. *B* has only an equitable

---

3. Cracknell: *Law Students' Companion*, 1974 Edn., Case 251, p. 76.
4. *Ibid.*

interest in his favour binding *A's* conscience. *C*, on the contrary, as a result of his agreement with *A*, gets the legal interest and has executed a document and obtained possession of the property. *B*'s interest is an equitable interest, whereas *C*'s interest is equitable with law in his favour. Naturally, therefore, in a conflict between *B* and *C, C* has a superior interest as compared to that of *B*. Thus equitable interest is not as strong as a legal interest and so, according to the maxim, the law shall prevail.

On this maxim are based the doctrines of Election, Marshalling and Set-off. In India, Sections 35, 48, 78, 79 and 81 of the Transfer of Property Act and Order 8, Rule 6 of the Civil Procedure Code illustrate the principle.

Both the above maxims are intimately connected and taken together they expose the well-known doctrine of priority from which flows the doctrine of "purchaser for valuable consideration and without notice".

5. WORKING OF THE MAXIMS

The rules, wherein the working of these two maxims can be observed, are expressed by Snell[5] as resolving into two broad categories: one—the general body of rules governing priorities, and second—the rule in *Dearle* v. *Hall*[6] or the rule as to notice. He has summarised them as follows:[7]

(1) In determining questions of priority, it is usually best to consider first whether the rule in *Dearle* v. *Hall*[8] applies, i.e. whether or not the conflict is between successive dealings with an equitable interest in real or personal property.

(2) If the rule in *Dearle* v. *Hall*[9] does not apply, the question will have to be settled according to the basic rule of order of creation, except so far as the operation of this rule is modified by the rules relating to—

   (*a*) the purchaser without notice;

   (*b*) fraud, estoppel and gross negligence;

   (*c*) registration; and

   (*d*) overreaching.

(3) If interests in land are concerned, registration and overreaching cover most of the grounds and usually make it unnecessary to look further. These two heads have reduced the doctrine of purchaser without notice to a position of relative unimportance. [10]

We shall consider these doctrines in turn.

---

5. *Snell's Principles of Equity*, pp. 44, 68.
6. (1828) 3 Russ 1.
7. *Ibid.*, p. 68.
8. (1828) 3 Russ 1.
9. *Ibid.*
10. (1828) 3 Russ 1, p. 68.

(*i*) Rule 1: The Fundamental Rule of "First Made, First Paid".—The basic rule is that estates and interests primarily rank in order of creation. This is expressed in the maxim, "*qui prior est tempore potior est jure*", he who is earlier in time is stronger in law, or the older is better.

In case of two legal mortgages of a legal estate in land created by grant of successive leases, the second would *prima facie* be postponed to the first. Between two competing equitable interests, the general rule is that he whose equity is fastened to the property earlier will get priority over the other. In other words, where neither claimant has a legal estate and both have equal equities, the first in time prevails over the other.

This can be illustrated better by considering the case of *Cave* v. *Cave*[11].

(*a*) *Prior Legal and Subsequent Equitable: Cave* v. *Cave*: Charles Cave was the sole trustee of a marriage settlement. In 1872 he used the funds, in breach of trust, to purchase land in the name of his brother Frederick Cave. In 1873, Frederick Cave created a legal mortgage in favour of Philip Chaplin and subsequently created an equitable mortgage in favour of John White. In 1879, Frederick became bankrupt and the beneficiaries under the marriage settlement, the plaintiffs in the action, claimed priority over the mortgages created in favour of Philip and John, the defendants.

(1) It was held that as Philip Chaplin did not have notice that the land was trust property, as a *bona fide* purchaser of a legal estate without notice, his legal mortgage took priority over the interests of the beneficiaries.[12]

(2) As between the equitable interests of the beneficiaries and the equitable mortgage of John, under the principle *qui prior est tempore potior est jure*, the interests of the beneficiaries took priority over the equitable mortgage held by John White.[13]

It happens with unfortunate frequency that a man having title to land, contrives by means of fraudulent concealment to get money from a number of different persons on the security of the land, then disappears, and the lenders are left to dispute among themselves as to the order in which they are to be paid out of the value of land which is insufficient to pay all of them. In such cases two rules have to be kept in mind. First: as between merely equitable rights, the oldest prevails. Secondly: no merely equitable right can be enforced against one who has acquired a legal right *bona fide*, for value and without notice. If these two rules be remembered, such cases will become easy of solution. If we start thinking of equitable interests as rights in land (proprietory rights), much will be incomprehensible.[14]

---

11. (1880) 15 Ch D 539.
12. But see *Northern Counties of England Fire Insurance Co. Case*, (1884) 26 Ch D 482 (wherein legal estate was postponed due to its connivance at the fraud which led to the creation of a subsequent equitable estate).
13. Cracknell: *Law Students' Companion*, 1974 Edn. Case 56, p. 18.
14. Maitland: *Lectures on Equity*, 1969 Edn., Chap. X, pp. 125-126.

(*b*) *Both having equitable rights*: *Samuel Allen & Sons Ltd.*[15], *In Re*, a company hired machinery from *A* under a hire purchase agreement. The condition was that the machinery would not pass to the company until all the instalments were paid up. In case of the company's failure to pay an instalment, *A* was given a right to remove the same. The machinery was fixed on the business premises of the company of which it was the legal owner. The legal interest in the machinery therefore vested in the company. The company thereafter created an equitable mortgage of the business premises in favour of *B*, who had no notice of the hire-purchase agreement between *A* and the company.

In a dispute between *A* and *B*, who should be given precedence? It was held that *A*'s right to remove the fixtures (machinery) was an equitable interest in the land and that as it had attached before *B*'s equitable mortgage was created, it had priority over *B*'s rights.[16]

(*c*) *Modification*: This basic rule of order of creation is qualified by the doctrine of purchaser without notice. And the doctrine demonstrates a fundamental distinction between legal estates and equitable interests.

A legal right being a right *in rem* can be enforced against any person, whether or not he has notice of it. Except where it is overreached or is void for want of registration, it is a *jus in rem*. Where a purchaser's conscience is in no way affected by the equitable right, equity follows the law. This is well illustrated by the case of *Pilcher* v. *Rawlins*[17].

(*d*) *Prior Equitable and Subsequent Legal: Pilcher* v. *Rawlins*[18]: In 1851, *P* and his co-trustees lent money, which they held on trust, to *R* on security of the mortgage of certain property. The documents of title to the property were delivered to *P*. By 1856, by which time he had become the sole surviving trustee, *P* reconveyed the property to *R*, in consideration of a payment to him by *R*. The deed of reconveyance discharged the mortgage on the property and *P* and *R*, who were both solicitors, made out an abstract of title which showed *R* as a fee-simple owner and omitted a reference to the mortgage and reconveyance. *R* then created a legal mortgage on the property to *S* and *L*. The money advanced to *S* and *L* on the security of the mortgage was shared by *P* and *R*. The beneficiaries under the trust, on discovering the fraud, claimed priority over *S* and *L*. Held, *S* and *L* as *bona fide* purchasers of the legal estate for value, without notice of the equitable interests of the beneficiaries, took free of those interests.[19]

---

15. (1907) 1 Ch 575.
16. Followed in *Morrison, Jones & Taylor, Ltd., Re*, (1914) 1 Ch 50. See *Hawks* v. *McArthur*, (1951) 1 All ER 22. But under Land Charges Act, 1925 and 1972, perhaps these may be registered as general equitable charges or equitable easements. (*Snell's Principles of Equity*, p. 46, note 8 and p. 58, note 93) .
17. (1872) 7 Ch App 259: (1872) 11 Eq 53 (Court of Appeal in Chancery).
18. *Ibid*. See also *Shamlal* v. *Banna*, (1882) 4 All 296.
19. Cracknell: *Law Students' Companion*, 1974 Edn., Case 234, p. 72.

James, L.J. stated in this case[20]:"I propose simply to apply myself to the case of a purchaser for valuable consideration, without notice, obtaining, upon the occasion of his purchase, and by means of his purchase deed, some legal estate, some legal right, some legal advantage; and according to my view of the established law of this court, such a purchaser's plea of a purchase for valuable consideration without notice is an absolute, unqualified, unanswerable defence and an unanswerable plea to the jurisdiction of this court. Such a purchaser may be interrogated and tested to any extent as to the valuable consideration which he has given in order to show the *bona fides* or *mala fides* of his purchase, and also the presence or absence of notice; but when once he has got through that ordeal and has satisfied the terms of the plea of purchase for valuable consideration without notice, then this court has no jurisdiction whatever to do anything more than to let him depart in possession of that legal estate, that legal right, that legal advantage, which he has obtained. In such a case the purchaser is entitled to hold that which, without breach of duty, he had had conveyed to him."[21]

Maitland remarks, how could it be otherwise? A purchaser in good faith has obtained a legal right. In a court of law that right is his: the law of the land gives it to him. On what ground of equity is it going to be taken from him ? He has not himself undertaken any obligation, he has not succeeded by voluntary (gratuitous) title to any obligation, he has done no wrong, he has acted honestly and with diligence. Equity cannot touch him, because, to use the old phrase, his conscience is unaffected by the trust.[22]

Cave v. *Cave*[23] is illustrative of both, the fundamental rule and its qualifications. It is the purchaser of a legal estate without notice, one has to note, on whom lies the burden of its proof. [24]

***(ii)* Characteristics of a bona fide purchaser for value without notice.**— It is necessary for the purchaser that he must have acquired the property *bona fide*, that is, honestly, without deception, fraud or collusion. If not, he loses priority. An equitable estate is not as strong as a legal estate. As mentioned by Maitland in his discussion on the subject, it is liable to be defeated by a claim of *bona fide* purchaser for value without notice. It then meets its Waterloo. Such a purchaser is equity's darling and in his presence the poor owner of his equitable estate is forgotten. The purchaser for value and without notice is the bogey that scares away equitable titles.

(1) The purchaser must have given value for the property. It is not necessary to show that the consideration was adequate. An existing debt is sufficient value.[25] But the consideration must be real, not a pretence. If no consideration is given, the person getting property is a

---

20. (1872) 7 Ch App 259, 268.
21. Cited by Maitland: *Lectures on Equity*, 1969 Edn., p. 114.
22. *Ibid.*, pp. 114-115.
23. (1880) 15 Ch D 639.
24. *Nisbet & Pott's Contract, Re,* (1906) 1 Ch 386.
25. *Thorndike* v. *Hunt*, (1859) 3 De G&J 563: 28 LJ Ch 417.

volunteer. And equity does not help a volunteer. Such a person takes an estate subject to equities attaching to it, *e.g. A* gifts his land to *P. P* gets a legal estate but in case an equitable interest is attached to the land, *P* will take the estate subject to it as he is a volunteer.

(2) The purchaser must have obtained a legal estate. If he obtains an equitable estate, he has nothing superior to equity from which he claims to be free. Therefore if he takes a legal estate he will be protected by the doctrine, even though his title is defective.

There are three qualifications to the second rule above. They are as follows:

(*a*) better right to a legal estate,

(*b*) subsequent acquisition of legal estate, and

(*c*) mere equities.

In *Thorndike* v. *Hunt*[26], one *T* had some money in trust for *A*, which he was ordered to deposit in court. He paid the amount and the money was treated as belonging to *A's* estate. It thereafter appeared that *A* was also a trustee for *B* and by misappropriating *B's* fund with him, he had paid the money into court. The question was whether *B* could follow the money into court. It was held that *B* could not, because *A* had thereby obtained a legal title. The Accountant-General held the money on *A*'s behalf. Thus, *B*'s right to follow the money was not greater than *A*'s right to retain it.

If a purchaser at the time of purchase comes into property without notice of prior encumbrance, and thus fails to get a better title than the former, he will nevertheless prevail over a prior equity if he subsequently gets in a legal estate without being a party to a breach of trust. Between him and the owner of prior equity, the equities are equal and there is no reason to deprive the purchaser of the advantage he reaps at law by his diligence.[27]

A purchaser of an equitable interest without notice takes it free from mere equities but subject to prior equitable interests.

***(iii)* Doctrine of Notice.**—Notice means the "knowledge" of a fact which would make a rational man act in the light of the knowledge so acquired.[28]

The doctrine states that a person who purchases an estate, though for value, after notice of a prior equitable claim, becomes a *mala fide* purchaser and takes subject to that right. He cannot beget in the legal estate and defeat such prior claim. Fraud or *mala fides* is the proper ground on which the court is governed in the case of notice.[29]

A purchaser must have had no notice of the equitable interest at the time of purchase. If he has and he purchases, he will hold subject to the charge. One who relies upon the seller's assurances that there is no charge on the property

---

26. *Thorndike* v. *Hunt*, (1859) 3 De G&J 563: 28 LJ Ch 417.
27. *Bailey* v. *Barnes*, (1894) 1 Ch 25.
28. *See* Section 3, Transfer of Property Act, 1882.
29. *Le Neve* v. *Le Neve*, (1937) 1 Amb 436.

acts at his own peril. A purchaser is affected by notice of an equity in the following three cases:[30]

(*a*) *Actual notice*: where the equity is within his own knowledge.[31] In actual notice knowledge of a fact is brought home directly to a party.

(*b*) *Constructive notice*: where the equity would have come to his own knowledge if proper inquiries had been made.[32] Here the knowledge is imparted by the courts on presumption.

(*c*) *Imputed notice*: where his agent as such in the course of the transaction has actual or constructive notice of the equity.

As can be seen from the foregoing examples, one has to note that a legal owner must have no notice *at the time of vesting* of the legal estate in him. His earlier ignorance of the notice is incapable of protecting him. At the same time, his subsequent knowledge of the notice cannot defeat his claim.

Rules as to notice.—Notice is an important information which sets a man thinking. On it rests the starting point of a legal action as contemplated by the legislature. It must be given to an interested person and should be clear, distinct and unambiguous. It should include important information and must be signed, dated and served on the proper person.

Notice to be actual must be given by the person interested in the property to a purchaser, clearly and distinctly, and in the course of negotiations. Vague reports do not bind a purchaser's conscience.

Constructive notice is "no more than evidence of notice". Presumptions regarding it are "so violent that the court will not allow even of its being controverted".

Bank of Bombay v. *Suleiman*[33], is an appropriate case illustrating this point. One *S* made a will and gave his immovable property to his son *A*. He appointed *A* as executor of his will too. By the same will, *S* gave Rs 30,000 to his second wife's son *B* and charged *A*'s property for this. This charge was exactly of the nature of an equitable estate in England and was binding on all, except a bona fide purchaser for value and without notice, as if it was an equitable interest.

A now mortgaged the property to Bank of Bombay. The bank in trying to recover the mortgaged amount argued that as they were unaware of the equitable charge upon the property when it was given in mortgage, the charge was not and could not be binding on them. The bank in fact did not know it, but had they inquired as to how *A* got in the estate (and it was their duty to do so which they did not discharge) they would have come to know of the charge of *B* on *A*'s property. But as they did not do so knowingly, they were held to have constructive notice of *B's* charge and therefore their mortgage was subject to *B*'s charge upon the mortgaged property in their hands. In cases where the

---

30. *Snell's Principles of Equity*, p. 50.
31. *Barnhart* v. *Greenshields*, (1853) Moo PC 18.
32. *Bailey* v. *Barnes*, (1894) 1 Ch 25.
33. 33 Bom 1 (PC).

purchaser has actual notice and in cases where he had deliberately or carelessly abstained from making those inquiries that a prudent purchaser would have made, he is fastened with the constructive notice of a thing. Thus a purchaser with notice of a mortgage will have constructive notice of the encumbrances referred to in the mortgage deed.[34]

In *Birch* v. *Ellames*[35], a mortgagee lent money on land. He knew that the title deeds were deposited with some other person but he abstained from making those inquiries that a prudent purchaser would have made. He was held to have notice of the charge that was in fact secured by the deposit. Registration of a charge under the Land Charges Act, 1972 is a notice. Moreover, a purchaser should not be satisfied with an abstract of the vendor's title but require him to produce them and he must verify them. If he fails to do so, again the notice will fasten upon him,[36] unless a reasonable excuse for non-production is given which did not involve the purchaser either in fraud or negligence. Not only must land deeds be investigated but the land itself must also be inspected, because if it is occupied by a third party, occupation amounts to constructive notice.

Imputed notice is a notice, actual or constructive to an agent. But the notice obtained by the agent must be in the capacity as an agent as such, in the same transaction, and it must be a material one. If a solicitor acting for both the parties in a transaction receives notice, it is imputed to each party unless there is fraud. Where there is a fraud by the agent his knowledge cannot be imputed to the principal.

Protection of this doctrine extends not only to the purchaser but also to any person claiming through him. The doctrine of notice is, therefore, not applicable in case of subsequent transferees from the *bona fide* purchaser for value without notice. The priority is therefore not lost as such purchasers are allowed shelter under the title of the first purchaser. Thus, where *A* is a purchaser with notice, if he has purchased the property from *B* who had obtained it without notice of an equitable interest, the doctrine does not affect *A*.[37] If it was otherwise, it would amount to clogging or stagnation of property which the law abhors. At the same time, trustees cannot misuse their position (by selling trust property to a *bona fide* purchaser for value without notice and then repurchasing the same having passed it through other hands) and benefit out of it.[38]

***(iv)* Fraud, Estoppel and Gross Negligence.**—Prima facie claims to priority are postponed where one assists illegally through fraud, estoppel or gross negligence. In other words, one who assists illegally must suffer. A prior legal interest may be postponed to a subsequent equitable interest, because here the equities are not equal, and the law prevails only where equities are equal. Similarly, a prior equitable interest may be postponed to a subsequent equitable

34. *Bisco* v. *Earl of Banbury*, (1676) 1 Ch Ca 287.
35. (1794) 2 Anstr 427.
36. *Spencer* v. *Clarke*, (1878) 9 Ch D 137.
37. *Wilkes* v. *Spooner*, (1911) 2 KB 473; *Harrison* v. *Forth*, (1695) Prec Ch 51; *Shamlal* v. *Banna*, (1882) 4 All 296.
38. *Barrow case*, (1880) 14 Ch 432.

interest because of the inequitable or negligent conduct of the former. An apt example of unequal equity is *Rice* v. *Rice*[39]. Other leading examples are *Grierson* v. *National Provincial Bank of England*[40] and *Northern Counties of England Fire Insurance Co.* v. *Whipp*[41]. In *Walker* v. *Linom*[42], due to the mortgagee's gross negligence, the mortgagor got a chance to create a subsequent mortgage and he was therefore postponed to a subsequent equitable owner.[43]

The facts of the *Northern Counties cases* were as under. *C*, the manager of a company, executed a legal mortgage of his own land to the company and handed over the title deeds to them which were placed in a safe of which a duplicate key was held by *C*, who later on removed the title deeds and executed a second mortgage to *W* by depositing the same with her. *W* was unaware of the first mortgage. Held:

(1) *The court will postpone the prior legal estate to a subsequent equitable estate.*—(*a*) Where the owner of the legal estate has assisted in or connived at the fraud which led to the creation of a subsequent equitable estate without notice of the prior legal estate, of which assistance or connivance, the omission to use ordinary care in the inquiry after or keeping title deeds may be, and in some cases has been, held to be sufficient evidence, where such conduct cannot otherwise be explained; and (*b*) where the owner of the legal estate has constituted the mortgagor his agent with authority to raise money, and the estate thus created has by the fraud or misconduct of the agent been represented as being the first estate.

(2) But the court *will not postpone the prior legal estate to the subsequent equitable estate on the ground of mere carelessness or want of prudence on the part of the legal owner.* (Per Fry, L.J.)

In this case the conduct of the company, although careless, was not evidence of fraud. The mortgage to the company therefore took priority over the mortgage to *W*.

(*v*) **Registration.**—Due to uncertainty and risk involved in the equitable doctrine of purchaser without notice, in England, it is replaced by provisions for the registration of rights. It is provided therefore that for certain transfer of properties, registered instruments are necessary and the registration amounts to a notice from the date of registration.[44] In the words of Snell, therefore, "the question is no longer the state of the purchaser's mind but the state of the register".[45] He whose charge is first registered has priority over the other. Notice

39. (1853) 2 Drew 73.
40. (1913) 2 Ch 18. See *Coleman* v. *L.C.&W. Bk. Ltd.*, (1916) 2 Ch 353.
41. (1884) 26 Ch D 482.
42. (1907) 2 Ch 104.
43. For Indian Law see *Imperial Bank of India* v. *U. Rai Gyaw Thu & Co.*, 51 Cal 86 (PC).
44. Law of Property Act, 1969; Land Charges Act, 1972.
45. *Snell's Principles of Equity*, p. 57.

actual or constructive is no bar to registration. Registration itself is a public notice.[46]

In India.—Under the Indian Registration Act, 1908, from April 1, 1930 registration of a document regarding immovable property is considered to be a constructive notice to all concerned.[47] When once a right in respect of property is duly registered, the subsequent charges and interests created thereon are subject to the right registered. But the following conditions must be fulfilled before this can so happen:

(1) The instrument must be compulsorily registrable, e.g. *A* promises *B* to sell him certain property. He prepares an instrument for this and gets it registered. Thereafter *A* sells the property to *C*. If the instrument between *A* and *B* is not compulsorily registrable it cannot be inferred that *A* had constructive notice. It may be that *C* may have that type of notice due to other reasons but here no such inference can be drawn.

(2) The instrument must have been registered in an appointed manner. Thus, though it is registered, if the details of registration are not duly entered in the register meant for it, such incomplete details cannot be as effective as a constructive notice. If after making proper inquiries into the registration office regarding prior charges upon the property, no details are forthcoming so as to give correct information, such incomplete details do not constitute notice. But if no inquiry is made at all, that conduct constitutes and results in having constructive notice.

(3) The purchase must have been made after having such notice.

Due to the Land Charges Act, 1952 the following are registrable:

(1) Suits pending before 1925.

(2) Writs.

(3) Instruments regarding disposal of property.

(4) Land Charges.

(*vi*) **Overreaching.**—Overreaching is a device (a conveyance) whereby the rights overreached are transferred from the land to the purchase money. They do not become valueless. Overreachable rights may be equitable as well as legal.

The object of this device is merely to prevent purchasers of property from being affected by notice of equitable interests relating to money lent on mortgage of the property; it does not affect the priority of such equitable interests *inter se.*[48]

---

46. Land Charges Act, 1972.
47. *See* Section 3, Transfer of Property Act and its explanations.
48. *Snell's Principles of Equity*, p. 62.

(*vii*) **Valuation of working of the maxims.**—*In England*[49]: In view of the above it will thus be seen that the maxim "where there is equal equity, the law shall prevail" has not been able to retain its earlier value and importance. Moreover, due to the Property Act, 1969 and the Land Charges Act, 1972 perplexing questions of priority are reduced to the minimum. Regarding the foregoing discussion about the two maxims and its rules, as expressed by Snell, we may say that before 1926 the rule of "first made, first paid" prevailed. But this rule has often been displaced by "where there is equal equity, the law shall prevail". If the subsequent legal mortgagee knows about the prior equitable mortgage, the rule of "first made, first paid" would be applied; but if the subsequent legal mortgagee has no actual or constructive notice, he will receive priority.

This so-called second rule is in fact no rule; it is the converse of the first or an exception to it. These maxims and the rules are unable to inform us as to when equities become equal and when they become unequal. There is no clear guidance as to what rule is to be applied and the strange fact is that it is only after the issues are drawn by the courts, does one come to know what rule has been applied.

Instances may be quoted wherein no maxim out of these two applies, e.g. if the prior legal mortgage falls outside the ambit of these two rules and its priority is postponed to a subsequent equitable mortgage, then what is the remedy? The question remains unanswered by these maxims.

Before 1926 there was no question of conflict between two legal mortgages, as, what remained after the first legal mortgage was an equitable right of redemption of which only an equitable mortgage could be made. The competition was therefore limited between (1) successive equitable mortgages, or (2) between prior equitable and subsequent legal mortgage, or (3) between first legal and subsequent equitable mortgage. Questions of priority ordinarily seem to be simple at first sight but are actually not so. A number of complications may arise therein, e.g. there are two successive mortgages of a property made, No. 1 and No. 2. The following questions may be posed:

A. If the subsequent mortgagee (No. 2) does not know about prior mortgage (No.1), can the rule first made, first paid be changed?

B. If the above situation has arisen due to negligence of No. 1 or No. 2, what difference does it make? or

C. If No. 1 has assisted the mortgagor in keeping mortgage No. 1 secret from No. 2, what would happen?

D. If one is a legal mortgage and the other is an equitable mortgage, what is the position?

Till 1925 the above questions were disposed of by applying the two maxims and the exceptions. But in the changed circumstances and the soaring land prices questions of priority need not arise, because prices have multiplied far beyond

49. Hanbury: *Modern Equity*, Chap. 29; *Snell's Principles of Equity*, Chap. 4.

ordinary imagination and it is possible that competing interests may be simultaneously satisfied.

In India: In India the principle contained in the maxim has been incorporated in Sections 40 and 78 of the Transfer of Property Act, 1882. Section 40 explains the case of prior equitable and subsequent legal estate and Section 70, the case of a prior legal and subsequent equitable estate. The provisions of the Transfer of Property Act, Section 40(2), Trusts Act, Sections 91 and 95 and Specific Relief Act, Section 27(*b*) when read together do protect a transferee who got the document executed and paid the amount in good faith and without notice. Under the Indian Registration Act, Section 47, when a person gets the document registered, the registration relates back to the date of its execution. Even though he had notice of the pre-existing contract after its presentation for registration but it was actually registered his position remains uneffected.[50] Section 40 runs thus:

> 40. ...*Or of obligation annexed to ownership but not amounting to interest or easement.*
>
> Where a third person is entitled to the benefit of an obligation arising out of contract, and annexed to the ownership of immovable property, but not amounting to an interest therein or easement thereon, such right or obligation may be enforced against a transferee with notice thereof or a gratuitous transferee of the property affected thereby, but not against a transferee for consideration and without notice of the right or obligation nor against such property in his hands.
>
> The illustration to the section runs thus:
>
> *A* contracts to sell Sultanpur to *B*. While the contract is still in force he sells Sultanpur to *C*, who has notice of the contract. *B* may enforce the contract against *C* to the same extent as against *A*.

"The ultimate para of Section 54 of the Transfer of Property Act expressly enunciates that a contract for the sale of immovable property *does not, of itself create any interest in, or charge on such property* but the ultimate and penultimate paras of Section 40 of the Transfer of Property Act make it clear that such a contract creates *an obligation annexed to the ownership of immovable property, not amounting to an interest in the property* but which obligation may be enforced against a transferee with notice of the contract or gratuitous transferee of the property." This is an instance of "the equitable ownership in property recognised....(and)....translated into Indian law—as an obligation annexed to......property".[51]

The illustration to Section 40 explains the scope of para (2) of the section. Many of the doctrines of English Equity have taken statutory form in India and have been incorporated in occasional provisions of various Indian statutes such as the Trusts Act, the Specific Relief Act and the Transfer of Property Act.

---

50. *Satyamandalini* v. *Shahadur Mondal*, AIR 1962 Cal 49.
51. *Bai Dosabai* v. *Mathurdas Govinddas*, (1980) 3 SCC 545.

Under the Trusts Act, it is an obligation in the nature of trust and there the subsequent transferee is bound by the obligation as a constructive trustee.

In *London and S.W. Rly. Co.* v. *Gomm*[52], a railway company conveyed land and the transferee covenanted to reconvey the same to the railway company at any *future time*, receiving back the purchase money. The covenant bound himself, his heirs and assigns. The covenant, though it created an equitable contingent interest, was found to be void as it contravened the rule against perpetuity of English law. But in India such agreements do not create any interest legal or equitable in property; *they only create obligations of fiduciary character,* which are enforceable. Further, they are not hit by the rule against perpetuity. The rule of perpetuity as laid down in the case of *Ram Baran* v. *Ram Mohit*[53], "concerns rights of property only and does not affect the making of contracts which do not create rights of property, even though the contract may have reference to land.[54]

On the maxim "where there are equal equities the first in time prevails" is based on the doctrine of notice, and Sections 48, 78 and 79 are instances of its expression. And, on the maxim "where there is equal equity, the law shall prevail" are based the doctrines of election, marshalling and set-off which are incorporated in Sections 35, 81 and 108 of the Transfer of Property Act.

Section 78 of the Transfer of Property Act runs thus:

> 78.'*Postponement of prior mortgagee.*—Where through the fraud, misrepresentation or gross neglect of a prior mortgagee, another person has been induced to advance money on the security of the mortgaged property, the prior mortgagee shall be postponed to the subsequent mortgagee.

These provisions have been discussed before. Briefly stating, there is no distinction between legal and equitable estates in India. There is no question of any conflict therefore. The general rule *qui prior est tempore potior est jure*— "where the equities are equal, the first in time prevails", governs the priorities. It is expressed in Section 48 of the Transfer of Property Act. Reading these provisions along with the provisions of the Registration Act, 1908, the following propositions can safely be enumerated in this regard:

(1) In case of successive transfers of the same property, the first in time prevails over the later *i.e.* the later in time must give way to the earlier. But in case of written transfers their priority is determined by the date of execution of the document and not by the date of registration of the document.

(2) According to Section 17 registration of certain documents is compulsory; while there are certain documents registration of which is optional (Section 18). When the registration is optional, questions of priorities arise, but when it is compulsory such questions do not arise.

---

52. (1882) 20 Ch D 562.
53. AIR 1967 SC 744 .
54. *S.W. Rly. Co.* v. *Associated Portland Cement Manufacturers*, (1910) 11 Ch 12.

(3) According to Section 50 of the Registration Act certain registered documents relating to land take effect against unregistered documents. When registration is optional a registered document though registered subsequently must take precedence over an unregistered document which is executed prior in time. Thus, a subsequent registered deed will have priority over a prior unregistered one. Of course, this is subject to the doctrine of notice.

(4) Where property under a prior unregistered document is delivered, the doctrine of notice (Section 3 of the Transfer of Property Act) will come into play and the subsequent transferee will lose his priority. This is because delivery of actual possession to the former transferee amounts to a notice to the subsequent transferee.

(5) Suppose for example that a subsequent transfer is made by a registered instrument and such a transferee has actual notice of the prior unregistered transaction. In such a case, the registered transferee will lose his priority, which position is very clear.

(6) A legal mortgage prevails over an equitable one in England, unless the holder of a legal mortgage has done or omitted to do something which disqualifies and therefore prevents him from asserting his priority. In India, as explained in Section 78 of the Transfer of Property Act, where a subsequent mortgage has been created through the fraud, misrepresentation or gross neglect of a prior mortgagee, the prior mortgagee shall be postponed to the subsequent mortgagee. *Northern Counties of England Fire Insurance Co.* v. *Whipp*, discussed above, is a leading decision on this point.

(7) Insofar as a mortgage by deposit of title deeds is concerned, in India it is considered as at par with other mortgages. If we look to Section 48 of the Registration Act, it will be found that special treatment has been given to such mortgages. The section says that such a mortgage under Section 58 of the Transfer of Property Act shall take effect against any mortgage deed subsequently executed and registered which relates to the same property. The apparent reason for this is that according to Section 58 (*f*) of the Act such a mortgage is a completed transfer and not a mere agreement to transfer. As laid down in *Imperial Bank of India* v. *U. Rai Gyaw Thu & Co.*[55], there is no distinction between a legal and an equitable mortgage in India. The provisions of Sections 78 to 80 of the Transfer of Property Act are therefore equally applicable to such a mortgage.

6. RULE 2: RULE OF NOTICE: DEARLE v. HALL[56]

This rule applies to successive dealings with equitable interest in any property, real or personal.

55. (1923) 1 Rang 637 (PC).
56. (1828) 3 Russ 1.

(*i*) **The Rule stated**: The rule is that "priority depends upon the order in which notice of the dealings was received by the person by whom the fund is distributable, or in the case of settled land, by the trustees of the settlement. Equitable titles have priority according to the priority of notice. If the notices are received substantially simultaneously, the dealings rank in the order in which they were made".[57]

(*ii*) **Exception**: Knowledge of prior assignment by the person advancing money results in the loss of his priority even if he gives notice first, but knowledge acquired after advancing is no bar to gaining priority.

(*iii*) **Facts of Dearle** v. **Hall**[58]**:** In his will, made in 1794, *PB* bequeathed his residuary estate to his executor on trust for sale and conversion for his son *ZB*. The interest payable to *ZB* amounted to £ 93 a year. In 1808, *ZB* assigned to Dearle an annuity of £ 37 a year, payable during *ZB*'s life and secured on *ZB*'s annuity of £ 93, *ZB* retaining his right to the same. If *ZB* failed to pay to *D*, his annuity of £ 93 was to be paid to *D* who was to take his £ 37 from the annuity charged and return the balance to *ZB*. Mr Unthank, the executor was unaware of this.

In 1812, *ZB* sold his life interest to *H* who had no notice of the earlier assignment to *D*. *H* gave written notice of his assignment to *D*. Held, the assignment to *H* took priority over *D's* assignment as *H* had been the first to give notice.

The idea underlying the rule, as it seems to be, is that by not giving notice the first assignee helps the assignor to make a subsequent assignment. The first assignee, therefore, becomes a party to a fraud to be practised upon the subsequent assignee. It is therefore just that his conscience is not pure and that he should be postponed. Here again, as stated before, a gratuitous assignee will not get priority because he, "though disappointed, is not defrauded". A volunteer can get no more than what the assignor was able to give.[59]

(*iv*) **Valuation and Criticism.**—The rule regulates priorities and does not create them, and it applies to equitable interests already created in any form of property, real or personal, but does not apply to shares in a company governed by the Companies Act. According to Snell, the principle behind the rule is lost sight of and at the present day its application has become absolute as was done in the case of *Dallas, Re*[60], wherein the creation of *B*'s subsequent charge was not due to the fault of the prior assignee *A* in giving notice earlier.

The criticism levelled against this rule is that Justice Plumer, M.R. while giving his decision in *Dearle* v. *Hall*, should have based it on the diligence or negligence of one or the other mortgagee. Had he based it on the negligence of

---

57. *Stocks* v. *Dobson*, (1853) 4 De GM&G 11, 17; *Calisher* v. *Jorbes*, (1871) 7 Ch App 109; *Johnstone* v. *Cox*, (1880) 16 Ch D 571; *Dallas, Re*, (1904) 2 Ch 385; *Snell's Principles Equity*, p. 63.

58. Cracknell: *Law Students' Companion*, 1974 Edn., Case No. 40, p. 25.

59. *Snell's Principles of Equity*, p. 63; *Fraser* v. *Imperial Bank*, (1912), 10 DLR 232; *Justice* v. *Wynne*, (1860) 12 Ir Ch R 289.

60. (1904) 2 Ch 385.

the other party, negligence would have been the reason for losing priority, but unfortunately he stressed upon the diligence of the mortgagee, which gave rise to this rule. Consequently the trustees sought refuge therein. This situation has been compared to "grabbing a plank in a shipwreck" i.e. *tabula in naufragio*.

The rule in *Dearle* v. *Hall* applies to interests already created but it does not apply to future interests. It applies to equitable assignments also,[61] but it does not apply to shares in a company.

The Law of Property Act, 1925 in England has made appropriate arrangements so that a mortgagee can know of prior charges. For this purpose, the land charges register must be examined and titles must be inspected. If no prior encumbrances or charges come to light he can proceed further. Of course, this arrangement also is not without its faults.[62]

(*v*) **In India.**—The rule in *Dearle* v. *Hall* does not apply in India and the priority of the assignee of an interest in property does not depend upon the principle of giving notice first, but is governed by the order of successive interests.

B. ASSIGNMENTS OF CHOSES-IN-ACTION

1. MEANING

A "chose" means a thing, and "action" is the right of a party to file a suit in a court of law to recover money or things.

A chose may be one in possession or one in action. Again, it may be legal because it is enforceable in a court of law, or it may be equitable because it is enforceable in a Court of Chancery only.

In the literal sense the expression means a thing recoverable by action, as contrasted with a chose in possession, i.e., a thing of which a person has not only ownership but also actual physical possession. The meaning of the expression has varied from time to time but it is now used to describe all personal rights of property which can be claimed or enforced only by action, and not by taking physical possession. It is used in respect of both corporeal and incorporeal personal property which is not in possession. Subject to exceptions, a chose-in-action may be bought, sold, given away, settled or left by will or become the subject of proceedings under the Married Women's Property Act, 1882, Section 17, just like any other interest in property.[63]

2. DEFINITION

Channel, J.,[64] defines chose-in-action as "a well-known legal expression used to describe all personal rights of property which can only be claimed or enforced by action, and not by taking physical possession".

---

61. Discussed in the following chapter.
62. For details *see* Hanbury: *Modern Equity*, 9th Edn., (1969), pp. 573-596.
63. *Halsbury's Laws of England*, p. 636.
64. In *Torkington* v. *Magee*, (1902) 2 KB 427. *See also* Hanbury: *Modern Equity*, 9th Edn., (1969), p. 636 and *Snell's Principles of Equity*, p. 69.

Debts due to specialty or by simple contract, whether debts of record or of judgment debts, mortgage debts, debentures and dividends, negotiable instruments including bills of exchange, promissory notes and cheques, stocks, shares in joint stock banks, policies of assurance of every kind, pensions, patents and copyrights, bills of lading, shares in partnership, right of action arising under contract and out of tort, lessee's right to be relieved against forfeiture, the right of re-entry for non-payment of rent and several others are included within this term.

3. ATTITUDE OF THE COMMON LAW

The Common Law rule made a chose-in-action unassignable, but it could be assigned by or to the king. This was possible if the debtor assented to the assignment. Reasons for this unassignability were twofold. According to Snell[65] assignment would be "the occasion of multiplying of contentions and suits, of great oppression of the people...and the subversion of the due and equal execution of justice".[66] Hanbury explains that this was "partly due to the fact that they were regarded as strictly personal and partly due to the fear of maintenance; any attempted assignment was viewed as an intrusion by a third party into a dispute between two others".[67]

One has to note at the outset that assignment of a bare right to sue is bad at law and at equity too; but there is "no rule of law which prevents the assignment of the fruits of an action".[68]

Balfour v. *Sea Fire Life Insurance Co.*[69] explains the situation succinctly and very clearly thus: "At Common Law, choses-in-action were not assignable and an assignee had to go to Equity to enforce his claims. If the thing in action was a legal claim, he had to file a bill to compel the assignor to permit him to sue in the name of the assignor, and equity would help him only if he had given valuable consideration for the assignment. But even before the Supreme Court of Judicature Act, 1873, the doctrine that there could not be an assignment at law of an existing debt had long been exploded". The words of Buller, J., in *Master* v. *Miller*[70] can be cited in support of this proposition. He said that "the good sense of the Common Law rule seemed to be very questionable to him". Equity, therefore, taking a less extreme view of the situation and considering each case on its merits gave effect to assignments not only of equitable things-in-action but also to legal things-in-action.

Thus in course of time strictness of the Common Law rule had to give way to the mercantile practice and statute-created exceptions and finally by the Judicature Act, 1873 and now by Section 136 of the Law of Property Act, 1925,

---

65. *Snell's Principles of Equity*, p. 69.
66. *Lampet case*, (1612) 10 Co Rep 46 b.
67. Hanbury: *Modern Equity*, p. 637.
68. *Glegg* v. *Bromley*, (1912) 3 KB 474. See also *Dawson* v. *G.N.R.*, (1905) 1 KB 260.
69. (1857) 3 CB (NS) 300.
70. (1791) 4 TR 320, 340; *Jowitt's Dictionary of English Law*, p. 367.

"any debt or other legal thing in action" was made assignable at law. This provision was extended to legal as well as equitable choses.[71]

4. KINDS OF ASSIGNMENTS

By way of useful contract Snell gives four categories of assignments: (*i*) statutory assignment of legal choses, (*ii*) statutory assignment of equitable choses, (*iii*) equitable assignment of legal choses, and (*iv*) equitable assignment of equitable choses.

5. REQUIREMENTS OF A STATUTORY ASSIGNMENT

The Law of Property Act, 1925, Section 136(1) provides that: "Any absolute assignment by writing under the hand of the assignor (not purporting to be by way of charge only) of any debt or other legal thing in action,[72] of which express notice in writing has been given to the debtor, trustee, or other person from whom the assignor would have been entitled to claim such debt or thing in action, is effectual in law...".

To analyse the section, (*i*) there must be a document in writing, (*ii*) it must be an absolute and complete assignment, (*iii*) the assignment should not be by way of charge only, and (*iv*) an express notice to this effect should be given to the debtor.

Thus a mere direction to the debtor is no assignment. A cheque is no assignment because it is but an order to a bank to pay and not an absolute assignment. Similarly, a charge is not an absolute assignment.[73] No consideration is required[74] and no particular document is necessary.

A notice of assignment to the debtor is a statutory requirement and the assignment is effective from the date of the notice received by the debtor. The consequences of an absolute assignment would be to pass on all the legal powers, rights and legal remedies to the assignee. Vexatious assignments and those in the nature of maintenance are not recognised at law. Such an assignment is subject to all prior equities. Notice given by the assignor or assignee, however, must be clear, express and unambiguous with date of assignment and the amount assigned. Even if the debtor is illiterate, a written notice is a must. If debtors are more than one, notice to all is necessary. If any of them if insolvent, notice must be given to the solvent debtors. The section is silent[75] as to who and at what time should give notice, but either the assignor or the assignee may give it. There is no time-limit fixed for giving it, but if it is not given the whole transaction becomes an equitable assignment. The effect of a statutory assignment would be that the assignee, now being the owner of the

---

71. See also *Fitzroy* v. *Cave*, 21 TLR 612.
72. Including equitable: see *Pain, Re*, (1919) 1 Ch 38, cited in Hanbury: *Modern Equity*, p. 638.
73. *Bank of Liverpool & Martins Ltd.* v. *Holland*, (1926) 42 TLR 29; *Jones* v. *Humphreys*, (1902) 1 KB 10.
74. *Fitzroy* v. *Cave*, 21 TLR 612.
75. *Ibid.*

chose at law can sue the debtor in his own name without joining the assignor. The benefits of giving a notice are discussed below.

6. BENEFITS OF GIVING NOTICE

Notice is the very basis of a right to sue. By giving it one gets a right *in rem* (without notice one gets a right *in personam*), and the assignment becomes effective and priority is obtained.[76] Moreover, it stops new equities from being created between the original creditor and debtor that become binding on the assignee. It also stops subsequent assignments from taking priority. In the absence of a notice it is very likely that the debtor may pay the amount to the original creditor; by notice this consequence is avoided. In case of insolvency of the original creditor it saves the assigned debt from being affected by it. It should be noted that an assignor cannot grant a better right than what he has and therefore a legal assignment is subject to all equitable rights, i.e., an assignee takes subject to all equities existing against the assignor up to the date of notice.[77] By notice, invalidity is cured and what is invalid becomes valid.

7. EQUITABLE ASSIGNMENT

An assignment not legally made is not void or ineffectual, but is an equitable one. As expressed by Lord Macnaghten in *Brandts* v. *Dunlop and Co.*[78]: "It may be addressed to the debtor. It may be couched in the language of command. It may be a courteous request. It may assume the form of mere permission. The language is immaterial if the meaning is plain. All that is necessary is that the debtor should be given to understand that the debt has been made over by the creditor to some third person." If the debtor ignores the notice, he will do so at his own peril. Since equity looks to the intent rather than the form, the form and mode of assignment are of no consequence. But the intention to assign must be explicit and direct because "you can have no charge in equity without an intention to charge".[79]

The consequence of assignment was that the assignee could sue in his own name in all the divisions of the High Court without joining the assignor as a party on either side.

The essentials of such an assignment are: (*i*) existence of some transaction exhibiting an assignment, (*ii*) an intention to assign, (*iii*) chose or thing to be an assigned must be certain, (*iv*) mode of assignment is immaterial, (*v*) it may not be in writing, (*vi*) the assignee must consent to the transaction, (*vii*) value is necessary, if the assignment is to take place in future or if it is for creation of a mere charge (as distinct from a complete transfer), but there is no reason why a man should not be able to give away an equitable interest as freely as he can give away a legal interest.

---

76. According to the rule in *Dearle* v. *Hall*, (1828) 3 Russ 1.
77. *Knapman, Re*, (1881) 18 Ch D 300.
78. 1905 AC 462.
79. *Hopkinson* v. *Forester*, 19 Eq 74.

William Brandt's Sons and Co. v. *Dunlop Rubber Co. Ltd.*[80]is a leading case on equitable assignment. The facts were that Dunlop Rubber Co., the defendants, owed money to K & Co., a firm of merchants. K & Co. in turn owed money to William Brandt's Sons & Co. bankers (hereinafter named W. Co.) K & Co. agreed with W. Co. that the money owing to K & Co. by the Dunlop Rubber Co. should be paid direct to W. Co. W. Co. forwarded to Dunlop Co. a notice in writing that K & Co. had assigned to them the right to receive the money owed by Dunlop Co. to K & Co., and requested Dunlop Co. to sign an undertaking to remit the money. Later, when K & Co. had become bankrupt, Dunlop Co. through inadvertence paid the money to someone other than W. Co.

Held, although the language of a formal assignment had not been used, it was immaterial if the meaning was plain. There was a valid equitable assignment of the debt to W. Co. Therefore Dunlop Co. "must pay the money over again, and pay it to the right person" (per Lord Macnaghten), i.e. W. Co.[81]

8. ASSIGNMENT OF FUTURE BENEFITS

In England assignment of future benefits is possible but consideration must be given in such cases or the interest must have been delivered in fact. If not, such assignments are ineffective. Formerly, the Common Law did not allow such assignments, but now it has been made possible.[82]

However, on principles of public policy equity did not allow certain assignments to be effective, as for example assigning the whole of a man's future and present income was ineffective. Public pay, alimony and maintenance and champerty are some of the important heads in respect of which such assignments were barred.

9. POSITION IN INDIA

An actionable claim has been defined in Section 3 of the Transfer of Property Act thus:

"Actionable claim" means,

(*a*) "a claim to any debt, other than a debt secured by mortgage of immovable property, or by hypothecation or pledge of moveable property", or

(*b*) a claim to "any beneficial interest in moveable property not in possession, either actual or constructive, of the claimant",

(*c*) "which the civil courts recognise as affording grounds for relief, whether such debt or beneficial interest be existent, accruing, conditional or contingent."

A debt is a certain, definite or a liquidated sum actually due and therefore *payable now* (termed as *existent debt*) or a sum that will become *payable in*

80. 1905 AC 454; *Kent & Sussex Saw Mill Ltd., Re*, 1947 Ch 177.

81. Cracknell: *Law Students' Companion*, 2nd Edn., 1974, Case 346.

82. For a list of such interests see *Snell's Principles of Equity*, pp. 81-82.

future by reason of a present obligation (termed as an *accruing debt*).[83] By "actually due" we mean "not actually payable until a later date".[84] This is termed as an accruing debt.[85] Thus all debts according to the definition can be assigned because they are actionable claims.

Insofar as beneficial interest is concerned all or "any beneficial interest in moveable property not in possession..." can be the subject of assignment. Thus, benefit of an executory contract for the purchase of goods[86] is a beneficial interest capable of assignment. But copyright,[87] right to recover damages for breach of contract, a claim to mesne profits, a mortgage debt, debentures, negotiable instruments and mercantile documents, a right of action arising out of a tort, a right to unliquidated damages, pensions and salaries, judgment debt and a decree are not actionable claims.[88] It should be noted that negotiable instruments and bills of exchange and insurance policies are included in the definition but since special statutes govern them, rules regarding actionable claims do not apply to them. They may be said, therefore, to form a special class or caste by themselves.

Looking to the above list, it can be noticed that in comparison to the scope and extent according to the English definition, the Indian definition is narrower.

The modes of assignment are contained in Sections 130 to 132 of the Transfer of Property Act and they combine features of legal as well as equitable assignment. Accordingly a transfer of actionable claim should be (*i*) in writing, (*ii*) signed by the transferor or his agent, (*iii*) the assignment may be with or without consideration, and (*iv*) it is complete on the execution of the instrument. It invests the assignee of all the rights and remedies of the transferor and at the same time, the claims which the debtor had against the transferor will now be available to him against the transferee. In short no particular words are necessary to make an assignment, provided the intention is clear.

As Section 132 explains, the transferee shall take it subject to all the liabilities and equities to which the transferor was subject in respect thereof at the date of the transfer.

10. DIFFERENCE BETWEEN INDIAN AND ENGLISH LAW

(*i*) English law recognises a distinction between legal and equitable assignment; Indian law does not.

(*ii*) Indian law allows conditional assignment; according to English law it should be absolute.

---

83. *Bhupati* v. *Fanindra*, 40 CWN 104.
84. *Haridas* v. *Baroda Kishore*, 27 Cal 38.
85. *Ibid*.
86. *Jafar Meher Ali* v. *Budge Jute Mill Co.*, 34 Cal 289.
87. *Dwarkaprasad Bhatia Case*, 1939 All LJ 71.
88. *Afzal* v. *Ram Kumar*, 12 Cal 610; *Dagdu* v. *Vanji*, 24 Bom 502; *Govindrajulu* v. *Ranga Rao*, 40 MLJ 124.

(*iii*) An assignment in India is complete and operates from the date of the transfer or from the moment of the execution of the deed. Notice to the debtor in India is given for the protection of the assignee (Section 131, Transfer of Property Act). Under English law, notice is the starting point of priority and the rule that until notice is given assignment can only be equitable, prevails there. It does not prevail in India. This rule is known as the rule in *Dearle* v. *Hall*[89].

(*iv*) Under English law, priority is determined by notice; under Indian law the date of execution of the instrument determines it.[90]

(*v*) The assignment, as the section says, may be with or without consideration in India; under English law, consideration is not essential for the assignment of an equitable or a legal[91] chose. This has not always been so in cases of legal choses.[92] Moreover, under our law actionable claim can be assigned only in the manner provided by the Transfer of Property Act, Section 130.[93]

Section 6 of the Transfer of Property Act, 1882 lays down what cannot be transferred. This is on principles of public policy.

---

89. 3 Russ 8, 27.
90. *Subramaniya Iyer* v. *Ramsuba Iyer*, 59 Mad 141.
91. *Holt* v. *Heatherfield Trust*, (1942) 2 KB 1: 58 TLR 274.
92. Hanbury: *Modern Equity*, p. 641.
93. *Holt* v. *Heatherfield Trust*, (1942) 2 KB 1: 58 TLR 274.

PART II

SPECIFIC EQUITIES, EQUITABLE DOCTRINES AND EQUITABLE RIGHTS

Chapter V
Penalties and Forfeitures

"Where a contract provides that on breach thereof, the party in breach shall pay a sum of money to the other party, the sum may be an agreed sum for damages, known as liquidated damages, or the sum may be a penalty to be held over the other party in terrorem."

—Snell's Principles of Equity, p. 534.

"Equity regarded the performance as the principle intent of the parties to the contract, and the penalty as a mere accessory,...according to the maxim 'Equity looks to the intent rather than to the form'."

—Maxims of Equity

"Penalty involves a payment or a loss of a sum of money; forfeiture involves the loss of an interest in property."

SYNOPSIS

A. PENALTY

1. NATURE, DEFINITION AND PRINCIPLE

Before 1863 there was a rule of Common Law that a person was absolutely bound by the obligations he had undertaken and he could not claim to be excused by the mere fact that performance had subsequently become impossible. *Paradine* v. *Jane*[1] and *Thiis* v. *Byres*,[2] are its leading examples. Similarly when the contract provided for a penalty or forfeiture those provisions were strictly enforced regardless of the circumstances, and were never relieved, consequently creating a positive injustice to the promisee.

1. (1647) Alyn 26.
2. (1876) 1 QBD 244.

During the reign of William and Anne the rigour of these rules was softened by passing two statutes[3] whereby relief could be granted by the law courts as well as the equity courts. The Judicature Acts reduced the importance of these statutes, and the scope of relief given by the Equity Courts thus widened and it applied not only to *money-bonds* but also to a number of other cases.

It is within the competence of the parties to a contract to provide therein as to the extent of liability arising out of its breach.[4] The loss so occasioned may be compensated by a sum liquidated or fixed therein. It may be that the sum so agreed may be far greater than the actual loss sustained; if so it is a penalty. But where the sum so agreed and provided is a genuine pre-estimate of the loss it is not penalty. Snell[5] puts it this way that in cases where a contract provides that on breach thereof, the defaulting party shall pay a sum of money to the other, the sum so agreed may be equal to the damage suffered or loss sustained by the party, or it may be a penalty to punish the defaulting party and called a sum *in terrorem*. A very early money-bond case referred to by Simpson in *Law Quarterly Review*[6] has been cited by Snell wherein it was provided that non-payment of the principal sum with interest within a fixed period would make the debtor liable for a greater sum, usually double. This is obviously a penalty clause and a proper subject for equity courts to intervene.

2. ANALYSIS

(*a*) *Existence of a breach.*—Where, however, there is no breach, the question of penalty need not arise. As expressed in *Associated Distributors Ltd.* v. *Hall*[7] (hire purchase agreement case), where an option was given in a contract to put an end to it and to pay the agreed penalty, such a sum cannot be considered to be a penalty because the hirer had exercised his option and thus had to pay the amount which he had made himself liable to pay. There is no breach; but according to Lord Denning and Lord Devlin[8] the question is still open.

(*b*) *Grounds of relief.*—The courts of equity gave relief against penalty on the ground that such a relief is the original intent of the case.[9] In such cases, therefore, the court looked to the intention rather than to the form. In *Sloman* v. *Walter*[10], where the agreement was to allow the use of a particular room when wanted and in default, to pay penalty stipulated in the bond, it was held that as the enjoyment of the object was the principal intent of the deed, and the penalty being only on accessional intent, it could not be recovered; but actual damage could be recovered.

(*c*) *Penalty and liquidated damages distinguished.*—To find out whether a particular provision in a contract is a penalty clause devised to punish a party or

3. 8&9 Will 3 C, 11, 1697 and 4&5 Anne C 3, 1705.
4. *Wallis* v. *Smith*, (1882) 21 Ch D 243.
5. *Snell's Principles of Equity*, 27th Edn., 1973, p. 534.
6. *A.W.B. Simpson case*, (1966) 82 ELQR 392.
7. (1938) 1 All ER 511 CA: (1938) 2 KB 83.
8. *Bridge* v. *Campbell Discount Co. Ltd.*, 1962 AC 600.
9. *Peachy* v. *Duke of Somerset*, (1742) 1 Stra 447.
10. (1784) 1 Bro CC 417.

is a genuine pre-estimate of the loss that would arise on its breach, the following rules have been framed by the courts.[11]

Ordinarily when the word penalty or liquidated damages is used by parties to a contract, they must be taken to mean what they say. But this cannot be considered to be final and conclusive.[12] The court therefore must find out whether the sum so named is penalty or liquidated damages. Penalty is a sum fixed *in terrorem* to punish the offending party for a default or by way of securing the performance of a collateral object, while liquidated damages is a genuine pre-estimate of damage reduced to dimensions which truly represent the loss. Liquidated damages can be fully recovered. Penalty is extravagant and unconscionable amount in relation to actual loss suffered or following from the breach.[13] As decided in *Kemble* v. *Farren*[14], when payment of a smaller sum is secured by a larger, that larger sum is penalty. But the largeness of the sum does not itself make it a penalty. Solution of the problem therefore depends upon construction of terms of the agreement and the surrounding circumstances of each case[15] *at the time of making the contract, but not at the time when the breach is made.* Breach of an agreement gives rise to a cause of action to recover the smaller amount, because, if it is otherwise, that is not a genuine pre-estimate of damages.

(*d*) *Exceptions*: (*i*) *Default in instalments.*—But where it is agreed that a loan received is to be returned within the appointed time by instalments and that on default in paying a single instalments as agreed, payment of all the remaining instalments would become due, that is not a penalty provision.

(*ii*) *Several breaches.*—The second exception to the penalty provision is expressed in the decision in *Dunlop Pneumatic Tyre Co.*[16] There it was agreed that "a single lump sum made payable by way of compensation on the occurrence of one or more of all or several events, some of which may occasion serious and others but trifling damage" will not be penal. There is thus a clear provision (of payment of lump sum) for penalty here, but it is no more so, because, where *every possible breach is incapable of being precisely ascertained*, the provision for payment of a particular sum is not necessarily a penalty provision.

(*iii*) *Pre-estimate almost an impossibility.*—Besides, the cases wherein the precise pre-estimate of damage is *almost an impossibility*, it may be probable that the pre-estimate of the damage stipulated by the parties was the true bargain between them. It must be noted that the latter two instances raise a presumption against penalty but such a presumption may also be rebutted.

---

11. *Snell's Principles of Equity*, 27th Edn., 1973, pp. 535-536.
12. *Price* v. *Green*, 16 M&W 346.
13. *Financing Ltd.* v. *Baldock*, (1963) 2 QB 104.
14. (1829) 6 Bing 141.
15. *Price* v. *Green*, 16 M&W 346.
16. *Dunlop Pneumatic Tyre Co. Ltd.* v. *New Garage and Motor Co. Ltd.*, 1915 AC 79. See also *Clydebank Co.* v. *D. Jose*, 1905 AC 6. For contra see *Newman, Re*, (1876) 4 Ch D 724.

3. SOME QUESTIONS

(*i*) *Damage exceeding penalty.*—A question that has been posed is, what would be the position if the damage exceeds the penalty? Can the plaintiff ignore the penalty clause? Is it not that his only right is to recover the agreed sum and no more? The answer to these questions has been given by Snell:[17] "Probably he can[18] (sue), although he clearly cannot do so where the contract shows that if there is a breach of the contract, *the right to recover the specified sum is to be his only right.*"[19]

(*ii*) *Misusing penalty clause.*—When it is agreed to perform or to abstain from doing a certain act, and in default to pay a penalty, can a party in default get rid of the agreement by just electing to pay penalty and consequently justifying his breach? Can he be compelled to act as agreed upon? The answer to this is obviously in the affirmative.[20] The courts cannot allow a party to escape from his liability. In contracts for sale by instalments, there is a provision for forfeiture of instalments when an instalment is not paid as agreed; in such cases the proviso being an integral part of the contract, the contract can be rescinded and the instalments paid can be retained by the vendor. This is not a penalty clause. In such cases, equity granted relief if the purchaser carried out the contract at the time of action.[21]

4. IN INDIA

Section 74 of the Indian Contract Act has abolished the distinction between penalty and liquidated damages as it exists under English law, and contains the equitable rule of the English law as to relief against penalty. It thus gets rid of the questions whether a particular amount is liquidated damages or penalty,[22] but the duty of the courts in India as well as in England is more or less the same for all practical purposes.[23] A court in India will not allow a party to escape from his contractual liabilities simply by paying a penalty in every case.[24] In India, therefore, the courts have powers to allow "reasonable compensation not exceeding the amount so named, or as the case may be, the penalty stipulated for". Under this section, actual proof of loss or damage is dispensed with and the party gets reasonable compensation, but the compensation will not exceed the amount named in the contract. The court is to carry out the primary contract between the parties and is not bound to carry out the secondary contract which comes into existence due to breach.[25]

---

17. *Snell's Principles of Equity*, 27th Edn., 1973, p. 536.
18. *Wall* v. *Rederiaktiebolaget Luggude*, (1915) 2 KB 66.
19. *Cellulose Acetate Silk W. Ltd* v. *Widnes Foundry, (1925) Ltd.*, 1933 AC 20 .
20. *French* v. *Macale*, (1842) 2 Dr&Ware 269.
21. *Stockloser* v. *Johnson*, (1954) 1 All ER 630 CA.
22. *Panna Singh* v. *Ajban Singh*, 33 CWN 949.
23. *Michel Habib* v. *Sk. Suleiman*, AIR 1941 PC 101.
24. Cf., *French* v. *Macale*, (1842) 2 Dr&Ware 269.
25. Per Justice Sundara Aiyer in *Muthu Krishnan case*, (1912) 36 Mad 229.

B. FORFEITURE

1. NATURE AND MEANING

In cases where on the failure of one party to perform the contract, a specific property is to be transferred by that party to the other, or where as a result of his having done or abstained from doing a particular act, the party loses some right, benefit, privilege or property, it is called a forfeiture.

2. BASIS AND EXTENSION OF RELIEF

Courts of equity relieved against this, but only in appropriate cases. Where the primary object of the bargain is to secure a stated result and the provision for forfeiture is added as security for the production of that result,[26] equity will grant relief against forfeiture for breach of covenant or condition. But where forfeiture is imposed not by act of parties but by statute, equity will give no relief. The most common instance of forfeiture lies in case of breach of a covenant in a lease. For example, the right of re-entry (on the lease property) of the landlord was considered as security for the payment of rent.

In granting such a relief, the appellant's conduct, graveness of the breach and the disparity between the value of the property forfeited and the damage caused by the breach would be inquired into by the court. Thus in a case where purchase money was payable by instalments and where there was a proviso that the vendor may rescind the contract and retain the instalment's already paid, it was held to be a forfeiture clause against which the court would not normally relieve, but relief could be granted if the purchaser was ready and willing to carry out the contract at the time of action.[27]

Relief against forfeiture also extended to cases of assignment of a lease, and non-payment of rent or fines, lease of land, hiring or lease of chattels; the underlying principle being that a forfeiture in substance was a mere security for the payment of a monetary sum. To ordinary breaches[28] of covenant this jurisdiction did not extend and forfeiture took place, but it is now conferred by statute.[29]

3. THREATENED FORFEITURE

As decided in *Barton case*[30], in case of threatened forfeiture where the lessor did not take possession nor commenced proceedings therefor, the court would not probably exercise this jurisdiction.

4. DISTINCTION: FORFEITURE AND PENALTY

The main difference in equity between forfeiture and penalty is that in the former, relief is *not always* given although compensation can be given, while in

---

26. *Snell's Principles of Equity*, 27th Edn., 1973, p. 537, citing *Siloh Spinners Ltd.* v. *Harding*, (1973) 2 WLR 28.
27. *Kilmer case*, 1913 AC 319.
28. E.g. a covenant to repair or to lay out a specific sum on repairs in given time.
29. *Snell's Principles of Equity*, 27th Edn., 1973, p. 538, note 38.
30. *Barton Thompson & Co. Ltd.* v. *Stapling Machines Co.*, 1966 Ch 499.

the latter, relief is *always given* if compensation can be given. Forfeiture involves loss of an interest in property. For example, in case of a lease there is generally a provision that on committing a breach of any covenant by the lessee the landlord may re-enter and the lease be forfeited. Insofar as penalty is concerned, in case of failure of performance the payment of a sum of money is stipulated.

5. IN INDIA

Section 111 of the Transfer of Property Act, 1882 incorporates the rule with regard to forfeitures and Sections 114 and 114-A incorporate the equitable rule of English law regarding relief against forfeiture for non-payment of rent.

Forfeiture is one of the eight ways to determine a lease as provided in Section 111(*g*). Forfeiture is incurred in three ways: where (*i*) a lessee breaks an express condition, providing for re-entry on land, (*ii*) where a lessee claims a title in the lease land or sets up a title thereof in a third person and renounces his character as lessee as such, and (*iii*) where he is adjudged an insolvent. In any of these cases the lessor must give a notice to the lessee of his intention to determine the lease. Notice by the landlord is thus a condition precedent to a forfeiture and the right of re-entry. On the fulfilment of anyone of the above three conditions, a lease does not automatically come to an end or become void. It only gives a right to the landlord to avoid the lease and to re-enter the land, and for this purpose to give notice to the lessee of his intention to do so.

Section 114 of the Transfer of Property Act incorporates the equitable rule of English law regarding relief against forfeiture of a lease. It lays down that in case of forfeiture of lease incurred due to non-payment of rent where the lessor sues to eject the lessee, the court will pass an order relieving the lessee against the forfeiture if he is prepared to pay within fifteen days the rent in arrears with interest due, and full costs of the suit, or gives security such as the court thinks sufficient. Thereupon the lessee shall hold the property as if the forfeiture had not occurred.[31]

This section indicates the principles that wherever compensation is an adequate remedy or an alternative, relief against forfeiture should be granted. The English principle in this regard is also the same.

In *Namdeo case*[32] it was observed that according to *Debendra case*[33], the court in granting such relief has no discretion and must grant relief to the tenant, but this is not so. Because "in exercising this discretion...under Section 114 a court in India is not bound by the practice of a Court of Chancery in England and I am not disposed to limit the discretion that it possesses. Those who seek equity must do equity, and I do not think merely because a tenant complies with the conditions laid down in Section 114 that he becomes entitled as of right to relief". Thus every case must be judged by relief. Besides he who comes in equity must come with clean hands and must do equity. It is the conduct of the

---

31. *Dharamtalla Properties* v. *Dhunbai*, AIR 1931 Cal 457.
32. *Namdeo Lokman Lodhi* v. *Narmadabai*, 1953 SCR 1009.
33. *Debendra Lal Khan* v. *F.M.A. Cohen*, 1927 ILR 54 Cal 485.

tenant that disqualifies him for such relief in equity. This view is affirmed in various cases.[34]

Section 114-A gives relief against forfeiture in certain other cases. The section contemplates covenants for repairs, maintenance or insurance of the property leased. It does not apply to breach of the covenant to pay rent and no relief is given by this section where the lessee incurs forfeiture by denying his landlord's title.

Where there are stipulations in contract it is the duty of the Court not to enforce the forfeiture clause, but only to award reasonable compensation which does not exceed the amount specified in the contract as liable to forfeiture. The award of compensation in all such cases should be reasonable.[35] If a stipulation for forfeiture amounts to penalty it is relieved against where the case is covered under Section 74 of the Indian Contract Act.[36] As held in *K.P. Subbarama Sastri* v. *K.S. Raghavan*[37], if on a proper construction of a contract it is found that the real agreement between the parties was to the effect that the whole amount was on the date of the bond a debt due but the creditor for the convenience of the debtor allowed it to be paid by instalments intimating that if default should be made in payment of any instalment he would withdraw the concession, then the stipulation as to the whole amount of the balance becoming payable would not be penal. If however, it appears that the debt itself arises or becomes due and payable by the debtor only on the respective dates fixed for the instalments, the stipulation that on default being made in the payment the whole of the balance should become due and payable would be in the nature of a penalty.[38]

Similarly where there was a clause in the agreement that special benefit of a share in the property at a lower price would be offered to a party under the agreement would not be available in case of default in payment of instalments of the price by the party within stipulated time, the stipulation was held to be valid and not a penalty clause.[39]

A well recognised exception in regard to penalty may be noted. The exception is that where a beneficial right is to arise under a contract, conveyance or a will, upon the performance of some act in a stated manner or at a stated time by the beneficiary, the act must be performed accordingly in order to obtain the enjoyment of the right, and there is no fraud, accident or surprise in the transaction, equity will not relieve against a breach of the terms.[40]

---

34. *Appayya Shetty* v. *Mohd. Beari*, 1916 ILR 39 Mad 834; *Ramakrishna Malhya* v. *Baburaya*, (1914) 24 IC 139 and *Rama Brahman* v. *Rami Reddi*, AIR 1928 Mad 250. See also *Stanhope* v. *Haworth*, (1886) 3 TLR 34.
35. *Fateh Chand* v. *Balkishan Das*, AIR 1963 SC 1405; *Naresh Chandra* v. *Calcutta Stock Exchange Ltd.*, (1971) 1 SCC 50: AIR 1971 SC 422.
36. *Maula Bux* v. *Union of India*, (1969) 2 SCC 554: AIR 1970 SC 1955.
37. (1987) 2 SCC 424, 427: AIR 1987 SC 1257.
38. Approving *P.K Achuthan* v. *State Bank of Travancore*, 1974 KLT 806.
39. *Sova Ray* v. *Gostha Gopal Dey*, (1988) 2 SCC 134: AIR 1988 SC 981.
40. *Simrathmull* v. *Nanjalingiah Gowder*, AIR 1963 SC 1182.

Insofar as the question of forfeiture of earnest money is concerned it may in certain circumstances amount to penalty.

Earnest money is a nominal sum of money sometimes given by the buyer to seller as a token that the parties are bound or are in earnest (eager or sincere to do something) about the bargain.[41] The amount is legally unnecessary but in practice in most cases of sale of immovable property it is given and taken.

If earnest money is given and the transaction proceed ahead, the same forms a part of purchase price. But if the transaction falls through due to buyer's fault or failure, the amount is forfeited. If the transaction goes through, the amount operates as a part payment.[42] If the amount of earnest is reasonable and if it is forfeited, it is not like imposing penalty.[43] But this depends upon circumstances of a case.

6. CASES OF CONCESSION AND PRIVILEGE DISTINGUISHED

Cases of penalties and forfeiture can be distinguished from cases of concession and privilege fixed by agreement. In such cases of concession and privilege, if a required condition is not fulfilled, no relief would be obtainable in case of loss of that concession or privilege. Decisions in *Shanmugam Pillai* v. *Anna Laxmi*[44] and *Burjorji* v. *Madhavlal*[45] explain this principle. For example, *A* covenants to pay Rs 25,000 to *B* within thirty days. If payment is made as agreed, *B* would give up the balance of Rs 40,000, the amount due, but if it is not so made by *A* within the stipulated time, he will have to pay the whole amount of Rs 40,000 and the concession would be cancelled. *A* in such cases acts against the agreement and therefore equity is not on his side. Even the courts of equity in such cases have no power to relieve *A* from the consequences of his failure to act according to the agreement.

---

41. Walker: *Oxford Companion to Law*, 1980, p. 387.
42. *Maula Bux*, supra.
43. *Hanuman Cotton Mills* v. *Tata Air Craft Ltd.*, (1969) 3 SCC 522: AIR 1970 SC 1986.
44. AIR 1950 FC 38.
45. AIR 1934 Bom 370.

Chapter VI
Mortgages, Liens and Merger

"A mortgage at Common Law was strictly an estate upon condition that the estate will be forfeited upon the breach of the condition... .Equity thus turned an absolute conveyance at Common Law into a real security or a pledge for the repayment of a debt."

—Williams on Real Property.

'Security' for the debt, 'Right to Redeem' and 'Right to Foreclose' are the essential characteristics of a mortgage.

SYNOPSIS

A. MORTGAGES

1. MEANING AND DEFINITION

What is generally understood by the term mortgage is a conveyance of land or other immovable or other property as security for the payment of money. Such mortgage is made to secure the repayment of money borrowed by the owner of the property mortgaged. In such a case the borrower incurs a debt or personal obligation to repay by whatever means. Where such a personal obligation is not incurred there is an express covenant for repayment. A mortgage at Common Law was strictly an "estate upon condition", that is, the estate was forfeited upon the breach of the condition.

A mortgage can be said to be a *conveyance* of some interest in land or other property "as a *security* for the payment of a *debt* or the *discharge of some other obligation* for which it is given".[1]

2. OBJECT

But insofar as a mortgage is a transfer of property, its object is to confer on the mortgagee a proprietory right, by exercising which he will be enabled to raise money payable to him; so that he shall have the means of securing himself from loss in the event of his debtor being personally unable to pay, or of attaining the desired end, where there is no personal liability to payment.[2] In other words, *the object of a mortgage is to secure the performance of the primary obligation.*

3. HISTORY

The history of mortgages goes back to Roman Law wherein due performance was secured by "pressurising the debtor's will or causing him inconvenience" by keeping him out of possession or ownership or forcing serfdom upon him so that he would repay the amount early. But this way of dealing with the debtor was hardly satisfactory and by efflux of time, a more concrete type of security whereunder irrespective of the debtor's will, the creditor could put the property to sale and recover his amount, came into vogue. Hypotheca of Roman Law was of this nature.

> "The term mortgage first appears in Glanville[3] in whose time either land or goods might be pledged as security for a debt. A pledge of land was effected by a conveyance thereof to the creditor to hold until the debt was paid, with an agreement either that the creditor should apply the rents and profits in reduction of the debt, or that he should receive them without any liability to account. In the latter case the transaction was called *mortuum vadium* (which in French is mort-deed and gage-pledge, whence mortgage); because although the debtor might redeem the land on payment of the principal sum, in the meantime it was dead or unprofitable to him. The

1. *Santley* v. *Wilde*, (1899) 2 Ch 475.
2. Joshua Williams: *Principles of the Law of Real Property*, 21st Edn., p. 544
3. Glanville Lib. x. c. pp. 6-8.

object of the *mortuum vadium* was to give the creditor the profits of the land in lieu of interest; the taking of which under the name of usury was anciently regarded as an unchristian abomination.[4] But these ancient methods of pledging lands seem to have fallen out of use at an early date, and to have been succeeded by a more stringent contract under which the land was given in pledge until a certain day fixed for payment, with a stipulation that on failure to pay at the appointed time the land should remain to the creditor in fee in the first instance with a proviso for re-entry on payment. Littleton, describing this, states that this is called a mortgage because, if the feoffer, do not pay (the feofee) then the land pledged is taken from him forever and so dead to him. The nature of this mortgage at law was that of a conveyance of land from one to another for an estate in fee, or other estate, which is to be determined or reconveyed on condition of the payment of money by the former on a certain day. If the condition was broken by non-payment of the money at the appointed time, the estate of the person to whom the land was so conveyed becomes absolute or discharged from the condition. So that, at law, he will be entitled to hold the land as his own, for all the estate limited to him. For in the courts of law the parties were held to the terms of their bargain by which the land was to be redeemed on a certain day, or if not, to be forfeited by the debtor."[5]

Courts of equity gave relief to the mortgagor against this strict construction of a mortgage. The relief was first given in cases of failure to pay at the appointed time by accident or of some *trifling default* and was afterwards extended to all cases of *forfeiture* of mortgaged land by failure to pay money when due. During the reign of Charles I this state of affairs was established.[6] Equity granted relief because it considered it unfair that the borrower should lose his land absolutely for default in payment. On its own principles and maxim that "equity looks to the intent rather than to the form", it enforced the original intention of the parties. It was also against the conscience of the lender that he should retain the property which he received from the borrower as a mere security. Equity thus turned *an absolute conveyance at Common Law into a real security or a pledge for the repayment of a debt*, so that if the borrower paid the principal amount with interest and costs within a reasonable time even after he had lost his legal right to redeem, equity granted him an equitable right to redeem, which came to be known as a *mortgagor's equity of redemption*. The effect of this kind of help to the mortgagor by equity caused Maitland to remark that the express words of the proviso for reconveyance as included in the mortgage deed become, "owing to the action of equity" a "long *suppressio veri* and *suggestio falsi*". It does not in the least explain the rights of the parties: it suggests that they are other than really they are.[7] The assurances given by the deed were thus left unaltered by equity, by granting the mortgagor a right to redeem by payment at any time before a sale or foreclosure of

4. Joshua Williams: *Principles of the Law of Real Property*, citing *Plowden on Usury* Part I.
5. Joshua Williams: *Principles of the Law of Real Property*. See also *Snell's Principles of Equity*, p. 376.
6. *How* v. *Vigures*, I Ch Rep 18.
7. Maitland: *Lectures on Equity*, 1969 Edn., p. 182.

the mortgage took place. *The right of redemption is thus a right given by equity contrary to an agreement.*[8]

4. CHARACTERISTICS OF A MORTGAGE

The first essential characteristic of a mortgage is the mortgagor's "right to redeem" which had its origin in the idea canvassed by equity that 'stipulation as to time for the payment' was a penalty and was therefore required to be relieved. This one-sided concession granted to a mortgagor, however, could not be allowed to continue indefinitely in point of time and the equity courts were required to set limits to their own generosity, because one has to be just before he professes to become generous. On this principle, after a reasonable time expired, the mortgagee was allowed to foreclose the right of redemption of a mortgagor who not only lost his legal right to redeem but also lost his equitable right to redeem. *This right to foreclose, according to Hanbury, is an equitable right given to a mortgagee to counterbalance the mortgagor's right to redeem and is the second essential characteristic of a mortgage.*

As the Common law judges strenuously resisted the introduction of this new principle and adhered in their courts to the principle of forfeiture,[9] the Judicature Act, 1873,[10] exclusively assigned the redemption and foreclosure of mortgages to the Chancery Division of the High Court.

5. MORTGAGOR'S RIGHT: EQUITY OF REDEMPTION

From the characteristics of mortgage enumerated above, it follows that a right to redeem cannot be fettered or circumvented even by express agreement of the parties, and the maxim "*modus et conventio vincunt legum*", that is "the agreement of parties overrides the law" has no application to mortgage. The mortgagor or anyone standing in his place, shall be admitted in equity to redeem a mortgage after the day fixed by the contract for redemption has gone by, and the estate has become forfeited at law.[11] As Coote has explained,[12] it was further laid down as a general rule, subject to very few exceptions, that wherever a conveyance of estate is originally intended as a security for money, whether this intention appears from the deed itself or by any other instrument or even by parole evidence,[12] it is always considered in equity as a mortgage and redeemable; even though there is an express agreement of the parties that it shall not be redeemable or that the right of redemption shall be confined to a particular time, or to a particular description of persons.[13] In other words, it was established that no agreement of the parties to a mortgage, that the mortgage should not be redeemable according to the rules of equity, should have any

---

8. *Salt* v. *Marquees of Northampton*, 1892 AC 1.
9. *Snell's Principles of Equity*, 27th Edn., p. 377.
10. Section 34(3).
11. *Tarn* v. *Turner*, 39 Ch D 456 cited in Joshua Williams: *Principles of Real Property*, p. 547. See *Hamzabi* v. *Syed Karimuddin*, (2001) 1 SCC 414 (Limits of the right discussed).
12. *Coote on Mortgages,* Chap. III, Section 3, cited in Joshua Williams: *Principles of Real Property*, p. 547; *see* also *England* v. *Cordington*, 1 Eden 169.
13. *Ibid*., Chap. III, Section 2.

effect in equity. Upon this principle it was held that any attempt to fetter the equity of redemption with any other condition than the payment of principal, interest and costs should be void.[14] This principle is summed up briefly in the phrase "*once a mortgage always a mortgage*".[15] Furthermore, it was held that in equity, the right of the mortgagee was to the money secured, and he held the land only as security for his money; so that in equity he had a mere charge for the amount due to him, even though he were absolute tenant in fee at law. It was therefore decided that the benefit of a mortgage should go along with the rest of the mortgagee's personal estate to his executor or administrator, not his heir.[16] And although at law the estate of a mortgagee in fee would go to his heir or devisee, yet in equity the heir or devisee was held a mere trustee thereof for the executor or administrator.[17] Consequently in equity the owner was regarded as the owner of the mortgaged land, subject only to the mortgagee's charge; and the mortgagor's equity of redemption was treated as an equitable estate in the land, of the same nature as other equitable estates.[18]

6. MODERN TREND

Thus, what was in the beginning an equitable right became an equitable estate, which amounts to ownership of the property subject to the mortgage and which a mortgagor could settle, devise, mortgage or otherwise dispose of in any way he liked.[19] Even a mortgagee can buy the equity of redemption, and nobody can prevent him.[20] And the collateral benefits if they continue beyond the redemption can be obtained by the mortgagee if they do not prevent free dealings with the property. As decided in *Kreglinger* v. *New Patagonia Meat Co.*[21], this is the modern trend. But as decided in *Shyam Singh Case*[22] since the sale agreement and agreement of repurchase were contained in two separate documents, although contemporaneously, executed, it was held that the transaction could not be treated to be a mortgage, though it is akin to mortgage if "not mortgage proper."

7. IN INDIA

(*a*) *History*.—The idea of a mortgage witnessed a similar evolution in India, and as a result of its intimate contact with English legal principles we have the Transfer of Property Act, 1882, Sections 58 to 104 whereof cover this topic. Under the Hindu and Muhamedan laws, the system of mortgages was in

---

14. *Jenning* v. *Ward*, 2 Vern 520; *Noakes & Co.* v. *Rice*, 1902 AC 24; *Howard* v. *Harris*, (1683) 1 Vern 33; *Samuel* v. *Jarrah Timber Corpn.*, 1904 AC 323.
15. Lord Nottingham in *Newcomb* v. *Bonham*, 1 Vern 7. *See* also *Achaldas Durgaji Oswal* v. *Ramvilas Gangabisan Heda*, (2003) 3 SCC 614; *Ramvilas G. Heda* v. *Achaldas D. Oswal*, AIR 2002 Bom 133 (More than a dozen cases cited on the print).
16. *Thornborough* v. *Baker*, 1 Ch Ca 283.
17. *Coote on Mortgages*, Chap. LXXIX, Section 1.
18. *Casborne* v. *Scarfe*, 1 Atk 603, 605.
19. *Snell's Principles of Equity*, pp. 378, 379.
20. *Reeve* v. *Lisle*, 1902 AC 461.
21. 1914 AC 25.
22. *Shyam Singh* v. *Daryao Singh*, (2003) 12 SCC 160.

vogue and it passed through a similar process of evolution as in Roman law. Mortgage by conditional sale and usufructuary mortgage, which resembled Pignus of Roman law, were known to Hindu law. Manusmriti[23] gives details[24] thereof. The ancient Hindu law did not make any distinction between pledge and mortgage. For both pledge and mortgage a common term, Adhi (आधि :) has been used in Smritis. The word Adhi came to be used because the article or immovable property goes under the Control (adhina) of the creditor. Manu uses the word Adamana for mortgage (Manu VIII 165) and Brihaspati employs the word bhogya (भोग्य) for mortgage.

In laying down the law on the topic of Adhi, the ancient Indian law givers have taken care to incorporate conditions reasonable to both the parties and they are comparable in several aspects to the present laws on the topic.[25]

In Muhamedan law a mortgage is called "bye-bil-wufa" and resembles an English mortgage. The Muslim religion prohibits charging of interest. To counter this religious restraint a mortgagee resold the mortgaged property to the mortgagor at a higher price. If the debtor did not repay the money obtained, the creditor (mortgagee) becomes the absolute owner thereof. The word "bye-bil-wufa" is an Arabic expression meaning a sale based on confidence, i.e. it is a sale with a condition to retransfer the property.[26]

Before the passing of the Transfer of Property Act, 1882 in India, the principles of English law along with the principles of equity were applied. The Transfer of Property Act, 1882 converted equitable rights into legal rights.[27]

(*b*) *Definition.*—Section 58 defines a mortgage as under: "A mortgage is the—

(*i*) transfer of an interest;

(*ii*) in the specific immovable property;

(*iii*) for the purpose of—

(*a*) securing the payment of money advanced or to be advanced by way of loan,

(*b*) an existing or future debt, or

(*c*) the performance of an engagement which may give rise to a pecuniary liability."

This definition is a very satisfactory one. Out of various interests in property three are prime and basic: right of possession, right of enjoyment and right to sell the property. In an outright sale, a person transfers all these rights which go to make the other an owner of the immovable property; in a mortgage he transfers any one of these, but not all.

23. Chap. 8, verse 143.
24. *See also* Sir William Jones: *Manusmriti*, Chap. 3, p. 142.
25. Rama Jois: *Legal and Constitutional History of India*, 1985 Edn., Part II, Ch. 5, pp. 115-130 (It gives interesting details on this topic).
26. For details *see* Mulla: *Transfer of Property Act*, 5th Edn., 1966, p. 364.
27. Lahiri: *Transfer of Property Act*, 8th Edn., 1965, p. 292.

A mortgage is different from a pledge. In a pledge the *ownership of goods or personal chattels* (not immovable property) remains with the pledgor; what is transferred to the pledgee is possession of the property. In a mortgage what is transferred is *an interest in specific immovable property* (not goods or personal chattels), the *ownership and possession* of the property being retained by the mortgagor except in case of an usufructuary mortgage.

A mortgage is different from a charge.[28]

(*c*) *Classification.*—The Transfer of Property Act recognises six kinds of mortgages: simple mortgage, mortgage by conditional sale, usufructuary mortgage, English mortgage, mortgage by deposit of title deeds and anomalous mortgage. Instead of reproducing their definitions,[29] we shall go through and discuss in brief their important features hereunder.

8. SIMPLE MORTGAGE

A simple mortgage which is made without delivering possession of the mortgaged property has the following ingredients:

(1) Possession and enjoyment of the property subject to mortgage remains with the mortgagor.

(2) The mortgagor binds himself personally to pay the mortgage money.

(3) In the event of his failing to pay, the mortgagee shall have a right to put the property to sale only through court and recover his money.

(4) Such a mortgage, irrespective of the amount of consideration, must be effected by a registered document.

In such a mortgage the mortgagee has two ways open to him: either to use his power of sale of the mortgaged property through sale and to recover his amount or to sue on the mortgage and obtain a money decree against the debtor. A simple mortgage has to be distinguished from a charge. As pointed out by Snell,[30] for most practical purposes a charge can be regarded as a species of mortgage; for whereas a mortgage is a conveyance of property, a charge merely gives the charge certain rights over the property as security for the loan. Where the amount is to be realised from the income of a definite and specified item of property and there is no right to put the property to sale, the transaction is only a charge and not a mortgage.

9. MORTGAGE BY CONDITIONAL SALE

In a mortgage by conditional sale there is:

(1) An ostensible sale of the mortgaged property.

(2) There is also a condition that in case of failure to pay the money on a certain date the sale shall become absolute, but on such payment

---

28. *Gajraj Jain* v. *State of Bihar*, (2004) 7 SCC 151.
29. *See* Sections 58(*b*) to 58(*g*) of the Transfer of Property Act, 1882.
30. *Snell's Principles of Equity*, p. 375. *See* also *Gajraj Jain* v. *State of Bihar*, (2004) 7 SCC 151.

being made the sale shall become void and the mortgagee (the buyer) shall retransfer the property to the seller (the mortgagor).

(3) Such a condition has to be embodied in the same document if the transaction is to be a mortgage.[31]

(4) The remedy of the mortgagee in such a transaction is a suit for foreclosure.

(5) If the consideration exceeds Rs 100 the registration of the document is compulsory.

Whether a transaction is a mortgage by conditional sale or a sale has to be decided with reference to the "intention of the parties",[32] which can be gathered from the document itself.[33] In every case the question is "what, upon a fair construction, is the meaning of the instrument. No extrinsic evidence or evidence *de hors* the document is allowed, as what the document expresses has to be accepted".

10. USUFRUCTUARY MORTGAGE[34]

The salient features of an usufructuary mortgage are:

(1) Delivery of possession of the property to the mortgagee or a binding to that effect.

(2) Till the amount obtained is repaid such possession is authorised to be retained.

(3) Rents and profits accruing from the property are to be appropriated in lieu of interest on the principal amount. On realisation of the amount the property is redeemed.

(4) The mortgagor has no personal liability.

(5) The mortgagee has no power either of sale or of foreclosure.

(6) Registration, if the consideration exceeds Rs 100, is compulsory.

Moreover, a binding to deliver possession of the mortgaged property must be plain and without any condition. The mortgaged property will remain with the creditor as long as the debt is not satisfied; but if the possession is for a definite number of years the transaction is not an usufructuary mortgage but an anomalous mortgage.

---

31. *Pandit Chunchun Jha* v. *Sk Ebadat Ali*, (1955) 1 SCR 174.

32. *Pandit Chunchun Jha* v. *Sk Ebadatali*, (1955) 1 SCR 174; *Bhasker Waman Joshi* v. *N.R. Agarwal*, (1960) 2 SCR 327. *See* also *State of Kerala* v. *Cochin Refineries Ltd.*, AIR 1968 SC 1361; *Balkishandas* v. *Legge*, 27 IA 58: 22 All 149; *Sachidananda Benerji, Asstt. Collector of Customs* v. *Sitaram Agarwala*, (1966) 2 SCR 1. See *Umabai* v. *Nilkanth Dhondiba Chavan*, (2005) 6 SCC 243 wherein a distinction between a mortgage by conditional sale and a sale with a condition of repurchase is restated.

33. *Alderson* v. *White*, (1858) 2 DG 97: 44 ER 924, 928.

34. See *A.D. Oswal* v. *R.G. Heda*, (2003) 3 SCC 614.

11. ENGLISH MORTGAGE

In an English mortgage:

(1) The mortgagor binds himself personally to repay the mortgage money on a certain date.

(2) There is transfer of the mortgaged property absolutely to the mortgagee.

(3) Possession is delivered.

(4) The property so transferred is to be retransferred to the mortgagor when there is repayment.

(5) The mortgagee's remedy is only a sale.

(6) Such a power of sale can be out of court.

It must be noted that like a simple mortgage, there is a personal undertaking to repay the amount. There is no personal undertaking in a mortgage by conditional sale, but in an English mortgage it is there. Similarly, there is a transfer of the mortgaged property absolutely in an English mortgage, but in a mortgage by conditional sale the transfer is an ostensible sale.

12. MORTGAGE BY DEPOSIT OF TITLE DEEDS

A mortgage by deposit of title deeds is restricted to the following towns: Calcutta, Bombay and Madras. Persons residing in these places can avail of its benefits. The recognition of this type of mortgage is for the benefit of the mercantile community to enable them to raise quick money.[35] Its essential characteristics are:

(1) There should be delivery of documents of title to the creditor with intent to create a security thereon. The property can be situate anywhere.

(2) Registration is not necessary, except that a memorandum evidencing the deposit of title deeds is required to be drawn and the terms of the mortgage are incorporated therein.

(3) No possession of property is delivered.

(4) The remedy available to the mortgagee is a suit for sale.

(5) Provisions in respect of simple mortgage are applicable to this type of mortgage also.

13. ANOMALOUS MORTGAGE

An anomalous mortgage is an admixture of any two or more types of mortgages mentioned above. However, it is not necessary that whenever a mortgage does not fall within any one of the five categories mentioned in Sections 58(*b*) to (*f*) it must necessarily be treated as an anomalous mortgage.

---

35. This was a practice prevalent in presidency towns and in moffusil before the passing of the Act. The Privy Council accepted it and experience has justified its retention. *See* Gour, H.S.: *The Law of Transfer*, 8th Edn., 1973, pp. 2301-2302.

This is so because the classification of mortgages by the Act is not an exhaustive one but projects only a cross-section of the common types of mortgages prevalent in India.

14. NATURE OF EQUITABLE MORTGAGES IN ENGLAND AND IN INDIA

In England, where a legal estate in property is conveyed as a security for payment of a debt there is a legal mortgage, and where the estate conveyed is equitable there is an equitable mortgage. What remains with the mortgagor after the first mortgage is made is the equity of redemption which is an equitable estate. This was the position prior to 1926, but even after 1926 there has not been any substantial change and the equitable mortgage continues to remain in vogue, because under the Law of Property Act, 1925, the mortgagor only grants a legal term of years to the mortgagee and retains with himself the fee-simple estate, whereon he can create still further legal mortgages. One should note that without transfer of interest, there is no question of there being a mortgage. A mere undertaking to create a mortgage is not sufficient to create any interest in immovable property.[36]

An equitable mortgage passes only an equitable interest in property unlike a legal mortgage which passes the entire legal interest in property to the mortgagee.

(*a*) *How it comes into being.*—(1) Where a legal mortgagor either by design or by accident does not fully convey the legal estate or does or refrains from doing something which falls short of conveying the legal estate, the resultant mortgage would be an equitable mortgage but not a legal one. This can happen in the following cases too:

(2) Where there is a written agreement to execute a mortgage, the agreement gives rise to a liability in equity which can be specifically enforced. Of course, in India this does not happen.

(3) Where there is a written declaration that the land of the mortgagor is charged with the repayment of a loan, an equitable mortgage comes into existence.

(4) Where title deeds to the property are deposited with intent to create a mortgage, the land concerned being the security for the payment of a debt, it is yet another instance wherein an equitable mortgage is created without a writing, on the principle of implied agreement and part performance.[37]

(*b*) *In India.*—In India all mortgages are legal mortgages.[38] Indian law knows no distinction between legal and equitable estates, rights and mortgages. The right of redemption of a mortgage is a legal right under Section 60 of the Transfer of Property Act, 1882. A mortgagor can therefore create a second mortgage on this right. As could be seen from the definition of mortgages in Section 58, a mortgagor in India does not transfer the whole interest in the

36. *Bank of India* v. *Abhay D. Narottam*, (2005) 11 SCC 520.
37. Maitland: *Lectures on Equity*, 1969 Edn., p. 198.
38. *Imperial Bank of India* v. *U. Rai Gyaw Thu & Co.*, (1923) 1 Rang 637 (PC).

property but retains a legal interest in the property which may be further subjected to a subsequent mortgage.

Under English law a legal mortgage takes precedence over an equitable mortgage subject to certain exceptions but in India this is not so, because, according to Section 48 of the Transfer of Property Act, all mortgages rank in order of the time of creation, subject to provisions of Sections 78 and 79.

Mortgage by deposit of title deeds in India differs from an English equitable mortgage, because, whereas the latter is an insufficient security[39] and can be postponed to a subsequent legal mortgage, the former is a sufficient security, a completed transfer, and takes effect and precedence as against any mortgage deed subsequently executed and registered.

A mortgage by deposit of title deeds in England is accompanied by a written memorandum and that memorandum alone determines the scope and extent of the security, as it is the memorandum only which governs the bargain. If the memorandum is merely the record of an already completed bargain, its position is not so strong. In India, if such a memorandum is an integral part of the transaction, it is required to be registered and it will not be allowed to be contradicted by extrinsic oral evidence.[40] Moreover on the ratio of *Pranjivandas Mehta* v. *Chan Ma Phee*[41] and per Lord Cairns in *Shaw* v. *Joster*[42] and *National Bank* v. *Nazir & Co.*,[43] per Justice Tayabji one may say that the question of registration depends on the question whether the written memo contains the real bargain between the parties or not. If it contains, it must be registered.

15. MORTGAGOR'S EQUITY OF REDEMPTION OR RIGHT OF REDEMPTION

(*a*) *Origin*.—The origin, nature and the elevation of the equity of redemption from an equitable right into an equitable estate has already been discussed in para 5 above.

(*b*) *Description*.—As could be seen from Section 60 of the Transfer of Property Act, *a right of redemption can be described as the mortgagor's right to get retransferred the mortgaged property, free from any encumbrance, on his repaying the mortgage debt with due interest, before his right to redeem is foreclosed or the property mortgaged is got sold by the mortgagee*. It is a right which requires the mortgagee to do three things on repayment of his money:—

(*i*) to deliver all the documents relating to the property;

(*ii*) to deliver possession of the property if he is in possession thereof; and

(*iii*) to retransfer the property as the mortgagor directs or to execute a registered acknowledgement in writing that no rights in derogation of the interest transferred subsist or exist.

---

39. "Equitable mortgages are not very safe things", Maitland: *Lectures on Equity*, 1969 Edn., p. 199.

40. *Obla* v. *Narayan*, (1930) 35 CWN 925 (PC); *Rachpal* v. *Bhagwan*, AIR 1950 SC 79.

41. (1916) LR 43 IA 122.

42. 1872 LR 5 HL 32.

43. 34 BLR 784, 751.

(*c*) *Nature.*—A right of redemption in India is a legal right (as discussed before) which a mortgagor can exercise by virtue of his residuary ownership in the property. It has been properly pointed out by Snell[44] that the mortgagor's equitable right to redeem, coupled with his other rights in the property, constitute his "*equity of redemption*". In other words, *it is the sum total of his residual rights and interests in the mortgaged property*. There can be no partial redemption (except in one case under Section 60) because the mortgage security is indivisible. If a piecemeal redemption is allowed the security may depreciate,[45] and the integrity of a mortgage may be broken.[46] Thus the indivisibility of the mortgage security is a statutory concept. The right to redeem, in India, subsists until a final decree of sale or order of foreclosure has been actually passed as per Rules 3 and 5 of Order 34 of the Civil Procedure Code.[47]

16. DOCTRINE OF CLOG ON REDEMPTION

Though equity of redemption under the English law in the same form is not recognised in India, the doctrine of clog on the right of redemption has been recognised.[48]

(*a*) *Description.*—A clog has been described as *any contrivance or method whereby the mortgagor's right of redemption is impaired*. Explaining this in *Noakes & Co.* v. *Rice*[49] it has been said:

> "There are three doctrines of the courts of equity in this country. The *first* is expressed in the maxim "*One a mortgage, always a mortgage*". The *second* is that the mortgagee shall not reserve to himself *any collateral advantage outside the mortgage contract; and the third is that a provision or stipulation which will have the effect of clogging or fettering the equity of redemption is void*. The third doctrine to which I have referred is only a corollary from the first, and might be expressed in this form '*once a mortgage, always a mortgage and nothing but a mortgage*.' The meaning is that the mortgagee shall not make any stipulation which will prevent a mortgagor who has paid principal, interest and costs from getting back his mortgaged property in the condition in which he parted with it."

This rule has been applicable in India too as could be observed from *Sherkhan case*[50] decided by the Privy Council. Thus any agreement which directly bars the mortgagor's right to redeem or a stipulation which directly or indirectly may have the effect of making the mortgage irredeemable or the

---

44. *Snell's Principles of Equity*, 27th Edn., 1973, p. 378.
45. *Nilkanth* v. *Suresh*, (1886) 12 IA 171.
46. *Ramchand* v. *Prabhu Dayal*, (1942) 69 IA 98.
47. *Achaldas Durgaji Oswal* v. *Ramvilas Gangabisan Heda*, (2003) 3 SCC 6140; *V.K. Palanippa Chettiar* v. *Ramaswamy Gounder*, (2001) 4 SCC 413. (Right of redemption extinguished by decree.)
48. *Ganga Dhar* v. *Shankar*, AIR 1958 SC 770.
49. 1902 AC 24, per Lord Davey.
50. *Mohd. Sherkhan* v. *Raja Seth Swamy Dayal*, (1921) 20 ALJ 476.

property being still subject to incumbrances after redemption, are clogs on the equity of redemption.[51]

(*b*) *Tests.*—The test whether a particular agreement or stipulation is a clog or not depends on the nature, import and scope of the stipulation and whether the same has been a part of the mortgage agreement itself. The needy mortgagor cannot bargain on equal terms with the mortgagee and it is to save him from pressures of the mortgagee that this rule has been made by equity. *James Fairlough case*[52] and *Reeve case*[53] in England, and *Shankardin case*[54] in India are leading examples on the topic.

(*c*) *Modern Trend.*—Courts in England were at one time inclined to rule even further than this that any benefit or advantage which may endure beyond the period of repayment of the debt with interest and costs (called "the price of redemption")[55] was invalid[56] but the modern trend is not so harsh; it restricts the rule to the clogging of equity and will not allow it to go further. Consequently, in *Kreglinger case*[57], Lord Mercey described this doctrine as an unruly dog, which if not chained and confined to its own kennel, was prone to wander into places where it ought not to be. It was observed in that case that if the collateral advantage is not unconscionable, unfair, extravagant or oppressive, or in the nature of penalty or inconsistent with the right to redeem, the same is valid.[58] This view finds expression in *Kanahayalal* v. *National Bank of India*[59] and is in line with the construction[60] of Section 60 of the Transfer of Property Act in India.

As to who can exercise this right and how, is laid down in Section 91 of the Transfer of Property Act. It can be exercised before it is foreclosed, or the mortgaged property is sold by the mortgagee or before it becomes time barred.

17. FORECLOSURE

As said by Hanbury, the right to foreclose is an equitable right given to the mortgagee to counterbalance the mortgagor's right to redeem. This was a proper move on the part of equity courts because one has to become just before he professes to become generous. Foreclosure can be effected only by an order of the court. The court thereby gives the mortgagor and all the parties interested in the equity of redemption an opportunity to redeem the mortgage. The mortgagor, who in such proceedings is already too late to redeem at law, shall be deprived even of his equitable right.[61] As Strahan puts it, it is simply the right

---

51. *Snell's Principles of Equity*, 27th Edn., p. 379.
52. 1912 AC 565.
53. *Reeve* v. *Lisle*, 1902 AC 461.
54. (1912) 34 All 620.
55. See *Snell's Principles of Equity*, pp. 410-413 for details.
56. *Noakes & Co.* v. *Rice*, 1902 AC 24; *Bradley* v. *Carritt*, 1903 AC 253.
57. 1914 AC 25.
58. *Biggs* v. *Hoddinott*, (1898) 2 Ch 307.
59. (1923) IA 162.
60. *Ambu Nair* v. *Kelu Nair*, (1930) 53 Mad 805.
61. *Snell's Principles of Equity*, p. 401.

to ask the court to withdraw its relief against a forfeiture which is created by the mortgage. In suitable cases, therefore, a court passes first of all a conditional order of foreclosure, called a *foreclosure nisi*, which if not complied with by the mortgagor will become absolute, and the mortgagor will be barred forever from redeeming his property. Resultantly the mortgagee will hold the land absolutely both at law and in equity. Section 67 of the Transfer of Property Act provides for this. The position of various mortgagees under the Act is that in case of a simple mortgagee and a usufructuary mortgagee, no foreclosure is allowed, while in case of a English mortgagee and a mortgagee by deposit of title deeds the remedy of sale is allowed. It is only in case of a mortgage by conditional sale that a foreclosure is allowed.

An anomalous mortgagee may have, according to the terms of the mortgage, both or any one of the two remedies—foreclosure or sale. A dismissal of the redemption suit on failure of the mortgagor to redeem operates to foreclose his right of redemption; and he will not be allowed to sue for redemption again, as it amounts to harassment of the mortgagee.[62]

18. OPENING THE FORECLOSURE

As said before, although the absolute foreclosure order appears to be final, a court will open a foreclosure in circumstances compelling and inducing it to do so. They are, as enumerated by Snell[63]: (*i*) an accident at the last moment preventing the mortgagor from raising the money, (*ii*) any special value of the property to the mortgagor, (*iii*) a marked disparity between the value of the property and the amount lent, (*iv*) the promptness of the application,[64] and (*v*) where the mortgagee pursues another remedy after obtaining an order of foreclosure absolute. It was for this reason that Maitland remarked that "one is not very safe in purchasing a foreclosed estate". In India no such provision for reopening a final decree of foreclosure exists as could be gathered from Order 34, Rule 3 of the Civil Procedure Code.

Besides suing a mortgagor personally and foreclosing his right of redemption, in India, a mortgagee has the remedies of a judicial sale, sale without intervention of court, appointment of a receiver and taking possession of the mortgaged property.

19. TACKING

Tacking is the union of two securities on the same property by the mortgagee who has a legal estate. This union is achieved in such a manner and with such a result that the intermediate equitable purchaser is prevented from claiming a title to redeem. This contrivance had the effect of modifying the rules of priorities. Putting this principle into practice resulted in injustice as when a subsequent equitable mortgagee might tack his right by getting in the legal estate and could squeeze out a second mortgagee. This is an extreme

---

62. *Biggs* v. *Hoddinott*, (1898) 2 Ch 307, 312.
63. *Snell's Principles of Equity*, p. 403.
64. *Campbell* v. *Holyland*, (1877) 7 Ch D 166.

and unjust extension of the principle underlying the maxim "where there is equal equity, the law shall prevail". This curious doctrine was therefore abolished in 1925,[65] and after 1925 a legal or equitable mortgage was allowed to tack further advances to rank in priority to intervening legal or equitable mortgages.[66] In India, tacking for the purpose of squeezing out an intermediate mortgagee is not recognised.[67] It is expressly prohibited by Section 93 of the Transfer of Property Act. The section enacts that when a third mortgagee pays off the first mortgagee, he is subrogated to the position of the first mortgagee. The section in such cases explains that the third mortgagee cannot join his own mortgage to the first and claim priority over the intermediate mortgagee. Tacking of this nature is prohibited but tacking further advances as set out in Section 79 of the Act is permitted. In short, what a third mortgagee gets by paying off the first mortgagee is not priority, but subrogation[68] or substitution.

20. CONSOLIDATION

The doctrine of consolidation had its origin in the maxim "he who seeks equity must do equity". Where distinct estates have been separately mortgaged by the same mortgagor to the same mortgagee, the mortgagee is in a better position as if the whole of the lands had been mortgaged to him for the total amounts advanced by him. He can therefore consolidate those mortgages against the mortgagor and refuse to allow him to redeem one without redeeming the other. In other words, when a party is entitled to the mortgages he can insist upon the mortgagor to redeem all at a time or none. Redemption here is allowed only upon equitable terms that is, when the mortgagor's right to redeem at law was lost and he seeks to enforce his equitable right to redeem, the mortgagee can subject the mortgagor to an equitable condition of redeeming all the mortgages, because otherwise a mortgagee would be exposed to the risk of deficiency of the other security. He is thus left to his luck, which is not fair.[69] The doctrine applies to real or personal property mortgaged and also to legal or equitable properties. This doctrine was abolished in England. The Transfer of Property Act, Section 61, in India, also enacts to this effect. Section 61 enacts against consolidation[70] but provides that if there is a contract to the contrary consolidation will be permitted.[71] But a mortgagee cannot compel a mortgagor to redeem all the mortgages as is provided in Section 67-A of the Transfer of Property Act. It must be noted that the old unamended section referred to separate mortgages of different properties but the amended section now covers the situation where the same property is mortgaged under successive mortgages.

---

65. Law of Property, 1925, Section 94(3).
66. Law of Property, 1925, Section 94.
67. *Gokulnath* v. *L.P. Lal*, (1878) 3 Cal 307.
68. *Imperial Bank of India* v. *U. Rai Gyaw Thu & Co.*, 51 Cal 86.
69. *Fischer on Mortgages*, p. 597.
70. *Shambhu Charan* v. *Harprasad*, (1962) SC CA 11.
71. *Aditya* v. *Rama Ratan*, 1930 PC 176.

As explained in *Jankinath* v. *Pramathnath*[72], such a situation may arise not due to consolidation but because of making a second mortgage of the same property to the same mortgagee.

21. MARSHALLING SECURITIES

To marshall means to arrange, to systematize, to methodize or to place in order.

The doctrine of marshalling represents the concept of natural justice and it is that a mortgagee cannot be allowed to act, either with design or with caprice, whim or rashness, in such a way as to prejudice the rights of the other. *Aldrich* v. *Cooper*[73] lays down the principle thus that "*it shall not depend upon the will of one creditor to disappoint another*". Moreover, "if a creditor has two funds, the interest of the debtor shall not be regarded, but the creditor having two funds shall take that which paying him will leave another fund for another creditor".[74] This idea has been incorporated in Section 81 of the Transfer of Property Act thus:

> 81. *Marshalling securities.*—If the owner of two or more properties mortgages them to one person and then mortgages one or more of the properties to another person, the subsequent mortgagee is, in the absence of a contract to the contrary, entitled to have the prior mortgage debt satisfied out of the property or properties not mortgaged to him, so far as the same will extend, but not so as to prejudice the rights of the prior mortgagee or of any other person who has for consideration acquired an interest in any of the properties.

The section is clear and enacts that where two mortgagees claim to be satisfied out of the same property, it is for the court to apply this doctrine of marshalling whereunder it will so arrange the securities that both the mortgagees are paid as far as possible. This could be done by directing the first mortgagee (at the instance of the subsequent mortgagee) to satisfy his claim first from the property not mortgaged to the subsequent mortgagee and then to extend his claim to the other. The result would be that it will leave the other security or so much of a part of it, not required for the satisfaction of the first, for the subsequent mortgagee. One has to note that the section includes the words "in the absence of a contract to the contrary", which means that this "right" of the mortgagee can be excluded by contract of the parties. Since the first mortgagee has two estates in his hands he, of his own will, cannot be allowed to act in a way to cause injustice and inflict loss to the other. But, if by marshalling the

72. 1940 PC 38, per Lord Roamer.

73. (1803) 8 Ves 382, per Lord Eldon. *See* also *Well* v. *Smith*, (1885) 30 Ch D 192; *Lenoy* v. *Duke of Athole*, 2 ATK 446.

74. *Annapurna* v. *Ramranjan*, 40 CWN 1173; *see* also *National Provincial Bank Ltd.* v. *Katz*, (1959) 3 All ER 740 (equity attempts to do justice among all beneficiaries on an equal footing).

securities the first mortgagee's interest is prejudiced or persons getting interest through him are put to a loss, this principle will not be applied.[75]

22. CONTRIBUTION

The doctrine of contribution is based on the maxim "equity delighteth in equality".[76] The principle underlying this doctrine is equality; for example, where several persons are debtors all shall be equal, and if the creditor does not make them to contribute equally the courts of equity will see that the object is achieved by making them to contribute equally. In other words, it involves the fixation of the proportion or share in which two or more owners of an estate, subject to a common charge, ought to contribute for its redemption. This principle is incorporated in Section 82 of the Transfer of Property Act. Dr Ghose[77] in his treatise has clearly explained thus:".....a mortgage debt is one and indivisible and if several distinct parcels of land are hypothecated to the creditor, which belong to two or more mortgagors, or subsequently pass to different owners, the creditor may, as a rule, proceed against any one of such parcels; and the only way to prevent a sale or foreclosure would be to pay the whole of the mortgage debt. It is but reasonable that in such a case, the person who is compelled to discharge the common burden should be permitted to seek indemnification from the others and no fairer rule can be suggested than that each of them should contribute according to the value of the property owned by him or the extent of his interest in it. For the law would not suffer the creditor to select his own victim, and from caprice or favouritism to turn a 'common burden' into a gross personal oppression". Principles of natural justice can be seen working here.

Section 82 of the Transfer of Property Act incorporates not only the case of a property once mortgaged and subsequently divided into several shares but also the case of a mortgage of several properties mortgaged. In other words, where the debt is one and the properties mortgaged are several, and where there are two properties and the debts are several the principle applies. It should be noted that contribution is regulated by the principle of marshalling and where there is a conflict between the two, principles of marshalling shall prevail. Section 82 will apply only up to the time the mortgage continues. Moreover, the liability created by contribution is not personal but it is attached to the property and the liability though statutory can be avoided or excluded by a contract, as the section itself provides. Looked at from a proper angle, one may say that contribution is marshalling in a different form. Leading cases on the principle are *Kidar Lall* v. *Hari Lall*[78] and *Narayan* v. *Nallammal*[79].

---

75. *Devkinandan* v. *Parmeshwari*, 1941 Punj LW 582. *See* also Lahiri: *Transfer of Property Act*, 8th Edn., 1965, p. 404 quoting *Jones on Mortgages*.
76. *Craythorne* v. *Swinburne*, (1807) 14 Ves 160.
77. *Law of Mortgages in India*, 8th Edn., p. 415.
78. 1952 SCR 179.
79. (1942) 2 MLJ 525.

23. SUBROGATION

(*a*) *Origin.*—The term subrogation is said to be derived from the Latin root *sub rogo subrogatum*—from sub and rogo to ask, meaning substitution. Dr Oglive explains that subrogation is a term of civil law meaning the substitution of one person in the place of another giving him his rights, but in the general sense it implies a succession of the kind either of a person to a person or a person to a thing.

(*b*) *Definition.*—The Law Commissioners in their report[80] say that technically the term is confined to cases where the right arises by operation of law. In Roman law, a creditor who lent money to the debtor for the purpose of paying off a mortgage on condition that he was to be substituted in the place of the mortgagee, was entitled to claim the benefit of the security discharged with his money;[81] and this right has been recognised in all modern systems derived from Roman law.... The principle of subrogation however ought to apply generally to all cases other than those of a mortgagor who pays off his own debt or of a mere volunteer.[82]

This doctrine is a doctrine of equity jurisprudence. As defined by Mukerjee, J. in *Bisseswar Prasad* v. *Lala Sarnam Singh*[83], it does not depend on privity of contract, express or implied, except in so far as equity may be supposed to be imported into the transaction and thus raise contract by implication. It is founded on the facts and circumstances of each particular case and on the principles of natural justice. While therefore the doctrine will be applied in general, (*i*) wherever any person other than a mere volunteer pays a debt or a demand which in equity or good conscience should have been satisfied by another, or (*ii*) where the liability of one person is discharged out of a fund belonging to another, or (*iii*) where one person is compelled for his own protection or that of some interest which he represents to pay a debt for which another is primarily liable, or (*iv*) wherever a denial of the right would be contrary to equity and good conscience, it will never be permitted, where the application of it would work injustice to the rights of those having equal or superior equities.

(*c*) *Test.*—The test of the right of subrogation[84] is found in an answer to the inquiry (*i*) whether the person who paid the mortgage debt is the one whose duty it was to pay it first of all; (*ii*) if the debt was not primarily his, and he only occupied the position of a surety to the mortgagor, he is entitled to be subrogated to the position of the mortgagee when he has paid the debt; (*iii*) but if the debt is the debt of the person who paid it, or is a debt which he has covenanted to pay, his payment of it raises no right of subrogation, but is simply a performance of his obligation or covenant. This important doctrine of equity, in simple language, means to say that one who removes another's burden is

---

80. 13th report in 1929.
81. See *Donatt's Civil Law*, Section 1774 and *Hunter's Roman Law*, pp. 441, 443.
82. See *Craythorne* v. *Swinburne*, (1807) 14 Ves 160, 162, per Sir S. Romilly in England.
83. 1907 Cal LJ 134, 137-138.
84. *Jones on Mortgages*, para 1119.

entitled to step into his shoes, the characteristic features being that reimbursement is the foundation of this principle and the encumbrance that is paid off is treated as alive and not as one extinguished.

(*d*) *Types.*—Subrogation is of two types: legal and conventional. Legal subrogation comes into existence when a mortgage debt is paid off by one who has to protect his interest. It is subrogation by law or legal subrogation.[85] Legal subrogation does not end the liability of the property; the liability herein is simply transferred in favour of one who pays off the mortgage debt. A conventional subrogation which may be said to be consensual subrogation or subrogation by agreement is by act of parties.[86]

Payment made to an infant for necessaries,[87] necessaries supplied to a deserted wife and the executor carrying on the business of his testator, are the well-known examples wherein subrogation on principles of equity have been allowed.

The Transfer of Property Act, Section 92 and the Indian Contract Act, Section 69 incorporate this principle.[88]

Subrogation can be achieved by redemption only and in no other way.[89] This right is available only from the date of redemption of the mortgaged property and not from the date of the right of redemption.

B. LIENS AND MERGER

24. LIENS

(*a*) *Definition.*—A common law lien is the right of a person to retain possession of the goods of another until his claims are satisfied.[90] Story defines it to the same effect[91] and explains that it is the right of a person to have his claim satisfied out of the property belonging to another. The main elements are right to possess and retain the property until the discharge of a charge. It is good against the world at large so long as it exists.

Lien is either legal or equitable and either particular or general. It differs from a mortgage or a pledge. The point of difference is that a lien does not give any *active right* in regard to the property; the right given is a *mere passive right* to possess.[92]

(*b*) *Legal and Equitable Lien.*—Legal lien is that which is recognized and enforced by the common law courts, while an equitable lien is that which is recognised and enforced in a court of equity only. A legal lien is lost when the

---

85. *Gokuldas* v. *Rambux*, (1884) 10 Cal 1036 (PC): 11 IA 126.
86. *Man Mohan* v. *Jankiprasad*, 1945 PC 23.
87. *Marlow* v. *Pitfield*, (1719) 1 P Wims 558. *See* Section 68 of Indian Contract Act, 1872.
88. *Hirasing* v. *Jaising*, 1937 All 588; *Kidari Lall* v. *Hari Lall*, 1952 SCJ 37.
89. *Gurudev* v. *Chandrika*, AIR 1944 PC 96.
90. *Snell's Principles of Equity* citing *Hammonds* v. *Barelay*, (1802) 2 East 227, 235.
91. Story: *Equity Jurisprudence*, 3rd Edn., p. 331.
92. *Barratt* v. *Gough Thomas (No. 2)*, 1951 Ch 242.

possession of the property subject to it is given up. It is however good against the whole world. Equitable lien, for its existence and continuance, does not depend upon retention of possession of the property subject to it; it affects everybody who obtains property with notice thereof. In other words "equitable lien confers a charge on property" and arises by "operation of equity from relationship between the parties rather than by act of parties. It exists independently of possession but will not avail against a purchaser for value of a legal estate without notice of it. It is enforceable by means of an order for sale".[93]

The distinction between a legal and an equitable lien is maintained in Indian Law too, as could be seen from the decision of the Privy Council in *Nippon Kaisha case*[94].

(*c*) *Lien and Pledge.*—A common law lien confers merely a right to possess and retain the property as security, which can be said to be a mere passive right to possess.[95] In a pledge there is a delivery of possession of property and a power of sale is its necessary concomitant.

(*d*) *Particular and General Lien.*—A particular lien is attached and confined to a particular charge whereas a general lien extends to all claims against the owner, whether or not in relation to particular goods, i.e., it stretches and expands to the general balance due.

(*e*) *Types of Lien.*—Liens are of diverse kinds, as already mentioned. Liens by custom and usage add to this list. The important liens may be listed as follows:

(1) solicitor's lien,

(2) banker's lien,

(3) agent's lien,

(4) vendor's lien,

(5) purchaser's lien

(6) bailee's lien,

(7) stockbroker's lien,

(8) factor's lien,

(9) trustee's lien,

(10) personal representative's lien,

(11) salvage lien,

(12) equitable lien,

(13) statutory lien,

(14) lessee's lien,

(15) lien of finder of goods, and

---

93. *Snell's Principles of Equity*, 27th Edn., p. 438.

94. *Nippon Kaisha* v. *Ramjiban*, (1938) 42 CWN 677 (PC).

95. *Barratt case*, (1951) Ch 242.

(16) pawnee's lien.

But these categories of liens are not exhaustive. Nos. 1, 4, 5, 9 and 10 may be cited as examples of equitable lien and Nos. 1, 2, 7 and 8 as those of general lien by custom or agreement. These liens may however, exist concurrently.

25. SOLICITOR'S LIEN

A solicitor has as per Common law a lien on his client's property in his possession and an equitable lien on his client's property recovered and preserved through him. The first kind of lien is a passive right to retain the property, while the second kind of lien is an active right which he can assert by taking steps to realise the property by sale. He has also a particular lien on his client's property for his costs of the suit (recognised by Section 28 of the Solicitors' Act, 1860).[96] He has a general lien on all deeds and documents (except a will) of his client with him and until he is paid they can be retained and withheld. This lien extends to the property of his client coming into the solicitor's hands as a solicitor, but not otherwise,[97] and is confined to his costs and does not include debts.

Members of the bar (advocates) are officers of the court. Remedy for an advocate in case of his unpaid remuneration is not to agitate before the High Court or the Supreme Court in a writ petition. Moreover an advocate has no lien over the papers of his client.[98]

26. BANKER'S LIEN

Regarding securities deposited, the banker has a general lien. It extends to the general balance of account. As laid down by Section 171 of the Indian Contract Act, bankers, factors, wharfingers, attorneys of the High Court and policy brokers have such a lien to retain the goods bailed to them.

27. AGENT'S LIEN

This has been incorporated under the Indian Contract Act, Section 221, whereby the agent is entitled to retain goods, papers and other property, whether moveable or immovable, of the principal received by him until his charges, etc. are paid out. The lien is lost as soon as the possession is parted with.[99]

28. BAILEE'S LIEN

Under Section 170 of the Indian Contract Act, when a bailee has done some work by his skill which is relevant to or in pursuance of a contract of bailment, he can retain them until he is suitably paid for it. Of course, this is subject to a

96. Now the Solicitors' Act, 1957, Section 72, replacing earlier provisions.

97. *Juller, ex p.*, (1881) 16 Ch D 617; *Tyabji Dahyabhai* v. *Jetha Devji and Co.*, (1927) 29 Bom LR 1196; *Sadanand* v. *Parashram*, (1928) 30 Bom LR 157.

98. *New India Assurance Co. Ltd.* v. *A.K. Saxena*, (2004) 1 SCC 117: (2004) 120 Comp Cas 284.

99. *Kishandas* v. *Ganesh Ram*, AIR 1950 Pat 481; *see* also *Ram Prasad* v. *State of M.P.*, (1969) 3 SCC 24: AIR 1970 SC 1818.

contract to the contrary. Thus artisans working on goods, packers, carriers and auctioneers are entitled to this kind of lien.[1]

29. SALVAGE LIEN

According to the doctrine of maritime law, salvors (those who by their assistance salvage the property, cargo or lives of persons in a ship), by the presumption of law have an implied contract with the owner of the ship whereby they have a retaining lien for their remuneration on the property rescued. The doctrine has been accepted in India, the most important features whereof are two: (*i*) bona fides of the person acting, and (*ii*) preservation of the estate in question.[2] The doctrine of salvage is different and therefore can be distinguished from subrogation.

30. PAWNEE'S LIEN

Section 173 of the Indian Contract Act lays down that "the pawnee may retain the goods pledged, not only for payment of the debt or the performance of the promise, but for the interest of the debt, and all necessary expenses incurred by him in respect of the possession or for the preservation of the goods pledged".

31. VENDOR'S LIEN

The concept of "vendor's trusteeship"[3] has been emphasised by the vendor's lien. This is not an ordinary trusteeship. Cotton, L.J. said that the vendor was a trustee only in a qualified sense. Lord Green, M.R. called him a quasi-trustee and Lord Cairns said that the trustee was entitled to protect his own interest in the property. A vendor becomes the trustee of the property sold to the vendee as the property passes at once to the purchaser, on a specifically enforceable contract for sale having been made. On such a contract having been made the seller has a lien on the property sold for unpaid purchase money. He can therefore retain it until the same is paid.[4] If the vendor parts with the possession both of property and the title deeds thereof, he still has an equitable lien on property in respect of the purchase money unpaid to him. The relationship between the parties contains a number of aspects and facets wherein they are hostile and the vendor self-interested. The terminology of trusteeship therefore must be received with reserve. Maitland explains this idea thus: "Usually there are two distinct acts in law; the agreement on the one hand, the conveyance on the other; and weeks or months elapse between the two".[5] According to him Austin did commit an error[6] when he said that "the mere agreement for sale

1. *Beaven* v. *Waters*, (1828) 3 Carr and P 520, per Best, J. *See* also *Skinner* v. *Jugar*, (1883) 8 All 1894.
2. *Dakshinamohan* v. *Saroda*, 21 Cal 142 PC.
3. *Snell's Principles of Equity*, p. 445; Hanbury: *Modern Equity*, p. 233; Maitland: *Lectures on Equity*, pp. 314-317. *See also* Jessel, M.R. in *Lysaght* v. *Edwards*, (1876) 2 Ch D 499.
4. *Mackreth* v. *Symmons*, (1808) 15 Ves 329.
5. Maitland: *Lectures on Equity*, 2nd Edn., 1969, p. 314.
6. *Ibid.*, p. 106, citing Austin: *Jurisprudence*, p. 388.

transfers the *dominium, the jus in re*". The most that it does is that it gives to the purchaser an equitable estate in land, a right good against those who claim under the vendor by gratuitous title, or who have or ought to have notice of it. The purchaser has only an equitable estate in the land, though one which is subject to the vendor's lien for the unpaid purchase money. The vendor has as yet the legal estate in the land, and anyone who purchases from the purchaser must purchase subject to those legal rights. Unless in the case of some very peculiar agreement the vendor may keep the legal estate, and may keep possession of the land until he is paid his price. If you say that the contract passess ownership, be careful to say that it does so only in equity.[7]

As laid down in *Mackreth case* this lien can be enforced against (*i*) the purchaser himself, (*ii*) his heirs or persons claiming through the purchaser as volunteers, (*iii*) subsequent purchasers for value but with notice of the lien, and (*iv*) the assignee in bankruptcy of the purchaser. The vendor may waive or abandon his lien and may lose it by laches or under the statutes of limitation.

32. VENDEE'S LIEN

Where a vendee pays the purchases money or a part of it in advance or by way of deposit to the vendor, he has also a lien on the estate in the vendor's hands. This lien exists not only when "the contract goes off for want of title, but also where he rescinds the contract under a condition enabling him to do so, or the vendor repudiates the contract;[8] but if the contract goes off through the purchaser's default, the lien is gone".[9] In order to bind the subsequent purchasers it is necessary that it should be registered.

When the lien comes into being under an express contract between the parties, it is a charge. As Strahan puts it, a lien and a charge are identical for all practical purposes.

33. IN INDIA

(*a*) *Charge.*—A charge is a general name for a burden attaching to a certain property making it security for the payment of a debt or the performance of an obligation. The term includes mortgages, liens and many security rights not having special names. Charges are of many kinds; a *fixed charge* attaches to specific property whereas a *floating charge* attaches to whichever property happens to be in the possession of the party at the time when the charge crystalizes. Some charges are capable of subsisting at law, including a rent charge in possession charged on land, a charge by way of legal mortgage and land tax or similar charge on land not created by an instrument, while others are equitable charges only, such as a mortgage by deposit of title deeds and equitable assignments by way of security.[10]

---

7. Maitland: *Lectures on Equity*, pp. 314-315. *See* also *Mackreth* v. *Symmons*, (1808) 15 Ves 329.
8. *Lee-Parker* v. *Izzet*, (1971) 1 WLR 1688.
9. *Snell's Principles of Equity*, 448.
10. Walker, David Maxwell: *The Oxford Companion to Law*, 1980, p. 206.

Section 100 defines a charge thus: "Where immovable property of one person is by act of the parties or operation of law made security for the payment of money to another, and the transaction does not amount to a mortgage, the latter person is said to have a charge on the property,...".

The section recognises that there can be charges both by operation of law and by act of parties. Charges by operation of law are, under Section 55(4)(*b*) which deals with vendee's charges for unpaid purchase money; under Section 55(6)(*b*) which deals with a purchaser's charge for the purchase amount paid in anticipation of delivery of property; under Section 73 with respect of surplus sale proceeds of a revenue sale; and under Section 82 for contribution.[11]

(*i*) *Vendor's lien*.—The right of recovery of unpaid purchase money, called, a non-possessory lien, or vendor's lien, can be enforced by him against the vendee and also against any person claiming through him with notice of sale. But the vendor cannot claim back the possession;[12] he can retain possession by virtue of it and when sued by the vendee for possession the court shall pass a conditional decree, decreeing possession only on payment of the unpaid purchase money.[13] This lien is, however, an equitable lien quite independent of the provisions of Sections 54 and 55 of the Transfer of Property Act. Being purely of personal character vendor's creditors cannot enforce it.[14] It can however be assigned, and the assignees can enforce it.[15]

This lien is available against the purchaser or any other person claiming through him with notice of the sale,[16] or against a transferee without consideration (*see* Section 40), but not against a purchaser's transferee for valuable consideration and without notice of the charge.[17]

(*ii*) *Lien: When lost*.—

(1) When the vendor accepts a collateral security from the vendee, the lien is lost, but by accepting an additional security it is not lost.[18] There should be evidence of the vendor's abandoning it.

(2) When the vendor by his conduct gives the vendee an impression that it will not be claimed, an estoppel is raised against him and the lien is lost.[19] But the lien is not lost because there is a recital in the conveyance that the consideration is fully paid up. This is so because it is the usual practice in India that although no

11. All under the Transfer of Property Act, 1882.
12. *Valaudha* v. *Govindswami*, 39 Mad 524.
13. *Pranadevi* v. *Satdeo Tiwari*, 111 IC 761; *Subramania* v. *Puran*, 27 Mad 28. For contra see *Kevaldas* v. *Naraindas*, 111 BLR 383.
14. *Motilal* v. *Bhagwandas*, 31 Mad 443.
15. *Dalchand* v. *Ganpat*, 1927 Nag 332.
16. *Ramanand* v. *Shivdas*, 43 All 314.
17. *Gurudayal* v. *Karan Singh*, 38 All 254.
18. *Grant* v. *Mil*, 2 V & B 306; *Webb* v. *Macpherson*, 31 Cal 57 PC.
19. *Kettlowel* v. *Walson*, 26 Ch D 501.

consideration is in fact paid before recital, the documents are executed.[20]

(3) When the purchase money has been left with the vendee for payment to the vendor's creditor, the lien cannot be enforced; but a mere direction by the vendor to the vendee cannot deprive him of his lien.

A vendee's lien is lost when he improperly refuses to accept delivery of property from the vendor.

(*b*) *Charge and Lien*.—A charge differs from a lien in that a charge can come into existence by act of parties or by operation of law, whereas a lien can be created only by operation of law. Moreover, a charge is only with respect to immovable property, whereas a lien can be with respect to movable as well as immovable property.

(*c*) *Charge and Mortgage*.—(*i*) A charge gives a right to payment out of a particular fund or property without transfer of the fund or property, whereas a mortgage is in essence, a transfer of an interest in specific immovable property. (*ii*) In other words, a charge is a *jus ed rem*, i.e., a right to a thing, whereas a mortgage is a *jus in rem*, i.e., a right against a property. (*iii*) Consequently, a mortgage prevails over subsequent transferees, while a charge cannot prevail against a transferee for consideration without notice of the charge. (*iv*) A charge can be a floating charge over all the assets of a company under the company law, while a mortgage can be created over a specific immovable property. (*v*) A mortgage, like a simple mortgagor, involves a personal liability, in a charge it is not so. (*vi*) A charge can be created either by operation of law or by act of parties, whereas a mortgage can be created only by act of parties. (*vii*) A mortgage gives the power of recovery of money by sale of the mortgaged premises whereas a charge directs the realisation of money from a particular property, without reference to a sale.[21]

(*d*) *Charge by act of parties and by operation of law*.—A charge by act of parties may be oral, if created by a document in writing it must be registered under Section 17(1-*b*) of the Registration Act, but if the amount secured is less than Rs 100, it need not be registered. The property charged must be definite and specified or else it would be void for uncertainty.[22] As said before, the principles of vendor's lien and vendee's lien are incorporated in Sections 55(4)(*b*) and 55(6)(*b*) of the Transfer of Property Act in India and they are similar to the corresponding equitable lien under the English law. Besides, Section 39 of the Transfer of Property Act speaks about the floating charge in respect of a Hindu widow's right of maintenance and Section 51 of the Act speaks about the equitable rule regarding improvements made on land by the holder of a defective title. Similarly, government revenue arrears under the local

---

20. *Meghraj* v. *Abdulla*, 12 ALJ 1032; *Timalrao* v. *Municipal Commr.*, 3 Bom 172 and per Lord Eldon in *Mackreth* v. *Simons*, 15 Ves 329.
21. Mukerji, J., in *Govinda Chandra* v. *Dwarka Nath*, (1908) 35 Cal 837.
22. *Mohini Debi* v. *Purnashashi*, (1932) 36 CWN 153.

Revenue Acts form a charge under the Transfer of Property Act. A trustee, under Section 32 of the Indian Trusts Act, has a right to reimburse himself from trust property for expenses properly incurred in the execution of his trust, and therefore Section 100 of the Transfer of Property Act rightly excludes this from charge. He can insist and can compel that his charges be paid first before disposition of trust property. While being a trustee he cannot sell or destroy the trust property, he can get it sold after he ceases to become a trustee.[23]

34. LIEN OF THE FINDER OF GOODS

A finder of goods has a right to retain the goods found until he receives suitable compensation; if a reward is offered, he can sue for the reward and retain the goods until the same is paid. This is provided in Section 168 of the Indian Contract Act and Section 169 gives him a right of sale when the goods are perishable. When the owner cannot be found in spite of reasonable inquiries and if found refuses to pay, the finder in such cases can sell the goods if his charges amount to two-thirds of the value of the goods.

35. MERGER

As explained by Blackstone, according to the common law rule in England, "whenever a greater estate and a lesser estate coincide and meet in one and the same person, without any intermediate estate, the less is immediately annihilated, or in the law phrase, is said to be merged, that is sunk or drowned, in the greater". As decided in *Forbes* v. *Moffat*[24], that means that when a charge and ownership of an estate are united in the same person, the charge is automatically extinguished. Of course, this depends upon the intention of the person in whom the interests are united and the same may be express or implied. Equity will find out this intention and consider what is most beneficial for him.

When a mortgage and the equity of redemption both come into the same hand such a question arises. The common law rule, as laid down by Blackstone and explained in *Jorbes case*, was that the merger was automatic irrespective of the intention of the person, but equity ruled that it depended on the person's intention and where merger was against that person's interest, equity presumed against the same.[25]

Now, after the Judicature Act, 1873, both at law and in equity, merger depends on intention.[26]

---

23. *Peary Mohan Mukerjee* v. *Narendra Nath*, (1901) 37 IA 27; *Abkan Sahib* v. *Soranbibi*, (1915) 38 Mad 260. See *Videocon Properties Ltd.* v. *Dr Bhalchandra Laboratories*, (2004) 3 SCC 711 (Discussed buyer's charge, when change attaches, till what time it ensures, nature of charge whether proprietary and whether it can be traced to third parties. Charge distinguished from contractual charge and equitable charge.)
24. (1811) 18 Ves 384.
25. *Ingle* v. *Vaugham Jenkins*, (1900) 2 Ch 368.
26. *Snell's Principles of Equity*, p. 406; *Nirmal Chandra* v. *Vimal Chand*, (2001) 5 SCC 51 (Mortgage of leased property by landlord to tenant. Merger of lease and mortgage.)

In India, the Transfer of Property Act before its amendment in 1929 accepted the rule laid down in *Toulmene* v. *Steere*[27] under which "extinguishment" (of a lesser estate into a bigger one) was the rule and "keeping alive" (both the estates, lesser and bigger) was the exception. But the Privy Council[28] declined to follow this rule of automatic merger. The amended Section 101 of the Transfer of Property Act, therefore, lays down that the court presumes that the person who discharges an incumbrance, kept it alive if it would be for his benefit, i.e., where a property is mortgaged once and there is a subsequent mortgage, the prior mortgagee if he purchases the equity of redemption will not bring about a merger because it would be in his own benefit to keep it alive. If he keeps it alive then and then the subsequent mortgagee will be able to redeem the prior mortgage, otherwise not. It is therefore the rule that there will be no merger and the application of the doctrine of intention is no longer required. Section 92 of the Transfer of Property Act lays down that the mortgagee's interest is not merged by reason of the fact that the mortgagee's interest and the mortgagor's equity of redemption have been united in the same person. Section 101 represents the converse case. According to Mulla, this right which is statutory can be waived by contract and therefore it is unnecessary to apply the equitable principle in India.

---

27. (1817) 3 Mer 210.
28. *Gokuldas* v. *Rambux*, (1884) 10 Cal 1036 (PC): 11 IA 126.

Chapter VII
Married Women, Infants, Idiots and Lunatics

"At common law, a wife's separate and distinct personality was considered to be merged into that of her husband who enjoyed power and domination over her... ."

"In India 'the wife got an honoured position on marriage', and as the old writers put it, 'a woman is half her husband and completes him, and the highest law for husband and wife was mutual fidelity'."

—*Vedic Index I*, pp. 484-486

Manu IX, p. 96; *Manu III*, pp. 55-56

"An infant is not absolutely incapable of binding himself by contract, but is, generally speaking, incapable of absolutely binding himself."

—An Irish judgment

SYNOPSIS

A. MARRIED WOMEN

1. HISTORY

To appreciate the modern law in respect of the legal position of married women, it is necessary to go through, though succinctly, into the history of the penetration, invasion and inroads upon the harshness of the Common law rules made, first by equity and later by statute.

At Common law, on marriage and during marriage, all rights of a woman were suspended, incorporated and consolidated into that of her husband with the result that she could neither acquire nor hold property independently of her husband. As the husband provided her with protection and cover and as he was considered to be the ablest and the fittest to govern the family, the wife's distinct and separate personality was considered to be merged into that of her husband who enjoyed power and domination over her. On marriage therefore the husband was entitled to all her property whether it belonged to her at the date of marriage or came to her after marriage. Consequently *she lost her property and distinct personality*. She could not contract with her husband. She could not sue or be sued either in tort or in contract without joining her husband as a party. Against her husband's neglect she was remediless. The husband had full power to alienate her chattels without her consent and to alienate her real property with her consent. He was entitled to receive rents and profits of her realty during coverture. If he survived the wife he could take the property absolutely. The wife was thus without remedy against such rigid practices of the Common law and was reduced to the status of a beneficiary under a trust or a mortgagor in a forfeited mortgage.

2. EQUITABLE RELIEF

But the courts of equity, although on the principle that "equity follows the law", in general protected the interests of the husband, thought it fit to depart from these rigid rules of Common law in three instances. This it did by innovating new ideas based on principles of natural justice and reciprocity.

(*a*) *Wife's equity to a settlement.*—If the husband wanted to enforce his rights regarding property of the wife and in doing so if he took proceedings and sought assistance from the courts of equity, the courts could compel him to make provision out of that property for his wife and children. This it did on the principle "he who seeks equity must do equity".[1] This principle was also pressed into service in a case where the wife died and her children initiated the action.[2]

(*b*) *Wife's separate estate.*—By ante-nuptial agreements when real or personal property was given or settled upon a woman, at Common law such agreements did not survive on marriage. But equity enforced such agreements in furtherance of their common intention and object. Similarly, where a husband abandoned his rights to the wife's property, where he gave his own property to her, or some stranger gifted property to the wife, that property together with her earnings, savings, pinmoney and cash investments in land formed her separate property, which she could dispose of without her husband's consent either *inter vivos* or by will,[3] whether the interest therein was in reversion or possession.[4] This idea was an innovation whereby the wife was considered to be a *femme sole*, capable of possessing independently of her husband's control, property within her complete control, for her separate use, without the intervention of trustees. An intention to reserve or keep apart such property was sufficient and no particular form of words was necessary to create the separate use.

By recognising and injecting into practice these two novel ideas, equity modified the Common law rights of a husband so that the position of a married woman in society could be raised to a respectable level. A married woman now could contract as her husband's agent and her debts could be satisfied out of her separate estate only. But one thing is to be noted here, that when she died during

1. *Elibank* v. *Montolieu*, (1801) 5 Ves 737.
2. *Murray* v. *Lord Elibank*, (1804) 10 Ves 84.
3. *Fettiplace* v. *Gorges*, (1789) 1 Ves Jun 46.
4. *Sturgis* v. *Corp.*, (1806) 13 Ves 190.

coverture and left her separate property undisposed, the husband's Common law right to this extent was revived.[5] The Married Women's Property Act, 1882 converted these equitable rights into legal rights which brought into vogue a popular aphorism that a husband could "break his wife's neck but not her watch" which was her separate property. By the Administration of Estates Act, 1925, Section 46 as amended[6] from time to time the husband's rights are now regulated. Neither spouse, however, has any rights consequent on the death intestate of the other spouse while a decree of judicial separation is in force and the separation is continuing, for the property of the intestate spouse devolves as if the other spouse were already dead.[7]

(*c*) *Restraint on anticipation.*—The third step to secure and protect the married woman's property rights against her husband's imperceptible but powerful persuasion or coercion was the invention by Lord Thurlow[8] of the doctrine of "restraint on anticipation". This doctrine was a creation of the equity courts and was especially brought into existence for guarding the wife's property. In course of time, the married woman's "separate property" became her "property"[9], and the fetters of "restraint on anticipation" attached by equity courts to it, which would otherwise be—in case of restraint on property of a man—void, as being repugnant to the nature of property, were modified as circumstances required in order to further the object for which it was created. This restraint was attached as soon as she married and would cease on her husband's death or on divorce. On remarriage it again attached. Thus it attached and reattached *toties quoties*[10]. As this restraint on anticipation, whereby a woman was prohibited or disabled during coverture from alienating the property or anticipating the future income out of the property, and which was recognised by the Married Women's Property Act, 1882, worked against her creditors, in 1935[11], new restraints were prevented from taking form and the existing restraints were abolished from December 16, 1949,[12] thus bringing and raising her position to that of a man. It has therefore been rightly said that on account of successive Married Women's Property Acts the old status of a married woman and the principle of the fictitious unity of the husband and wife now no more exists; they stand abrogated and therefore the subject can be said to be obsolete here being a fit subject for discussion under the Law of Property generally.

(*d*) *Modern position.*—As presented by Snell[13] the modern position in general is that a married women is now,

---

5. Before 1926 the husband took such rights.
6. By the Intestates' Estates Act, 1957, the Family Provision Act, 1966 and the Family Law Reforms Act, 1969.
7. Matrimonial Proceedings & Property Act, 1970, Section 40(1), cited in *Snell's Principles of Equity*, 27th Edn., 1973, p. 516.
8. In *Pybus* v. *Smith*, (1791) 3 Bro CC 340; *Brandon* v. *Robinson*, (1811) LC 18 Ves 429 at Nathan No. 72 on p. 314.
9. *See* Law Reforms (Married Women and Tortfeasors) Act, 1935. Ss. 1 and 2.
10. For detailed account see *Snell's Principles of Equity*, 24th Edn., 1954, pp. 457, 462.
11. Law Reforms (Married Women and Tortfeasors) Act, 1935.
12. Married Woman (Restraint upon Anticipation) Act, 1949.
13. *Snell's Principles of Equity*, 27th Edn., 1973, p. 517. For detailed account *see* p. 517-530.

(*i*) capable of acquiring, holding and disposing of, any property;

(*ii*) capable of rendering herself and being rendered, liable in respect of any tort, contract, debt or obligation;

(*iii*) capable of suing and being sued, either in tort or in contract or otherwise; and

(*iv*) subject to the law relating to bankruptcy and to the enforcement of judgements and orders, in all respects as if she were a *femme sole*. Moreover, she is no longer able, as her husband's agent of necessity, to pledge his credit or borrow money on his credit.

3. IN INDIA

The fictitious principle of unity of persons between husband and wife as recognised in England in the beginning and abrogated at present, is not accepted in India[14] as is evident from the Indian Succession Act, 1925, Section 20. The section provides:

"20. *Interests and powers not acquired nor lost by marriage*.—(1) No person shall, by marriage, acquire any interest in the property of the person whom he or she marries, or become capable of doing any act in respect of his or her property which he or she could have done if unmarried.

(2) This section—

(*a*) shall not apply to any marriage contracted before the first day of January, 1866;

(*b*) shall not apply and shall be deemed never to have applied to any marriage, one or both of the parties to which professed at the time of the marriage the Hindu, Muhammadan, Buddhist, Sikh or Jain religion."

The Transfer of Property Act, Section 10, which enacts that a condition restraining alienation is void provides in case of a married woman by making an exception, that property may be transferred for the benefit of a woman (not being Hindu, Muhammadan, or Buddhist) with a condition that she shall not have power during her marriage to transfer or charge the same or her beneficial interest therein.

Non-Hindus and Non-Muhammadans.—Limited to persons other than Hindus and Muhammadans, the Married Women's Property Act, 1874, by its Sections 4, 7, 8, 9 and 10, provides on this point as follows.

Purpose.—The preamble states that, "And whereas by force of the said Acts all women to whose marriages it applies are absolute owners of all property vested in or acquired by them, and their husbands do not by their marriage acquire any interest in such property, but the said Act does not protect such husbands from liabilities on account of the debts of their wives contracted

14. *Proby* v. *Proby*, 5 Cal 357.

before marriage and does not expressly provide for enforcement of claims by or against such wives".

Separate property.—According to Section 4, a married woman's earnings, together with all the savings therefrom and investments thereof, from any employment, occupation or trade carried on by her or through the exercise of any literary, artistic or scientific skill, shall be her separate property.

A married woman, according to Section 7, can sue and be sued in her own name with regard to the separate property in the same way as if she were unmarried. Section 8 provides for liability in respect of contracts based on such property and at the same time it enacts a proviso for restraint on anticipation and explains that no person who enters into a contract with her will be entitled to recover anything by attachment and sale or otherwise out of any property which has been transferred to a woman or for her benefit on condition that she shall have no power during her marriage, to transfer or charge the same or her beneficial interest therein. Sections 9 and 10 provide for the husband's non-liability in respect of the wife's ante-nuptial debts or unless he intermeddles therein, for any breach of trust or devastation committed by her.

Sections 56, 58 and 68 of the Indian Trusts Act also refer to and provide with regard to restraint on anticipation. A Muhammadan woman on her marriage does not merge her separate existence or entity into that of her husband, but retains it. She can therefore deal with her separate property in any way she likes and her husband has no control over it. This is so because of the fact that the doctrine of coverture is not recognised under Muhammadan law. Thus a Muhammadan marriage does not invest a husband with power over the property of his wife.

The position of a Hindu woman in regard to her personal property may be succinctly stated as follows:

"From the commencement of the Rigvedic age marriage was a well-established institution.[15] The wife got an honoured position on marriage and as the old writers put it, "*a woman is half her husband and completes him*"[16], and the highest law for husband and wife was "mutual fidelity".[17] Stridhana or woman's peculiar literally means woman's property.[18] In its etymological sense it includes all kinds of property of which a woman has become the owner. In modern Hindu law it denotes not only the specific kinds of property enumerated in the Smritis but also other species of property acquired or owned by a woman over which she has either absolute control or control subject only to her husband's dominion.[19] It devolves on her own heirs."

---

15. C. H. I. Vol. I, 88, Madlik, 396; *Mahabharat, Adi Parva* Ch. 122 cited by Mayne: *Hindu Law*, 10th Edn., 1938, Chap. IV, p. 105.
16. *Vedic Index I*, 484—6; *Manu IX*, 96.
17. *Manu III*, 55—76.
18. Jolly, *Tagore Law Lectures*, p. 228.
19. Mayne: *Hindu Law*, 10th Edn., 1938, Chap. XVI, p. 734 by S. Srinivas Iyenagar.

This shows that unlike the English law, a woman's right to hold separate property was recognised from the very early times.[20]

Stridhana can be of a number of kinds, namely—

(1) What is given before the nuptial fire (अध्याग्नि).

(2) What a woman receives while she is conducted from her father's house to her husband's dwelling (अध्यवाहनिक).

(3) What is bestowed in token of love (प्रीतिदत्त or भर्तृदाय).

(4) What is obtained through affection from, mother-in-law, father-in-law and also what is termed as, (पादवंदनिका), what is obtained at the time of bowing at the feet of elders.

(5) What is gifted by father, mother or brother.

(6) Gifts subsequent, that is that which is received from her husband's family or her father's family subsequent to marriage (अन्वधेयक).

(7) Gifts on supersession (अधिवेदनिका), a gift on her husband's marriage to another wife.

(8) Gifts by bandhus (बंधुदत्त), gifts by relations of her mother or father.

(9) शुल्क or the fee which a girl receives as the price of household furniture, conveyance, milch cattle and ornaments. Moreover, according to Devala (देवल) cited in स्मृतिचंद्रिका, "Her subsistence (वृत्ति), ornaments, fee or शुल्क or her gains (लाभम्) are the separate property of a woman".[21]

(10) All saving made by stridhana and all purchases made by it are of course stridhana.

(11) All gifts made by strangers, whether during covertrue or when she is a widow, will be stridhana.

(12) Money or property given to a woman absolutely in lieu of maintenance and all income of her husband's estate and investments and purchases out of it are stridhana.[22]

From the above it is clear that the doctrine of coverture is accepted in Hindu law. A woman has a right to hold separate property and she has complete control over it. During maidenhood, coverture and widowhood she has unrestricted power over stridhana acquired through gifts and bequests from relations but regarding other types of stridhana, during coverture a married woman cannot dispose of it without her husband's consent. After her husband's death her power over this is absolute, so that she can give it by transfer *inter vivos* or through a will. Before the Hindu Succession Act, 1954, she could inherit her husband's properties and had a widow's estate or a limited property therein. She could not dispose of the corpus of the property and on her death the

---

20. Mayne: *Hindu Law*, 10th Edn., 1938, Chap. XVI, p. 734 by S. Srinivas Iyenagar., p. 735.

21. *Ibid.* , pp. 737-738 .

22. Mayne: *Hindu Law*, 10th Edn., 1938, Chap. XVI, p. 734 by S. Srinivas Iyengar, pp. 744-745 .

property did not go her heirs, but to the reversioners. But now under Section 14 of the Hindu Succession Act, 1956, a woman takes through inheritance her husband's property as an absolute owner, except some land tenures in U.P. in certain cases, where her life interest is still retained.

Thus under Muhammadan law, a wife has complete control over her separate property and it is independent of her husband's control. Under Hindu law also the position is very clear that she is the full owner of her separate property. Regarding the non-Hindu and non-Muhammadan women, the Indian Succession Act, 1925, Section 20, the Transfer of Property Act, 1882, Section 10 and the Married Women's Property Act, 1874, Sections 4, 7, 8, 9 and 10 clear the position which comes as near as that under the English law.

B. INFANTS

1. JURISDICTION

The origin of the jurisdiction of the Chancery Courts over infants or minors, though a subject of much discussion,[23] remains undisputed that from the earliest times it was exercised by the Court of Wards on the prerogative of the crown as *parens patriae*. In course of time it was delegated to the Chancellor.[24] The Court of Probate also had such jurisdiction.

Guardianship is a right, a duty and a trust. The persons having the care of a minor and the custody of the estate of an infant are called their guardians. Under the Common law a father is his child's natural guardian up to the age of 21 years. A mother is the guardian of her illegitimate child and she has the same right as the father. It is very difficult to remove a natural guardian unless a very strong case is made out against him. Where a natural guardian is insolvent or his conduct is loathsome or he is ill-treating the child, he can be removed. The court will thereafter appoint a guardian who will protect the person and property of the infant.

2. PURPOSE AND PROCEDURE

The purpose of such jurisdiction was to protect minors and lunatics against their mental unripeness, defects and deficiencies. Appointment of a guardian is therefore of paramount importance. As a delegation of the rights and duties of the Crown, the Court of Chancery supervises the person and property of infants. In short, the courts have authority to appoint and remove guardians, to maintain infants, to get infants married and to manage and dispose of their property.

As Snell[25] notes, in the list of matters specially assigned to the Chancery Division by the Judicature Act, 1873, "the wardship of the infants and the care of infants' estates" were of great importance and in matters "relating to the custody and education of infants the rules of equity should prevail over the rules of Common law".

---

23. Family Law Reforms Act, 1969, Sections 1(2), 12.
24. *Snell's Principles of Equity*, 27th Edn., 1973, p. 531; *Official Solicitor* v. *K.*, 1965 AC 201.
25. *Ibid.*

A father has a right to appoint the guardian by his deed or will but when the court appoints one, the father's wishes ought to be regarded as far as possible.

A ward of court is a person who is under a guardian appointed by the court. All dealings with the person and property of the ward of court are subject to sanction and approval of the court. Disregard of the court in this connection will amount to contempt of the court. For example, to marry a ward without the courts's previous permission is a gross disrespect to the court. Not only the persons committing the contempt but those who aid and abet it are liable to punishment.[26]

As a natural guardian a father has a legal right to control and direct the education and to bring up and maintain his child. Courts will not interfere with this parental authority except when the guardian forfeits this right by his conduct or tries to remove the child being the ward of court, out of the court's jurisdiction without its permission. As regards the maintenance, marriage and management and disposal of the property of the ward, the court has complete power of superintendence and vigilant care.

By the Law Reform (Miscellaneous Provisions) Act, 1949 it is now provided in England for making an infant a ward of court even though no property was involved. This goes to explain that the jurisdiction is now concerned more with the welfare of an infant than with his property. This is a changed trend. According to Snell[27] since the Probate, Divorce and Admiralty Division has been replaced by the Family Division of the High Court, the Chancery jurisdiction over the infants was transferred to that division from October 1, 1971. As a result this subject now falls outside the scope of this book.[28]

3. IN INDIA

Unless the personal law of an infant or a party provides in this regard the law on this point is represented by the Guardians and Wards Act, 1890, the Indian Majority Act, 1875 and Section 491 of the Criminal Procedure Code, 1973. The British Minors Act, 1874 (on which is based our Guardians and Wards Act) is now repealed. Hindu law determines who is entitled to an infant's custody and care, but since the subject has been codified the Hindu Minority and Guardianship Act, 1956 governs the same. Under Muhammadan law, the father, paternal grandfather, their executors and executors of such executors are near guardians who are entitled to management of an infant's property. The rest of the persons being remote guardians, are not entitled to it. A court in India may appoint a guardian for an infant or for his property or for both, but in doing so it will look to the welfare of the child. The proposed guardian's age, sex, character, religion, nearness of relation and wishes of the deceased parents and near relations are matters which will be looked into for this purpose.

---

26. *Eyre* v. *Countess of Shaftsbury*, (1772) 2 P Wms 103, *see also* Guardianship of Infants Act, 1925 in England.
27. *Manu III*, 55—76.
28. *Snell's Principles of Equity*, 27th Edn., 1973, p. 531.

The High Courts in India can appoint guardians of the person or property of minors, lunatics and idiots, irrespective of the Guardians and Wards Act. This power is conferred upon the High Courts by the Letters Patent establishing them. Under Article 226 of the Constitution of India, High Courts can issue a writ in the nature of habeas corpus for production of any person detained within its jurisdiction. Under Section 491 of the CrPC, High Courts can also direct to set free a minor who has been illegally or improperly detained in private custody within the limits of its appellate criminal jurisdiction. A person seeking to recover the custody of a minor may proceed under Section 25 of Guardians and Wards Act, or by a regular suit or under Section 498 of the CrPC.

C. PERSONS OF UNSOUND MIND

Under the Mental Health Act, 1959, "idiots and lunatics", being incapable by reason of mental disorder to manage their person and property, are now known as "patients" or "mental patients".[29] Lunatics are persons *non compos mentis*.

Jurisdiction over such persons and their property was the prerogative of the Crown and it existed long before the existence of the Chancery Courts. Originally it is based on the so-called statute of the crown known as *De Praerogativa Regis* dating between 1255 and 1290. As noted by Holdsworth[30] the ninth and tenth chapters related to idiots and lunatics.[31] The Crown by sign manual especially delegated his authority to the Lord Chancellor. From his decision an appeal lay to the King in Council and to none else.[32] In 1851 a court of appeal was established and in 1853 the Lunacy Regulation Act was passed, which was reenacted with some modifications as the Lunacy Act, 1890. This jurisdiction was continued as before by the Judicature Act, 1873 and it was then entrusted to the High Court of Justice or court of appeal. It is now exercised by the Lord Chancellor, the Master of Rolls and the Lord Justices.[33] In practice, nearly all the work is done by an office of the Supreme Court, called the Court of Protection (formerly the Management and Administration Department) under a Master and a Deputy Master, subject to appeal to the judge, and thence to the court of appeal and the House of Lords. The jurisdiction is exercisable over any person "incapable, by reason of mental disorder, of managing and administering his property and affairs".[34]

Insofar as the interest of a lunatic in trust property is concerned, the Chancery Division will exercise its jurisdiction only when the following three conditions are fulfilled. It will then be rendered unnecessary to file proceedings in the Court of Protection.

---

29. Section 101, Mental Health Act, 1959, in England.
30. *History of English Law*, p. 473.
31. *Ibid.*, p. 533, cited in *Snell's Principles of Equity*.
32. *Story's Equity Jurisprudence*, p. 560.
33. See *Smith's Principles of Equity*, 4th Edn., p. 475; *Snell's Principles of Equity*, 27th Edn., p. 533.
34. Sections 100 and 111 of the Mental Health Act, 1959.

(*a*) The income from the fund is so small that all of it will be used for maintaining him.

(*b*) Proceedings in this regard before the Courts of Protection are not contemplated.

(*c*) Proceedings in Chancery Courts are already pending.

IN INDIA

The Indian Lunacy Act, 1912, which is mostly based on English law, covers this subject and its provisions can be broadly divided into—

(*a*) the reception, care and treatment and discharge of a lunatic,

(*b*) judicial inquisition as to lunacy, and

(*c*) custody of the lunatic and management of his estate.

In presidency towns the High Courts of Bombay, Calcutta and Madras have jurisdiction, and outside the presidency towns the magistrates (as defined therein) have such jurisdiction. Upon an application by any relative of the lunatic or by the Advocate General, the court may make an order for inquisition to find out whether the alleged lunatic is of unsound mind or is incapable of managing himself and his affairs. It will also conduct inquiry as to the time during which he has been of unsound mind, as to his relatives and as to the property belonging to him. After he is adjudged a lunatic, orders for management of his property and his custody will follow. A manager appointed for his property shall not sell, charge, gift, exchange, mortgage or lease for more than ten years, the property of the lunatic. But the court for just reasons and for the benefit of the lunatic has such powers provided the money so secured, obtained or raised is to be applied or has been applied to paying out the lunatic's debts, or in discharging the incumbrances on his property or for maintenance of the lunatic or his dependents. When the unsoundness of mind has ceased, the proceeding in lunacy shall also cease or be set aside. Outside the presidency towns an application in this regard can be made by the husband or wife of the alleged lunatic, or by the nearest relative of the alleged lunatic. If there is no husband or wife, or if the husband or wife is prevented due to lunacy or is absent from India, the nearest relative can apply.

Chapter VIII
Accident, Set-off, Fraud and Undue Influence

ACCIDENT

"The doctrine cannot be precisely formulated, since of its very nature it contemplates the undefined case: the case where through the happening of some unforeseen event, or through the omission or misstatement of some term, an obligation good in its essence stands in danger of being thrown away. The cause of the defect must be purely accidental, in the sense that it could not have been foreseen by reasonable prudence. Equity is not procurator fatuorum, and no man has a claim to be relieved from his own weakness, unless he was from the first at a disadvantage or his disability was deliberately exploited. Out of this doctrine grew the equitable jurisdiction in regard to mistake, and, as a corollary, the rectification and rescission of documents."

—C.K. Allen: *Law in the Making*

FRAUD

" . . . . *Equity did not pose as pure morality. It could not, for example, reject a defence based on a strict statutory rule merely because it was morally unmeritorious. It could sometimes find a way round technical common law rules in the interest of conscience . . . . But for the most part equitable fraud came within the domain of things of confidence, resolving itself into cases—Generically undue influence and catching bargains—where there was some special relationship of trust or confidence between the parties."*

—C.K. Allen: *Law in the Making*, pp. 411-412

SYNOPSIS

A. Accident
  1. Nature of Jurisdiction
  2. Types of Relief
     (*a*) Documents lost or destroyed
     (*b*) Erroneous payments
     (*c*) Defective execution of powers

B. Set-off

C. Mistake
  In India

D. Fraud
  1. Actual Fraud
  2. Doctrine of Constructive Fraud
  3. Types of Fraud
  4. Jurisdiction
  5. Distinction
  6. Undue Influence
  7. Abuse of Confidence
  8. Unconscionable Bargains
     Requirements for proving incidents of fraud
  9. Fraud on Power

A. ACCIDENT

1. NATURE OF JURISDICTION

Due to the rigid application of the Common law rules in case of accident, mistake, misrepresentation, undue influence and fraud, courts of equity in their concurrent jurisdiction intervened and granted relief. "There were many frauds which the stiff old procedure of the courts of law could not adequately meet and 'accident', in particular, the accidental loss of a document, was a proper occasion for the Chancellor's interference. No one could set any very strict limit to his power, but the best hint to its extent that could be given in the sixteenth century was given by the words 'fraud, accident and breach of confidence'. On the other hand, the Chancellor was not to interfere where a court of Common law offered an adequate remedy".[1]

In cases of accident or mistake when a bond, or document under seal, or title deeds, or a negotiable or a non-negotiable instrument was lost or destroyed, there could be no profert (production) and over (reading) of the document. To prevent injustice in such cases from taking shape, equity courts came forward. Executors were relieved when the estates in their hand were lost without their default, but unless they could show that they had duly administered them, or that they were lost due to some accident without their fault, they were answerable for their loss or destruction. If goods of the deceased are stolen,[2] or being perishable, depreciate,[3] or are reduced in value by act of parliament,[4] the executors were not liable, but they were liable for their *devastavit*.[5] At the same time one has to note that accident was no excuse for not fulfilling obligations of a contract.

2. TYPES OF RELIEF

In cases of accident equity granted relief in the following three instances—

(*a*) where a document was lost or destroyed by accident,

(*b*) where payments are erroneously made but in good faith and accidently, and

(*c*) where there was an imperfect or defective execution of powers.

An accident for this purpose has been defined as an uncontrollable, unforeseeable and injurious occurrence, which is not attributable to mistake, neglect or misconduct.

(*a*) *Documents lost or destroyed* —Lost or destroyed documents could not be offered or produced in evidence as support of title or interest. In order to get relief in equity for this purpose a special loss or inconvenience to the party concerned was to be shown. For this a desire to get into possession of some property or a desire to assert a right or claim in future was to be shown which moved the conscience of the Chancellor to intervene. In India, Section 65(*c*) of the Indian Evidence Act, 1872 makes provisions for offering secondary evidence in such cases and acceptance of such evidence is a secondary evidence of the original registered document.[6] Order 7, Rule 16 of the Civil Procedure Code lays down the procedure in this respect.

---

1. Maitland: *Lectures on Equity*, 1969 Edn., p. 7.
2. *Jones* v. *Lewis*, (1750) 2 Ves Sen 240.
3. *Clough* v. *Bond*, (1837) 3 Mys & CR 490.
4. *Davies* v. *Wattier*, (1823) 1 Sim & St 463.
5. *Snell's Principles of Equity*, 27th Edn., 1973, p. 340.
6. *Nani Bai* v. *Gita bai*, AIR 1958 SC 706.

(*b*) *Erroneous payments.*—Insofar as administration of estates of a deceased person was concerned, equity exercised a concurrent jurisdiction over such matters. Where the executor or administrator pays off a debt or legacy completely misconceiving a deed erroneously in an honest belief that the property in question is sufficient to discharge all the debts or legatees, and it later on turns out that it is not so, because some new claims so far unknown have come to light, or because there is a depreciation in the value of the property, equity in such unforeseen and injurious occurrence granted relief. But it must be noted that mistake of law is not an accident.[7] Similarly, accident is no excuse for not fulfilling the obligations of a contract and equity did not intervene in such cases, e.g., a lessee had to pay his rent even if the premises were destroyed.

In India, the Indian Succession Act, 1925, Section 359 provides that when the executor or administrator has paid away the assets in legacies and he is afterwards obliged to discharge a debt of which he had no previous notice he is entitled to call upon each legatee to refund in proportion.

As in England so in India, no relief is granted by equity in case of positive contracts because it is presumed by equity that the parties must have contracted subject to those future events or contingencies. Section 13 of the Specific Relief Act, 1963 makes provision to this effect.

(*c*) *Defective execution of powers.*—A power is an authority vested in a person to deal with or dispose of property not his own.[8] In order that equity could intervene and grant relief in suitable cases, first of all it is necessary that power must be exercised or executed. If it is not executed, equity cannot help. For example, properties are transferred by *P* to *Q* with a power of appointment granted to *Q* which he was to exercise. Now, if *Q* does not exercise this power or exercises it in a manner unauthorised by the instrument creating the power, in each case the power will prima facie be treated as unexercised and consequently the object of the power will take nothing. This was the rule at Common law. In the above example if *Q* was required to exercise the power by deed but he exercises it through a will, the exercise though technically improper, was treated by equity as proper and effective. Now the Law of Property Act, 1925, Sections 159(2) and (3) has made provision to this effect and dispensed with the requirements of two witnesses and the requirement of a deed if the appointment complies with the terms of the power. To the same effect are the provisions in Section 2(2) of the Wills Act, 1963.

One has to note further that a defect such as this should not go to the root, or in other words it should not hit the very essence and substance of the power. Where consent to the execution of power is necessary but it is executed without obtaining consent, equity cannot help, unless it was impossible to obtain the same. Thus accident would be relieved against all the formal defects (by equity supplying the same) which do not go to the root and therefore are not of the

---

7. *Milliard case*, 4 Ch D 389.
8. *Jreme* v. *Clement*, (1881) 18 Ch D 499.

essence of the transaction and which are not irremediable by the statute.[9] Such relief was granted only in assistance of certain favoured persons provided a clear expression of an intention to execute power is manifested: they were purchasers for value, creditors, charities, children and wives. This was so because these persons are regarded to have supplied good consideration and therefore a sort of moral obligation. But in case of husbands, illegitimate children, remote relations and volunteers, no such consideration existed and therefore no relief was granted by equity.[10]

Abridging the foregoing details we may note that accident will not be relieved against where (*a*) there is a positive contract to the effect, the injury in the case not being unforeseen, (*b*) the concerned parties themselves are thoughtless and unprepared against future uncertain events, (*c*) the accident took place due to the gross negligence of the applicant, (*d*) the party seeking relief has an expectancy only and not a vested right, and (*e*) the party against whom the relief is applied for has equal equities.

B. SET-OFF

See under maxim 3, para (*b*)(*viii*) in Chap. III.

C. MISTAKE

As Snell's editors Meggary and Baker note in their 27th Edition (at p. 539): "Mistake is not now regarded as exclusively resting on equitable principles, but has been absorbed by the Common law; and the remainder of the jurisdiction of equity to grant relief against accidents is of little importance." It is therefore not very necessary to discuss those principles here but we may consider the Indian position.

IN INDIA

Sections 20, 21 and 22 of the Indian Contract Act incorporate the law relating to the effect of mistake on contracts:

> 20. Where *both the parties* to an agreement are under a mistake as to matter of fact essential to the agreement, the agreement is void.
>
> 21. A contract is not voidable because it was caused by a mistake as to any law in force in India. But a mistake as to a law not in force in India has the same effect as a mistake of fact.
>
> 22. A contract is not voidable merely because it was caused by one of the parties to it being under a mistake as to a matter of fact.

Thus a contract is vitiated by a mutual mistake and the same should be essential to the agreement.[11] Mistake of law does not make a contract voidable,

---

9. *Cockerell* v. *Cholmeley*, (1830) 1 Russ & M 418.
10. *Mansell case,* 2 Bro CC 450.
11. See *Raffles* v. *Wichelhaus*, (1864) 2 H&R 906; *Cooper* v. *Phibbs*, (1867) 2 HC 149; *Kalyanpur Lime Works Ltd.* v. *State of Bihar*, AIR 1954 SC 165.

it does not afford a relief. *Ignorantia juris non excusat.* If a mistake of law was allowed as a defence or a ground of relief one does not know or cannot imagine how far it would be carried. But to this maxim there are three well-known exceptions:

(*a*) The maxim applies to the general law of the land and not to a mere private right.[12]

(*b*) Mistake as to a law not in force in India has the same effect as a mistake of fact.[13]

(*c*) Mistake as to a plain and established rule of law raising a presumption of undue influence, fraud and the like.

In all these cases, equitable relief as could be contemplated by the relevant sections of the Indian Contract Act may be given.

Section 72 of the Contract Act lays down:

> 72. A person to whom money has been paid, or anything delivered, by mistake or under coercion, must repay or return it.

The right granted under this section is a statutory right. The question of granting equitable relief is therefore solved by it, but this right cannot be rejected on equitable considerations, unless the plaintiff by estoppel or other statutory bars, disentitles himself. Such relief is available in case of money paid under coercion. The word 'coercion' does not have the same meaning as defined in Section 15 of the Contract Act but it should be taken in the ordinary and general sense: for example, money paid under protest in order to obtain a release of property under attachment can be recovered under this section.[14]

Sections 18(*a*) and 26 of the Specific Relief Act, 1963 also afford relief in case of mistake.

In case of "family arrangements" where the members of a family claim an interest in the family property, claims which if not settled or set at rest at the earliest would create disputes that tarnish the reputation of the family, rules of equity and justice are applied. In arriving at such compromises full disclosure of the facts has to be made by all, and the claims advanced must be bona fide and honest. One should not take advantage of the ignorance of the other party. Moreover, there should be no imposition or surprise exercised by one over the other. In short, the claims must be bona fide, the solidarity of the right being of no worth. Leading English authorities on this point are *Westby* v. *Westby*[15], *Stapilton* v. *Stapilton*[16] and *Gordon* v. *Gordon*[17]. The Privy Council in the

---

12. *Cooper* v. *Phibbs*, (1867) 2 HC 149.
13. Section 21, Indian Contract Act, 1872.
14. *Kanhayalal* v. *National Bank*, (1923) 40 Cal 598 (PC).
15. (1842) 2 D&W 503.
16. (1739) 1 Atk 2.
17. (1816) 3 Swan 400.

case of *Cashin* v. *Cashin*[18] has explained the principle in the following words:

> "Where family arrangements have been fairly entered into, without concealment or imposition on either side, with no suppression of what is true, or suggestion of what is false, then although the parties may have greatly *misunderstood* their situation, and mistaken their rights, a court of equity will not disturb the quiet, which is the consequence of that arrangement; but when the transaction has been unfair, a court of equity would have very great difficulty in permitting such a contract to bind the parties."

Minors cannot challenge an arrangement when they come of age unless there was a fraud.[19] A person not authorised in this behalf cannot enter into such an agreement and call them a family settlement or family arrangement.[20] Section 15(*c*) of the Specific Relief Act, 1963 also provides in this connection, that a compromise of doubtful rights between members of the same family may be enforced by any person beneficially entitled thereunder.

D. FRAUD

Fraud is far-reaching—for centuries the rule has been that fraud unravels all.[21] The idea of fraud in equity embraces a very large cross-section of human behaviour. It includes fraud in law or actual fraud and fraud in equity or constructive or equitable fraud.

1. ACTUAL FRAUD

Actual fraud has been defined as a false statement of fact, made before another, without belief in its truth or recklessly, whether it be true or false, with the intention that the person before whom it is made may rely upon it and act to his disadvantage or loss. Fraud is thus composed of (*a*) a false misrepresentation,[22] or (*b*) a concealment of a material fact fitted to deceive. As decided in *Polhil* v. *Walter*[23] it consists in knowingly asserting that which is false to the injury of another. It is not necessary that the person representing should profit out of it, but there is always a design to do evil present therein.[24] It is practised by either suppressing the truth (*suppressio veri*) or by suggesting the untruth (*suggestio falsi*) or by the combination of both. It is therefore "something said, done or omitted with the design of perpetrating what the party must have known to be a positive fraud".

18. AIR 1938 PC 103.
19. *Binda* v. *Lalita*, (1936) 41 CWN 161 (PC).
20. *Pratap* v. *Sant Kaur*, (1938) 42 CWN 817 (PC).
21. *Master* v. *Miller*, (1791) 4 TR 320.
22. *Derry* v. *Peek*, (1889) 14 AC 337.
23. (1832) 3 B & Eld 116, per Creswell, J.
24. *Nocton* v. *Ashburton*, 1914 AC 932: 30 TLR 602 HL.

2. DOCTRINE OF CONSTRUCTIVE FRAUD

Constructive fraud encompasses all types of behaviour or conduct which falls short of the standard demanded by equity courts. This extension of the Common law definition and its practice was so wide that it prevented Lord Chancellor Hardwicke from defining it, because, in his own words, "Fraud is infinite and were a court of equity once to lay down rules, how far they would go and no further in extending their relief against it, or to define strictly the species of evidence of it, the jurisdiction would be cramped and perpetually eluded by new schemes which the fertility of man's invention would contrive".[25]

As Walker puts it, at Common law in England, fraud was limited to actual deceit. Equity, however, gave a more extended meaning to the concept of fraud, by developing the doctrine that if one man enters into a transaction with another in circumstances in which the latter is not a free agent and not fully able to look after his own interests, the latter is entitled to the protection of the court and may rescind the transaction. This principle applies where a confidential or fiduciary relationship exists between the parties, where a party has placed himself in such a position that it has become his duty to act fairly towards and have regard to the interest of the other party, where the bargain appears clearly unconscionable and inequitable, and where the principle of undue influence applies.[26]

3. TYPES OF FRAUD

It has therefore been rightly described by John Tiley[27] that "the equitable jurisdiction to intervene on the ground of fraud is very broad. It ranges from the doctrine of fraud on power to fraud inducing a contract. It covers conduct of a sort that offends conscience once a relationship has been established (e.g., under the doctrine of equitable estoppel) as well as untruths inducing the formation of the relationship. The interference with the normal rules of priority between interests in property is another example of this jurisdiction. . . . The expression "equitable fraud" may, however, still be used to indicate the doctrine whereby equity will prevent the abuse of a confidential relationship".[28]

In *Earl of Chesterfield* v. *Janssen*[29], however, the same Lord Chancellor tried to lay down the classification of fraud as—(*a*) fraud in which evil design is actual and plain, (*b*) bargains which are unequitable and unconscientious, (*c*) taking advantage of the weakness, ignorance and necessity of another, (*d*) imposition and deceit on the other persons, not parties to the agreement, and

---

25. Parkes: *History of the Court of Chancery*, p. 508, quoted in *Snell's Principles of Equity*, 27th Edn., 1973, p. 546. A letter to Lord Kames dated June 30, 1759 by Lord Chancellor Hardwicke.
26. *The Oxford Companion to Law*, 1980 Edn., p. 489.
27. *A Casebook of Equity & Succession*, 1968 Edn., p. 44.
28. *Ibid*.
29. (1750) 2 Ves Sen 125.

(*e*) catching bargains with heirs, reversioners and expectants, and mixed cases of these species. In his own words:

"1. Fraud, which is *dolus malus*, may be actual, arising from facts and circumstances of imposition; which is the plainest case.

2. It may be apparent from the intrinsic nature and subject of the bargain itself; such as no man in his senses and not under delusion would make on the one hand and as no honest and fair man would accept on the other; which are unequitable and unconscientious bargains; and of such even the Common law has taken notice; for which if it would not look a little ludicrous might be cited, *James* v. *Morgan* [(1663) 1 Lev 111].

3. A third kind of fraud is, which may be presumed from the circumstances and condition of the parties contracting and this goes farther than the rule of law; which is, that it must be proved not presumed; but it is wisely established in this court to prevent taking *surreptitious advantage of the weakness or necessity of another*; which knowingly to do is equally against the conscience as to *take advantage of his ignorance*: a person is equally unable to judge for himself in one as the other.

4. A fourth kind of fraud may be collected or inferred in the consideration of this court from the nature and circumstances of the transaction, as being an *imposition and deceit on the other persons not parties to the fraudulent agreement*. It may sound odd that an agreement may be infected by being a deceit on others not parties: but such there are, against such there has been relief. Of this kind have been marriage-brokerage contracts; neither of the parties herein being deceived: but they tend necessarily to the deceit on one party to the marriage, or of the parent, or of the friend. So in a clandestine, private agreement to return part of the portion of the wife or provision stipulated for the husband to the parent or guardian. In most of these it is done with their eyes open, and knowing that they do: but if there is fraud therein, the court holds it infected thereby, and relieves. So where a debtor enters into a deed of composition with his creditors for 10s. in the pound, or any other rate, attended with a proviso that all creditors pound, or any other rate, attended with a proviso that all creditors executed this within a certain period, if the debtor privately agrees with one creditor to induce him to sign this deed, that he will pay or secure a greater sum in respect of this particular debt: in this there can be no particular deceit on the debtor, who is party thereto: but it tends to deceit of the other creditors, who relied on an equal composition, and did it out of compassion to the debtor. This court therefore relieves against all such underhand bargains [*Spurret* v. *Spiller*, (1740) 1 Atk 105: 1 Wms 768]. So of premiums contracted to be given for preferring or recommending to a public office or employment: none of the parties are defrauded; but the persons, having the legal appointment of these offices are or may be deceived thereby: or if any person agreeing to take the premium has authority to appoint the officer, it tends to public mischief by introducing an unworthy object for an unworthy consideration. These cases show what courts of equity mean, when they profess to go on reasons drawn from public utility . . . (If the word politics is taken in its

original meaning these are not political arguments. In its true original meaning, it comprehends everything that concerns the government of the country; of which the administration of justice makes a considerable part). To apply this and in this sense, is relief in a court of equity founded on public utility. Particular persons in contracts shall not only transact *bona fide* between themselves but shall not transact *mala fide* in respect of other persons, who stand in such a relation to either as to be affected by the contract or the consequences of it; and as the rest of mankind beside the parties contracting are concerned, it is probably said to be governed on public policy.

5. The last head of fraud, on which there has been relief, is that which infects catching bargains with heirs, reversioners or expectants, in the life of the father, against which relief always extended. These have been mixed cases compounded of all or several species of fraud; there being sometimes proof of actual fraud which is always decisive. There is always fraud presumed or inferred from the circumstances or conditions of the parties contracting: weakness on one side, usury on the other, or extortion or advantage taken of that weakness . . . . "[30].

Fraud is anathema to all equitable principles and any affair tainted with fraud cannot be perpetuated or saved by application of any equitable doctrine including res judicata. Once fraud is proved, it will deprive the person of all advantages or benefits obtained thereby.[31]

4. JURISDICTION

Courts of Chancery and Common law courts exercised a concurrent jurisdiction in cases of actual fraud from the earliest times. For some of these cases, the greater freedom which in early days the court of chancery exercised in admitting the testimony of parties to the proceedings, made it a more suitable tribunal. Moreover its remedies were more elastic. Operating *in personam* as a court of conscience it could order the defendant, not indeed, in those days, to pay damages as such, but to make restitution, or to compensate the plaintiff by putting him in as good a position pecuniarily as that in which he was before.[32]

In its exclusive jurisdiction it dealt with cases which did not involve an element of *dolus malus* and thus the term "fraud" in chancery courts came to be used to describe what fell short of deceit, but imported a breach of duty to which equity had attached its sanction.

5. DISTINCTION

The fundamental distinction between actual and constructive fraud may be drawn as, that in the former there is necessarily "a design to do evil", in the

30. Per Lord Chancellor Hardwicke in *Earl of Chesterfield* v. *Janssen, High Court of Chancery*, (1750) 2 Ves Sen 125: Atk 301: Wils Ch 286: 1 W&T LC 248, quoted in John Tiley: *Casebook on Equity & Succession*, Chap. 4.

31. *Ram Preeti Yadav* v. *U.P. Board of High School and Intermediate Education*, (2003) 8 SCC 311.

32. *Nocton* v. *Ashburton*, 1914 AC 932 (HL).

latter it is not so; but equity would not allow that position to stand or prevail as it would do greater injustice by opening the door for all possible evils in other cases. As could be seen from what has been said before, equitable fraud is but an extension of the legal doctrine of actual fraud. We may thus lay down the definition of equitable fraud as something said, done or omitted which from the viewpoint of equity would operate to the prejudice of public welfare and of an individual even though a design to do evil is absent.

Fraud in equity therefore resolves itself into the following chief species:

(1) Undue Influence.

(2) Abuse of Confidence.

(3) Unconscionable Bargains.

(4) Fraud on Power.

6. UNDUE INFLUENCE

Undue influence has been said to be constructive fraud. It is either express or presumed. The latter category arises out of fiduciary relationships. In *Mehboobkhan* v. *Abdulrahim*[33] it has been laid down that "undue influence is said to be a subtle species of fraud whereby mastery is obtained over the mind of the victim by insidious approaches and seductive artifices. Sometimes the result is brought about by fear, coercion, importunity or other domination calculated to prevent expression of the victim's true mind. It is a constraint undermining free agency overcoming the powers of resistance, bringing about a submission to an overmastering and unfair persuasion to the detriment of the other". Equity granting relief not only in such cases where the actual proof of undue influence was available but also in cases where such influence was presumed. *Huguenin* v. *Baseley*[34], *Allcard* v. *Skinner*[35] and *Inche Noriah* v. *Sk. Allie*[36] are leading cases on the point.[37] Such bargains were set aside by equity. Where sales are made at an excessive price or purchases are made at an undervalue such presumption arises. Undue influence is presumed to arise between a parent and a child, a guardian and his ward, a trustee and a beneficiary, a spiritual adviser and his follower, an advocate and his client and a doctor and his patient. But it should be noted that it is no monopoly of equity courts to save people from consequences of their own follies.[38] In other words, *extravagant liberality and immoderate folly do not themselves provide a passport to equitable relief.*[39]

But where it can be proved that the will was exercised spontaneously by the donor without anybody's advice or that the exercise of it was by the donor as a

---

33. AIR 1964 Raj 250.
34. 1807 14 Ves 237.
35. (1887) 36 Ch D 145.
36. 1929 AC 127: AIR 1929 PC 3.
37. *See* also *Tungabai Kumbhojkar* v. *Yeshwant Jag*, AIR 1945 PC 8.
38. *Allcard* v. *Skinner*, (1887) 36 Ch D 145.
39. Sir Raymond Evershed, M. R. in *Tufton* v. *Sperni*, (1952) 2 TLR 516.

free person, no presumption of exercise of undue influence can stand. Moreover, steps to obtain relief by the party, whose will, was so overpowered and guided should be taken during the period so long as such influence exists. If steps are taken after that period is over, they should be within a reasonable time. In India, Section 16 of the Indian Contract Act provides in this regard, its first part laying down the general principle about undue influence and the second part laying down a presumption against such persons who are capable of dominating the will of others,[40] thereby guiding and streamlining it in a direction desired by them. The third part of Section 16 explains that since such dominating persons are able to suppress the evidence of undue influence it lies on them to prove that the contract was not obtained by them through undue influence. The court under Section 19-A may set aside the contract, or the contract may be voidable at the option of the party whose consent was so obtained.

In English law[41] there is a modern trend to recognise the economic situation and circumstances wherein the parties are placed, as a variety of coercion and duress[42] liable to such relief.

7. ABUSE OF CONFIDENCE

It is difficult exactly to distinguish and therefore draw a line between the permissive forms of coercion and persuasion on the one hand and undue influence on the other. The line of distinction between them is regulated by public policy. Similarly, the principles of undue influence and abuse of confidence may seem to overlap but as Snell notes, they do not coincide. In the case of a person who is in a fiduciary position to the other and thereby obtains and procures a benefit for himself from that position in disregard of that duty, the transaction will be set aside.[43] Similarly, a trustee purchasing from the beneficiary at an undervalue is liable to be proceeded against under this principle.

8. UNCONSCIONABLE BARGAINS

Bargains against morality, which are improper and unreasonable and unconsiderable in particular circumstances are unconscionable bargains.[44] They resolve themselves into the following sections—

(*a*) bargains with the ignorant and the poor, who are without independent advice;

(*b*) bargains with expectant heirs;

(*c*) money-lending transactions;

(*d*) transactions contrary to the policy of the law.

---

40. *Mohd. Buksh* v. *Hosseini*, (1888) 15 Cal 684 (PC).
41. See *Law Quarterly Review*, 1979, Vol. 95, pp. 475-77; Anson: *Law of Contract*, 25th Edn., 1979, p. 270
42. Doctrine of economic duress, *North Ocean Shipping Co.*, (1978) 3 All ER 1170.
43. *Nocton* v. *Ashburton*, 1914 AC 932.
44. *See also* Walker, D. M.: *The Oxford Companion to Law*, 1980 Edn., p. 1247.

An expectant heir is a person who is expecting either some reversionary interest or a benefit under a will or intestacy of a person still alive. If a bargain is made with a person, the person enforcing the contract has to prove that he did not misuse or take advantage of the circumstances, situation and the urgent need of the expectant heir so that he was induced to sacrifice his future. He must have paid a fair price without exercising any kind of oppression or extortion. "Fraud here does not mean deceit or circumvention; it means an unconscientious use of the power arising out of the *circumstances* and conditions; and when the relation of the parties is such as prima facie to raise such presumption, the transaction cannot stand unless the person claiming the benefit of it is able to repeal the presumption by contrary evidence, proving it to have been in fact fair, just and reasonable".[45] Here again application to the court for help (to set aside the transaction) must be made within a reasonable time after coming into possession of the property. If the transaction is confirmed, it will not be relieved against.[46]

Post-obit Bonds.—Under such bonds a borrower agrees to pay a lump sum, higher than the amount obtained by borrowing, if and only if he gets some property on the death of some definite person.[47]

The doctrine of unconscionable bargains has nothing of fraud in it, but looking from the point of view of reasonableness and the unequal position of the parties, it is very plain that a party in a dominating position cannot be allowed to extract undue profit or benefit by transacting a hard and cruel bargain. Sales of reversions at undervalue are also fitting examples of the situation. The court in such cases will not set aside the whole transaction but order the repayment of what is due, *ex aequo et bono*, i.e., the sum actually advanced with reasonable interest.

Pardanashin woman.—In India the position of a pardanashin woman is open to undue influence.[48] Such a woman observes a pardah, i.e., a complete seclusion from others. To observe pardah is a custom in some castes or classes in India. As the woman does not come out in society, she is not in contact with persons in society, meaning thereby that she is in contact with only a few persons and these persons can easily influence her. Her position therefore is to a certain extent analogous to that of the expectant heir who by force of circumstances is susceptible to force, advice, persuasion and influence. Law therefore throws around her a special cloak of protection whereby those who deal with her have to prove affirmatively and conclusively that the deed was not only executed by, but was explained to and was readily understood by her; she signing it, not under duress but as a free and independent agent.[49] But it is not absolutely necessary to prove that she had

---

45. *Earl of Aylesford* v. *Morris*, (1873) 8 Ch 484.
46. *Earl of Chesterfield* v. *Janssen*, (1750) 8 Ch App 484.
47. *Ibid.* Walker, D.M.: *The Oxford Companion to Law*, 1980 Edn., p. 972. In Gujarat an aphorism explains this. It is बाप मरे बमणा —It means that the borrower will pay the double amount on his father's death. Only on this condition he borrows.
48. *Kaminisundari* v. *Kali Prossunno Ghose*, (1885) 12 Cal 225: 12 IA 215.
49. *Kalibux* v. *Ramgopal*, (1914) 36 All 81 (PC); *Ismail* v. *Hufizboo*, (1906) 33 Cal 773, 783 (PC).

independent and disinterested advice from outside.[50] In short, she must have understood the bargain "substantially" so that it may be said to be her own "mental or conscious act".[51]

There is no such class as a quasi-pardanashin woman and therefore the question of protection of law depends upon the facts and merits of each case.[52] A woman who comes out in society as often as needed, goes to the court, gives evidence, fixes rents with tenants and collects rents and communicates with men other than members of the family in matters of business, is not pardanashin lady.

In money-lending transactions where the terms of the loan were unreasonable, equity relieved against the transaction and the lender had to remain satisfied with the repayment of the amount advanced plus a fair interest. This situation of unconscionable money-lending transaction prevailed and existed up to the pre-1900 period. After the coming into operation of the Money-lenders Act, 1900 and 1927, the equitable doctrine of catching bargains with expectant heirs has lost importance because the transactions are regulated by the Act, particularly in case of those whose business is to lend money. Banking and insurance companies are excluded from its scope. The Act also provides for reopening settled accounts if the transaction is harsh and unconscionable.[53] Under the Act, money-lenders are required to take a licence,[54] and an unlicenced money-lender cannot sue the borrower.

In India, the Usurious Loans Act, 1918 governs the transactions of money-lending. It is based on the analogy of English law. States in India have also passed their own Acts to this effect. If the transactions is substantially unfair and the interest is excessive, the transaction may be reopened or set aside. It is for the court to decide whether the interest is excessive or not. Thus the equitable relief as provided in England is available in India through the Central and States' legislation on money-lending business.

Requirements for proving incidents of fraud.—As held by the Supreme Court in *A.C. Ananthaswamy* v. *Boraiah*[55] it must be proved that the representation made was false to the knowledge of the party making it or that the party could have no reasonable belief that it was true. Level of proof required in such a case is extremely high. An ambiguous statement cannot per se make the representor guilty of fraud. Where the only fraud alleged is a bare non-service of summons then such a suit to set aside the decree on alleged ground of fraud is not maintainable. The present case is a matter of non-service of summons and passing of an ex parte decree thereon, and therefore no case of fraud is made out.

---

50. *Kalibux* v. *Ramgopal*, (1914) 36 All 81 (PC); *Ismail* v. *Hufizboo*, (1906) 33 Cal 773, 783 (PC), *Faridunnisa* v. *Mukhtar*, (1925) 30 CWN 337 (PC).
51. *Faridunnisa* v. *Mukhtar*, (1925) 30 CWN 337 (PC).
52. *Hodges* v. *Delhi & London Bank*, (1901) 23 All 137 (PC).
53. *B.S. Lyle Ltd.* v. *Peasson*, (1941) 2 KB 391.
54. Section 1, Money-lenders Act, 1927.
55. (2004) 8 SCC 588.

As explained in *Chesterfield* v. *Janssen*[56], imposition and deceit on other persons not parties to the contract are relieved by equity in so far as they constitute fraud on third parties or upon the public generally. Under this category are included, marriage brokage contracts, payment to a parent to consent to the marriage of his child (called वर विक्रय sale of a bridegroom or कन्या विक्रय sale of a bride), loans to a woman to swell her dowry and thus deceive her husband, rewards for influencing a testator and contracts in restraint of trade and a clandestine deed by a debtor with one of his creditors to the disadvantage of other creditors. Being against public policy such agreements are void but on principles of public interest suitable relief may be granted by equity.

9. FRAUD ON POWER

A power is an authority vested in a person to deal with or dispose of property not his own.[57] Where the power is special the donee is to exercise it subject to restrictions as to its objects or persons. It should thus be exercised *bona fide* for the end designed and not for any purpose foreign to the power. One who exercises it beyond the scope of the instrument or for a purpose not justified by it commits a fraud on power, which equity will relieve. As pointed out by Snell, there are three main types of such fraud. Here also it should be noted that the word 'fraud' has a special connotation or meaning, differing widely from actual fraud. The three main categories are (*a*) appointment made with a corrupt purpose,[58] (*b*) or for purposes foreign to the power,[59] or (*c*) for the benefit of non-objects.[60] Such appointments are void and will be set aside, but a *bona fide* purchaser for value from such an appointee has been protected (up to the value of appointee's share only) by the Law of Property Act, 1925. Section 157 lays down that the purchaser must show that he purchased after 1925, for value, without notice of the fraud and that the appointee from whom he purchased was not less than 25 years. There are certain well-recognised exceptions to the fraud on power, as revocation of power, release of power and power to jointure.[61]

---

56. (1750) 2 Ves Sen 125.
57. Walker D.M.: *The Oxford Companion to Law*, 1980 Edn., pp. 973-974.
58. *Lord Hinchinbroke* v. *Seymour*, (1789) 1 Bro CC 395.
59. *Dick, Re*, 1953 Ch 343.
60. *Nicholson's Settlement, Re*, 1939 Ch 11.
61. For details see *Snell's Principles of Equity*, 27th Edn., 1973, pp. 559-60.

Chapter IX
Administration of Assets, Equitable Estoppel and Five Great Doctrines

"Prepare for death if here at night you roam,
And sign your will before you sup from home."

—Dr Samuel Johnson: "*London*"

"Estoppel is a rule of equity flowing out of fairness striking on behaviour deficient in good faith. It operates as a check on spurious conducting by preventing the inducer from taking advantage and assailing forfeiture already accomplished. It is invoked and applied to aid the law in administration of justice. But for it great many injustices may have been perpetrated."

—Sahai, J., in *Indira Bai* v. *Nand Kishore*, (1990) 4 SCC 668 at 670.

"There is no estoppel against a statute."

—K.N. Saikia, J., in *Plasma Machine Mfg. Co.* v. *Collector of Central Excise*, 1991 Supp (1) SCC 57 at 59.

SYNOPSIS

A. ADMINISTRATION OF ASSETS

1. ASSETS: MEANING OF

The administration of assets is the function that an heir, executor or an administrator is required to discharge. The word 'asset' has been derived from the french word 'assez' (meaning 'enough') and the Latin word "*ad satis*" (meaning 'to sufficiency'). As the connotation of the word denotes, assets is the property of the deceased which is available to meet the deceased person's debts and other liabilities. These assets include personalty as well as realty. So that an executor or administrator can administrate well, it is necessary that the assets be collected and realised and are available for the payment of debts and distribution of the surplus among the beneficiaries entitled under the will or intestacy.

The combination of three functions—

(*a*) collection,

(*b*) payment, and

(*c*) distribution,

is called "administration of assets". These are the duties, therefore, of the deceased's personal representatives, i.e., his executors (appointed by the deceased) and otherwise his administrators (appointed by court). As expressed by Bowen, L.J. in *Stanhope* v. *Stanhope*[1], the executor or administrator "does not act for a dead man or in his name but for the estate of the dead man". Snell has rightly pointed out[2] that the administration is normally conducted by the personal representatives out of court, but difficult or complex administrations may take place in court.

2. JURISDICTION

Formerly, i.e., before 1925, ecclesiastical courts, courts of probate and the High Court dealt with the problem of administration of the assets of a testator or intestate. At the end of the seventeenth century the chancery courts practically took over this jurisdiction from the ecclesiastical courts and slowly but certainly acquired a concurrent jurisdiction with the Common law courts. In the beginning it followed, and in suitable cases supplemented, the law of the courts but gradually and steadily it modified this law and developed its own rules. As has been pointed out[3], "its success in acquiring jurisdiction was in large part due to its superior administrative machinery and not least its ability to take complicated accounts. A Common law court would merely resolve the particular dispute brought before it by the parties to it, whereas the Court of Chancery looked at the estate as a whole; if it interfered at all, it would administer the entire estate for the benefit of all the creditors and beneficiaries alike. The result is that the law of administration of assets, though based in part on the principles of ecclesiastical and Common law, is largely equitable".

3. THE RULES

Before 1926, only the chattels or personality of the deceased were available for the payment of debts. Realty was usually not available for the deceased's creditors. Chattels were the legal assets of the deceased. The executor had complete control and power over these assets and could give a valid discharge in case of debts due to the testator and in case of a sale, mortgage or a pledge[4] by him, the purchaser obtained a valid legal title. Moreover, against his giving away without consideration any part of the assets to the donee, creditors and legatees had no claim or remedy at Common law. Looked at from this point of view at equity courts, the equitable estates were also available for distribution. Equitable estates included also the realty of the deceased.

The Administration of Estates Act, 1925 superseded the foregoing old rules and made available the real as well as the personal estate of the deceased for payment and distribution. Personal representative has been defined therein to include "the executor, original or by representation, or administrator for the time being of a deceased person" and for liability regarding estate taxes, an "executor

1. (1886) 11 PD 103.
2. *Snell's Principles of Equity*, 27th Edn., 1973, p. 295.
3. *Ibid.*, p. 296.
4. *Oceanic Steam Navigation Co.*, (1880) 16 Ch D 236.

de son tort" is also included. Chattels real (i.e., leaseholds) and land in possession, remainder or reversion, and every interest in or over land, to which the deceased was entitled at his death is included in asset. With some exceptions, "real estate held on trust, including settled land, realty appointed by the deceased's will under power of appointment and an entailed interest disposed of by the will" formed part of the real estate. In so far as payment of debts is concerned, all real and personal estates whether they be legal or equitable, form part of his assets. Any real or personal estate appointed by him under his will under a general power of appointment is a part of his assets.

4. COLLECTION

The personal representative has to take possession of the property and for this purpose he is to collect the same by suitable means within a reasonable period. He must first pay, before he proceeds further, from the ready money available for the following—

(*a*) funeral expenses,

(*b*) testamentary and administrative expenses, and

(*c*) debts and liabilities, so far as the ready money amount permit according to the rules in this behalf.

The residue is to be distributed in the manner provided in Section 46 as amended from time to time, or is to be held in trust as the section requires.

So far as the powers of disposition are concerned, an administrator derives his title solely from the grant of letters of administration from the court; whereas an executor derives the title from the instrument of the will itself, so that where an administrator has no power before a grant is made, the executor has wide powers as per the instrument even before his title is confirmed by the grant of probate by the court. Powers of disposition of a personal representative are wide as conferred by the Land Transfer Act, 1897 and the Administration of Estates Act, 1925. The latter Act provides for the protection of purchasers from the personal representatives for money or money's worth. With certain exceptions the personal representatives can conduct and carry on the business of their testator, though *virtue officii* they cannot.

5. PAYMENT

Within the executor's year[5] the personal representative has to pay the debts of the deceased with interest and perform "all enforceable contracts" of the deceased, even though to break them and pay damages would be more beneficial to the estate. All the debts are to be paid without distinction. Partiality and preference in payment will make him personally liable. The Act[6] lays down rules as to the order in which they must be paid[7], the funeral and other

---

5. Administration of Estates Act, 1925, S. 44—Generally one year from the death of the deceased.
6. Administration of Estates Act, 1925.
7. For details see *Snell's Principles of Equity*, pp. 310 to 322.

administrative expenses taking priority. If the estate is able to pay debts but is unable to pay administrative charges, it is termed insolvent and in such cases the court will make a suitable inquiry to find out whether it is so or not. Formerly a person entitled to land could require the personal representative to pay it off, out of the deceased's estate but now by a series of statutes known as the Locke Kings Act or the Real Estate Charges Acts and the Administration of Estates Act, 1925, the beneficiary takes the property subject to the charge, and if the charge exceeds the value of the property he is not allowed to call on the estate to pay off the charge. The rule, of course, is subject to certain details.

6. DISTRIBUTION

After the debts of the deceased have been paid off and liabilities discharged, the remaining estate has to be distributed to the persons beneficially entitled, provided, of course, no proceedings under the Inheritance (Family Provision) Act, 1938 are pending. But in no case can a personal representative be compelled to distribute before the expiration of the executor's year. After this is cleared off, he holds the residue in trust for the residuary legatees or next of kin.

7. IN INDIA

In India, the Indian Succession Act, 1925, by Part IX, Sections 217 to 369 makes provisions with regard to probate, letters of administration and administration of assets of the deceased.

For Administration suit and its details see Civil Procedure Code, Order 20, Rule 13. The Indian Succession Act contains provisions relating to executors and administrators and their powers, duties and liabilities.

B. EQUITABLE ESTOPPEL

[*See* maxim 3, para (*b*)(*vi*) in Chap. III]

C. FIVE GREAT DOCTRINES

1. Conversion [*See* maxim 8, para (*b*)(*i*) in Chap. III]
2. Reconversion [*See* maxim 8, para (*b*)(*i*) in Chap. III]
3. Election [*See* maxim 3, part (*b*)(*ii*) in Chap. III]
4. Performance [*See* maxim 9 para (*b*)(*i*) in Chap. III]
5. Satisfaction [*See* maxim 9 para (*b*)(*i*) in Chap. III]

PART III
TRUSTS

Chapter X
History of the Trusts

"Invention of trust has been 'a most powerful instrument of social experimentation'."

"The trust has given us a liberal substitute for a law about personified institutions . . . (and) a liberal supplement for a necessarily meagre law of corporations."

—C.K. Allen: *Law in the Making*, pp. 415-416,
citing Maitland: *Lectures on Equity*

"A trust is the binding of the conscience of one to the intention of another."

—Bacon.

"A trust is the very centre and kernel of equity."

—Hanbury: *Modern Equity*

"Of all the exploits of equity the largest and the most important is the invention and development of the trust. It is an 'institute' of great elasticity and generality; as elastic as general as contract . . . it involves the conception of obligation and ownership."

"The modern trust developed from the ancient use."

—Maitland: *Lectures on Equity*, p. 23

"Parents of trusts were FRAUD and FEAR and a court of conscience was the nurse."

—A.G.V. Sands, (1669) 2 Freem 129

SYNOPSIS

1. CONCEPT OF A TRUST

All efforts for defining a trust have remained unfruitful in so far as no complete definition of it has been produced. According to D. Hanbury, therefore, it is better to describe what a trust is and to compare the idea with other like concepts in order to understand its nature. A trust may be described as an *equitable obligation* binding a person (called trustee) to deal with the property over which he has control (called the trust property) for the benefit of persons (called the beneficiaries or *cestuis que trust*) of whom he may himself be one and anyone of whom may enforce the obligation.[1]

---

1. Underhill: *Law of Trusts*, 12th Edn., 1970, p. 3.

From the above descriptive definition it is very clear that a trust is an obligation—An equitable obligation binding a person's conscience. It is concerned with property which is to be held in confidence and managed for the benefit of certain persons called beneficiaries.

2. HOW A TRUST ARISES

A trust may come into being in various ways but a very simple way in which it arises may be, when *A* transfers his property to *B* for the 'use' of and in trust for *X*. *A* is the owner of property, *X* is the beneficiary and *B* is a trustee in whom confidence by the owner of the property is reposed. According to Common law, *A* was the legal owner and *B* was to look after the property and manage it for the benefit of *X*. These were *B*'s moral obligations. English Common law could not enforce this arrangement because enforcing moral obligations was not within its competence which was its prominent drawback. In the equity courts also it was quite difficult in the beginning to enforce this obligation as 'equity followed the law', but in course of time ingenuity of the chancery lawyers and judges found a way out, so that *B* was recognised as the legal owner and an obligation was attached to his title whereby his conscience was bound to carry out the moral obligations in favour of *X*. *B* was thus bound to hold and manage the property, and not to give it away to anybody or damage it. If he did it, he was punishable. In other words, equity converted moral obligation into equitable obligation by dissociating beneficial interest from legal title and gave the essence or the kernel to *X* and the husk to *B*. *A trust thus arises when beneficial interest is dissociated from legal title and confidence is reposed in the legal titleholder.*

3. ORIGIN

(a) In English law.—Regarding the origin of trust, opinions are divided. Some authorities hold that the English trust is connected with the Roman *Fidei Commissum* while others hold that it is of indigenous growth. Maitland maintains that it did not come from outside England but developed from ancient use. Story holds the opposite view. Pomeroy joins Maitland and explains that "these essential differences are as marked as their superficial similarity and it is a grave error to represent the entire equity jurisprudence concerning uses and trusts as derived from Roman law".

Maitland supports his thesis by advancing the following arguments.[2]

(*i*) The word "use" is not derived from Latin *usus* but from the Latin word *opus*. Owing to the similarity of terminology and its pronounciation one may be tempted to draw an inference that the term "use" is derived from *usus*, but it is not so. In Latin *ad opus* means "on behalf of" and this terminology was in vogue as could be seen from the ancient Lombard and Frank legal documents. It was due to the transliteration of the phrase *ad upus* that it was alternatively used for *usus*. Maitland points out that in the 13th Century when land was held

2. *Lectures on Equity*, 1969 Edn., pp. 23-32.

permanently by one man on behalf of another, the term *ad opus* came to acquire its modern connotation and significance.

(*ii*) The Roman terminology *fidei commissum* was used in Roman law to express the obligation of the heir to execute the last wishes of the deceased. In other words, the appointed heir who got property in trust for another was termed *fidei commissum*. The expression thus belonged to the land of testament, whereas the English word "use" had its origin in an agreement, *inter vivos*, between the parties as a result of which one person held the property of another for the benefit of a third person. Thus " . . . . use, trust or confidence originates in an agreement. As to the want of valuable consideration for the trustee's promise, it might, I think, fairly be said that even if there is no benefit to the promisor, the trustee, there is at all the events detriment to the promisee, the trustor, since he parts with legal rights with property and with possession. Men ought to fulfil their promises, their agreements; and they ought to be compelled to do so, that is the principle . . . "[3]

(*iii*) From the very beginning the chancellors seem to have treated the rights of a *cestui que use* as analogous to an estate in land. They brought to bear upon it the rules of the English land law as regards such matters as descent and the like.[4] The Roman "*fidei commissarius*"[5] (the beneficiary) had no such right of ownership.

(**b**) **In Roman law**.—Under Roman law, a citizen while appointing a testamentary heir had but a limited choice in so far as he could not appoint an alien, not a posthumous child outside his family, nor a woman, to inherit his property. This was quite unfair. A method, therefore, was found out to bypass the State rules, statutes and prohibitory orders. They appointed a qualified person as heir according to law, and as prearranged with him under a request or direction, this qualified person would transfer the property to the person who was to be the real object of the bounty. This subsequent transfer was in the form of a gift which the person receiving was not prohibited to receive. The qualified person was thus to hold the property in trust for another until he transferred it to the real object. The inheritance so given was termed *fidei commissum*, the heir or trustee was termed as *fiduciarius* and the beneficiary the *fidei commissarius*.

4. USE AND FIDEI COMMISSUM

These two concepts under two different legal systems had between them their own similarities, of course, not praiseworthy. (*i*) Both were designed as an instrument or a device to get rid of the clutches of the prevailing law, and (*ii*) in both, it was left to the heir's or the trustee's sense of honour and confidence to hold and use or transfer the land for the benefit of another.

But the distinctions between these are also noteworthy. The Privy Council accepted the same in *Abdul Hamid case*[6].

3. Maitland: *Lectures on Equity*, p. 29.
4. *Ibid.*, p. 32.
5. Pomeroy: *Equity Jurisprudence*, p. 891.
6. *Abdul Hamid* v. *De Saram*, 1946 App Cas 208.

(*i*) The essence of a trust lies in the distinction between legal and equitable ownership whereas in a *fidei commissum* no such double estate idea or division of ownership existed.

(*ii*) The legal and equitable ownership which rests in two different persons in a trust, is simultaneous and concurrent while in a *fidei commissum* the legal ownership begins where the fiduciary ownership ends.

(*iii*) In a trust the interest of a beneficiary is quite ineffective and impotent against a *bona fide* purchaser of an estate for value without notice. In *fidei commissum* this is not so. There, once an interest is vested in the *fidei commissarios*, it holds good against the whole world and a *fiduciarius* (trustee/heir) cannot destroy it or cannot burden it by a transfer as a charge.

5. USE DEVELOPS INTO A TRUST

The history of the growth of trust falls into two natural divisions: the period before the Statute of Uses and the period after the Statute of Uses, 1536.

(a) **Before 1535.**—After the Norman conquest by William the Bastard, the Duke of Normandy, better known as William the Conqueror,[7] a controversy of Norman versus Anglo-Saxon law came to surface. William had brought with him the feudal law. He made certain that every acre of English land was held, directly or indirectly, from the king. He had the political foresight to avoid decentralization which feudalism had introduced in the rest of Europe. He got compiled the famous "Doonesday Book" by referring to which his agents could find out at once who the owner of the land was. He did not destroy the Germanic legal system of Anglo-Saxon England but gradually got both of them merged just as the two languages merged to form the English tongue.[8] The merger of the two systems gave England its Common law.[9] Under this system, the king was the supreme lord and the feudal lords held the lands distributed by the king on his behalf and at his pleasure. In turn, these lords also distributed the land received by them to their friends and followers, which consequently resulted in a feudalistic arrangement wherein the immediate superior at the top was the feudal lord, subject to the king, and the lowest link in the chain was the poor helpless life tenant, whose position was no better than a serf in so far as the lord had complete control over his person and property.[10] In the beginning the land held by the life tenants was inalienable, non-transferable and non-hereditary, but after a prolonged battle and owing to the force of circumstances, concessions were wrenched out which made the land hereditary and transferable but in no case was it absolutely transferable without the king's prior approval, as in principle, all lands belonged to him. This position held good roughly up to the end of the twelfth century.

The thirteenth century witnessed for the first time an incident wherein land was conveyed by one person to the other, the first holding the same for the use

---

7. R.A. Wormser: *The Story of the Law,* 1961 Edn., pp. 238-239
8. *Ibid.*, Part VII, 'William Begins a New System', pp. 240-242.
9. William ruled from 1066 to 1087.
10. Story: *Equity Jurisprudence*, 3rd Edn., p. 396.

of another. The monasteries had their rule that no monk or man was to have any wealth or property at all. But it was impossible to run them unless they had some means to live upon. And this was supplied by a device, by which land was conveyed to the borough community to the use of the Franciscan friars. English Common law had a similar provision so that no land could be conveyed to religious houses and monasteries by reason of the Statute of Mortmain.[11] But in spite of this so many Englishmen had sought to save their souls by making donations to the church that it seemed as though all the land of England, sooner or later, might pass into the hands of the church corporations. This in turn increased the power of the church.

As the above contrivance worked well people were tempted to use it more and more. The growing power of the church was a serious challenge to the king's powers and the powers of the feudal lords.

This popular device, which was originally used for conveying lands to religious houses, was in the 14th Century employed profitably[12] to get rid of (*i*) the feudal burdens of wardship and marriage, (*ii*) the law of forfeiture for treason and escheat for felony, (*iii*) the Statute of Mortmain, and (*iv*) one's own creditors, (*v*) lastly, by means of this device, one could give oneself the power of making something very like a will of lands. The use was thus a cloak for the real owner.

In the 15th Century the use became popular for transfer of land for all purposes. The ordinary Common law lawyers found this system very distasteful. Common law itself did not and could not recognise and enforce it as it was too vague as an agreement and did not fulfil the requirements of a contract. It therefore fell within the province of the Chancellor who enforced it efficiently. The Chancellor enforced it not as a contract but as a confidence binding the conscience of the feoffee who was to hold the land for the *cestui que use* (the person called beneficiary) and a remedy was given to the beneficiary to enforce it. The right of the beneficiary was recognised as an equitable ownership in land-an equitable estate in the land, which in course of time was available against all except a *bona fide* purchaser for value without notice of the equitable interest. Common law lawyers rejected the 'deed to a use' entirely and prevailed upon the Parliament to enact the Statute of Uses, which converted a deed to the use of another into actual title in that other. Thus the feoffee could not serve the purpose of a cloak to the real owner and the use, in the words of Snell, became the land.

(**b**) **After 1535.**—With the passing of the Statute of Uses the second period in the development of use into a trust began. The statute was designed to put an end to the use. For example, when land was conveyed to *X* to the use of *Y*, the statute deprived *X* of any interest in the land and the equitable interest of *Y* was recognised by it as a legal estate. The statute however did not apply to personal chattels, leaseholds and copyholds, but it applied only to freeholds. It also did

---

11. 'Mortmain' means 'dead hand'. Land was no longer to be transferred in such a way that it would be forever owned by a dead hand.
12. Maitland: *Lectures on Equity*, 1969 Edn., p. 27.

not apply where there were duties to be performed by the trustee, the person to whom the land was conveyed, and it did not recognise a use upon use,[13] i.e., where land was conveyed by *X* to *Y* to the use of *Z* to the use of *P*; *Z* was considered to be the legal owner and *P* got nothing. This gave a fresh and further chance to equity courts to decide in favour of the second[14] use, under the argument that the statute when applied to the first use, recognised the holder of the first use as a legal owner and thus the statute was exhausted in its application. The result would be that in the above example *Z* would be the legal owner and *P* the holder of an equitable estate. The second use came to be known as trust due to the invention of the chancery lawyers. In the words of Lord Hardwicke[15], the net result of passing the "statute, made upon great consideration, and introduced into a solemn and a pompous manner by this strict construction, had no other effect than add at most three words to a conveyance", i.e., 'to the use'.

In 1660, military tenures were abolished and the 17th and the 18th Centuries saw its smooth working with the extension of the doctrine to chattels, funds of every kind, actionable claims and money, till we come to the Law of Property Act, 1925 which repealed all the previous enactments relating to trusts.[16] From January 1, 1926, a trust of any property can be created by an instrument without the aid of a use. Thus *A* can convey property to *B* in trust for *C*. At present trusts in England are created by way of settlements, and the beneficial interest of such a trust may be enjoyed by a number of persons in succession.

6. IN INDIA

In India the law regarding trusts has been incorporated in the Indian Trusts Act, 1882. Recapitulating succinctly what has been said before regarding the essential characteristics of a trust in England, we can say that there are two kinds of estates, legal and equitable, of which two different persons can be the owners and these owners can well transfer their respective interests to any person or persons. This peculiar position of double ownership is the distinctive and original feature of an English trust. Justice Peacock[17] and Justice Markby[18] were of the opinion that no such precise idea as expressed by the English "use" and the Roman "*fidei commissum*" existed or was ever known to Hindu or Muslim law. But Macpherson, J.[19] opined to the contrary and said that a number of trusts for religious and charitable purposes were enforced by the courts in India and gift made to an idol tantamounted to a trust, which was beyond doubt.

13. *Tyrrel case*, (1557) Dyer's Rep 155(*a*).
14. *Sambach* v. *Dalston*, (1634) Tothil 188.
15. *Hopkins* v. *Hopkins*, (1938) 1 Atk 581.
16. The Statute of Uses, 1535, the Trustees Act, 1850, the Trustees Act, 1888, the Trust Investment Act, 1889, and the Trustees Act, 1893.
17. *Kumar Asimkrishna Dev* v. *Kumar Kumarkrishna*, BLR (Original Cases) 36.
18. *Krishna Ramini Dasi* v. *Anand Krishna Bose*, BLR (Original Cases) 231.
19. In appeal in these cases.

In *Ganendra Mohan Tagore* v. *Upendra Mohan Tagore*[20], it has been clearly expressed by Frier, J. that the double-ownership idea was unknown to Hindu and Mahomedan law but that is not a ground for drawing a baseless conclusion that trusts were unknown to Hindu and Mahomedan law. On the contrary, the variety of fiduciary relationship and the meticulous way in which they have been expressed in Indian law are quite unparalleled.[21] This proposition also finds support in his speech by Stokes on the Trusts Bill in the Legislative Council in the year 1881. Before 1882, trusts under Hindu law and Mahomedan law were enforced, but in doing so principles of English equity, justice and good conscience were applied where necessary.[22]

It is true that before 1882, no systematic effort was made to present the law relating to trusts which was scattered in different provisions in various other enactments. A commission[23] for this purpose was appointed, which gave its report on November 15, 1879 and in 1882 it was passed as an Act called the Indian Trusts Act, 1882.

7. INSTITUTION OF TRUST—ITS BENEFITS AND HAZARDS[24]

Trusts grew out of Fraud and Fear and their nurse was the court of Conscience. They are the product of evasion of law by society. However it is not an overstatement when one says that trust implies power and big trusts imply and generate "big power, a group power".

No doubt trusts have contributed to the progress and development of society in every sphere. In several striking passages Maitland has vigorously emphasized that the English trust has "supplied a personalized substitute for the far more comprehensive use of corporate devices in German law".

Maitland was true when he said that the personalized English concept of a trust was more useful to society than the impersonal collectivized German concept of an association (*verein*). Charitable trust therefore should be confined not to corporations but to natural persons, because men are more conscientious when they are acting in their own names than when they are using the name of a corporation (or associations of foundations, etc.).

Besides, the giant trusts (corporations) wield a great hidden group power, so far not satisfactorily controlled by the State. One may, therefore, join W. Friedmann when he says that: "Ironically enough, the immense sociological and juristic aspects of the problem of group power within the State have largely remained hidden behind accidents of legal form, especially in the Anglo-American system". The greatest problem is "the social and political danger of the assumption that an association, corporate or unincorporated, merely by being in form private rather than public, should still enjoy the far-reaching immunity from judicial or other official control which the courts have accorded

20. BLR (OC) 134.
21. *Ibid.*
22. *Kahandas Narandas, Re*, (1880) 5 Bom 154.
23. Whitley Stokes, C.A. Turner and Raymond West were its members.
24. Based on W. Friedmann: *Law in a Changing Society*, Chaps. 9 and 10, pp. 231-254, 268.

it". *Giant trusts are thus a constant source of hidden power, which if not properly controlled by the State, would result into a continuous menace and challenge to the social, political and economic life of the country, as is the experience of the Western world. Ransacked as a subject of research "Use of Trust Power" would expose equally shocking results in India too.*[25]

As a solution to the riddle of abuses of group power eight types of controls or remedies have been suggested:

(*i*) Total socialization,

(*ii*) Mixed public and private enterprise,

(*iii*) Cooperatives,

(*iv*) Mixed companies,

(*v*) Partnership of capital and labour,

(*vi*) Regulatory public authorities,

(*vii*) Anti-trust law, and

(*viii*) Social restraints.

To examine these is not within the scope here, but it would be profitable to look to Friedmann when he explains how this can be achieved: (*i*) By safeguarding of "due process" in the personal, political and social life of the individual, and (*ii*) by response of law largely in terms of judicial interpretation and extension of reviewability of unfair practices and lack of procedural safeguards in the affairs of association, this is possible. Of course, continuous administrative supervision over private institutions (unions, associations, foundations and the like representing group power-congeries) would jeopardize that minimum freedom without which democracies can slide to the brink of totalitarianism. No country can be an exception to this, much less India.

---

25. *Cf.* The Scandal about Indira Pratibha Pratishthan and other trusts by the then Chief Minister of Maharashtra State. U.S. Stall Corporation, Standard Oil Company, American Tobacco Company are the American examples of notorious Trusts. The Sherman Anti-Trust Act, 1890, outlawed many of their practices and The American Supreme Court decreed dissolution of such Trusts. (Walker D.M.: *The Oxford Companion to Law*, 1980 Edn., pp. 1241, 1267.

Chapter XI
Definition and Distinctions

"There is no trust where obligation is absent."

—*Allahabad Bank* v. *CIT*, 1954 SCR 195

"As between trustee and beneficiary, the law recognises the truth of the matter; as between these two, the property belongs to the latter and not to the former. But as between the trustee and third persons, the fiction prevails. The trustee is clothed with the rights of his beneficiary and is so enabled to personate or represent him in dealings with the world at large."

—Salmond

The Indian beneficiary is not an equitable owner, he has only "rights" against the trustees.

—Indian Trusts Act, 1882, Section 3

"Put not your trust in money, put your money in trust."

—An Adage

SYNOPSIS

1. THE PROBLEM OF DEFINITION

All efforts to produce a logical and satisfactory definition of trust have so far remained unsuccessful, as has been noted by Snell[1], Hanbury[2] and others. Hanbury goes to the extent of laying down that: "It is not thought that a dissection and criticism of earlier definitions are very rewarding; rather it is better to describe than to define a trust, and than to distinguish it from related but distinguishable concepts".[3]

In spite, however, we may venture to state Underhill's[4] definition of a trust, which was adopted in *Marshall case* and *Green case*[5]. Accordingly, a trust is "an equitable obligation binding a person (who is called a trustee) to deal with

1. *Snell's Principles of Equity*, p. 87.
2. Hanbury: *Modern Equity*, p. 85.
3. *Ibid.*
4. *Law of Trust*, 12th Edn., 1970, p. 3.
5. Cited by *Snell's Principles of Equity*, p. 87.

property over which he has control (called the trust property), for the benefit of persons (called the beneficiaries), of whom he may himself be one, and anyone of whom may enforce the obligation".

Professor Keeton,[6] defines a trust as a "relationship which arises wherever a person called the trustee is compelled in equity to hold the property, whether real or personal, and whether by legal or equitable title, for the benefit of some persons (of whom he may be one and who are termed *cestui que trust*) or for some object permitted by law, in such a way that the real benefit of the property accrues, not to trustee, but to the beneficiaries or other objects of the trust".

Lewin's classical definition[7] cannot be overlooked. According to him, it is: "A confidence reposed in some other, not issuing out of the land, but as a thing collateral, annexed in privity to the estate of the land, and to the person touching the land, for which the *cestui que trust* has no remedy but by subpoena in the chancery".

Story defines it to be an equitable right, title or interest in property, real or personal, distinct from the legal ownership thereof. Smith defines it as a duty deemed in equity to rest on the conscience of the legal owner. Snell calls it a beneficial interest in, or a beneficial ownership of, real or personal property unattended by the legal ownership.

Underhill's definition is narrow, in the sense that it cannot contain in itself trusts for charitable purposes or purpose trusts which lack human beneficiaries and yet may be valid as trusts, and other trusts which lack beneficiaries who can enforce them, e.g., trusts of imperfect obligations or honorary trusts. Keeton's definition that a person is compelled to hold property in trust for another seems far from the elementary rule that no one can be compelled to undertake a trust. As the definition connotes, the legal title vests in the trustee but he is the nominal owner as the real benefit does not accrue to him, while a beneficiary has the equitable title in him and is a beneficial owner, as the real benefit accrues to him. The question, therefore, as to who is the actual or real owner is still open and unsolved.[8] Against Lewin's definition Maitland remarks that it comes from Lord Coke upon Littleton[9] and he levels the following objections against it:[10]

(*i*) To say that a trust is a confidence is not very useful; for if we go on to ask what is confidence, we shall probably be told that it is a trust. This hardly explains anything.

(*ii*) Moreover, the definition stressed that wherever there is a trust, some reliance or confidence is reposed by one into another, but this is true only in case of a trustor who puts confidence in the trustee; the beneficiary does not place confidence in the trustee. Going further,

6. *Law of Trusts*, 9th Edn., 1968, p. 5.
7. *Lewin on Trusts*, 13th Edn., p.11, cited in Maitland: *Lectures in Equity,* p. 43.
8. See *Snell's Principles of Equity*, p. 88.
9. P. 272(*b*), Maitland: *Lectures in Equity*, citing Coke.
10. Maitland: *Lectures in Equity*, pp. 44-45.

there may be cases where no reliance is placed in the trustee, *e.g.* where I constitute myself a trustee of this watch for my eldest daughter. My daughter knows nothing of the trust and she has not been placing trust in me, yet there is a trust.

Maitland himself tried to present a definition but he was not satisfied with it. We may consequently reiterate that no satisfactory definition of a trust is available and more so when we know that contrary to the general rule, there may be trustees of a trust even though no property is vested in them, as is often the case with Settled Land Act trustees.

2. THE INDIAN TRUSTS ACT, 1882

Section 3 of the Indian Trusts Act, 1882 defines a trust. But one has to note that the Act is confined to private trusts (Section 1). It does not apply to public trusts or private religious or charitable endowments.[11] By this enactment, Indian courts have now not to go in search of English principles and precedents as the Act provides readymade principles. The Act does not affect the rule of Mahomedan law as to waqf, or the mutual relations of the members of an undivided family,[12] as determined by the customary or personal law, or to trusts to distribute prizes taken in war among the captors, and nothing in the second chapter of this Act applies to trusts created before the said day, i.e., the first day of March, 1882. It applies to the whole of India except the State of Jammu and Kashmir and the Andaman and Nicobar islands [Section 1]. The Act has repealed the Statute of Frauds (Sections 7, 8, 9, 10 and 11] and the Trustees' and Mortgagees' Powers Act, 1866 (Sections 2 to 5 and 32 to 37) and the Specific Relief Act, 1877 (Section 12, i.e. its first illustration) [Section 2].

3. DEFINITION OF TRUST: SECTION 3

The definition rendered by the Act runs as follows:

3. A trust is an *obligation annexed to the ownership of property*, and arising out of a confidence reposed in and accepted by the owner, or declared and accepted by him, *for the benefit of another*, or of another and the owner;

The person who reposes or declares the confidence is called the "*author of the trust*"; the person who accepts the confidence is called the "*trustee*"; the person for whose benefit the confidence is accepted is called "*beneficiary*"; the subject-matter of the trust is called "*trust property*" or "*trust money*"; the "*beneficial interest*" or "*interest*" of the beneficiary is his right against the trustee as owner of the trust property: and the instrument, if any, by which the trust is declared is called the "*instrument of trust*";

"a breach of any duty imposed on a trustee, as such, by any law for the time being in force, is called "*a breach of trust*".

---

11. *Thayarammal* v. *Kanakammal*, (2005) 1 SCC 457: AIR 2005 SC 1588. Section 1, *see also* Bombay Public Trusts Act, 1940 and various Religious Endowments Acts of different States.
12. *Perrazu* v. *Subbarayudu*, 44 Mad 656 (PC) 71 explains the reason as to why this is so.

The above definition is quite good but the question of its comparison with other foregoing well-known definitions is out of place because this definition covers only a specific field in the concept of trusts, private express trusts, and the section itself clears it. To say, therefore, that the definition is defective is to close one's eyes to the express provisions of the section.

The definition in Section 3 is said to be definition of Lewin with certain improvements thereon. In the beginning, it emphasises upon obligation, laying down that a trust is an obligation annexed to the ownership of property for the benefit of another. There is no trust where such obligation is absent.[13] Secondly, the beneficiary has no interest in the trust property but has only a right against the trustee who is the owner of the property. And lastly, the settlor himself can be a trustee. Besides, as the definition lays down, there must be four certainties in a trust:

(*i*) the *intention* of the settlor to create a trust must be express and clear,

(*ii*) the *purpose* for which the trust is to be created,

(*iii*) the *property* that is to be held in trust, and

(*iv*) the *beneficiaries* who are to benefit from the trust must be certain and definite.

A trust involves a transfer of property from the settlor to the trustee. Where the property is immovable property given under a will or by a non-testamentary instrument, it should be in writing, signed by the settlor and registered. In case of movable property the above method is safe, or else transfer of ownership of the property along with a parol declaration to give it in trust would be sufficient. A dedication by a Hindu for religious or charitable purposes is neither a "gift" nor a "trust" in the strict legal sense. Religious endowment does not create title in respect of the property dedicated in anybody's favour.[14] Moreover, the author must be competent to transfer, the property must be transferable and the trustee must also be capable of holding the property. Where a trust involves use of discretion by the trustee he must be competent to contract. As the definition lays down that a trust arises "out of a confidence reposed in and accepted by the owner", it refers to express trusts only. Implied or constructive trusts, described as "obligations in the nature of trusts" in Chapter IX of the Act are not within the purview of the definition. In other words, resulting and constructive trusts under English law are not within this definition of trust under Section 3.[15]

In this connection an interesting case should be noted.[16] Facts in brief may be stated as under:

Election to the State Legislature or the House of the People are held under the Constitution on the basis of adult suffrage. Applicant was elected as a Member of Parliament and was inducted into the Ministry of State. He

13. *Allahabad Bank Ltd.* v. *CIT*, 1954 SCR 195: AIR 1953 SC 476.
14. *Thayarammal* v. *Kanakammal*, (2005) 1 SCC 457.
15. *Tan Bug* v. *Collector of Bombay*, AIR 1946 Bom 216.
16. *Common Cause, A Regd. Society* v. *Union of India*, (1999) 6 SCC 667: 1999 SCC (Cri) 1196; *Common Cause, A Regd. Society* v. *Union of India*, (1996) 6 SCC 530 & (1996) 6 SCC 593.

was allocated Department of Petroleum & Natural gas. As per rules of this department (the President of India makes such rules) he was to look into the work of distribution of petroleum products. This arrangement was for smooth and better administration. As a consequence to this arrangement neither a "trust" as ordinarily understood or as defined under the Trusts Act, was created in favour of the petitioner nor did he become a "trustee" in that sense. He therefore cannot assume the role of a trustee, nor does a "trust" come into existence in respect of the Government properties. Therefore the Court's direction regarding investigation by CBI into the offence of criminal breach of trust against the minister cannot be sustained.

The court observed further that after election and after becoming a minister, he holds a *sacred trust* which is on behalf of people. This concept is a philosophical concept and reflects the image of virtue in its highest conceivable perfection. This philosophy cannot be employed for the determination of the offence of "Criminal Breach of Trust" which is defined in the Indian Penal Code. Whether the offence has been committed or not has to be determined according to the definition of that offence.

4. IDEA OF DOUBLE OWNERSHIP AND SECTION 3

As explained before, the idea of double-ownership or double-estate is a peculiar and distinctive feature of an English trust so that a beneficial interest is dissociated from a legal title. The trustee is the nominal owner, or a legal owner who has a direct and absolute dominion over property, while a beneficiary, is the beneficial or equitable owner for whose purpose and benefit the trustee has to hold and manage the trust property. One has to note that the duties of a trustee regarding "using" his rights are *positive*, and not negative. As Maitland[17] puts it: "One is not made a trustee by being bound *not* to use one's rights in some particular manner. On every owner of lands or goods there lies the duty of not using them in various ways. The law of torts largely consists of rules which limit the general rights of owners. I must not dig a quarry in my land so as to cause the subsidence of my neighbour's land. If I do this I commit a wrong and give my neighbour a cause of action; but of course I am not a trustee of my land for him". Thus the trustee has rights but they are to be used not for his own purpose but for the accomplishment of a certain purpose and for the benefit of a *cestui que trust*. He is bound to use these rights. One more thing is to be remembered here that a trustee is the legal owner but that does not mean that he should have a legal estate in all cases. In cases where the subject matter of a trust is a mere personal right (e.g. a benefit of a contract or a debt), or where the settlor has only equitable rights (as when a beneficiary of a trust makes a settlement of his interest), the trustee does not have anything more than what the settlor commands. Thus personal or equitable rights become the subject of a trust. A trustee, in the words of Snell, is the 'nominal owner' and in the words of Salmond,[18] his ownership is matter of form rather than substance, and

17. Maitland: *Lectures in Equity*, p. 44.
18. *Jurisprudence*, p. 256.

nominal rather than real. The property is rather fictitiously attributed to him for certain purposes. But the specific result of this is, that as between a trustee and the beneficiary, the law recognises the truth of the matter, the property belongs not to the former but to the latter; as between the trustee and third persons the fictitious ownership of the trustee (the fiction of law) prevails. The trustee is clothed with the rights of his beneficiaries and is so enabled to personate or represent him in dealing with the world at large. Thus both the ownerships are to serve a definite but a different purpose and one may be transferred or encumbered without affecting the other.[19]

In India.—As decided in *Tagore* v. *Tagore*[20], the double-ownership idea is unknown in India. Equitable ownership is not recognised in India and the trustee is the owner of the trust property when it is vested in him. The Indian beneficiary is not an equitable owner but he has only "rights" against the trustees (Section 3). The beneficial interest or interest of the beneficiary cannot be a subject-matter of trust in India as Section 8 of the Act clearly lays down.

> 8. *Subject of trust.*—The subject-matter of a trust must be property transferable to the beneficiary.

It must not be merely beneficial interest under a subsisting trust. This is a basic and definite difference between the English and the Indian Law of Trusts.

The rights of the beneficiary as explained by Section 55 onwards in Chapter VI of the Indian Trusts Act, are to call upon the trustees to administer the trust property properly and to transfer the same in suitable cases. Section 58 also lays down that the beneficiary's beneficial interest can be transferred by him when he is competent to do so. He can mortgage his interest[21] and assign[22] the same also.

5. TRUST DISTINGUISHED FROM OTHER RELATIONS

Trusts resemble certain other legal conceptions namely, bailments, agency, contracts and powers and administration of the deceased person's estate. As Snell explains, out of these the first three categories were enforceable in Common law courts whereas trust was enforceable in equity courts and the administration of estates fell within the competence of the ecclesiastical courts.[23]

(a) **Bailments.**—Blackstone's definition of a bailment as "a delivery of goods in trust" is a fruitful source of confusion.[24]

It is a delivery of goods by *A* to *B* for a limited purpose with an express or implied condition that on fulfilment of the purpose, *B* will return the goods to *A* as directed by him. Delivery of the goods for a limited purpose (which implies a definite or suitable period for the accomplishment of the limited purpose)

---

19. For distinction between legal and equitable ownership *see* Salmond: *Jurisprudence*, 12th Edn., 1966, pp. 260-262.
20. (1872) BLR 377 (PC).
21. *Hemchandra* v. *Surdhani*, (1940) 54 CWN 253 (PC).
22. *Moolla* v. *A.O.*, (1936) 40 CWN 1253 (PC).
23. *Snell's Principles of Equity*, 27th Edn., 1973, p. 89
24. Hanbury: *Modern Equity*, p. 86.

without transferring ownership from *A* to *B* is the important feature of bailment. Bailment resembles a trust, in that in both one person has possession over the other's property for that other's benefit. It may be described as a species of trust therefore. The contrast between the two lies in the fact that:

(*i*) Bailment was recognised at Common law and consequently the rights and obligations of a bailee are legal, whereas a trust is merely equitable, the trustees having equitable rights.

(*ii*) Only personal chattels can be bailed, while any property may be held in trust.

(*iii*) A bailee has only a special property in the bailment, the bailor keeping general property with himself, whereas a trustee has the general property in the trust with himself. In other words, a bailor gives to the bailee only a limited or special property for the time being, while a trustee is the full legal owner, subject to obligations attached to the property in trust with him.

(*iv*) A bailee selling without authority the goods bailed to him can pass no good title as against the bailor but an unauthorised sale by a trustee will confer a good title upon a *bona fide* purchaser for value, acquiring the legal interest without notice of the trust.[25]

(*v*) Only a bailor can enforce the duties of the bailee, an obligation under a trust can be enforced by anyone entitled to its benefits.

(*vi*) A bailor uses his special rights for his own benefit but a trustee is bound to exercise them on behalf of and for the benefit of another.

A trust is therefore fundamentally distinguishable from a bailment[26] and a bailee is not a trustee express or implied within the meaning of the Indian Trusts Act, 1882.[26]

(b) Agency.—An agent and a trustee both administer property on behalf of another and they cannot become the beneficial owner thereof, i.e., each is subject to fiduciary obligations towards his principal or beneficiaries. As Hanbury[27] puts it, the position of a principal and agent resembles that of a beneficiary and trustee. Agents, like trustees, must act personally in the business of the agency and are accountable to their principals, as are trustees to beneficiaries, for any profit made out of the property or business entrusted to them.[28] The relation in each case is a fiduciary one. But the difference lies in this that:

(*i*) Trusts are governed by equity, agency by Common law.

(*ii*) Agency normally arises by contract between the principal and agent (except in case of agency of necessity) whereas in most trusts no such contractual relationship between trustees and beneficiaries exists.

---

25. Maitland: *Lectures in Equity*, 1969 Edn., p. 47.
26. *Ramasami* v. *Kamal Ammal*, (1921) 45 Mad 173.
27. *Modern Equity*, p. 87.
28. Hanbury: *Principles of Agency*, 2nd Edn., pp. 3-10; Bowstead: *Agency*, 13th Edn., p. 6.

(*iii*) Property of agency does not vest in the agent whereas a trustee has property vested in him.

(*iv*) While an agent can make his principal liable, a trustee cannot involve his beneficiaries in liability.[29]

(*v*) An agent always acts on behalf of his principal and is subject to his control. A trustee is not subject to such a control either from the settlor or from the beneficiaries.

(*vi*) An agent when he goes beyond his powers and out of his sphere cannot pass a legal title to a *bona fide* purchaser for value without notice of the trust.

(*vii*) An agent derives his authority to act by delegation from his principal, whereas a trustee derives such an authority from the instrument of trust. In short, the principle is that when ownership of property is vested in one for a specific purpose for the benefit of another, there he is a trustee.[30] But where only a power of management is given to one and the ownership is retained by the other, there he is only an agent.[31]

(**c**) **Contracts.**—Contract and Trust are quite different concepts, but there are basic similarities in so far as the commonest origin of a trust obligation is a transaction between two persons, and in contract also its obligation is the result of an agreement between two persons. As to the distinction between them, (*i*) a contract, as Hanbury[32] lays down, is a *common law personal obligation* resulting from an agreement, a trust is an *equitable proprietory relation* which can arise independently of an agreement. However, the trust may arise as a result of an agreement for consideration, in which case there may be both—a trust and a contract.[33] Where money is lent on agreed terms for payment to specific persons and to return to the lender if not so paid, such money is impressed with a trust for those persons.[34] (*ii*) A contract is enforceable at Common law; it is a bilateral act, it springs from an offer and acceptance, it gives a right *in personam*, a stranger to a contract can have neither the benefit of it nor its liability, and contracts without consideration cannot be enforced. On the other hand, a trust being a matter of confidence, was enforced by equity courts: it may be a purely unilateral act (where the settlor himself is a trustee), there is no offer and the trustee's acceptance is presumed unless he disclaims a trust, it almost gives a right *in rem*, its benefit is claimed not by the trustor (unless he is also a beneficiary) but by the *cestui que trust* who is not a party to the contract, and lastly, the consideration supplied in contract and trust are of different nature, as in equity the issues of a prospective marriage are treated to be within the "marriage consideration". In the sense in which Common law

---

29. *Snell's Principles of Equity*, pp. 89-90.
30. *Annappa* v. *Krishna*, 1936 Bom 412.
31. *Kalipad* v. *Haridasi*, 1938 Cal 673; *Maloji Rao* v. *Keshav*, 1939 Bom 126.
32. Hanbury: *Modern Equity*, p. 88.
33. *Quistclose Investments Ltd.* v. *Rolls Razor Ltd.*, (1968) 3 WLR 1097.
34. *Barclays Bank Ltd.* v. *Quistclose Investments Ltd.*, 1970 AC 567.

understands the word consideration in a contract, the issues are no party to the consideration.

In the recent English case of *Beswick* v. *Beswick*[35], specific performance for the benefit of a third party was granted by the House of Lords. Thus, as Hanbury[36] notes, a few cases have enabled the third party to obtain the benefits due to him under the contract by finding that one of the contracting parties contracted as trustees for him. Of course, not much encouragement has been given to the development of this doctrine. The House of Lords has recently, as seen above, extended the scope of the remedy of specific performance so as to enable a party to a contract to obtain performance for the benefit of a third party, thus rendering the Common law doctrine of privity of contract (an unfortunate inheritance from the past) "unnecessary", Common law "inadequate", and the trust concept "irrelevant".[37]

Much of the discussion on the question of distinguishing trust from contract has centred on the problem of the introduction of the so-called trust concept as a way of permitting a third party to enforce a contract entered into by others for his benefit. This is a recent development.[38]

Pooley v. *Budd*[39] is a leading case on the point.

(d) Powers.—A power is an authority vested in a person to deal with or dispose of property not his own. The person giving the power is the 'donor' and the person receiving the same is called the donee of the power. Power is neither legal or equitable, imperative or discretionary, general or special. A general power does not restrict a donee's choice whereas a special power restricts his choice of appointment within a certain class of persons. The substantial distinction between a power and a trust is that a mere power is discretionary, while a trust is imperative. When I hold Rs 50,000 upon trust to divide it among a certain class of persons, I have no choice but I am bound to carry out the trust, and in default the court will compel me to do so. In the event of my failure to act either by design or by accident, the property will pass to the persons in default of appointment.[40] In other words, benefits to be given or claimed under trust do not depend upon a trustee's fancy, whereas execution of power is left to the free will of the donee. Moreover, the beneficiaries can compel the trustee to act and to hand over the benefits to them, but in case of power no such compulsion is possible against the donee of power. Where the donor exhibits an intention that the property in any event must go to the objects of power, the power is a trust power which must be exercised; if it is not so, there is a mere power of

35. 1968 AC 58; John Tiley: *A Casebook on Equity and Succession*, p. 82. *See also* F.E. Dowrick, (1956) 19 MLR 374.
36. Hanbury: *Modern Equity*, p. 631.
37. Hanbury: *Modern Equity*, p. 635.
38. For detailed discussion *see* Law of Property Act, 1925, S. 56, discussed in *Snell's Principles of Equity*, 1973 Edn., pp. 91, 92, 93.
39. Rolls Court (1851) 14 B 34; John Tiley: *A Casebook on Equity and Succession*, pp. 98-100.
40. *Mcphail* v. *Doulton*, 1971 AC 424.

appointment.[41] Thus the distinction rests on the intention of the donor as exhibited in the instrument.

(e) **Debts.**—(*i*) A debtor has the duty to pay money to the creditor, a trustee has to hold the trust property in trust for the beneficiary.

(*ii*) A debtor's obligation, like that of an agent, is personal, the trust is proprietory.

(*iii*) A debtor is not a trustee for his creditor, because he has not to 'use' any right for his creditor's benefit (except when a debtor becomes the creditor's personal representative), a trustee is bound to exercise his rights for the benefit of his *cestui que trust*.

(*iv*) A debtor can spend or use the money obtained or do anything he likes with it, but a trustee has no right to deal with the trust property according to his own fancy.

(*v*) On a debtor's (e.g. banker) bankruptcy, money cannot be followed but must be claimed as a creditor in bankruptcy. In case of a trust if the trustee goes bankrupt, the trust property can be followed and recovered so far as it can be traced.[42]

(*vi*) A debtor is bound to repay the money even if it is stolen, whereas a trustee is not liable for accidental loss.

(*vii*) A trust and a debt may coexist, as where a loan to be held by the borrower on trust is repayable if the purpose for which the money was lent is carried out, and may be held in trust for the lender if performance is impossible.[43]

(f) Conditions and Charges.—Trusts and Conditions are similar in this respect that in both, the owner of the property is subject to obligation. This obligation could not be enforced by Common law courts but the courts of equity enforced it.

(*i*) An owner of property can create a trust, but no other person can do so. In condition, the person disposing the property to *A* may attach a condition to it that *A* shall dispose of his own property in a certain manner.

(*ii*) A condition may impose an obligation therefor the value of which may exceed the property received in gift, whereas in a trust a trustee's obligation is always limited to the value of the trust property.

> "If *A* gives property to *B* on condition that he do something in favour of *C*, then if the court construes the gift as a condition, the following is the result: if the condition is subsequent and becomes impossible to perform, the interest given to *B* becomes absolute and *C* has no right, whether the condition is attached to real or personal property; similarly if a condition precedent attached to personal property becomes impossible of

---

41. *Snell's Principle of Equity*, p. 96.
42. *Official Assignee* v. *Bhat*, (1933) 60 IA 203.
43. Hanbury: *Modern Equity*, pp. 88-89.

performance. Further, if *B* observes the condition the property vests in him absolutely. On the other hand, if the court construes the gift as trust, *B* will be bound to give benefit to *C* notwithstanding the impossibility of performing the obligation precisely according to its terms."[44]

It is therefore difficult to find out whether a gift of property is subject to a trust or whether it is conditional upon, or charged with, a duty of making certain payments. The difficulties of construction in cases of this type are well-illustrated by *Quistclose Investments Ltd.* v. *Rolls Razor Ltd.*[45]

A charge differs from a trust in the following cases.[46]

(*i*) Once the party subject to the charge has fulfilled the charge he holds the property beneficially,[47] *aliter* (otherwise) as a trustee who may have to hold the property on a resulting trust.[48]

(*ii*) A trustee who occupies trust property must account for rents and profits: *aliter* as a person holding property subject to a charge.[49]

But a charge is similar to a trust in the following respects.[50]

(*i*) Neither a person subject to a charge nor a trustee is under a personal obligation to make up any deficiency caused by insufficiency[51] of assets.

(*ii*) Both a charge and a trust create equitable interest which give way to the *bona fide* purchaser for value of the legal estate without notice.[52]

(g) Mortgages.—A mortgage is the result of a contract whereas a trust is the result of confidence. A mortgagee does not hold the mortgaged property as a trustee for the mortgagor; a trustee has to hold the trust property for the beneficiary's benefit. On the contrary, a mortgagee has an interest quite adverse to the mortgagor, which the trustee cannot have. The former can use or get sold the mortgaged property in suitable cases while the latter cannot use the trust property himself. One has to take note that a mortgagee, when he is paid by the mortgagor, becomes a trustee for the mortgagor because though he has every right to secure repayment of his money, that right cannot go beyond it. He becomes a trustee also for the excess amount with him when the mortgaged property is sold and he has been reimbursed out of the sale proceeds.

(h) Administration.—Administration of assets and trusts have certain similarities too Trusts were the invention of the Chancellor, whereas

44. Nathan and Marshall: *Equity Through the Cases*, 1961 Edn., p. 197, citing Thomas: *Conditions in Favour of Third Parties*, (1952) 11 CLJ; *A.G.* v. *Cordwainer's Co.*, (1833) MR/MY & K 534.
45. (1968) 3 WLR 1097.
46. Nathan and Marshall: *Equity Through the Cases*, p. 211.
47. *Oliver, Re*, 62 LT 633.
48. *West, Re, George* v. *Grose*, (1900) 1 Ch 84.
49. *Oliver, Re*, 62 LT 633.
50. Nathan and Marshall: *Equity Through the Cases*, p. 201.
51. *Cowley, Re*, (1885) 53 LT 494.
52. *Parker* v. *Judkin*, (1931) 1 Ch 475.

administration of the assets of a deceased person was originally regulated by ecclesiastical courts. As the Chancery Courts had also a supplementary jurisdiction in this respect the position of the administrators became more and more assimilated to that of the trustees. Moreover, like a trustee, an administrator is bound to convey the surplus of assets in his hands after the debts have been paid off. Most of the rules applicable to trustees have been made applicable to administrators also. Like trustees therefore, an administrator cannot have an interest adverse to the property, cannot make a profit out of the property in his charge, is not liable unless he commits any wilful default, and can claim a discharge from his office when the mission is completed.

Apart from these similarities, (*i*) an executor or administrator, merely as such, is not a trustee for the legatee or the next of kin. As Snell[53] puts it, "the function of personal representatives is to wind up, and the function of *a trustee* is to hold".

(*ii*) Personal representatives have usually the whole ownership of the property administered and the beneficiaries have only a right to compel them the due administration. Under a trust, the trustees have only the bare ownership while the beneficiaries have the beneficial interest in them.

(*iii*) For the breach of trust and for a claim to the personal estate, the time-limits are also different except in case of fraud to which neither limit applies. Moreover, a trustee cannot plead limitation statutes where he himself is guilty of fraud or conversion.

(*iv*) A personal representative can pay his own debt or debt of others in preference to other creditors, but a trustee cannot do so.

(*v*) One of the several personal representatives can pass a good title to the purchase of the pure personality whereas the trustees must act jointly.

---

53. *Snell's Principles of Equity*, p. 96.

Chapter XII

Classification of Trusts

"There is one good, general and infallible rule that goes to both these kinds of trusts; it is a rule that never deceives and to which there is no exception, and that is: THE LAW NEVER IMPLIES, THE COURT NEVER PRESUMES A TRUST, BUT IN CASE OF ABSOLUTE NECESSITY."

—Nottingham, L.C.
in *Cook* v. *Fountain*, (1676) 3 Swans 585

"The names given to various types of trusts are not terms of art, but they are commonly assumed to be so. The categories are not exclusive."

—Hanbury: *Modern Equity*

"A constructive trust is the formula through which the conscience of equity finds expression."

—Cardozo

SYNOPSIS

1. GENERAL

There is a divergence of opinion[1] on the question of classification of trusts and rightly enough, it is possible, because classification involves an angle from which, and a reason or purpose for which, a situation is surveyed.

---

1. Nottingham, L.C. expresses in *Cook* v. *Fountain*, (1676) 3 Swan 585, that trusts are either express, implied or presumptive. Lord Esher, M.R., Bowen, L.J. and Kay, L.J. in *Solar* v. *Ashwell*, (1893) 2 QBD 390, say that they are either express or constructive and in *Re I. Lanover, S.E.*,. 1926 Ch 626, Ashbury, J. expresses that trusts are either express, by act of parties, or implied, i.e. constructive, which is either resulting or non-resulting. *See* Nathan & Marshall: *Equity Through the Cases*, Chap. 5, pp. 210-213.

Following Lewin, Maitland[2] classifies trusts according to the mode of their creation. Trusts are created either (*i*) by the act of a party, or (*ii*) by operation of law. Express and implied trusts come under the first classification and resulting or constructive trusts in the second.

As Hanbury[3] notes, the names given to various types of trusts are not terms of art, but they are commonly (even in statutes) assumed to be so. The categories are not exclusive; some trusts could appear in more than one category. According to him trusts are either (*a*) express, (*b*) implied, (*c*) resulting, or (*d*) constructive. Express trusts may be (*i*) executed, or (*ii*) executory and, (*i*) completely constituted, or (*ii*) incompletely constituted. Snell practically accepts this classification adding (*i*) private and public, (*ii*) simple and special, and (*iii*) perfect and imperfect trusts to the list.[4]

(1) Viewed at from the *mode of their creation* we have express or declared trusts, implied or presumed trusts and constructive trusts. Resulting trusts, precatory trusts and secret trusts are also a species of any of the above-mentioned three main classes, which we shall consider.

(2) According to the *nature and duties of the trustees*, trusts may be classified into two categories: simple trusts and special trusts.

(3) Considering the trusts *with reference to their objects*, there are two divisions of trusts: private trusts and public trusts or charitable trusts.

(4) Lastly, *from the viewpoint of supplying consideration*, trusts are divided into: trusts for value, voluntary trusts and trusts of imperfect obligations or illusory trusts.

(5) All the varieties of trust fall into two broad divisions: trusts created by the act of parties and those created by the operation of law.

It will be fruitful, therefore, to cast the above broad divisions into a tabular form to facilitate understanding.

2. TABLES OF CLASSIFICATION

Table I

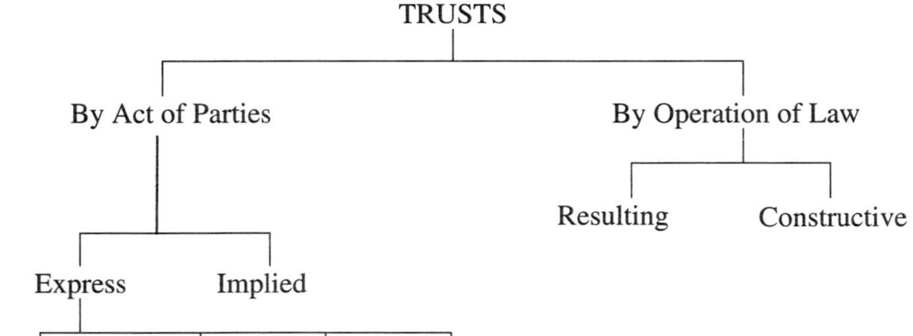

2. Maitland: *Lectures on Equity*, 1969 Edn., p. 53.
3. Hanbury: *Modern Equity*, p. 98.
4. *Snell's Principles of Equity*, pp. 98-100

Table II

Classification according to nature of duties, objects, mode of creation and consideration.

TRUSTS

(*a*) According to nature of duties of trustees

(*i*) Simple

(*ii*) Special

(*b*) According to objects

(*i*) Private

(*ii*) Public or Charitable

(*c*) According to the mode of creation

(*i*) Express or declared trust

(A) Executed

(B) Executory

(*ii*) Implied or presumed

(*iii*) Constructive

(*iv*) Resulting

(*v*) Precatory

(*vi*) Secret

} These may fall in any one of the above categories (*i*), (*ii*) or (*iii*)

(*d*) According to consideration

(*i*) Trust for value

(*ii*) Voluntary trust

(*iii*) Trust of imperfect obligations or illusory trust

(*e*) Rest

(*i*) Completely and incompletely constituted trust

(*ii*) Trusts of perfect and imperfect obligations

(*iii*) Protective and discretionary trusts which may fall in any one or more of the above divisions

Note.—The categories are not exclusive and they may overlap.

Table III

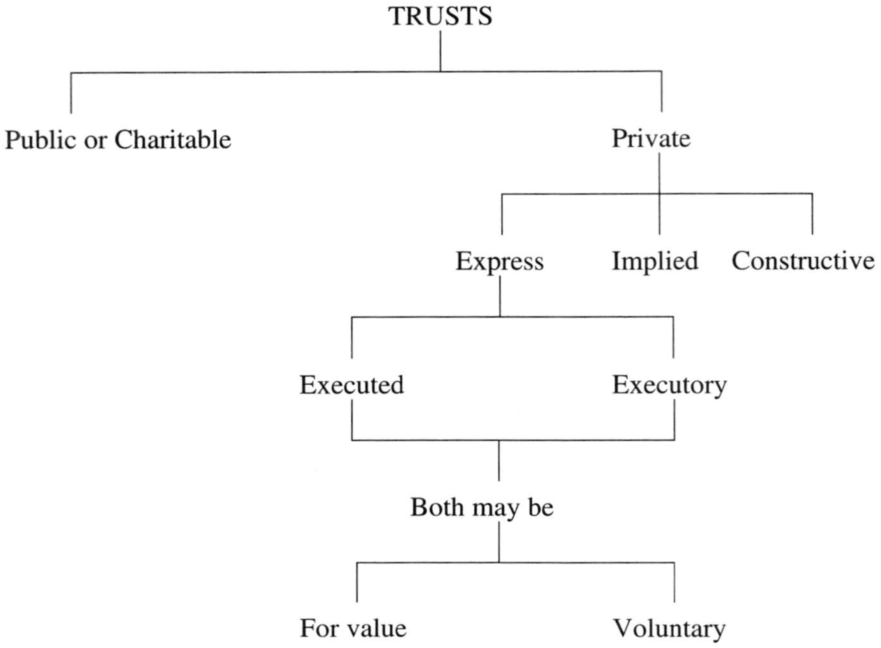

3. EXPRESS TRUSTS

In the words of Lord Brougham in *Fitzgerald* v. *Steward*[5], an express trust is one "created, not by facts and circumstances, but by express words". As per Lord Esher, M.R., " . . . If there is created in expressed terms, whether written or verbal, a trust, and a person is in terms nominated to be the trustee of that trust . . . such a trust is in equity called an express trust".[6] In short, a trust created by an express declaration of the person in whom the property is vested is an express trust.[7] For example, *A* declares himself a trustee of 'Blackacre' for *B*. Similarly where *A* conveys the land to *C* in trust for *B*, the same result follows. Express trusts are termed declared trusts also.

4. IMPLIED TRUSTS

Such trusts are raised or created by act of construction of law. It arises from the presumed intention of the owner of the property. As expressed by Nottingham, L.C. in *Cook* v. *Fountain*[8], "express trusts are declared either by word or in writing; and these declarations appear either by direct and manifest proof, or violent and necessary presumption. The last are commonly called

5. (1831) 2 Russ & M 457, 460.
6. *Solar* v. *Ashwell*, (1893) 2 QBD 390.
7. *Snell's Principles of Equity*, p. 98.
8. Nathan & Marshall: *A Casebook on Equity and Succession*, No. 46; (1676) 3 Swans 585.

presumptive trusts . . . so the trust, if there be any, must either be implied by the law or presumed by the court. There is one good, general and infallible rule that goes to both these kinds of trusts; it is a rule that never deceives and to which there is no exception, and that is: the law never implies, the court never presumes a trust, but in case of absolute necessity".

Where *A* purchases land and conveys it to *X*, there is *prima facie* an implied trust and *X* holds it as a trustee for *A*.

Thus the distinction between an express and an implied trust is thin insofar as in the former, the words creating a trust are clear, while in the latter they are less clear.

5. CONSTRUCTIVE TRUSTS[9]

Constructive trusts arise by operation of law. In certain circumstances the legal owner of property must hold it on trust for another according to principles of equity. It is not possible in such circumstances to observe formalities. When it would be an abuse of confidence for the owner of property to hold the same for his own benefit, a trust is imposed upon him irrespective of his intention. Such a trust is called a constructive trust, e.g., a trustee getting renewal of a lease of land held by him as a trustee is bound by this trust. As Cardozo said, a constructive trust is the formula through which the conscience of equity finds expression.[10]

The most accurate and lucid distinctions have been brought out by *Lewin on Trusts*[11]. "An *implied trust* is one declared by a party not directly, but only by implication; as where a testator devises an estate to *A* and his heirs, 'not doubting' that he will there out pay an annuity of £ 20 per annum to *B* for his life, in which case *A* is the trustee for *B* to the extent of the annuity. Trusts by operation of law are such as are not declared by a party at all, either directly or indirectly, but result from the effect of a rule of equity and are either (1) *resulting trusts*, as where an estate is devised to *A* and his heirs upon a trust to sell and pay the testator's debts, in which case the surplus of the beneficial interest is a resulting trust in favour of the testator's heir; or (2) *constructive trusts*, which the court elicits by a construction put upon certain acts of parties, as when a tenant for life of leasehold renews the lease on his own account, in which case the law gives the benefit of the renewed lease to those who were interested in the old lease".

The term has been used in different senses. It is applied to fiduciary and quasi-fiduciary relationships other than that subsisting between trustee and beneficiary.[12] The obligation incumbent on a trustee who has made a profit however innocently, through his office, is of this nature and the trustee is to hold

---

9. Hanbury: *Modern Equity*, p. 101; *Snell's Principles of Equity*, p, 99.
10. *HPA International* v. *Bhagwandas Fateh Chand Daswani*, (2004) 6 SCC 537 (Property acquired with notice of existing contract. Parties are bound by it). Ss. 91, 90 & 92.
11. 12th Edn., p. 124; 15th Edn., p. 16, cited in *Re Llanover Settled Trusts*, Nathan & Marshall: *A Casebook on Equity and Succession*, No. 47, 1961 Edn.
12. Maitland: *Lectures on Equity*, p. 80.

such profit for the benefit of the beneficiaries.[13] The position of a stranger to the trust who meddles with the trust property in such a way that equity will regard him *a trustee de son tort*[14] is also of this nature wherein a constructive trust is created. In *Eves* v. *Eves*[15] Lord Denning has therefore rightly said that . . . "a few years ago even equity would not have helped. But things have altered now. Equity is not past the age of child-bearing. One of her latest progeny is a constructive trust of a new model".

Principle of unjust enrichment.—Such trusts are enforced on one principle and that is, to prevent unjust enrichment of one person at the expense of another. In America, this has become one of the weapons in the form of an equitable remedy of a proprietary nature, available to prevent unjust enrichment, whenever the quasi-contractual remedy is inadequate.[16]

Before coming to the provisions of the Indian Trusts Act, 1882, it is necessary that the concept of the divisions (*a*) and (*e*) under Table II are made clear first, the express trust and its subdivisions to be discussed in the course of discussion of the statutory provisions of the Indian Trusts Act.

6. PRIVATE AND PUBLIC TRUSTS

A private trust primarily confers the benefit of the trust on certain persons or a class of them. It is possible that in doing so it may incidentally confer some benefit on the public at large, e.g., there may be a trust for the benefit of *X* individually or for his sons or descendants.

A public trust, as the very name connotes, confers a benefit on the public at large. Trusts to promote public welfare or education are public trusts and they may incidentally confer a benefit on an individual, or a class of them. The division of trusts into private and public are related to the end or purpose or object which they are supposed to serve. A public trust may be a charitable trust or a purpose trust or a religious trust, but it must, to justify its existence, serve some considerable portion of the public answering a definite description[17], because it is for the benefit of the community or of an appreciably important section of the community.[18] A trust which has no such element is not a public trust.[19]

A private trust may be enforced by any of the beneficiaries while a public trust only by the Attorney-General.

---

13. *Boardman* v. *Phipps*, (1967) 2 AC 46; Nathan and Marshall: *A Casebook on Equity and Succession*, No. 78.
14. *Carl-Zeiss Stiftlung* v. *Herbert Smith & Co.*, (1969) 2 WLR 427.
15. (1975) 3 All ER 768, 771.
16. Hanbury: *Modern Equity*, pp. 101-2; *K.S. Satyanarayana* v. *V.R. Narayana Rao*, (1999) 6 SCC 104: AIR 1999 SC 2544.
17. *Nabi Shirazi* v. *Province of Bengal*, ILR 1942 Cal 211.
18. *Verge* v. *Somerville*, 1924 AC 496; *Keren* v. *Inland Revenue Commr.*, 1932 AC 650.
19. *Cambay Municipality* v. *Ratilal Ambalal Reshamwala*, 1995 Supp (2) SCC 591.

7. SIMPLE AND SPECIAL TRUSTS

Where *A* vests his property in *B* for the benefit of *C* and *A* has not laid down the nature of the trust, what results is a simple trust. The beneficiary in such a trust has a right to be put in possession of the trust property and consequently call upon the trustee to execute a conveyance of the legal estate. The simple reason is that here a trustee has no duties to perform. The trust is also termed a bare trust[20] and it is for the law to construe its nature.

A special trust imposes duties on trustees for the execution of the purpose pointed out by the settlor. Thus where there is a trust for sale, the trustee is not a mere depository of the trust but he has to take pains and perform his duties. Where these duties are ordinary and of a mechanical character involving routine intelligence, the trust is called a *ministerial trust.* But where the duties involve special intelligence and a greater element of judgment and discretion, it is called a Discretionary trust. The beneficiary in such a trust cannot order a particular part of the income from the trustees as he can do in a simple trust, because it all depends upon the discretion of the trustees.[21]

8. TRUSTS OF PERFECT AND IMPERFECT OBLIGATION

Such a trust is also called an Honorary trust. The distinguishing feature of this type of trust is that it cannot be enforced by or on behalf of the *cestui que trust.* A trust for the preservation of the independence and integrity of newspapers[22], or for the maintenance of good understanding between nations[23], or for pursuing inquiries into a new alphabet[24] (made by George Bernard Shaw) are void because the purpose involved therein is abstract and impersonal.[25] As Snell notes, acceptance of certain other trusts for the purpose of maintenance of a tomb or individual animals by courts, branding them as "exceptional or anomalous" trusts, shows unfortunate "concessions to human weakness or sentiment". He also observes that "an individual trust cannot be tortured into a valid power"[26] even though the settlor's wishes or purpose could be achieved thereby. Thus a trust, the object of which is "certain" and which can be "enforced", is not a trust of imperfect obligation but a valid trust.

9. RESULTING TRUST

(a) When comes into existence.—What Hornman, J. expressed in the *Gillingham Bus Disaster case*[27] in regard to a resulting trust appears to be the

---

20. *Tomlinson* v. *Glyns Executor and Trustee Co.*, 1970 Ch 112.
21. *Gulbenkian's Settlements* (No. 2), *Re*, 1970 Ch. 408.
22. *Astor's S.T., Re*, 1952 Ch 534; Nathan and Marshall: *A Casebook on Equity and Succession*, No. 27.
23. *Ibid.*
24. *Shaw, Re*, (1957) 1 WLR 729: (1958) 1 All ER 245; Nathan and Marshall: *A Casebook on Equity and Succession*, No. 29.
25. *Denley's Trust, Re*, (1969) 1 Ch 373.
26. *Snell's Principles of Equity*, p. 100.
27. *Gillingham Bus Disaster Fund, Re, Bowman* v. *Official Solicitor*, (1958) 3 WLR 325: 1959 Ch 62; Nathan and Marshall: *A Casebook on Equity and Succession*, No. 92.

best description thereof. Such a trust arises, according to him, where the expectation of the settlor "is for some unforeseen reason cheated of fruition and" (*ii*) "is an inference of law based on an after-knowledge of the event". As expressed by Hanbury[28], "resulting trusts occur where equity regards property which is held by *T* (a trustee) as belonging in equity to the person who has transferred it to, or caused it to be vested in *T*. . . . There is no doctrinal unity to resulting trusts." Creation of such a trust is not dependent on compliance with formalities and is also not subject to all rules regarding express trusts. In such a trust the beneficial interest in the property results or reverts to the creator.[29]

(*b*) *Types.*—According to Maitland[30], resulting trusts are of two kinds: (*i*) where there is a gift and the question is whether the donee takes beneficially or merely as a trustee, and (*ii*) where a person buys something but the conveyance of it is at his instance made not to him but to someone else, i.e., cases of 'purchases in the name of third parties'. In expressing this Maitland followed Lewin[31], who said that resulting trusts may be subdivided thus:

(*i*) where a person being himself both legally and equitably entitled makes a conveyance or bequest of the legal estate and there is no ground for the inference that he meant to dispose of the equitable interest.

(*ii*) where a purchaser of property takes a conveyance of the legal estate in the name of a third person, but there is nothing to indicate an intention of not appropriating to himself the beneficial interest.

(*c*) *Important features.*—The important thing here is that in a resulting trust there is a disposition of the legal interest but not of the equitable interest. The consequence of this will be that the equitable interest, or so much thereof as is left undisposed of, will result, if arising out of the settlor's reality, to himself or his personal representatives. The second important feature of such a trust is that the intention of excluding the person invested with the legal estate from the enjoyment of the property may be expressed or may not be expressed. Such trust is also called an implied trust because it is founded on an unexpressed but presumed intention of the party creating it. Where the rule of perpetuities is defeated such a trust comes into being.

(*d*) *Distinction from Constructive Trust.*—Coming to the distinctions between a resulting and a constructive trust, it may be said that the former arises because of incomplete disposition by the settlor, and it arises in case of a gift or from purchases in the name of third parties; the latter arises out of fiduciary relationship between the parties and in such cases even a stranger is bound by the trust.

---

28. *Modern Equity*, 1969 Edn., Chap. 12, p. 204.
29. See *Canbank Financial Services Ltd.* v. *Custodian*, (2004) 8 SCC 355 (situation wherein it arises).
30. *Lectures on Equity*, 1969 Edn., pp. 75, 78.
31. *Lewin on Trusts*, 13th Edn., Chap. VI.

(*e*) *Varieties of Resulting Trusts.*—As has been said, such a trust is the result of an incomplete disposition or a result of unclear intention as to the disposition (which is very difficult to find[32]), whereby legal estate is vested in the donee but as to the enjoyment of the beneficial interest there is insufficient clarity and the donee is thereby excluded from it. Thus in cases (*i*) where property is conveyed upon trust but a trust is not declared[33], (*ii*) where trust-property conveyed to the trustee is not completely exhausted[34], (*iii*) where a trust fails as it offends some rule of law[35], a trustee cannot set up a plea that he should get the benefit of the trust as there is nobody else who should get its benefit. The trust-property in such cases, or so much of it as remains unspent and unexhausted, must return to the settlor or to his legal representatives if he is dead. This is so because there is an intention expressed to exclude the donee. (*iv*) In the same way, when property is given upon trust but the beneficiaries are not specified at all, or (*v*) where property is purchased by *A* and transferred to *B* without consideration[36], *B* should hold it in trust for *A* as a trust results from the circumstances of the case. It must be noted that in the above case, the intention that *B* is to be a trustee is not expressed but still *B* has to hold it as a trustee. But this rule is liable to be rebutted either by extrinsic evidence of a donor's intention in this regard in favour of the donee, or by the doctrine of advancement. In England the Law of Property Act, 1925 does not allow a resulting trust to arise under the circumstance. (*vi*) Moreover, where a trust is created for *X*'s maintenance and *X* dies without spending anything, a resulting trust for the settlor will ensue. (*vii*) Even in cases of conveyance to a stranger or in the name of the purchaser and others jointly or in other's name without the purchaser's name, a trust results to the purchaser[37], which presumption, if rebutted by evidence, the nominal purchaser will take the estate fully. (*viii*) On the contrary, a conveyance to the purchaser's wife or child stands on a different footing because here the presumption is that the purchaser wanted to benefit them. Thus the relation between the nominal purchaser and the person who advanced money for the purchase is a circumstance of great and vital importance, which raises a presumption of advancement which will rebut a presumption of the resulting trust. *Dyer case*[38] is a leading one on this point. But again the presumption of advancement is also liable to be rebutted and defeated by proper evidence as to contemporaneous and subsequent acts and declarations of the purchaser himself.

(*f*) *Modern position.*—As Hanbury exposes[39], *the principle of these cases is not that any new equity arises to create a resulting trust, but that the beneficial interest has never left the settlor.* But many difficulties may be involved. What

---

32. *Sanderson's Trust*, 3 K & J 497; *Andrew's Trust, Re, Caester* v. *Andrew*, (1905) 2 Ch 49.
33. Section 83 of Indian Trusts Act, Illustration (*a*).
34. *Ibid.*, Illustration (*c*).
35. *Ibid.*, Illustration (*d*).
36. Section 83 of Indian Trusts Act, Illustration (*a*).
37. *Ibid.*
38. *Dyer* v. *Dyer*, (1788) 2 Cox 92. Other equally important cases are *Sanderson case*, 3 K & J 497; *Andrew case*, (1905) 2 Ch 49 and *R.* v. *Denison*, (1889) 1 V & B 260.
39. *Modern Equity*, Chap. 12, pp. 204-217.

would be the position if property were settled on a widow determinable on her remarriage, and the "remarriage" were annulled? Could she claim once more—rather reclaim the property from the settlor's estate? Logic should not here be pushed further than the occasion demanded. Different branches of law rely on different policy considerations and there is no one clear ruling on the effect of a void marriage and the annulment of a voidable one.

But, at the same time, equity will refuse to lend its aid to cases wherein illegality is a part of the evidence on which a resulting trust will or will not be found to exist.[40]

The resulting trust may be invoked as a device of equitable surgery, to provide a solution in cases where unskilful draftsmanship leaves the beneficial interest wholly or partially undisposed of.[41] The principle of *unjust enrichment* is also one of the reasons why such trusts are enforced in modern times.[42]

10. PRECATORY TRUSTS

(a) Meaning and origin.—The word precatory is obtained from the Latin root *precarius* meaning entreaty and the archaic English meaning is—that which depends on the will or pleasure of another. The meaning of the word is characterised by a lack of security or stability that threatens with danger.[43]

A trust must have three certainties:[44] certainty of intention, of subject-matter and of objects, so that a trustee must be under an imperative obligation. That obligation can be inferred from the nature and manner of the gift considered as a whole. No technical words are required to create a trust and the question in each case would depend upon whether on the proper construction of the words used, the settlor or testator has manifested an intention to create a trust. However, no expressions or terms which are insufficient to express a definite intention can create a trust. For example, I desire, will, request, entreat, beseech, recommend, hope, do not doubt, etc. are ineffectual.

But, as Hanbury notes, the courts have not been consistent on such questions of construction. In the past the court of chancery seems to have been eager to catch at any phrase which could possibly be twisted into an expression of trust.[45] This created a dissatisfaction and an adverse reaction and the court had to discard that tendency (but not completely even up to this time) to discover a trust.[46]

The reason for such an inclination of the chancery court was very clear. According to the rules of ecclesiastical courts, an executor who administered an estate was entitled to keep for himself any surplus that was undisposed of. In

---

40. *Emery's Investment Trusts, Re*, 1959 Ch 410; *Chettiar* v. *Chettiar*, 1962 AC 294; *Ayerst* v. *Jenkins*, 1873 LR 16 Eq 275.
41. *Modern Equity*, Chap. 12, pp. 204-217.
42. *Ibid.*, pp. 101-2.
43. A Merrium Webster: *Webster's Seventh New Collegiate Dictionary*, p. 668
44. Lord Langdale in *Knight* v. *Knight*, (1840) 3 Bear 148.
45. Maitland: *Lectures on Equity*, p. 65.
46. See *Williams, Re*, (1897) 2 Ch 12; *Comiskey* v. *Bowring*, 1905 AC 84.

1830 however the Executors Act provided that the same should be held in trust for the next of kin.

(*b*) *A turning point.*—In the middle of the 19th century stricter construction was placed upon expressions of this type of precatory words. *Lambe* v. *Eames*[47] marks the "turning of the tide" but the process was gradual and slow.

Such a trust is considered to be a species of an express trust, as noted by Hanbury[48] and Underhill[49], because they are expressed, though in ambiguous and uncertain language.

It was after hearing many old cases being cited that James, L.J. in *Lambe case* remarked: "I could not help feeling that it was the officious kindness of the court of chancery in interpreting trusts where in many cases the father of the family never meant to create trusts, must have been a very cruel kindness indeed". *Re Adams*[50] is a leading case on the point where a trust was held to exist by the chancery court (where it was not so intended).

(*c*) *Ratio of modern decisions.*— In view of the modern decisions[51], it is not enough in such cases where precatory words are used, to say *that they do not create a trust*, because if according to reported decisions[52], a particular expression is held to create a trust, the use of that identical expression today will also create a trust. So one has to read his will or trust twice to understand what it means.[53]

11. SECRET TRUST

(*a*) *Meaning.*—In a secret trust the settlor's intention to create a trust is either expressed in disregard of the formal requirements of the statute, or if expressed with due regard to the formalities, it becomes ineffectual ultimately at law. A trust may be created by act *inter vivos*, or it may be created, declared and transferred by a will. In both the cases you cannot create a trust without observing certain formalities and more so when a trust is created by any instrument of a testamentary character that is not a valid will. In other words, in such cases one makes a testamentary disposition without observing those formalities which the law requires him to observe in case of all such dispositions. Maitland[54] has given fine examples in this connection.

(*b*) *Illustrations.*—(*i*) If I make a devise to *T*, *saying nothing of any trust*, and I then make a declaration that *T* is to hold it in trust for *X*, but this declaration is not made with the formalities required by the Wills Act, and is not communicated to and assented to by *T* during my lifetime; then on my death *T* will take the land beneficially, unburdened by any trust. (*ii*) If on the other hand,

47. (1871) LR 6 Ch App 597.
48. *Modern Equity*, p. 124.
49. *Underhill on Trusts and Trustees*, 6th Edn., p. 9.
50. *Adams and the Kensington Vestry, Re*, (1884) 27 Ch D 394.
51. *Steel's Will Trusts, Re*, 1948 Ch 603.
52. *Shelley* v. *Shelley*, 1868 LR 6 Esq 540.
53. See *Snell*, Chap. 2, p.111.
54. *Lectures on Equity*, p. 61.

I devise to T "upon trust", but do not mention what trust, and then by some paper which is not a valid will declare that the trust is for *X*, then on my death my heir-at-law, or my residuary devisee, if I have one, will be equitably entitled to the land that *I* devised to *T*. *T* cannot establish a trust and *T* cannot retain the beneficial interest for himself, for I have made clear on the face my will that I did not intend him to have it. (*iii*) *If during my lifetime I communicate to T* my intention that he should hold merely as a trustee for *X* and *T* assents to hold in that character, he is bound[55] to execute the testator's intention.[56] (*iv*) If the direction has not been communicated in my lifetime to *T* there is no trust in favour of *X*.[57]

(*c*) *Types.*—Secret trusts are of two kinds (*i*) fully secret trust (*ii*) half secret trust.

(*d*) *Definitions.*—A fully secret trust is one where *neither the existence* of a trust *nor its terms are disclosed* by the will or other instrument.[58]

A half secret trust is one where the existence of the trust is disclosed by the will or other instrument but the terms are not.[59]

(*e*) *Explanation.*—Example (*i*) illustrates a fully secret trust, while (*ii*) illustrates a half secret trust. Examples (*iii*) and (*iv*) connote a further development in the situation and its result.

It will be noticed that in both the types of trusts the property is transferred to a person and the transfers are not clothed with due formalities. This situation provides an allurement and a handle to the devisee to keep the property for himself either as an absolute owner or a beneficiary[60] on the pretext that the legal formalities for creation of a will or disposition of property as provided by the Statute of Frauds have not been observed. But equity in such cases will not allow this to happen on the principle that no man can be allowed to profit from his own fraud and the Statute of Frauds cannot be allowed to be used as a shield for covering dishonest and fraudulent intentions.

Varieties of such trusts could be seen in the case of transfer *inter vivos*, testamentary dispositions and a transfer obtained upon a fraudulent representation to the owner, secretly giving him an assurance to hold the property in trust. Such holding of property rightly binds the conscience of the holder from the point of view of equity and therefore he is converted into a trustee who can be compelled to execute the disappointed intention.[61]

Some writers consider a secret trust as a species of constructive trust[62], others consider it as a species of express trust, but Snell[63] points out that it is still

55. *Drakeford* v. *Wilks*, (1747) 3 Alk 539.
56. Cf. *Kalicharan* v. *Ramchandra*, (1903) 30 Cal 783. *See* also *Tee* v. *Ferris*, 69 Eng Rep 819.
57. *Boyes*, *Re*, (1884) 26 Ch D 531.
58. Nathan & Marshall: *A Casebook on Equity and Succession*, Chap. 10.
59. *Ibid.*
60. *Rochefoucauld* v. *Boustead*, (1897) 1 Ch 196.
61. *Scott* v. *Tyler*, (1787) 2 Dick 725; *McCormick* v. *Grogan*, (1869) 4 HL 82.
62. Nathan & Marshall: *A Casebook on Equity and Succession*, Chap. 10, p. 431.
63. *Snell's Principles of Equity*, 1969 Edn., Chap. 2, p.110.

unsettled whether it is a species of a constructive or a species of an express trust. In either view, he says, there are difficulties. A fully secret trust, however, appears to be a clear example of a constructive trust and a half secret trust within certain limits can be said to be an example of an express trust. But *Blackwell* v. *Blackwell*[64] equates the half secret with the secret trust (i.e, constructive).

(*f*) *Basis of the secret trust.*—The title of a beneficiary under a fully secret trust as well as under a half secret trust arises outside the will and is not testamentary. If that is so, Section 9 of the Wills Act, 1837 is irrelevant. The section says that "No will shall be valid unless it shall be in writing and . . . signed at the foot or end thereof by the testator, or by some other person in his presence and by his direction and such signature shall be made or acknowledged by the testator in the presence of two or more witnesses present at the same time and such witnesses shall attest and shall subscribe the will in the presence of the testator, but no form of attestation shall be necessary".

12. TRUSTS FOR VALUE

Where consideration has been paid by the beneficiaries to the settlor in order to bring a trust in existence, the resultant trust is one for value. For example, *A* creates a trust in favour of *P* if she marries *A*, marriage being a valuable consideration. Similarly, in a debtor creating a trust in favour of his creditors for payment of their dues if they reduce these debts by 5 per cent the transaction results in a trust for value. As Maitland expresses, in such cases formalities are of minor importance, since if the transaction cannot take place by way of "trust executed" it can be enforced as a contract by a court of equity.[65]

13. VOLUNTARY TRUSTS

The law as to voluntary trusts has been laid down in *Milroy* v. *Lord*[66]:

> "In order to render a voluntary settlement valid and effectual, the settlor must have done everything, which according to the nature of the property comprised in the settlement was necessary to be done in order to transfer the property and render the settlement binding upon him. He may, of course, do this by actually transferring the property to the persons for whom he intends to provide, and the proviso will then be effectual, and it will be equally effectual if he transfers the property to a trustee for the purposes of the settlement, or declares that he himself holds it in trust for those purposes. But in order to render the settlement binding, one or other of these modes must be resorted to, for there is no equity to perfect an imperfect gift."

In a voluntary trust one must note that no consideration is moving from the beneficiary to the settlor or no detriment is suffered by the beneficiary. If the trust is executed it comes into force at once and the beneficiaries can enforce the

---

64. (1929) AC 318. *See* Nathan, p. 451.
65. Citing *Lewin on Trusts*, 13th Edn., pp. 61, 66.
66. (1862) 4 De GF & J 264; Nathan & Marshall: *A Casebook on Equity and Succession*, No. 67.

same at once. If it is executory, it cannot be enforced at once, on the principle that "Equity will not aid a volunteer". In such a case the settlor must do what is necessary for him to do to bring into operation.

But even here if the agreement to create a trust was for consideration, the same can be enforced but in that case it will be trust for value. The word "consideration" includes marriage consideration, and consideration other than marriage. Even the trustees of the above parties who paid consideration can enforce such trusts.

14. ILLUSORY TRUSTS

(a) Nature.—Trusts require certainties, that of words, that of subject-matter and that of objects, so that there will be ascertainable persons who can insist upon its enforcement. If there are no beneficiaries, as is the case with purpose trusts and in "monument" and "animal cases"[67], the trustees so called will have arbitrary powers and nobody can compel them to act according to the purpose of the trust. Likewise, a trust for an abstract purpose or for purposes where the benefit to individuals is "indirect or intangible" which does not give the *cestui que trust* any *locus standi* to enforce the trust is void, being not a trust in favour of ascertainable beneficiaries. The ultimate object of such trusts is the settlor's own convenience and benefit rather than that of the beneficiaries. That is why such trusts are called illusory trusts or trusts of imperfect obligation.

(*b*) *Benefits enjoyed by a purpose trust.*—A trust is obligatory, it is not a matter of choice or discretion in the trustees; moreover, it must have a human beneficiary who can enforce it. This dictum of Sir William Grant[68] may be confusing but it is authoritative. In general, therefore, trusts for purposes are valid if they are charitable. If not, they would be a burden on society in so far as the power they concentrate and wield and the freedom enjoyed by them not only from the rules of certainty, enforceability by beneficiaries and perpetual duration, but also freedom from taxation are all a matter of envy for others. One has to note that so far as taxation is concerned there is not a halfway house with these privileges: either a purpose trust is charitable and enjoys all these privileges, or it is private and enjoys none.[69]

(*c*) *Where such trusts arise.*—There are three situations wherein such a trust arises: (*i*) trusts for advancement of purposes not charitable, (*ii*) trusts for payment of creditors, and (*iii*) trust of money voted by Parliament, for execution whereof the officers in charge are responsible to the Government and to none else. About (*i*) we have discussed before. For (*iii*) it may be said that it stands on quite a different footing from (*i*) and (*ii*), and is quite distinctive from the general principle of trust.

A trust of this nature, wherein money or property is transferred by the debtor to a trustee, upon trust for his creditors, can be enforced by the

---

67. For detailed discussion *see* Hanbury: *Modern Equity*, pp. 195-203 and 242-251.
68. *Moris* v. *Bishop of Durham*, (1804) 9 Ves Jr 399, cited in Hanbury: *Modern Equity*, p. 196.
69. *Ibid.*

beneficiaries and is irrevocable. This proposition is backed by the general rule that in the absence of a power of revocation is settlor cannot revoke even a voluntary settlement once it is completely constituted. But to this there is an important exception that such a trust might be revoked by the debtor and in that case the beneficiaries will not always have the right to compel the enforcement of the trust. It is for this reason that such trusts are called illusory. As Leach, M.R. said[70], such a deed creating a trust in favour of creditors had the same effect as if the debtor had delivered money to an agent to pay his creditors, and, before any payment made by the agent, or communication by him to the creditors, had recalled the money so delivered. Lord Brougham said in *Garrard case*[71] that it was "an arrangement (rather than a conveyance vesting a trust in *A*) by the debtor for his own personal convenience and accommodation". The creditors are not a party to it and they have not waived any right of action, they are not injured by it and therefore the debtor has complete control over it. This situation points to one plain and undisputable fact that the implementation and execution of this type of trusts depends solely upon the goodwill, honesty and integrity of the debtor where he of his own accord has created a trust. But in spite of this, the following are the circumstances wherefrom an inference of a binding and irrevocable trust in favour of creditors could be drawn.

(*d*) *When it becomes irrevocable*.—(*i*) *As against executing creditor*: Where the creditor himself is a party to execution of the deed the same will be irrevocable as against him and he will be able to enforce it.[72]

(*ii*) *As against assenting creditor*.—When a deed is made known to the creditors and they assent to it or acquiesce therein and thereby delay pressing their claims, the same is irrevocable as to them.[73] Of course, mere communication short of assent or action on it by creditors is of no consequence.

(*iii*) *After debtor's death*.—The right to revoke the trust being personal, becomes irrevocable after a debtor dies.[74]

(*iv*) *Intention to create a trust*.—If the intention of the maker is firm and final so as to make good previous lapses and breaches by him[75] in paying his debts, the trust is final and irrevocable. Here, its maker's intention is to escape the consequences of his previous breaches. In short, where due to debtor's firm intention the relationship of a trustee and *cestui que trust* is established, the trust is irrevocable.

---

70. *Acton* v. *Woodgate*, (1833) 2 My & K 492.
71. (1831) 2 Russ & M 451.
72. *Mackinnon* v. *Stewart*, (1850) 1 Sim (NS) 76.
73. *Acton case*, (1833) 2 My & K 492.
74. *Synnot* v. *Simpson*, (1854) 5 HLC 121.
75. *New Prance & G. Trustee*, (1897) 2 KB 19.

Chapter XIII

Creation of Trusts

"The doctrine of precatory trusts is a creature of Equity, by whose aid the intention of testators . . . have too frequently been defeated."

—Lopes, L.J. in *Hill* v. *H*, (1897) 1 QB 483, cited in
C. K. Allen: *Law in the Making*, p. 417

"The legal meaning and the popular meaning of the word 'charitable' are so far apart that it is necessary almost to dismiss the popular meaning from the mind as misleading before setting out to determine whether a gift is charitable within the legal meaning of the word . . . The legal significance is clearly narrower than the popular."

—*Lewin on Trusts*, 15th Edn., p. 15

"The whole law relating to charitable trusts has been well described as a 'wilderness'[1]*, and it provides one of the worst examples in our law of endless technical distinctions which have no relation to reality or common sense, and which again and again succeed only in frustrating the intentions, to the prejudice of the public interest, of benevolent minded testators. Faith and Hope are highly necessary virtues in all courts of law, but in the Chancery Division charity is the least, and not the greatest, of these."*

—C. K. Allen: *Law in the Making*, p. 419

SYNOPSIS

1. N. Bentwich: *The Wilderness of Legal Charity*, 49 LQR 520.

A. EXPRESS PRIVATE TRUST

1. GENERAL[2]

The Statute of Uses, 1535, in England, abolished uses but it failed to put a stop to a "use upon use"—an idea which in the course of time found momentum in practice, consequently resulting into a trust whereunder legal and beneficial interests in a property were dissociated. Later on, the statute itself was repealed and replaced by the Law of Property Act, 1925, and today, private trusts in England find expression in one of these forms: (*a*) bare trust, (*b*) trust for sale, and (*c*) a trust under the Settled Land Act, 1925 by means of a vesting deed and a trust instrument. In case of a settlement made by a will, the will is the trust instrument and the vesting assent is the assent of the testator's personal representatives.

A trust may be by act of parties or by operation of law. Trusts by act of parties are either express or implied and an express trust may be private or public.

2. TEXT

3. *Interpretations-clause—"trust": "author of the trust": "trustee": "beneficiary": "trust-property": "beneficial interest": "instrument of trust"*.—A "trust" is an obligation annexed to the ownership of property, and arising out of a confidence reposed in and accepted by the owner, or declared and accepted by him, for the benefit of another, or of another and the owner;

the person who reposes or declares the confidence is called the "author of the trust"; the person who accepts the confidence is called the "trustee"; the person for whose benefit the confidence is accepted is called the "beneficiary"; the subject-matter of the trust is called "trust-property" or "trust-money"; the "beneficial interest" or "interest" of the beneficiary is his right against the trustee as owner of the trust-property; and the instrument, if any, by which the trust is declared is called the "instrument of trust";

a breach of any duty imposed on a trustee, as such, by any law for the time being in force, is called a "breach of trust";

and in this Act, unless there be something repugnant in the subject or context, "registered" means registered under the law for the registration of documents for the time being in force; a person is said to have "notice" of a fact either when he actually knows that fact, or when, but for wilful abstention from inquiry or gross negligence, he would have known it, or when information of

2. *See* Chap. 10, *supra*.

the facts is given to or obtained by his agent, under the circumstances mentioned in the Indian Contract Act, 1872, Section 229; and all expressions used herein and defined in the Indian Contract Act, 1872, shall be deemed to have the meanings respectively attributed to them by that Act.

4. *Lawful purpose.*—A trust may be created for any lawful purpose. The purpose of a trust is lawful unless it is (*a*) forbidden by law, or (*b*) is of such a nature that, if permitted, it would defeat the provisions of any law, or (*c*) is fraudulent, or (*d*) involves or implies injury to the person or property of another, or (*e*) the court regards it as immoral or opposed to public policy.

Every trust of which the purpose is unlawful is void. And where a trust is created for two purposes, of which one is lawful and the other unlawful, and the two purposes cannot be separated, the whole trust is void.

Explanation.—In this section the expression "law" includes, where the trust-property is immovable and situate in a foreign country, the law of such country.

Illustrations

(*a*) *A* conveys property to *B* in trust to apply the profits to the nurture of female foundlings to be trained up as prostitutes. The trust is void.

(*b*) *A* bequeaths property to *B* in trust to employ it in carrying on a smuggling business, and out of the profits thereof to support *A*'s children. The trust is void.

(*c*) *A*, while in insolvent circumstances, transfers property to *B* in trust for *A* during his life, and after his death for *B*. *A* is declared an insolvent. The trust for *A* is invalid as against his creditors.

5. *Trust of immovable property.*—No trust in relation to immovable property is valid unless declared by a non-testamentary instrument in writing signed by the author of the trust or the trustee and registered, or by the will of the author of the trust or of the trustee.

Trust of movable property.—No trust in relation to movable property is valid unless declared as aforesaid, or unless the ownership of the property is transferred to the trustee.

These rules do not apply where they would operate so as to effectuate a fraud.

6. *Creation of trust.*—Subject to the provisions of Section 5, a trust is created when the author of the trust indicates with reasonable certainty by any words or acts (*a*) an intention on his part to create thereby a trust, (*b*) the purpose of the trust, (*c*) the beneficiary, and (*d*) the trust-property, and (unless the trust is declared by will or the author of the trust is himself to be the trustee) transfers the trust-property to the trustee.

Illustrations

(*a*) *A* bequeaths certain property to *B*, "having the fullest confidence that he will dispose of it for the benefit of" *C*. This creates a trust so far as regards *A* and *C*.

(*b*) *A* bequeaths certain property to *B* "hoping he will continue it in the family". This does not create a trust, as the beneficiary is not indicated with reasonable certainty.

(*c*) *A* bequeaths certain property to *B*, requesting him to distribute it among such members of *C*'s family as *B* should think most deserving. This does not create a trust, for the beneficiaries are not indicated with reasonable certainty.

(*d*) *A* bequeaths certain property to *B*, desiring him to divide the bulk of it among *C*'s children. This does not create a trust, for the trust-property is not indicated with sufficient certainty.

(*e*) *A* bequeaths a shop and stock-in-trade to *B*, on condition that he pays *A*'s debts and a legacy to *C*. This is a condition, not a trust for *A*'s creditors and *C*.

7. *Who may create trusts.*—A trust may be created—

(*a*) by every person competent to contract, and

(*b*) with the permission of a principal Civil Court of original jurisdiction, by or on behalf of a minor;

but subject in each case to the law for the time being in force as to the circumstances and extent in and to which the author of the trust may dispose of the trust-property.

8. *Subject of trust.*—The subject-matter of a trust must be property transferable to the beneficiary.

It must not be a merely beneficial interest under a subsisting trust.

9. *Who may be beneficiary.*—Every person capable of holding property may be a beneficiary.

Disclaimer by beneficiary.—A proposed beneficiary may renounce his interest under the trust by disclaimer addressed to the trustee, or by setting up, with notice of the trust, a claim inconsistent therewith.

10. *Who may be trustee.*—Every person capable of holding property may be a trustee; but, where the trust involves the exercise of discretion, he cannot execute it unless he is competent to contract.

No one bound to accept trust.—No one is bound to accept a trust.

Acceptance of trust.—A trust is accepted by any words or acts of the trustee indicating with reasonable certainty such acceptance.

Disclaimer of trust.—Instead of accepting a trust, the intended trustee may, within a reasonable period, disclaim it, and such disclaimer shall prevent the trust-property from vesting in him.

A disclaimer by one of two or more co-trustees vests the trust-property in the other or others, and makes him or them sole trustee or trustees from the date of the creation of the trust.

Illustrations

(*a*) *A* bequeaths certain property to *B* and *C*, his executors, as trustees for *D*. *B* and *C* prove *A*'s will. This is in itself an acceptance of the trust, and *B* and *C* hold the property in trust for *D*.

(*b*) *A* transfers certain property to *B* in trust to sell it and to pay out of the proceeds *A*'s debts. *B* accepts the trust and sells the property. So far as regards *B*, a trust of the proceeds is created for *A*'s creditors.

(*c*) *A* bequeaths a lakh of rupees to *B* upon certain trusts and appoints him his executor. *B* severs the lakh from the general assets and appropriates it to the specific purpose. This is an acceptance of the trust.

3. PARTIES TO A TRUST[3] (SECTION 3)

An express trust is the creation of the acts and declarations of the party.

The equitable ownership in property recognised by Equity in England is translated into Indian law as "an obligation annexed to the ownership of property, not amounting to an interest in the property", but an obligation which may be enforced against a transferee with notice or a gratuitous transferee.[4]

The Indian Trusts Act, 1882, Section 3, defines a trust as an obligation annexed to the ownership of property, and arising out of a confidence reposed in and accepted by the owner, or declared and accepted by him, for the benefit of another, or of another and the owner. This we have seen in Chapter XI. The section further states that the person who reposes or declares the confidence is called the "*author of the trust*"; the person so accepting the confidence is called the "*trustee*"; and the person for whose benefit the confidence is accepted is the "*beneficiary*".

For the constitution of an express private trust, there must be three parties: (*i*) the author of the trust, called a settlor, (*ii*) the trustee, and (*iii*) the *cestui que trust* or the beneficiary.

4. WHO MAY CREATE TRUST (SECTION 7)

The capacity to create a trust is, generally speaking, co-extensive with the ability to hold and dispose of a legal or equitable interest in property. As laid down by the Trusts Act, Section 7:

"A trust may be created—

(*a*) by every person competent to contract, and

(*b*) with the permission of a principal Civil Court of original jurisdiction, by or on behalf of a minor, but subject in each case to the law for the time being in force as to the circumstances and extent in and to which the author of the trust may dispose of the trust-property."

As to competency, every person *sui juris*, i.e., of full age and legal capacity and of sound mind, is competent to contract. This is laid down by Section 7(*a*). As per clause (*b*) of the section even a minor, or any person on behalf of the minor, can create a trust. Under this clause creation of a trust is subject to approval and permission of the High Court or a District Court.

5. WHO MAY BE BENEFICIARY (SECTION 9)

Every person capable of holding property may be a beneficiary (Section 9). This means that even a minor, or a child in its mother's womb (*en ventre sa mere*), may be a beneficiary. Of course, in giving property to such an unborn

3. Chap. 2 of the Indian Trusts Act, 1882.
4. *Bai Dosabai* v. *Mathurdas Govinddas*, (1980) 3 SCC 545.

person, the rule as to perpetuities (Section 14 of the Transfer of Property Act) should not be broken.

6. WHO MAY BE TRUSTEE (SECTIONS 10 AND 60)

As laid down by Section 10,

> "Every person capable of holding property may be a trustee; but where the trust involves the exercise of discretion, he cannot execute it unless he is competent to contract."

Thus a minor can be a trustee but where the question of using discretion arises he is considered not competent to become a trustee. Besides, as per Section 60 of the Act, "the beneficiary has a right (subject to the provisions of the instrument of trust) that the trust-property shall be properly protected and held and administered by proper persons, and by a proper number of such persons". The following are not proper persons within the meaning of this section:

(*a*) a person domiciled abroad;

(*b*) an alien enemy;

(*c*) a person having an interest inconsistent with that of the beneficiary;

(*d*) a person in insolvent circumstances; and

(*e*) unless the personal law of the beneficiary allows otherwise, a woman and a minor. (Section 60)

Reading Section 10 with Section 60 it is clear that though a minor can be a trustee, if the beneficiaries object to his being such and the court does not consider him to be a proper person, he cannot be one. A married woman's position is also the same. If the personal law of the beneficiary allows a minor or a woman to be a trustee, the section has no application, e.g., under Hindu and Muslim laws a minor can be a trustee. That a married woman is not a proper person as a trustee is now no longer acceptable. Keeping this in view the Law Commission of India in its seventeenth report dated 6th January, 1961, has recommended the deletion of these words.

7. WHEN IS A TRUST CREATED (SECTION 6)

Subject to the provisions of Section 5, a trust is created when the author of the trust *indicates with reasonable certainty* by any words or acts,

(*a*) an *intention* on his part to create thereby a trust,

(*b*) the *purpose* of the trust,

(*c*) the *beneficiary*, and

(*d*) the *trust-property*, and

(*e*) unless the trust is declared by will or the author of the trust is himself to be a trustee transfers the trust-property to the trustee. As laid down by the section, the following are necessary for creation of a trust:

(*i*) intention,

(*ii*) trust-property,

(*iii*) beneficiaries,

(*iv*) purpose of the trust, and

(*v*) transfer of trust-property to trustees[5] which may be a transfer *inter vivos* or under a will.

8. RULE OF THREE CERTAINTIES

In *Knight* v. *Knight*[6], Lord Langdale, M.R., has laid down that three things are necessary for the creation of a trust:

(*i*) certainty of words,

(*ii*) certainty of subject-matter, and

(*iii*) certainty of object.

(*a*) *Certainty of intention.*—Certainty being an essential requirement for the constitution of a trust, the words expressing a trust must be so used that on the whole they ought to be construed as imperative. Moreover, if on the whole it can be gathered that a trust was intended, no particular form of expression is necessary. As Snell puts it, "a trust may well be created, although there may be an absence of any expression in terms importing confidence".[7] The word 'trust' may not be used and yet a trust may exist because the court looks to the intent rather than the form.

Law on this point and other certainties is the same in England and in India[8], and Section 6 lays down this fact. If the intention to create a trust, the purpose of it, the beneficiaries to it, and the trust-property are indicated by the settlor (or trustor) along with a transfer of the trust-property to the trustee, all with reasonable certainty, there is nothing that can stop a trust from taking form. But if the "intention" in the declaration of trust is lacking[9], no trust can arise and the transferee takes the property beneficially for himself.

As Nathan[10] notes, "on the assumption that there is certainty of subject-matter[11] and of objects,[12] the court will hold a precatory trust to have been created if it considers that the precatory expressions used, studied in relation to the will as a whole, impose an obligation". In other words, where precatory words are used in a gift from which it is not easy to find out whether the donor wanted to give an absolute gift to the donee or not, or whether he intended that the donee should hold the gift in trust and dispose of it in accordance with the

5. *Kumari Chandan* v. *Longa Bai*, AIR 1998 MP 1; *see* also Ch. XIII, in A, para 2, for removal of "nominated trustees".
6. (1840) 3 Bear 148.
7. *Page* v. *Cox*, (1852) 10 Here 163.
8. *Mussorie Bank* v. *Raynor*, 4 All 500 (PC): 9 IA 70.
9. *Chambers* v. *Chambers*, (1944) 48 CWN 621 (PC): AIR 1944 PC 78.
10. *Nathan's Equity through the Cases*, Chap. 6, p. 219.
11. *Wynne* v. *Hawkins*, (1782) 1 Bro CC 179; *Fox* v. *Fox*, (1859) 27 Bear 301, *per* Romilly, M.R.
12. *Morice* v. *Bishop of Durham*, (1805) 10 Ves 522; *Nathan's Equity Through the Cases,* No. 52.

instructions contained in the will, the court will find out an answer to this from an examination of the whole of the instrument.[13]

(*b*) *Certainty of subject-matter* (*Section 8*).—The subject-matter of a trust must be property transferable to the beneficiary.

Property of any kind, movable or immovable, that is legally transferable can be the subject of trust. But a mere beneficial interest under a subsisting trust (which can be settled in trust in England) cannot be a subject-matter of trust in India. This is a departure from English law as in India equitable interest is not recognised. It therefore follows that a trust of "mere expectancy" which is not transferable according to Section 6 of the Transfer of Property Act, is not possible in India. Similarly, a chance of being an heir apparent to succeed a contingent interest of a reversioner, a public office, pay of a public office, pension of a government servant or any other interest restricted to enjoyment personally, cannot be a subject of trust.

In England, 'any' property which is alienable may be a subject-matter of trust unless public policy or the statute prohibits its transfer. By 'any' is meant, all property which is legal, equitable, real, personal, at home or abroad, in possession or action, whether a remainder, a reversion or an expectancy.[14]

For creation of trust the owner of the property must fully divest himself of the property. In a recent case[15] the owner of the property executed a trust expressing a desire to construct a Dharmshala in order to perpetuate the memories of himself and his family members. The executant however, did not divest herself of rights of the property and transferred the same to the trustees. The court decided that the document cannot be said to have created a trust in present.

The subject-matter of a trust must be certain or the "bulk"[16] of property bound by the trust must be definite; if not, the trust cannot arise. The subject-matter falls under two heads: (*a*) the trust-property, and (*b*) the beneficial interest. Thus if the settlor leaves all his houses to trustees but keeps it uncertain as to which of the houses or how many each beneficiary is to have, the trust fails and there will be a resulting trust for the settlor.[17] Similarly, if some part of the interest for the beneficiaries is certain while some other part is uncertain, that uncertain part fails and the principal beneficiary takes the whole.[18] Out of the three kinds of uncertainties in this regard, as noted by Snell[19], the first may be cured by applying the maxim "equality is equity", the second kind of uncertainty where the settlor gives the trustee a discretion to apply the trust fund among a certain class of persons is no uncertainty, while the third kind of uncertainty arises where one beneficiary is given the whole of the beneficial

13. For further details and modern trend *see* Chap. 12, topic 10, *supra*.
14. Underhill: *Law of Trusts and Trustees*.
15. *Kumari Chandan* v. *Longa Bai*, AIR 1998 MP 1.
16. *Palmer* v. *Simmonds*, (1854) 2 Drew 221.
17. *Doyle* v. *A.G.*, (1735) 2 Eq Ca Abr 194.
18. *Curtis* v. *Rippon*, (1820) 21 RR 327.
19. *Snell's Principles of Equity*, 27th Edn., p. 113.

interest and others an uncertain part of it; the direction for the uncertain part fails and the principal beneficiary takes the whole.[20] In *Sprange case*[20], the wife bewilled her husband, Thomas Sprange to £ 300 lying in joint stock annuities, for his sole use and at his death "the *remaining part of what is left, that he does not want for his own wants and use*", to be divided between 3 other beneficiaries. In the result Thomas was entitled to £ 300 absolutely.

(*c*) *Certainty of object.*—Certainty of object or the beneficiaries is also necessary for the validity of a trust, except where the trust is for the benefit of "charity". A non-charitable trust, as laid down by Grant, M.R., in *Morice case*[21], therefore fails if the object is uncertain. In that case Grant, M.R. said that "there can be no trust over the exercise of which this court will not assume a control: *for an uncontrollable power of disposition would be ownership and no trust.* If there be a clear trust but for uncertain objects, the property that is the subject of the trust is undisposed of and the benefit of such trust must result to those to whom the law gives the ownership in default of disposition by the former owner. But this doctrine does not hold good with regard to trusts for charity. *Every other trust must have a definite object*".

Where a trust fails for uncertainty of object, the donee does not and cannot take for his own benefit, but holds for the settlor or his legal representatives as a trustee, *i.e.*, a resulting trust arises here.[22]

Summarising the situation regarding the three certainties, Lord Eldon has said that the trust must be of such a nature that it can be under the control and review of the court if there is maladministration. And unless the subject and objects can be ascertained upon principles familiar in other cases, the court can neither reform maladministration nor direct due administration.[23]

(*d*) *Illustrations.*—(1) In *Bhaidas* v. *Bai Gulam*[24], a Hindu testator bequeathed estate to his wife as a sole executrix, constituting her the owner and directed that *whatever remained* of the property after her death should go to the testator's two daughters in such a manner *as she*, the executrix, *may like*. The trust for daughters failed for uncertainty of the subject-matter as "whatever may remain" was uncertain. This case is similar to *Sprange case*[25].

(2) In *Allahabad Bank Ltd.* v. *CIT*[26], the appellant-bank purported to create a trust for payment of pensions to its staff members. By a deed it transferred a fund to three persons, named as "present trustees". The deed provided for applying the trust fund income to the payment of such pensions and in such manner as the bank or its authorised officer shall direct. The bank retained the

---

20. *Curtis* v. *Rippon*, (1820) 21 ER 327; *Parnall* v. *Parnall*, (1878) 9 Ch D 96; *Sprange* v. *Bernard*, (1789) 2 Bro CC 585; *Nathan's Equity Through the Cases*, No. 51.
21. *Morice* v. *Bishop of Durham*, (1805) 10 Ves 522.
22. *See* also *Boyes, Re*, (1884) 26 Ch D 531.
23. *Morice* v. *Bishop of Durham*, (1805) 10 Ves 522; *Chhotabhai* v. *Gnanchandra*, AIR 1935 PC 97.
24. (1921) 46 Bom 153 (PC): AIR 1922 PC 193.
25. *Sprange* v. *Bernard*, (1789) 2 Bro CC 585.
26. AIR 1953 SC 476: 1954 SCR 195.

sole discretion of granting, withdrawing, modifying or determining the pension. It was held that since it was not at all obligatory upon the bank to grant any pensions or to continue them, the deed of trust did not constitute a trust. This was so because a trust is obligatory. Moreover, the beneficiaries were not and could not be indicated with reasonable certainty, and hence the deed was void for uncertainty.

(3) Where *X* bequeaths certain property upon *Y*, "having the fullest confidence that he will dispose it of, for *Z*'s benefit", a valid trust is created.

(4) Where *X* bequeaths to *Y* certain property requesting him to hold and distribute it among such members of *Z*'s family as *Y* should think most deserving, no valid trust arises as the beneficiaries are not created with reasonable certainty.

(5) A shop and its stock-in-trade are conveyed to *P* on condition that *P* is to pay *A*'s debts and to grant a legacy to *Q*. This is not a trust but a condition.

(6) *Ogden*[27], *In Re*, a testator bequeathed a portion of his residuary estate to *P*, to be distributed by him among such political federations or bodies in the United Kingdom, having as their objects or one of their objects the promotion of liberal principles in politics, as he (*P*) shall in his absolute discretion select and in such shares and proportions as he shall in the like discretion think fit. As evidence was given that *P* could enlist all such institutions which qualified, the gift was upheld.[28] The onus is on those who allege the validity of the trust to show that its objects are certain.

(*e*) *Lawful purpose and transfer of trust-property*.—Section 6 of the Trusts Act, 1882 adds two further essentials to the abovesaid three certainties. They are:

(*iv*) the purpose of the trust, and

(*v*) the transfer of the trust-property to the trustee.[29]

If the trust is to be operative the purpose of the trust, the ultimate intention of creating the trust, must be lawful. If it is otherwise, the trust cannot operate though it exists. This is laid down by Section 4.

Lawful purpose.—A trust may be created for any lawful purpose. The purpose of a trust is lawful unless it is

(*a*) forbidden by law, or

(*b*) is of such a nature that, if permitted, it would defeat the provisions of any law, or

(*c*) is fraudulent, or

(*d*) involves or implies injury to the person or property of another, or

(*e*) the court regards it as immoral or opposed to public policy.

---

27. 1933 Ch 678; *Kirloy* v. *Parker*, 1966 IR 309.
28. *Ogden, Re*, was followed in *I.R.C.* v. *Broadway Cottage Trust*, 1955 Ch 20.
29. See *Kumari Chandan* v. *Longa Bai*, AIR 1998 MP 1, *supra*.

The above two essentials are by way of abundant caution, as their absence does not stop a trust from coming into existence, or does not make the trust uncertain. It is for those who want to avoid a trust to prove its unlawfulness. Moreover, the transfer of property is a necessary element but not so in all cases because where the author himself is a trustee, the question of transfer need not arise; it is a question of change of status, i.e., from an absolute owner to a trustee. Similarly, where a trust is incorporated into an instrument of will it takes effect after the death of the settlor. The trust-property in such a case is automatically vested in the trustee on a settlor's death and the settlor is quite unable (because he is already dead) here to transfer the property to the trustee. It is by operation of law that property is transferred in such a case. A mere agreement to create a trust or an expression of intention to create a trust, as when I put a cheque of Rs 10,000 into my son's hand saying that I give it to him and then take it back from him I express an intention to give it to him after my death, does not create a valid trust.[30]

Suppose the property is not transferred. Should a trust fail in such a case? The answer is that in case of a voluntary trust, it fails because there is no transfer but in case of a trust for value it will not fail because consideration has been provided for creating a trust and the settlor in such cases will be compelled to do so. If the trustees are not named they shall have to be named. On the principle that "equity will not allow a trust to fail for want of a trustee", the settlor will be compelled.

So far as the purpose is concerned, a trust which postpones the enjoyment of the property for an indefinite period or prevents its alienation forever, being in breach of the rule against perpetuities, is void. A trust seeking to alter the ordinary law of descent or succession or violating the rules for valid disposition of property (Section 14, Transfer of Property Act; Section 114, Indian Succession Act) is void. A trust to defraud creditors, a trust in restraint of marriage or for future illegitimate children are in the same way void being against public policy. But a trust for an illegitimate child in existence is valid.[31] If a trust is directed to more than one purpose, all of which are unlawful, the trust is void, but if some of them only are unlawful, and the unlawful can be severed from the lawful, the lawful purpose will take effect.

Chambers v. *Chambers*[32] must be considered to be a representative decision as it deals with most of the certainties. Here *C*, a businessman (i.e., company), transferred a certain amount by book entries to his wife. His wife was informed that the amount so transferred constituted a gift and she could not draw more than10 per cent of the capital in any one year. On *C* transferring a certain amount from his wife's gift account subsequently, it was held that there was no trust for three reasons:

(*i*) there was no declaration of trust by *C*;

30. *Jones* v. *Lock*, (1865) 1 Ch App 25.
31. *Blodwell* v. *Edwards*, (1596) 78 ER 758.
32. (1944) 48 CWN 621 (PC): AIR 1944 PC 78.

(*ii*) there was no parting with the property by *C*; and

(*iii*) there were no ascertained funds for the trust.

9. NECESSARY FORMALITIES FOR CREATION OF A TRUST (SECTION 5)

In England, as Maitland expresses, a trust may be created without deed, without writing, without formalities of any kind, by a mere word of mouth; and no particular words are necessary. But this was the position before the Statute of Frauds, 1677. After the enactment of this statute, a trust must be 'manifested and proved' by some writing and signed by the author; or else they shall be utterly void. A trust may be *inter vivos*, which takes effect immediately, or it may be ambulatory (which can be revoked) as it is expressed in a will, a testamentary instrument validly executed.

In India, Section 5 lays down the formalities as under:

> "5. *Trust of Immovable Property*.—No trust in relation to immovable property is valid unless declared by a non-testamentary instrument in writing signed by the author of the trust or the trustee and registered, or by the will of the author of the trust or of the trustee."

Trust of Movable Property.—No trust in relation to movable property is valid unless declared as aforesaid, or unless the ownership of the property is transferred to the trustee. These rules do not apply where they would operate so as to effectuate a fraud.

As laid down by the section, the immovable property must be transferred; mere vesting is not enough. Movables must actually be transferred. Registration of a will as contemplated by the first part of Section 5 is compulsory. A trust when declared in a will must comply with the provisions of the Indian Succession Act, 1925, except where the testator is a Mahomedan. An uncertain trust and a trust void for want of registration may be made prefect by 12 years' adverse possession by the trustees and action against them for remedy is barred thereafter.[33]

A mere beneficial interest cannot be a subject-matter of trust. Here the Indian law departs from the English law whereunder a beneficial interest may also be subjected to a trust. The trust-property may be in actual possession of the settlor or it may be vested in him which he will obtain on the death of a third person, but in no case can an expectancy be made a subject-matter of trust.

As provided by the last para of Section 5, "these rules do not apply where they would operate so as to effectuate a fraud", property obtained by fraudulent representation will be held in trust. In one Bombay case, a father executed a gift deed in his daughters' favour, who by an unregistered writing stipulated with the father that they would be bound to restore the property at any time the father liked to revoke the gift. Held, that the daughters held as trustees the gift of the father and the writing though unregistered was admissible in evidence to show that a fraud was effectuated and Section 5 would not apply to effectuate a fraud.

33. *Hemchand* v. *Pyarelal*, (1942) 47 CWN 46(PC): AIR 1942 PC 64.

10. EXECUTED AND EXECUTORY TRUST

An express trust may be (*i*) executed, or (*ii*) executory. Plainly speaking, no technical words are necessary to create a trust. But words have their own meaning and technical words have technical meanings. When in a trust technical words are used, they will be understood in their technical sense. This brings us to the distinction between executed and executory trusts.

An executed trust, as the very word and its tense connote, is a trust wherein everything that was required to be done for bringing the trust into existence has been done and completed by the settlor. He has fully and finally declared a trust by the instrument laying down with reasonable certainty all that was necessary. In such cases he can be said *to be his own conveyancer.*

But a trust is executory where something remains to be done by the settlor to complete it. Where, therefore, a declaration of trust takes the form of an agreement or direction for the subsequent execution of a proper trust instrument, the trust so declared is an executory trust (Strahan). It arises mainly in marriage articles and in wills.

Where *A* conveys property to *X* to hold in trust for *B* and declares a trust, transferring the property to *X*, laying down *B*'s interest, the trust is a fully operative, express and executed trust taking effect immediately. For such trusts, when an occasion for interpretation arises, the words therein are strictly and technically construed on the principle "equity follows the law". When executory trusts are interpreted, the language of the will is subordinated to the intent of the settlor and will be construed favourably so as to strengthen the intention of the settlor on the ground that "the sketch being a sketch, equity will not catch at technical phrases and defeat what is believed to be his (settlor's) intention". (Maitland)

The difference between the two may be expressed thus:

(*a*) A trust is executed when nothing is left to be done, whereas something remains to be done in an executory trust.

(*b*) The former arises where the settlor has been his own conveyancer, the latter arises chiefly in marriage articles and in wills.

(*c*) In the former, while interpreting it the language will be strictly construed, because 'equity follows the law'; in the latter, the language will be subordinated to the intent of the settlor on the principle that "equity looks to the intent rather than to the form".[34]

11. COMPLETELY AND INCOMPLETELY CONSTITUTED TRUST

A trust if incomplete cannot be termed a trust. The expression therefore connotes not a category of trusts but rather a rule for distinguishing what is a trust from something that is not so. The nomenclature is therefore misleading.

To be valid as a trust, the settlor must vest the property in the trustee, and a mere declaration without vesting is of no consequence. Where land is to be

---

34. In *Glenorchy* v. *Bosville*, (1733) Cas Talb 3, this distinction is brought out.

given in trust there must be a written declaration to that effect. So, where property is vested in a trustee, it will be a completely constituted trust, otherwise it will be an incompletely constituted trust. If a declaration of vesting is backed by valuable consideration it will be enforced by equity as contrary to convey property because, "equity looks on that as done which ought to be done".[35] Such promises are construed by equity (if backed by valuable consideration) as a declaration of trust. If not backed by consideration such a promise amounts to a voluntary promise which cannot be enforced, because equity will not assist a volunteer. If the subject-matter of a trust is a legal estate the settlor must do all that the law requires him to transfer it to the trustee to effectuate a trust. In other words, if the subject-matter is freehold property it should be conveyed by a deed of grant, if it is leasehold there should be a deed of assignment, if it is movable property there must be a deed of a delivery thereof and if it is registered shares a proper form of transfer must be used. This boils down to the fact that an imperfect gift is no declaration of trust.[36] As was stated by Lord Eldon, L.C., in *Ellison case*[37], if you want the assistance of the court to constitute you *cestui que trust*, and the instrument is voluntary, you shall not have the assistance because there is no equity to perfect an imperfect gift[38], but if there is a complete transfer of property, though it is voluntary, yet the legal conveyance being effectually made the equitable interest will be enforced by the court.

12. DISCRETIONARY TRUST

It is a trust wherein trustees are invested with a discretion as to how much benefit is to be given to a beneficiary. The discretion vested in trustees must be exercised by them so that as and when the income from the trust is available they will exercise the discretionary powers of distribution of the benefit, and the beneficiary has therefore no more than a hope that the discretion will be exercised in his favour. Before 1969, in England such trusts were used as tools for mitigating the burden of estate duty but now the Finance Act, 1969 has minimised such advantages by taxing the actual benefits received. In such a trust, since all possible *sui juris* beneficiaries as a whole are between them entitled to the whole of the income, they by joining together can dispose of the whole of the income.[39]

13. PROTECTIVE TRUST

A protective trust combines in itself the advantages of determinable interests with those of discretionary interests. Where an interest of a principal beneficiary has been determined on bankruptcy, etc., a discretionary trust of his part of the income (benefit) arises in his favour or in favour of any other person entitled to the same on his death. During the period such a trust subsists he will not receive the income or any part of it, and the disbursement thereof will be

35. *Ellison* v. *Ellison*, (1802) 6 Ves 656.
36. *Richards* v. *Delbridge*, (1874) LR 18 Eq 11.
37. *Ellison* v. *Ellison*, (1802) 6 Ves 656.
38. *Milroy* v. *Lord*, (1862) 31 Ch 798.
39. *Smith, Re, Public Trustee* v. *Aspinall*, 1928 Ch 915.

within the absolute discretion of the trustees (*see* Section 33 of the Trustees Act, 1925 in England). On the extinguishment of the principal beneficiary's right, the discretionary trust comes to an end and the determinable interest also comes to an end.

A protective trust, as explained by Nathan[40], contains three parts as per Section 33:

(*a*) a life or lesser interest determinable on certain events;

(*b*) a forfeiture clause specifying the determining events;

(*c*) a discretionary trust which arises after forfeiture.

As to when a forfeiture occurs is a matter of construction[41] of the instrument by the court, but the effect of the forfeiture clause is to determine the principal beneficiary's life interest and to bring a discretionary trust into operation. In *Gourju case*[42], "trading with enemy" brought forfeiture, but a discretionary trust may arise independently[43] of Section 33 of the Trustees Act, 1925.

14. PURPOSE TRUST

In the previous chapter we have come across such trusts under the caption "trusts of perfect and imperfect obligations". According to Maitland, private trusts fall into two categories:[44]

(*a*) wherein a trustee is to exercise his rights on behalf of some other person, and

(*b*) wherein a trustee is to exercise his rights for the accomplishment of a particular purpose.

This second class of trust is known as a purpose trust. Since there is no *cestui que trust* here who can enforce the trust, it is sometimes called a trust of imperfect obligation. But then, such a trust is valid if the purpose be legal. Such a trust is enforced not by any person but by the Attorney-General. As Maitland says, if there be any *cestui que trust*, it is the public. But one has to note that charitable trusts are not trusts of imperfect obligation, and moreover they differ from a purpose trust. A purpose trust is the genus and a charitable trust is its species. We may also say that a purpose trust is for some definite and lawful purpose other than a charitable purpose.

(*a*) *Distinction from a Charitable Trust.*—A purpose trust can be distinguished from a charitable[45] trust in following respects:

(*i*) The former though valid cannot be enforced by anyone[46], whereas the latter can be enforced in the Attorney-General's name.

---

40. Nathan's *Equity Through the Cases*, pp. 310-319.
41. *Hall, Re, Public Trustee* v. *Montgomery*, 1944 Ch 46.
42. 1943 Ch 24.
43. *Smith, Re, Public Trustee* v. *Aspinall*, 1928 Ch 915.
44. Maitland: *Lectures on Equity*, pp. 50-53.
45. *Cf.* Hanbury: *Modern Equity*, pp. 195-203, 252; *Snell's Principles of Equity*, p. 142.
46. *Dean, Re*, (1889) 41 Ch D 552 (a trust for hounds and horses).

(*ii*) The former is bound to fail for uncertainty of object, while the latter will not so fail and the cy pres doctrine will come to its help.

(*iii*) The former if violates the rule against perpetuity will fail, the latter is not so affected.

(*iv*) A charitable trust is a purpose trust, but a purpose trust is not a charitable trust.

(*v*) A charitable trust enjoys complete tax concession, whereas a non-charitable purpose trust does not.[47]

Compared to a purpose trust, the position of a charitable trust is far more favourable.

(*b*) *A Purpose Trust or a 'Power Trust'*[48].—Power without accountability is the second name of tyranny. And in this brief resume we shall see ways to curb it because it results into a surreptitiously looming danger eroding the economic, social and political life of a country.

A purpose trust is non-charitable and breaks the rule of three certainties. One does not know who the beneficiaries are and the trust cannot be enforced. As has been said, "a purpose trust, even of the limited kind now allowed, cannot be upheld for an indefinite or perpetual period".[49] As Snell has noted, this is an unfortunate 'concession to human weakness or sentiment' and 'an invalid trust cannot be tortured into a valid power'.[50] The reasons for this are more than clear. Such trusts arise under a guise of unincorporated associations, which are not persons and therefore cannot be beneficiaries. In *Macaulay* v. *O'Donnel*[51], its validity was attempted to be established, but with no sufficient satisfaction on all points. Though in that very year, in *Re Price case*[52], a trust the purpose whereof was specific and non-charitable and did not hurt the rule of perpetuities, was held to be a valid one, in 1959, in *Leaby case*[53], it was ruled that such a trust was invalid as it lacked human beneficiaries, and the fact that the 'property is spent' does not provide an answer to the basic uncertainty of beneficiaries.

Such trusts are therefore closer to power, and they must be construed as such. If done so, many or most of the problems would disappear, because 'no one enforces a power'.

Whether a purpose trust should be upheld is a teasing question requiring urgent solution.

In view of the arguments in favour of and against the problem, it is submitted that though such a trust is not qualified as a chartiable trust, it serves society and the community. To such trusts are granted certain tax concessions in

---

47. *Cf.* Hanbury: *Modern Equity*, p. 200.
48. *Ibid.*, p. 197.
49. *Ibid.*
50. *Snell's Principles of Equity*, p. 100.
51. 1943 Ch 435.
52. 1943 Ch 422.
53. *Leaby* v. *A.G.*, 1959 AC 457.

western countries. As this position is unwillingly tolerated its result would be 'out of harmony with the principles of our law'. Though the trust breaks certain rules as to private trust, it serves the community and therefore the issue of fiscal privileges enjoyed by it cannot be joined with arguments not upholding it.

If the above arguments in favour of upholding the purpose, non-charitable, rule-breaker trusts are accepted, the immediate consequence would be to create a new category of trust. But this cannot be allowed and if allowed it would be a premium to useless and capricious trust. In *Brown case*[54], the purpose of a trust was "to block up almost all the rooms of the house and coach-house for 20 years and subject thereto, to a devisee in fee". This was held to be void and the 'sealing' of the rooms was "unsealed".

A safer way between the two extremes would be to impose certain limitations upon them so that they would not be termed and accepted as trust, but as power. Friedmann has tried to show that such trusts are like "legal cloaks of corporated power"[55], wielding enormous and uncontrollable power without the courts having power to reform or review their administration[56] or maladministration. They spell and exercise by their enormous wealth and specialised knowledge sometimes a disastrous influence on the economic, social and political life of the community and slip into a disservice to society, a purpose never intended by the trust. Such trusts may not spend money and nobody can force them to do so, and when they spend money nobody can check them as to how and to what end they are to do so. For these reasons, they should not be upheld.

Hanbury[57] has shown that there should be two limitations on such power trusts (they cannot be accepted as purpose trusts). One is the limitation as to time within which they have to achieve the purpose, and the second the limitation as to spending the amount completely at the end of the time-limit. If any sum remains unspent it should revert to the settlor or his successors. Such limitations have been imposed in Canada and other countries should not lag behind in following suit.

---

54. *Brown* v. *Burdett*, (1882) 21 Ch D 667.
55. *Law in a Changing Society*, Chap. 9, p. 231.
56. As the cover story of *India Today*, a fortnightly, of October 1981, pages 16 to 28 goes, the recent Rs 30 crores (original plan for Rs 125 crores) A.R. Antulay's "trading in trusts" scandal is a fitting illustration of acquisition of "power without accountability" through trust. It is the biggest political scandal which dwarfed the souvenir scandal of 1977 and which is qualitatively different from the comparatively minor scandals of two union ministers, T.T. Krishnamachari and K.D. Malaviya. "Will a splash of perfume remove the stench emanating from a rotten political system where power has been conditioned to grow not out of the people but out of filthy lucre? This has not only shook the foundations of the social, political and economic life of the country but has also brought down to the dust the established moral values of the Indian society, by shouting from the rooftops shamelessly that "if you are technically correct, you are morally correct too". (Also see *Jana Satta*, *Gujarat Samachar*, *Times of India*, dailies, dated 2-9-1981); see *R.S. Nayak* v. *A.R. Antulay*, (1986) 2 SCC 716: 1986 SCC (Cri) 256.
57. *Modern Equity*, pp. 202-203.

For secret trust, precatory trust and trust in favour of creditors (all of them being variations of a private express trust), *see* Chapter 12, *supra*.

B. EXPRESS PUBLIC (OR CHARITABLE) TRUST

1. GENERAL

Charitable trusts are purpose trusts and their assets are vested in trustees or a corporation. To obtain the status of a charitable trust what is important is the nature of purpose only. Moreover, it is the way in which the finite number of ascertainable persons, i.e., the beneficiaries, are benefited that makes such a trust charitable.[58]

The distinction between a private and a public trust is that whereas in the former the beneficiaries are specific individuals, in the latter they are the general public or a class thereof. While in the former the beneficiaries are persons who are ascertained or capable of being ascertained, in the latter they constitute a body which is incapable of ascertainment.[59]

In *Cambay Municipality case*[60], a dharmashala was constructed on municipal land with funds provided by a private citizen. This cannot be said to be a public trust since it lacks the ingredients of a public trust. The case lays down test of a public trust.[61]

Since charitable trusts are immune from the validity of the general rule regarding trusts, their definition becomes far more vital and important. Their object is never capable of complete achievement and they are immune from the rule of perpetuities and from taxation. A gift, if it is so worded that it does not commence within the perpetuity period, is caught by the rule of perpetuity unless saved by the "wait and see" provisions of the Act[62] in England. Similarly when a gift to charity is shifted from a charity to an individual, it is caught by the rule but a gift from one charity to another is outside it. A charitable trust will not fail for uncertainty and the reason is that when the donor "has confined himself to charity", the absence of selection of a particular charitable object will not render a trust uncertain because the scheme of the donor will be carried out even by applying the cy pres doctrine. At one time equity leaned in favour of such a trust but since times have changed, it has not remained now a matter of pride. As the idea of such a trust was abused in 1601, a Statute of Charitable

---

58. *Sarisbrick, Re*, 1951 Ch 622.
59. *Deokinandan* v. *Murlidhar*, AIR 1957 SC 133 quoted in *Dolagovinda Sethi* v. *Kanika Museum*, AIR 1989 Ori 60; also see *Jai Narayan Jai Govind* v. *Controller of Estate Duty*, (1963) 49 ITR (Ed) 105; *State of Madras* v. *Subramaniaswami*, (1961) 74 Mad LW 388; *Sri Ram* v. *Prabhu Dayal*, AIR 1972 Raj 180.
60. *Cambay Municipality* v. *Ratilal Ambalal Reshamwala*, 1995 Supp (2) SCC 591. *see* also *Seth Chand Ratan* v. *Pandit Durga Prasad*, (2003) 5 SCC 399; *Shankar Ramachandra Abhyankar* v. *Krishnaji Dattatreya Bapat*, (1969) 2 SCC 74.
61. *Mulla Gulam Ali & Safiabai D. Trust* v. *Deelip Kumar & Co.*, (2003) 11 SCC 772 (Character of public trust is not taken away by the fact control of its administration is vested in a particular group of people. In case of that administration remedy lies in Section 92 of CPC, 1908.)
62. Perpetuities and Accumulations Act, 1964, in England.

Uses was passed, the preamble whereof gave instances of charitable objects and since then it has remained a guiding factor till it was struck off from the statute-book by the Charities Act, 1960. Before that, in *CIT* v. *Pemsel*[63], Lord Macnaughten laid down a classification of objects which has won wide acceptance.[64] Still, however, no satisfactory and comprehensive definition of charity has been laid down either by the Legislature or by judicial utterance.[65] But it must be said that a charitable trust is charitable as well as public.

Since public charitable trusts receive a favoured treatment[66] a question came for decision in *M.P. Shanti Verma Jain case*[67], whether assessee trust was a public trust or a private trust. The trust deed narrated philosophy of Jain Dharma. The object of the trust was to propagate Jain Dharma and help its followers. Medical aid was also to be rendered to persons devoted to Jain Dharma. Non-Jains were to be given medical aid only if families managing the trust showed sympathy. The trust in question was thus set up to propagate Jain religion and serve its followers. Consequently its income was not exempted. The trust was not a public charitable trust.

Courts' general parens patriae jurisdiction over Religious and Charitable trusts.—In *Executive Officer, Ardhanareswarar Temple* v. *R. Sathyamoorthy*[68], a question arose as to when the "Executors and Trustees" under the will cease to be executors and become trustees and eligible for assessment as trustees. The answer to this query depends on the construction of the will as to when the testator intended the trust to come into being.

In this case the will contained a provision that the executors and trustees should pay off the debts of the author of the will, pay off funeral and other expenses connected with it, pay off government dues and after obtaining letters of administration give away property bequeathed to relevant persons. Till this period they should administer the property and the residue of the property should be used for the charitable purpose shown in the will. In this situation the trust comes into being only when all the instructions given by the author of the trust have been carried out. After this whatever property remains with the trustees, forms the corpus of the trust. All the instruction were executed upto February 1964. The court observed that from the date of death or from the date of probate the executors and trustees did not hold the property in trust and during 1964-1965 they did not get any income from the trust. Consequently they are not liable to assessment of income tax. The court further observed:

> "If one keeps in view the provisions of Sections 2(13), 18, 20, 29, 36 and 66 of the Bombay Public Trusts Act, 1950, it would appear that under

63. Known as *Pemsel case*, 1891 AC 531.
64. Hanbury: *Modern Equity*, Chap. 15, pp. 252-255.
65. *Snell's Principles of Equity*, Chap. 3, p. 142.
66. *Agastyar Trust* v. *Commr. & Secy. to Govt. Revenue Department*, (2005) 3 SCC 516, entitled to (exemption) but see *CIT* v. *Thanthi Trust*, (2001) 2 SCC 707 applicability of S. 13(1)(*bb*), Income Tax Act, *CIT* v. *Programme for Community Organisation*, (2001) 248 ITR 1.
67. *State of Kerala* v. *M.P. Shanti Verma Jain*, (1998) 5 SCC 63: AIR 1998 SC 2208.
68. (1999) 3 SCC 115: AIR 1999 SC 958.

the will the testator was very particular that all properties that she had not bequeathed specifically under the will should be converted into cash and the money so collected could be donated for charitable purposes. This direction in the will is of great significance and understanding as to what stage the trust comes into existence. It all depends on the construction of the will as to when the testator desired the trust to come into being. For that one has also to see when the functions of the executors administering the estate of the testator come to an end. Keeping in view Sections 302, 317 and 366 of the Succession Act, 1925, and examining the said clause 20 of the will together with other clauses one finds that the trust was to come into being only after funeral and other expenses were met, legatees were paid and properties were converted into cash by the executors and trustees; that administration of the estate would come to an end and all the amount thus lying with the executors and trustees would form the corpus of the trust. Functions of the trustees and executors as imposed upon them did not come to an end till February 1964 and therefore cannot be said that there was any trust created under the will till that time. Section 168(3) of the Act makes it clear that the executors will continue to be assessed until the estate is distributed among the beneficiaries according to their several interests. Thus courts have a general *parens patriae* jurisdiction over religious and charitable trusts".[69]

2. DEFINITION

No satisfactory and comprehensive definition of charity has been possible so far,[70] for, a rigid definition would be too restrictive and would not include in itself a number of desirable objects. The courts are oscillating between two extreme types of cases wherein either a liberal interpretation of "charity" is made, so that such trusts may not become void, or it is strictly construed, so that no tax relief would be available to trusts which are not really charitable. Its popular meaning differs from its legal meaning. An object which is charitable in a popular sense but which benefits individuals only is not therefore charitable in the legal sense, It is therefore necessary to describe it rather than to definite it. For this purpose recourse may be made to the House of Lords' decision in *CIT* v. *Pemsel*[71].

Land was conveyed in 1813 to trustees on trust to apply a proportion of the rents and profits for missionary establishments commonly known as the Moravian Church of which Pemsel was the treasurer. It was claimed that the gift was for "charitable purposes" under the Income Tax Act, 1842 and hence exempt from income tax. Held, since the trust contemplated purposes which had no relation to the relief of poverty, the purposes were not charitable within the meaning of the 1842 Act and thus income tax was payable. (This case is noteworthy chiefly because of the definition of charity given by Lord

---

69. *Ibid*, affirming *K.R. Patel* v. *CIT*, (1999) 7 SCC 26: (1999) 239 ITR 738.
70. Lord Evershed in *Cole, Re*, 1958 Ch 877.
71. Known as *Pemsel case*, 1891 AC 531.

Macnaghten. "How far then, it may be does the popular meaning of the word 'charity' correspond with its legal meaning? 'Charity' in the legal sense comprises four principal divisions: trusts for the relief of poverty; trusts for the advancement of education; trusts for the advancement of religion; and trusts for other purposes beneficial to the community, not falling under any of the preceding heads.")

3. REQUIREMENTS OF A CHARITABLE TRUST

A trust to be charitable must satisfy the following three requirements:

(*a*) charitable nature,

(*b*) public benefit,

(*c*) exclusively charitable.

Moreover, as laid down in a *Bombay case*[72], there must be in such a trust the following certainties:

(*a*) a declaration of trust binding the settlor,

(*b*) the settlor must set apart certain properties and must deprive himself of the ownership thereof, and

(*c*) there must be a statement of objects for which property is to be held.[73]

4. CHARITABLE OBJECTS CLASSIFIED

The best classification of charitable objects is found in *Pemsel case*[74], given by Lord Macnaghten, which comprises four principal divisions:

(*i*) trusts for the relief of *poverty*;

(*ii*) trusts for the advancement of *education*;

(*iii*) trusts for the advancement of *religion*; and

(*iv*) trusts for other purposes *beneficial to the community* not falling under any of the preceding heads.

5. WHAT IS A CHARITABLE OBJECT?

A charitable object, according to Mukhopadhyaya[75], must have the following three peculiarities, that is,

(*i*) indefiniteness,

(*ii*) meritoriousness, and

(*iii*) perpetuity.

A charity must benefit an indefinite number of individuals; it must refer to a definite class or community or a section of the public, but they must be well-

---

72. *Hanmantram Ramnath* v. *CIT*, AIR 1947 Bom 115: 48 BLR 532.

73. See *Dolagovinda Sethi* v. *Kanika Museum*, AIR 1989 Ori 60 at p. 66 wherein requirements of a public trust are enumerated.

74. *CIT* v. *Pemsel*, 1891 AC 531.

75. *Mukhopadhyaya on Perpetuities*.

defined[76] and not private individuals or a fluctuating body. This element distinguishes a charity from a private trust. The next element is that of altruism and altruism is always meritorious. The word charity implies an instilled virtue as its motivating power. Charity, whether in bountiful generosity to the poor or in that of kindness and indulgence in one's opinion of others, still retains a hint of its early meaning of brotherly love and compassion. Altruism is devotion to the interests of others, and suggests not only an ethical principle as one's guiding motive but also the absence of any selfishness or self-interest.[77] Here the beneficiaries must not be able to claim the benefit personally but they regard the pursuance of such an object as a mark of respect and reverence due to the pursuer. Lastly, the object is of a perpetual nature, that is, it is never capable of complete accomplishment and consequently it is permanent in duration. Thus the aim of charity is general public utility, but this does not mean that something should be given free of charge or at a price less than the cost price. A charitable object does not depend upon the donor's opinion about it and at the same time every object of public general utility is not necessarily charitable. According to English law, therefore, that purpose is charitable which is contained or enlisted in the Statute of Elizabeth[78] or which by analogies is deemed or decided to be within the spirit and intendment of the statute.[79]

6. EXAMPLES

(a) Poverty.—The word is not capable of being subjected to a definition. It is a comparative idea with reference to worldly needs. Thus poverty is the condition of one who does not have enough to live on; it is most comprehensive, denoting either a total lack of material possessions or a state in which one must forego many of the necessities and all of the luxuries of life; as the monk took the threefold vow of poverty, chastity and obedience, and during the last years of his life Mozart lived in the uttermost poverty. Destitution connotes a state of extreme poverty, in which one lacks the bare means of subsistence, and suggests dependence on charity to provide food and shelter.[80] Poverty therefore does not mean destitution.

Encouragement of poor emigrants[81], or provision of flats at economic rents for the benefit of aged persons of small means,[82] are included in charity but to provide dwellings for the working classes or a mutual benefit fund with no test of poverty are not charitable.[83] Similarly, a trust to provide comfortable

76. *Ahmedabad Rana Caste Assn.* v. *CIT*, (1971) 3 SCC 475: AIR 1972 SC 273 following *CIT* v. *Andhra Chamber of Commerce*, AIR 1965 SC 1281.
77. Funk & Wagnall: *Standard Handbook of Synonyms and Antonyms.*
78. 43 Eliz 1, C 4, 1601.
79. See *Chaturbhuj Vallabhdas* v. *CIT*, AIR 1946 Bom 337: 48 BLR 83; *CIT* v. *Breach Candy Swimming Bath Trust*, AIR 1955 Bom 250: ILR 1955 Bom 268. See *Church of North India* v. *Lavajibhai Ratanjibhai*, (2005) 10 SCC 760; *Vinayak Dev, Idagunji* v. *Shivaram*, (2005) 6 SCC 641.
80. Funk & Wagnall: *Standard Handbook of Synonyms and Antonyms*, p. 326.
81. *Davies* v. *Perpetual Trustee Co. Ltd.*, 1959 AC 439.
82. *Paylings W.T., Re*, (1969) 1 WLR 1595.
83. *Snell's Principles of Equity*, p. 146.

circumstances for those who are used to them is doubtful of being enlisted as charitable because "needy" is not the same thing as "used to comfort". Gifts to the 'working classes' or for the benefit of the employees of a company are now unlikely to be held charitable unless the qualification of poverty is clearly stated.[84] As Hanbury notes, the requirement of *public* benefit has been reduced in the field of poverty almost to a vanishing-point. It is still true to say that a gift to a group of individuals *chosen* because they are poor is not charitable, provided the object of the gift is not to relieve their poverty.[85] That is why Justice Harman has pointed out that "to amuse the poor would not be to relieve them".[86] The rule has to be stated so widely due to the "poor relations"[87] cases, holding gifts to one's poor relations as a class to be charitable. He expects that poor relations cases will be treated as exceptions rather than the rule, and the exceptions will not be extended.[88]

Thus if a trust be brought under any of the other three heads then there should be no objection that it may incidentally benefit the rich as well as the poor;[89] but if it cannot be brought under any head save that of the relief of poverty, then the benefits contemplated by the trust must be directed to that end.

(*b*) *Education.*—As has been said, education is the systematic development and cultivation of the mind and other natural powers. "It begins in the nursery," as said by John Lubbock, "and goes on at school, but does not end there. It continues through life, whether we will or not,"[90] Moral development is included in education in its fullest and noblest sense. Any full education must be the result in great part of instruction, training and personal association.[91] It has therefore rightly been noted by Snell[92], that its meaning is not confined to education given by a master or a mistress in class in a formal institution. But some element of instruction and improvement there must be; the mere increase of public knowledge or acquisition of experience is not enough. Education can take many forms. Schools and universities are its obvious examples. But education of a less academic sort is not excluded. The following may be cited as its examples:

(*i*) foundation of a lectureship in a university;

(*ii*) for cultivation of the skills of self-control, elocution, oratory, department and the arts of personal contact;

(*iii*) for the production of a dictionary, the publication of law reports, finding the Bacon—Shakespeare manuscripts;

---

84. Hanbury: *Modern Equity*, p. 264.
85. *I.R.C.* v. *Baddeley*, (1953) 1 WLR 84.
86. *Ibid.*
87. See *Scarisbrick, Re*, 1951 Ch 622: Nathan & Marshall: *Equity Through the Cases*, No. 77.
88. Hanbury: *Modern Equity*, pp. 264-265.
89. *Verge* v. *Somerville*, 1924 AC 496.
90. Funk and Wagnall: *Standard Handbook of Synonyms and Antonyms*, p. 170, citing *Use of Life.*
91. *Ibid.*
92. *Snell's Principles of Equity*, p. 146; Hanbury: *Modern Equity*, pp. 258-261.

(*iv*) for teaching business management, or education in the art of government.

Thus there are in fact very few aspects of the education of the young that would be regarded as education. It is natural therefore that it excludes research. As Wilberforce, J., said in *Hopkins, Re* [93]:

> "In order to be charitable, research must either be of *educational value* to the researcher, or must be so directed as to lead to something which will pass into the *store of educational material*, or so as to improve *the sum of communicable knowledge in* the area which education may cover."

Research of a purely private character is thus excluded.

But the following purposes have been held not to be charitable:

(*i*) founding a college for training spiritualistic mediums;

(*ii*) preserving a useless collection of pictures and furniture as museum;

(*iii*) political propaganda masquerading;

(*iv*) education of pickpockets in a thieves' kitchen to make them fit for their profession; or

(*v*) a public library devoted entirely to works of pornography.[94]

The concept of education must mix with public benefit or else it has no relevance to charity. As has been observed by Hanbury[95] a trust to educate one's own children is not charitable; it is educational but it is not sufficiently public. The same is true of a trust to educate one's relations.[96] It was remarked in that case that the "founder's kin" provisions belonged "more to history than to doctrine". Relations are neither the whole community nor a sufficient section of it. In this connection a sect a locality, or a sect in a locality is a sufficient section but under the heading community, e.g., "Welsh people" will be a sufficient section only if it is identifiable as a section. There is a distinction between a group of people identified by virtue of their character as individuals (e.g., children or employees of a particular person; their common quality is personal), and a group of people identified by virtue of membership of a class (e.g., inhabitants of a parish; the common quality which identifies them is impersonal). On the other end of the scale, a trust will be held not charitable if it is for a "fluctuating body of private individuals". A section of the community must have some coherence. If all this is not taken into account and the beneficiaries are defined too capriciously, the gift must fail for uncertainty because there is some limit to the rule that a charitable trust will not fail for uncertainty. The task of the draftsman in steering clear of these various

93. 1965 Ch 669.
94. *Snell's Principles of Equity*, p. 147.
95. Hanbury: *Modern Equity*, pp. 259-61.
96. *Caffoor Trustees* v. *CIT*, 1961 AC 584

obstacles is surely a formidable one, because it is not easy to be sure in advance of what constitutes a 'section' of the community.[1]

(*c*) *Religion*[2].—The word *religion* applies to any system of religious belief and worship and the conscientious devotion to it. Religion is a genus and denomination, sect, faith, creed, communion, church and cult are but its species. A denomination refers to a body of people having a name and set of beliefs that distinguish them from the larger body of which they are a part, as the Baptist denomination. A sect is a group of people who follow a particular leader or teacher and also the doctrines of the group. A communion is a religious group, perhaps comprising several bodies or churches, having a common essential faith.[3] In one sentence, in the words of Dr Hanbury, within the pale of religion shades of doctrines are immaterial. Thus a trust for the advancement of religion is naturally not confined to the Chiristian religion only but the idea extends and attracts within its sweep the furtherance of any religion provided it is not subversive of all religion and morality. Consequently, (*i*) trusts for the religious order or for community[4] (e.g. a monastery or a convent), (*ii*) trusts for saying of masses for the dead, (*iii*) a gift simply for God's work, (*iv*) a trust for the repair of the whole churchyard, are all held to be charitable. But (*i*) a trust for establishing "a catholic daily newspaper" and (*ii*) the upkeep of a particular vault or tomb in a churchyard are held not to be charitable.

As Hanbury notes, "in religious toleration equity lagged behind the criminal law. For some decades after it ceased to be a criminal offence to hold and propagate certain religious beliefs or to deny all beliefs, equity would prevent a trust for such purposes from being carried out at all." *Bowman* v. *Secular Society*[5] and *Bourne* v. *Keane*[6], are the two leading cases which mark the purposes in this field. It was in *Thornton* v. *Howe case*[7], that Romilly, M.R. remarked that the privilege of charity is not, of course, confined to Christianity. As Cross, J., once remarked, "as between different religions the law stands neutral, but it assumes that any religion is at least likely to be better than none".[8] But as with education, so with religion, there are limits. Nor is every moral philosophy a religion. The constitutional possession of religious doctrine by a society is not sufficient in itself to make that society charitable; there must be the *intention to advance* religion in some positive manner. On this ground both Masonry and Theosophy have failed to qualify.[9] Again, doctrines adverse to the very foundations of all religion, and a gift to propagate arguments calculated to disprove all religious beliefs could not be upheld as a trust for the advancement of religion. Of course, looking from another angle of rationalism and moral philosophy, it may be educational under certain

1. Hanbury: *Modern Equity*, p. 261.
2. *Snell's Principles of Equity*, pp. 147-148; Hanbury: *Modern Equity*, pp. 261-263.
3. Funk and Wagnall: *Standard Handbook of Synonyms and Antonyms*, p. 360.
4. *Banfield, Re*, (1968) 1 WLR 846.
5. 1917 AC 406.
6. 1919 AC 815.
7. (1862) 31 Beav 14.
8. *Noville Estates* v. *Madden*, 1962 Ch 832.
9. *United Grand Lodge of AFAM, England* v. *Holborn B. C.*, (1957) 1 WLR 1080.

circumstances.[10] Finally, as laid down in *Glimour* v. *Coats*[11] by the House of Lords, proof of public benefits was necessary to constitute a charity; and that benefit to the public was not proved by doctrine alone. Neither religious doctrine, nor edification by example, nor the eligibility of all Roman Catholic women to enter the convent were sufficient to satisfy it. In that case, therefore, the community of cloistered nuns was held to be non-charitable. Still, however, it must be noted that many 'satellite' purposes[12] have been freely admitted into the realm of religious charity in the United Kingdom.

(*d*) *Beneficial to the community.*—This expression is of very wide import but it should not be taken to include every object of general public utility. "Beneficial" means "beneficial in a way that the law regards as charitable". Though the inspirations of the donors are "infinitely variegated" this becomes a test of the legal status of charity and has to be approached objectively from two main points.

What the donor thought or what other people think is not the issue here; "beneficial to the community" is something that has to be decided by the courts in the light of all relevant evidence available. The second point is that the legal test of charity is governed by the spirit and intendment of the preamble of the statute and valuable analogies created therefrom. Thus, under this fourth head an element of "public" as well as "benefit" is required.

Provision of a fire brigade, or crematorium, or of hospitals, whether voluntary or from paying patients, publication of law reports, provision for a library, provision for prizes for sports are instances of this fourth division, but a political purpose would stand outside the equity of the statute. A trust for the protection and benefit of animals generally is charitable provided it involves a benefit to the community[13], but, surprisingly enough, a gift for total suppression of vivisection which was once held charitable on the ground that it promoted humanitarian views, is now established as not being charitable as it leads to disadvantage of mankind.[14]

Social and recreational activities may be considered under this head. Under the Recreational Charities Act, 1958, which extends the definition of charity without restricting the purposes, activities and facilities in the interests of social welfare are includible under this head.[15] It must be mentioned that most of the inclusions under this head are for earning exemption from taxation. As to political trusts, there can be no such class of trusts but if a trust is purely for a political purpose it is non-charitable. A trust whose ultimate and predominant

---

10. Hanbury: *Modern Equity*, pp. 262-263. cf. *Stemson's W.T., Re*, (1969) 3 WLR 21.
11. 1949 AC 426.
12. Hanbury: *Modern Equity*, pp. 262-263, cf. *Stemson's W.T., Re*, (1969) 3 WLR 21.
13. *Wedgwood, Re*, (1915) 1 Ch 113.
14. *National Anti-Vivisection Society* v. *I.R.C.*, 1948 AC 31. *Commr. of Endowments* v. *Vittal Rao*, (2005) 4 SCC 120 (more fact that premises are being used as dharmashala for several years cannot lead to inference that the premises belong to public trust.)
15. For details see *Snell's Principles of Equity*, pp. 149-156; Hanbury: *Modern Equity*, pp. 266-271.

purpose is benefit to society must not fail simply because politics may be involved in its fulfilment. The *National Anti-Vivisection Society case*[16] is an example of this kind.

7. INCIDENTS OF A CHARITABLE TRUST

An express private trust and an express public or charitable trust though governed mostly by the same rules, due to a striking peculiarity of its nature, a charitable trust receives a different treatment at the hands of the court so far as the questions of interpretation and concessions are concerned. A private trust benefits an individual or individuals but a charitable one benefits the public or a definite section of the public. It is because of this reason that a charitable trust receives a favoured treatment. The points of comparison in this regard are uncertainty of object, failing of the object and the permanent duration of the trust conflicting with the rule against perpetuity and the rule against inalienability.

(*a*) *When is a charity favoured*

(1) A private trust fails for uncertainty of the object unless a power of selection and apportionment among a definitely prescribed class of beneficiaries is given by the trustor to the trustee[17]; but a charitable trust does not fail for uncertainty. Once the intention of the donor confining himself to charity is clear the absence of selection of a particular charitable object will not render a trust uncertain. There are no compulsions for the donor as to how to express his intention. Interpretation by the court, therefore, in such cases will make it possible for a trust to exist. Where the intention is not clear (apart from the mode in which it is expressed) or is not exclusively charitable,[18] or is mixed up with other purposes of shadowy and indefinite nature, or where a discretion is vested in a trustee, or the description includes purposes which may or may not be charitable and where the purpose is not obligatory, the gift will fail for uncertainty because there is a limit beyond which a court cannot go and uphold the trust.[19] Thus, where a private trust fails at the very first instance for uncertainty, a charitable trust will not easily yield because of the favourable treatment accorded to it by the court.

(2) Where the object selected by the settlor fails but the general charitable intention is clear a cypres doctrine will be applied by the courts and the trust will survive; but in case of private trusts the doctrine does not apply.

(3) As seen before, a charitable trust is of a permanent duration. This being so it is not affected by the rule against perpetuity. In charity, property is devoted forever and this prevents its alienation but the trust does not fail. A private trust has not won such concessions.

---

16. *National Anti-Vivisection Society* v. *I.R.C.*, 1948 AC 31.
17. *A.G.* v. *New Zealand Insurance Co.*, (1936) 41 CWN 321 (PC).
18. *Hunter* v. *A.G.*, 1899 AC 309; *Mills* v. *Farmer*, (1815) 1 Meriv 55.
19. See *Osmund, Re*, (1944) 1 All ER 262 (CA).

(4) Moreover, a charitable trust is exempted from taxation and this is the greatest favour in present times when taxation is at its highest; a private trust is not so exempted. A gift from one charity to another is outside the rule of perpetuities, while a private trust doing this would be caught by the rule against perpetuity.[20]

(5) Where the donor has capacity and disposable estate, defects in conveyancing in a charitable trust are supplied, i.e., an imperfect conveyance which will not be executed in case of a private individual will be perfected and executed in case of a charity.[21]

(6) In a charitable trust a majority of trustees will bind the minority, whereas in a private trust, trustees must act unanimously.

A charitable trust is thus more favoured than a private trust.

(*b*) *When less favoured*

It is not that public trusts are everywhere favoured in comparison to private trusts. There are circumstances wherein they are less favoured and even treated on a par with private individuals.

A trust must have a lawful purpose. But this rule is applied more strictly to charities and, consequently, charities for superstitious purposes[22] are void. Where the purpose is against the political and moral sense of the country,[23] the trusts are void. The *Anti-Vivisection Society case*[24] is a noteworthy example for this. In case of private trusts no such questions as to the nature and character of the beneficiaries can arise.

In the following circumstances charities are treated on a par with private individuals. Where a testator fails to name a trustee or if one named by him dies, equity would supply the want of a trustee.[25] Where purposes of a trust are legal as well as illegal and the legal purposes can be separated from the illegal ones, the trust will be exempted *pro tanto*. Section 10 of the Indian Limitation Act applies equally to a public as well as a private trust. If there is a gift to an individual as well as a charity, and both are left indefinite, the gift is bound to fail, but if the individual is definite and the charity is indefinite, the gift is not to fail. Where a gift given is construed in words ambiguous having both legal and illegal sense, the legal interpretation will prevail on the principle that it is better for a thing to have effect than to be made void.

8. THE CY-PRES DOCTRINE

The Latin word cy-pres means—for a purpose resembling "as nearly as possible" the purpose originally proposed. It means approximation. Cy-pres

---

20. *Royal College of Surgeons* v. *N.P. Bank*, (1952) 1 All ER 984 (HL). *See* also *State of Kerala* v. *M.P. Shanti Verma Jain*, (1998) 5 SCC 63: AIR 1998 SC 2208.
21. *Alt* v. *Strathden*, (1894) 3 Ch 265.
22. *Bourne* v. *Keane*, 1919 AC 815.
23. *Heath* v. *Chapman*, 2 Drew 417.
24. 1948 AC 31, overruling *Cross* v. *London Anti-Vivisection Board*, (1895) 2 Ch 501.
25. *Ibid*.

(from *ici-pres* or, probably) is a doctrine evolved in English in relation to charitable trusts whereby, if a gift is clearly for charitable purposes only, it will not be allowed to fail because the precise object to be benefited, or the mode of application of the fund is uncertain. It must be evident that the truster had a general charitable intent, but the precise purpose is impossible, or has never existed, or has ceased to exist before the testator's death, or the purpose or institution has ceased to exist after the gift has taken effect, or in certain other cases where the question of general charitable intent is less material. If the conditions are satisfied the court will settle a scheme for the application of the funds to another purpose as near as possible to that prescribed by the truster.[26]

According to Hanbury[27] the word has several connotations. In connection with charities, the cypres application of a fund means the application of that fund to objects or purposes which are not precisely those the donor provided for, but which as nearly as possible fit his intentions. It is obvious that such a power of altering the terms of such a trust will only be used where it is impossible or impracticable to give literal effect to them as laid down in the trust.[28] At the same time there must be present in the gift the necessary wider or paramount intention for this purpose.[29] Thus a gift may be saved from initial failure by the presence of a wider or paramount charitable intention to which it is possible to give effect.

Once there is an effective devotion of funds to charity, those funds will remain devoted forever unless there is in the gift an effective provision for devolution. Save in the special case, the possibility of a lapse or a resulting trust is excluded. Cypres is available without there being width of charitable intent. Its jurisdiction depends upon the Charities Act, 1960, Section 13. In such cases the court will frame a scheme and it will be carried out.[30]

Where there is a surplus of funds after the specified charitable object has been carried out, the same will be applied cypres, provided a paramount intention of charity appears.[31] A court has no authority to sanction any deviation from the donor's expressed intention so far as it can be given effect. Similarly, because the court considers the application of the trust property or its income to another purpose which would be more expedient or beneficial, it has no authority to do so.[32]

The principle underlying this doctrine has also been summarised in *Mayor of Lyons* v. *A.G.*[33], an Indian case.

---

26. Walker, *The Oxford Companion to Law*, 1980, p. 329, from L. Sheridan and V. Delany, *The Cy-pres Doctrine*.
27. *Modern Equity*, pp. 279-87.
28. *A.G.* v. *Ironmonger's*, (1840) 10 Cl & F 908.
29. *Ibid.*
30. *Ratilal* v. *State of Bombay*, AIR 1954 SC 388.
31. *Campden Charities, Re*, (1881) 18 Ch D 310; *A.G. of Bengal* v. *S. Webb-Johnson*, AIR 1925 Cal 797; *Shankarnarayan* v. *H.R.E. Board, Madras*, (1948) 74 IA 230: ILR 1948 Mad 585.
32. *Ratilal* v. *State of Bombay*, AIR 1954 SC 388.
33. (1876) 1 Cal 303 (PC): 3 IA 32: 1 MIA 272. *See* also *Strahan's Digest of Equity*, p. 209.

Hanbury[34] has therefore rightly pointed out that "such a power of altering purposes must be hedged around with safeguards, but in recent years, especially in connection with trusts with long outmoded purposes, it has been found necessary to relax them. Application of cypres is justified in varying circumstances". He from this point of view, divides such cases into two parts: "first, where the problems arise at the commencement of a charitable trust, to which the width of a charitable intent provides the answer; secondly, problems that only arise subsequently, to which perpetual dedication to charity provides the answer".

9. POSITION IN INDIA

(*a*) *What trusts are charitable.*—Looking to the provisions of the various Acts[35] in this connection one must come to the conclusion that the meaning and scope of the words public or charitable are very much the same in India they are in England. Moreover, it is generally acknowledged that in order to be charitable a trust must be either for the relief of poverty, or for the advancement of education or religion, or for any other purpose beneficial to the community as in England.

In *Section 18 of the Transfer of Property Act, 1882, charity* has been classified under the following four principal divisions:

(*i*) advancement of *religion*;

(*ii*) advancement of *knowledge*;

(*iii*) advancement of *commerce, health and safety of the public*; and

(*iv*) advancement of *any other object beneficial to mankind.*

Illustrations of *Section 118 of the Indian Succession Act* indicate and explain the nature of charitable objects and purposes. A *charitable purpose* under Section 9 of the *Bombay Public Trusts Act*, 1950, includes:

(*i*) relief of poverty or distress;

(*ii*) education;

(*iii*) medical relief and the advancement of any other object of general public utility, but does not include a purpose which relates (*A*) exclusively to sports, or (*B*) exclusively to religious teaching or worship.

As for example, the following have been held to be charitable or religious purposes:

(*i*) gift of property to temple or to idol[36];

(*ii*) gift for the maintenance of priests[37];

---

34. *Modern Equity*, p. 280. For details of the doctrine see *Snell's Principles of Equity*, pp. 160-165, Hanbury: *Modern Equity*, pp. 279-287 and leading case Nos. 85 to 89 in Nathan & Marshall: *Equity Through the Cases*.

35. Section 9, Bombay Public Trusts Act, 1950; Section 2, Charitable Endowments Act, 1890; Religious Endowments Act, 1863; Charitable and Religious Trusts Act, 1920; Section 118, Indian Succession Act, 1925; Section 18, Transfer of Property Act, 1882; and Section 4, Indian Income Tax Act, 1922.

36. *Thakersy Devraj* v. *Harbhan Narsy*, 8 Bom 432; *Bhugavati P. Sen* v. *Guru Prasanna Sen*, 25 Cal 112.

37. *Ibid.*

(*iii*) gift to a dignitary of a church[38];

(*iv*) gift for building wells, haudas (troughs)[39], sarais[40], sadavrata[41], hospitals[42], schools and universities[43], for feeding the poor and to supply buttermilk to the poor[44];

(*v*) gift for keeping a choultry in repair.[45]

In this connection one is to note what Sections 10 and 11 of the Bombay Public Trusts Act, 1950 provide. As per Section 10: "Notwithstanding any law, custom or usage, a public trust shall not be void only on the ground that the persons or objects for the benefit of whom or which it is created are unascertained or unascertainable." Thus a charity created for such objects as "dharma, dharmada, punyadan, punyakarya" is not void only on the ground that the objects for which it is created are unascertained or unascertainable.

As Section 11 goes: "A public trust created for purposes some of which are charitable or religious and some of which are not, shall not be deemed to be void in respect to the charitable or religious purpose only on the ground that it is void with respect to the non-charitable or non-religious purpose." Thus a gift for saying mass, as it advances religion, is validly charitable.

(*b*) *General Public Utility*.—The test of an object of general public utility or an object beneficial to the community, is not whether the testator believed it to be so, but *whether the court considers it to be beneficial to the public having regard to the nature and character of the trust and at the same time in so deciding the court would be guided by Indian ideas and particularly the common opinion amongst the community to which the interested parties belong*.[46]

(*c*) *Charity*.—The word charity without any further qualification has a recognised meaning in law. It amounts to a general charitable intention for objects well-recognised as charitable in law. It is not an indefinite word so as to include a public or private charity or benevolent or philanthrophic objects. The words "*charity*", "*charitable objects*" or "*charitable purpose*" are defined in various sections of different Acts of the Indian Legislature and in all of them the idea of *public benefit* is clearly involved.[47] One of the tests to be applied is whether the gift in question is valid in law. If the gift to charity is valid in law it is a relevant factor to be considered in deciding if it is a charitable purpose

38. *Thakersy Devraj* v. *Harbhan Narsy*, 8 Bom 432; *Bhugavati P. Sen* v. *Guru Prasanna Sen*, 25 Cal 112.
39. *Jamnabai* v. *Khimji*, 14 Bom 1.
40. *Jugal Kishore* v. *Laxman*, 23 Bom 659; *Ramkrishna Mission* v. *Dogar Singh*, 1984 All 72.
41. *Jamnabai* v. *Khimji*, 14 Bom 1.
42. *Fanindra Kumar case*, 6 CWN 321.
43. *Manorama* v. *Kalicharan*, 31 Cal 166: 8 CWN 273.
44. *Draivia Sundram* v. *Subramania*, ILR 1945 Mad 854: AIR 1945 Mad 217; *Municipality of Taloda* v. *Charity Commr.*, AIR 1968 SC 418: (1968) 1 SCR 652.
45. *Gulam* v. *Ajia*, 4 Mad HC 44.
46. *Trustees of Tribune Press* v. *CIT*, (1939) 66 IA 231: AIR 1939 PC 208: (1939) 43 CWN 1065 (PC).
47. *Chamber of Commerce* v. *CIT*, 1936 ALJ 1085: AIR 1936 All 764.

within the meaning of the Income Tax Act.[48] Charity defined under the Indian Income Tax Act, it must be noted, is of much wider application than charity as understood in English law under Statute of Elizabeth. Similarly, the expression "*any other object of general public utility*" in the definition of "charitable purposes" in the Act is of the widest connotation. It is sufficient if a well-defined section of the public benefit by the object.[49]

Thus (*i*) the establishment of a dispensary[50] or a hospital, (*ii*) of school or college for spread of education,[51] (*iii*) provisions for scholarships and similar objects of education,[52] (*iv*) for feeding of poor Brahmins, (*v*) help to poor widows and orphans, (*vi*) providing accommodation for persons visiting Benaras and other places, (*vii*) providing food to pilgrims, (*viii*) help to sick and distressed, (*ix*) *seva* and worship of deities,[53] (*x*) provision for sadhus and saints[54], (*xi*) maintenance of a newspaper for supplying the province with an organ of educated public opinion,[55] (*xii*) organisation for the development of handspinning and khaddar,[56] (*xiii*) performance of *shraddhas*, reading of sacred books to masses, establishment of sarai or a resting place, construction of tanks and ponds,[57] *goshalas* can all be the objects of charity. In short, all the purposes coming within the sweep of charitable or charitable and religious[58] purposes are qualified to get exemptions under the Income Tax Act.

The dominant purpose of the trust must be charitable,[59] matter of control and management thereof being immaterial.[60] But if the object is the promotion and development of motor trade and industry carried on for profit[61] or if the object is to protect the business interest of the association[62] members, the trust is not charitable because the income of the property or its benefit does not enure to

---

48. *Chaturbhuj Vallabhdas* v. *CIT*, AIR 1946 Bom 337: 48 BLR 63.
49. *CIT* v. *Breach Candy Swimming Bath Trust*, ILR 1955 Bom 268: AIR 1955 Bom 250.
50. *Haridasi* v. *Secry. of State*, 7 Cal 304 (PC): 8 IA 46.
51. Ibid., *CIT* v. *Sreeram-Surajmall Charity Trust*, (1971) 79 ITR 649 (Cal); *Bhupti* v. *Ramlal*, 37 Cal 128: 14 CWN 18; *Vedapatshala* v. *State of T.N.*, (1981) 94 LW 137; *Rajammal* v. *Authorised Officer Land Reforms*, (1984) 1 MLJ 270 (red parayanam in a temple).
52. Ibid., *CIT* v. *Sreeram -Surajmall Charity Trust*, (1971) 79 ITR 649 (Cal); *Bhupti* v. *Ramlal*, 37 Cal 128: 14 CWN 18; *Vedapatshala* v. *State of T.N.*, (1981) 94 LW 137; *Rajammal* v. *Authorised Officer Land Reforms*, 1984 (1) MLJ 270 (red parayanam in a temple).
53. Ibid., *CIT* v. *Sreeram-Surajmall Charity Trust*, (1971) 79 ITR 649 (Cal); *Bhupti* v. *Ramlal*, 37 Cal 128: 14 CWN 18; *Vedapatshala* v. *State of T.N.*, (1981) 94 LW 137; *Rajammal* v. *Authorised Officer Land Reforms*, (1984) 1 MLJ 270 (parayanam in a temple).
54. *Purmanundass* v. *Venayekrao*, 7 Bom 19 (PC): 9 IA 86.
55. *Trustees of Tribune Press* v. *CIT*, AIR 1939 PC 208.
56. *All-India Spinners' Assn.* v. *CIT*, (1944) 49 CWN 1 (PC): AIR 1944 PC 88.
57. *Venkata Krishna Rao* v. *Sub-Collector, Ongole*, AIR 1969 SC 563.
58. See *Mayor of Lyons* v. *A.G.*, 1 MIA 175: (1876) 1 Cal 303 (PC).
59. *CIT* v. *D.D. Deshpandey*, (1976) 102 ITR 390 (DB)(Bom); *Trustees of the Charity Fund* v. *CIT*, AIR 1959 SC 1060.
60. *Ganeshi Devi Rami Devi Charity Trust* v. *CIT*, (1969) 71 ITR 696 (Cal); *CIT* v. *Ahmedabad Rana Caste Assn.*, (1968) 70 ITR 503 (Guj).
61. *CIT* v. *Calcutta Motor Dealers' Assn.*, (1977) TLR 604 (Cal).
62. *Madras Hotels Assn.* v. *CIT*, (1977) TLR 1375 (Mad); *Chamber of Commerce* v. *CIT*, 1936 ALJ 1085.

benefit the public[63], i.e., a well-defined section of the public,[64] but it benefits only certain individuals connected with it who can claim its benefit. For a trust to be charitable there must be altruism.[65] But that does not mean that the benefit must reach mankind at large; if the benefit is obtained by a section of a community sufficiently defined and identifiable by some common quality of a public or impersonal nature, it is enough.[66]

In deciding whether a Hindu endowment is for a religious purpose or for a charitable one, Hindu law and Hindu notions are very valuable and they would be followed.[67]

The concept of "charity" under the Muslim law is even more wider than under the English and the Hindu laws.

(*d*) *Cases.*—It would be sufficient for this topic to cite the substance of two Indian cases, *Mayor of Lyons* v. *A.G.*[68] and *Trustee of the Tribune Press* v. *CIT*[69].

The ratio of the first decision is that if the charity in the abstract is the substance of the gift and the particular disposition is merely the mode thereof which may not be capable of execution, the gift does not fail. Thus if the gift is confined to charity but the method of application shown in the deed is not possible of execution, it cannot fail. This is the doctrine. But this doctrine will not be applied (*i*) where the donor's desires are highly undesirable, impracticable or impossible of literal execution. In such a case the court cannot substitute the same. (*ii*) Moreover, where a donor's paramount intention of charity is clear and manifest and yet that cannot be carried into effect, the gift will fail, creating a resulting trust in favour of the donor.[70] In short, if there is a general intention, the failure of the particular form in which the charity is to be executed shall not destroy the whole. In applying this doctrine, regard must be had to the other objects of the testator's bounty, but primary attention must be paid to the objects akin or near to the original one.[71]

Thus the doctrine should receive an extended application to give effect to the true intent and aim of the donor in spite of his lapses, his ignorance and his failure to understand the situation.[72] Where a charitable gift is made upon a condition precedent it fails if the condition is not satisfied and the doctrine does

---

63. *Ganeshi Devi Rami Devi Charity Trust* v. *CIT*, (1969) 71 ITR 696 (Cal).
64. *Ahmedabad Rana Caste Assn.* v. *CIT*, (1971) 3 SCC 475: ILR (1973) Bom 545.
65. *Chamber of Commerce* v. *CIT*, AIR 1936 All 764.
66. *Laxmi Narain Lath Trust* v. *CIT*, (1971) 1 ITJ 562: AIR 1966 Raj 154; *CIT* v. *Walchand Diamond Jubilee Trust*, AIR 1959 Bom 148; *CIT* v. *Programme for Community Organisation*, (2001) 248 ITR 1 (accumulation of income wholly for charitable or religious purposes—determination.); *CIT* v. *Thanthi Trust*, (2001) 2 SCC 707 (Charitable object not directly accomplished.)
67. For details see *Mayne's Hindu Law*, 11th Edn., p. 192; *Saraswati Ammal* v. *Rajgopal Ammal*, AIR 1953 SC 491. *See* also *Mayne's Hindu Law*, 13th Edn., 1991, pp. 1158, 1160
68. (1876) 1 Cal 303 (PC): 3 IA 32: 1 MIA 272.
69. AIR 1939 PC 208.
70. *Commr.* v. *Dy. Commr.*, (1937) 41 CWN 1072 (PC): AIR 1937 PC 240.
71. *A.G.* v. *Fardoonji*, 13 BLR 341.
72. 65 IC 820: 37 MLJ 489.

not apply. To attract the application of the doctrine an absolute declaration of intention to give to charity must be established.[73]

One has to remember here that it is the court's duty to give effect to the donor's intention if it is not against public policy. In *Sir Currimbhoy, Ebrahim Re*,[74] it was rightly held that the court would not consider whether the directions of the donor were wise or whether a more beneficial application of the donor's property might not be found.

In the second case, Sardar Dayal Singh created a trust "to maintain the Tribune Press and newspaper in an efficient condition, keeping up the liberal policy of the newspaper and placing it on a footing of permanency. On applying for exemption of income tax under Section 4(3)(*i*) of the Indian Income Tax Act, it was held (by the Judicial Committee) that the appellants were entitled to exemption as the dominant purpose of the trust was "supplying the province with an organ of educated public opinion", which was an object of "public utility", and hence "charitable" within the meaning of the provisions of the Income Tax Act. *The test of an object of general public utility is not whether the testator considered it to be so, but whether the court considers it to be beneficial to the public, having regard to the nature and character of the trust.* In the present case this must be determined with reference to the policy and character of the newspaper as it existed at the time when the testator created the trust, and it is not necessary to enquire as to the manner in which the trust has been or is being carried out since the date of the testator's death. In *Mehrwan Homi Irani case*[75] a lease of immovable property belonging to public trust, for a period exceeding the statutory period was made. A question arose as to relevant considerations for grant of permission to agreement for such lease under Section 36(1) of the Bombay Public Trust Act, 1950. The court observed that it must be seen whether such an agreement is capable of advancing or fulfilling the object of the trust. If it is not in the best interest of the trust it should not be allowed. The case was therefore, remanded to the Charity Commissioner for deciding it afresh. The English decisions establish that political propaganda is not an object of general public utility, but in the present case, *the dominant object of the testator was to benefit the public* of upper India by providing them with an English newspaper—the dissemination of news and ventilation of opinion upon all matters of public interest. Though politics and legislation were discussed in the paper, that was not its dominant purpose. *The object of supplying the province with the organ of educated public opinion should therefore be held to be an object of general public utility.*

---

73. *Santona Roy* v. *A.G., Bengal*, (1920) 25 CWN 343; *Kuruppannan (R.K.)* v. *Tirumalai*, AIR 1962 Mad 500; *Ratilal Panachand* v. *State of Bombay*, AIR 1954 SC 388: 1954 SCR 1055.
74. 12 BLR 1040.
75. *Mehrwan Homi Irani* v. *Charity Commr., Bombay*, (2001) 5 SCC 305: AIR 2001 SC 2350.

Chapter XIV

Trustees—Their duties and liabilities

Between a paid trustee and an unpaid trustee "there is no difference as to the standard of diligence expected; indeed it would be a brave amateur trustee who attempted to excuse himself for lack of diligence on the ground that he was not being paid".

—Hanbury: *Modern Equity*, p. 294

"The office of trustee is... an office of honorary service and not an office of profit—so much so, indeed, that if a trustee makes a profit out of his trusteeship he gets into serious trouble."

—Evershed, M.R., in *Dale* v. *I.R.C.*, 1954 AC 11 (1953 HL)

" ... . *In other words, the receipt of a profit for the performance of the duties of a trustee is repugnant to the nature of trusteeship... .The fiduciary duty may arise, not only from trust but also ex lege and ex conventione. The duty was... acknowledged in the jurisprudence of all civilised communities... . It applies to all judicial factors appointed by the courts... and to partners and to agents under a contract of agency and, of course, to trustees under a settlement or under a will... . Some who are entitled to the duty are never entitled to remuneration; some are ex lege entitled to payment for their services; some are entitled to payment ex conventione; and some are entitled to payment if the settlor or testator so directs. The rule is the same for all: it is not that reward for the services is repugnant to fiduciary duty, but that he who has the duty shall not take any secret remuneration or any financial benefit not authorised by the law, or by his contract, or by the trust-deed under which he acts, as the case may be."*

—Lord Normand in *Dale* v. *I.R.C.*, 1954 AC 11 (1953 HL)

SYNOPSIS

A. DUTIES

1. TEXT OF SECTIONS 11 TO 22

11. *Trustee to execute trust.*—The trustee is bound to fulfil the purpose of the trust, and to obey the directions of the author of the trust given at the time of its creation, except as modified by the consent of all the beneficiaries being competent to contract.

Where the beneyficiary is incompetent to contract, his consent may, for the purposes of this section, be given by a principal Civil Court of original jurisdiction.

Nothing in this section shall be deemed to require a trustee to obey any direction when to do so would be impracticable, illegal or manifestly injurious to the beneficiaries.

Explanation.—Unless a contrary intention be expressed, the purpose of a trust for the payment of debts shall be deemed to be (*a*) to pay only the debts of the author of the trust existing and recoverable at the date of the instrument of trust, or, when such instrument is a will, at the date of his death, and (*b*) in the case of debts not bearing interest, to make such payment without interest.

Illustrations

(*a*) *A*, a trustee, is simply authorized to sell certain land by public auction. He cannot sell the land by private contract.

(*b*) *A*, a trustee of certain land for *X*, *Y* and *Z*, is authorized to sell the land to *B* for a specified sum. *X*, *Y* and *Z*, being competent to contract, consent that *A* may sell the land to *C* for a less sum. *A* may sell the land accordingly.

(*c*) *A*, a trustee for *B* and her children, is directed by the author of the trust to lend, on *B*'s request, trust-property to *B*'s husband, *C*, on the security of his bond. *C* becomes insolvent and *B* requests *A* to make the loan. *A* may refuse to make it.

12. *Trustee to inform himself of state of trust-property.*—A trustee is bound to acquaint himself, as soon as possible, with the nature and circumstances of the trust-property; to obtain, where necessary, a transfer of the trust-property to himself; and (subject to the provisions of the instrument of trust) to get in trust-moneys invested on insufficient or hazardous security.

Illustrations

(*a*) The trust-property is a debt outstanding on personal security. The instrument of trust gives the trustee no discretionary power to leave the debt so outstanding. The trustee's duty is to recover the debt without unnecessary delay.

(*b*) The trust-property is money in the hands of one or two co-trustees. No discretionary power is given by the instrument of trust. The other co-trustee must not allow the former to retain the money for a longer period than circumstances of the case required.

13. *Trustee to protect title to trust-property.*—A trustee is bound to maintain and defend all such suits, and (subject to the provisions of the instrument of trust) to take such other steps as, regard being had to the nature and amount or value of the trust-property, may be reasonably requisite for the preservation of the trust-property and the assertion or protection of the title thereto.

Illustration

The trust-property is immovable property which has been given to the author of the trust by an unregistered instrument. Subject to the provisions of the Indian Registration Act, 1877, the trustee's duty is to cause the instrument to be registered.

14. *Trustee not to set up title adverse to beneficiary.*—The trustee must not for himself or another set up or aid any title to the trust-property adverse to the interest of the beneficiary.

15. *Care required from trustee.*—A trustee is bound to deal with the trust-property as carefully as a man of ordinary prudence would deal with such property if it were his own; and, in the absence of a contract to the contrary, a trustee so dealing is not responsible for the loss, destruction or deterioration of the trust-property.

Illustrations

(*a*) *A*, living in Calcutta, is a trustee for *B*, living in Bombay. *A* remits trust-funds to *B* by bills drawn by a person of undoubted credit in favour of the trustee as such, and payable at Bombay. The bills are dishonoured. *A* is not bound to make good the loss.

(*b*) *A*, a trustee of leasehold property, directs the tenant to pay the rents on account of the trust to a banker *B*, then in credit. The rents are accordingly paid to *B*, and *A* leaves the money with *B*, only till wanted. Before the money is drawn out, *B* becomes insolvent. *A*, having had no reason to believe that *B* was in insolvent circumstances, is not bound to make good the loss.

(*c*) *A*, a trustee to two debts for *B*, releases one and compounds the other, in good faith, and reasonably believing that it is for *B*'s interest to do so. *A* is not bound to make good any loss caused thereby to *B*.

(*d*) *A*, a trustee directed to sell the trust-property by auction, sells the same, but does not advertise the sale and otherwise fails in reasonable diligence in inviting competition. *A* is bound to make good the loss caused thereby to the beneficiary.

(*e*) *A*, a trustee for *B*, in execution of his trust, sells the trust-property, but for want of due diligence on his part fails to receive part of the purchase-money. *A* is bound to make good the loss thereby caused to *B*.

(*f*) *A*, a trustee for *B* of a policy of insurance, has funds in hand for payment of the premiums. *A* neglects to pay the premiums, and the policy is consequently forfeited. *A* is bound to make good the loss to *B*.

(*g*) *A* bequeaths certain moneys to *B* and *C* as trustees, and authorizes them to continue trust-moneys upon the personal security of a certain firm in which *A* had himself invested them. *A* dies, and a change takes place in the firm. *B* and *C* must not permit the moneys to remain upon the personal security of the new firm.

(*h*) *A*, a trustee for *B*, allows the trust to be executed solely by his co-trustee, *C*. *C* misapplies the trust-property. *A* is personally answerable for the loss resulting to *B*.

16. *Conversion of perishable property.*—Where the trust is created for the benefit of several persons in succession, and the trust-property is of a wasting nature or a future or reversionary interest, the trustee is bound, unless an intention to the contrary may be inferred from the instrument of trust, to convert the property into property of a permanent and immediately profitable character.

Illustrations

(*a*) *A* bequeaths to *B* all his property in trust for *C* during his life, and on this death for *D*, and on *D*'s death for *E*. *A*'s property consists of three leasehold houses, and there is nothing in *A*'s will to show that he intended the houses to be enjoyed in specie. *B* should sell the houses, and invest the proceeds in accordance with Section 20.

(*b*) *A* bequeaths to *B* his three leasehold houses in Calcutta and all the furniture therein in trust for *C* during his life, and on his death for *D*, and on *D*'s death for *E*. Here an intention that the houses and furniture should be enjoyed in specie appears clearly, and *B* should not sell them.

17. *Trustee to be impartial.*—Where there are more beneficiaries than one, the trustee is bound to be impartial, and must not execute the trust for the advantage of one at the expense of another.

Where the trustee has a discretionary power, nothing in this section shall be deemed to authorize the Court to control the exercise reasonably and in good faith of such discretion.

Illustration

A, a trustee for *B*, *C* and *D*, is empowered to choose between several specified modes of investing the trust-property. *A* in good faith chooses one of these modes. The Court will not interfere, although the result of the choice may be to vary the relative right to *B*, *C* and *D*.

18. *Trustee to prevent waste.*—Where the trust is created for the benefit of several persons in succession and one of them is in possession of the trust-property, if he commits, or threatens to commit, any act which is destructive or permanently injurious thereto, the trustee is bound to take measures to prevent such act.

19. *Accounts and information.*—A trustee is bound (*a*) to keep clear and accurate accounts of the trust-property, and (*b*) at all reasonable times, at the request of the beneficiary, to furnish him with full and accurate information as to the amount and state of the trust-property.

20. *Investment of trust-money.*—Where the trust-property consists of money and cannot be applied immediately or at an early date to the purposes of the trust, the trustee is bound (subject to any direction contained in the instrument of trust) to invest the money on the following securities, and on no others—

(*a*) in promissory notes, debentures, stock or other securities of any State Government or of the Central Government or of the United Kingdom of Great Britain and Ireland:

Provided that securities, both the principal whereof and the interest whereon shall have been fully and unconditionally guaranteed by any such Government shall be deemed, for the purposes of this clause, to be securities of such Government;

(*b*) in bonds, debentures and annuities charged or secured by the Parliament of the United Kingdom before the fifteenth day of August, 1947 on the revenues of India or of the Governor-General-in-Council or of any Province:

Provided that, after the fifteenth day of February, 1916, no money shall be invested in any such annuity being a terminable annuity unless a sinking fund has been established in connection with such annuity; but nothing in this proviso shall apply to investments made before the date aforesaid;

(*bb*) in India three-and-a-half per cent stock, India three per cent stock, India two-and-a-half per cent stock or any other capital stock, which before the 15th day of August, 1947, was issued by the Secretary of State for India-in-Council under the authority of an Act of Parliament of the United Kingdom and charged on the revenues of India or which was issued by the Secretary of State on behalf of the Governor-General-in-Council under the provisions of Part XIII of the Government of India Act, 1935;

(*c*) in stock or debentures of, or shares in, Railway or other Companies the interest whereon shall have been guaranteed by the Secretary of State for India-in-Council or by the Central Government or in debentures of the Bombay Provincial Co-operative Bank, Limited, the interest whereon shall have been guaranteed, by the Secretary of State for India-in-Council or the State Government of Bombay;

(*d*) in debentures or other securities for money issued, under the authority of any Central Act or Provincial Act or State Act, by or on behalf of any municipal body, port trust or city improvement trust in any Presidency Town, or in Rangoon Town, or by or on behalf of the trustees of the port of Karachi:

Provided that after the 31st day of March, 1948, no money shall be invested in any securities issued by or on behalf of a municipal body, port trust or city improvement trust in Rangoon town, or by or on behalf of the trustees of the port of Karachi;

(*e*) on a first mortgage of immovable property situate in any part of territories to which this Act extends:

Provided that the property is not a leasehold for a term of years and that the value of the property exceeds by one-third, or, if consisting of buildings, exceeds by one-half, the mortgage money;

(*ee*) in units issued by the Unit Trust of India under any unit scheme made under Scheme 21 of the Unit Trust of India Act, 1963 (52 of 1963); or

(*f*) on any other security expressly authorized by the instrument of trust, or by the Central Government by notification in the Official Gazette or by any rule which the High Court may from time to time prescribe in this behalf:

Provided that, where there is a person competent to contract and entitled in possession to receive the income of the trust-property for his life, or for any greater estate, no investment on any security mentioned or referred to in clauses (*d*), (*e*) and (*f*) shall be made without his consent in writing.

20-A. *Power to purchase redeemable stock at a premium.*—(1) A trustee may invest in any of the securities mentioned or referred to in Section 20, notwithstanding that the same may be redeemable and that the price exceeds the redemption value:

Provided that a trustee may not purchase at a price exceeding its redemption value any security mentioned or referred to in clauses (*c*) and (*d*) of Section 20 which is liable to be redeemed within fifteen years of the date of purchase at par or at some other fixed rate, or purchase any such security as is mentioned or referred to in the said clauses which is liable to be redeemed at par or at some other fixed rate at a price exceeding fifteen per centum above par or such other fixed rate.

(2) A trustee may retain until redemption any redeemable stock, fund or security which may have been purchased in accordance with this section.

21. *Mortagage of land pledged to Government under Act 26 of 1871. Deposit in Government Savings Bank.*—Nothing in Section 20 shall apply to investments made before this Act comes into force, or shall be deemed to preclude an investment on a mortgage of immovable property already pledged as security for an advance under the Land Improvement Act, 1871 (26 of 1871), or, in case the trust-money does not exceed three thousand rupees, a deposit thereof in a Government Savings Bank.

22. *Sale by trustee directed to sell within specified time.*—Where a trustee directed to sell within a specified time extends such time, the burden of proving, as between himself and the beneficiary, that the latter is not prejudiced by the extension lies upon the trustee, unless the extension has been authorised by a principal Civil Court of original jurisdiction.

Illustration

A bequeaths property to *B*, directing him with all convenient speed and within five years to sell it, and apply the proceeds for the benefit of *C*. In the exercise of reasonable discretion, *B* postpones the sale for six years. The sale is not thereby rendered invalid, but *C*, alleging that he has been injured by the postponement, institutes a suit against *B* to obtain compensation. In such suit the burden of proving that *C* has not been injured lies on *B*.

2. ONEROUS NATURE OF OFFICE

According to Professor Issac, a noted author on Trusts, Trusteeship has become a readily available tool for every purpose of organisation, financing, risk-shifting, credit operations, settling disputes and liquidation of business affairs. Maitland the other renowned writer on equity, observed that one of the exploits of Equity, the largest and the most important, is the innovation and the development of the trust. The trust has been and is being applied for all purposes mentioned by Professor Issac, and many others as a device to accomplish different purposes. Trusteeship is an institution of elasticity and generality. The broad base of the concept of property or its management rested in one person and obligation imposed for its enjoyment by others is accepted in Hindu Jurisprudence.[1]

The office of a trustee is an onerous one. So much so that Hanbury has remarked that " ... there is little to be said as to his rights". Hardwicke, L.C., was so much moved by the "cares of office" of a trustee and his position that in *Knight* v. *Earl of Plymouth*[2], it made him remark as under:

> "A trust is an office necessary in the concerns between man and man, and... if faithfully discharged, attended with no small degree of trouble and anxiety" so that "it is an act of great kindness in anyone to accept".[3]

A trustee must act exclusively in the interest of the trust. *He stands to gain nothing* from his work unless the trust instrument so provides. He is required to observe the highest standard of integrity, and a *reasonable standard of business efficiency* in the management of the affairs of the trust; and he is subjected to *onerous personal liability* if he fails to reach the standards set. Nor may he compete in business with the trust; or be in a position in which his personal interests conflict with those of the trust. He may thus be forced to forego opportunities which would be available to him if he were not a trustee.[4]

A question may be asked, that if this were so why do people consent to become trustees? Hanbury[5] in this regard divides the class into two types: professionals and non-professionals. The professionals (e.g., solicitors and banks) charge for what they do, while the non-professionals do not, because they act out of feelings of duty to the settlor. Trusts involve administration and it comprises collection, investment, distribution, accounting, tax payment, etc., and these too depend upon the size of the trust. According to Hanbury, even non-professional trustees, when they have to act efficiently, take the help of professional agents like solicitors, stockbrokers and accountants or taxation experts. It is therefore advisable to appoint professionals or experts as trustees so that technical matters will not be overlooked. At the same time there is some disadvantage in such appointments because such professional trustees are too "official" and never take the slightest of risk in respect of a breach of trust however beneficial such a course may be in the interests of the family. One has also to note that there are certain other persons (e.g., agents, partners, etc.) who though not trustees are under special duties because of their fiduciary position.[6]

We have to keep before us these general principles when we embark upon a discussion of the duties of trustees because they apply in England as well as in India with equal force.

---

1. Quoted in *Mahesh Chandra* v. *Regional Manager, U.P. Financial Corpn.*, (1993) 2 SCC 279: (1993) 78 Comp Cas 1: (1993) 2 GLH 337.
2. 1747 Dick 120.
3. *Snell's Principles of Equity*, p. 204.
4. *Phipps* v. *Boardman*, (1967) 2 AC 46. See also *Snell's Principles of Equity*, pp. 204-205.
5. Hanbury: *Modern Equity*, p. 292.
6. *Ibid.*

Regarding nominated trustees, their removal from office by State Government "at any time" under Section 6 is covered by the Doctrine of pleasure. Where this doctrine applies, there the principles of natural justice would not apply.[7]

3. STANDARDS APPLICABLE TO TRUSTEES

At this juncture a distinction must be made between duties of trustees and their power or discretions.

A duty is an obligation which must be carried out; there is no option, it is imperative and must be performed with the utmost diligence,[8] or *exacta diligentia.*

But a power is discretionary. It may be exercised or it may not. As Salmond observes, it is that which I can do effectively. I am vested with a discretion here to do or not to do a particular thing, and in this field the law actively assists me in making my will effective. A power, as defined by Salmond, is an ability conferred upon a person by law to alter, by his own will, directed to that end, the rights, duties, liabilities or other legal relations, either of himself or of others. A power or discretion given by statute to trustees is in no way different from that which is given by the instrument of trust. A trustee while exercising his power must do so honestly and while managing trust affairs must take "all those precautions which an ordinary prudent man of business would take in managing similar affairs of his own".[9] As to judicial control of the discretionary powers of trustees, as decided in *Tempest* v. *Lord Camoys*[10] Jessel, M.R., said that in case of pure discretion to trustees the court does not enforce the exercise of a power against the wish of the trustees, but it does prevent them from exercising it improperly.

And now comes the most interesting and subtle distinction between an ordinary prudent man's behaviour and the scope of the exercise of a trustee's discretion. As Lord Watson pointed out in *Learoyd* v. *Whiteley*[11] a trustee is under a duty to invest; he has a discretion in the selection of investments, but in the exercise of this discretion he is less free than a prudent man would be in investing his own money; for "businessmen of ordinary prudence may, and frequently do, select investments which are more or less of a speculative character; but it is the duty of a trustee to confine himself to the class of investments which are permitted by the trust and likewise to avoid all investments of that class which are attended with hazard". If he properly performs his duties, powers and discretions, he is not liable for loss to or depreciation of the trust-property arising from factors beyond his control.[12]

---

7. *Krishna* v. *State of Maharashtra*, (2001) 2 SCC 441: AIR 2001 SC 695.
8. Hanbury: *Modern Equity*, p. 293; *Snell's Principles of Equity*, p. 204.
9. *Per* Lord Blackburn in *Speight* v. *Gaunt*, (1883) 9 App Cas 1.
10. (1882) 21 Ch D 571. See also *Gisborne* v. *Gisborne*, (1877) 2 App Cas 300.
11. (1887) 12 App Cas 727. Cited in Hanbury: *Modern Equity*, p. 293.
12. *Lucking's W.T., Re*, (1968) 1 WLR 866.

In the last hundred years England has seen that due to the appointment of professionals as persons doing the administrative work of a trust, the duties of trustees in their strict application have been mitigated. The courts and statute have helped in this pacification process so that the requirement of a trustee to act personally has been relaxed, and the exculpating clauses excluding trustees' personal liability have become statutory. Section 61 of the Trustees Act, 1925, in England, therefore, gives the court a discretion to excuse a trustee who has acted honestly and reasonably and ought fairly to be excused. But it must be remembered that the standard of diligence expected of an unpaid trustee is no less (but equal) than that expected of a paid trustee; the only difference between these two types of trustees being that while an unpaid trustee has an opportunity of taking shelter behind Section 61 of the Trustees Act, a paid trustee will not have such a shelter or to such an extent.[13]

The relationship between trustee and beneficiary is not that of a debtor and creditor.[14] No relationship of trustee and beneficiary exists between the State Electricity Board and its consumers on security deposits made by consumers with the Board for supply of electricity by the Board. The Board is also not a constructive trustee. The object of security deposit is to secure the payment of consumption charges.[15]

Duties of a trustee.—As seen, a duty is an obligation of an imperative nature exacting the utmost diligence. Duties are of two types: positive and negative: positive duties oblige one to do something, negative ones oblige to abstain from doing something. Negative duties are considered to be disabilities. The failure to perform a duty is a breach of trust. The Indian Trusts Act, 1882 lays down the duties of a trustee under Sections 11 to 22 and his liabilities under Sections 23 to 30.

4. TO EXECUTE TRUST (SECTION 11)

As laid down by the section, a trustee—

(*a*) is bound to fulfil the purpose of the trust; and

(*b*) to obey the author's directions contained in the instrument.

Where the directions of the author are illegal, impracticable or manifestly injurious to the beneficiaries, they need not be obeyed. Besides, where all the beneficiaries are competent to contract and they collectively consent to modify the directions or where a court allows a departure from them, the original directions need not be followed. A trust is obligatory and the fulfilment of its purpose in the directed manner is the fundamental duty of a trustee. This finds expression in an adage giving homely truth in a condensed manner, that "he who pays the piper, calls the tune", or "one who pays, dictates". Where such directions are given after a trust has been created they are ineffective and of no

---

13. *Learoyd* v. *Whiteley*, (1887) 12 App Cas 727. Cited in Hanbury: *Modern Equity*, p. 293.
14. *Nawab Mir Barkat Ali* v. *CED*, (1996) 10 SCC 685: (1996) 222 ITR 612.
15. *Ferro Alloys Corpn. Ltd.* v. *A.P. State Electricity Board*, 1993 Supp (4) SCC 136: AIR 1993 SC 2005.

consequence, because on creation of a trust its property is transferred to the trustee and the owner loses all control over it. This is clearly laid down by the section itself by the expression "directions... given at the time of its creation".

The Explanation appended to Section 11 explains the duty of a trustee where the purpose of the trust is for the payment of a debt. There his duty will be to—

(*i*) pay only those debts of the author of the trust which exist and are recoverable at the date of the instrument;

(*ii*) where such instrument creating a trust is a will, the trustee is to pay those debts which exist and are recoverable at the date of the author's death. The reason for this is very clear in that a will speaks from the death of a person and is effective only thereafter; and

(*iii*) in case of debts not bearing interest, a trustee is to make payments without interest.

The gist of Section 11 which lays down a general principle can be stated this way, that a trustee is to execute the trust as far as it is practicable, legally and beneficially, for the *cestui que trust*; the beneficiaries, if all of them are *sui juris* and of one mind, can control the trust and the principal Civil Court of original jurisdiction can permit a departure from the author's original directions in the following cases, as explained and accepted in *New case, Re*,[16] by Romer, L. J.:

(*i*) where circumstances exist which are not foreseen by the author (and therefore not provided for);

(*ii*) where the trustees are embarrassed by emergency; and

(*iii*) where consent of all the beneficiaries cannot be obtained as all of them are not *sui juris* or not in existence.[17]

This was incorporated in the statute-book in England in Section 57 of the Trustees Act, 1925, but with a warning that such a recasted arrangement which is shown to be "beneficial to the estate or to beneficiaries" will not be the sole criterion on which the court's jurisdiction is founded.[18] Every case has its own special circumstances and it will be decided accordingly.

Section 11 of the Indian Trusts Act, 1882 incorporates within its sweep only a part of Chapman's decision[19] in para 2 thereof, which explains that "where the beneficiary is incompetent to contract, his consent may, for the purposes of this section, be given by a principal Civil Court of original jurisdiction".

Maitland[20] has very ably summed up the general rules regarding the duties of a trustee thus:

---

16. (1901) 2 Ch 534.
17. See *Nathan's Equity Through the Cases*, S. 4, p. 546.
18. *Chapman* v. *Chapman*, 1954 AC 429.
19. *Ibid.*
20. *Lectures on Equity*, p. 93.

(*a*) A trustee is *bound to do* anything that he is expressly bidden to do by the instrument creating the trust.

(*b*) A trustee may *safely do* anything that he is expressly authorised to do by that instrument.

(*c*) A trustee is *bound to refrain* from doing anything that is expressly forbidden by that instrument (supposing that the provisions of the instrument in question are in no way invalid or unlawful).

(*d*) Within these limits a trustee must play the part of a prudent owner and a prudent man of business.

That is the standard by which his conduct will be judged.

5. ACQUAINTANCE WITH TRUST-PROPERTY (SECTION 12)

The second duty of a trustee is (*i*) to acquaint himself with the nature and circumstances of the trust-property as soon as possible after his appointment. (*ii*) He must also obtain a transfer of such property to himself, and (*iii*) get in trust-moneys invested on insufficient or hazardous securities. For example, if the trust-money is a debt or a chose-in-action, a trustee should take immediate steps to recover it or to reduce it into possession immediately unless he can show a well-founded justification for his delay or default. If there are two or more trustees, it is not advisable for one trustee to allow the property to remain under the sole control of one trustee but it should be reduced into the joint control of all.[21]

6. TO PROTECT TITLE TO TRUST-PROPERTY (SECTION 13)

It is the most fundamental duty of a trustee to secure and place the trust-property in a state of security. He has to maintain and defend suits for the assertion and protection of its title and for this purpose must take all reasonable and possible steps suitable to the occasion. A trust-property if it is given to the author of the trust by an unregistered deed, it is his duty to get such instrument registered. This situation of a trustee requires the utmost diligence, *exacta diligentia*, and fidelity on his part. And in doing so he cannot deviate from the letter of the trust.

7. NOT TO SET UP ADVERSE TITLE (SECTION 14)

Fidelity is the very foundation of a trust. Consequently a trustee cannot and must not, for himself or for another, set up or aid any title to the trust-property adverse to the interest of the beneficiary. His interest should not conflict with that of the beneficiary and if it is so, he cannot be allowed to do so unless he obtains a proper discharge from trust with which he has clothed himself.[22] In other words, he cannot impeach the trust,[23] others may. But in that case he cannot join them or aid them; he has to defend the trust-property and assert his

---

21. *Cf.* Section 26(*b*), Indian Trusts Act and *see* illustration (*b*) to Section 12.
22. *Shrinivas* v. *V. Ayangar*, 13 BLR 520; *Venkatraman* v. *Jayamal*, AIR 1963 Mad 353.
23. *Asharam* v. *Ludheshvar*, AIR 1931 Nag 335 (FB).

title thereto. If the trust is invalid it is for the beneficiaries to set up their claim against it, but it does not befit a trustee to do so.[24] A trustee consequently cannot mix his own property with that of the trust. If he does so, a burden lies heavily upon him to prove that any particular property belongs to him as distinct from the trust-property.[25]

8. TO EXERCISE REASONABLE CARE (SECTION 15)

Section 15 informs about the care required of a trustee in dealing with trust-property. We have in this chapter explained the standards required of a trustee. He is to observe the highest standard of integrity and a reasonable standard of business efficiency in the management of the affairs of the trust, and if he fails to reach the standards set, he will be subjected to onerous personal liability[26] as the section and its Illustrations (*d*) to (*h*) explain. As has been ably observed by Maitland, a trustee should do that which he is bidden to do and should refrain from doing that which he is forbidden to do.[27] In using his discretion the conduct of a prudent and reasonable man is the standard by which he will be judged; if he fails to reach that, he is held liable. As to what a reasonable man or a person of ordinary prudence would do under the circumstances is a question of fact to be answered by the court on evidence; it is not for the trustee to decide. If he can prove his diligence and the care exercised, he will not be liable. A trustee's discretion is subject, in India, to control by the principal Civil Court of original jurisdiction as provided in Sections 15, 36 and 49 of the Act.[28] Whether a trust is gratuitous or for remuneration, the liability is the same.[29] One has to note that in England, equity courts distinguish between duties and discretions. Duties are *imposed upon* while the discretions are *invested in*, the trustee. Thus, as regards duties, utmost diligence is the only formidable protection and "mere hardship" is no defence;[30] but as regards discretion, the standard is the *amount of* diligence one would bestow on one's own property.[31] Still, however, in both the cases failure to reach the expected standard amounts to a breach of duty.

Strahan in his digest of equity[32] has rightly pointed out that it is a question of fact whether in a particular case reasonable care has been exercised or not, and it can be proved only by evidence. But it is a dangerous practice to decide a question of fact by help of precedents as to what amounts to reasonable care. If this is allowed it would go to establish a "doctrine of constructive want of care" similar to the venerable but exploded doctrine of constructive fraud.

---

24. *Ardeshar* v. *Shirinbai*, 1 BLR 721.
25. *Narayan B. Gosavi* v. *G.V. Gosavi*, AIR 1960 SC 100.
26. *Phipps* v. *Boardman*, (1967) 2 AC 46.
27. Maitland: *Lectures on Equity*, p. 93.
28. *Nilam Tirupati Rayudu* v. *V.L. Narsama*, 38 Mad 71.
29. *Jobson* v. *Palmer*, (1893) 1 Ch 71.
30. *Caffrey* v. *Darby*, (1801) 6 Ves G 488.
31. *Webb* v. *Jones*, 39 Ch D 660. See also *Speight* v. *Gaunt*, (1883) 9 App Cas 1.
32. Strahan & Kenrick: *Digest of Equity*, 3rd Edn., p. 111, cited in Maitland: *Lectures on Equity*, p. 94.

A financial corporation granting loan on hypothecation of property of the loanee is a trustee of the property hypothecated and should act as a prudent owner, bona fide and in good faith while resorting to coercive method such as sale of the property hypothecated in case of default in repayment.[33] Trusteeship has nowadays become a readily available tool for every purpose of organisation and trusteeship is an institution of elasticity and generality.

Thus where the property of the debtor stands transferred to a Financial Corporation for management or possession thereof which includes right to sell or further mortgage, etc., the Corporation or its officers or employees stand in the shoes of the debtor as trustee and the property *cesti que trust*.[34] The very idea is reiterated in N. Surya Narayan Iyer's book[35] as under:

> "Where the trustee is empowered to sell any trust-property... by public auction or private contract and either at one time or at several times... ." The duty of trustee is to obtain the best price. He should therefore use reasonable diligence in inviting competition to that end. Contracts entered into by trustees bona fide would not be invalidated or cancelled by a court, but a trustee should not act in haste unmindful of the consequences.

Where in a trust for sale and payment of creditors the trustee sold at a gross undervaluation showing a preference to one of the creditors, he was held guilty of breach of trust. If the purchaser is privy to fraud the property itself can be recovered from him.[36]

In short, for the trustee, "as is the job, so is the care" to be exercised.[37]

9. TO CONVERT PERISHABLE PROPERTY (SECTION 16)

Section 16 of the Indian Trusts Act embodies the well-known rule in *Howe* v. *Earl of Dartmouth*[38]. It lays down that unless there is a specific intention in the instrument of trust that the property should be enjoyed in specie, it is the duty of a trustee to convert perishable property into that of a permanent and profitable character.

Hanbury[39] has explained the reasons for the rule thus:

> "The rules governing investment by trustees are an attempt to strike a balance between the provision of income for the life tenant and the preservation of the capital for the remainderman.[40] So long as those rules

---

33. *Mahesh Chandra* v. *Regional Manager, U.P. Financial Corpn.*, (1993) 2 SCC 279: (1993) 78 Comp Cas 1: (1993) 2 GLH 337.
34. *Ibid.*
35. N. Surya Narayan Iyer: *Indian Trusts Act*, 3rd Edn., 1987, p. 275 quoted in the case of *Mahesh Chandra*, supra.
36. (1993) 2 SCC 279, *supra.*
37. See *Official Trustee of T.N.* v. *Udavum Karankal*, 1993 Supp (3) SCC 509, 517, 518, *infra*. See also *John D'Souza* v. *Edward Ani*, (1994) 2 SCC 64: (1994) DLT 229 (Care required of his client's will by an advocate, he being a trustee thereof).
38. 1 W&T: (1802) 7 Ves 137; Nathan: *Equity Through the Cases*, No. 131.
39. *Modern Equity*, pp. 328-330.
40. For details *see* "The Economics of Investment" in Hanbury: *Modern Equity*, pp. 314-316.

are observed, a trustee is usually under no duty to rearrange the investments so as to balance equally the interests of the life tenant and remainderman. Nor if there are unauthorised investments in the fund, are the trustees under any duty to covert them into authorised investments. However, the fund if invested, the normal rule is that the tenant for life takes all the income; the remainderman's interest is in the capital. The capital is not of course available until the life tenant's death; but he may if he wishes, deal with or dispose of his reversionary interest in the fund... . A duty to convert and reinvest in authorised investments may arise by reason of the existence of an express trust to sell or to convert, or by statute, or in the case of a bequest of residuary personality, under the rule in *Howe* v. *Earl of Dartmouth...* . The rule establishes that independently of any provision in the will, there is a duty to convert where residuary personality is settled by will in favour of persons who are to enjoy it in succession. The trustees should convert all such parts of it as are of a wasting or future or reversionary nature or consist of unauthorised securities, into property of a permanent or income-bearing character."[41]

It must be noted that this rule has but limited application and it does not apply to property settled *inter vivos*, nor to specific as opposed to residuary bequests. Nor does it apply to freehold lands nor to leaseholds held for a term exceeding sixty years.

This rule in thus a part of the *economics of investment* and the Illustrations to Section 16 explain it. The section and the Illustrations thus lay down an equitable principle so that the benefit of the trust-property may not be exhausted by [in Illustration (*a*) to the section] *B* or *C*, but may be left available to all the beneficiaries equally and equitably. The burden of proof always rests on the person who asserts that the principle is not applicable.

10. TO BE IMPARTIAL (SECTION 17)

Where there are more beneficiaries than one, he cannot execute the trust in favour of one at the expense of another. He has to be impartial. He has not to pick and choose between beneficiaries; that is not given to him. He should not favour a tenant for life by investing in more productive but less secure property. He has to hold the scales evenly between the beneficiaries. The rule in *Howe case* is applicable here too, for it is a trustee's duty to hold an even hand between all their beneficiaries.[42]

11. TO PREVENT WASTE (SECTION 18)

Where out of several beneficiaries in succession, one in possession of the property commits or threatens to commit waste, the trustee must prevent it, as it is his duty. The meaning is very plain that a life tenant cannot behave in a manner prejudicial to the interests of the remainderman. Such acts either of destruction or of depreciation of the value of the trust-property are known as

41. Hanbury: *Modern Equity*, pp. 328-330.
42. Fry, L.J., in *Lepine, Re*, (1892) 1 Ch 210.

waste, which a trustee is bound to prevent unless they are permissive in their character.[43]

12. ACCOUNTS AND INFORMATION (SECTION 19)

A trustee is bound to maintain clear, accurate and proper accounts of trust-property and must be prepared to produce it on demand by the beneficiaries. He should not 'conceal' anything.[44] He is also bound to render such accounts in respect of the state of the trust-property. He is at the same time entitled under Section 35 to get his accounts settled and examined on completion of his office and to an acknowledgement from the beneficiaries that there is nothing due by him to the trust. He cannot advance his illiteracy or incapability as a defence for his fault. Consequently, as decided in *Lakhmichand* v. *Jaykuvarbai*[45], he becomes *prima facie* liable for the loss that thereby occurs.

A trustee should not mix trust-property with any private property. If he does so it lies heavily upon him to prove that a particular property is his.[46]

Besides this, a trustee is not only liable for moneys received in his possession but also liable for moneys which might have come into his possession had he acted with suitable alertness and diligence.[47]

13. INVESTMENT OF TRUST-MONEY (SECTIONS 20, 20-A, 21 AND 22)

Sections 20, 20-A and 21 of the Act cast a duty upon the trustee to invest[48] the trust-property, if it is money not immediately needed, into the securities mentioned therein and in no others. Where a trustee is directed to sell within[49] a specified time he should do so unless he has valid and justifiable reasons to act otherwise. Section 22 in this respect is more a power to a trustee than a duty; it is a power to sell within a specified time conferred upon him by a direction contained in the deed, but it is his duty to sell.

As we have seen, the duties of trustees are many. Those who are asked to become trustees "are bound to inquire of what the property consists that is proposed to be handed over to them and what are the trusts. They ought also to look into the trust documents and papers to ascertain what notices appear among them of incumbrances and other matters affecting the trust".[50] In carrying out the trusts they must take due care of the trust-property by investing it prudently and in the manner directed; they must give information to the beneficiaries when required and in some cases submit to their directions; they must comply with any directions of the court and when in difficulty seek its aid; and finally they

43. See *Lalit Mohan* v. *Kishan Mohan Laxmichand*, (1904) 6 Bom LR 907.
44. *Walker* v. *Symmonds*, (1818) 19 AA 155.
45. 6 BLR 907.
46. *Narayan* v. *Gopal*, AIR 1960 SC 100, 114.
47. *Vasudevan* v. *Bhavadasan*, AIR 1934 Mad 115.
48. *Littlehale case*, (1970) 3 Bro CC 73.
49. *Fry* v. *Fry*, (1859) 27 Beav 144.
50. *Hallows* v. *Lloyd*, (1888) 39 Ch D 686, *per* Kekewich, J., cited in *Snell's Principles of Equity*, p. 205.

must make no profit out of the trust unless authorised.[51] In other words, on appointment trustees must make themselves acquainted with the state and details of the trust-property, check that the trust fund is invested in accordance with the provisions of the trust deed and that the securities are in proper custody. They should not wait until the trust-property is formally vested in them. The discharge of their duties will obviously depend upon circumstances but the duty to protect the trust assets is a stringent one is also a continuous one. It is enforced very stringently too.[52] As would be seen from the sections, the most important or basic duties of trustees are duties of collecting, of investing and of distributing the assets according to claims, and to provide accounts and information with due regard to the principle of equality. A trustee should not keep unnecessary cash with him which is not required for immediate expenses. This should be avoided.[53]

14. POSITIVE AND NEGATIVE DUTIES

As said before, duties are either positive or negative. Positive duties impose an obligation to do something, negative duties ask a trustee to refrain from doing something. Looking from this point of view, and as Strahan has pointed out, subject to the *absolute duty* of a trustee to carry out the directions of the settlor as contained in the instrument of trust (Section 11 of the Indian Trusts Act), the following are the positive duties—

(*i*) to preserve the trust-property, this being a stringent and a continuous duty (*cf.* Sections 12, 13, 16, 18 and 20, Indian Trusts Act),

(*ii*) to transfer the income and the corpus to the persons entitle thereto (*cf.* Sections 55 and 56, Indian Trusts Act), and

(*iii*) to render accounts and supply information (*cf.* Section 57, Indian Trusts Act).

The negative duties are as follows—

(*i*) not to make a profit out of the trust-property (*cf.* Sections 50 and 51, Indian Trusts Act),

(*ii*) as a general rule not to purchase trust-property from himself or from his co-trustees (*cf.* Sections 52 and 53, Indian Trusts Act), and

(*iii*) as a general rule, not to delegate his duties (*cf.* Section 47, Indian Trusts Act).

B. LIABILITIES

1. TEXT OF SECTIONS 23 TO 30

23. *Liability for breach of trust.*—Where the trustee commits a breach of trust, he is liable to make good the loss which the trust-property or the

51. *Snell's Principles of Equity*, p. 205.
52. Hanbury: *Modern Equity*, pp. 310-312.
53. *Ratilal* v. *State of Bombay*, AIR 1954 SC 388.

beneficiary has thereby sustained, unless the beneficiary has by fraud induced the trustee to commit the breach, or the beneficiary, being competent to contract, has himself, without coercion or undue influence having been brought to bear on him, concurred in the breach, or subsequently acquiesced therein, with full knowledge of the facts of the case and of his rights as against the trustee.

A trustee committing a breach of trust is not liable to pay interest except in the following cases:—

(*a*) where he has actually received interest;

(*b*) where the breach consists in unreasonable delay in paying trust-money to the beneficiary;

(*c*) where the trustee ought to have received interest, but has not done so;

(*d*) where he may be fairly presumed to have received interest.

He is liable in case (*a*), to account for the interest actually received, and, in cases (*b*), (*c*) and (*d*), to account for simple interest at the rate of six per cent per annum, unless the Court otherwise directs.

(*e*) where the breach consists in failure to invest trust-money and to accumulate the interest or dividends thereon, he is liable to account for compound interest (with half-yearly rests) at the same rate;

(*f*) where the breach consists in the employment of trust-property or the proceeds thereof in trade or business, he is liable to account, at the option of the beneficiary, either for compound interest (with half-yearly rests) at the same rate, or for the net profits made by such employment.

Illustrations

(*a*) *A* trustee improperly leaves trust-property outstanding, and it is consequently lost: he is liable to make good the property lost, but he is not liable to pay interest thereon.

(*b*) *A* bequeaths a house to *B* in trust to sell it and pay the proceeds to *C*. *B* neglects to sell the house for a great length of time, whereby the house is deteriorated and its market price falls. *B* is answerable to *C* for the loss.

(*c*) *A* trustee is guilty of unreasonable delay in investing trust-money in accordance with Section 20, or in paying it to the beneficiary. The trustee is liable to pay interest thereon for the period of the delay.

(*d*) The duty of the trustee is to invest trust-money in any of the securities mentioned in Section 20, clause (*a*), (*b*), (*c*) or (*d*). Instead of so doing, he retains the money in his hands. He is liable, at the option of the beneficiary, to be charged either with the amount of the principal money and interest, or with the amount of such securities as he might have purchased with the trust-money when the investment should have been made, and the intermediate dividends and interest thereon.

(*e*) The instrument of trust directs the trustee to invest trust-money either in any of such securities or on mortgage of immovable property. The trustee does neither. He is liable for the principal money and interest.

(*f*) The instrument of trust directs the trustee to invest trust-money in any of such securities and to accumulate the dividends thereon. The trustee disregards the direction. He is liable, at the option of the beneficiary, to be charged either with the amount of the principal money and compound interest, or with the amount of such securities as he might have purchased with the trust-money when the investment should have been made, together with the amount of the accumulation which would have arisen from a proper investment of the intermediate dividends.

(*g*) Trust-property is invested in one of the securities mentioned in Section 20, clause (*a*), (*b*), (*c*) or (*d*). The trustee sells such security for some purpose not authorized by the terms of the instrument of trust. He is liable, at the option of the beneficiary, either to replace the security with the intermediate dividends and interest thereon, or to account for the proceeds of the sale with interest thereon.

(*h*) The trust-property consists of land. The trustee sells the land to a purchaser for a consideration without notice of the trust. The trustee is liable, at the option of the beneficiary, to purchase other land of equal value to be settled upon the like trust, or to be charged with the proceeds of the sale with interest.

24. *No set-off allowed to trustee.*—A trustee who is liable for a loss occasioned by a breach of trust in respect of one portion of the trust-property cannot set-off against his liability a gain which has accrued to another portion of the trust-property through another and distinct breach of trust.

25. *Non-liability for predecessor's default.*—Where a trustee succeeds another, he is not, as such, liable for the acts or defaults of his predecessor.

26. *Non-liability for co-trustee's default.*—Subject to the provisions of Sections 13 and 15, one trustee is not, as such, liable for a breach of trust committed by his co-trustee:

Provided that, in the absence of an express declaration to the contrary in the instrument of trust, a trustee is so liable—

(*a*) where he has delivered trust-property to his co-trustee without seeing to its proper application;

(*b*) where he allows his co-trustee to receive trust-property and fails to make due enquiry as to the co-trustee's dealings therewith, or allows him to retain it longer than the circumstances of the case reasonably require;

(*c*) where he becomes aware of a breach of trust committed or intended by his co-trustee, and either actively conceals it or does not within a reasonable time take proper steps to protect the beneficiary's interest.

Joining in receipt for conformity.—A co-trustee who joins in signing a receipt for trust-property and proves that he has not received the same is not answerable, by reason of such signature only, for loss or misapplication of the property by his co-trustee.

Illustration

A bequeaths certain property to *B* and *C*, and directs them to sell it and invest the proceeds for the benefit of *D*. *B* and *C* accordingly sell the property, and the purchase-money is received by *B* and retained in his hands. *C* pays no attention to the matter for two years and then calls on *B* to make the investment. *B* is unable to do so, becomes insolvent, and the purchase-money is lost. *C* may be compelled to make good the amount.

27. *Several liabilities of co-trustees.*—Where co-trustees jointly commit a breach of trust, or where one of them by his neglect enables the other to commit

a breach of trust, each is liable to the beneficiary for the whole of the loss occasioned by such breach.

Contribution as between co-trustees.—But as between the trustees themselves, if one be less guilty than another and has had to refund the loss, the former may compel the latter, or his legal representative to the extent of the assets he has received, to make good such loss; and if all be equally guilty, any one or more of the trustees who has had to refund the loss may compel the others to contribute.

Nothing in this section shall be deemed to authorize a trustee who has been guilty of fraud to institute a suit to compel contribution.

28. *Non-liability of trustee paying without notice of transfer by beneficiary.*—When any beneficiary's interest becomes vested in another person, and the trustee, not having notice of the vesting, pays or delivers trust-property to the person who would have been entitled thereto in the absence of such vesting, the trustee is not liable for the property so paid or delivered.

29. *Liability of trustee where beneficiary's interest is forfeited to the Government.*—When the beneficiary's interest is forfeited or awarded by legal adjudication to the Government, the trustee is bound to hold the trust-property to the extent of such interest for the benefit of such person in such manner as the State Government may direct in this behalf.

30. *Indemnity of trustees.*—Subject to the provisions of the instrument of trust and of Sections 23 and 26, trustees shall be respectively chargeable only for such moneys, stocks, funds and securities as they respectively actually receive, and shall not be answerable the one for the other of them, nor for any banker, broker or other person in whose hands any trust-property may be placed, nor for the insufficiency or deficiency of any stocks, funds or securities, nor otherwise for involuntary losses.

2. BREACH OF TRUST[54]

(*a*) *Meaning and definition.*—Simply stated, a breach of trust is failing to do what a trust requires a trustee to do. But it is not only by commission of an act that a breach ensues, but also by an omission to do so. As has been aptly said, "Breaches of trust are almost infinitely various. They range from the fraudulent conversion of trust funds to purely technical failures of duty which harm nobody, and transactions (such as some investments in unauthorised securities) which result in a substantial profit for the trust."[55] It is better therefore to say that a trustee may commit 'judicious' breaches of trust.[56]

A breach of trust, as defined by Keeton, consists in (*i*) some improper act, (*ii*) neglect, (*iii*) default, or (*iv*) omission of a trustee in respect of trust-property or beneficiary's interest therein. It may be active or passive. Active breach results from action; passive, from omission. In other words, any act by a trustee

54. *Townley* v. *Sherborne*, (1634) BR 35.
55. *Snell's Principles of Equity*, p. 272.
56. *Perrins* v. *Bellamy*, (1899) 1 Ch 797, Lord Lindley quoting Selwyn, L.J.

in reference to the trust-property in contravention of the duties imposed on him by the trust, or in excess of those duties, and any neglect or omission on his part to fulfil those duties and the concurrence or acquiescence by one of the several trustees in a similar act, neglect or omission on the part of a co-trustee constitutes a breach of trust. But when (*i*) the provisions of the trust deed relieve a trustee, or (*ii*) the statute so relieves him, or (*iii*) where it is occasioned by necessity, or (*iv*) authorised, and (*v*) condoned by beneficiaries, and where (*vi*) it is due to an innocent mistake, a trustee is relieved from the liability ensuing therefrom.[57] In one sentence a trustee is liable for a breach of trust if there was in him an intention to prejudice, or an act or default which prejudiced, the trust.[58]

(*b*) *Section 23.*—As laid down by the section, a trustee is liable for breach of trust. Liability presupposes existence of duty and a trustee is under an imperative duty to execute the trust. As has been said, it has been the constant habit of courts of equity to charge trustees for breach of trust and to charge their representatives also, whether they derive benefit therefrom or not. The section clearly states that such a trustee is liable to make good the loss occasioned to the trust-property or to the interest of beneficiaries. But a trustee will not incur liability if (*i*) he was induced by fraud of the beneficiaries[59], or (*ii*) the beneficiaries have concurred therein, or (*iii*) have subsequently acquiesced therein with full knowledge of their rights and the facts.

The liability of a trustee for breach of trust does not depend upon benefit received by him, but upon an act or omission. Remaining passive is equally a breach of trust where a trustee is required to act. Equity will not tolerate this passivism or set a premium upon inactivity of a trustee. Breach of any of the duties as detailed in Sections 11 to 20 will result in breach of trust.[60] Section 23, Illustrations, (*a*) to (*g*) explain that (*i*) where a trustee improperly leaves the trust-property outstanding, which is consequently lost, (*ii*) where on account of his neglect, sale of a trust-property is unduly delayed and a consequent loss in the form of fall of price ensues, (*iii*) where unreasonable delay in investing trust funds invites a loss of interest to trust-property or to the beneficiary, (*iv*) where a loss results from retaining trust money in trustee's hands, while they could have been invested in government securities as explained in Section 20, and (*v*) where a loss results from his selling of the trust land which he should not have done; in all such cases he is liable for breach of trust.

(*c*) *Measure of liability.*—The measure of liability for breach is the loss caused to the estate which will have to be paid with interest as explained in Section 23. A point to be noted here is that the loss caused to the trust-property must be attributable to, or must be capable of being connected with, the breach

57. *Halsbury's Laws of England*, Vol. 26, pp. 184-185.
58. *Townley* v. *Sherborne*, (1634) BR 35. See *Mahesh Chandra* v. *Regional Manager, U.P. Financial Corpn.*, (1993) 2 SCC 279: (1993) 78 Comp Cas 1: (1993) 2 Guj LH 337.
59. *Overton* v. *Banister*, (1844) 3 Hare 503.
60. *Tirupatiraidu case*, ILR 38 Mad 71.

of trust by the trustee, i.e., a causal connection must be established between the act or omission of a trustee and the loss resulted.

In *Official Trustee of T.N.* v. *Udavum Karankal*[61], a question was raised whether the Official Trustee had acted in undue haste and in an irresponsible manner in proceeding to demolish the building without obtaining specific orders of the court, to the detriment of the trust. As the facts go predecessor of Official Trustee obtained sanction from the High Court for conversion of tiled roof of marriage hall belonging to the trust into RCC roof and for providing other amenities at a cost of Rs 6 lacs, to augment trust income. Official Trustee, however, after obtaining opinion of architect, decided to demolish the entire structure and re-erect the same at a cost of Rs 10 lacs. He accordingly demolished the structure and applied to the High Court for sanction of the revised plan. High Court rejected the application and directed that expenditure in excess of Rs 6 lacs involved be borne by the Official Trustee himself. The case therefore came in appeal before the Supreme Court. The Supreme Court held that to the extent that the Official Trustee did not take the permission of the High Court before proceeding to demolish the existing structure, he did not commit a breach of trust. Nevertheless, he could not, in the circumstances of the case, be made personally liable for the breach. His intention in promoting the revised proposal was in the interest of the trust and his bona fides could not be impeached. He had acted on professional advice that the building had become old and dilapidated and that from the point of view of augmenting the income of the trust, a new structure was desirable. The additional expenditure involved was also within reasonable bounds. Hence the High Court was not justified in fastening personal liability on the Official Trustee for the additional expenditure involved. Order of the High Court was therefore set aside.

(*d*) *No set-off: Section 24.*—In case there are more than one transactions and a loss results in one and a gain in another, a trustee cannot be allowed to set-off the loss against the gain obtained and thus cover his neglect or default and get out of the liability. But if gain and loss both are in one and the same transaction it can be adjusted.[62] In other words, the measure of a trustee's liability is the whole loss or the whole gain, e.g., if he wrongfully sells stock and applies the proceeds for his purpose, he is liable for the amount necessary to replace the whole stock.[63] There can be no adjustment between two distinct breaches of trust. Not only this, but he is also liable to pay interest thereon as laid down by the section.

(*e*) *Liability for Interest: Section 23.*—No interest is payable by a trustee except in the following cases—

(*i*) where he has actually received it;[64]

(*ii*) where he has delayed payments to the beneficiary;

61. 1993 Supp (3) SCC 509, 517, 518: AIR 1993 SC 1472.
62. *Fletcher* v. *Green*, 33 Beav 426.
63. *Sadler* v. *Lea*, 6 Beav 824.
64. *Emmet case*, 17 Ch D 142.

(*iii*) where he ought to have received interest, but has not done so;

(*iv*) where he may be fairly presumed to have received it, e.g., if he has employed trust-property in private trade;[65]

(*v*) where he fails to invest trust money[66] (a gross misconduct amounting to a direct breach of trust); and

(*vi*) where he employs the trust-property in trade or business.

In all such cases a trustee is liable to make good the loss to the trust-property along with the interest at the rate of six per cent. It must be noted that the rate of 6% interest is very low and it must be raised substantially as the occasion demands. The old rate of 6% therefore requires a suitable amendment by the Parliament.

For following the trust-property or its proceeds into the hands of a trustee or his legal representatives, there is no bar of the Limitation Act.[67]

(*f*) *Co-Trustees*: *Liability and Non-liability* (*Sections 25, 26, 27, 28, 29* and *30*).—As provided by Section 26, one trustee is not liable as such for a breach of trust committed by his co-trustee; but this non-liability is there only when he behaves in accordance with the provisions of Sections 13 and 15.

If there is no express declaration about such liability in the instrument of trust, a trustee is so liable for his co-trustee's default in the following cases—

(*i*) where he delivers property to co-trustee without seeing to its proper application;

(*ii*) where he allows his co-trustee to receive the trust-property, but fails to inquire into the dealings made by the co-trustee; or

(*iii*) where he allows him to retain it for a period longer than required; or

(*iv*) where he actively conceals or does not take proper steps to protect the property from his co-trustee's breach of trust, either committed or intended.[68]

The gist of the section may be expressed thus that a trustee must properly delegate, he must employ fit and proper persons, the delegation should not last for a period longer than necessary, and he must look into the acts of the agent and check whether he properly performs them or not. Thus a trustee is liable for his co-trustee's acts if he has allowed things to take place knowingly, the result whereof is fraud; and he actively involves himself therein. But where he is not so involved, there is no liability.

A trustee succeeding another is not liable for the acts or defaults of his predecessor (Section 25). And he is not even liable for default of his co-trustees.

---

65. *See* Section 10, Indian Limitation Act.
66. See *Hukum Chand* v. *Fulchand*, AIR 1955 SC 1692.
67. *Ibid.*
68. Based on the decision of *Wilkins* v. *Hogg*, 3 Gift 116.

The law as to liability of a trustee for the default of his co-trustee is discussed in the leading cases of *Townley* v. *Sherborne* and *Brice* v. *Stokes* in England.[69]

Co-trustees jointly committing a breach of trust, or enabling one to commit such a breach, make each one liable to the beneficiary for the whole of the loss so occasioned. Each is therefore liable to contribute equally towards the loss.[70] On the analogy that there is no contribution between joint tort feasors,[71] a trustee who has committed a fraud is not entitled to contribution from his co-trustee (Section 27). When one of the co-trustees committing a breach of trust becomes a beneficiary thereafter, he will be liable for the loss occasioned by his breach to the extent of his interest in the trust-property.[72] Where a loss is occasioned due to wrong advice of a trustee on whom others are entitled to rely, the trustee so advising will have to indemnify his co-trustees. Section 27 explains this.

Section 28 lays down the non-liability of a trustee paying without notice of transfer by a beneficiary. Section 29 provides one more liability of a trustee to hold the trust-property for the benefit of persons directed by the State Government, in case of forfeiture of the beneficiary's interest. Section 30 limits the liabilities of trustees to such moneys, stocks, funds and securities as they actually receive and they shall not be answerable for the acts of a banker, broker or any person in whose hands trust-property may be placed, nor for insufficiency or deficiency of any stocks, funds or securities, nor otherwise for involuntary losses. This section therefore provides an indemnity for trustees.

---

69. (1634) BR 35 and (1805) 11 Ves 319.
70. *Jackson* v. *Dickinson*, (1903) 1 Ch 947.
71. *Merryweather* v. *Nixon*, (1799) 8 TR 186.
72. Such a trustee's beneficial interest will be impounded in accordance with the rule in *Dacre, Re*, (1916) 1 Ch 344.

Chapter XV

Trustees—Their rights and powers

"At one period the 'conscience' of the trustee was so severely scrutinized that ordinary honest execution of a trust became a matter of considerable difficulty; and it was not till 1887 that doctrines... (e.g., 'overrighteousness of equity') were tempered with common sense, not to say mercy."

—*Learoyd* v. *Whiteley*, 12 App Cas 727

C.K. Allen: *Law in the Making*, cited at p. 418.

SYNOPSIS

A. RIGHTS

1. TEXT OF SECTIONS 31 TO 35

31. *Right to title-deed.*—A trustee is entitled to have in his possession the instrument of trust and all the documents of title (if any) relating solely to the trust-property.

32. *Right to reimbursement of expenses.*—Every trustee may reimburse himself, or pay or discharge out of the trust-property, all expenses properly incurred in or about the execution of the trust, or the realization, preservation or benefit of the trust-property, or the protection or support of the beneficiary.

If he pays such expenses out of his own pocket he has a first charge upon the trust-property for such expenses and interest thereon; but such charge (unless the expenses have been incurred with the sanction of a Principal Civil Court of original jurisdiction) shall be enforced only by prohibiting any disposition of the trust-property without previous payment of such expenses and interest.

If the trust-property fails, the trustee is entitled to recover from the beneficiary personally on whose behalf he acted, and at whose request, expressed or implied, he made the payment of the amount of such expenses.

Right to be recouped for erroneous overpayment.—Where a trustee has by mistake made an over-payment to the beneficiary, he may reimburse the trust-property out of the beneficiary's interest. If such interest fails, the trustee is entitled to recover from the beneficiary personally the amount of such over-payment.

33. *Right to indemnity from gainer by breach of trust.*—A person other than a trustee who has gained an advantage from a breach of trust must indemnify the trustee to the extent of the amount actually received by such person under the breach; and where he is a beneficiary the trustee has a charge on his interest for such amount.

Nothing in this section shall be deemed to entitle a trustee to be indemnified who has, in committing the breach of trust, been guilty of fraud.

34. *Right to apply to court for opinion in management of trust-property.*— Any trustee may, without instituting a suit, apply by petition to a principal Civil Court of original jurisdiction for its opinion, advice or direction on any present questions respecting the management or administration of the trust-property other than questions of detail, difficulty or importance, not proper in the opinion of the Court for summary disposal.

A copy of such petition shall be served upon, and the hearing thereof may be attended by, such of the persons interested in the application as the Court thinks fit.

The trustee stating in good faith the facts in such petition and acting upon the opinion, advice or direction given by the Court shall be deemed, so far as regards his own responsibility, to have discharged his duty as such trustee in the subject-matter of the application.

The costs of every application under this section shall be in the discretion of the Court to which it is made.

35. *Right to settlement of accounts.*—When the duties of a trustee, as such, are completed, he is entitled to have the accounts of his administration of the trust-property examined and settled; and, where nothing is due to the beneficiary under the trust, to an acknowledgment in writing to that effect.

2. ABOUT RIGHTS AND POWERS

In the strict sense of the term, to ascribe a right to a person is to imply that some other person is under a corresponding duty. Used in a wider sense, to say that a man has a right to something is roughly to say that it is his right to obtain it. This may entail that others ought to provide him with it, or that they ought not to prevent him from getting it, or merely that it would not be wrong for him to get it. Thus in the strictest sense *rights constitute the correlatives of duties*; in its generic sense it connotes and may be defined as *any advantage or benefit conferred upon a person by a rule of law*. Of rights in this sense there are four distinct kinds: (*i*) rights (in the strict sense), (*ii*) liberties, (*iii*) powers, and (*iv*) immunities.[1]

1. Salmond: *Jurisprudence*, Chap. 7.

We are concerned here with the rights and powers of trustees. A right exists when law *limits the liberty of others* in my behalf, and a power exists when law *actively assists me* in making my will effective. In other words, what others *ought to do* towards me is my right; what *I may do innocently is* my liberty; but *what I can do effectively is my power.*

The rights and powers of trustees have been laid down in Chapter IV, Sections 31 to 45 of the Indian Trusts Act. Accordingly a trustee is entitled (*i*) to have the title deeds of the trust-property in his possession, (*ii*) to be reimbursed of the expenses incurred in respect of the property of the trust, (*iii*) to seek the court's opinion, (*iv*) to have the accounts of the trust-property examined and settled, and (*v*) to be indemnified from the gainer by breach of trust.

Apart from the above rights, one has to remember that a trustee has one supreme and extraordinary right, and that is a right conferred by law upon him that he can give a valid title to a *bona fide* purchaser from him without notice even though his act of alienation may be one resulting from his breach of trust. He has also those rights which a trust instrument confers upon him or which are given to him or recognised by equity, which he is to exercise for the benefit of the beneficiaries. The Indian Trusts Act gives him the following rights.

3. RIGHTS TO TITLE DEED (SECTION 31)

In the eyes of the law, a trustee is the owner of the trust estate and therefore he is entitled to have in his possession the instrument of trust and all the other documents of title relating solely to the trust-property. When a trust is created there must be a transfer of property to the trustee or else no trust can come into existence. When the title deeds relating to property are not delivered up to the trustee, a trustee has a right to secure them so that the same may not be used otherwise and so that he can be safe and the property secured.

4. RIGHT TO REIMBURSEMENT OF EXPENSES (SECTION 32)

It is the right of a trustee to be reimbursed from the trust-property, as regards all expenses properly incurred in connection with the execution of the trust, or realization, preservation, protection of the trust-property and support of the beneficiary. Such expenses if incurred out of his pocket shall be the first charge over the trust-property and before such property is disposed of this charge must be settled. If the trust-property fails to pay for these expenses, they would be recovered from the beneficiary personally. The same is the case with overpayment made erroneously to the beneficiary by a trustee.

In order that a trustee may recover the expenses from the beneficiary personally, the beneficiary must be *sui juris* and must not have disclaimed his beneficial interest in the trust. As expressed by Lord Elden, such a charge being in respect of expenses incurred in respect of due discharge of duties of the office of a trustee, it is not considered to be a profit obtained by the trustee from his office and, therefore, even though the instrument does not provide for it, it shall be reimbursed.[2] To be recoverable, such charges must fulfil two conditions: (*i*) they must be in the execution of the trust, and (*ii*) they must be reasonable and not speculative or oppressive. Only the good faith of a trustee, short of the above two conditions left unfulfilled, is not helpful to him.

5. RIGHT TO INDEMNITY AGAINST BENEFICIARY PERSONALLY (SECTION 32)

As pointed out by Nathan[3], a trustee's right of indemnity in respect of expenses properly incurred, e.g., in respect of costs, a call on shares, solicitor's, stockbroker's or auctioneer's charges, is a right of indemnity against the *trust-estate*, not against the *beneficiary*. Hence the trustees of an ordinary club are entitled to be indemnified by the club property, not by the club members.[4] But in the following circumstances a trustee's indemnity extends beyond the estate to the beneficiary personally.

First, where the trustee accepted the trust at the request of the beneficiary. Secondly, where the beneficiary was the creator of the trust. Thirdly, where the beneficiary is a sole beneficiary *sui juris* and entitled absolutely,[5] and fourthly, where there is apparently also a personal indemnity against several beneficiaries, provided they are all *sui juris* and collectively entitled absolutely and the expense was incurred at the request of all of them. Section 32, para 3 implies this position.

6. RIGHT TO INDEMNITY FROM GAINER BY BREACH OF TRUST (SECTION 33)

A person gaining an advantage from a breach of trust must indemnify the trustee to the extent of the benefit obtained by him from the breach. Such a person must not be a trustee but if he is a beneficiary, his beneficial interest will stand charged for such amount. A trustee committing a fraud and obtaining a benefit from his breach of trust is not entitled to be indemnified.

7. RIGHT TO SEEK COURT'S DIRECTION (SECTION 34)

Opinion, advice or direction of a principal Civil Court of original jurisdiction can be sought by a trustee by an application in that regard, on any present questions of management or administration of trust-property. And a trustee so acting according to court's opinion shall be deemed to have discharged his duties in that respect. But on questions of detail, difficulty or importance, no such petition for court's advice can be filed. It is for the court to decide whether the questions are worth summary disposal or otherwise. Section 34 is an enabling section. It does not take away powers from trustees.[6] Under this section the court will not decide as to who is entitled to be a trustee.[7]

---

2. *Warral* v. *Harford*, 8 Ves 8; *Bennet* v. *Wyndham*, 4 DF & J 259.
3. *Equity Through the Cases*, p. 617.
4. *Wise* v. *Perpetual Trustee Co.*, 1903 AC 139.
5. *Hardoon* v. *Belilios*, 1901 AC 118.
6. *D.K. Sain* v. *Smt Nandarani Dassi*, AIR 1970 Cal 292.
7. *Krishna Kumar Keosa* v. *Krishanlal*, AIR 1979 J&K 13.

8. RIGHT TO SETTLEMENT OF ACCOUNTS (SECTION 35)

On completion of his duties as a trustee, he is entitled to have the trust accounts examined and settled and to obtain an acknowledgment that nothing is due to the beneficiary under the trust.

B. POWERS

1. TEXT OF SECTIONS 36 TO 45

36. *General authority of trustee.*—In addition to the powers expressly conferred by this Act and by the instrument of trust, and subject to the restrictions, if any, contained in such instrument, and to the provisions of Section 17, a trustee may do all acts which are reasonable and proper for the realization, protection or benefit of the trust-property, and for the protection or support of a beneficiary who is not competent to contract.[8]

Except with the permission of a principal Civil Court of original jurisdiction, no trustees shall lease trust-property for a term exceeding twenty-one years from the date of executing the lease, nor without reserving the best yearly rent that can be reasonably obtained.[9]

37. *Power to sell in lots, and either by public auction or private contract.*—Where the trustee is empowered to sell any trust-property, he may sell the same subject to prior charges or not, and either together or in lots, by public auction or private contract, and either at one time or at several times, unless the instrument of trust otherwise directs.

38. *Power to sell under special conditions: Power to buy-in and re-sell.*—The trustee making any such sale may insert such reasonable stipulations either as to title or evidence of title, or otherwise, in any conditions of sale or contract for sale, as he thinks fit; and may also buy-in the property or any part thereof at any sale by auction, and rescind or vary any contract for sale, and re-sell the property so bought in, or as to which the contract is so rescinded, without being responsible to the beneficiary for any loss occasioned thereby.

Time allowed for selling trust-property.—Where a trustee is directed to sell trust-property or to invest trust-money in the purchase of property, he may exercise a reasonable discretion as to the time of effecting the sale or purchase.

Illustrations

(*a*) *A* bequeaths property to *B*, directing him to sell it with all convenient speed and pay the proceeds to *C*. This does not render an immediate sale imperative.

---

8. *CIT* v. *Palghat Shadi Mahal Trust*, (2002) 9 SCC 685 (Provision in the trust deed entitling the general body of trustees to decide the meaning and scope of the clauses contained therein—its scope discussed.)
9. *Mehrwan Homi Irani* v. *Charity Commr., Bombay*, (2001) 5 SCC 305. (Lease for a period exceeding the statutory period; relevant considerations for grant of such lease of Bombay Public Trusts Act, 1950.)

(*b*) *A* bequeaths property to *B*, directing him to sell it at such time and in such manner as he shall think fit and invest the proceeds for the benefit of *C*. This does not authorize *B*, as between him and *C*, to postpone the sale to an indefinite period.

39. *Power to convey.*—For the purpose of completing any such sale, the trustee shall have power to convey or otherwise dispose of the property sold in such manner as may be necessary.

40. *Power to vary investments.*—A trustee may, at his discretion, call in any trust-property invested in any security and invest the same on any of the securities mentioned or referred to in Section 20, and from time to time vary any such investments for others of the same nature:

Provided that, where there is a person competent to contract and entitled at the time to receive the income of the trust-property for his life, or for any greater estate, no such change of investment shall be made without his consent in writing.

41. *Power to apply property of minors, etc., for their maintenance, etc.*—Where any property is held by a trustee in trust for a minor, such trustee may, at his discretion, pay to the guardians (if any) of such minor, or otherwise apply for or towards his maintenance or education or advancement in life, or the reasonable expenses of his religious worship, marriage or funeral, the whole or any part of the income to which he may be entitled in respect of such property; and such trustee shall accumulate all the residue of such income by way of compound interest by investing the same and the resulting income thereof from time to time in any of the securities mentioned, or referred to in Section 20, for the benefit of the person who shall ultimately become entitled to the property from which such accumulations have arisen:

Provided that such trustee may, at any time, if he thinks fit, apply the whole or any part of such accumulations as if the same were part of the income arising in the then current year.

Where the income of the trust-property is insufficient for the minor's maintenance or education or advancement in life, or the reasonable expenses of his religious worship, marriage or funeral, the trustee may, with the permission of a principal Civil Court of original jurisdiction, but not otherwise, apply the whole or any part of such property for or towards such maintenance, education, advancement or expenses.

Nothing in this section shall be deemed to affect the provisions of any local law for the time being in force relating to the person and property of minors.

42. *Power to give receipts.*—Any trustee or trustees may give a receipt in writing for any money, securities or other moveable property payable, transferable or deliverable to them or him by reason, or in the exercise, of any trust or power; and, in the absence of fraud, such receipt shall discharge the person paying, transferring or delivering, the same therefrom, and from seeing to the application thereof, or being accountable for any loss or misapplication thereof.

43. *Power to compound, etc.*—Two or more trustees acting together may, if and as they think fit—

(*a*) accept any composition or any security for any debt or for any property claimed;

(*b*) allow any time for payment of any debt;

(*c*) compromise, compound, abandon, submit to arbitration or otherwise settle any debt, account, claim or thing whatever relating to the trust; and,

(*d*) for any of those purposes, enter into, give, execute and do such agreements, instruments of composition or arrangement, releases and other things as to them seem expedient, without being responsible for any loss occasioned by any act or thing so done by them in good faith.

The powers conferred by this section on two or more trustees acting together may be exercised by a sole acting trustee when by the instrument of trust, if any, a sole trustee is authorized to execute the trusts and powers thereof.

This section applies only if and as far as a contrary intention is not expressed in the instrument of trust, if any, and shall have effect subject to the terms of that instrument and to the provisions therein contained.

This section applies only to trusts created after this Act comes into force.

44. *Power to several trustees of whom one disclaims or dies.*—When an authority to deal with the trust-property is given to several trustees and one of them disclaims or dies, the authority may be exercised by the continuing trustees, unless from the terms of the instrument of trust it is apparent that the authority is to be exercised by a number in excess of the number of the remaining trustees.

45. *Suspension of trustee's powers by decree.*—Where a decree has been made in suit for the execution of a trust, the trustee must not exercise any of his powers except in conformity with such decree, or with the sanction of the Court by which the decree has been made, or, where an appeal against the decree is pending, of the Appellate Court.

2. POWERS AND DUTIES

In the preceding chapter we have noticed that powers are different from duties in so far as powers are discretionary while duties are imperative. The difference between them lies in the nature of the act one is obliged to do. A duty is to be performed, according to Strahan, whether one likes it or not, or whether it is wise to do so or not. In powers or discretions, one is bound to think and exercise his judgment as to whether it is wise to do a thing or not and to act accordingly.

3. NATURE OF POWERS

For proper and efficient discharge of their duties by trustees, vesting of power in them is necessary. Exercise of power depends upon the nature of a trust and the character and situation of the beneficiary. In case of special trusts and in case of beneficiaries not being *sui juris* the exercise of power is bound to vary. In case of absolute power to the trustee the court cannot compel him to exercise it, but the court will see that it is not exercised improperly in case it is proposed to be exercised. In case of power coupled with duty, its proper and timely exercise will be compelled[10] by a court but the manner and method of its exercise cannot be a matter of control by the court. Powers must be exercised for the benefit of a trust and its exercise must be *bona fide*, reasonable and impartial. The Indian Trusts Act, 1882 lays down the powers of a trustee in Sections 36 to 45.

4. GENERAL AUTHORITY OF A TRUSTEE (SECTION 36)

Over and above the powers given to a trustee by the instrument of trust and by this Act, a trustee has been given a general authority by this Act by virtue of which he "may do all acts which are reasonable and proper" for

(*i*) the realization, protection or benefit of the *trust-property*, and

(*ii*) for the protection and support of a *beneficiary who is not competent to* contract.

Of course this general authority is subject to the following restrictions: (*i*) restrictions contained in the instrument, (*ii*) provisions of Section 17 (a trustee to be impartial), and (*iii*) restriction as to leasing of trust-property.

The underlying principle behind granting such wide powers to a trustee is very clear. For this purpose one has to anticipate and foresee that a time may come or occasions may arise during the administration of a trust which demand proper but immediate decision; and it is very likely that on that decision, depends the benefit or loss to, either the trust-property or to the beneficiary.[11] In cases of emergency or necessity, when it is not possible to obtain sanction of a trustee's action from the beneficiaries (*i*) because they are not *sui juris*, or (*ii*) because they are away, or (*iii*) because they suffer from a disability which prevents them from consenting, or (*iv*) because they have not come into existence and therefore no sanction can be obtained at all, or (*v*) because seeking opinion from a court is very expensive and time-consuming and by the time the opinion is obtained the opportunity is lost, in all such cases liberty of reasonable action is granted to the trustee which he may utilise taking into consideration the importance of the situation. But a trustee cannot do acts which are unreasonable, unnecessary and problematical. He may get the property of trust repaired[12] or may make improvements[13] therein but cannot make merely ornamental improvements. He can improve but cannot rebuild residential property. He can thus do all proper and reasonable acts suitable for the realization, protection and benefit of the property and for the protection and support of the beneficiaries who are not *sui juris*. These two points, benefit to the property and protection and support of the beneficiary, are the guiding principles on which he may act. Still, however, in such cases a trustee is not to act capriciously but has to

10. *See* Section 49, Indian Trusts Act, 1882.
11. *Ward* v. *Ward*, (1843) 2 HLC 784.
12. *Bellinger* v. *Bellinger*, *Re*, (1898) 1 Ch 534.
13. *Dalim Kumar Sain* v. *Smt Nandarani Dassi*, AIR 1970 Cal 292, 310.

exercise his sound discretion. In one case, a resolution by other trustees condemning the managing trustee without affording him an opportunity to explain himself. The resolution lacks legality, since the principles of natural justice are not observed by other trustees.[14]

5. STATUTORY POWERS OF A TRUSTEE

These statutory powers are enlisted in Sections 37 to 45. They are (*i*) power to sell; (*ii*) power to sell under special circumstances; (*iii*) power to convey; (*iv*) power to vary investments; (*v*) power to apply property of minors, etc., for their maintenance; (*vi*) power to give receipts; and (*vii*) power to compound. Sections 44 and 45 provide for joint power and suspension of a trustee's power.

6. POWER TO SELL IN LOTS, ETC. (SECTIONS 37, 38 AND 39)

As decided in *Murlidhar Narayan* v. *Dattajirao*[15], there is no express power conferred by the Indian Trusts Act upon the trustee to sell the trust-property. A trustee as such, therefore, has no right to sell the trust-property. If he sells it the vendee's title will be impeachable and challenged either by a beneficiary or anyone claiming through him. But, if he is empowered to sell as Sections 37 and 38 say, he may sell the property in lots, by auction or on any special condition. He can thus convey the property under Section 39 and complete the sale. While selling the trust-property he has to act in a manner most advantageous to the trust estate and must use all due diligence with reference to the time for sale, the manner of sale and the value of the property in question. He may sell subject to prior charges or not, either together or in lots, by public auction or private contract and either at one time or at several times. If the trust deed provides otherwise those directions have to be followed. As Section 38 provides, he can buy in and resell and may insert special conditions but in all such cases of sale and investment of trust money in purchase of property he must exercise reasonable discretion as to the time of effecting the sale or purchase. As the Illustrations to Section 38 connote, an immediate sale may not be imperative but a trustee cannot postpone the sale for an indefinite period.

As decided in *Shirinbai M. Dalal, Re*[16], *Manilal Hargovan, Re*,[17] and *De Souza* v. *Daphtary*[18], circumstances may arise which the author of the trust did not contemplate and therefore the instrument of the trust cannot direct or does not provide; in such a situation of real emergency the court under its extraordinary jurisdiction will accord sanction to the acts of trustees, which are beneficial to and necessary for, the protection of the trust estate. It has been cautioned that this kind of jurisdiction is of an extremely delicate nature and therefore it must be made use of with the greatest possible care and caution. In

---

14. *P. Narasimha Bhat* v. *B. Shankaranarayana Rao*, (2002) 10 SCC 200: AIR 2002 SC 2379.
15. 53 Bom LR 883: AIR 1952 Bom 106.
16. 21 BLR 41: 43 Bom 519.
17. 25 Bom 353: 3 Bom LR 411.
18. 25 BLR 617.

short, what is termed as "expedient" for the management or administration of the trust-property must be sanctioned by the court.

7. POWER TO VARY INVESTMENTS (SECTION 40)

We have seen in the previous chapter that a trustee has a duty to convert perishable property into income-bearing property and this is intimately connected with the economics of investment. Section 40 of the Indian Trusts Act in this regard gives power to a trustee to vary investments. To invest means "to employ money in the purchase of anything from which interest or profit is expected". A trustee while investing has to bear in mind one thing, and that is, the investment must produce income and maintain the capital. Thus a purchase of a house for occupation is held not to be an investment.[19] It is for this reason that power is usually given expressly to a trustee to make such a purchase.[20] The Indian Trusts Act, 1882, Section 40 gives power to a trustee to vary investments and thus gives the trustee an area of choice within the principle of advantageous investments or the economics of investment.

As the section goes, a trustee at his discretion can call in the trust-property already invested and reinvest the same in any of the securities mentioned under Section 20. He can do so from time to time. But where the beneficiary is competent to contract and is entitled to the trust income for his life or is entitled to any greater estate, his consent in writing is a must for the trustee varying investments. This means that where the beneficiary is a minor, a trustee can vary investments, but when the beneficiary becomes competent to contract a trustee cannot exercise this power without written consent of the beneficiary.

8. POWER WITH REGARD TO MAINTENANCE OF MINOR BENEFICIARIES (SECTION 41)

A trustee has power to pay to the guardians of a minor beneficiary, either the whole of the income of the trust-property or a part of it, as is suitable to the occasion for the minor's maintenance, education, advancement in life, religious worship, marriage or funeral. And whatever remains from the income thereafter may be invested by him as required under Section 20 of the Act. If the income accruing from the trust-property is insufficient for the purpose, the trust-property or the corpus may be so applied with the previous permission of the court.

9. POWER TO GIVE RECEIPTS (SECTION 42)

A trustee can pass a valid receipt for the money, etc., received by him and the receipt so obtained shall discharge the payer from all the liabilities with regard to it thereafter.

---

19. *Power, Re*, 1947 Ch 572; *Peczenik S.T., Re*, (1964) 1 WLR 720.
20. Hanbury: *Modern Equity*, Chap. 17.

10. POWER TO COMPOUND (SECTION 43)

Two or more trustees jointly or a sole trustee so authorised, may accept any composition or any security for any debt or property, allow time for payment of any debt, compromise, compound, abandon, submit to arbitration or settle any debt, account, claim or thing relating to the trust and for this purpose do everything that is necessary. In so acting if they have observed good faith they will be free from any liability.

11. VESTING AND SUSPENSION OF POWER (SECTIONS 44 AND 45)

Authority given to several trustees to act may be exercised by the continuing trustees when one of them dies or disclaims, unless there is an indication to the contrary in the trust deed (Section 44). In case a decree is made for execution of a trust, a trustee is not to exercise any of his powers except in conformity with such decree. But he can do so with the permission of the court that has given the decree or an appeal court where an appeal against the decree is pending.

Chapter XVI

Trustees—Their disabilities

"A trustee cannot delegate his trust. If confidence has been reposed in him by a dead man he cannot throw upon the shoulders of somebody else that which has been placed on his shoulders. On the other hand, in the administration of a trust, a trustee cannot do everything for himself, he must to a certain extent make use of the arms, legs, eyes and hands of other persons and the limit within which he is confined is that a trustee may follow the ordinary course of business provided that he runs no needless risk in doing so."

—Bowen, L.J., in *Speight* v. *Gaunt*, (1883) 9 App Cas 1

"It is not usual for trusts to be administered in court, for the court exercises a general controlling influence over all trustees, and has power to give directions and determine questions affecting the trustees and beneficiaries without making an order for administration . . . notwithstanding that the trustees claim to exercise their discretion without the interference of the court."

"However wide the language of such (power) clauses they give the trustee an absolute discretion in appearance only; as in the case of all discretionary powers, he must act honestly and with ordinary prudence."

—*Re Lucking's W.T.*[1], (1968) 1 WLR 866, 874

SYNOPSIS

1. Text of Sections 46 to 54
2. Trustees cannot Renounce (Section 46)
3. Trustees cannot Delegate (Section 47)
4. Co-trustees cannot act Singly (Sections 48 and 49)
5. No right to Remuneration (Section 50)
6. Not to use Trust-property (Section 51)
7. Trustees must not be Purchasers (Section 52 and 53)
8. Co-trustees cannot lend to one of themselves (Section 54)

1. TEXT OF SECTIONS 46 TO 54

46. *Trustee cannot renounce after acceptance.*—A trustee who has accepted the trust cannot afterwards renounce it except (*a*) with the permission of a principal Civil Court of original jurisdiction, or (*b*) if the beneficiary is competent to contract, with his consent, or (*c*) by virtue of a special power in the instrument of trust.

47. *Trustee cannot delegate.*—A trustee cannot delegate his office or any of his duties either to a co-trustee or to a stranger, unless (*a*) the instrument of trust so provides, or (*b*) the delegation is in the regular course of business, or (*c*) the

1. *Snell's Principles of Equity*, pp. 204, 216, 226.

delegation is necessary, or (*d*) the beneficiary, being competent to contract, consents to the delegation.

Explanation.—The appointment of an attorney or proxy to do an act merely ministerial and involving no independent discretion is not a delegation within the meaning of this section.

Illustrations

(*a*) *A* bequeaths certain property to *B* and *C* on certain trusts to be executed by them or the survivor of them or the assigns of such survivor. *B* dies. *C* may bequeath the trust-property to *D* and *E* upon the trusts of *A*'s will.

(*b*) *A* is trustee of certain property with power to sell the same. *A* may employ an auctioneer to effect the sale.

(*c*) *A* bequeaths to *B* fifty houses let at monthly rents in trust to collect the rents and pay them to *C*. *B* may employ a proper person to collect these rents.

48. *Co-trustees cannot act singly.*—When there are more trustees than one, all must join in the execution of the trust, except where the instrument of trust otherwise provides.

49. *Control of discretionary power.*—Where a discretionary power conferred on a trustee is not exercised reasonably and in good faith, such power may be controlled by a principal Civil Court of original jurisdiction.

50. *Trustee may not charge for services.*—In the absence of express directions to the contrary contained in the instrument of trust or of a contract to the contrary entered into with the beneficiary or the court at the time of accepting the trust, a trustee has no right to remuneration for his trouble, skill and loss of time in executing the trust.

Nothing in this section applies to any Official Trustee, Administrator-General, Public Curator, or person holding a certificate of administration.

51. *Trustee may not use trust-property for his own profit.*—A trustee may not use or deal with the trust-property for his own profit or for any other purpose unconnected with the trust.

52. *Trustee for sale or his agent may not buy.*—No trustee whose duty it is to sell trust-property, and no agent employed by such trustee for the purpose of the sale, may, directly or indirectly, buy the same or any interest therein, on his own account or as agent for a third person.

53. *Trustee may not buy beneficiary's interest without permission.*—No trustee, and no person who has recently ceased to be a trustee, may, without the permission of a principal Civil Court of original jurisdiction, buy or become mortgagee or lessee of the trust-property or any part thereof; and such permission shall not be given unless the proposed purchase, mortgage or lease is manifestly for the advantage of the beneficiary.

Trustee for purchase.—And no trustee whose duty it is to buy or to obtain a mortgage or lease of particular property for the beneficiary may buy it, or any part thereof, or obtain a mortgage or lease of it, or any part thereof, for himself.

54. *Co-trustees may not lend to one of themselves.*—A trustee or co-trustee whose duty it is to invest trust-money on mortgage or personal security must not invest it on a mortgage by, or on the personal security of, himself or one of his co-trustees.

2. TRUSTEES CANNOT RENOUNCE (SECTION 46)

Nobody can be compelled to accept the office of trustee against his will.[2] A person appointed as trustee who wishes to disclaim should do so by deed, as this provides a clear evidence of the disclaimer.[3] However, a disclaimer may be implied; apathy will be evidence of an intention to disclaim, provided the apathy is consistent. But if the trustee meddles with the estate, his conduct will be construed as an acceptance. Once he has disclaimed he can no longer accept. Once he has accepted he can no longer disclaim, but he may retire.[4]

The first trustees are appointed either by the settlor or by the testator by a deed or will as the case may be. After once accepting the trust responsibility, it is not given to the trustee to at once disclaim the trust, because it is an obligatory office, an office of confidence and trust. But this does not mean that he can be compelled to work there forever. Section 46 of the Indian Trusts Act, therefore, lays down clearly that: "A trustee who has accepted the trust cannot afterwards renounce it". But he can do so only in three cases, and they are (*i*) by court's permission, (*ii*) by consent of beneficiaries competent to contract, and (*iii*) by a provision in the trust-deed. The object of the section is to indicate the obligatory and onerous nature of the office which once accepted cannot be abruptly forsaken or abdicated. The section therefore covers the question of office of a trustee with which his functions and duties are intimately connected.

The office of a trustee is attached with the duties of a trustee and those duties are either positive or negative. Chapter V, Sections 46 to 54 of the Indian Trusts Act enumerate these negative duties, which call upon a trustee not to do certain things which he is capable of doing, because, on the whole, it is in the interest of the trust and the beneficiaries that a trustee should refrain from doing certain things damaging to the trust. Thus by accepting the office, a trustee imposes upon himself these disabilities. On one side there is abrupt disclaimer by a trustee and on the other there is interest of the trust and the confidence reposed in a trustee by the author. Between these two ends, the law takes the middle course so that the working of the office which is of a continuous nature may not suffer but can go on smoothly, systematically and in an efficient manner. It is for this reason that a trustee is not allowed a premature and an unlawful retirement. If he does so the responsibility lies heavily upon him and he gets into trouble.

---

2. But a person can, of course, become a constructive or resulting trustee against his will.
3. *Holder* v. *Holder*, 1968 Ch 353 (an executor).
4. Hanbury: *Modern Equity*, p. 296.

3. TRUSTEES CANNOT DELEGATE (SECTION 47)

As expressed by Lord Langdale in *Turner* v. *Carney*[5], a person entrusted with a fiduciary duty does not fulfil it if he simply lays it on the shoulders of someone else: he remains liable for the other person's default. This is the basic rule. But an inflexible view of this rule was never accepted and therefore there are exceptions recognised in English law. In 1754 *per* Lord Hardwicke in *Ex p. Belchier*[6] and thereafter in two famous cases of *Speight* v. *Gaunt*[7] and *Learoyd* v. *Whiteley*[8] delegation was made permissible if the trustees could show that it was reasonably necessary in the circumstances or was in accordance with ordinary business practice. By the Trustees Act, 1925 in England this has been accepted but the principle of acceptance of the need for delegation rests on a different line of thinking. Now delegation is accepted there as a normal method of performing the duties incidental to trusteeship.[9] Section 23(1) of the Trustees Act in England has now widened the powers of the trustees to delegate and "revolutionised the position of a trustee or an executor so far as regards the employment of agents. No doubt he should use his discretion in selecting an agent and should employ him to do acts within the scope of the usual business of an agent".[10]

In India the law is more or less the same on this point as has been laid down by Section 47 of the Indian Trusts Act, 1882. A trustee under this section cannot delegate (*i*) his office, or (*ii*) any of his duties either to a co-trustee or to a stranger[11] unless—

(*i*) it is so *provided* by the trust-deed, or

(*ii*) it is in the *regular course of business*, or

(*iii*) the delegation is *necessary*, or

(*iv*) it is *consented* to by the competent beneficiary.

The above proposition is further explained and reiterated in *Srivastava & Sons case*.[12] In this case the co-trustees delegated their powers to one co-trustee to act on behalf of all. A question was posed whether this is permissible? If yes, when it is permissible. The Supreme Court observed: Although as a rule trustees must execute the duties of their office jointly. This general principle is, however, subject to the following exceptions. Thus one trustee may act for all—

(*i*) Where the trust-deed allows the trust to be executed by one or more or by a majority of trustees;

5. (1841) 5 Beav 515.
6. 1754 Amb 218.
7. (1883) 9 App Cas 1.
8. (1887) 12 App Cas 727.
9. Section 23(1), Trustees Act, 1925.
10. *Vickery, Re*, (1931) 1 Ch 572; Hanbury: *Modern Equity*, pp. 346-348.
11. *Atmaram Ranchod* v. *Gulamhusein*, 13 Guj LR 828 (FB): AIR 1973 Guj 113.
12. *J.P. Srivastava & Sons (P) Ltd.* v. *Gwalior Sugar Co. Ltd.*, (2005) 1 SCC 172: (2004) 122 Comp Cas 696.

(*ii*) Where there is express sanction or approval of the Act by the co-trustees;

(*iii*) Where the delegation of power is necessary;

(*iv*) Where the beneficiaries competent to contract consent to the delegation;

(*v*) Where the delegation to a co-trustee is in regular course of the business;

(*vi*) Where the co-trustee merely gives effect to decision taken by the trustee jointly.

The section has given an Explanation that if an act by an agent is only of a ministerial nature, not involving use of independent discretion, that cannot be said to be a delegation.

The section thus first states the general principle '*delegatus non potest delegare*' and then lays down exceptions to it so that in proper cases delegation could be made. A trustee delegating his duties in contravention of these provisions will be liable for a breach of trust and the acts of a delegate will not only become void[13] but he also will be liable as a constructive trustee to the beneficiary.[14]

In India, the general rule that a delegate cannot delegate his powers has been relaxed by the section as it has been relaxed in England by the Trustees Act, 1925, Section 23. Thus a trustee can obtain professional assistance and an expert's advice and also get the ministerial or clerical work done by employing an agent, because a trustee is not supposed to be an expert in all matters. A necessity to employ an agent may arise, and the same may be a legal necessity or a moral necessity.

In employing an agent a trustee should follow the ordinary course of business and should run no risk.[15] His conduct in this respect would be compared to that of an ordinary prudent person in his own affairs. It is the measure by which a trustee's conduct would be measured.[16] If it falls below that standard, he will be responsible.

Where a trustee leaves trust funds to an agent who afterwards mis-appropriates them or where he advances more money than usual on mortgage property and leaves valuation of the property in the hands of his agent leaving him alone without supervision, or where he leases out property on his agent's recommendations, at a lower and inadequate rent, he will be liable because he did not exercise the care that a prudent person takes in ordinary course of business in his own affairs.

13. *Alexander* v. *Alexander*, 2 Ves 643.
14. *Mara* v. *Brown*, (1896) 1 Ch 199 (CA).
15. *Speight* v. *Gaunt*, (1883) 9 App Cas 1 and *Weall, Re*, (1889) 42 Ch D 674.
16. *Ibid.*

But where a trustee entrusts a bank with the work of collecting interest on securities, or where money is remitted through a bank, the trustee will not be liable, this being the most regular, convenient and the safest mode that a prudent person would employ. Obtaining advice on taxation matters from experts and to hand over taxation work to them is the only mode and method that a reasonable person would employ and, moreover, it is all the more necessary to do so as he does not possess expert knowledge; in such matters therefore he will not become liable if something goes wrong and a loss occurs to the trust-property.

The question of a trustee's liability in such cases revolves round one point, and that is whether the delegation made by him was proper or not. If it was proper he is not liable, if otherwise, he is liable. A delegation to be proper must pass through the following tests—

(*i*) circumstances must justify the delegation;

(*ii*) the trustee in employing an agent must have behaved as a prudent person behaves or acts in ordinary course of business in his own matters;

(*iii*) agent employed by him should be proper and fit for the job, well-versed and competent in his profession; and

(*iv*) the delegation so far as its nature, duration and scope permits, should not last for a period longer than required.

If this is done, he is free from liability

4. CO-TRUSTEES CANNOT ACT SINGLY (SECTIONS 48 AND 49)

Where there are more trustees than one, all must join in the execution of the trust, except where the instrument of trust otherwise provides.[17] Section 48 accepts the principle that each trustee should be active in the administration of the trust and that a "sleeping" trustee is not recognised. Hanbury[18] points out that a trustee who concurs with his co-trustees has, in so agreeing, as much 'acted' as those others, and thus will be equally liable with them to beneficiaries who suffer loss if a breach results. Nor will the concurring trustee necessarily escape liability when his co-trustee was a solicitor, though he may escape if, after considering the matter, he reasonably deferred to what could legitimately be regarded as superior knowledge. But blind trust cannot safely be placed in a co-trustee. For although there is no rule that trustees are vicariously liable for the acts of co-trustees, a non-active trustee may himself be liable for neglecting to take steps necessary to have prevented the breach.[19]

The above position points to one basic proposition of law that when the administration of a trust is vested in co-trustees they are one single unit, they

---

17. *J.P. Srivastava & Sons (P) Ltd.* v. *Gwalior Sugar Co. Ltd.*, (2005) 1 SCC 172 (Delegation of powers to one co-trustee to act singly on behalf of all—when permissible.) *see* also *P. Punnaiah* v. *Jaypore Sugar Co. Ltd.*, (1994) 4 SCC 341. (Cases cited).
18. *Modern Equity*, pp. 294-295.
19. Hanbury : *Modern Equity*, p. 294-95.

form a collective entity and therefore they must act jointly[20] unless the instrument of trust provides otherwise. "A trustee cannot act singly" is therefore a corollary of the well-known rule that "a trustee cannot delegate". As explained by Maitland their powers, interests and authority are equal and undivided. At the same time one must note that all of them are suffering from the same disability that "a trustee cannot delegate" and, therefore, they must act jointly and not singly. Moreover, all trustees are entrusted with the trust office alike by the author of the trust and therefore each one must exercise his individual discretion and judgment, without remaining a "sleeping" trustee.

Their office being a joint one they cannot act by majority[21] unless they are trustees of a charitable trust. A trustee cannot advance a defence that he was outvoted by a majority or that he was bound to act according to the majority decision, because a majority binds neither a dissenting minority nor the trust estate.

In *Re Mayo*[22], for instance, one trustee of a trust for sale wished to sell, two of them wished to postpone. The trustees were by virtue of the trust to sell under a *duty* to sell, but possessed *power* to postpone. Simonds, J., held that their duty to sell prevailed unless they were unanimous in exercising their power to postpone. They were not unanimous on this point; the view of the single trustee who wished to sell prevailed, and the other two were directed to join in the sale.[23] *Luke's* case points to the same dictum that to bind a trust, the decision or the act must be the act of all.[24]

Control of trust-property is, therefore, the control of all as a result of which breach of trust or misappropriation of one brings liability for all.[25] In so far as money receipt is concerned, it should be a joint receipt of all. Co-trustees as a rule must join while passing a money receipt but this does not make them liable unless they allow the money received by one to remain in his hands for a longer period than necessary so as to give him a chance to misapply or to misappropriate the same. This position of co-trustees is distinctly different from that of co-executors.[26] In co-executors the law, taking into consideration their wide powers, draws an inference that all those who sign a money receipt are liable for the amount. Section 48 of the Act implies and incorporates this situation. As seen in *Re Mayo case*, if the co-trustees do not exercise their discretionary power reasonably, and in good faith, it can be controlled and guided by the court on suitable occasions. This is what is explained by Section 49 of the Act. Moreover, a trustee cannot exercise his powers arbitrarily and sell

---

20. *Atmaram Ranchhodbhai* v. *Gulamhusein*, 13 Guj LR 828 (FB).
21. *Manmohandas* v. *Janki Prasad*, 47 BLR (PC) 250: AIR 1945 PC 23.
22. 1943 Ch 302.
23. See also *Luke* v. *South Kensington Hotel*, (1879) 11 Ch D 121; Hanbury: *Modern Equity*, p. 295.
24. *Kunhan* v. *Narayan*, 20 MLJ 201.
25. *Ranganathan* v. *Periakuppan*, AIR 1957 SC 815.
26. *Townley* v. *Sherborne*, (1634) BR 35; *Brice* v. *Stocks*, (1805) 11 Ves 319.

the trust-property for Rs 25,000 when he had an offer of Rs 35,000. In such cases,[27] the court would definitely control them.

5. NO RIGHT TO REMUNERATION (SECTION 50)

A trustee has no right to charge remuneration for his services, i.e., trouble, skill and loss of time in executing the trust. But, as the section goes, if the instrument of trust so directs, or if the trustee has contracted with the beneficiary for this purpose or if it is so contracted with the court at the time of accepting the trust, a trustee may charge for his services. The section altogether does not put a ban or does not prohibit a trustee from charging but says that a "trustee may not charge for services".

English law speaks similarly. It says that a trustee acting voluntarily is not paid; it does not matter whether his services are of a personal nature or of a professional nature. "It follows, therefore, that a trustee can only claim remuneration if he can show a specific entitlement to it". But "it will appear that the basic principle (serving without charging) is much honoured in its breach".[28] According to English law, if the remuneration is authorised by the trust instrument, or the statute, or the court, or for litigious work by solicitor trustees, or authorized by contract, the same can be charged.[29]

This principle of no remuneration follows from the larger principle that a trustee cannot extract profit from his office as a trustee.

Section 50 provides this and also explains the exceptions to this position wherein a trustee can get remuneration. Thus a trustee can get out-of-pocket expenses, which include the payment of agent's fees wherever their employment is justified, calls on shares and the proper costs of litigation. To an official trustee, administrator-general, public curator or persons holding a certificate of administration, this section does not apply. They are therefore entitled to remuneration. Such expenses are a charge upon the property and in some cases against the beneficiaries personally. As Section 32 of the Act provides, a trustee is entitled to reimbursement and indemnity for all expenses properly incurred in the execution of the trust and for the benefit of trust-property and the beneficiaries.

In *K.T. Doctor* v. *CIT*[30] a question was raised whether the concept of lifting the veil can be resorted to in case of Trusts. The court observed that the lifting of or piercing of veil is an exercise which is not permissible in the field of law of trusts. It is permissible in the case of a company with a view to find out the real persons behind the corporate body, but in the case of trustees, they are under legal obligation to carry out the objects of the trust and to act in accordance with the deed of trust subject to overall provisions of the Indian Trusts Act and if they

---

27. *M.V. Ramasubbiar* v. *Manicka Narasimachari*, (1979) 2 SCC 65: AIR 1979 SC 671, 673.
28. Hanbury: *Modern Equity*, p. 366.
29. *Cradoc* v. *Piper*, (1849) 1 Mac & G 664, *followed* in *Shivramdas* v. *Nerurkar*, 39 BLR 633: AIR 1937 Bom 374.
30. ITR 269/1978, dt. 9-1-1980: GLT XVII 59-60.

fail in their duty or if they do not carry out certain activities as trustees, they are accountable in their capacity as trustees.[31]

6. NOT TO USE TRUST-PROPERTY (SECTION 51)

As provided by Section 51, a trustee may not *use* or *deal with* the trust-property (*i*) for his own profit, or (*ii*) for any other purpose unconnected with the trust.

All the acts of a trustee must be directed towards and must point to one thing, and that is, benefit to the trust and the beneficiary. This section is thus concerned with the acts of a trustee or his dealings with the trust-property which should not be for his own benefit or profit or for any other purpose unconnected with the trust. Looking from a different angle, we may say that a trustee must not put himself in a situation whereby his duty as a trustee and his personal interest may come into conflict. If he goes ahead in this fashion unrestrained, he will definitely gain from the trust-property or would make a profit out of it, either by investing the trust money with him for his personal benefit in his personal business or by using the trust-property for his personal gain. Benefit thus gained by a trustee by bypassing his disabilities, by committing a breach of trust, will not, as a general rule, be allowed to remain with him and he will have to account for it or to hold it for the beneficiaries, because this is an unjust enrichment secured by misusing his position as such. This general rule is an immutable one and it applies not only to express trustees but also to all those persons who are in a fiduciary position. Thus no one can extract an undue advantage from his fiduciary position. This general rule is the legitimate origin or source of the following two sub-rules:

(*i*) that a trustee may not buy beneficiary interest (Sections 52 and 53), and

(*ii*) that a trustee may not charge for his services (Section 50).

In *Chandler* v. *Bradley*[32], trust moneys were lent on a mortgage. The mortgagor being of an eccentric character, devised the equity of redemption of the mortgage to the mortgagee-trustee. It was held that the devise of the equity of redemption belonged to the trust as it was by reason of the trust that the trustee was in that position. This explains that a benefit obtained by a trustee by using his office as such is not his, but belongs to the beneficiary. Hanbury[33] has explained this position very neatly under the heading "Incidental Rights" by trustees as under:

"Accordingly, profits may come to a trustee in many ways. Those which come to him by reason of his being a trustee must be handed over to the beneficiaries; indeed the rule applies to many fiduciary agents who are not trustees.[34] It is often said that a fiduciary who is required to account for such a

---

31. ITR 269/1978, dt. 9-1-1980: GLT XVII 59-60.
32. (1897) 1 Ch 315.
33. *Modern Equity*, Chap. 20, pp. 366-372.
34. *Aberdeen Town Council* v. *Aberdeen University*, (1877) 2 App Cas 544; *Macadam, Re*, 1946 Ch 73.

profit becomes a constructive trustee. But such statements often repeat the fallacy of arguments because the main question for consideration in such cases is the liability or accountability of the trustee rather than the trust. This is so even though the courts have sometimes found a trust, and though the property in question was sometimes vested in the defendant. In none of them, however, did the question arise whether the defendant was a trustee as *opposed* to being accountable."

A duty to account is a personal liability; a constructive trust is a proprietary remedy. In short, the liability to account is a different question from that of a constructive trust.

On the same principle, the rule in *Keech* v. *Sandford*[35] prevents a trustee from keeping for his own benefit a renewal of a lease which he was able to obtain for himself by reason of his being a trustee of the original lease; and even though the trustee had tried unsuccessfully to obtain a renewal for the benefit of his infant *cestui que trust*. Where trustees have obtained remunerative directorship by virtue of their position as trustees, they were held liable to account for the remuneration.[36] Thus incidental profits coming to trustees in a variety of ways must always be disgorged. Whenever it can be shown that the trustee has so arranged matters as to obtain an advantage whether in money or money's worth to himself personally through the execution of his trust, he will not be permitted to retain, but will be compelled to make it over to his constituent.[37] In *Brown* v. *I.R.C.*[38], a Scottish solicitor was compelled to account for interest earned by deposits of his clients' money.

The same principle holds good where a trustee competes with the trust business. This is really a situation wherein a trustee places himself in a position where his duty and interest may conflict. As declared in *Re Thomson*[39], one possible area of conflict is where the trustee operates in business in competition with the trust. The rule applies to other fiduciaries who are not trustees. A partner cannot compete with the partnership business unless he has consent of the other partners. It is a question of fact in each case whether or not the activity is in conflict with the fiduciary duty.

Summarising the situation, we must say that a trustee must not use his position as a trustee to obtain any secret profit either by arrangement or by any other contrivance surreptitiously. But where a beneficiary abandons the profit from a trust and the trustee obtains it by his own labour, the trustee can keep it with himself and need not hold it in trust for the beneficiary.[40] Similarly, he should not make use of the trust-property or deal with it in a manner profitable to him and he should not deal with the trust-property for any other purpose unconnected with the trust. When he does so, he has to account for the profit

35. 1726 Sel Cas King 61.
36. *Macadam, Re*, 1946 Ch 73.
37. *Huntingdon Copper Co. case*, (1872) 4 R.
38. 1965 AC 244.
39. (1930) 1 Ch 203; Hanbury; *Modern Equity*, p. 371.
40. *Harihar Prasad Singh* v. *Maharaja Kesho Prasad Singh*, AIR 1925 Pat 68 (FB).

thus obtained. In the last chapter about trust, you will see that the Indian law has made attempts to enumerate broadly circumstances under which a person may be placed in the position of a trustee in reference to another. These "obligations in the nature of trusts" are not different from the implied and constructive trusts found in the decision of the English equity courts.[41] (For details as to fiduciary relationship and its types and instances *see* Chapter 20 *infra.*)

7. TRUSTEES MUST NOT BE PURCHASERS (SECTIONS 52 AND 53)

No trustee whose duty it is to sell trust-property, nor his agent employed for the purchase may, (*i*) buy the trust-property, or (*ii*) any interest therein, on his own account or as agent for third person (Section 52). As laid down by Section 53 no trustee, and any person who has recently ceased to be a trustee, may without court's permission, (*i*) buy, or (*ii*) become a mortgagee or lessee of the trust-property or any part thereof, unless the transaction is manifestly for the advantage of the beneficiary. (*iii*) Similarly, no trustee whose duty it is to buy or to obtain a mortgage or lease for the beneficiary may do so for himself (Section 53).

A trustee, as the sections lay down, may not place himself in a position where *trafficking in the trust-property* may prove to be an irresistible temptation. The general rule is that trustees are not to become the owners or lessees of trust-property. This rule is independent of any question of inadequacy of any price, or unfairness or undue advantage; the sale may have been at auction and the trustee may have taken the bidding well above the reserve price, *but he is still caught by the rule which derives from his status and position and not from his conduct in the particular case.*[42] Nor does it matter that he left the decision to sell and the manner of sale wholly to his co-trustee; nor that he retired from the trust before making an offer. *His responsibility as trustee is such that he must not contemplate the purchase at all.*[43] Even after retirement, for a considerable period the rule affects a trustee.[44] Even if a person in a fiduciary position is otherwise entitled to purchase, yet, if he effects the purchase secretly in another person's name, such a purchase cannot be allowed to stand.[45]

But the rule is not an inflexible one; in proper cases it has been relaxed in England.[46] A beneficiary is given a generous time to discover the position and the rule cannot be got around by sales to nominees or a purchaser with notice of the circumstances. In the words of Snell,[47] "that a trustee may not purchase the trust-property" has never been the true rule, which is that a purchase of trust-

41. *Thomson, Re*, 1930 Ch 203; *Boardman* v. *Phipps*, (1967) 2 AC 46; *Reading* v. *Attorney-General*, 1951 AC 507; Hanbury: *Modern Equity*, pp. 369 to 378; M.C. Setalvad: *Common Law in India*, pp. 60-61.
42. *Campbell* v. *Walker*, (1800) 5 Ves Jr 678; *Lacey*, ex p., (1802) 6 Ves Jr 625.
43. Hanbury: *Modern Equity*, p. 368.
44. Hanbury: *Modern Equity*, p. 369.
45. *Peari Mohan* v. *Manohar*, 23 BLR 913, 914-15 (PC): AIR 1922 PC 235.
46. *Holder* v. *Holder*, 1968 Ch 353.
47. *Snell's Principles of Equity*, p. 239.

property by a trustee is voidable at the instance of any beneficiary. It is the absolute right of the beneficiary to have the conveyance set aside within a reasonable time after he discovers the circumstances; and it matters not whether the purchase by the trustee was from himself alone, as sole trustee, or from his co-trustee". The burden lies on the trustee to show that every possible advantage has been gained for the trust.[48]

We may, for the purpose of proper understanding, divide the subject under two heads:

(*a*) cases wherein a trustee purchases or attempts to do so from himself and

(*b*) cases wherein the purchase is the result of an agreement between the trustee and the beneficiary.

The general rule regarding (*a*) has been explained above while that regarding (*b*) has been stated thus by Hanbury[49]:

> "Equity's view is less stringent when dealing with a purchase by a trustee of the beneficial interest of a beneficiary. This is a type of transaction which is carefully watched; the onus is on the trustee to show 'that he gave full value, and that all information was laid before the *cestui que trust* when it was sold'. The principles of undue influence apply; but it is open to a trustee in this type of case to show that the whole transaction was conducted at arm's length. This must however be distinctly proved."

When can a Trustee purchase?

We can now summarise and say that (*i*) where the sale is by a public auction and the trustee has obtained court's permission, (*ii*) where a trustee is a bare trustee (i.e., not actual but a nominal trustee) and has not to perform any duties, (*iii*) where he has disclaimed his office of trusteeship, (*iv*) where there is an offer from a beneficiary to sell and there is a fair dealing between them[50], and (*v*) where a trustee has given more than a market price for the trust-property[51], he can purchase it.

But on the principle laid down in the well-known decisions of *Keech* v. *Sandford*[52] and *Fox* v. *Mackreth*[53], a trustee can sell trust-property to a joint stock company of which he is a shareholder. Besides, when there are repeated requests from beneficiaries and with great unwillingness a trustee purchases the property of the trust[54], in both these types of cases the sale cannot be set aside.

---

48. *Plowright* v. *Lambert*, (1885) 52 LT 646.
49. *Modern Equity*, p. 369.
50. *Dovgan* v. *McPherson*, 1902 AC 197.
51. *Lacey*, ex p., 6 Ves 625.
52. 1726 Sel Cas King 61.
53. (1788) 2 Bro CC 400.
54. *Morse* v. *Royal*, 12 Ves 355.

But it must be noted that the onus lies in such cases on the trustee to prove that the transaction was fair, bona fide and with disclosure of the facts.[55]

Fox v. *Mackreth*[56] and *Pooley* v. *Quilter*[57] are the leading cases explaining the above principle. In the first case, Mackreth, the trustee himself, purchased the trust-property for a certain price. Before the contract of sale was completed he sold it to a third party at a higher price. Fox, the beneficiary, sued Mackreth for recovery of the profit earned by him and it was held that Mackreth should return the profits and in the meantime must hold it for the beneficiary in a constructive trust.[58] In the second case, *P*, a creditor of *H*, a bankrupt, sold his claim against *H* to *W*. *P* later discovered that *W* had purchased as trustee for *Q*, the assignee in bankruptcy of *H*. *P* sought to have the sale to *W* set aside. Held, the sale must be set aside and *Q* must refund to the bankrupt's estate dividends received by him. The rules as to a purchase by a trustee from him *cestui que trust* applied with still greater force to a purchase, for his own benefit, by an assignee of a bankrupt's estate from a creditor of the estate. It is therefore most fittingly remarked by Lord Eldon in *Ex p. Lacey case*[59] that, *it is "not that a trustee cannot buy from his cestui que trust, but that he shall not buy* from himself".

Section 53 is very clear and lays down a situation that a trustee may not buy or become a lessee[60] or mortgagee unless the court so permits, and the court will permit only in those cases where the transaction is apparently for the advantage of the beneficiary. So in the second head (*b*) of the principle explained before, the prohibition is not absolute but it is less stringent. It appears that Section 53 is not so clearly worded as to cover situations of both the types (*a*) and (*b*), but covers situations as explained under head (*b*) only.

8. CO-TRUSTEES CANNOT LEND TO ONE OF THEMSELVES (SECTION 54)

A trustee or co-trustee whose duty it is to invest trust money on mortgage or personal security must not invest it on a mortgage, or on the personal security of himself or one of his co-trustees.

This situation is similar and in fact closer to the one discussed under the preceding disability that trustees must not be purchasers. The same principles therefore must apply.

SUMMARY

A trust is an obligatory affair; its office is fraught with duties, discretions, disabilities, rights and powers. A duty is imperative. It has to be performed and

55. *Coaks* v. *Boswell*, 11 AC 232.
56. (1788) 2 Bro CC 400.
57. (1858) 2 De G & J 327; Cracknell: *Law Students' Companion*, Case No. 242.
58. See *Jankiram Ayyar* v. *Nilkamba Ayyar*, 1954 MLJ 486.
59. (1802) 6 Ves Jr 625.
60. See *Madhavrao Jiwajirao Scindia* v. *Sambhajirao Chandrojirao Angre*, (1988) 1 SCC 692: 1988 SCC (Cri) 234: 1988 Cri LJ 853.

no option exists there. Positive duties demand certain acts while negative duties require abstinence from a trustee. Negative duties are what are termed as disabilities. Accordingly,

(*i*) a trustee cannot renounce his office;

(*ii*) cannot delegate his office;

(*iii*) cannot act singly (if there are two or more trustees);

(*iv*) may not charge for his services;

(*v*) may not use trust-property;

(*vi*) cannot set up an adverse title to trust-property;

(*vii*) must not misuse his position as a trustee to get an advantage from the trust-property or dealings therewith;

(*viii*) cannot profit out of a trust;

(*ix*) cannot compete with the trust business;

(*x*) may not buy trust-property either from himself or from a co-trustee;

(*xi*) may not buy beneficiary interest without court's prior permission; and

(*xii*) may not lend money to one of co-trustees.

Chapter XVII
Rights and Liabilities of the Beneficiary

"I think that principle is repeatedly acted upon; and where a legacy is directed to accumulate for a certain period, or where the payment is postponed the legatee, if he has an absolute indefeasible interest in the legacy, is not bound to wait until the expiration of that period, but may require payment the moment he is competent to give a valid discharge."

—Lord Langdale, M.R., in *Saunders* v. *Vautier*, (1841) 4 Beav 115

"A trustee commits a breach of trust if he fails to do what his duty requires, or if he does what he is not entitled to do."

"Breaches of trust are almost infinitely various. They range from the fraudulent conversion of trust funds to purely technical failures of duty which harm nobody and transactions (such as some investments in unauthorised securities) which result in a substantial profit for the trust."

—*Snell's Principles of Equity*, Chap. 9, p. 272

"It is not for the trustee to dictate to the cestui que trust in what shape he will make his claim."

—Maitland: *Lectures on Equity*, Chap. XIV, p. 221

SYNOPSIS

1. TEXT OF SECTIONS 55 TO 69

55. *Rights to rents and profits.*—The beneficiary has, subject to the provisions of the instrument of trust, a right to the rents and profits of the trust-property.

56. *Right to specific execution.*—The beneficiary is entitled to have the intention of the author of the trust specifically executed to the extent of the beneficiary's interest;

Right to transfer of possession.—and, where there is only one beneficiary and he is competent to contract, or where there are several beneficiaries and they are competent to contract and all are of one mind, he or they may require the trustee to transfer the trust-property to him or them, or to such person as he or they may direct.

When property has been transferred or bequeathed for the benefit of a married woman, so that she shall not have power to deprive herself of her beneficial interest, nothing in the second clause of this section applies to such property during her marriage.

Illustrations

(*a*) Certain Government securities are given to trustees upon trust to accumulate the interest until *A* attains the age of 24, and then to transfer the gross amount to him. *A* on attaining majority may, as the person exclusively interested in the trust-property, require the trustees to transfer it immediately to him.

(*b*) *A* bequeaths Rs 10,000 to trustees upon trust to purchase an annuity for *B*, who has attained his majority and is otherwise competent to contract. *B* may claim Rs 10,000.

(*c*) *A* transfers certain property to *B* and directs him to sell or invest it for the benefit of *C*, who is competent to contract. *C* may elect to take the property in its original character.

57. *Right to inspect and take copies of instrument of trust, accounts, etc.*—The beneficiary has a right, as against the trustee and all persons claiming under him with notice of the trust, to inspect and take copies of the instrument of trust, the documents of title relating solely to the trust-property, the accounts of the trust property and the vouchers (if any) by which they are supported, and the cases submitted and opinions taken by the trustee for his guidance in the discharge of his duty.

58. *Right to transfer beneficial interest.*—The beneficiary, if competent to contract, may transfer his interest, but subject to the law for the time being in force as to the circumstances and extent in and to which he may dispose of such interest:

Provided that when property is transferred or bequeathed for the benefit of a married woman, so that she shall not have power to deprive herself of her beneficial interest, nothing in this section shall authorize her to transfer such interest during her marriage.

59. *Right to sue for execution of trust.*—Where no trustees are appointed or all the trustees die, disclaim, or are discharged, or where for any other reason the execution of a trust by the trustee is or becomes impracticable, the beneficiary may institute a suit for the execution of the trust, and the trust shall, so far as may be possible, be executed by the Court until the appointment of a trustee or new trustee.

60. *Right to proper trustees.*—The beneficiary has a right (subject to the provisions of the instrument of trust) that the trust-property shall be properly

protected and held and administered by proper persons and by a proper number of such persons.

Explanation I.—The following are not proper persons within the meaning of this section:—

A person domiciled abroad; an alien enemy; a person having an interest inconsistent with that of the beneficiary; a person in insolvent circumstances; and, unless the personal law of the beneficiary allows otherwise, a married woman and a minor.

Explanation II.—When the administration of the trust involves the receipt and custody of money, the number of trustees should be two at least.

Illustrations

(*a*) *A*, one of several beneficiaries, proves that *B*, the trustee, has improperly disposed of part of the trust-property, or that the property is in danger from *B*'s being in insolvent circumstances, or that he is incapacitated from acting as trustee. *A* may obtain a receiver of the trust-property.

(*b*) *A* bequeaths certain jewels to *B* in trust for *C*. *B* dies during *A's* lifetime; then *A* dies. *C* is entitled to have the property conveyed to a trustee for him.

(*c*) *A* conveys certain property to four trustees in trust for *B*. Three of the trustees die. *B* may institute a suit to have three new trustees appointed in the place of the deceased trustees.

(*d*) *A* conveys certain property to three trustees in trust for *B*. All the trustees disclaim. *B* may institute a suit to have three trustees appointed in place of the trustees so disclaiming.

(*e*) *A*, a trustee for *B*, refuses to act, or goes to reside permanently out of India or is declared an insolvent, or compounds with his creditors, or suffers a co-trustee to commit a breach of trust. *B* may institute a suit to have *A* removed and a new trustee appointed in his place.

61. *Right to compel to any act of duty.*—The beneficiary has a right that his trustee shall be compelled to perform any particular act of his duty as such, and restrained from committing any contemplated or probable breach of trust.

Illustrations

(*a*) *A* contracts with *B* to pay him monthly Rs 100 for the benefit of *C*. *B* writes and signs a letter declaring that he will hold in trust for *C* the money so to be paid. *A* fails to pay the money in accordance with his contract. *C* may compel *B* on a proper indemnity to allow *C* to sue on the contract in *B*'s name.

(*b*) *A* is trustee of certain land, with a power to sell the same and pay the proceeds to *B* and *C* equally. *A* is about to make an improvident sale of the land. *B* may sue on behalf of himself and *C* for an injunction to restrain *A* from making the sale.

62. *Wrongful purchase by trustee.*—Where a trustee has wrongfully bought trust-property, the beneficiary has a right to have the property declared subject to the trust or retransferred by the trustee, if it remains in his hands unsold, or, if it has been bought from him by any person with notice of the trust, by such person. But in such case the beneficiary must repay the purchase-money paid by the trustee, with interest, and such other expenses (if any) as he has properly incurred in the preservation of the property; and the trustee or purchaser must

(*a*) account for the net profits of the property, (*b*) be charged with an occupation-rent, if he has been in actual possession of the property, and (*c*) allow the beneficiary to deduct a proportionate part of the purchase money if the property has been deteriorated by the acts or omissions of the trustee or purchaser.

Nothing in this section—

(*a*) impairs the rights of lessees and others who, before the institution of a suit to have the property declared subject to the trust or retransferred, have contracted in good faith with the trustee or purchaser; or

(*b*) entitles the beneficiary to have the property declared subject to the trust or retransferred where he, being competent to contract, has himself, without coercion or undue influence having been brought to bear on him, ratified the sale to the trustee with full knowledge of the facts of the case and of his rights as against the trustee.

63. *Following trust-property—into the hands of third persons; into that into which it has been converted.*—Where trust-property comes into the hands of a third person inconsistently with the trust, the beneficiary may require him to admit formally, or may institute a suit for a declaration, that the property is comprised in the trust.

Where the trustee has disposed of trust-property and the money or other property which he has received therefor can be traced in his hands, or the hands of his legal representative or legatee, the beneficiary has, in respect thereof, rights as nearly as may be the same as his rights in respect of the original trust-property.

Illustrations

(*a*) *A*, a trustee for *B* of Rs 10,000, wrongfully invests Rs 10,000, in the purchase of certain land. *B* is entitled to the land.

(*b*) *A*, a trustee, wrongfully purchases land in his own name, partly with his own money, partly with money subject to a trust for *B*. *B* is entitled to a charge on the land for the amount of the trust money so misemployed.

64. *Saving of rights of certain transferees.*—Nothing in Section 63 entitles the beneficiary to any right in respect of property in the hands of—

(*a*) a transferee in good faith for consideration without having notice of the trust, either when the purchase-money was paid, or when the conveyance was executed; or

(*b*) a transferee for consideration from such a transferee.

A judgment-creditor of the trustee attaching and purchasing trust-property is not a transferee for consideration within the meaning of this section.

Nothing in Section 63 applies to money, currency notes and negotiable instruments in the hands of a bona fide holder to whom they have passed in circulation, or shall be deemed to affect the Indian Contract Act, 1872 (9 of 1872), Section 108, or the liability of a person to whom a debt or charge is transferred.

65. *Acquisition by trustee of trust-property wrongfully converted.*—Where a trustee wrongfully sells or otherwise transfers trust-property and afterwards himself becomes the owner of the property, the property again becomes subject to the trust, notwithstanding any want of notice on the part of intervening transferees in good faith for consideration.

66. *Right in case of blended property.*—Where the trustee wrongfully mingles the trust-property with his own, the beneficiary is entitled to a charge on the whole fund for the amount due to him.

67. *Wrongful employment by partner-trustee of trust-property for partnership purposes.*—If a partner, being a trustee, wrongfully employs trust-property in the business or on the account of the partnership, no other partner is liable therefor in his personal capacity to the beneficiaries, unless he had notice of the breach of trust.

The partners having such notice are jointly and severally liable for the breach of trust.

Illustrations

(*a*) *A* and *B* are partners. *A* dies, having bequeathed all his property to *B* in trust for *Z*, and appointed *B* his sole executor. *B*, instead of winding up the affairs of the partnership, retains all the assets in the business. *Z* may compel him, as partner, to account for so much of the profits as are derived from *A*'s share of the capital. *B* is also answerable to *Z* for the improper employment of *A*'s assets.

(*b*) *A*, a trader, bequeaths his property to *B* in trust for *C*, appoints *B* his sole executor, and dies. *B* enters into partnership with *X* and *Y* in the same trade, and employs *A*'s assets in the partnership business. *B* gives an indemnity to *X* and *Y* against the claims of *C*. Here *X* and *Y* are jointly liable with *B* to *C* as having knowingly become parties to the breach of trust committed by *B*.

68. *Liability of beneficiary joining in breach of trust.*—Where one of several beneficiaries—

(*a*) joins in committing breach of trust, or

(*b*) knowingly obtains any advantage therefrom, without the consent of the other beneficiaries, or

(*c*) becomes aware of a breach of trust committed or intended to be committed, and either actually conceals it, or does not within a reasonable time take proper steps to protect the interests of the other beneficiaries, or

(*d*) has deceived the trustee and thereby induced him to commit a breach of trust,

the other beneficiaries are entitled to have all his beneficial interest impounded as against him and all who claim under him (otherwise than as transferees for consideration without notice of the breach) until the loss caused by the breach has been compensated.

When property has been transferred or bequeathed for the benefit of a married woman, so that she shall not have power to deprive herself of her beneficial interest, nothing in this section applies to such property during her marriage.

69. *Rights and liabilities of beneficiary's transferee.*—Every person to whom a beneficiary transfers his interest has the rights, and is subject to the liabilities, of the beneficiary in respect of such interest at the date of the transfer.

2. GENERAL

A trust is controlled not only by the instrument of trust and the court, but also by the beneficiaries and the rules of equity. As Snell observes, a trustee is, in a sense, a servant of the beneficiary and in carrying out his duties and in exercising his powers or discretions which are confined to him, he is guided by the instrument of trust and the rules of equity; he is bound and entitled to use his own judgment and is not ordinarily obliged to consult the wishes or to accede to the importunities of the beneficiary. In suitable cases the court will also guide him and control his actions.[1] In other words a trustee is the owner of trust property for the purpose of its administration and for no other purpose. The beneficiary has a right to obtain his beneficial interest or interest against the trustees as owner of the trust property.[2] Thus one may say that there is a fourfold control on the trustees and the rights and powers of the beneficiaries may be viewed in this background. One has to remember that some of the rights and liabilities of the beneficiaries have already been considered while discussing what has been termed as the duties, disabilities and the liabilities of the trustees. Sections 55 to 69 of the Indian Trusts Act lay down some more rights and liabilities of the beneficiaries. The result would be some overlapping here and there, but this defect of overlapping is originally associated with the English law. The rights of the beneficiaries are (*i*) right to rents and profits (Section 55); (*ii*) right to specific execution of the trust (Section 56); (*iii*) right to transfer of possession of trust property (Section 56); (*iv*) right to inspect and take copies of the instrument of trust, accounts, etc. (Section 57); (*v*) right to transfer his beneficial interest (Section 58); (*vi*) right to sue for execution of trust (Section 59); (*vii*) right to proper trustees (Section 60); (*viii*) right to compel his trustee to any act of duty (Section 61); (*ix*) right to recover trust-property from the trustee (Sections 62, 63 and 65); (*x*) right of following the trust-fund (Section 63); (*xi*) right in case of blended property (Section 66); and (*xii*) right to hold a partner-trustee of trust-property liable for partnership business (Section 67).

A beneficiary is liable when the joins in breach of trust with the trustees (Section 68).

A. RIGHTS OF THE BENEFICIARY

(i) Right to Rents and Profits (Section 55)

A beneficiary is entitled to the rents and profits of the trust-property. This right lasts so long as the trust-property exists or so long as the trust is not validly

1. *Butt* v. *Kelson*, 1952 Ch 197.
2. *State Bank of India* v. *Special Secy., Land*, 1995 Supp (4) SCC 30.

terminated and it is controlled by the instrument of trust. Section 62 of the Act makes a trustee liable for breach of trust and consequently to account for the net profits, occupation rent the deterioration of the trust-property, as the case may be.

(ii) Right to Specific Execution (Section 56)

The beneficiary is entitled to have the intention of the author of the trust specially executed to the extent of his interest. A trustee is thus bound to carry out the specific execution of the author's intention.

He is a servant of the trust and therefore when a *sui juris* beneficiary requires him to transfer the trust-property to himself, he is bound to obey the directions even though it is not in consonance with those of the author of the trust. The section further provides that in case of more than one beneficiary, if all of them are *sui juris* and they all are of one mind, they may require the trustee to deliver the trust-property to them or to such persons as they direct. The main condition in both these cases is that a beneficiary or beneficiaries must be entitled to the *whole* of the beneficial interest. As expressed by Hanbury[3], any adult beneficiary *sui juris* may deal with his equitable interest under the trust in any way he wishes; and may consent to the trustee dealing with the trust-funds in a way which affects his interest.[4]

(iii) Right to terminate a trust (Section 56)

From the above provision of Section 56 it is clear that adult beneficiaries who together are absolutely entitled to the trust-property may terminate the trust and demand that the fund be handed over to them; but not if any interests are outstanding.[5] Illustration (*a*) to Section 56 of the Act is based on the well-known rule laid down in *Saunders* v. *Vautier*[6]. Beneficiaries may wish to do so for various reasons. In *Saunders case*, the beneficiary wished to terminate an accumulation which was to continue until he reached the age of 25; he was able to claim the fund at 21. Moreover, if property is given to *A* for life and then to *B*, and both *A* and *B* are adults, they may each wish to have capital immediately available and may agree to split up the fund. As noted by Hanbury, the most potent fact that persuades them to do so at the present time is the possibility of avoiding liability for estate duty on the death of *A*.[7] Thus by a timely decision to divide and share each will gain and the loser is the Revenue. Therefore, as Nathan's editor O.R. Marshall points out:[8] "If property is given to a person of full age, any restriction on his enjoyment of it is inconsistent with his absolute interest. Hence a beneficiary *sui juris* and entitled absolutely can call for a transfer. . . and he may do so even if the settlor purports to remove this right. So

---

3. *Modern Equity*, p. 379.
4. *Saunders* v. *Vautier*, (1841) CR & Ph 240.
5. Hanbury: *Modern Equity*, p. 379.
6. (1841) CR & Ph 240. See also *Gosting* v. *Gosting*, 1859 Johns 265.
7. Hanbury: *Modern Equity*, p. 380, citing Beattie: *Elements of Estate Duty*, 6th Edn. For Methods of Division, *see* Hanbury: *Modern Equity*, pp. 380-382.
8. Nathan: *Equity Through the Cases*, pp. 546-547.

also several beneficiaries who are all *sui juris* and between them entitled absolutely may call for a transfer, if they act together. Even beneficiaries who are entitled in succession can combine to call for a transfer provided they are *sui juris* and are collectively entitled absolutely. The rule in *Saunders* v. *Vautier* operates also in favour of a charity.[9] But it does not apply where other persons have an interest in the accumulation of income which the beneficiaries are seeking to stop. Nor does it give beneficiaries the right to control the trustee in the exercise of any discretion conferred upon him by statute or the trust instrument.''[10]

A married woman who is a sole beneficiary has no such right to terminate a trust, which is an exception to this rule. But this disability requires to be removed in view of the recommendations of the Law Commission.

(iv) Right to inspect and take copies of trust instrument, etc. (Section 57)

The beneficiary has a right as against a trustee and other persons claiming under him (*a*) to inspect the instrument of trust, (*b*) the documents of title relating solely to the trust-property, (*c*) the vouchers (if any) by which they are supported, and (*d*) the cases submitted and opinion taken by the trustee from the court.

The idea underlying this right is that the beneficiary must be in complete know of the trust and its administration. As the trustee has a right to have the custody of the documents relating to the trust-property, so the beneficiary has a corresponding right to look into the documents, i.e., the instrument of trust and documents of title to trust-property and to obtain copies (of course, by payment of due charges) thereof. Opinion of the court sought and obtained by a trustee must also be shown to the beneficiaries and their copies given if they want it. Thus by exercising this right a beneficiary will be able to have a full and accurate account of the trust-funds, its administration, the trust-property and its title deeds, which will enable him to safeguard his interest and prevent a breach of trust which may be in the offing. A beneficiary may take inspection through his solicitor.[11]

(v) Right to Transfer Beneficial Interest (Section 58)

Section 58 gives the beneficiary a right to transfer his beneficial interest. For this purpose the beneficiary must be competent to contract (*sui juris*). He can transfer his interest if he is the full owner of the interest but this right is circumscribed by his personal law and the general law of the land in this regard. This he can do without intervention of the trustees. Section 56 gives him a right to get transfer of possession from trustees and this section gives him a further right in continuation of that right, and that is of transfer of his interest to others. A beneficial interest indisputably can be transferred. For the said purpose the

9. *Wharton* v. *Masterman*, 1895 AC 186. But see *Levy, Re*, (1960) 1 All ER 42 (CA) for contra opinion that the principle does not apply to a bequest to charity.
10. *Brockbank, Re,* 1948 Ch 206. See also *Snell's Principles of Equity*, pp. 224-225.
11. *Kemp* v. *Burn*, (1863) 4 Giff 348.

only requirement will be the essence of the trust. Such a right being absolute the transferee derives his right, title and interest therein.[12] He can, therefore, also assign his interest,[13] and the assignee shall have the right and is subject to the liabilities of the beneficiary in respect of such interest (Section 69).

One must also note that Sections 56 and 58 both make a common provision in respect of a married woman, so that when property is transferred for her benefit (she being a sole trustee) these sections do not enable her to transfer the property to anyone which deprives her of her beneficial interest therein. This is a discriminatory disability imposed upon a female beneficiary which requires to be removed as recommended by the Law Commission.

(vi) Right to Sue for Execution of Trust (Section 59)

Where the execution of a trust becomes impracticable due to non-appointment, death, disclaimer or discharge of a trustee or for any other reason, the beneficiary may file a suit for execution of the trust. Under the circumstances, and until a new trustee is appointed, the court will execute the trust. This provision is but the logical corollary-in-action of the well-known equitable maxim "equity will not allow a trust to fail for want of a trustee"[14] or "a trust never fails for want of a trustee". The intention of the author of the trust will not be allowed to fall flat because of the want of trustees due to peculiar circumstances and the court will carry on the trust execution.

(vii) Right to Proper Trustees (Section 60)

It is the right of a beneficiary that the trust-property is held, protected and administered by proper persons and by a proper number of persons.

In so far as proper persons are concerned the following are not proper persons within the meaning of this section:

(*a*) a person domiciled abroad,

(*b*) an alien enemy,

(*c*) a person having a conflicting interest with that of the beneficiary,

(*d*) a person in insolvent circumstances,

(*e*) unless the personal law of the beneficiary allows otherwise, a married woman, and

(*f*) a minor.

The section at the outset makes it clear that in making an appointment the court considers the wishes of a settlor and the beneficiaries, whether the interests of the proposed trustee conflict with those of the settlor or of the beneficiaries, or whether the appointment will promote or impede the execution of the trust.[15] The court will not appoint a person under disability or those who are not proper

12. *Canbank Financial Services Ltd.* v. *Custodian*, (2004) 8 SCC 355: (2004) 122 Comp Cas 263.

13. *See* Chapter on Priorities and Assignments.

14. See *A.G.* v. *Lady Downing*, Wilm 21, 22.

15. *Snell's Principles of Equity*, p. 196.

persons. Beneficiaries, solicitor, husband or wife are not proper persons because their interest and duty conflict, but as observed by Snell, where such an appointment is advantageous to the trust, the court will make it though it may be slow to do so.

Where the trust-property is not properly protected or administered or held by a trustee, and where this is due to his deliberate conduct or as a result of his negligence or misconduct, the court, if it is satisfied that the continuance of the trustee is not in the interest of the trust, may remove him even though proof of such a charge or disqualification is not forthcoming. In short, a trustee should not be ambitious of a trust, when he can get nothing but trouble by it.[16] As decided in *Re Tempest*[17] by Lord Justice Turner, (*a*) where the instrument of trust specifically informs not to appoint a particular person as a trustee, the court will not override the author's wishes, (*b*) a court cannot appoint a trustee taking into account interests of certain beneficiaries only and in contravention of the author's wishes, (*c*) a court must take into account the nature of the trust, the function of the trustee and the interest of the beneficiaries and whether the appointment will promote the trust or impede it, before it makes any such appointment.

Where receipt and custody of money is involved, the number of trustees should be at least two, as the section itself lays down. It is therefore provided in the section that not only must 'proper persons' be appointed to the trust, but also that a proper number of such persons be appointed thereto where required.

(viii) Right to compel to any act of duty (Section 61)

A trustee can be compelled to perform his duties because there is no discretion therein for him. He may also be restrained by the beneficiary from committing any contemplated or probable breach of trust.[18] This section is connected with the conduct of the trustee in reference to the trust administration. If he is slack and indifferent or misconducts himself, thereby causing loss to the trust-property by his act or omission, e.g., by not defending the trust-property, not preventing a trespass or delaying in renewing a lease, he can be compelled to do so and can be proceeded against by the beneficiary under this section. With the court's permission the beneficiary can use the name of the trust and file a suit under this section.

B. REMEDIES OF THE BENEFICIARY

(i) General

Sections 62 to 67which now follow are intimately connected with the breach of trust by a trustee which he may commit in various ways, namely, by wrongfully purchasing trust-property (Section 62), by holding the trust-funds inconsistently with the trust (Section 63), by acquiring trust-property wrongfully

16. Lord Nottingham in *Uvedale* v. *Ettrick*, 2 Ch Cas 130.
17. LR 1 Ch 485.
18. *Balls* v. *Strutt*, 1 Hare 146; *Bowen* v. *Phillips*, (1897) 1 Ch 174.

converted (Section 65), by blending trust-property wrongfully with his own (Section 66) and by wrongful employment of trust-property for his partnership business (Section 67). We shall have to consider this conduct of a trustee in the background of the rights and remedies available to a beneficiary.

A beneficiary may adopt a breach of trust and accept all the benefits arising therefrom or may condone the breach and bear the consequences thereof. This type of conduct suggests that the beneficiary has nothing to complain about since he has reconciled with the situation. But where a breach of trust is neither adopted nor condoned the question of action and relief may arise. It is also so where there are more than one beneficiaries and all are not competent to contract or are not prepared to condone or adopt. It does not lie in the trustee to say that the breach has benefitted the trust and therefore the court must accept the benefit and reject the breach. A breach of trust is an evil in itself and therefore such dangerous doctrines must be rejected by all means.[19] For every breach of trust a beneficiary has a twofold remedy:

(*a*) relief against the trustee himself personally, called a personal remedy against the trustee; and

(*b*) relief against the trust-property or the property into which the trust-property has been converted. This is called a *proprietary remedy* against the trust-property.

As Snell points out[20], in case of a threatened or actual breach of trust, there are four heads of remedies to be considered, namely—

(*a*) an injunction to restrain the breach;

(*b*) a personal remedy against the trustee;

(*c*) a proprietary remedy against the trust-property; and

(*d*) (probably) a personal remedy against those who have received the trust-property.

This topic of a trustee dealing wrongfully with the trust-property and the rights and remedies of the beneficiary to proceed against him to recover the property, in whatever form it may have been, is an important one, as explained by Sections 62 to 67. Let us take one concrete example.

(*a*) *T* is a trustee. *B* is a beneficiary. *X* is the trust-property. *T* in breach of trust sells *X* to a third party *T-1*, for Rs 30,000.

Under the circumstances if *B* either by his act or omission does not adopt or condone the breach he may sue *T* and recover the loss to the trust.

(*b*) Now if *T-1* transfers the property *X* to *W* and *W* to *Y* and so on, the beneficiary may exercise his right to follow the trust-property into subsequent hands in whatever form it may be.

19. *Mariyam Bibi* v. *Natharsa Rawther Trust*, AIR 1978 Mad 272.
20. *Snell's Principles of Equity*, p. 272.

(ii) Right to action against trustee personally (Personal Remedy)

We have to keep in mind Section 23 here whereunder a trustee is liable to account not only for what he might receive but for his willful default and also for the interest thereon. Personal liability of a trustee is essentially a liability for his own acts and defaults and not for those of others. The subject of breach of trust has been considered before and accordingly a trustee has to compensate the trust for the loss caused by him. His personal liability is therefore of a compensatory nature, and it is enforced against him irrespective of his fraud, intention, efficiency or otherwise and it does not depend on the nature of his lapse or default whether it is of a serious nature or not. The ultimate aim of enforcing such a liability is not to punish a trustee but to compensate the loss caused to the trust. In the foregoing example therefore neither worries as to who has purchased the trust-property from the trustee nor who files a suit against *T-1*, because he can recover the loss from the trustee.

Thus, as laid down in Section 67, a partner-trustee employing trust-funds in his partnership business is himself liable in his personal capacity to the beneficiary. Of course, if other partners have notice of the breach of trust and allow this situation to take place, they are jointly and severally liable for the breach of trust. The personal liability of a trustee in case of more trustees than one, is joint and several. In case of fraud even a bankrupt trustee is not discharged.[21]

(iii) Difference between a proprietary and a personal remedy

A proprietary remedy available to the beneficiary is more powerful than a personal remedy because of the following reasons:

(*a*) The plaintiff's demand does not depend, in the former, on the solvency of the defendant; so that if the defendants become insolvent, even then the property can be recovered by the plaintiff and he obtains priority in comparison to the rights of other creditors. In the latter it is not so.

(*b*) A plaintiff in the former is entitled to the accretions to the property and its higher value, in the latter the question does not arise.

(*c*) A plaintiff pursuing a proprietary remedy can receive interest from the date the defendant obtained it; in case of personal remedy interest is granted from the date of the decision.

(*d*) Proprietary remedy generates a right *in rem* whereas a personal remedy gives a right *in personam* only, which is narrower than a right *in rem.*

Sections 62 and 65 explain a beneficiary's *right to recover trust-property from the trustee* and Section 63 his *right to recover trust-property from alienee.*

Where therefore (*a*) a trustee wrongfully buys trust-property (Section 62), or (*b*) after wrongfully disposing of the trust-property he thereafter acquires the

---

21. *Mora* v. *Brumt*, (1896) 1 Ch 199.

same for himself (Section 65), in both these cases the beneficiary gets the right to trace the property in its original character in the trustee's hands.

Where a trustee wrongfully alienates trust-property (Section 63), a personal remedy against him is quite inapt; a proprietary remedy is therefore a proper one. But this will not avail against a transferee in good faith for consideration and without having notice of the trust (Section 64).[22]

(iv) Right of "following trust-property" (Sections 63, 64, 65 and 66)

In a proprietary remedy the plaintiff claims his right to a particular property or a part of it with the defendant. But if the property in question is not in the same form, or if it is sold away and with its proceeds the defendant has purchased some other property, or if he has blended the property with his own, how far can the plaintiff press his claim and succeed? According to Keeton, (*a*) if the trust-property is not in its original form but its proceeds with the trustees can be identified, or (*b*) if the property or its proceeds are with a third party, or (*c*) with another beneficiary and can be identified, the same can be recovered to that extent. Moreover, the property must be such that can be "followed" and the beneficiary must have a right to follow. Also, the ''following'' should not produce an inequitable result. In short, the property to be followed must be identifiable and there must exist a nexus between the right to follow and the property followed.

Under Section 63, a beneficiary can follow the trust-property (*a*) into the hands of third person where it has come into his hand inconsistently with the trust. A transferee in good faith for consideration and without notice is an exception to this. The transferee must have such character either when the purchase money was paid or when the conveyance was executed. (*b*) He can also follow the property into the hands of a transferee for consideration from such a transferee [as said in (*a*) above]. But (*c*) a beneficiary cannot follow money, currency notes and negotiable instruments into the hands of a bona fide holder to whom they have passed in circumstances, and (*d*) nothing in Section 63 shall affect the liability of a person to whom a debt or a charge is transferred. (*e*) Moreover, the section explains that a judgment creditor of a trustee attaching and purchasing trust-property is not a transferee for consideration[23] (Section 63-64). (*f*) The beneficiary may require the transferee either to formally admit that the property is comprised in the trust, or may institute a suit for a declaration. (*g*) If the transferee of the trust-property is a volunteer the property can be followed into his hands irrespective of the fact of his having notice of the trust or not.[24] (*h*) A person purchasing trust-property without notice from a purchaser with notice may put forward and plead his own bona fides as a defence and it will constitute a good defence. (*i*) One more important point is that as between a trustee and his beneficiary a suit to follow trust-property is not barred by limitation. (*j*) Money, currency notes,

22. *Thorndike* v. *Hunt*, (1859) 3 De G & J 563.
23. *Dayal* v. *Jivraj*, 1 Bom 237.
24. *Spurgeon* v. *Collier*, 1 Edn. 55.

etc., cannot be followed (Section 64). But this idea has not gained ground in England and it is therefore rejected. The reason for rejection seems to be that the basis on which money, etc., has been excluded from being followed is not due to the nature of the property concerned but of its having passed into the hands of a bona fide holder. Therefore, subject to the exceptions contained in Section 64, they can be followed and this idea is well supported by the decisions in *Thorndike* v. *Hunt*[25] and *Re Hallett Estate*[26]. (*k*) If the trustee committing a breach of trust makes good the loss so made out of his estate and thereafter becomes bankrupt, his conduct of transferring the funds to repay the loss will not be taken as a fraudulent preference by him.[27] (*l*) This right to follow trust-property which is converted and is in the hands of a trustee or his legal representative or a legatee is available so long as the trust-property exists or is in an "identifiable" state or can be "earmarked", e.g., where *A*, a trustee, wrongfully invests trust-funds in purchasing land, a beneficiary is entitled to the land. (*m*) Where a trustee first sells wrongfully (i.e., converts) the trust-property and then becomes an owner of the same by acquiring it, the property so acquired will again become subject to the trust, notwithstanding any want of notice on the part of an intervening transferee in good faith or consideration (Section 65). (*n*) A beneficiary will have a charge on the whole fund where a trustee wrongfully mingles the trust-property with his own. In England, the beneficiary is entitled to the "whole" or "all" unless the trustee can prove it to be his own; in India he has only "a charge" thereon to the extent of the amount due[28] (Section 66). (*o*) A trustee may blend trust-property either by purchasing property partly with his funds and partly with the trust-fund; or by paying trust-funds into his own banking account, thus making it difficult to identify. In such cases the dispute would be decided on the principles laid down in *Re Hallett Estate case* and the rule in *Clayton case*[29] (that "a person will be presumed to draw out first the money he first paid in") will not be applied to such a situation because it is productive of unexpected and unjust results here.

(v) Equities attached to "Right of following Trust-Property"-(Section 62)

Where a trustee wrongfully purchases trust-property, as explained by Section 62, a beneficiary whose right it is to recover the same and to get it re-transferred from the trustee must, according to the provisions of Section 62 and also on the maxim that one who seeks equity must do equity, repay the purchase money with interest and expenses properly incurred by the trustee. At the same time the trustee must also account for (*a*) the net profits of the property, he will (*b*) be charged with the occupation rent of the property in his possession, and also he (*c*) should allow the beneficiary to deduct *pro rata* purchase money for the deterioration of the property. Of course, the section saves the rights of a lessee by enacting exceptions therein.

---

25. (1859) 3 De G & J 563.
26. (1880) 13 Ch D 696.
27. *Lister* v. *Stubbs*, 45 Ch D 1.
28. *Ghosh* v. *Macintosh*, 4 Cal 908; *Lipton* v. *White*, 15 Ves 432.
29. (1816) 1 Mer 572.

C. LIABILITY OF THE BENEFICIARY (SECTION 68)

(i) Impounding of Beneficial Interest

Section 68 fixes the liability of a beneficiary joining the breach of trust. Where a beneficiary (*a*) joins in committing the breach, or (*b*) knowingly obtains an advantage therefrom without the consent of the other beneficiaries, or (*c*) does not take proper steps to protect the interests of the other beneficiaries when he knows of a breach of trust, committed or intended, and conceals the same, or (*d*) has deceived the trustee and induced him to commit a breach thereby, he will render his interest in the trust-property liable to be impounded until the loss caused is compensated. When all the beneficiaries join the breach, all are liable under this section and the trustee is in a stronger position so far as his defence for liability is concerned.

Impounding a beneficiary's interest means that it will be applied so far as it will go towards providing an indemnity to the trustee in respect of the breach.[30] In other words, it means not allowing the beneficiary (or all who claim under him) to receive any part of the trust-fund till the loss is compensated. Legal interest cannot be impounded; it is the equitable interest that is impounded. Interest of a feme covert not having power of anticipation is an exception to this liability. Moreover, it is important to note that impounding cannot operate as against bona fide transferees for valuable consideration (Section 68).

Looking from a different angle, a beneficiary who was *sui juris* and with full knowledge of facts and its consequences concurred or acquiesced in the breach, cannot proceed against a trustee for breach of trust.[31] But concurrence implies capacity and so, unless guilty of fraud, a beneficiary who concurred in the breach can successfully proceed against the trustee if at the time of the breach he was an infant, or even being of full age was under undue influence of his parents and they were profiting from the breach.[32] Thus participation in, or consent to, a breach of trust where there was freedom of decision or release or acquiescence by the beneficiary in the breach and its after-effects, give the trustee an opportunity to come out, without blot, of his liability. A beneficiary getting an advantage from the breach has to compensate and therefore must indemnify the trustee to the extent of the benefit received. Till then the trustee will have charge on the beneficiary's interest for such amount. Section 68 gives a remedy to the beneficiary to proceed against another defaulting beneficiary.

(ii) Bar to remedies for breach of trust

A beneficiary's right of action, i.e., his remedy, is lost in one of the following ways—

(*a*) by lapse of time, i.e., by law of limitation;

(*b*) by continued acquiescence in the breach; or

30. Hanbury: *Modern Equity,* p. 406.

31. See *Re Panling's Settlement Trusts*, 1964 Ch 303.

32. For details *see* Hanbury: *Modern Equity*, pp. 403-414 and *Snell's Principles of Equity*, pp. 278-283.

(*c*) by concurrence therein; or

(*d*) by subsequent confirmation of the breach; or

(*e*) by release of the trustee from his liability (*see* Section 23 of the Indian Trusts Act).

Section 69 imposes the same liabilities and gives the same rights to the transferee of a beneficiary.

Chapter XVIII

Appointment and Discharge of Trustees

"*. . . in cases of positive misconduct, courts of equity have no difficulty in interposing to remove trustees who have abused their trust. . . In exercising so delicate a jurisdiction as that of removing trustees. . . their main guide must be the welfare of the beneficiaries.*"

—*Story on Equity,* Section 1289, quoted in *Letterstedt* v. *Broers, Nathan: Equity Through the* Cases, No. 114, p. 498

SYNOPSIS

1. TEXT OF SECTIONS 70 TO 76

70. *Office how vacated.*—The office of a trustee is vacated by his death or by his discharge from his office.

71. *Discharge of trustee.*—The trustee may be discharged from his office only as follows:—

(*a*) by the extinction of the trust;

(*b*) by the completion of his duties under the trust;

(*c*) by such means as may be prescribed by the instrument of trust;

(*d*) by appointment under this Act of a new trustee is his place;

(*e*) by consent of himself and the beneficiary, or, where there are more beneficiaries than one, all the beneficiaries being competent to contract; or

(*f*) by the Court to which a petition for his discharge is presented under this Act.

72. *Petition to be discharged from trust.*—Notwithstanding the provisions of Section 11, every trustee may apply by petition to a principal Civil Court of original jurisdiction to be discharged from his office; and if the Court finds that there is sufficient reason for such discharge, it may discharge him accordingly, and direct his costs to be paid out of the trust-property. But where there is no such reason, the Court shall not discharge him, unless a proper person can be found to take his place.

73. *Appointment of new trustees on death, etc.*—Whenever any person appointed a trustee disclaims, or any trustee, either original or substituted, dies,

or is for a continuous period of six months absent from India, or leaves India for the purpose of residing abroad, or is declared an insolvent, or desires to be discharged from the trust, or refuses or becomes, in the opinion of a principal Civil Court of original jurisdiction, unfit or personally incapable to act in the trust, or accepts an inconsistent trust, a new trustee may be appointed in his place by—

(*a*) the person nominated for that purpose by the instrument of trust (if any), or

(*b*) if there be no such person, or no such person able and willing to act, the author of the trust if he be alive and competent to contract, or the surviving or continuing trustees or trustee for the time being, or legal representative of the last surviving and continuing trustee, or (with the consent of the Court) the retiring trustees, if they all retire simultaneously, or (with the like consent) the last retiring trustee.

Every such appointment shall be by writing under the hand of the person making it.

On an appointment of a new trustee the number of trustees may be increased.

The Official Trustee may, with his consent and by the order of the Court, be appointed under this section, in any case in which only one trustee is to be appointed and such trustee is to be the sole trustee.

The provisions of this section relative to a trustee who is dead include the case of a person nominated trustee in a will but dying before the testator, and those relative to a continuing trustee include a refusing or retiring trustee if willing to act in the execution of the power.

74. *Appointment by Court.*—Whenever any such vacancy or disqualification occurs and it is found impracticable to appoint a new trustee under Section 73, the beneficiary may, without instituting a suit, apply by petition to a principal Civil Court of original jurisdiction for the appointment of a trustee or a new trustee, and the Court may appoint a trustee or a new trustee accordingly.

Rule for selecting new trustees.—In appointing new trustees, the Court shall have regard—(*a*) to the wishes of the author of the trust as expressed in or to be inferred from the instrument of trust; (*b*) to the wishes of the person, if any, empowered to appoint new trustees; (*c*) to the question whether the appointment will promote or impede the execution of the trust; and (*d*) where there are more beneficiaries than one, to the interests of all such beneficiaries.

75. *Vesting of trust-property in new trustees.*—Whenever any new trustee is appointed under Section 73 or Section 74, all the trust-property for the time being vested in the surviving or continuing trustees or trustee, or in the legal representative of any trustee, shall become vested in such new trustee, either solely or jointly with the surviving or continuing trustees or trustee, as the case may require.

Powers of new trustees.—Every new trustee so appointed, and every trustee appointed by a Court either before or after the passing of this Act, shall have the same powers, authorities and discretions, and shall in all respects act, as if he had been originally nominated a trustee by the author of the trust.

76. *Survival of trust.*—On the death or discharge of one of several co-trustees, the trust survives and the trust-property passes to the others, unless the instrument of trust expressly declares otherwise.

2. INITIAL TRUSTEES

The ability to be a trustee is co-extensive with the capacity to hold property[1] and accordingly, an alien may be a trustee according to English law. There a woman may also become a trustee. Since every person capable of holding property may be a trustee, a married woman subject to the provisions under Section 60 in India can also be a trustee even without her husband's consent and would herself be liable for a breach of trust. Her husband will not be liable for the breach unless he intermeddles in the affairs or the administration of the trust. An infant cannot be a trustee because he is not vested with discretion but where the trust does not involve using of discretion and where the personal law of the beneficiary does not prohibit, an infant can be a trustee.[2] That a married woman is not proper as a trustee is a provision which requires reconsideration in the light of the facts of advanced education of women and her position and status of equality in society.

The first trustees will ordinarily be appointed by the settlor or testator in the deed or will creating the trust. Provided that the deed is effective to constitute the trust or the disposition in the will is adequate to identify the testator's assets as trust assets, a trust will not fail for want of trustees.[3]

Since a trust will not fail if the settlor or testator has failed to appoint trustees, or if the appointed trustees refuse to act or are unable to act, or have ceased to exist, still, however, a trust may be so framed that, as decided in *Re Lysaght Hill case*[4], its operation is conditional upon specific trustees undertaking the trust as where there was a charitable trust for medical students who were to be selected and closely supervised by the Royal College of Surgeons as trustees.[5]

The Indian Trusts Act, 1882 in Sections 10 and 70 to 76 makes provision for the qualification, appointment and discharge of trustees. Accordingly, a person appointed as a trustee may accept the appointment or may not. It depends upon his own free will to accept the appointment or not because no one can be compelled to be a trustee or is bound to be a trustee (Section 10). But once

1. Section 10, Indian Trusts Act, 1882.
2. Section 60, Indian Trusts Act, 1882.
3. Hanbury: *Modern Equity*, p. 297.
4. *Snell's Principles of Equity*, p. 191, citing *Re Lysaght Hill* v. *Royal College of Surgeons*, 1966 Ch 191.
5. *Ibid.*

trusteeship is accepted, one is bound to carry out its duties, because a trust is obligatory and a trustee has got to act.

It may happen that the sole trustee or the trustees first appointed may disclaim the trust,[6] or decline to act as trustees. If the trust contains provisions for the discharge of such trustees and new appointment of fresh trustees, the emergent situation can be met successfully by acting according to the instructions in the deed. But where no such provisions are forthcoming or if they are, they are incomplete or ineffective, the situation requires a solution which can be arrived at by the help of law.

3. VACATION OF OFFICE (SECTION 70)

As provided by Section 70, the office of a trustee is vacated by his death or by his discharge from his office.

4. DISCHARGE OF TRUSTEE (SECTION 71)

A trustee may be discharged from his office—

(*i*) by the extinction of the trust,

(*ii*) by completion of his duties under the trust,

(*iii*) by such means as are prescribed in the trust instrument,

(*iv*) by appointment of new trustee in his place,

(*v*) by consent of himself and the beneficiary or beneficiaries, as the case may be, or

(*vi*) by the court in response to a petition presented by him under Section 72 of the Act.

5. PETITION FOR DISCHARGE (SECTION 72)

Even though a trustee is bound to carry out the trust and to obey the directions of the author of the trust, he may present a petition to a court for his discharge. On finding that the reasons advanced by the trustee are valid and sufficient, *i.e.,* disability to give attention to trust administration due to continuous illness, or for some other reasons beyond his control, the court will discharge him accordingly and order the costs of the petition to be paid out of the trust-property. If the reasons are not sufficient, he will not be discharged unless and until a proper person to take his place is found. Where there are sufficient reasons for discharge, the court will give an immediate discharge and order the costs to be paid from the trust-property, but where there are no sufficient reasons, the release of a trustee will not be immediate and would be delayed until a proper person is found; the costs in such a situation will have to be borne by the trustee himself. One more point to be noted here is that in the latter situation the property remains vested in the first trustee till a new appointment is made.

---

6. Section 10, Indian Trusts Act, 1882.

6. REMOVAL OF A TRUSTEE (SECTION 73)

In *Letterstedt* v. *Broers*[7], it was expressed by Lord Blackburn that "friction or hostility between the trustees and the immediate possessor of the trust estate is not of itself a reason for the removal of the trustees", but since there was very little to guide their Lordships, they were compelled to have recourse to general principles.

"As Story says,: 'But in cases of positive misconduct, courts of equity have no difficulty in interposing to remove trustees who have abused their trust; it is not indeed every mistake or neglect of duty, or inaccuracy of conduct of trustees, which will induce courts of equity to adopt such a course. But the acts or omissions must be such as to endanger the trust-property or (*i*) to show a want of honesty, or (*ii*) a want of proper capacity to execute the duties, or (*iii*) want of reasonable fidelity.' . . . . In exercising so delicate a jurisdiction as that of removing trustees. . . their main guide must be the welfare of the beneficiaries."[8]

In India, Section 73 makes provision for removal of trustees[9] in cases (*i*) where any trustee is absent from India for a continuous period of six months, or (*ii*) leaves India for the purpose of residing abroad, or (*iii*) is declared an insolvent, or (*iv*) being old and infirm is unfit or personally incapable to act as a trustee, or (*v*) accepts an inconsistent trust. All these categories can be properly included under the second category in the preceding para. Cases of want of honesty and want of reasonable fidelity are many. But in all such cases the trustees are removed, they do not retire, because retirement is voluntary and at one's request, whereas removal is compulsory and against one's desire or wishes. Section 71 enumerates situations wherein a retirement is granted, while Section 73 operates when trustees are removed and new appointments are made.[10]

7. APPOINTMENT OF NEW TRUSTEES (SECTION 73)

As the section explains, new trustees in place of initial or first trustees or other trustees can be made,

(*i*) by the person nominated for that purpose by the instrument of trust, or

(*ii*) by the author of the trust if he be alive and competent to contract, or

(*iii*) by the surviving or continuing trustees or trustee, or

(*iv*) by the legal representative of the last surviving and continuing trustee, or

---

7. (1884) 9 App Cas 371; Nathan: *Equity Through the Cases*, No. 114, p. 497.

8. *Id.*, at p. 498.

9. *Krishna* v. *State of Maharashtra*, (2001) 2 SCC 441. (According to Nagpur Improvement Trust Act, 1936, Section 6, 4(1)(*c*) and 10, a nominated trustee can be removed from the office of the State Government "at any time". And this is covered by the doctrine of pleasure.

10. However, it must be remembered that before condemning the majority trustee, he should be given an opportunity to say whatever he has to say. If this, is not done, that amounts to violation of the principles of natural justice—See *P. Narasimha Bhat* v. *B. Shankaranarayana Rao*, (2002) 10 SCC 200: AIR 2000 SC 2379.

(*v*) with the consent of the court by the retiring trustees, if they all retire simultaneously, or

(*vi*) with the consent of the court, by the last retiring trustee.

The power to nominate a trustee, as said above, is to be exercised in the order given; each preceding person having a superior or preferential power than the one following. If no appointment of a trustee can be made under Section 73, the court will appoint trustees under Section 74 on the application of the beneficiary for that purpose.

8. SELECTION OF NEW TRUSTEES: RULES (SECTION 74)

In appointing new trustees the court shall have regard to—

(*i*) the wishes of the author of the trust, as expressed or to be inferred from the instrument of trust;

(*ii*) the wishes of the person (if any) empowered to appoint new trustees;

(*iii*) the question whether it will promote or impede the execution of the trust; and

(*iv*) to the interest of all the beneficiaries where there are more than one.

These rules were expressed by Turner, L.J., in *Re Tempest*[11] and the Indian law runs on its close analogy. In doing so, he said, the court acts upon and exercises its discretion which is not arbitrary, but based on general rules and principles, which are not very easy to apply to the varying circumstances of each particular case. But the following rules apply to all cases of appointment of new trustees.

The first rule is "that the court will have regard to the wishes of the persons by whom the trust has been created. If the author of the trust has in terms declared that a particular person, or a person filling a particular character, should not be a trustee of the instrument, there cannot, as I apprehend, be the least doubt that the court would not appoint to the office a person whose appointment was so prohibited, and I do not think that upon a question of this description any distinction can be drawn between express declarations and demonstrated intention".[12]

The next rule is "that the court will not appoint a person to be a trustee with a view to the interest of some of the persons interested under the trust, in opposition either to wishes of the testator or to the interest of others of the *cestui que trust*. . . It is of the essence of the duty of every trustee to hold an even hand between the parties interested under the trust. Every trustee is duty-bound to look to the interests of all, and not of any particular member or class of members of his *cestui que trust*".

---

11. 1 Ch App 485 (Turner & Knight Bruce, L., JJ.); Nathan: *Equity Through the Cases,* No. 113, pp. 492-493.
12. *Ibid.*

The last rule is "that a court in appointing a trustee will have regard to the question whether his appointment will promote or impede the execution of the trust, for the very purpose of the appointment is that the trust may be better carried into execution".[13]

It was, therefore, rightly said by Warrington, J. in *Re Wrightson*[14], "that you must find something which induces a court to think either that the trust property will not be safe, or that the trust will not be properly executed in the interest of the beneficiaries". In the same way, bankruptcy of a trustee is, as a general rule, a ground for his removal[15] but as decided in *Satya Kinkar case*[16] in India, wherein *Barker case*[17] was followed, bankruptcy would not *ipso facto* discharge him from his office. He remains competent to work unless he is removed by the court.[18]

9. RESULT OF NEW APPOINTMENT (SECTIONS 75 AND 76)

The consequence of the new appointment of a trustee under Section 73 or 74 would be that the trust property which was so far vested in the surviving or continuing trustees would now be vested in the new trustee, either solely or jointly with the surviving or continuing trustees or trustee. The newly-appointed trustee shall have the same powers, authorities and discretions in regard to trust administration as the originally nominated trustee and he will act accordingly. As Section 76 provides, on the death or discharge of one of several co-trustees the trust survives and the trust property passes to the others unless provided otherwise by the trust.[19]

---

13. 1 Ch App 485 (Turner & Knight Bruce, L., JJ.); Nathan: *Equity Through the Cases,* No. 113, pp. 492 493.
14. (1908) 1 Ch D 789, 803.
15. *Barker's Trusts, Re,* (1875) 1 Ch D 43.
16. *Satya Kinkar* v. *Kiron Chandra,* AIR 1954 Cal 432.
17. *Barker's Trusts, Re,* (1875) 1 Ch D 43.
18. *Satya Kinkar* v. *Kiron Chandra,* AIR 1954 Cal 432.
19. See *Jarat Kumari Dassi* v. *Shubhakaran Khemani,* AIR 1960 Cal 489.

Chapter XIX

Extinction of Trusts

"... It is not the province of the court of justice to decide on what terms or conditions a man of competent understanding may choose to dispose of his property. If he thoroughly understands what he is about, it is not the duty of a court of justice to set aside a settlement which he chooses to execute on the ground that it contains clauses which are not proper."

—Jessel, M.R., in
Dutton v. *Thompson*, (1883) 23 Ch D 278

SYNOPSIS

1. TEXT OF SECTIONS 77 TO 79

77. *Trust how extinguished.*—A trust is extinguished—

(*a*) when its purpose is completely fulfilled; or

(*b*) when its purpose becomes unlawful; or

(*c*) when the fulfilment of its purpose becomes impossible by destruction of the trust-property or otherwise; or

(*d*) when the trust, being revocable, is expressly revoked.

78. *Revocation of trust.*—A trust created by will may be revoked at the pleasure of the testator.

A trust otherwise created can be revoked only—

(*a*) where all the beneficiaries are competent to contract—by their consent;

(*b*) where the trust has been declared by a non-testamentary instrument or by word of mouth—in exercise of a power of revocation expressly reserved to the author of the trust; or

(*c*) where the trust is for the payment of the debts of the author of the trust, and has not been communicated to the creditors—at the pleasure of the author of the trust.

Illustration

A conveys property to *B* in trust to sell the same and pay out of the proceeds the claims of *A's* creditors. *A* reserves no power of revocation. If no communication has been made to the creditors, *A* may revoke the trust. But if the creditors are parties to the arrangement, the trust cannot be revoked without their consent.

79. *Revocation not to defeat what trustees have duly done.*—No trust can be revoked by the author of the trust so as to defeat or prejudice what the trustees may have duly done in execution of the trust.

2. EXTINCTION (SECTION 77)

The Indian Trusts Act, 1882 makes provision for the extinction of trusts under Sections 77, 78 and 79. Section 77 lays down four situations when a trust is extinguished. Accordingly, a trust is extinguished—

(*i*) when its purpose *is completely fulfilled*; or

(*ii*) when its purpose *becomes unlawful*; or

(*iii*) when the fulfilment of its purpose *becomes impossible* by destruction of the trust property or otherwise; or

(*iv*) when the trust, being revocable, *is expressly revoked.*

A valid express trust, whether it be private or public, comes to an end in any one of the abovesaid four situations. It is natural that the life of a public trust is longer than that of a private one but from the viewpoint of extinction of trust there is no such difference.

Suppose a trust is created for *A* and property is transferred to *X* as a trustee to hold it in trust and to apply it for the maintenance and education of *A* up to graduation and to hand over the corpus to *A* after he attains majority. Under the circumstances after graduation of *A* and on his attaining majority the trust has fulfilled its purpose completely. Accordingly, it must come to an end under Section 77(*a*) when its purpose is fulfilled. In the above example if there was a provision that after *A*'s graduation the remaining property will go to certain persons, the purpose is not fulfilled unless and until the residue reaches its ultimate and proper destination.

To be legal, a trust must have a lawful object or purpose. A purpose lawful at the initial stage may become unlawful afterwards due to some new legislation coming into force. The purpose, therefore, cannot be accomplished, being unlawful. In such cases a trust is extinguished from the date when its purpose became unlawful. Thus while an initial unlawfulness does not allow a trust to come into existence, a supervening unlawfulness turns a lawful purpose into an unlawful one whereby a trust is extinguished under Section 77(*b*).

Similarly, under Section 77(*c*) when the fulfilment of the purpose becomes impossible by destruction of the trust property or otherwise, a trust is extinguished. In the first example where a trust is created for *A*, if he dies, the trust comes to an end. Similarly, when there is a litigation by *Z* against *X* in regard to his claim to trust property and *Z* becomes successful in getting the property, the trust is extinguished as there is no trust property now. The destruction of the trust property may take place in any other way also, *e.g.*, on account of flood, lightning and other natural calamities.

In the last instance a trust is extinguished when it is revoked (Section 77).

3. REVOCATION (SECTIONS 78 AND 79)

Section 78 enumerates the circumstances when a trust may be revoked. A trust created by a will may be revoked at any time at the pleasure of the testator, for a will is inherently ambulatory. But a trust which is created otherwise than by will may be revoked—

(*i*) by consent of all the beneficiaries where all of them are competent to contract;

(*ii*) by expressly providing in the instrument of trust for a power of revocation: by exercising such a power a trust may be revoked;

(*iii*) when its purpose is the payment of author's debts, it can be revoked at any time prior to communication of the arrangement to the creditors.

(*a*) *Meaning.*—To revoke is to annul something by recalling or taking back, and to annul is to make void legally. To revoke is, therefore, to make void legally a document by recalling it or taking it back.[1] It may mean the undoing of a thing already granted in writing by making it legally ineffective. So long as the trust created has not become fully operative, it remains within the settlor's competence to withdraw any part of the property from trust or to vary its terms etc., but once it starts operating without assistance or interference from the settlor, he has no right to make any variation therein, as he is then divested of all his powers, and interests in and dominion over the trust. He consequently cannot revoke it. In other words a settlor cannot revoke a completely constituted trust unless the settlement reserves a power of revocation.

(*b*) *Power of Revocation.*—As explained by Snell,[2] there are cases where a trust even though completely constituted may be revoked by the settlor, or set aside by third parties. These cases fall under four heads,[3] of which revocation is one.

A settlor cannot revoke a completely constituted trust unless a power to do so is reserved in the instrument. One should note that a mere absence of power of revocation from a voluntary trust or the presence of it by unusual provisions is not any ground for setting it aside, provided that those provisions were brought to the settlor's notice and were understood by him. "It is not the province of the court of justice to decide on what terms or conditions a man of competent understanding may choose to dispose of his property. If he thoroughly understands what he is about, it is not the duty of a court of justice to set aside a settlement which he chooses to execute on the ground that it contains clauses which are not proper."[4]

Other grounds for revocation may be (*i*) fraud or undue influence in obtaining the settlement, or (*ii*) the execution of the settlement under a

---

1. Funk and Wagnalls: *Standard Handbook of Synonyms, Antonyms & Prepositions,* p. 107.
2. *Snell's Principles of Equity*, pp. 126-127.
3. (*i*) Revocation, (*ii*) Conveyance to defraud creditors, (*iii*) Voluntary conveyance to defraud a subsequent purchaser, and (*iv*) Bankruptcy of the settlor.
4. *Per* Jessel, M.R., in *Dutton* v. *Thompson*, (1883) 23 Ch D 278.

fundamental mistake or misapprehension as to its effect,[5] or (*iii*) illusory trusts may also be revoked by the settlor.[6]

One who seeks to set it aside on the above grounds must discharge the onus of proving it. If the settlor is proved to be a free agent, it cannot be set aside, but a settlement for value can very rarely be set aside, for marriage is a valuable consideration.

(*c*) *Trust created by a will.*—A trust created by a will can be revoked at any time by the author, during his lifetime but thereafter it cannot be, because after the author's death the will begins to speak and the trust immediately comes into existence.

A trust for the payment of its author's debts can also be revoked at any time before it is communicated to the creditors (because up to that time it is simply an uncommunicated arrangement and not really a trust).[7]

(*d*) *Trust created otherwise.*—A trust created by a non-testamentary instrument may be revoked by means of a power of revocation expressly reserved by the author in that instrument or it may be revoked when all the beneficiaries are competent to contract and they so consent.

When a trust is revoked, the revocation will not affect the acts of the trustees duly done in execution of the trust so as to defeat or prejudice those acts (Section 79).

---

5. *Strauss* v. *Sutro*, 1948 LJR 33; *Bullock* v. *Lloyds Bank Ltd.*, 1955 Ch 317.
6. *See* Chap. 12, *supra*.
7. *See* Chap. 12, *supra*.

Chapter XX
Obligations in the Nature of Trust

"A constructive trust is the extension of a court's conscience, its foundations are vesting of property in the defendant and the principle of unjust enrichment; absence of confidence has no relevance."

SYNOPSIS

1. TEXT OF SECTIONS 80 TO 96*

80. *Where obligation in nature of trust is created.*—An obligation in the nature of a trust is created in the following cases.

83. *Trust incapable of execution or executed without exhausting trust-property.*—Where a trust is incapable of being executed, or where the trust is completely executed without exhausting the trust-property, the trustee, in the absence of a direction to the contrary, must hold the trust-property, or so much thereof as is unexhausted, for the benefit of the author of the trust or his legal representative.

Illustrations

(*a*) *A* conveys certain land to *B*—

"upon trust", and no trust is declared; or

"upon trust to be thereafter declared", and no such declaration is ever made; or

upon trusts that are too vague to be executed; or

upon trusts that become incapable of taking effect; or

"in trust for *C*", and *C* renounces his interest under the trust.

In each of these cases *B* holds that land for the benefit of *A*.

(*b*) *A* transfers Rs 10,000 in the four per cent to *B*, in trusts to pay the interest annually accruing due to *C* for her life. *A* dies. Then *C* dies. *B* holds the fund for the benefit of *A*'s legal representative.

(*c*) *A* conveys land to *B* upon trust to sell it and apply one moiety of the proceeds for certain charitable purposes, and the other for the maintenance of the worship of an idol. *B* sells the land, but the charitable purposes wholly fail, and the maintenance of the worship does not exhaust the second moiety of the proceeds. *B* holds the first moiety and the part unapplied of the second moiety for the benefit of *A* or his legal representative.

---

*. Ss. 81, 82 and 94 have been repealed by Benami Transactions (Prohibition) Act, 1988—*See* Chap. 3, maxim 9, *ante*.

(*d*) *A* bequeaths Rs 10,000 to *B*, to be laid out, in buying land to be conveyed for purposes which either wholly or partially fail to take effect. *B* holds for the benefit of *A*'s legal representative the undisposed of interest in the money or land if purchased.

84. *Transfer for illegal purpose.*—Where the owner of property transfers it to another for an illegal purpose and such purpose is not carried into execution, or the transferor is not as guilty as the transferee, or the effect of permitting the transferee to retain the property might be to defeat the provisions of any law, the transferee must hold the property for the benefit of the transferor.

85. *Bequest for illegal purpose.*—Where a testator bequeaths certain property upon trust and the purpose of the trust appears on the face of the will to be unlawful, or during the testator's lifetime the legatee agrees with him to apply the property for an unlawful purpose, the legatee must hold the property for the benefit of the testator's legal representative.

Bequest of which revocation is prevented by coercion.—Where property is bequeathed and the revocation of the bequest is prevented by coercion, the legatee must hold the property for the benefit of the testator's legal representative.

86. *Transfer pursuant to rescindable contract.*—Where property is transferred in pursuance of a contract which is liable to rescission or induced by fraud or mistake, the transferee must, on receiving notice to that effect, hold the property for the benefit of the transferor, subject to repayment by the latter of the consideration actually paid.

87. *Debtor becoming creditor's representative.*—Where a debtor becomes the executor or other legal representative of his creditor, he must hold the debt for the benefit of the persons interested therein.

88. *Advantage gained by fiduciary.*—Where a trustee, executor, partner, agent, director of a company, legal adviser, or other person bound in a fiduciary character to protect the interests of another person, by availing himself of his character, gains for himself any pecuniary advantage, or where any person so bound enters into any dealings under circumstances in which his own interests are, or may be, adverse to those of such other person and thereby gains for himself a pecuniary advantage, he must hold for the benefit of such other person the advantage so gained.

Illustrations

(*a*) *A*, an executor, buys at an undervalue from *B*, a legatee, his claim under the will. *B* is ignorant of the value of the bequest. *A* must hold for the benefit to *B* the difference between the price and value.

(*b*) *A*, a trustee, uses the trust-property for the purpose of his own business. *A* holds for the benefit of his beneficiary the profits arising from such user.

(*c*) *A*, a trustee, retires from his trust in consideration of his successor paying him a sum of money. *A* holds such money for the benefit of his beneficiary.

(*d*) *A*, a partner, buys land in his own name with funds belonging to the partnership. *A* holds such land for the benefit of the partnership.

(*e*) *A*, a partner, employed on behalf of himself and his co-partners is negotiating the terms of a lease, clandestinely stipulates with the lessor for payment to himself of a lakh of rupees. *A* holds the lakh for the benefit of the partnership.

(*f*) *A* and *B* are partners. *A* dies. *B*, instead of winding up the affairs of the partnership, retains all the assets in the business. *B* must account to *A*'s legal representative for the profits arising from *A*'s share of the capital.

(*g*) *A*, an agent employed to obtain a lease for *B*, obtains the lease for himself. *A* holds the lease for the benefit of *B*.

(*h*) *A*, a guardian, buys up for himself incumbrances on his ward *B*'s estate at an undervalue. *A* holds for the benefit of *B* the incumbrances so bought, and can only charge him with what he has actually paid.

89. *Advantage gained by exercise of undue influence.*—Where, by the exercise of undue influence, any advantage is gained in derogation of the interest of another, the person gaining such advantage without consideration, or with notice that such influence has been exercised, must hold the advantage for the benefit of the person whose interests have been so prejudiced.

90. *Advantage gained by qualified owner.*—Where a tenant for life, co-owner, mortgagee or other qualified owner of any property, by availing himself of his position as such, gains an advantage in derogation of the rights of the other persons interested in the property, or where any such owner, as representing all persons interested in such property, gains any advantage, he must hold, for the benefit of all persons so interested, the advantage so gained, but subject to repayment by such persons of their due share of the expenses properly incurred, and to an indemnity by the same persons against liabilities properly contracted, in gaining such advantage.

Illustrations

(*a*) *A*, the tenant for life of leasehold property, renews the lease in his own name and for his own benefit. *A* holds the renewed lease for the benefit of all those interested in the old lease.

(*b*) A village belongs to a Hindu family. *A*, one of its members, pays *Nazrana* to Government and thereby procures his name to be entered as the inamdar of the village. *A* holds the village for the benefit of himself and the other members.

(*c*) *A* mortgages land to *B*, who enters into possession. *B* allows the government revenue to fall into arrears with a view to the land being put up for sale and his becoming himself the purchaser of it. The land is accordingly sold to *B*. Subject to the repayment of the amount due on the mortgage and of his expenses properly incurred as mortgagee, *B* holds the land for the benefit of *A*.

91. *Property acquired with notice of existing contract.*—Where a person acquires property with notice that another person has entered into an existing contract affecting that property, of which specific performance could be enforced, the former must hold the property for the benefit of the latter to the extent necessary to give effect to the contract.

92. *Purchase by person contracting to buy property to be held on trust.*—Where a person contracts to buy property to be held on trust for certain beneficiaries and buys the property accordingly, he must hold the property for their benefit to the extent necessary to give effect to the contract.

93. *Advantage secretly gained by one of several compounding creditors.*—Where creditors compound the debts due to them, and one of such creditors, by a secret arrangement with the debtor, gains an undue advantage over his co-creditors, he must hold for the benefit of such creditors the advantage so gained.

95. *Obligor's duties, liabilities and disabilities.*—The person holding property in accordance with any of the preceding sections of this Chapter must, so far as may be, perform the same duties, and is subject, so far as may be, to the same liabilities and disabilities, as if he were a trustee of the property for the person for whose benefit he holds it:

Provided that (*a*) where he rightfully cultivates the property or employs it in trade or business, he is entitled to reasonable remuneration for his trouble, skill and loss of time in such cultivation or employment; and (*b*) where he holds the property by virtue of a contract with the person for whose benefit he holds it, or with any one through whom such person claims, he may, without the permission of the Court, buy or become lessee or mortgagee of the property or any part thereof.

96. *Saving of rights of bona fide purchasers.*—Nothing contained in this Chapter shall impair the rights of transferees in good faith for consideration, or create an obligation in evasion of any law for the time being in force.

Sections 81 to 94 in this chapter relate to certain obligations in the nature of trusts. The Indian Trusts Act, 1882 does not use the terms "resulting" and "constructive" trusts but these sections are virtually its examples. Sections 81 to 85 explain the circumstances wherein a *resulting trust* is created and Sections 86 to 94 put forward the instances wherein a *constructive trust* comes into existence.

2. (a) RESULTING TRUSTS (SECTIONS 83-85)

As has been explained before, there is no doctrinal unity to resulting trusts and hence creation of such a trust is not dependent on compliance with formalities and is also not subject to all rules of express trust. In such a trust the beneficial interest in the property results or reverts to its creator. The essential principles regarding this type of trust have been discussed in Chapter 12, para 9. The instances of such trusts collected by the Indian Trusts Act under Sections 83 to 85 may be reproduced as follows:

(*i*) Where a trust is incapable of execution or where it is completely executed and some property remains still, the trustee must hold such property in trust called a resulting trust. Illustrations to the section make this clear (Section 83). But a resulting trust cannot arise "only in the absence of a contract to the contrary".[1]

(*ii*) Where property is transferred to another for an illegal purpose and the same is not carried[2] out and the transferor is not as guilty as the

1. *Fazalbhoy Currimbhoy* v. *Official Trustee of Maharashtra*, (1979) 3 SCC 189, 195.
2. *Petherpermal* v. *Muniandi*, 35 IA 98.

transferee, there results a trust as contemplated by the section (Section 84).

(*iii*) Where a bequest is made for an illegal purpose, the same must be held in trust by the legatee without any action to carry out the purpose. The same result follows where a bequeath made is prevented by coercion from being revoked (Section 85). This section and Section 84 must be read with Section 4 of the Act.

(b) CONSTRUCTIVE TRUSTS (SECTIONS 86-94)

(*i*) *General.*—Such trusts arise by operation of law. In certain circumstances the legal owner of property must hold it in trust for another according to principles of equity. It is not possible in such circumstances to observe formalities. When it would be an abuse of confidence for the owner of property to hold the same for his own benefit, a trust is imposed upon him irrespective of his intention. Such trusts are called constructive trusts and they are enforced on one principle and that is, to prevent unjust enrichment of one person at the expense of another. A somewhat elaborate discussion of this will be found in Chapter 12, para 5, but it would be fruitful to note some important aspects of this type of trust. No satisfactory definition of such trust, as Snell says, has been so far produced; its concept not having assumed a complete form and its limitations being not clear. But one thing is clear that it arises out of an obligation imposed on conscience, says Keeton. We may say that it is an extension of "conscience" of the equity courts. In other words, it is a method of exposing the conscience by equity courts. There are various types of constructive trusts. Where a person is a legal owner of property but according to conscience he is not entitled to its beneficial interest, where property should have been with *Y*, but it is with *X* due to a peculiar situation and where a person intermeddles with the trust affairs and either gains or inflicts a loss to the trust, in all such circumstances he is bound by conscience and he is said to be a constructive trustee.

(*ii*) *Constructive Trust: A Remedy or a Trust?*—On this point the answers differ. According to English law, it is a variety of trusts and fiduciary relations between the parties are necessary for its existence. According to American law, it is a remedy and not an independent trust. Before finding an answer to this question we must note that the area of operation and the limitations or scope of the constructive, resulting and implied trusts are not clear and they may overlap. Now suppose *A* transfers property to *C*, a trustee, for *B*'s benefit for *B*'s lifetime. *B* dies and therefore the property will revert to *A*, the author, and in his absence to his legal representatives. What is the justification for this position? Is it because of the implied intention of the testator, or because it was a case of a resulting trust, or because it is fair and just to do so? The reason may be any one of these. English law, in such a situation, takes it as a trust in the hands of *C*. But this solution does not provide answers to the following questions:

(*i*) Are fiduciary relations necessary for such a trust to arise?

(*ii*) Where such relations do not exist, does a trust arise?

(*iii*) By what test would you determine the rights and duties of its parties?

(*iv*) Is it not a novel experiment found out by the courts to supply a remedy in cases demanding justice?

American law considers this as a remedy springing from the court's desire to supply one in case of unjust enrichment. Out of the two views, English and American, the latter offers a better and reasonable approach.

Such a trust arises only where a property is vested in or transferred to the defendant and not otherwise. At this juncture one has to note that in a constructive trust there may not be a position of confidence existing between the parties and yet the law imposes obligations on the parties exactly similar to trust obligations. Why so? Because the situation demands a solution, and a just solution is the answer. Just as a quasi-contract (obligation in the nature of a contract) arises in spite of absence of proposal, acceptance, consent and consideration, so a constructive trust (obligation in the nature of a trust) arises even in the absence of a position of confidence as required by Section 3 of the Trusts Act.

(*iii*) *Instances.*—The Indian Trusts Act has collected those instances in Sections 86 to 93 wherein such trusts arise and they can be briefly laid down as under:

(*i*) Where property is obtained by one under a contract which is liable to rescission, or induced by fraud or mistake, he must hold the same for the transferor's benefit provided the transferor is prepared to do equity and return the consideration actually paid (Section 86). This is on the principle that the transferee has got the legal estate but not the equitable estate.[3] One should read with this section Section 19 of the Indian Contract Act and Section 35 of the Specific Relief Act.

(*ii*) Where a debtor becomes the creditor's representative there arises a constructive trust because on the principles laid down in *Ingle* v. *Richards*[4], a debt which an executor owes to the estate will be considered as an asset in his hands because his debt is not extinguished in equity because of his appointment as such (Section 87).

(*iii*) Where a person standing in a fiduciary position with another, instead of protecting the interest of that other, gains as such for himself or enters into dealings whereby he gains for himself and where therefore his duties and interest conflict, he must hold that pecuniary advantage in trust for that other person (Section 88). Illustrations to the section amply explain these situations. A trustee, executor, partner, agent, director of a company, legal adviser, co-decree holder and co-mortgagee are its illustrations.

Whether or not under the situations as above a trust arises and therefore a liability to account is imposed upon such person in fiduciary character, or it is because on the principle of unjust enrichment that a liability to account for the advantages received is imposed, is an interesting question and its elaborate discussion is provided in

3. *Rochefocauld, Re*, (1897) 1 Ch 196.
4. (1860) 28 Bav 366.

Hanbury[5] under the topic "Incidental Profits". *Boardman* v. *Phipps*[6] is a leading case on the point wherein trustees were compelled to account for profits gained by their position as trustees. Paragraph 6 of Chapter 16 may be seen in this regard.[7]

---

5. *Modern Equity*, pp. 369 to 378.
6. (1967) 2 AC 46.
7. Also see *Sangramsinh P. Gaekwad* v. *Shantadevi P. Gaekwad*, (2005) 11 SCC 314: (2005) 123 Comp Cas 566. (*see* next chapter)

PART III-A
FIDUCIARY RELATIONSHIPS

Chapter XXI
Fiduciary Relationship

SYNOPSIS

1. General

Section 88 of the Trust Act requires a fiduciary not to gain an advantage of his position. If he acts in contravention of the provisions of the section and gains or obtains an advantage for himself, he should hold the same for that other person who has reposed confidence in him to protect his interests. The section gives Illustrations of this situation. However, it has to be noted that the section does not define a "fiduciary". Fiduciary relationship arises not from trust only but *ex lege* and *ex conventione* also.

2. Definition

As Walker defines it:

> "A 'fiduciary' is a person in a position of trust, or occupying a position of power and confidence with respect to another such that he is obliged by various rules of law to act solely in the interest of the other, whose rights he has to protect. He may not make any profit or advantage from the relationship without full disclosure. The category includes trustees, Company promoters and directors, guardians, solicitors and clients and others similarly placed."[1]

"A fiduciary relationship", as observed by Anantnarayanan, J., "may arise in the context of a *jural relationship*. Where *confidence is reposed* by one in another and that leads to a transaction in which there is a *conflict of interest and duty* in the person in whom such confidence is reposed, fiduciary relationship immediately springs into existence."[2]

The term "fiduciary" is derived from the Roman Law, and, means (as a noun) a person holding the character of a trustee, or a character analogous to that of a trustee, in respect of the trust or confidence involved in it and the scrupulous good faith and candour which it requires. As an adjective it means the nature of trust; analogous to trust; related to or founded upon trust or confidence. For example, executor of estate, receiver in bankruptcy, trustee. A trustee for example, possesses a fiduciary responsibility to the beneficiaries of

---

1. *Oxford Companion to Law*, 1980, p. 469.
2. *Nellie Wapshare* v. *Pierce Lasha & Co. Ltd.*, AIR 1960 Mad 410.

the trust to follow the terms of the trust and requirements of applicable state law.[3]

3. Trust and a Fiduciary Relationship

There are two things in which an analogy exists between fiduciary relationship and a trust. And it is because of this that it is commonly understood that fiduciary relationship is a trust. The first point on which an analogy can be traced is about following the property. In case of a trust the trust property in the hands of trustee can be followed by the beneficiary as against the creditors of a trustee, when the trustee goes bankrupt. This feature is present in case of fiduciary relationship generally. That is, a similar remedy would be available.[4] The second similarity is in case of remedy for a wrong. The same remedy as is available against a trustee in respect of a wrong, when it arises in regard to trust property, is available in case of a wrong in case of fiduciary relationship.

Though there is a similarity in these two incidents one cannot say that a fiduciary relation is necessarily a trust. On the contrary the fiduciary relation is a genus, while a trust is one of its species.

There are certain obligations which are not but akin to trust. Such obligations establish fiduciary relationship. A fiduciary relationship exists—

(*i*) Where one person obtains property or other advantage which justice or equity requires should belong to another; or

(*ii*) When a person reposes a trust, confidence or reliance on another; or

(*iii*) Where a person has a legal title and/or control over property or other advantage while the beneficial ownership rests in another; or

(*iv*) Where one person has discretionary power to change the legal position of another and that discretion exists because someone has entrusted the fiduciary to exercise it.

Thus, a fiduciary is a person who undertakes to act in the interest of another person. It is immaterial that the understanding is gratuitous or whether it is in the form of a contract. Such a relationship is sometimes expressed as a relationship of trust or confidential relationship, viz, trustee and beneficiary, agent and principal, solicitor and client, employee and employer, director and company, and partners. The critical feature of these relationships is that the fiduciary undertakes or agrees to act for or on behalf of or in the interest of another person in exercise of a power or discretion which will affect the interests of that other person in a legal or practical sense.[5]

There are two types of relationship between individuals, or, on facts arising from obligations. Examples for the former are the relationship between

---

3. Black's Law Dictionary quoted in *V.M. Francis* v. *Central Bank of India*, (1992) 74 Comp Cas 765 (Ker).
4. See *Re West of England South Wales Dt. Bank, ex p. Dale & Co.*, (1879) 11 Ch D 772.
5. See *Hospital Products Ltd.* v. *United States Surgical Corpn.*, (1984) 156 CLR 4 (High Court of Australia).

individuals, such as trustee and beneficiary or director and company; and for the latter, is the obligation imposed not to do an act as an employee acting in violation of employer's trade secrets. Breach of fiduciary obligations takes place where there is a conflict of interest and duty or where undue influence is exercised or where confidential information is misused.[6]

4. When Arises

Whenever two persons stand in such a situation that confidence is necessarily reposed by one in the other, there arises a presumption as to fiduciary relationship which grows naturally out of that confidence. Such a confidential situation may arise from a contract or by some gratuitous undertaking, or it may be upon previous request or undertaken without any authority.[7]

5. Its Nature

It is an inflexible and settled rule of equity that a person in a fiduciary position will not be allowed to misuse his office and gain out of it. His interest should not conflict with the interest of those whose interest he is bound to protect. Here self-interest and self-preference are made subordinate to loyalty towards others. Principle of equity is ingrained in this relationship.[8] In other words such a person should not be *auctor in rem suam*, that is, he should not be an agent for his own advantage.

As said before, this relationship springs into existence out of circumstances; it is a confidential relationship which is the product of equity in the interests of good conscience and justice.

The fiduciary who gains on account of his position against the interests of his confider is bound to account for the same.[9] This principle is not, as said by Lord Herschell in *Bray* v. *Ford*[10], founded upon morality; it is rather based upon consideration of human nature: human beings being selfish by nature, and some rule is required to check that selfishness. If it is not checked one would act as an agent for one's own advantage.[11]

Fiduciary relationship covers a wide variety of different relations, having very few features in common. It is therefore to be found out from circumstances.

Elaborating the principle laid down in *Bray* v. *Ford*[12] by Lord Herschell, Lord Wright explains it as under:[13]

> "That question can be briefly stated to be whether an agent, a director, a trustee or other person in an analogous fiduciary position, when a demand is

6. Taxmann's Law Dictionary by D.P. Mittal, pp. 249-250.
7. *Lyell* v. *Kennedy*, (1889) 14 AC 437.
8. *Krishna Mohan Kul* v. *Pratima Maity*, (2004) 9 SCC 468 (Onus of proof is reversed in fiduciary relationship.)
9. See *Regal (Hastings) Ltd.* v. *Gulliver*, (1942) 1 All ER 378.
10. (1896) AC 44.
11. See *Jayasingh* v. *Krishna*, (1985) 4 SCC 162: AIR 1985 SC 1646.
12. In *Regal (Hastings) Ltd.* v. *Gulliver*, (1942) 1 All ER 378.
13. (1896) AC 44.

made upon him by the person to whom he stands in the fiduciary relationship to account for profits acquired by him by reason of his fiduciary position, and by reason of the opportunity of knowledge or either resulting from it, is entitled to defeat the claim upon any ground save that he made the profits with the knowledge and assent of the other person. The most usual and typical case of this nature is that of principal and agent. The rule in such cases is compendiously expressed to be that an agent must account for not profits secretly (that is, without the knowledge of his principal) acquired by him in the course of his agency. The authorities show how manifold and various are the applications of the rule. It does not depend on fraud or corruption."

6. Object of Section

As held in *S.P. Gaekwad case*[14] by reason of Section 88 a person bound in fiduciary character is required to protect the interests of other persons, but the heart and soul thereof is,—as between two persons if one is bound to protect the interests of the other and if the former availing of that relationship makes a pecuniary gain for himself, Section 88 would be attracted. What is sought to be prevented by a person holding such fiduciary benefit is unjust enrichment or unjust benefit derived from another, which is against conscience that he should keep. Thus when a person makes a pecuniary gain by a transaction, the *Cestique trust* created thereunder must be restored back.

7. Important Aspects

Some important aspects of this relationship may be laid down as under:

Office of fiduciary being *onerous* one the fiduciary has to take care—*A fiduciary* cannot get remuneration unless so provided. This is so because his office is gratuitous. He has to maintain a reasonable standard of business efficiency—(*See* the duties of a trustee and compare). The nature of the office of fiduciary is such that he *cannot be a purchaser* of the property under his control. Vishwanath Shastri, J., has explained this principle as: "A transaction by a person occupying a fiduciary position under circumstances in which his own interests are or may be adverse to those of the persons who own the property and whose interests he is bound to protect is always guarded by the courts with utmost jealousy. If such a transaction is impeached. . . The purchaser must show that there has been no fraud or concealment or advantage taken by him of information acquired by him by virtue of his position.[15] His duty of office is so onerous, demanding and exacting that one may say that he must never think of purchasing the trust property at all. Akin to this the general rule for fiduciary is that he may not profit at the expense of the beneficiary. If at all he benefits, the profit belongs to the beneficiary. He must therefore account for it and return it to the beneficiary since it is inequitable in him to retain it. Last, but not the least, is

---

14. *Sangramsinh P. Gaekwad* v. *Shantadevi P. Gaekwad*, (2005) 11 SCC 314: (2005) 123 Comp Cas 566.
15. *Eswara Gowd* v. *Samasekhar Gowd*, 1956 Andh WR 911.

good faith. Good faith and honesty lie at the root of all fiduciary relations. Transactions devoid of good faith are quite unfair and therefore liable to be set aside. Personal interest of a fiduciary should not conflict with that of his beneficiary. This is what Viscount Sankey in *Regal (Hastings) Ltd.* v. *Gulliver*[16] and Anant Narayanan, J. in *Nellie Wapshare*[17] observed. In short, as observed by the Supreme Court[18], honesty and protection of confidence are very very important for a fiduciary. Summing up, it may be said that good faith, honesty, no profit from one's office and position, no purchase of beneficiary's interest and no remuneration for working as a fiduciary are some of the important rules for a fiduciary.

8. Types

Section 88 applies to a trustee, executor, partner, agent, director of a company, legal adviser or *other persons bound in fiduciary character.* Kinds of these other persons bound by fiduciary character may be enumerated as under:

(1) Trustee (*see* their duties and liabilities),[19]

(2) Director of a company,[20]

(3) Partner,[21]

(4) Agent,[22]

In *Sankara Kurup case*[23] an agent was employed to purchase property on behalf of his principal. He does so in his own name. Consequently, upon conveyance or transfer of the property to the agent, he stands as a trustee for the principal. The property in the hands of the agent is for the principal and the agent stands in the fiduciary capacity for the beneficial interest he had for the property as a trustee.

(5) Executor,[24]

(6) Legal Adviser,

(7) Manager of a joint family,[25]

---

16. (1942) 1 All ER 378.
17. AIR 1960 Mad 410.
18. *Controller of Estate Duty* v. *Aloke Mitra*, (1981) 2 SCC 121: AIR 1981 SC 102.
19. Illustrations (*b*), (*c*) to S. 88.
20. *Coop. Co. Ltd.* v. *Bhagwandas & Co.*, AIR 1930 All 615; *Commr. of Agricultural Income Tax* v. *Shree Hanuman Sugar Mills Ltd.*, AIR 1965 Pat 58.
21. Illustrations (*d*), (*e*), (*f*) to S. 88; *Mathura Dutt Bhatt* v. *Prem Bhallabh Khulba*, AIR 1961 All 19; *Ram Narayanan* v. *Kashinath*, AIR 1954 Pat 63; *Gopinath* v. *Satish Chandra*, AIR 1964 All 53.
22. Illustration (*g*) to S. 88; *P.V. Sankara Kurup* v. *Leelavathi Nambiar*, (1994) 6 SCC 68, 70, 71: AIR 1994 SC 2694.
23. *Ibid.*
24. Illustration (*a*) to S. 88; *Re Mackay* v. *Gould*, (1906) 1 Ch 25; *Venkatsubramania* v. *Sivagurunath*, 1938 Mad 64.
25. *N.C.T. Chidambaram* v. *C.A.C. Subramaniam*, AIR 1982 Mad 228.

(8) Donor and donee,[26]

(9) Parent and child,[27]

(10) Religious, medical and other advisers,

(11) Guardian and Ward,[28]

(12) Licensees appointed on remuneration to purchase stocks on behalf of government,[29]

(13) Confidential Transactions wherein confidence is reposed,[30] and which are indicated by—

(*a*) Undue influence,[31]

(*b*) Control over property,

(*c*) Cases of unjust enrichment,[32]

(*d*) Confidential information,[33]

(*e*) Commitment of job,[34]

(14) Tenant for life,[35]

(15) Co-owner,[36]

(16) Mortgagee,[37]

(17) Other qualified owners of property,[38]

(18) De facto guardian,[39]

(19) Receiver,[40]

(20) Insurance Company,[41]

(21) Trustee de son tort,[42]

(22) Co-heir,[43]

---

26. *Thakur Raghunathji Maharaj* v. *Ramesh Chandra*, (2001) 5 SCC 18: (2001) All LT 1369: (2001) Andh LT 20 (SC); *Krishna Mohan Kul* v. *Pratima Maity*, (2004) 9 SCC 468: AIR 2003 SC 4351.
27. *Brahma Raj Singh* v. *B.R. Devi*, AIR 1982 HP 57.
28. Illustration (*h*) to S. 88.
29. *State of Madras* v. *Jayalaxmi Rice Mills Contractors*, AIR 1959 AP 352.
30. *Subhas Chandra* v. *Ganga Prasad*, AIR 1967 SC 878; *Debi Prasad* v. *Chhote Lal*, AIR 1966 All 438; *Hodgson* v. *Marks*, (1971) 2 All ER 684; *Smith* v. *Kay*, (1859) 7 HLC 749.
31. *See* S. 89, *Debi Prasad* v. *Chhotey Lal*, AIR 1966 All 438.
32. *Boardman* v. *Phipps*, (1967) 2 AC 46.
33. *Regal (Hastings) Ltd.* v. *Gulliver*, (1942) All ER 378.
34. *Reading* v. *R.*, (1949) KB 232.
35. *Rajendra Prasad* v. *R.P. Sao*, AIR 1985 Pat 104; *See* S. 90.
36. *Ibid.*
37. *Ibid.*
38. *Ibid.*
39. *Abdul Wajid* v. *Oosman Abdul Rubb*, 1943 Mad 154.
40. *Seerangathuni* v. *Vaithilinga*, 1921 Mad 528.
41. *Ramkrishna Iyer* v. *S.I. General Assurance Co.*, 1942 Mad 210.
42. *Moosabhai* v. *Yacob Bhai*, 29 Bom 267.
43. *Kadir Bathummal* v. *Meera M. Ammal*, (1945) 1 MLJ 338: 1945 Mad 303.

(23) Benamidar,[44]

—arises out of employment commission or charge or business. It includes the employer and the employee, the Crown and its servants, officers, the government and the company directors, agents, solicitors and promoters.

(24) By Commitment of job.[45]

(25) Relationship induced by profit

—by unjust enrichment.[46]

(26) Sharebroker and customer[47]

(27) Directors and shareholders[48]

9. Broad Categories

These transactions may fall in various broad categories, like commercial transactions, confidential transactions, domestic transactions, jural transactions, professional transactions, public transactions and trusteeship transactions.

(*i*) Similarly, advantages gained by exercise of undue influence or by a qualified owner[49] must be held in trust for the benefit of that other (Sections 89-90). *Huguenin* v. *Baseley*[50] and *Allcard* v. *Skinner*[51] are leading instances on the point. A tenant for life, co-owner,[52] mortgagee[53] and co-sharer are the instances of this situation and they are illustrated in the examples attached to the section. *Sorabjee* v. *Dwarkadas*[54] may be cited as a leading case on this point.[55] Section 63 of the Transfer of Property Act, it must be noted, should be read subject to Section 90 of the Trusts Act, i.e., a mortgagor is not only entitled to accession to his property but also entitled to acquisitions made by the mortgagee for his own benefit in circumstances which bring him within Section 90 of the Indian Trusts Act.

(*ii*) Where property is acquired by a person with notice of an existing contract which is capable of specific performance, he must hold the

44. In view of Benami Transactions (Prohibition) Act, 1988, the benamidar's position is no longer the same as it was before the Act.
45. *Reading* v. *R.*, (1949) KB 232.
46. *Boardman* v. *Phipps*, (1967) 2 AC 46 at p. 51.
47. *Canbank Financial Services* v. *Custodian*, (2004) 5 SCC 653.
48. See *Dale & Carrington Invt. (P) Ltd.* v. *P.K. Prathapan*, (2005) 1 SCC 212 (Consequences of breach of fiduciary duties. Relationship inter se between Directors and with shareholders); *Sangram Singh P. Gaekwad* v. *Shantadevi P. Gaekwad*, (2005) 11 SCC 314. (cases cited) (Fiduciary relationship between directors and shareholders, if any).
49. *Namdeo Shripati Nale* v. *Bapu Ganapati Jagtap*, (1997) 5 SCC 185.
50. (1807) 15 Ves 180.
51. (1887) 36 Ch D 145.
52. *Mohd. Israfil* v. *Mohd Israil*, AIR 1971 Pat 350.
53. *Mahabir Singh* v. *Rameshwar Singh*, AIR 1979 Pat 46.
54. (1932) 36 CWN 947 (PC).
55. *See* also *Sataded* v. *Kamal*, AIR 1953 Pat 27 and *Mrutunjay* v. *Narmada*, AIR 1961 SC 1353.

same in trust under Section 91. One must note that here a contract raises a trust.[56]

(*iii*) Where a person buys property which he knows is to be held on trust, he is subjected to a constructive trust under Section 92.

(*iv*) Advantage secretly gained by one of co-compounding creditors must also be held in trust under Section 93.

Section 95 fixes the obligee (trustee) holding property in accordance with any of the preceding sections, with duties, liabilities and disabilities as those of the actual trustee. Such a person is entitled to suitable remuneration as the occasion demands. But the rights of a *bona fide* transferee in good faith and for consideration are not impaired by these provisions.

56. *HPA International* v. *Bhagwandas Fateh Chand Daswani*, (2004) 6 SCC 537.

PART IV
SPECIFIC RELIEF OR EQUITABLE REMEDIES

Chapter XXII
Equitable Remedies—Nature and Scope

"One of the most striking characteristics of equity has been its inventiveness in providing a diversity of remedies. . ."

"The remedies at law were thus both circumscribed and impersonal. The law acted in pursuance only to a limited extent. . . Equity supplemented the limited range of legal remedies by providing a wide range of new remedies. . . These remedies gradually evolved and became settled in their rules and principles."

—*Snell's Principles of Equity*, p. 569

"Throughout these several departments of jurisdiction runs the common principle that the Chancellor addresses himself directly to the conscience of the individual, acting in personam by means of a subpoena and being therefore independent of territorial limits of jurisdiction."

—C.K. Allen: *Law in the Making*, p. 413

SYNOPSIS

1. GENERAL

Specific relief, as form of judicial redress, belongs to the law of procedure, and in a body of written law arranged according to the natural affinities of the subject-matter would find its place as a distinct part or other division of the Civil Procedure Code. This has not happened in India because some centuries ago, the King's ordinary civil courts of law had but limited remedies and in many cases the King's justice was in default. It is now familiar learning to all students of legal history that in the early stages of judicial institutions we constantly find that the power of courts to enforce decisions or even to compel the appearance of parties is rudimentary if not wholly wanting. There is, therefore, nothing to be surprised at in the limited scope of common law remedies in the Middle Ages. The question why it was not enlarged until the latter part of the nineteenth century has its own historical reasons. Meanwhile, the Chancellor, exercising the King's reserved power of doing justice in an extraordinary way where the ordinary means failed, had undertaken to make the defect good. It is only in quite recent times that the courts have acquired power to do without any concurrence of a party in default that which he ought to have done.[1]

Hence were derived both the strength and the weakness of the courts of equity. They could do much that a court of common law could not do; but they had to justify their action on the ground that the suitor showed some special

1. Pollock & Mulla: *Indian Contract Act and Specific Relief Act*, 9th Edn., 1972, pp. 805-806. See also *Snell's Principles of Equity*, p. 569.

cause for seeking a kind of relief which was originally conceived as extraordinary. This was especially so in cases where the plaintiff had a legal right, a right for which the Common Law provided some remedy, but was inadequate in the sense of not being capable of doing full justice in the case. The doctrine and practice of specific performance belong to this class.[2]

The word 'specific' in the expression specific relief implies a precise reference to one particular thing or to certain details among several. It may therefore be said to be a definite or an exact positive remedy.[3] It aims consequently at the exact fulfilment of an obligation and is directed straightaway to the obtaining of the very thing which a person is entitled under a contract and of which he had been deprived. In words of Dr Banerjee it is directed to the obtaining of the very thing that a party is under the law entitled to ask for, whether it be an act or a forbearance. Specific relief thus though more exact is very delicate and more difficult to administer and requires more skill and care on the part of a judge; and hence the guidance in the form of this legislation in India.

2. BASIS OF EQUITABLE RELIEF

Inadequacy of the remedies at law and the elastic willingness of equity to use its discretion[4] directly with reference to the conscience of the individual were the two main foundations of equitable relief. For this purpose the equity courts invented the working principles, called the maxims, and in granting relief it relied on the same, mainly—

(*i*) he who comes to equity must come with clean hands;

(*ii*) he who seeks equity must do equity; and

(*iii*) delay defeats equity.

The Specific Relief Act, 1963[5] in India relies on the English principles of equity in granting or refusing such relief.

3. EQUITABLE REMEDIES

As said before, equity supplemented the limited range of legal remedies by acting *in personam* and by providing a wide range of new remedies. They were—

(*i*) specific performance;

(*ii*) delivery up and cancellation of documents;

(*iii*) rescission of contracts and rectification of instruments;

(*iv*) ordering accounts in proper cases;

(*v*) issuing injunctions; and

---

2. Pollock & Mulla: *Indian Contract Act and Specific Relief Act*, 9th Edn., 1972, pp. 805-806. See also *Snell's Principles of Equity*, p. 569.
3. *Funk & Wagnalls*: *Standard Handbook of Synonyms, Antonyms & Prepositions*, pp. 190-191.
4. See *Ajit Prasad Jain* v. *N.K. Widhani*, AIR 1990 Del 42.
5. Originally Specific Relief Act, 1877.

(*vi*) appointment of receivers.

Besides, discovery of documents, suits for perpetuation of testimony, *quia timet action* (a remedy granted to the petitioner because "he fears what he will suffer in the future"), bills of peace and new *exeat regno* (whereby a person who owed an equitable claim to the petitioner was restrained from proceeding outside the country without first giving security for the sum claimed) were the main remedies.

4. SPECIFIC RELIEF ACT, 1963: SCHEME

The Specific Relief Act, 1963 in India grants the following remedies, dividing them as specific relief (Sections 5 to 35) and preventive relief (Sections 36 to 42):

(*i*) recovering possession of property (Sections 5-8);

(*ii*) specific performance of contracts (Sections 9-25);

(*iii*) rectification of instruments (Section 26);

(*iv*) rescission of contracts (Sections 27-30);

(*v*) cancellation of instruments (Sections 31-33);

(*vi*) declaratory decrees (Sections 34-35); and

(*vii*) injunctions (Sections 36-42)

5. SPECIFIC RELIEF

Common Law relief or legal relief was mainly compensatory while equitable relief was specific. As noted by Woodroffe:[6] "The remedies for the non-performance of a duty enforceable by law are either compensatory or specific. *Compensatory remedy is by the award of damages which is often useless and inadequate.* Useless where the person ordered to pay them is insolvent, and inadequate where for instance the duty is to transfer particular immovable property or a movable property to which special interest is attached. The specific remedy is enforced by directing the party in default to do or forbear the very thing which he is bound to do or forbear, and in case of disobedience, by imprisonment or attachment of his property, or both.

When no one is in default, it is enforced by making such declarations and orders as the nature of the case may require". Specific performance can be distinguished from injunctions. The former, as noted by Story, is directed to compelling performance of an active duty and is concerned mainly with contracts, whereas the latter is generally directed to preventing the violation of a negative duty and deals not only with contract but also with torts and many other equitable subjects. As Maitland observes, specific performance applies to agreements for sale of land or lease of land as a matter of course; its application outside these lines is somewhat exceptional and discretionary.

---

6. Whitely Stokes quoted in *Woodroffe on Injunctions.*

6. SECTIONS 1-4

The Specific Relief Act, 1963 was not meant to be an exhaustive code with all kinds of specific reliefs incorporated therein, but refers to only that branch of reliefs which could be obtained in civil suits. In its essence, the law of specific relief is, a part of the law of procedure, for, specific relief is a form of a judicial redress.[7] It is adjective law.[8] That is why the Act starts by stating its object, "to define and amend the law relating to certain kinds of specific reliefs". Specific reliefs obtainable in criminal and revenue courts is outside the precincts of this Act. The Act is therefore not exhaustive.[9] When a case is governed by any section of the Act, the court must in the first instance examine the language of the section and find out its natural meaning.[10] It will be seen that the Act is based on the rules and practice of the English Law in relation to the doctrine of specific performance and the sections must be interpreted in that light, but where there is an express divergence by the section then it will be strictly adhered to, whatever may be the English Law on the point.[11]

The Act extends to the whole of India except the State of Jammu and Kashmir. Illustrations to the sections, it will be seen, have been removed as they do not serve any useful purpose in clarifying the provisions.

Relief in general means the remedy a court of justice may afford to some actual or apprehended wrong or injury[12] and the Act gives relief for the purpose of enforcing individual civil rights and not for the mere purpose of enforcing a penal law (Section 4). This means that enforcement of a penal law must not be the sole object of the suit. Moreover grant of relief of declaration tending to affect the free flow of capital and mercantile business would be unjust.[13] Section 3, one must note, recognises the fiduciary character of personal obligation created by a contract of sale.[14] The jurisdiction to order specific performance of a contract is based on the existence of a valid and enforceable contract; where it is not so, the specific performance will not be ordered.[15]

---

7. *Ali Hasan* v. *Rajkumar Haldar*, AIR 1943 Cal 417, 426: 208 IC 473: 47 CWN 557: 77 CLJ 216.
8. *Radhey Shyam* v. *Kiran Bala Dasi*, AIR 1971 Cal 314: 74 CWN 573; Banerjee: *Law of Specific Relief*, 9th edn., 1992, p. 3.
9. *Hungerford Investment Trust Ltd.* v. *Haridas Mundhra*, (1972) 3 SCC 684; *Ashok Kumar Srivastav* v. *National Insurance Co. Ltd.*, (1998) 4 SCC 361: 1998 SCC (L&S) 1137: (1998) 2 LLT 699.
10. *Bank of England* v. *Vagliano Bros.*, 1891 AC 107; *Ramdas Vithaldas Durbar* v. *S. Amerchand & Co.*, AIR 1916 PC 7: 43 IA 164; *Ardeshir Mama* v. *Flora Sassoon*, (1928) 55 IA 360: AIR 1928 PC 208.
11. *Akshayalingam Pillai* v. *Avayambala Ammal*, 64 MLJ 536: AIR 1933 Mad 386; *Ramnath* v. *Shimoga Bank Ltd.*, A. No. 120 (Mys HC) 1948-49, quoted in *Indian Digest*, 1951: AIR 1951 Mys 59.
12. *Sarsuti* v. *Kunj Behari Lal*, ILR (1883) 3 All 345.
13. *American Express Bank Ltd.* v. *Calcutta Steel Co.*, (1993) 2 SCC 199, 213.
14. *Narandas Karasandas* v. *S.A. Kamtam*, (1977) 3 SCC 247: (1977) 2 SCR 341.
15. *Mayawanti* v. *Kaushalya Devi*, (1990) 3 SCC 1.

Chapter XXIII
Recovering Possession of Property

"Suits under both the sections are mutually exclusive; if a suit is brought under Section 9 (new Section 6) for recovery of possession, question of title cannot be raised or determined, while in a suit under Section 8 (new Section 5) a plaintiff sues to establish his title for recovery of possession."

Ananta Kumar Sarkar v. *Meghu Kurmi*,
(1957) 61 Cal WN 347

"Scope and Object of Section 9 is:

(*i*) *to restore a person dispossessed otherwise than in due course of law (and) Fazal Hussain* v. *Abdul Latif*, AIR 1955 NUC Ajmer 334.

(*ii*) *to discourage people from taking law into their own hands however good their title may be."*

M.C. Batra v. *Lakshmi Insurance Co. Ltd.*,
AIR 1956 All 709.

SYNOPSIS

1. RECOVERY OF PROPERTY

Sections 5 to 8 make provisions for recovering possession of property, movable and immovable. The procedure for the purpose is laid down in the Civil Procedure Code, Order 21, Rules 35 and 36. Section 7 speaks about a suit by a person dispossessed of immovable property and Section 8 explains that a person holding movable property not as an owner may be compelled in suitable cases to deliver it to the person entitled to its immediate possession.

Possession, as Salmond has explained, is a very vital relationship which needs protection from every system of law. All things we need to use and consume must be in our possession. It is, therefore, the most basic relationship between men and things. One must however note that the provision in Specific Relief Act is founded more on public policy than on Jurisprudence.[1]

1. *Krishna Kishore Firm* v. *Govt. of A.P.*, (1991) 1 SCC 184: AIR 1990 SC 2292. See *Sudhir Jaggi* v. *Sunil Akash Sinha Choudhury*, (2004) 7 SCC 515 (Concept of possession and test to determine it discussed and case law reviewed.)

The question is, what relief is afforded by law to a person who has been deprived of his property (and therefore wants to recover the property); the manner of acquisition and the extent of his interest therein being questions different from this. Where property is vested in law the person dispossessed of it has stronger reasons for getting specific relief and it will be for the defendant to show cause why the relief should not be granted against him. Where the property is vested in equity it will be for the plaintiff to explain why he should be granted specific relief. Putting the situation in a different way, when a person is deprived of his property or of any interest or right therein, he is entitled to have it back and enjoy or use the very interest or right thereto, as it is his own, and no amount of money compensation is adequate to satisfy his loss. Remembering this general basic principle we now look to the provisions of the Act in this regard.

2. TEXT OF SECTIONS 5 TO 8

Recovering Possession of Property

5. Recovery of specific immovable property.—A person entitled to the possession of specific immovable property may recover it in the manner provided by the Code of Civil Procedure, 1908 (5 of 1908).

6. Suit by person dispossessed of immovable property.—(1) If any person is dispossessed without his consent of immovable property otherwise than in due course of law, he or any person claiming through him may, by suit, recover possession thereof, notwithstanding any other title that may be set up in such suit.

(2) No suit under this section shall be brought—

(*a*) after the expiry of six months from the date of dispossession; or

(*b*) against the Government.

(3) No appeal shall lie from any order or decree passed in any suit instituted under this section, nor shall any review of any such order or decree be allowed.

(4) Nothing in this section shall bar any person from suit to establish his title to such property and to recover possession thereof.

7. Recovery of specific movable property.—A person entitled to the possession of specific movable property may recover it in the manner provided by the Code of Civil Procedure, 1908 (5 of 1908).

Explanation I.—A trustee may sue under this section for the possession of movable property to the beneficial interest in which the person for whom he is trustee is entitled.

Explanation II.—A special or temporary right to the present possession of movable property is sufficient to support a suit under this section.

8. Liability of person in possession, not as owner, to deliver to person entitled to immediate possession.—Any person having the possession or control of a particular article of movable property, of which he is not the owner, may be compelled specifically to deliver it to the person entitled to its immediate possession, in any of the following cases—

(*a*) when the thing claimed is held by the defendant as the agent or trustee of the plaintiff;

(*b*) when compensation in money would not afford the plaintiff adequate relief for the loss of the thing claimed;

(*c*) when it would be extremely difficult to ascertain the actual damage caused by its loss;

(*d*) when the possession of the thing claimed has been wrongfully transferred from the plaintiff.

Explanation.—Unless and until the contrary is proved, the court shall, in respect of any article of movable property claimed under clause (*b*) or clause (*c*) of this section, presume—

(*a*) that compensation in money would not afford the plaintiff adequate relief for the loss of the thing claimed, or, as the case may be;

(*b*) that it would be extremely difficult to ascertain the actual damage caused by its loss.

3. RECOVERY OF SPECIFIC IMMOVABLE PROPERTY (SECTIONS 5 AND 6)

Although provision in Specific Relief Act empowering a person or tenant to recover possession if he has been evicted forcibly by landlord, may be judicial and not lawful or a tenant holding over is not in lawful possession unless landlord agrees or acquiesces expressly or impliedly but that does not alter the legal position about possession of a person not legal, yet not without interest. The provision in Specific Relief Act, it should be remembered, is founded more on public policy than on jurisprudence.[2]

In *Indian Iron & Steel Co. Ltd. case*[3] there was a title suit for possession and for restraining the occupant-defendant from pulling down the structures on the site. The structures did not belong to the owner of the title. Under the circumstances decree although upheld, the plaintiff was directed to pay compensation to the defendant, for such structures.

The object of the provisions is to discourage people from taking the law into their own hands. The sections provide a speedy and summary remedy through a medium of civil court for restoration of possession to the dispossessed. Section 5 thus provides for a suit for ejectment *on the basis of title*[4] and Section 6 gives a remedy without *establishing title*, provided the suit is brought within six months of the date of dispossession. The sections thus give remedy in the alternative.[5]

The object of Section 6 is to discourage forcible dispossession and to enable the person dispossessed to recover possession by merely providing previous possession and wrongful dispossession without proving title, but that is not the only remedy.[6] He may bring a suit for possession on the basis of his title.[7]

A suit for possession simpliciter (Section 5) differs from a suit for possession under Section 6 in this that in the latter case a plaintiff need only prove dispossession within six months and the defendant cannot plead a superior title. But in the former the plaintiff can be defeated if the defendant

2. *Krishna Kishore Firm* v. *Govt. of A.P.*, (1991) 1 SCC 184: AIR 1990 SC 2292; See also *Express Newspapers (P) Ltd.* v. *Union of India*, (1986) 1 SCC 133.
3. *Indian Iron & Steel Co. Ltd.* v. *Chhaganlal Marwari*, 1994 Supp (3) SCC 719.
4. *Lachman* v. *Shambhu Narain*, ILR (1911) 33 All 174: 7 IC 495; *Prataprai N. Kothari* v. *John Braganza*, (1999) 4 SCC 403: AIR 1999 SC 1666.
5. *East India Hotels Ltd.* v. *Syndicate Bank*, 1992 Supp (2) SCC 29.
6. *Ibid.*
7. Pollock and Mulla: *Indian Contract Act & Specific Relief Act*, p. 814.

proves his superior title to the land.[8] Sections 5 and 6 are not mutually exclusive.

In *Alexander case*[9], the plaintiff brought a suit for possession of lands alleging his possession for 70 years and forcible dispossession by the defendants. The defendant denied this forcible possession and pleaded that a suit for possession did not lie without proof of title and a prior trespasser could not eject a later trespasser, and a mere possessory suit after the expiry of six months was not possible under Section 6 of the Specific Relief Act. In appeal the High Court held that the plaintiff was in possession before the suit and could maintain a suit based on prior possession without proof of title and therefore could eject the defendants. The High Court's decision was upheld in appeal to the Supreme Court.

As observed in *Rama Gowda case*[10] occupant in "settled possession" cannot be dispossessed without recourse to law. This judgment gives meaning of settled possession, possessory title and tests for it.

Possessory title: Possessory title is good against all the world but the rightful owner. A person in possession of land in assumed character as owner and exercising peaceably the ordinary right of ownership has a perfectly good title against all the world but the rightful owner. When the facts disclose no title in either party, possession alone decides. *Possessio Contra Omnes Valet Praeter Eur Cui Ins Sit Possessionis.*—i.e. he that hath possession or prior peaceful settled possession is itself evidence of title. Law presumes the possession to go with the title unless rebutted.

Settled Possession: *Meaning and tests*: The settled possession must be (*i*) effective, (*ii*) undisturbed and (*iii*) to the knowledge of the owner or without any attempt at concealment by the trespasser. The phrase does not carry any special charm or magic in it; nor it is a ritualistic formula which can be confined in a straight-jacket.

The Supreme Court in *Puran Singh case*[11] has laid down tests which may be adopted as a working rule for determining the attributes of "settled possession." (para 9).

In India possession of land cannot be obtained by using force; law does not allow it. Possession can be obtained through Court. A person in possession of land can defend his possession even by using force and law will aid him. This is because the other person is a trespasser. Even injunction can be obtained against him.

A settled possession gives right to possession, such that even the rightful owner may only recover it by taking recourse to law.[12]

---

8. *Yar Muhammad* v. *Lakshmidas*, AIR 1959 All 1; see also *Mohd. Sharif K. Rangawala* v. *Amibai A. Rangawala*, AIR 1984 Guj 90: (1983) 2 GLR 1481.
9. *Nair Service Society Ltd.* v. *K.C. Alexander*, AIR 1968 SC 1165.
10. *Rame Gowda* v. *M. Varadappa Naidu*, (2004) 1 SCC 769.
11. (1975) 4 SCC 518, 527 at para 12.
12. *See* also *Sopan Sukhdeo Sable* v. *Asstt. Charity Commr.*, (2004) 3 SCC 137: (2004) 2 CHN 152. See *K.K. Verma* v. *Union of India*, AIR 1954 Bom 358.

In *Ramesh Chand Ardawatiya* v. *Anil Panjwani*,[13] the owner of property contracts with plaintiff to sell his land and gives possession to the plaintiff. The possession remains peaceful and plaintiff make part-payment giving assurance that the remaining amount would be paid at the time of registration of the sale deed. A third party who has no better title than the plaintiff's, during this period makes construction on that land. The plaintiff by filing a suit against him obtains stay order from court but the fellow takes no notice of stay order. The remedy of the plaintiff at this juncture is to get declaration from the court that he is the possessor of the property and his title is possessory title. However he cannot obtain a declaration that he is the owner of the property. The plaintiff is also entitled to a mandatory and permanent preventive injunction against that third party.[14]

Where a person gives purely a gratuitous permission and is dispossessed of immovable property, he has a right to reclaim the possession even without the knowledge of the person in possession.[15]

Section 6 is a reproduction of Section 15 of the Indian Limitation Act, 1859, provisions whereof are based on the Writ of Assizes in England. Its object is to resolve the *status quo ante*. In England a rightful owner of property has a right of re-entry on his property if he can do it in a peaceful and reasonable manner, but the Indian law differs from this in that even a rightful owner cannot by self-help regain his possession. If he does so it is a wrong. He must take the help of court in such cases.

Section 6 thus provides a summary remedy to the plaintiff to seek restoration of possession from defendant within 6 months of illegal recovery of possession by the defendant without referring to the title of the plaintiff and defendant.[16] It is purely a possessory suit wherein status of the party is irrelevant. In such type of suits the plaintiff is not required to prove his title or a superior right to possession as compared to the defendant and has only to show that he was in possession of the immovable property and he was illegally dispossessed within a period of 6 months prior to the date of the suit.[17] Once the plaintiff proves case he becomes entitled to succeed and can get status quo ante and restoration of possession of the suit premises through the assistance of the court.[18] The question in such cases is about "prior possession" and the question of title does not arise under this section. As held

13. (2003) 7 SCC 350: AIR 2003 SC 2508.
14. *See* also *Prataprai N. Kothari* v. *John Braganza*, (1999) 4 SCC 403: AIR 1999 SC 1666.
15. *Anima Mallick* v. *Ajoy Kumar Roy*, (2000) 4 SCC 119.
16. *Sanjay Kumar Pandey* v. *Gulbahar Sheikh*, (2004) 4 SCC 664; *Deva* v. *Sajjan Kumar*, (2003) 7 SCC 481 (Suit for possession of Land encroached on.); *Rachakonda Venkat Rao* v. *R. Satya Bai*, (2003) 7 SCC 452 (for properties in joint possession); *S.R. Ejaz* v. *T.N. Handloom Weavers' Coop. Society Ltd.*, (2002) 3 SCC 137; *Sayed Muhammed Mashur Kunhi Koya Thangal* v. *Badagara Jumayath Palli Dharas Committee*, (2004) 7 SCC 708; *Shubh Shanti Services Ltd.* v. *Manjula S. Agarwalla*, (2005) 5 SCC 30 (retrieving company's property wrongfully withheld by office employee).
17. *Mahabir Prasad Jain* v. *Ganga Singh*, (1999) 8 SCC 274.
18. *Mansukhlal Dhanraj Jain* v. *Eknath Vithal Ogale*, (1995) 2 SCC 665: AIR 1995 SC 1102.

in *Jagat Singh case*[19] this section is a reproduction of a provision of the Roman Law under which by an *interdictum de vi* a person wrongfully dispossessed from property could recover it by proving previous possession, without being required to prove his title.

The main elements of Section 6 are:

(*i*) That the possession of the plaintiff must be "juridical" and he must establish it. "Juridical possession" is the same thing as legal possession in a more impressive form. It is a possession based on some right and not a possession obtained by force or fraud. Such possession, however cannot be equated with lawful possession. For example a tenant holding possession after expiry of his lease has a juridical possession, however that cannot be termed as lawful possession.[20]

As observed by the Supreme Court in Mahale case[21] where a person is in settled possession of property, even on the assumption that he had no right to remain on the property, he cannot be dispossessed by the owner of the property except by recourse to law.[22]

This means that possession here cannot mean merely juridical possession or the same under a valid title; it includes possession which is excusable.

The expression "due course of law" means such an exercise of powers by duly constituted tribunal or court in accordance with the procedure established by law under such safeguards for the protection of individual rights.[23]

(*ii*) That he must have been dispossessed against his will and without due process of law. The plaintiff in such a case has to prove his previous possession. The suit under this section is a possessory suit; it does not refer to title of the plaintiff and the defendant.[24] If the suit is brought after six months, the plaintiff can recover only if he proves his title to the land.[25] The purpose behind Section 6 is to restrain a person from using force and to dispossess a person without his consent otherwise than in due course of law.[26]

(*iii*) That a plaintiff must file a suit within six months. The plaintiff in such a case has to prove his previous possession. If the suit is brought after

---

19. *Nagar Palika* v. *Jagat Singh*, (1995) 3 SCC 426: (1995) 3 Punj LR 224.
20. *M.C. Chockalingam* v. *V. Manickavasagam*, (1974) 1 SCC 48: AIR 1974 SC 104; *Lallu Yashwant Singh* v. *Rao Jagdish Singh*, AIR 1968 SC 620.
21. *Krishna Ram Mahale* v. *Shobha Venkat Rao*, (1989) 4 SCC 131.
22. *East India Hotels Ltd.* v. *Syndicate Bank*, 1992 Supp (2) SCC 29.
23. *Ibid.*
24. *Ibid.*
25. *Mansukhlal Dhanraj Jain* v. *Eknath Vithal Ogale*, (1995) 2 SCC 665: AIR 1995 SC 1102.
26. *Krishna Ram Mahale* v. *Shobha Venkat Rao*, (1989) 4 SCC 131: 1989 MPLJ 767; *East India Hotels Ltd.* v. *Syndicate Bank*, supra; See *Chocka Lingam* v. *Manickavasagam*, (1974) 1 SCC 48.

six months, the plaintiff can recover only if he proves his title to the land.[27] Moreover, one has to note that a person dispossessed is entitled to regain his possession; the better title of the dispossessor is of no relevance as it is not in issue. It therefore follows that a decision under this section does not make or mar the original title of either party.

Under this section court can grant interim relief of restoration of possession, however, the power has to be exercised carefully, wisely and in exceptional circumstances only.[28] The only prohibition under the provisions of Section 6 is not to use force and not to use any unlawful means for dispossessing a person. The position of a licensee remaining in occupation after the expiry of the term of licence is no better than a tresspasser and if the true owner comes into possession of the premises without using any force or on account of fire or other act of vis major, it would not be in the interest of justice to grant a decree for possession in favour of such licensee under Section 6 of the Act.[29]

If the suit is one for possession against a trespasser (i.e., one who has no title to the land) what should a plaintiff prove: should he prove his title to the land or would proof of previous possession suffice? The answer is yes. In such circumstances it is not necessary for plaintiff to establish his title. This is because a trespasser has no right to disturb peaceful possession of long time of any person on any land and he cannot reap benefit of his illegal act.[30] The Supreme Court has accepted this view in *K.C. Alexander case*.[31] But one has to note that in a suit against the trespasser after six months the period should not be so long as to allow a trespasser's possession to ripen into prescriptive title.[32]

In a suit for recovery of possession by licensee forcibly dispossessed by the Municipal Corporation it was held that in such a case the licensee forcibly dispossessed has two remedies open to him:

(*i*) to file a suit under Section 64 of the Easements Act, and

(*ii*) to file a suit under Section 6 of the Specific Relief Act. One remedy does not bar the other.[33]

---

27. *Mansukhlal Dhanraj Jain* v. *Eknath Vithal Ogale*, (1995) 2 SCC 665: AIR 1995 SC 1102.

28. *Ramesh Devchand Pala* v. *Jayavantkumar Gordhandas Madani*, AIR 1998 Guj 120.

29. *East India Hotels Ltd.*, supra, *Ramesh Chand Ardawatiya* v. *Anil Panjwani*, (2003) 7 SCC 350: AIR 2003 SC 2508.

30. *Lallu Yeshwant Singh* v. *Rao Jagdish Singh*, AIR 1968 SC 620: (1968) 2 SCR 203; *Midnapur Zamindari Co. Ltd.* v. *N.N. Roy*, AIR 1924 PC 144: 51 IA 293: 23 ALJ 76; *Ram Rattan* v. *State of U.P.*, (1977) 1 SCC 188: 1977 SCC (Cri) 85; *State of U.P.* v. *Maharaja Dharmander Prasad Singh*, (1989) 2 SCC 505 at pp. 516-517, paras 30-31.

31. *Nair Service Society Ltd.* v. *K.C. Alexander*, AIR 1968 SC 1165; see also *Naziruddin* v. *Abeda Khatun*, (1989) 1 Gau LR 177, 179; *Sankar Goala* v. *Mufiauddin*, (1988) 1 Cur CC 393.

32. *Narayan* v. *T. Mathayi*, AIR 1966 Ker 179.

33. *M.S. Baliga (dead, by his LRs)* v. *Mangalore City Corpn.*, AIR 1998 Kant 76; see also *Beharilal* v. *Bhuri Devi*, (1997) 2 SCC 279: AIR 1997 SC 1879.

In *S.R. Ejaz case*[34] a tenant was forcibly dispossessed. He filed a police complaint, but to no result; the police remained inactive. He therefore filed a writ in High Court which ordered the CB/CID to inquire into the matter. The government gave permission to inquire. However for reasons best known to government it withdrew the criminal proceedings. This goes to prove that the tenant was in possession, and he was forcibly dispossessed.

This procedure took fifteen years. If this matter even if it is remanded, it would not serve the purpose of law. The purpose of the law is thus frustrated. The court observed:

"If such actions by the mighty or powerful are condoned in a democratic country nobody would be safe nor can the citizens protect their properties. Law frowns upon such conduct. The court accords legitimacy and legality only to possession taken in due course of law. If such actions are condoned the Fundamental Rights guaranteed under the Constitution of India or the legal rights would be given a go-by either by the authority or by rich and influential persons or by musclemen. "Law of Jungle" will prevail and "might would be right" instead of "right being might".

No suit against the government can be brought under this section but one must bring a regular suit and prove one's title. An order under this section is not appealable nor reviewable except where jurisdiction is wrongly assumed.

4. RECOVERY OF SPECIFIC MOVABLE PROPERTY (Sections 7 and 8)

(*a*) *History*.—These sections embody the English rules as to detinue.

There are three specific torts in respect of the possession of goods[35]: trespass, detention of goods or detinue and conversion. Detinue is a kind of conversion. It consists in wrongfully detaining from the plaintiff goods to the immediate possession of which he is entitled.[36] An action in detinue would lie only for some specific article of movable property capable of being recovered in specie and of being seized and delivered up to the winning party. The elements of detinue may be laid down as: (*i*) existence of some specific article of movable property, (*ii*) plaintiff's immediate right to such property, (*iii*) defendant's possession and unjust detention of the property. When the defendant has got possession of the plaintiff's goods (whether wrongfully in the first instance, or by keeping them wrongfully after having lawfully obtained possession) the plaintiff can sue either for wrongful detention or for conversion, but generally an action for detention is brought where the defendant is at the time of action brought in wrongful possession of specific goods such as a horse or a picture, which the plaintiff wished to have returned to him.[37] Thus a plaintiff may

---

34. *S.R. Ejaz* v. *T.N. Handloom Weavers' Coop. Society Ltd.*, (2002) 3 SCC 137: AIR 2002 SC 1152.
35. *Underhills's Law of Torts*, 13th Edn., p. 92.
36. *Ibid.*
37. *Ibid.*, p. 96.

demand the specific delivery of property or, on failing thereto, he may demand the value and also damages for detention of the property. Specific delivery of the article was not available up to 1854, in England, but due to the intervention of equity the same was made available in suitable cases where the article sought to be obtained had a peculiar value or some association or importance attached thereto. After 1854 this was granted without help from the equity courts, and in 1873-75 by the Judicature Acts the form of detinue was abolished, but the name has so far survived.

(*b*) *Comments.*—As the section provides, possession of specific movable property may be recovered not only by a person entitled to its possession but also by a trustee for his beneficiary and to be so entitled, a special or temporary right to the present possession of movable property is sufficient to support a suit under this section. *Donald* v. *Suckling*[38] and *Oliver* v. *Oliver*[39] are leading English cases on the point. In *Ramnath Gagoi* v. *Pitambar Deb Goswami*[40], *A* leaves an elephant in charge of *B*, *C* wrongfully takes away the elephant from *B*. *B* may sue *C* for possession of the elephant. Likewise, the railway as bailee of goods[41] is entitled to recover them from a person who takes them from its possession forcibly or fraudulently. If such goods are pledged it can be recovered from the pledgee of such person too by the railway.[42] As said before, the requisites of Section 7 are the same as the rules for detinue and the nature and quality of the property is immaterial. It is not necessary that the plaintiff must be an owner; he may be a limited owner, or he may have a special or a temporary right to possess. Thus immediate right to possess the property as against the defendant is material.

Illustrations to Section 10 of the old Act which have been dropped in this new enactment would be informative in order to understand the scope of this section. The same may be reproduced as under:

(*a*) *A* bequeaths land to *B* for his life with remainder to *C*. *A* dies. *B* enters on the land but *C*, without *B*'s consent obtains possession of title deeds. *B* may recover them from *C*.

(*b*) *A* pledges certain jewels to *B* to secure a loan. *B* disposes of them before he is entitled to do so. *A* without having paid or tendered the amount of the loan sues *B* for possession of the jewels. The suit should be dismissed as *A* is not *entitled to their possession*, whatever right he may have to secure their safe custody.

38. (1866) 1 QB 585: 14 LT 772.

39. (1861) 11 CBNS 139: 5 LT 287; *Ramnath Gagoi* v. *Pitambar Deb Goswami*, ILR (1916) 43 Cal 733: 31 IC 430: AIR 1916 Cal 788. See Pollock and Mulla: *Indian Contract Act & Specific Relief Act*, p. 820.

40. (1861) 11 CBNS 139: 5 LT 287; *Ramnath Gagoi* v. *Pitambar Deb Goswami*, ILR (1916) 43 Cal 733: 31 IC 430: AIR 1916 Cal 788. See Pollock and Mulla: *Indian Contract Act & Specific Relief Act*, p. 820.

41. Section 18 of the Indian Contract Act.

42. *Purshottam Das* v. *Union of India*, AIR 1967 All 549: ILR (1967) 1 All 398; *Sagarmal Megh Raj* v. *Abdul Hafeez*, 1964 MLJ (Cri) 623.

(*c*) *A* receives a letter addressed to him by *B*. *B* gets back the letter without *A*'s consent. *A* has such a property therein as entitles him to recover it from *B*.

(*d*) *A* deposits books and papers for safe custody with *B*. *B* loses them and *C* finds them, but refuses to deliver them to *B* when demanded. *B* may recover them from *C*, subject to *C*'s right (if any) under Section 168 of the Indian Contract Act, 1872.

(*e*) *A*, warehouse keeper, is charged with the delivery of certain goods to *Z*, which *B* takes out of *A*'s possession. *A* may sue *B* for the goods.

A thief steals certain articles and pledges them with *X* (a pledgee). Such a pledge does not confer any title to the pledgee so as to have possession and control thereof. Its true owner can recover them and the pledgee cannot claim compensation or resist the owner's claim.[43] The articles of dowry given to wife can also be claimed by the wife under Dowry Prohibition Act.[44] This is so on the principle that the wife is the person entitled to the possession.

"Specific movable property" means property which is ascertained and ascertainable, but not its equivalent.[45] A dead body is not movable property. No suit under this section is therefore maintainable.[46] Share Certificates[47] and Government Securities[48] are specific movable properties, but money[49] is not movable property.

That the plaintiff is not entitled to possession of the property or that the property claimed by the plaintiff belongs to a third person (defence of *jus tertii*) are not considered as valid defences.[50] It should be remembered that the plaintiff must succeed or fail on his own case and cannot take advantage of weakness in defendant's case to get a decree. The Supreme Court would not interfere in such cases.[51]

Section 8 speaks of the liability of a person in possession of movable property not as owner, to deliver the same to the person entitled to its immediate possession—

(*i*) when he holds it as the agent or trustee of the plaintiff;

(*ii*) when compensation is an inadequate relief for the loss to the plaintiff;

(*iii*) when ascertainment of actual damage caused is extremely difficult;

(*iv*) when possession of the thing is wrongfully transferred from the plaintiff.

---

43. *Sagar Mal Megh Raj* v. *Abdul Hafeez*, 1964 MLJ (CR) 623.
44. *Kamini Savhani* v. *Puma Chandra Sahoo*, AIR 1987 Ori 134.
45. *Fadu Jhala* v. *Gour Mohan Jhala*, 19 Cal 544.
46. *Ma Kin* v. *U. Ba*, AIR 1930 Rang 143: 121 IC 775: ILR 7 Rang 603.
47. *Gopal Chandra Bose* v. *Surendra Nath Dutt*, 12 BLR 513.
48. 12 CWN 1010.
49. *Bhubaneshwar* v. *Dwarkeshwar*, AIR 1921 Cal 77.
50. *Armory* v. *De la mirie*, 1 Stra 504.
51. *Punjab Urban Planning and Development Authority* v. *Shiv Saraswati Iron & Steel Re-Rolling Mills*, (1998) 4 SCC 539.

In cases covered under clause (*ii*) or (*iii*) the court presumes that the compensation is not an adequate relief and that the ascertainment of the damage caused is extremely difficult, unless it is proved otherwise.

(*c*) *Difference between Section 7 and Section 8.*—Sections 7 and 8 speak of the recovery of specific movable property but there is a difference between them which is as follows:

(1) It can be seen that relief given by Section 7 is (*i*) of a general nature, (*ii*) independent of the nature of property, and (*iii*) relation between the parties. The relief afforded by Section 8 is of a special character and depends upon the nature of property and the relationship existing between the parties, as can be seen from its clauses.

(2) Relief claimed under Section 7 is for possession of the movable property and *in alternative* for compensation equal to *the value* of property, whereas the relief sought under Section 8 is for the very property *i.e.*, for delivery of the specific movable property.

(3) Under Section 7, a suit to recover possession can be maintained even against the owner of property if the plaintiff has vested in him the immediate right to possess it. Section 8 does not contemplate a suit against the owner.

Leading cases on the sections are *Wood* v. *Rowcliffe*[52] and *Falcke* v. *Gray*.[53]

(*d*) *Burden of Proof.*—The section contemplates in other words the restitution of chattels. Pollock and Mulla in their earlier editions of the treatise[54] on contract and specific relief remarked that the burden of proof thrown on the plaintiff under a more logically developed system would be on the defendant to show cause why it should not be just and equitable to award specific restitution. These remarks were approved by the Madras High Court in *G.J. Subbarayulu* v. *Annamalai Chettiar*[55] and led to the enactment of the explanation which now clarifies that the burden of proof in clauses (*a*) and (*d*) rests on the plaintiff, while the burden under clauses (*b*) and (*c*) rests on the defendant who has to prove that the compensation would be an adequate relief and that it would not be extremely difficult to ascertain the actual damage caused by the loss of the chattel.

It must be noted that a plaintiff under this section has to prove that the defendant is in possession; if he cannot, he will not get a decree.[56]

---

52. (1844) 3 Hare 304.
53. (1859) 4 Drew 651: 62 ER 250.
54. *Indian Contract Act and Specific Relief Act*, 9th Edn., 1972, p. 821.
55. ILR (1946) Mad 174: AIR 1945 Mad 281.
56. For execution of decree under this section *see* Order 21, Rule 31 of Civil Procedure Code, 1908.

Chapter XXIV
Specific Performance of Contracts

"Two great remedies it invented, remedies peculiar to itself—the decree for specific performance of a contract, and the injunction."

* * * *

"On the whole I think that specific performance applies to agreements for sale or lease of lands as a matter of course; its application outside these limits is somewhat exceptional and discretionary."

Maitland: *Lectures on Equity*, pp. 301, 304

"In India we are free from these anomalies."

—Pollock and Mulla: *Indian Contract Act and Specific Relief Act*, p. 823

SYNOPSIS

12. Parties to an action for Specific Performance (Sections 15, 16, 17 and 19)
    (*a*) For whom contracts may be specifically enforced (Section 15)
    (*b*) For whom Specific Performance cannot be enforced (Sections 16 and 17)
    (*c*) Persons against whom contracts may be enforced (Section 19)
13. When contract cannot be enforced except with a variation (Section 18)
14. Discretion and Powers of the Court (Sections 20 to 24)
    (*a*) Compensatory Relief (Sections 21 to 24)
    (*b*) Other Reliefs (Sections 24 and 22)
    (*c*) Liquidation of damages not a bar to specific performance (Section 23)

1. INTRODUCTION

The jurisdiction of the English court of chancery to decree specific performance of contracts was founded on the want of an adequate remedy at law. As Pollock and Mulla[1] note: "If the conception of equitable remedies had been maintained with logical strictness, the court would have held itself bound to examine each individual case with an open mind before deciding whether an extraordinary remedy was called for. But after the court of chancery was recognised as a regular and ordinary court it was impossible to affect such an attitude, and it became the settled rule that in certain classes of cases the nature of the case itself was ground enough for the court's interference." At one time contract for the sale or letting of land was presumed to be a subject-matter fit for the exercise of this jurisdiction but in the modern doctrine of the courts of equity it has been extended to contracts of other species only when exceptional circumstances make it proper to do so. As to why this doctrine does not in general extend to sale of goods is that regularly, a complete contract for the sale of ascertained goods transfers the property at once to the buyer, who thereupon has all the ordinary legal rights and remedies of an owner.[2] Another and more extensive reason is that where the goods are of a kind purchasable in the market, whether the contract is for specific goods or not, compensation in money is an adequate remedy; the successful plaintiff can, if he chooses, employ the damage awarded to him in buying goods equivalent to those contracted for.

Further, it was held[3] that if the vendor of property was compellable in a court of equity to perform his contract, he must also be entitled to come to the court, though merely seeking payment of his purchase money; this was commonly accounted for as being required by the principle of "mutuality" in order to give a right corresponding with that which is given to a purchaser.[4]

The attitude of English law and lawyers that the remedy of specific performance applied only to suits for land (sale or letting) as if there were no other kinds of contracts in the world, has been criticised by Pollock and Mulla.[5]

---

1. *Indian Contract Act and Specific Relief Act*, 9th Edn., 1972, p. 823.
2. *See* Sections 19 and 20 of the Sale of Goods Act, 1930.
3. Lord Cranworth in *Webb* v. *Direct London & Portsmouth Ry. Co.*, (1852) 1 De GM & G 521: 42 ER 654.
4. Pollock & Mulla: *Indian Contract Act and Specific Relief Act*, p. 823.
5. *Ibid.*

In India, we are free from these anomalies but they also express their disapproval towards the language employed by the framers of the Act, saying that "one could wish, however, that the Specific Relief Act had not in many places adopted the language of the old-fashioned English books". In applying this law, they say, the best thing to do is to forget all the technicalities as thoroughly as possible for Indian purposes. Where there is an express divergence of the English principles and those laid down in this Act, the Act will be strictly adhered to, whatever be the English law.[6]

2. PURPOSE OF SPECIFIC RELIEF

Specific performance of contract is an equitable relief. Where the court finds that grant of such relief would be in equitable it is not obliged to grant it merely because it is lawful to do so.[7] The purpose of this kind of relief or remedy is to serve the ends of justice.[8] It consists in doing the very act which one has agreed to do, or to omit. It consists of both, the negative stipulations and the positive. Negative stipulations are called injunctions. As remarked by Pollock and Mulla, the *order* for specific performance falls into two parts: the first can be of a declaratory nature and the second contains consequential directions.

Common Law allowed, so to say, a party to a contract to break it at his pleasure and to pay compensation without being responsible for anything more; but equity did not approve of this. It required from the offending party's conscience a strict adherence to and performance of that which he could not without manifest wrong or fraud, refuse. Moreover, as the legal relief was compensatory it was inadequate and unsuitable to the situation. Here, equity intervened and granted specific relief. Specific performance was not one-sided, but was "a mutual remedy". It must be noted that the defence of 'mutuality' has been abolished by the Specific Relief Act in India.

3. SCHEME OF THE TOPIC

The Specific Relief Act has dealt with the topic of specific performance of contracts in Sections 9 to 25 under the following sub-headings:

(*a*) Defences to specific performance (Section 9)

(*b*) Contracts which can be specifically enforced (Sections 10-13)

---

6. *Ardeshir Mama* v. *Flora Sassoon*, (1928) 55 IA 360: ILR (1928) 52 Bom 597: AIR 1928 PC 208.

7. *Nirmala Anand* v. *Advent Corpn. (P) Ltd.*, (2002) 5 SCC 481; *Beg Raj Singh* v. *State of U.P.*, (2003) 1 SCC 726 (Considering subsequent or intervening events between commencement of litigation and date of decision, a litigant though entitled to relief in law, may yet be denied relief in equity.); *see* also *Hemalatha Gargya* v. *CIT*, (2003) 9 SCC 510. (Cases cited for impermissibility); *E. Palanisamy* v. *Palanisamy*, (2003) 1 SCC 123 (Considerations of equity not applicable; *See* also *National Insurance Co. Ltd.* v. *Savitri Devi*, (2004) 1 SCC 596; *National Insurance Co. Ltd.* v. *Ram Kali*, (2004) 1 SCC 565; *Punjab National Bank* v. *Virendra Kumar Goel*, (2004) 1 SCC 565; *Punjab National Bank* v. *Virender Kumar Goel*, (2004) 2 SCC 193 (In breach of contract (VRS) no equitable relief allowed.)

8. *Cf.* Maitland: *Lectures on Equity*, Chap. XX, p. 301.

(*c*) Contracts which cannot be specifically enforced (Section 14)

(*d*) Persons for or against whom contracts may be specifically enforced Sections (15—19)

(*e*) Discretions and powers of courts (Sections 20—24)

(*f*) Applicability to awards and directions to execute settlements (Section 25)

4. TEXT OF SECTIONS 9 TO 25

Specific Performance of Contracts

9. Defences respecting suits for relief based on contract.—Except as otherwise provided herein, where any relief is claimed under this Chapter in respect of a contract, the person against whom the relief is claimed may plead by way of defence any ground which is available to him under any law relating to contracts.

Contracts which can be Specifically Enforced

10. Cases in which specific performance of contract enforceable.—Except as otherwise provided in this Chapter, the specific performance of any contract may, in the discretion of the court, be enforced—

(*a*) when there exists no standard for ascertaining the actual damage caused by the non-performance of the act agreed to be done; or

(*b*) when the act agreed to be done is such that compensation in money for its non-performance would not afford adequate relief.

Explanation.—Unless and until the contrary is proved, the court shall presume—

(*i*) that the breach of a contract to transfer immovable property cannot be adequately relieved by compensation in money; and

(*ii*) that the breach of a contract to transfer movable property can be so relieved except in the following cases—

(*a*) where the property is not an ordinary article of commerce, or is of special value or interest to the plaintiff, or consists of goods which are not easily obtainable in the market;

(*b*) where the property is held by the defendant as the agent or trustee of the plaintiff.

11. Cases in which specific performance of contracts connected with trusts enforceable.—(1) Except as otherwise provided in this Act, specific performance of a contract may, in the discretion of the court, be enforced when the act agreed to be done is in the performance wholly or partly of a trust.

(2) A contract made by a trustee in excess of his powers or in breach of trust cannot be specifically enforced.

12. Specific performance of part of contract.—(1) Except as otherwise hereinafter provided in this section, the court shall not direct the specific performance of a part of a contract.

(2) Where a party to a contract is unable to perform the whole of his part of it, but the part which must be left unperformed bears only a small proportion to the whole in value and admits of compensation in money, the court may, at the suit of either party, direct the specific performance of so much of the contract as can be performed, and award compensation in money for the deficiency.

(3) Where a party to a contract is unable to perform the whole of his part of it, and the part which must be left unperformed either—

(*a*) forms a considerable part of the whole, though admitting of compensation in money; or (*b*) does not admit of compensation in money;

he is not entitled to obtain a decree for specific performance; but the court may, at the suit of the other party, direct the party in default to perform specifically so much of his part of the contract as he can perform, if the other party:—

(*i*) in a case falling under clause (*a*), pays or has paid the agreed consideration for the whole of the contract reduced by the consideration for the part which must be left unperformed and in a case falling under clause (*b*) pays or has paid the consideration for the whole of the contract without any abatement; and

(*ii*) in either case, relinquishes all claims to the performance of the remaining part of the contract and all rights to compensation, either for the deficiency or for the loss or damage sustained by him through the default of the defendant.

(4) When a part of a contract which, taken by itself, can and ought to be specifically performed, stands on a separate and independent footing from another part of the same contract which cannot or ought not to be specifically performed, the court may direct specific performance of the former part.

Explanation.—For the purposes of this section, a party to a contract shall be deemed to be unable to perform the whole of his part of it if a portion of its subject-matter existing at the date of the contract has ceased to exist at the time of its performance.

13. Rights of purchaser or lessee against person with no title or imperfect title.—(1) Where a person contracts to sell or let certain immovable property having no title or only an imperfect title, the purchaser or lessee (subject to the other provisions of this Chapter), has the following rights, namely—

(*a*) if the vendor or lessor has subsequently to the contract acquired any interest in the property, the purchaser or lessee may compel him to make good the contract out of such interest;

(*b*) where the concurrence of other persons is necessary for validating the title, and they are bound to concur at the request of the vendor or lessor, the purchaser or lessee may compel him to procure such concurrence, and when a conveyance by other persons is necessary to validate the title and they are bound to convey at the request of the vendor or lessor, the purchaser or lessee may compel him to procure such conveyance;

(*c*) where the vendor professes to sell unencumbered property, but the property is mortgaged for an amount not exceeding the purchase money and the vendor has in fact only a right to redeem it the purchaser may compel him to redeem the mortgage and to obtain a valid discharge, and, where necessary, also a conveyance from the mortgagee;

(*d*) where the vendor or lessor sues for specific performance of the contract and the suit is dismissed on the ground of his want of title or imperfect title, the defendant has a right to a return of his deposit, if any, with interest thereon, to his costs of the suit, and to a lien for such deposit interest and costs on the interest, if any, of the vendor or lessor in the property which is the subject-matter of the contract.

(2) The provisions of sub-section (1) shall also apply, as far as may be, to contracts for the sale or hire of movable property.

Contracts which cannot be Specifically Enforced

14. Contracts not specifically enforceable.—(1) The following contracts cannot be specifically enforced, namely—

(*a*) a contract for the non-performance of which compensation in money is an adequate relief;

(*b*) a contract which runs into such minute or numerous details or which is so dependent on the personal qualifications or volition of the parties, or otherwise from its nature is such, that the court cannot enforce specific performance of its material terms;

(*c*) a contract which is in its nature determinable;

(*d*) a contract the performance of which involves the performance of a continuous duty which the court cannot supervise.

(2) Save as provided by the Arbitration Act, 1940 (10 of 1940), no contract to refer present or future differences to arbitration shall be specifically enforced; but if any person who has made such a contract (other than an arbitration agreement to which the provisions of the said Act apply) and has refused to perform it, sues in respect of any subject which he has contracted to refer, the existence of such contract shall bar the suit.

(3) Notwithstanding anything contained in clause (*a*) or clause (*c*) or clause (*d*) of sub-section (1), the court may enforce specific performance in the following cases—

(*a*) where the suit is for the enforcement of a contract,—

(*i*) to execute a mortgage or furnish any other security for securing the repayment of any loan which the borrower is not willing to repay at once:

Provided that where only a part of loan has been advanced the lender is willing to advance the remaining part of the loan in terms of the contract; or

(*ii*) to take up and pay for any debentures of a company;

(*b*) where the suit is for,—

(*i*) the execution of a formal deed of partnership, the parties having commenced to carry on the business of the partnership; or

(*ii*) the purchase of a share of a partner in a firm;

(*c*) where the suit is for the enforcement of contract for the construction of any building or the execution of any other work on land:

Provided that the following conditions are fulfilled, namely—

(*i*) the building or other work is described in the contract in terms sufficiently precise to enable the court to determine the exact nature of the building or work;

(*ii*) the plaintiff has a substantial interest in the performance of the contract and the interest is of such a nature that compensation in money for non-performance of the contract is not an adequate relief; and

(*iii*) the defendant has, in pursuance of the contract, obtained possession of the whole or any part of the land on which the building is to be constructed or other work is to be executed.

Persons for or against whom Contracts may be Specifically Enforced

15. Who may obtain specific performance.—Except as otherwise provided by this Chapter, the specific performance of a contract may be obtained by—

(*a*) any party thereto;

(*b*) the representative in interest or the principal, of any party thereto:

Provided that where the learning, skill, solvency or any personal quality of such party is a material ingredient in the contract, or where the contract provides that his interest shall not be assigned, his representative in interest or his principal shall not be entitled to specific performance of the contract, unless such party has already performed his part of the contract, or the performance thereof by his representative in interest, or his principal, has been accepted by the other party;

(*c*) where the contract is a settlement on marriage, or a compromise of doubtful rights between members of the same family, any person beneficially entitled thereunder;

(*d*) where the contract has been entered into by a tenant for life in due exercise of a power, the remainder man;

(*e*) a reversioner in possession, where the agreement is a covenant entered into with his predecessor in title and the reversioner is entitled to the benefit of such covenant;

(*f*) a reversioner in remainder, where the agreement is such a covenant, and the reversioner is entitled to the benefit thereof and will sustain material injury by reason of its breach;

(*g*) when a company has entered into a contract and subsequently becomes amalgamated with another company, the new company which arises out of the amalgamation;

(*h*) when the promoters of a company have, before its incorporation, entered into a contract for the purposes of the company, and such contract is warranted by the terms of the incorporation, the company:

Provided that the company has accepted the contract and has communicated such acceptance to the other party to the contract.

16. Personal bars to relief.—Specific performance of a contract cannot be enforced in favour of a person—

(*a*) who would not be entitled to recover compensation for its breach; or

(*b*) who has become incapable of performing, or violates any essential term of, the contract that on his part remains to be performed, or acts in fraud of the contract, or wilfully acts at variance with, or in subversion of, the relation intended to be established by the contract; or

(*c*) who fails to aver and prove that he has performed or has always been ready and willing to perform the essential terms of the contract which are to be performed by him, other than terms of performance of which has been prevented or waived by the defendant.

Explanation.—For the purposes of clause (*c*),—

(*i*) where a contract involves the payment of money, it is not essential for the plaintiff to actually tender to the defendant or to deposit in court any money except when so directed by the court;

(*ii*) the plaintiff must aver performance of, or readiness and willingness to perform, the contract according to its true construction.

17. Contract to sell or let property by one who has no title, not specifically enforceable.—(1) A contract to sell or let any immovable property cannot be specifically enforced in favour of a vendor or lessor—

(*a*) who, knowing himself not to have any title to the property, has contracted to sell or let the property;

(*b*) who, though he entered into the contract believing that he had a good title to the property, cannot at the time fixed by the parties or by the court for the completion of the sale or letting, give the purchaser or lessee a title free from reasonable doubt.

(2) The provisions of sub-section (1) shall also apply, as far as may be, to contracts for the sale or hire of movable property.

18. Non-enforcement except with variation.—Where a plaintiff seeks specific performance of a contract in writing, to which the defendant sets up a variation, the plaintiff cannot obtain the performance sought, with the variation so set up, in the following cases, namely—

(*a*) where by fraud, mistake of fact or misrepresentation, the written contract of which performance is sought is in its terms or effect different from what the parties agreed to, or does not contain all the terms agreed to between the parties on the basis of which the defendant entered into the contract;

(*b*) where the object of the parties was to produce a certain legal result which the contract as framed is not calculated to produce;

(*c*) where the parties have, subsequently to the execution of the contract, varied its terms.

19. Relief against parties and persons claiming under them by subsequent title.—Except as otherwise provided by this Chapter, specific performance of a contract may be enforced against—

(*a*) either party thereto;

(*b*) any other person claiming under him by a title arising subsequently to the contract, except a transferee for value who has paid his money in good faith and without notice of the original contract;

(*c*) any person claiming under a title which, though prior to the contract and known to the plaintiff, might have been displaced by the defendant;

(*d*) when a company has entered into a contract and subsequently becomes amalgamated with another company, the new company which arises out of the amalgamation;

(*e*) when the promoters of a company have, before its incorporation entered into a contract for the purpose of the company and such contract is warranted by the terms of the incorporation, the company:

Provided that the company has accepted the contract and communicated such acceptance to the other party to the contract.

Discretion and Powers of Court

20. Discretion as to decreeing specific performance.—(1) The jurisdiction to decree specific performance is discretionary, and the court is not bound to grant such relief merely because it is lawful to do so; but the discretion of the court is not arbitrary but sound and reasonable, guided by judicial principles and capable of correction by a court of appeal.

(2) The following are cases in which the court may properly exercise discretion not to decree specific performance—

(*a*) where the terms of the contract or the conduct of the parties at the time of entering into the contract or the other circumstances under which the contract was entered into are such that the contract, though not voidable, gives the plaintiff an unfair advantage over the defendant; or

(*b*) where the performance of the contract would involve some hardship on the defendant which he did not foresee, whereas its non-performance would involve no such hardship on the plaintiff;

(*c*) where the defendant entered into the contract under circumstances which though not rendering the contract voidable, makes it inequitable to enforce specific performance.

Explanation 1.—Mere inadequacy of consideration, or the mere fact that the contract is onerous to the defendant or improvident in its nature, shall not be deemed to constitute an unfair advantage within the meaning of clause (*a*) or hardship within the meaning of clause (*b*).

Explanation 2.—The question whether the performance of a contract would involve hardship on the defendant within the meaning of clause (*b*) shall, except in cases where the hardship has resulted from any act of the plaintiff, subsequent to the contract, be determined with reference to the circumstances existing at the time of the contract.

(3) The court may properly exercise discretion to decree specific performance in any case where the plaintiff has done substantial acts or suffered losses in consequence of a contract capable of specific performance.

(4) The court shall not refuse to any party specific performance of a contract merely on the ground that the contract is not enforceable at the instance of the other party.

21. Power to award compensation in certain cases.—(1) In a suit for specific performance of a contract, the plaintiff may also claim compensation for its breach, either in addition to, or in substitution of, such performance.

(2) If, in any such suit, the court decides that specific performance ought not to be granted, but that there is a contract between the parties which has been broken by the defendant, and that the plaintiff is entitled to compensation for that breach, it shall award him such compensation accordingly.

(3) If, in any such suit, the court decides that specific performance ought to be granted, but that it is not sufficient to satisfy the justice of the case, and that some compensation for breach of the contract should also be made to the plaintiff, it shall award him such compensation accordingly.

(4) In determining the amount of any compensation awarded under this section, the court shall be guided by the principles specified in Section 73 of the Indian Contract Act, 1872 (9 of 1872).

(5) No compensation shall be awarded under this section unless the plaintiff has claimed such compensation in his plaint:

Provided that where the plaintiff has not claimed any such compensation in the plaint, the court shall, at any stage of the proceeding, allow him to amend the plaint on such terms as may be just, for including a claim for such compensation.

Explanation.—The circumstance that the contract has become incapable of specific performance does not preclude the court from exercising the jurisdiction conferred by this section.

22. Power to grant relief for possession, partition, refund of earnest money, etc.—(1) Notwithstanding anything to the contrary contained in the Code of Civil Procedure, 1908 (5 of 1908), any person suing for the specific performance of a contract for the transfer of immovable property may, in an appropriate case, ask for—

(*a*) possession, or partition and separate possession, of the property, in addition to such performance; or

(*b*) any other relief to which he may be entitled, including the refund of any earnest money or deposit paid or made by him, in case his claim for specific performance is refused.

(2) No relief under clause (*a*) or clause (*b*) of sub-section (1) shall be granted by the court unless it has been specifically claimed:

Provided that where the plaintiff has not claimed any such relief in the plaint, the court shall, at any stage of the proceeding, allow him to amend the plaint on such terms as may be just for including a claim for such relief.

(3) The power of the court to grant relief under clause (*b*) of sub-section (1) shall be without prejudice to its powers to award compensation under Section 21.

23. Liquidation of damages not a bar to specific performance.—(1) A contract, otherwise proper to be specifically enforced, may be so enforced, though a sum be named in it as the amount to be paid in case of its breach and the party in default is willing to pay the same, if the court, having regard to the terms of the contract and other attending circumstances, is satisfied that the sum was named only for the purpose of securing the performance of the contract and not for the purpose of giving to the party in default an option of paying money in lieu of specific performance.

(2) When enforcing specific performance under this section, the court shall not also decree payment of the sum so named in the contract.

24. Bar of suit for compensation for breach after dismissal of suit for specific performance.—The dismissal of a suit for specific performance of a contract or part thereof shall bar the plaintiff's right to sue for compensation for the breach of such contract or part, as the case may be, but shall not bar his right to sue for any other relief to which he may be entitled, by reason of such breach.

Enforcement of Awards and Directions to Execute Settlements

25. Application of preceding sections to certain awards and testamentary directions to execute settlements.—The provisions of this Chapter as to contracts shall apply to awards to which the Arbitration Act, 1940 (10 of 1940); does not apply and to directions in a will or codicil to execute particular settlement.

5. GENERAL PRINCIPLES FOR GRANTING SPECIFIC PERFORMANCE

In England, inadequacy of the Common Law remedies in general[9] and incompleteness of the compensatory remedy in special became the foundation of equitable remedies of which specific performance was one. Granting specific performance started from land cases and by and by it spread its tentacles to other kinds of contracts too. As observed by Maitland, it "applies to agreements for sale or lease of lands as a matter of course; its application outside these limits is somewhat exceptional and discretionary".[10] The discretionary jurisdiction of the Supreme Court cannot be availed of in cases where there is no concluded contract.[11] The basic idea underlying the grant of specific performance is that there should be a valid contract of which specific performance could be decreed; not that there should be a breach.[12] The equitable principles which regulated the grant of specific performance by the Separate Court of Equity which existed in England at one time have been given statutory form in India.[13] They are as under:

Grant of Specific performance is an equitable relief regulated by Section 20 of the Specific Relief Act, 1963.[14] In order that a decree for specific performance of a contract may be passed it is necessary to consider whether such a relief can be granted in view of Section 16 of the Act. It is for the appellant to prove that Section 16 does not prohibit granting such a decree while it is for the respondent to prove otherwise.[15]

In respect of specific performance of agreement of sale of immovable property, the same must be identifiable in order to avail relief under the Act.[16]

As observed by the Supreme Court in *Kaulashwari Devi* v. *Nawal Kishore*, in view of Section 52 of the Transfer of Property Act, 1882 (doctrine of Lis Pendens) transfer during pendency of a suit for specific performance does not affect the right of the plaintiff.[17]

(*a*) *Remedy in Personam.*—As explained by Hanbury, the decree of specific performance issues against the defendant personally and he will be compelled to carry out his obligation if he is within the court's jurisdiction. As the

---

9. *Hutton* v. *Watling*, 1948 Ch 26: (1947) 2 All ER 641 (Ch D).
10. Maitland: *Lectures on Equity*, p. 304. *Bommaka Nagabhushana Reddy* v. *W. Srinivasa Rao*, (2002) 9 SCC 664 ("An agreement for sale of property" and "a promise to transfer a property" held, is a same thing.)
11. *M.V. Shankar Bhat* v. *Claude Pinto*, (2003) 4 SCC 86.
12. *Hasham* v. *Zenab*, 1960 AC 316: (1958) 3 All ER 719 (PC).
13. *M.L. Devender Singh* v. *Syed Khaja*, (1973) 2 SCC 515: AIR 1973 SC 2457.
14. *A.C. Arulappan* v. *Ahalya Naik*, (2001) 6 SCC 600.
15. *Thakamma Mathew* v. *M. Azamathulla Khan*, 1993 Supp (4) SCC 492, 497, 498: AIR 1993 SC 1120: (1993) 21 ALR 170.
16. *Nahar Singh* v. *Harnak Singh*, (1996) 6 SCC 699.
17. 1995 Supp (1) SCC 141: 1995 SCC (Cri) 60.

defendant's conscience was bound by the agreement, he was compelled to act even though the subject-matter fell outside the court's jurisdiction.[18] This tendency to expand jurisdiction has been restricted and checked nowadays in England. In India, according to some writers, no such jurisdiction is recognised, while according to some the courts have but a limited power of making a decree *in personam.*[19]

(*b*) *Remedy of damages inadequate.*—It is a fundamental rule that specific performance will not be granted where the plaintiff would be adequately compensated by the common law remedy of damages.[20] In other words, where pecuniary damages are adequate or will put the plaintiff in a similar position as if the contract had been specifically performed, equity will not interfere to grant specific performance.[21] But as decided in *Jeewan Lal Daga* v. *Nilmani Chaudhuri*[22], specific performance of an agreement to execute a mortgage will be ordered where money has been actually advanced.

(*c*) *Reciprocal Remedy.*—This remedy is a mutual or a reciprocal remedy and can be obtained as effectively by the vendor as the vendee. On the same principle, contracts for minors and against minors will not be specifically enforced. In *Mir Sarwarjan* v. *Fakhruddin Mohd Chowdhuri*[23], a Mahomadan minor, on coming of age, sued the vendor for specific performance of a contract for sale. Dismissing the case the Privy Council held that since it was not within the competence of the guardian of a minor to bind the minor or his estate for the purchase of immovable property, the contract was short of mutuality or reciprocity and consequently no specific performance thereof could be obtained by the minor. Thus, this remedy is mutual and *mutuality refers to the time* when the contract was entered into. Advantage to the minor is of no consequence here.

(*d*) *Enforceable (Valid) Contract.*—The basis of specific performance is a valid contract.[24] The doctrine of part performance of a contract is an expression of this basic idea. *Maddison* v. *Alderson*[25] and *Wakeham* v. *Mackenzie*[26] are the leading examples on the point. The acts of part performance done must be referable to the contract and it must be such as to render it a fraud in the defendant to take advantage of the contract not being in writing. It must be noted that Section 53-A of the Transfer of Property Act (part performance) in India requires a contract to be in writing. In short, in the words of Lord Selborne

---

18. *Penn* v. *Baltimore (Lord)*, (1750) 1 Ves Sen 444: 27 ER 1132 cited in Hanbury: *Modern Equity*, p. 34.
19. For details *see* Mulla: *Civil Procedure Code*, 13th Edn., 1965, pp. 133—136 and Maxim 12 in Chap. III *Supra.*
20. *Hutton* v. *Watling*, 1948 Ch 26: (1947) 2 All ER 641 (Ch D).
21. *Harnett* v. *Yielding*, (1805) 2 Sch & Lef 549 (Ireland).
22. AIR 1928 PC 80: 55 IA 107.
23. ILR (1912) 39 Cal 232 (PC): 39 IA 1.
24. *Hasham* v. *Zenab*, 1960 AC 316: (1958) 3 All ER 719 (PC); *Mayawanti* v. *Kaushalya Devi*, (1990) 3 SCC 1 (Defence of no contract exists, and is available to defendant).
25. (1883) 8 AC 467: 49 LT 303 (HL).
26. (1968) 1 WLR 1175: (1968) 2 All ER 783 (Ch D).

in *Maddison* v. *Alderson*[27], the gist of the situation is that "the defendant is really 'charged' upon the equities resulting from the acts in execution of the contract and not upon the contract itself".[28]

(*e*) *Contracts without consideration.*—Specific performance would not be awarded to a party who has given no consideration. A contract to be valid must be supported by consideration.

(*f*) *No Part Performance.*—The court will not usually decree specific performance of any part of a contract unless it can decree performance of the whole. But in case of a divisible contract parts whereof express several, separate, independent and distinct contracts, such a performance can be decreed.[29]

Question of granting specific performance of a part of the contract arose in *Surya Narain case*.[30] In this case a house which was mutated in joint names of two brothers was agreed to be sold by the appellant. Both the brothers were in possession and enjoyment thereof. The neighbour to whom the entire property was sold sought specific performance and it was granted. This was not correct. In appeal however, having regard to the principles of equity and justice partial performance of the contract was allowed and specific performance of half of the share of the appellant's brother was granted. Discussing the provisions of S. 20(1) the court remarked that the circumstances specified in S. 20 are only illustrative and not exhaustive. The court would take into consideration the circumstances in each case, the conduct of the parties and the respective interest of the contract.

(*g*) *Discretionary Remedy.*—As observed by the Supreme Court of India the jurisdiction of the court to decree specific relief is discretionary[31] and must be exercised on sound and reasonable grounds "guided by judicial principles and capable of correction by a court of appeal". This jurisdiction cannot be curtailed or taken away by merely fixing a sum even as liquidated damages. This is made perfectly clear by the provisions of Section 23 (Section 20 old Act) of the Act of 1963, so that the court has to determine on the facts and circumstances of each case before it, whether specific performance of a contract to convey a property ought to be granted.[32] Mulla and Pollock also note in their commentary[33], this discretion in England is intimately bound up with the historical limits of the

---

27. (1883) 8 AC 467: 49 LT 303 (HL).
28. Hanbury: *Modern Equity*, Chap. 2.
29. *William Graham* v. *Krishna Chandra Dey*, AIR 1925 PC 45: 52 IA 90.
30. *Surya Narain Upadhyaya* v. *Ram Roop Pandey*, 1995 Supp (4) SCC 542: AIR 1994 SC 105; *Ravi Singhal* v. *Manali Singhal*, (2001) 8 SCC 1.
31. *Olympus Superstructures (P) Ltd.* v. *Meena Vijay Khetan*, (1999) 5 SCC 651: AIR 1999 SC 2102; *K. Narendra* v. *Riviera Apartments (P) Ltd.*, (1999) 5 SCC 77: AIR 1999 SC 2309; *V. Muthusami* v. *Angammal*, (2002) 3 SCC 316: AIR 2002 SC 1279.
32. *M.L. Devender Singh* v. *Syed Khaja*, (1973) 2 SCC 515: AIR 1973 SC 2457; *Sardar Singh* v. *Krishna Devi*, (1994) 4 SCC 18; *Kallathil Shreedharan* v. *Komath Pandyala Prasanna*, (1996) 6 SCC 218; *Lourdu Mari David* v. *Louis Chinnaya Arogiaswamy*, (1996) 5 SCC 589: AIR 1996 SC 699.
33. *Indian Contract Act and Specific Relief Act*, pp. 869-870.

jurisdiction of judges. "Everyone who came to a court of equity was bound to show that he had no remedy, or no adequate remedy in the ordinary jurisdiction of a court of common law. Failing this his suit would be dismissed 'for want of equity'. Now a claim for specific performance assumes the existence of an actionable contract. Therefore the plaintiff had always to face the question: why is not the common law right to recover damages good enough for your case? and the court was in strictness always on the defensive against a charge of trespassing on the domain of the common law. The court of chancery did indeed establish the presumption that specific performance was the proper remedy on a contract to convey land, but it was only a presumption liable to be displaced; there is no absolute right to this remedy".

In exercising the discretion the court will take into account the circumstances of the case, the conduct of the parties and their respective interests under the contract.[34] The discretion is thus not arbitrary but is controlled by certain rules of certainty, fairness and justice between the parties.[35] Consequently where it has been exercised perversely, arbitrarily or against judicial principles, it will be interfered with.[36]

(*h*) *Contracts of personal services*.—Cannot be specifically enforced.[37]

(*i*) *Continuous Supervision*.—Specific performance of a contract involving continuous supervision of the court will not be granted.

(*j*) *Sale of Goods cases*.—Here the damages would generally afford an adequate remedy and therefore no specific performance will be granted. The reason is that since the specific goods contracted for can be had from the market such performance is uncalled for. But if the contrary is proved as provided in Section 10, explanation, specific performance will be ordered.

(*k*) *Specific Performance Refused*.—There are also cases wherein though compensation is not an adequate relief, the court will not decree specific performance of a contract. A person seeking enforcement must reach court within reasonable time.[38]

6. APPLICABILITY OF ENGLISH PRINCIPLES IN INDIA

The above general principles have been incorporated in the Specific Relief Act.[39] Where there are *specific provisions* in the Act regarding particular situations, the provisions of the Act prevail, and *in cases of divergence* between

---

34. *Oxford* v. *Provand*, (1868) LR 2 PC 135: 16 ER 472 (PC); *Jethalal Nanshah Modi* v. *Bachu*, (1945) 47 BLR 463: AIR 1945 Bom 481; *G. Rasaiah* v. *C. Balarami Reddi*, AIR 1989 AP 179.
35. *G. Rasaiah* v. *C. Balarami*, AIR 1989 AP 179; *K. Narendra* v. *Riviera Apartments* (*P*) *Ltd.*, (1999) 5 SCC 77: AIR 1999 SC 2309.
36. *Pujari Narasappa* v. *Sk. Hazrat*, AIR 1960 Mys 59; *Mademsetty Satyanarayana* v. *G. Yelloji Rao*, AIR 1965 SC 1405; *Malins* v. *Freeman*, (1837) 2 Keen 25: 48 ER 537; also see (1994) 6 SCC 18: (1996) 6 SCC 218 and (1996) 5 SCC 589 in foot note 32 *supra*.
37. *Page One Records Ltd.* v. *Britton*, (1968) 1 WLR 157: (1967) 3 All ER 822 (Ch D).
38. *Veerayee Ammal* v. *Seeni Ammal*, (2002) 1 SCC 134.
39. *Parmanand* v. *Bajrang*, (2001) 7 SCC 705 (unless defendant has been given opportunity to adduce evidence, his suit ought not to be decreed or dismissed.)

the provisions and the principles abovesaid the general English principles must give way to the specific provision of the Act as laid down in *William Graham* v. *Krishna Chandra Dey*[40] by the Privy Council. Moreover, as expressed in *Ardeshir Mama* v. *Flora Sassoon*[41], at the time of codification of the above principles where *a reference* has been made to English rules, that must be a guide in interpretation and application of the provisions of the Act. But where the *Act is silent* on a particular situation, the English principles and practice are a valuable guide.[42] Besides, the principles of equity, justice and good conscience will apply in situations and in the fields where the *Act does not apply*.

7. DIFFERENCE OF THE ACT WITH ENGLISH GENERAL PRINCIPLES

The Specific Relief Act has at many places avoided the complications of the English law and provided clear provisions for the same as in cases of specific performance with abatement or compensation under Section 12(2) and in cases of serious deficiency under Section 12(3). The defence of 'mutuality' prevailing in England has been abolished by the Act. If a suit is brought for specific performance all remedies must be sought therein. It is for this reason that Section 24 provides that on dismissal of such a suit no suit for compensation for breach of agreement shall lie. This is not so in England. Besides, the doctrine of laches with its bedroll of cases is not applicable in India in view of the provisions of the Limitation Act, 1963, Article 54 whereby such a suit must be brought within three years from the date fixed for performance or from the date when the plaintiff has notice that performance is refused.

8. DEFENCES TO AN ACTION FOR SPECIFIC PERFORMANCE (SECTION 9)

General.—A defence is denial of the plaintiff's claim. A defendant may advance a plea of total denial of the plaintiff's claim on account of contract having been induced and therefore vitiated by mistake, fraud and undue influence or on the ground that the contract is one which cannot be specifically enforced. And these we have considered before. We shall now look into the various other defences that equity provided and the Specific Relief Act lays down. As expressed by Snell[43] in his *Principles of Equity*, those defences may be—

(*a*) no effective contract

(*b*) absence of writing or part performance

(*c*) plaintiff's misrepresentation

(*d*) mistake

(*e*) misdescription

---

40. AIR 1925 PC 45: 52 IA 90.
41. AIR 1928 PC 208: 55 IA 360.
42. *Akshayalingam Pillai* v. *Avayambala Ammal*, AIR 1933 Mad 386.
43. 27th Edn., 1972, Part VII, Chap. 1, pp. 583-600.

(*f*) default by plaintiff

(*g*) lapse of time

(*h*) trickiness

(*i*) great hardship

(*j*) Illegality

(*k*) defective title.

In such a suit the defendant may plead any ground available to him under any law relating to contracts such as incapacity of parties, absence of a concluded contract, coercion, fraud, misrepresentation, mistake, illegality or want of authority to enter into the contract[44] and so on.

Section 9 in this regard provides that:

> "Except as otherwise provided herein, where any relief is claimed under this chapter in respect of a contract, the person against whom the relief is claimed may plead by way of defence any ground which is available to him under any law relating to contracts."

As the defences are scattered over various sections, we shall take them serially in a logical and chronological order.

(*a*) *No effective contract*

Specific performance presupposes the existence of a complete and definite contract. The statutory requirement of a written evidence of the contract, it must be noted, "is a weapon of defence, not offence and does not make any signed instrument a valid contract by reason of the signature, if it is not such according to the good faith and real intention of the parties".[45] This means that to be enforceable at law that agreement should not be void because of uncertainty or illegality.[46] It should also not be voidable because of lack of consent, or presence of fraud, mistake, misrepresentation or undue influence. An incomplete contract is also a good defence.[47]

Uncertainty.—Want of certainty is a ground for resisting specific performance. Certainty must be with regard to terms, parties, value, date and description of the subject-matter. The uncertainty in a contract which may arise in different ways must be determined at the commencement of the action, because it is at that time that the non-compliance with the terms of the contract must be incapable of justification. It is well known that there cannot be a contract to make a contract. If the parties leave the essential terms of the agreement undetermined, the same cannot be enforced for uncertainty, but if the agreement is otherwise complete leaving certain details (non-essential)

---

44. Pollock and Mulla: *Indian Contract Act and Specific Relief Act*, p. 825.

45. *Jervis* v. *Berridge*, (1873) 8 Ch App 351: 28 LT 481.

46. *Douglas* v. *Baynes*, 1908 AC 477: 99 LT 599 (PC).

47. *Bishandayal & Sons* v. *State of Orissa*, (2001) 1 SCC 555; *Zorawar Singh* v. *Sarwan Singh*, (2002) 4 SCC 460 (Defence of bona fide purchaser, for value, without notice raised.) *C. Bala Subba Reddy* v. *Laxmi Narasamma*, (2002) 10 SCC 247: AIR 2002 SC 390.

incomplete, the court will find out or ascertain them from the evidence produced and enforce the contract, because what is essentially required is the reasonable certainty.[48] But one must note that the evidence produced has to explain the terms; it cannot be allowed to alter or vary the terms of a written agreement.[49] Section 14(1) (*b*) of the Specific Relief Act expresses this when it speaks of a contract which "from its nature is such that a court cannot enforce specific performance of its terms". Section 29 of the Indian Contract Act also expresses that an agreement, the meaning of which is not certain, or capable of being made certain, is void. Mulla has dealt with these under the heading "Vague Contracts".[50]

(*b*) *Defective Title*

It is a good defence by the purchaser to show that the vendor cannot make a good title to the property in accordance with the contract he made. In the same way, where the property is encumbered or its title is doubtful, a suit for specific performance can be resisted. In suitable cases, therefore, the purchaser may be relieved or discharged from the contract or may repudiate the contract because the court will not compel a purchaser to buy a lawsuit, a term which means not a bare possibility of proceedings, but "a reasonable, decent probability of litigation".[51]

Section 17 of the Act lays down the Indian law on the point. It applies to both movable as well as immovable property and to sales and leases. The section says:

"(1) A contract to sell or let any immovable property cannot be specifically enforced in favour of a vendor or lessor—

(*a*) who, knowing himself not to have any title to the property, has contracted to sell or let the property;

(*b*) who, though he entered into the contract believing that he had *a good title* to the property, cannot, at the time fixed by the parties or by the court for the completion of the sale or letting, give the purchaser or lessee a *title free from reasonable doubt.*

(2) The provisions of sub-section (1) shall also apply, as far as may be, to contracts for the sale or hire of movable property."

The section thus deals with the case wherein the seller or lessor has either (*i*) no title to the property sold or let out, or (*ii*) where he cannot give the purchaser or lessee a title free from reasonable doubt, and (*iii*) where prior to such sale or letting he has made a settlement of the subject-matter of the contract.

In this connection Section 55(2) of the Transfer of Property Act explains that a seller impliedly contracts that he has an interest in the property, the same

48. *Sheo Kumar* v. *Gyan Nath*, AIR 1955 All 408, 412.
49. *Gajkumar* v. *Luchhmanram*, (1911) 14 Cal LJ 627: 10 IC 503.
50. Pollock and Mulla: *Indian Contract Act and Specific Relief Act*, p. 848.
51. *George* v. *Thomas*, (1904) 90 LT 505: 52 WR 416.

subsists, and that he has power to transfer the same. The title must be in the vendor himself and Section 13 of the Specific Relief Act therefore expressly lays down the rights of the purchaser or lessee against the vendor who has no title or imperfect title. The suit for specific performance can therefore be resisted where the vendor's title is either defective, doubtful, encumbered or bad. One has to note that the defect in the title must be substantial and the doubt a very serious doubt. Section 17(1) (*a*) is in conformity with the view of Lord Knight Bruce, V.C. in *Adams* v. *Broke*[52] that subsequent acquisition of title will not entitle the vendor to enforce the specific performance even though the time fixed for completion has not passed. This view has been confirmed by the Nagpur High Court in *Kisanlal Rudmal Agarwal* v. *Namdeo Krushnaji Dhangar*[53].

In the following cases, it must be noted, the title is not considered to be open to doubt—

(*i*) where the doubt raised is *mala fide* and unsupported by any proof;

(*ii*) where the probability of litigation is not great;

(*iii*) where there is an adverse decision of the inferior court regarding title which the superior court thinks to be clearly wrong; and

(*iv*) where the question depends upon the general rule of construction of words against the special context and the court is in favour of title.

In short, defective title is a good ground for resisting specific performance, subject to the exceptions mentioned above.

(*c*) *Mistake and Misrepresentation*

Sections 20 and 22 of the Specific Relief Act and Section 18 of the Indian Contract Act lay down the effects of mistake and misrepresentation on the contract.

(*d*) *Great Hardship*

A contracts to buy a piece of land from *X*. There is no right of way existing to it and nothing is mentioned in the contract above it. No right of way can be shown to exist also. Such a contract cannot be specifically enforced because if performance is decreed, it would create great hardship for *A* in so far as access to the land is concerned. And this defect is incurable. Hardship is therefore a good defence here,[54] and it must be taken at the earliest stage.[55]

It must therefore be said that as a general rule if the contract is otherwise valid or legal it does not lie in the mouth of the defendant to say that specific performance thereof should be refused because it involves hardship to him. But

52. (1842) 1 Y & C Ch Cas 627: 62 ER 1046.
53. AIR 1943 Nag 299.
54. Cf. *Kamini Sundari Chaodhrani* v. *Kali Prossunno Ghose*, (1885) 12 Cal 225 (PC): 12 IA 215. Facts have been given under the next topic.
55. *A. Maria Angelena* v. *A.G. Balkis Bee*, (2002) 9 SCC 597.

in genuine cases of hardship the court would definitely not allow specific performance.[56] And this is what is provided by Section 20(2)(*b*).

What is hardship.—When we say that hardship is a good defence we must also understand in what cases and how it comes into existence and what it means. Firstly, hardship is not the same as onerousness, because what is onerous is mentally burdensome or oppressive. But hardship may be said to be an untoward event or a difficulty or inconvenience usually of a lingering character for which the sufferer is not deemed directly responsible. A contract mixed with hardship is almost unconscionable. But where it is the creation of the plaintiff himself as when he induces another to strike a contract by use of misrepresentation or fraud and obtains an unfair advantage from that other[57], hardship and unfair advantage are good defences and the court will not decree a specific performance of such a contract. Secondly, as the section provides, the hardship must be one which the defendant could not foresee.[58] Moreover, the hardship must not be such as flows from the terms of the contract; it must be something existing side by side or collateral,[59] which grows from outside the contract without the default or some other act of the defendant. Where the defendant knowingly enters into a contract involving hardship, he would have no defence of hardship.[60] The court in deciding such cases will look to the facts of the case, its circumstances and the relative position of the parties at the time of making the contract, because hardship arising subsequent to the formation of a contract cannot be advanced as a defence against specific performance, unless it has arisen due to some act of the plaintiff.[61] At the same time, the court will not look into the hardship of the defendant only, but will look into that of the plaintiff too and after weighing the facts and consequences it will decree or refuse the specific performance; not before. Explanation 2 to Section 20(2)(*b*) enlightens the position mentioned above.[62]

(*e*) *Unfairness*

As Section 20(2) (*a*) provides, the court may properly exercise its discretion not to decree specific performance where (*i*) the terms of the contract, or (*ii*) the conduct of the parties at the time of entering into the contract, or (*iii*) the other circumstances under which the contract was entered into, are such that the contract, though not voidable, gives the plaintiff an unfair advantage over the defendant. Where *A* sells land to *B* for protection of which an embarkment is to be maintained by *A*, and *A* does not disclose this to *B* but conceals this position knowingly, the court will not grant specific performance to *A* because by so decreeing *A* will gain an unfair advantage over *B*. What is unfair is far from just. Similarly, where a *pardanashin* lady obtained a loan from her own *mukhtar* at

56. *Preston* v. *Luck*, (1884) 27 Ch D 497: 33 WR 317 (CA).
57. *Davis* v. *Maung Shwe Goh*, 38 Cal 805 (PC): 38 IA 155.
58. *Janakdhari Lal* v. *Gossain Lal Bhaya Gaywal*, ILR (1910) 37 Cal 107: 1 IC 871.
59. Halsbury: *Laws of England*, 2nd Edn., Vol. 31, para 421, p. 370.
60. *Radha Kanta Pal* v. *United Bank of India Ltd.*, AIR 1955 Cal 217.
61. *Peer Mohammed.* v. *Mahmod*, ILR (1905) 29 Bom 234: 6 Bom LR 1013: 7 Bom LR 200.
62. *K. Narendra* v. *Riviera Apartments (P) Ltd.*, (1999) 5 SCC 77: AIR 1999 SC 2309 (applicability of the doctrine of comparative hardship to the parities).

an excessive rate of interest, the security being ample, it was decided by the Privy Council that as the bargain was hard and unconscionable the rate of interest in the contract could not be enforced in equity.[63]

Unfairness arises from the terms of the contract or from the conduct of the parties or from other circumstances attending the contract. It expresses itself in various ways. It must arise at the time of entering into the contract, but it may arise subsequent to it also, as when a contract to sell at a price to be fixed at a future date is made or some precondition is to be fulfilled before the contract becomes absolute. The time when the contract becomes absolute (when price is fixed or condition is fulfilled) is the time with reference to which the fairness is to be judged; the date of execution of the contract not being material to judge the fairness. Unfairness arising from surrounding circumstances may take place from mental weakness, or due to age, sex, poverty, illiteracy, or intoxication of the parties or from any other circumstance giving unfair advantage to the plaintiff.

(*f*) *Inadequacy of Consideration*

Mere inadequacy of consideration is no ground for resisting specific performance because "the value of all things contracted for is measured by the appetite of the contractors and therefore the just value is that which they be contended to give". At the same time, a voluntary contract cannot be decreed on the principle that "equity will not aid a volunteer". If the inadequacy leads to some fraud or undue advantage by the plaintiff, that is a ground for resisting specific performance. Similarly, inadequacy which may amount to mere hardship is no ground for relief, but if the inadequacy is such as shocks the conscience it is a good ground for resisting specific performance.

Explanation 1 to Section 20(2) therefore provides that *mere inadequacy* of consideration or the mere fact that the contract is *onerous* to the defendant or improvident in its nature, shall not be deemed to constitute an unfair advantage within the meaning of clause (*a*) or hardship within the meaning of clause (*b*).

The inadequacy of consideration to be a good defence must be such as to shock the conscience of a person or to lead by itself to an evidence of fraud or undue advantage; or when weighed with other surrounding circumstances forms an evidence of fraud or undue advantage. Here one thing must be noted that, as decided in *Ganga Baksh* v. *Jagat Bahadur Singh*[64], the adequacy or inadequacy of consideration has to be determined with reference to the state of things or circumstances surrounding or existing at the time when the contract was made and not with reference to subsequent events. Thus inadequacy of consideration, to be a good defence, must exist at the time when the contract was made, must be shocking to the conscience, cannot emanate from mere onerousness of the contract, is not obtainable by a volunteer and taken by itself or taking the existing or surrounding circumstances of the contract into consideration must lead to some fraud or undue advantage obtained by the plaintiff.

---

63. *Kamini Sundari Chaodhrani* v. *Kali Prossunno Ghose*, (1885) 12 Cal 225 (PC): 12 IA 215.
64. (1895) 22 IA 153: ILR (1896) 23 Cal 15 PC.

(g) Delay and Laches

Section 54 of the Limitation Act, 1963 has prescribed a period for filing a suit for specific performance of contracts and accordingly all such suits must be brought within 3 years from the date fixed for performance, or if no such date is fixed, when the plaintiff has notice that performance is refused.

It is very plain that a suit for specific performance must be brought *within the time* when time is the essence of the contract. Time may be made to be the essence of the contract by express provision in the contract. This is so in mercantile contracts. Besides, if the nature of the contract is such or if the terms thereof are such, it may be apparent that time is the essence of the contract. Thus where time is such, a suit for specific performance must be brought within that time but where time is not such no party can insist for performance within a particular period of time. But performance can be insisted upon within a *reasonable time*, according to law. And what is reasonable time is a question of fact. If a suit for specific performance is not brought within a reasonable period of time a decree for specific performance will not be granted.[65]

The basic requisites for the plaintiff's success in a suit for specific performance of a contract are (*i*) his performance or his *readiness and willingness all along to perform the terms of the contract*, and (*ii*) his readiness and willingness to do all matters to be thereafter done. A failure of the plaintiff in any of these respects will afford a good defence to the opposite side.[66] In other words, he has to allege and if the fact is traversed, he must prove his continuous readiness and willingness from the date of the contract to the time of the hearings to perform the contract on his part.[67]

Article 54 of the Limitation Act, 1963 provides that a suit for specific performance must be brought within "three years from the date fixed for performance, or if no such date is fixed, when the plaintiff has notice that performance is refused". This provision of the Limitation Act makes the doctrine of laches inapplicable in India to this kind of litigation. Like England we have no rules in the Limitation Act on the subject of delay and laches. But from the decided cases there should be no difficulty in laying them down as below.

A. RULES

(1) Even if mere delay does not disentitle a plaintiff to claim specific performance of a contract, nevertheless, delay is one of the factors to be considered while granting the discretionary relief.[68]

(2) Whether lapse of time destroys the plaintiff's right has to be considered with reference to the other prevailing circumstances. If the plaintiff has been in

---

65. *Binda Prasad* v. *Kishori Saran*, AIR 1929 PC 195: 116 IC 388; *Veerayee Ammal* v. *Seeni Ammal*, (2002) 1 SCC 134.
66. 37 IC 257 (DB): (1916) 24 Cal LJ 90.
67. *Dau Alakhram* v. *Kulwantin Bai*, ILR 1950 Nag 386: AIR 1950 Nag 238.
68. *Sultan* v. *Sharfan*, 113 IC 140 (DB): AIR 1929 Lah 249.

substantial possession of the benefits of the contract and has always been claiming the completion of the legal estate, delay, if properly explained, will not affect his rights to claim specific performance.[69]

(3) Inordinate and unexplained delay coupled with the change of conditions is sufficient ground for refusing specific performance and dismissing the suit.[70]

(4) In no case does mere delay or lapse of time deprive the plaintiff of his right to specific performance unless it be held that—

(*i*) there has been abandonment,

(*ii*) acquiescence,

(*iii*) waiver, or

(*iv*) at the least an alteration in the position of the defendant in that the other party has been put in a situation in which it would not be reasonable to place him if the remedy was afterwards to be asserted.[71]

(5) The court may exercise its discretion and not decree specific performance where the circumstances under which the contract is made are such as to give the plaintiff an unfair advantage over the defendant. Mere delay by itself is no ground for refusing relief but when it raises the presumption of an abandonment of the plaintiff's claim or has caused—

(*i*) a hardship to the opposite party; or

(*ii*) something to his prejudice,

the courts are entitled to exercise their discretion and refuse the relief prayed for.[72]

(6) Where delay does not amount to waiver, abandonment or acquiescence, and which in no way alters the position of the defendant, it does not disentitle the plaintiff to sue for specific performance. Thus when the suit is within time and the delay is not so great as to induce the court to hold that the plaintiff has forfeited his right under the agreement, the court will not refuse equitable relief.[73]

(7) Where status quo position of the parties was changed, as when there was a change in value of property, and it had occurred by reason of delay attributable to the plaintiff, specific performance was rightly refused.[74]

(8) In cases of serious laches specific performance is refused, but where the plaintiff was guilty of delay of over two years in filing suit[75], or where he

---

69. ILR 1952 Cal 198. *See* also *Union of India* v. *Kishorilal Bablani*, (1999) 1 SCC 729: AIR 1999 SC 517.
70. *Sultan* v. *Sharfan*, 113 Ind Cas 140 (DB): AIR 1929 Lah 249; *Dau Alakhram* v. *Kulwantin Bai*, ILR 1950 Nag 386: AIR 1950 Nag 238.
71. *Allah Ditta* v. *Jamna Das*, 117 Ind Cas 225 (DB): AIR 1929 Lah 679: 44 Ind Cas 244: (1918) 4 Pat LW 192.
72. *Rami Reddi* v. *Pattabhirami Reddi*, 169 Ind Cas 12 (DB): AIR 1937 Mad 124.
73. *Jaugal Singh* v. *Gulam Mahomed*, 67 Ind Cas 700 (DB): 32 PWR 1922: AIR 1922 Lah 461.
74. *Bahadur Singh* v. *Suresh Chandra Roy*, 34 CLJ 364 (DB): AIR 1921 Cal 179.
75. *Narooshankar Pranshanker* v. *Rajumal Bhagwandas*, AIR 1921 Sind 197: 15 Sind LR 21.

delayed till the end of the limitation period unnecessarily[76], specific performance was refused.

(9) But one has to note that mere laches or delay, even if it is up to the hilt of the limitation period, is not always evidence of waiver and abandonment.[77] To operate as a bar to relief the delay should be such as to amount to a waiver or abandonment of the plaintiff's right by acquiescence or where by his conduct or neglect he has though perhaps not waived his remedy yet put the other party in a situation in which it would not be reasonable to place him, if the remedy were afterwards to be asserted.

When such is not the case, any lapse of time short of the period allowed under the Limitation Act should not disentitle the claimant to relief which he is otherwise entitled.[78]

B. TIME WHEN ESSENCE OF THE CONTRACT[79]

In *Burjorji case*[80] the Privy Council laid down the principles governing contracts of sale of land and when times is or is not of the essence of the contract. Following this decision it has been held by the Indian courts that time in contracts for sale of immovable property is not of the essence of the contract unless the nature of the property and surrounding circumstances make it so. Equity treats the limits of the time as subordinate to the main purpose of the parties.[81] After *Burjorji case*[82], again in *Paul Couvreur* v. *M.G. Shapiro*[83], the Privy Council again had the occasion to consider the question as to time being of the essence of the contract and it was held that (*i*) reasonable time for getting a permit applies to a contract which fails to be carried out within a reasonable time, and (*ii*) where the contract fails to be completed within a fixed period and therefore time is of the essence of the contract, to allow the purchaser reasonable time beyond the fixed period to enable him to do what by the terms of the contract he was required to do, would amount to making a new contract for the parties. In *Gomathinayagam Pillai case*[84], the Supreme Court after reviewing the authorities laid down the law as below:

(1) There is a presumption in the case of immovable property that time is not the essence of the contract.

---

76. *Marudanayagam Pillai* v. *Munusamy Pillai*, AIR 1917 Mad 8: 37 IC 776: 58 Ind Cas 23. See also *Ram Charan Lal* v. *Karim-un-Nissa Bibi*, 26 Ind Cas 121 (DB): (1914) 27 Mad LJ 482: ILR (1915) 37 All 12 where delay of 20 months disentitled the plaintiff to sue for specific performance.

77. 23 Ind Cas 56 (DB). See *Lalit Kumar Jain* v. *Jaipur Traders Corpn. (P) Ltd.*, (2002) 5 SCC 383.

78. *Kissen Gopal Sadaney* v. *Kally Prosonno Sett*, ILR (1906) 33 Cal 633, 636.

79. Pollock and Mulla: *Indian Contract Act and Specific Relief Act*, pp. 825-826.

80. *Jamshed Khodaram Irani* v. *Burjorji Dhunjibhai*, (1916) 43 IA 26: AIR 1915 PC 83: 32 IC 246.

81. *Gomathinayagam Pillai* v. *Pillaniswami Nadar*, (1967) 1 SCR 227: AIR 1967 SC 868.

82. *Jamshed Khodaram Irani* v. *Burjorji Dhunjibhai*, (1916) 43 IA 26: AIR 1915 PC 83: 32 IC 246.

83. AIR 1948 PC 192: 1948 Mad WN 121.

84. (1967) 1 SCR 227: AIR 1967 SC 868.

In the matter of enforcement of the agreement or agreement of reconveyance, time is not always the essence of the contract unless the agreement specifically stipulates and there are special facts and circumstances in support thereof. It must be specifically pleaded and issue raised so that the other party has a right to lead evidence.[85]

(2) Even where a contract contains a stipulation making time the essence of the contract, the presumption applies and more so where time for performance has been extended more than once.

(3) Similarly, incorporating a clause imposing penalty in case of default does not by itself evidence an intention to make time the essence.[86] In a case where a promisor has an option either to do or to abstain from doing on payment of the sum of money, court may treat covenants to perform or to pay as alternative where specific performance would work unreasonable results.[87] Where stipulation in a contract is uncertain and ambiguous specific performance cannot be granted.[88]

It was further expressed that intention to make time of the essence of the contract must be in unmistakable language. It may be inferred from the nature of the property agreed to be sold, the conduct of the parties and the surrounding circumstances at or before the contract. As observed in *Chaturvedi case* High Court cannot make the essence of the contract an issue if it was not an issue in the trial court.[89]

In case of contracts the object whereof is commercial enterprise, the court is strongly inclined to hold time to be essential, e.g., agreement to purchase land for construction of a factory.[90] It must be once again remembered that to allow this defence is discretionary and it may be refused too in suitable cases where delay had led the other party to change his position thinking that the plaintiff has abandoned his rights.

(*h*) *Other Defences*

Moreover, where the plaintiff has not performed his part or where he has not been continuously ready and willing to perform his part, where compensation is an adequate relief (Section 14), where the plaintiff is not competent to sue (Section 15), where the plaintiff, by his conduct, has disqualified himself for the relief (Section 16), where the defendant is a person against whom specific performance cannot be obtained or enforced (Section 19) and where he is incapable of performing his part due to some statutory bar or due to impossibility arising out of destruction of the subject-matter of the contract—a good defence for resisting the specific performance is constituted.

---

85. *Bibi Jaibunisha* v. *Jagdish Pandit*, (1997) 4 SCC 481.
86. (1967) 1 SCR 227: AIR 1967 SC 868.
87. *Mayawanti* v. *Kaushalya Devi*, (1990) 3 SCC 1.
88. *Ibid.*
89. *Govind Prasad Chaturvedi* v. *Hari Dutt Shastri*, (1977) 2 SCC 539: (1977) 2 SCR 877.
90. *Sri Ram Cotton Pressing Factory (P) Ltd.* v. *K.E. Narayanswami Naidu*, AIR 1965 Mad 352.

9. CONTRACTS WHICH CAN BE SPECIFICALLY ENFORCED (SECTIONS 10 TO 13)

While the negative proposition that "no agreement which is not a contract shall be enforced in specie" is true, its converse that "all contracts shall be enforced in specie" is not universally true.[91] The act therefore speaks of contracts which may be specifically enforced and those which cannot be specifically enforced (Sections 10-14).

No one is allowed to depart from the contract at his pleasure because as expressed by Jessel, M.R. "No principle can be more sacred than that a man shall be compelled to perform his contract". Where persons voluntarily, without any fraud, accident or mistake, enter into contracts, the jurisdiction of the court of equity ought to be exercised.[92]

Where there is a concluded and complete contract.[93] Where it is in writing, fair and certain, where it is upon adequate consideration and capable of being enforced and where its nature is such as requires enforcement in specie,[94] the contract would be enforced. Specific performance is thus a conscience attempt on the part of the court to do complete justice between the parties with regard to all the juridical relations growing out of the contract.

The section for its enforcement requires fulfilment of the following conditions:

(*a*) the suit must relate to specific performance of a contract;

(*b*) it must fall within clause (*a*) or clause (*b*) of Section 10;

(*c*) it must be a fit case for specific performance; and

(*d*) it should not be barred for specific performance, as per other sections of this chapter.

Sections 10 to 13 explain where specific performance is enforced either in full or in part, either of a contract or contracts connected with trusts, and in doing so they explain the very general principles which we have noted before. It must also be noted that Section 14(3) grants specific performance in six cases.

Section 10.—Section 10 of the Act lays down the following equitable rules—

(*i*) that the specific performance of a contract is within the discretion of the court;

(*ii*) it will be granted where there exists no standard for ascertaining the actual damage [Section 10, clause (*a*)]. As decided in *Falcke* v. *Gray*[95], where a rare China vase or an old and rare manuscript is

91. Banerjee: *Law of Specific Relief*, 9th Edn., 1992, pp. 108-109.

92. *Leech* v. *Schweder*, (1874) 9 Ch App 463; Cf. *Davis* v. *Maung Shwe*, ILR 38 Cal 805 (PC): 13 Bom LR 704: Banerjee: *Law of Specific Relief*, 9th Edn., p. 109. *See* also *V. Pechimuthu* v. *Gowrammal*, (2001) 7 SCC 617. *Veerayee Ammal* v. *Seeni Ammal*, (2002) 1 SCC 134.

93. *S.V.R. Mudaliar* v. *Rajabu F. Buhari*, (1995) 4 SCC 15: AIR 1995 SC 1607.

94. *Induben Ashokrao Nalvade* v. *Dhirajlal Shivlal Surati*, 1995 Supp (3) SCC 541.

95. (1859) 4 Drew 651: 62 ER 250.

agreed to be sold, there is no standard for ascertaining the actual damage that would be caused by its non-performance and therefore the contract will be specifically enforced. As is the case with a China vase (a movable property) so is the case with land or a house or shares of a particular company or construction of a building,[1] but the goods or chattel must have a particular value or association, or some antiquity, unusual beauty, variety and distinction attached to it from the buyer's viewpoint. As Story[2] writes the grounds of such a rule is utter-uncertainty of any calculation of damages as they must, in such a case, be, in a great measure conjectural. Thus all contracts concerning unique and precious articles, heirlooms, or paintings, old furniture and the like, in which there are no details to furnish a criterion nor any other means of estimating the *pretium affectionis* which constitutes the real value to the owner, and which is beyond the competency of the court to decide, writes Pomeroy[3] may be specifically enforced. The leading cases on this point are *Pusey* v. *Pusey*[4] and *Duke of Somerset* v. *Cooxson*[5];

(*iii*) as clause (*b*) of Section 10 provides, specific relief will also be granted where compensation is not an adequate relief;

(*iv*) as is further provided by the explanation, the court in such cases will presume that unless and until the contrary is proved in case of sale of immovable property, compensation is not an adequate relief;

(*v*) in case of movable property, compensation is an adequate relief [Explanation (*ii*)]; Where compensation for non-performance is laid down in the contract itself, the court must abide by it.[6]

(*vi*) But in the following cases the court presumes that compensation is not an adequate relief and hence specific performance will be granted—

(*a*) where the movable property is not an ordinary article of commerce, or

(*b*) is of special value or interest to the plaintiff, or

(*c*) it consists of goods not easily available in the market [Explanation (*ii*)(*a*), or]

(*d*) where the defendant holds the property as the agent or trustee of the plaintiff [Explanation (*ii*) (*b*)]

In *Cohen* v. *Roche*[7], the plaintiff failed to recover in specie certain antique furniture though it was of some beauty and distinction because he was merely a

---

1. *Storer* v. *Great Western Rly. Co.*, (1842) 2 Y & C Ch Cas 48: 63 ER 21.
2. Story: *Equity*, S. 722(*a*).
3. *Pomeroy,* Sp. Cs 34, p. 101: Cited in Banerjee: *Law of Specific Relief*, 9th Edn., 1992, at pp. 115-116.
4. (1864) 1 Ver 273 (a horn with inscription thereon).
5. (1935) 3 P wms 390 (a thing of antiquity and curiosity).
6. *Surjit Kaur* v. *Naurata Singh* (Section 12)—(2000) 7 SCC 379.
7. (1927) 1 KB 169: 136 LT 219.

dealer who had bought it for resale. Similarly, any stock for which there is a regular market is not a proper subject for specific performance.[8]

Section 11.—Section 11 provides for cases in which specific performance of contracts connected with trusts are enforceable. For this purpose it may be said that—(*i*) to grant specific performance of such contracts rests solely within the discretion of the court as the word "may" suggests [Section 11(1)]. No specific performance is granted where (*ii*) a trustee contracts in excess of his powers or (*iii*) in breach of a trust [Section 11(2)]. Behind this lies the simple reason that a court will not aid the use of excess powers of a trustee nor aid his breach of trust by granting specific performance of a contract connected with trust.

For example, *A* is a trustee of land with powers to lease it for seven years. He contracts with *B* to lease the land for 7 years and to renew the contract after its expiry. This contract cannot be specifically enforced as it is in excess of *A*'s powers as a trustee.[9] Thus a trustee selling trust property at a price below its market value and the directors of a company selling property without proper sanctions, are instances of misuse of trust and excess use of powers. Such contracts cannot be specifically enforced.

Section 12.—This section is in relation to specific performance of a part of contract. It explains that (*i*) specific performance of a part of contract shall not be granted [Section 12(1)]. (*ii*) Where a part of contract cannot be specifically performed but its non-performance admits of compensation and the part left unperformed is of small value, the court will allow specific performance of so much of the contract as can be performed and will allow compensation for the rest [Section 12(2)]. (*iii*) When a party is unable to perform the whole of his part of the contract and the part so left unperformed is (*a*) a considerable one and admits of compensation, or (*b*) is such that it does not admit of compensation, the plaintiff cannot get specific performance.[10]

But in cases falling under (*a*) above, the consideration paid will be abated or reduced suitably and in cases under (*b*) above there will be no abatement and the whole of the consideration must be paid. In both these cases the plaintiff will have to let go all his claims to performance or for compensation for the part left unperformed as the case may be [Section 12(3)].[11] (*iv*) When a contract consists of two parts: one, which ought to be performed and the other standing apart and being independent of the first cannot or ought not to be specifically performed, the first part must be specifically performed [Section 12(4)]. (*v*) Ceasing of a part of the subject-matter of the contract at the date of its performance raises a

---

8. *Tej Singh* v. *State of U.P.*, AIR 1981 All 103 (waste coal ash); for contrary opinion see *U.P. State Electricity Board* v. *Ram Barai Prasad*, AIR 1985 All 265.
9. *Mohd. Esmat Khan* v. *Nunda Dulal*, 16 IC 390; see *Mortlock* v. *Buller*, (1804) 10 Ves 292: 32 ER 857.
10. Under Section 12 of the J&K Specific Relief Act, 1999, the court may direct the party in default to perform specifically so much of his part of the contract as he can perform. *Manzoor Ahmed Magray* v. *Ghulam Hassan Aram*, (1999) 7 SCC 703.
11. *Rachakonda Narayana* v. *Ponthala Parvathamma*, (2001) 8 SCC 173 (benefit of S. 12(3) claim at appellate state permissible.

presumption in favour of a party that he is unable to perform it [Explanation to Section 12(4)].

Section 12, as noted by Mulla, constitutes a complete code in respect of a claim for specific performance of a part of a contract.[12] But here he sounds a note of caution that in the area of "specific performance with compensation" English cases would have to be applied with great care. Strong remarks have been made by eminent English judges on the unfortunate adventures of the courts of equity in "making bargains for the contracting parties which they never would have made for themselves".[13]

General principles as to compensation have been ably summed up in *Rutherford case*[14] as cited by Mulla. The question for the court is always whether the contract can be executed in substance. "*If a vendor sues* and is in a position to convey substantially what the purchaser has contracted to get, the court will decree specific performance with compensation for any small and immaterial deficiency provided the vendor has not, by misrepresentation or otherwise, disentitled himself to his remedy. Another possible case arises where a vendor claims specific performance and *the court refuses it* unless the purchaser is willing to consent to a decree on terms that the vendor will make compensation to the purchaser who agrees to such a decree on condition that he is compensated. *If it is the purchaser who is suing,* the court holds him to have an even larger right. Subject to considerations of hardship he may elect to take all he can get, and to have a proportionate abatement of the purchase money. But this right applies only to a deficiency in the subject-matter described in the contract".[15]

The explanation includes the cases that fall under Section 56 of the Contract Act.

In case of sale of immovable property by a single owner to several purchasers, no specific performance can be decreed against the vendor at the suit of only some of them if others do not join it claiming performance. The section, therefore, would not apply to such a case.

Section 13.—This section provides regarding the rights of a purchaser or lessee against persons with no title or imperfect title. As the section provides, where a person contracts to purchase or to obtain a lease of immovable property from a person who has no title or only an imperfect title to it, he will have the following rights:

(*i*) He can compel the vendor or lessor to make good the contract when he acquires any interest in the property subsequent to the contract [Section 13(1)(*a*)].

12. *Indian Contract Act and Specific Relief Act*, pp. 833-34.
13. *Re Arnold, Arnold* v. *Arnold*, (1880) 14 Ch D 270; 42 LT 705, cited in *ibid.*
14. *Rutherford* v. *Acton-Adams*, 1915 AC 866: 113 LT 931 (PC); *Arun Prakash* v. *Tulsi Charan*, 1949 AC 510.
15. Pollock and Mulla: *Indian Contract Act and Specific Relief Act*, p. 834.

(*ii*) He can compel him to procure concurrence or conveyance from the other person when it is necessary for validating the title and the persons are bound to concur [Section 13(1)(*b*)].

(*iii*) He can compel him to redeem the property and to get a valid discharge if it is mortgaged and also compel him to make a conveyance from the mortgagee if necessary [Section 13(1)(*c*)].

(*iv*) A purchaser or lessee will have a right to return of his deposit with interest, to costs of the suit and to a lien for all these three items on the vendor's interest or on his property subjected to contract, in case vendor's or lessee's suit for specific performance is dismissed for want of his title or imperfect title [Section 13(1)(*d*)].

(*v*) The above rules apply to contracts for sale or hire of movable property.

As is provided, where a party enters into a contract regarding property which he has no power to dispose of, but subsequently acquires that power, he can be compelled to perform the contract he entered into.[16] But the purchaser cannot afford to remain negligent and the rule of *caveat emptor* applies to him.[17]

This section should not be confused with Section 43 of the Transfer of Property Act. In *Silla Chandra Sekharam* v. *Ramchandra Sahu*[18], the Supreme Court explained that the expression "subsequently to the sale or lease" in Section 18 of the old Specific Relief Act (Section 13 here) means subsequently to the *contract to sell or let* and not subsequently to *the execution of the sale deed or lease deed.* The above expression should preferably be construed in a way that there are no overlappings between the provisions of clause (*a*) of Section 13 and Section 43 of the Transfer of Property Act as the legislature does not ordinarily intend to make duplicate provisions for similar situations. Sub-section (1)(*a*) is really plain justice.[19] A seller's obligation is determined by what he has contracted for, and one may bind oneself to sell that which he has not, but expects to have it in time to perform the promise, taking the risk of failure. There is nothing extraordinary here therefore to compel him at a suitable time to perform that which he has undertaken to perform.

Section 43 of the Transfer of Property Act refers to the sale or lease and under it property is conveyed first and title is acquired afterwards, whereas Section 13 refers to the performance of a contract and the vendor is required to convey the property contracted for, when acquired by him. Thus Section 13 refers to facts during the pendency of a contract.

It must be noted that the main principle is laid down by Section 13(1)(*a*) and sub-clauses (*b*) and (*c*) declare the consequences of the principle. In so far

16. *Halroyd* v. *Marshall*, (1862) 10 HLC 191; *Ehsanul Haq* v. *Mohd. Umar*, AIR 1973 All 425.

17. *Gour Chandra Das* v. *Prasanna Kumar Chandra*, ILR (1906) 33 Cal 812: 10 Cal WN 788; *Gajapathi* v. *Alagia*, ILR (1886) 9 Mad 89: 9 Ind Jur 419.

18. (1964) 7 SCR 858: AIR 1964 SC 1789.

19. Pollock and Mulla: *Indian Contract Act and Specific Relief Act*, p. 840.

as return of deposit is concerned the principles laid down in *Howe* v. *Smith*[20] by Cotton, L.J. apply in India.[21] Similarly, where a contract for sale goes off by default of a purchaser the vendor is entitled to retain the deposit.[22]

The provisions of sub-section (1) apply to immovable property but they may be applied to contracts for sale or hire of movable property also, as provided by sub-section (2).

10. WHAT SHOULD A PLAINTIFF PROVE

As Section 16(*c*) provides, in a suit for specific performance the plaintiff has to prove the following things:

(*i*) That there was a concluded contract between himself and the defendant.[23] If he cannot prove it, decree for specific performance cannot be granted.[24]

(*ii*) That he has performed or has always been ready and willing to perform the essential terms of the contract which are to be performed by him.[25]

(*iii*) That he is ready and willing to do everything on his part in future too, *i.e.*, he has to prove his continuous readiness and willingness to perform the contract as it really was and not as he alleges it to be.[26] His readiness and willingness would be inferred from his conduct, and that is a question of fact in each case.[27]

Readiness to perform according to Fry consists of (*a*) past acts as well as (*b*) future acts including all conditions precedent, the express and essential terms, the implied and essential terms and all the representations made on the faith of which the contract was entered into, but for the non-essential terms or the terms of a collateral contract no such performance need be shown.

---

20. (1884) 27 Ch D 89: 50 LT 573 (CA).
21. *Natesa Aiyar* v. *Appavu Padayachi*, ILR (1915) 38 Mad 178: 24 Mad LJ 488: 19 IC 462.
22. *Naresh Chandra Guha* v. *Ram Chandra Samanta*, AIR 1952 Cal 93.
23. *S.V.R. Mudaliar* v. *Rajabu F. Buhari*, (1995) 4 SCC 15: AIR 1995 SC 1607.
24. *Ganesh Shet* v. *Dr C.S.G.K. Setty*, (1998) 5 SCC 381.
25. *Balraj Taneja* v. *Sunil Madan*, (1999) 8 SCC 396: (1999) 90 RD 600: (1999) 81 DLT 779 (a condition precedent); *Syed Dastagir* v. *T.R. Gopalakrishna Setty*, (1999) 6 SCC 337: AIR 1999 SC 3029 (using special phraseology not necessary.) *Surjit Kaur* v. *Naurata Singh*, (2000) 7 SCC 379 (refusing to access part performance. There is no readiness & willingness). *Ajaib Singh* v. *Tulsi Devi*, (2000) 6 SCC 566: AIR 2000 SC 2493 (Readiness & willingness is there.); *Boramma* v. *Krishna Gowda*, (2000) 9 SCC 214 (Readiness & willingness at the time of filing suit but not thereafter); *Bishan Dayal & Sons* v. *State of Orissa*, (2001) 1 SCC 555: AIR 2001 SC 544 (no readiness & willingness); *Pushparani S. Sundaram* v. *Pauline Manomani James*, (2002) 9 SCC 582 (readiness & willingness must be proved; it may be inferred from circumstances also); *Manjunath Anandappa* v. *Tammanasa*, (2003) 10 SCC 390: AIR 2003 SC 1391 (what amounts to readiness & willingness); *P.D'Souza* v. *Shondrilo Naidu*, (2004) 6 SCC 649 (onus of proving. It should exist and continue from the date of contract to the hearing of the suit.); *Shanti Prasad Devi* v. *Shankar Mahto*, (2005) 5 SCC 543: AIR 2005 SC 2905 (clauses of contract uncertain. Specific performance cannot be granted.)
26. *Ardeshir Mama* v. *Flora Sassoon*, (1928) 32 CWN 953 (PC): (1928) 55 IA 360: AIR 1928 PC 208.
27. *Bindeshri Prasad* v. *Jairam Gir*, ILR (1887) 9 All 705 (PC): 14 IA 173; *Bank of India Ltd.* v. *Jamsetji A.H. Chinoy*, AIR 1950 PC 90: 77 IA 76.

"Aver" and "Prove" are two entirely different words with two different connotations. "Aver" means to ascertain or to mention something in the plaint, while "prove" connotes that what has been asserted in the plaint has to be proved by presenting evidence. As expressed in *Palthur H. Saheb case*,[28] it is therefore imperative on the part of the plaintiff to aver in the plaint that he has performed his part or that he has been always ready and willing to perform the essential terms of the contract which are to be performed by him. In judging this readiness and willingness the Court has to look to the totality of circumstances, a literal compliance with the terms is not imperative, nor it is a requirement of law.[29] The plaintiff in such cases may be directed suitably so that interest of both the parties are safeguarded.[30] However the performance of the essential terms must be full and not of a part only.[31] A plaintiff failing to fulfil any of the two obligations enjoined by the law will not be allowed to succeed.[32] This is because "he who seeks equity, must do equity". The Court has no power to relax this rule. The burden of proving readiness and willingness up to the date of trial lies on the plaintiff;[33] it is his duty. There is no particular form prescribed for expressing readiness and willingness.[34] The plaint in this respect should not be construed in a pedantic manner in order to non-suit the plaintiff.[35] The averment of the plaintiff's readiness and willingness, if it is not initially made due to counsel's mistake, may be allowed to be made later on by amending the plaint. Such an amendment does not tantamount to adding a new cause of action; it merely completes the prayer already made.[36]

As observed by the Supreme Court of India where a subsequent purchaser had deemed notice from fact of possession of previous purchaser, he would be deemed to be a non-bonafide purchaser with notice, and consequently specific performance of sale agreement of previous purchaser was decreed.[37] Where there are clear recitals in an agreement of sale of whole building the same cannot be whittled down by inaccuracy in the recitals.[38] In case where there was an agreement to sell share of a joint holder of property, the submission that the property will have to be partitioned or that it was scattered at different places

---

28. *P.H. Saheb* v. *Bapanna Annapumamma*, AIR 1986 Kar 109.
29. *Mithukhan* v. *Pipariawali*, AIR 1986 MP 39, *relying on R.C. Chandiok* v. *Chuni Lal Sabharwal*, (1970) 3 SCC 140: AIR 1971 SC 1238.
30. *C.L. Jain* v. *Gopi Chand*, AIR 1990 Del 380.
31. *Byomkesh Banerjee* v. *Nani Gopal Banik*, AIR 1987 Cal 92.
32. *Jagannath Misra* v. *Umar Misra*, (1984) 1 Cri LJ 223; *Abdul Khader* v. *P.K. Sara Bai*, (1989) 4 SCC 313: AIR 1990 SC 682.
33. *Saral Kumar Chatterjee* v. *Madhusudan*, AIR 1964 Cal 556.
34. *K. Sambasiva Rao* v. *P. Bangaru Raju*, AIR 1985 AP 392.
35. *Naval Kishore* v. *Kuleshwari Devi*, 1986 BLJ 268: (1986) 34 BLJR 418.
36. *Gajanan, J. Joshi* v. *P.M. Kalwar*, (1990) 1 BLJ 650; *Oscar Lovis* v. *Sarodha*, (1990) 1 KLT 469; *Joga Singh* v. *Pakhar Ram*, AIR 1990 P&H 314.
37. *Ram Bilas Ojha* v. *Bishwa Muni*, (1979) 1 SCC 21: AIR 1978 SC 1094; *Govinddas* v. *Shantibai*, (1973) 3 SCC 418: AIR 1972 SC 1520.
38. *Induben Ashokrao Nalvade* v. *Dhirajlal Shivlal Surati*, 1995 Supp (3) SCC 541.

was held not to be a legal difficulty.[39] Performance of contract in a "reasonable time" is a question of fact in each case.[40] Finally to grant specific performance or not is a question depending upon facts and circumstances of a case. Where a plaintiff in seeking specific performance obtains an unfair advantage over the defendant, the same would not be granted by the court.[41]

11. CONTRACTS WHICH CANNOT BE SPECIFICALLY ENFORCED

General.—As discussed before, where pecuniary compensation was not an adequate relief specific performance was decreed. Looking at the proposition the other way, it could be said that if compensation is an adequate relief, specific performance will not be decreed. But this is not all and it is not so simple as to close the discussion, because there are situations wherein, on the general principles, specific performance should have been granted by the Chancery Courts in England even though they have declined to grant it. Those cases have been grouped by Snell[42] under the following headings:

(*i*) Illegal or immoral contracts

(*ii*) Agreements without consideration

(*iii*) Contracts for transient interests

(*iv*) Contracts involving personal skill

(*v*) Contracts requiring personal supervision

(*vi*) Contracts to transfer goodwill alone

(*vii*) Divisible contracts

(*viii*) Contracts for arbitration

(*ix*) Contracts wanting in mutuality

(*x*) Contracts to exercise a testamentary power of disposition.

Section 14 of the Specific Relief Act when viewed with Sections 11, 12 and 13 enlists the contracts which cannot be specifically enforced, as under:

(*i*) Contracts where compensation is an adequate relief [Section 14(1)(*a*)]

(*ii*) Contracts running into minute or numerous details [Section 14(1)(*b*)]

(*iii*) Contracts dependent upon personal qualifications [Section 14(1)(*b*)]

(*iv*) Contracts dependent upon volition of the parties [Section 14(1)(*b*)]

(*v*) Contracts which from their very nature are such that they cannot be specifically enforced [Section 14 (1) (*b*)]

(*vi*) Contracts in their nature determinable [Section 14(1)(*c*)][43]

---

39. *Kartar Singh* v. *Harjinder Singh*, (1990) 3 SCC 517: AIR 1990 SC 854.

40. *Hungerford Investment Trust Ltd.* v. *Haridas Mundhra*, (1992) 3 SCC 684: (1972) 3 SCR 690.

41. *Sandhya Rani Sarkar* v. *Sudha Rani Devi*, (1978) 2 SCC 116: AIR 1978 SC 537; *B.R. Mulani* v. *Dr A.B. Aswathanarayana*, 1993 Supp (4) SCC 743: AIR 1993 SC 1318.

42. *Snell's Principles of Equity*, pp. 578, 583. *See* also *Subhadra Rani Pal Choudhary* v. *Sheirly Weigal Nain*, (2005) 5 SCC 230.

43. *Indian Oil Corpn. Ltd.* v. *Amritsar Gas Service*, (1991) 1 SCC 533.

(*vii*) Contracts requiring continuous supervision of the court [Section 14(1)(*d*)][44]

(*viii*) Agreements to refer to arbitration [Section 14(2)]

(*ix*) Agreements to lend money or to mortgage [Section 14(3)(*a*)]

(*x*) Agreements to form partnership [Section 14(3)(*b*)]

(*xi*) Contracts to build or repair [Section 14(3) (*c*)]

(*xii*) Contracts made by trustees in excess of their powers [Section 11(2)]

(*xiii*) A part of contract cannot be specifically enforced [Section 12(1)]

(*xiv*) A contract whose material part of the subject-matter has ceased to exist [Section 13(4) explanation].

Equity will not compel the specific performance of an illegal contract in England even though it is legal in the country of its origin, *e.g.*, agreement between husband and wife for future separation. An agreement for immediate separation was once believed to be contrary to the policy of law but now it is not so and will be enforced if it was by way of matrimonial or other proceedings. Section 9 of the Specific Relief Act, 1963 provides this by way of defence available to a party under any law relating to contracts. With the legality of contract are connected the questions regarding consideration, consent, capacity, legality of the object and formalities, but since they are peculiar to the Contract Act we must leave them. It would therefore suffice to say that a contract entered into by a minor misrepresenting his age[45], a contract entered into by a trustee that necessitates a breach of trust[46], are contracts the specific performance whereof would not be granted as they are not valid at law. Similarly, agreements without consideration will not be enforced. Agreements for transient interests or interests which are not lasting or enduring will not be specifically enforced. Where there is no concluded contract, its specific performance cannot be granted.[47]

(*a*) *Contracts involving personal skill.*—There is a limit to courts' power in granting specific performance and it is discernible in case of contracts to do acts involving personal skill, knowledge, inclination and qualification. Courts cannot control the mind and the ideas of an individual. Their scope becomes limited here. In *Lumley* v. *Wagner*[48], a singer agreed with a theatrical manager to sing at his theatre for a particular period. In a suit for specific performance against her the court could not compel her to sing as it depended on personal inclination, but it must be noted that she was enjoined from singing elsewhere. As noted by Snell[49], the threat of committal might induce her to perform but the court could

44. *Her Highness Maharani Shantidevi P. Gaikwad* v. *Savjibhai Haribhai Patel*, (2001) 5 SCC 101.
45. *Ajudhia Prasad* v. *Chandan Lal*, AIR 1937 All 610.
46. *Willmott* v. *Barber*, (1880) 15 Ch D 96: 43 LT 95 (CA).
47. *Ganesh Shet* v. *Dr G.S.G.K. Setty*, (1998) 5 SCC 381; *M.V. Shankar Bhat* v. *Claude Pinto*, (2003) 4 SCC 86.
48. (1852) 1 De GM & G 604: 42 ER 687.
49. *Snell's Principles of Equity*, p. 580.

not control imperfections of performance or judge whether they were natural or self-induced.[50] It is for such reasons that a contract to report cases for a series of law reports[51], or an infant's apprenticeship deed, are not specifically enforced. It is true that in such cases of breach, money compensation is wholly inadequate, the real ground behind it being the inability of the court in executing its decree. In the words of Professor Langdell, if a contract consists in giving, equity can enforce a specific reparation of a breach of it, but if it consists in doing something, it cannot enforce it. Similarly, a contract of employment by or against an employer[52], or a contract of personal service[53] cannot be specifically enforced. The cases of *Executive Committee of Vaish Degree College* v. *Lakshmi Narain*[54] and the *Kayastha Pathshala, Allahabad*[55] reiterate the same principle. In the first case it was held that a court would not normally give a declaration that the contract subsists and the employee even after having been removed from service can be deemed to be in service against the will of the employer. Of course, this rule is subject to three exceptions. In the second case[56] the employee, a teacher in educational institution taught for one or two years. He was afterwards suspended and was out of teaching job for about 25 years. The Supreme Court held that his reinstatement is not justifiable and salary of three years as damages would suffice. In educational institutions, the court cannot focus only on the individual forgetting all else. The court must have regard to varying circumstances in the academic atmosphere and radically changed position of the individual sought to be reinstated. Specific enforcement and reinstatement in service in such cases are rarely made because to do so, in the words of Dr. Hanbury[57], would be difficult if the defendant proves recalcitrant, and it is contrary to public policy to compel one person to submit to the orders of another. The courts, said Fry, L.J. in *De. Francesco case*[58], "are bound to be jealous, lest they should turn contracts of service into contracts of slavery". Conversely, equity will not compel an employer to keep a servant. The proper and exclusive remedy for wrongful dismissal is an action for damages.[59] Under this heading may be included the

---

50. *C.H. Giles and Co. Ltd.* v. *Morris*, (1972) 1 WLR 307: (1972) 1 All ER 960 (Ch D).
51. *Clarke* v. *Price*, (1819) 2 Wils Ch 157: 37 ER 270.
52. *Calcutta Chemical Co. Ltd.* v. *D.K. Barman*, AIR 1969 Pat 371.
53. *S. Dutt (Dr)*.v. *University of Delhi*, AIR 1958 SC 1050; *Bool Chand (Dr)* v. *Chancellor, Kurukshetra University*, AIR 1968 SC 292: (1968) 1 SCR 434: 68 Punj LR 1031: (1968) 2 LLJ 135; *Vidya Ram Mishra* v. *Managing Committee, Shri Jai Narayan College*, (1972) 1 SCC 623: AIR 1972 SC 1450 (College & its teacher); *S.R. Tewari* v. *District Board, Agra*, AIR 1964 SC 1680: (1964) 3 SCR 55 (action can be declared ultra vires); *Pearlite Liners (P) Ltd.* v. *Manorama Sirsi*, (2004) 3 SCC 172.
54. (1976) 2 SCC 58: 1976 SCC (L&S) 176.
55. *Kayastha Pathshala, Allahabad* v. *Rajendra Prasad*, 1989 Supp (2) SCC 732: 1990 SCC (L&S) 86.
56. 1989 Supp (2) SCC 732: 1990 SCC (L&S) 86.
57. Hanbury: *Modern Equity*, p. 45.
58. *De Francesco* v. *Barnum (No.2)*, (1890) 45 Ch D 430: 63 LT 438.
59. *Bool Chand (Dr)* v. *Chancellor, Kurukshetra University*, AIR 1968 SC 292: (1968) 1 SCR 434; *Nandganj Sihori Sugar Co. Ltd.* v. *Badri Nath Dixit*, (1991) 3 SCC 54: AIR 1991 SC 1525.

cases of personal service[60], contract of employment, contracts to marry, to paint a picture, to sing, to report cases, or to write a book.

A contract for personal service, where there is a relation of master and servant and the relations are strained cannot be enforced.[61]

As observed in *Jitendra Nath case*[62] a contract of employment for personal service cannot be enforced specifically, and more so when the services are of trust and confidence.[63] Similarly contracts for the purposes of pleasure, for pursuit of science or for the purpose of charity[64], contracts wherein an employee is demoted or wherein he is dismissed from Zilla Parishad Service,[65] no specific enforcement is possible; the proper remedy for the plaintiff being to seek damages.[66] A party to an illegal contract cannot enforce his rights thereunder.[67]

Statutory Servants

However whenever a Court is satisfied that a departure from this principle is desirable and called for it will grant a declaration that the employers action in determining the employee's services is illegal and *ultra vires*.[68] This will compel the employer to reinstate or re-employ the servant. Thus to this general rule that there can be no specific enforcement of a contract of employment for personal service, the following are the exceptions which impels the court to grant specific performance of a contract—

(*a*) a public servant dismissed from service in contravention of Article 311 of the Constitution;

(*b*) a dismissed worker under Industrial Law or by Labour or Industrial Tribunal; and

(*c*) when a statutory body acts in breach of a mandatory obligation imposed by statute.[69]

In such cases the Court may grant an injunction and further compel the employer to reinstate the employee. Such an order is made because there is a breach of statutory obligation on the part of the employer. However no such relief can be claimed against a non-statutory body.[70]

---

60. *Steel Industries Kerala Ltd.* v. *S.M. Rebello*, (1985) 2 SCC 363; *Jitendra Nath* v. *Empire of India and Ceylone Tea Co.*, (1989) 3 SCC 582: 1989 SCC (L&S) 552.
61. *Pearlite Liners (P) Ltd.* v. *Manorama Sirsi*, (2004) 3 SCC 172: (2004) 3 MPLJ 367.
62. (1989) 3 SCC 582: 1989 SCC (L&S) 552.
63. *Madan* v. *Kamaldhari*, AIR 1930 Pat 121: 127 IC 281.
64. *Rigby* v. *Connol*, (1880) 14 Ch D 482.
65. *Zilla Parishad, Gorakhpur* v. *Ramanuj Sahai*, 1986 Lab IC 319.
66. *Vidya Ram Mishra* v. *Managing Committee, Shri Jai Narain College*, (1972) 1 SCC 623: AIR 1972 SC 1450.
67. *ITC Ltd.* v. *George Joseph Fernandes*, (1989) 2 SCC 1: AIR 1989 SC 839.
68. *S.R. Tewari* v. *District Board, Agra*, AIR 1964 SC 1680: (1964) 3 SCR 55; *Sirsi Municipality* v. *Cecelia Kom Francis Tellis*, (1973) 1 SCC 409: 1973 SCC (L&S) 207.
69. *Indian Airlines* v. *Sukhdeo Rai*, (1971) 2 SCC 192: AIR 1971 SC 1828; *Executive Committee of Vaish Degree College* v. *Lakshmi Narain*, (1976) 2 SCC 58: 1976 SCC (L&S) 176; for details *see* Banerjee S.C.: *Law of Specific Relief*, Ch II, Edn. 9, 1992, pp. 194-198.
70. *Agarwal Digambar* v. *B.P. Shrivastava*, 1984 Lab IC 2591 (All) (DB).

In case of Government servants the only relief would be by way of appeal to superior officers. They cannot get injunction in their favour but may claim damages for the actual loss caused to them by the dismissal.[71]

(*b*) *Contracts involving personal supervision.*—Such contracts require continuous, constant and possibly ineffective, supervision of successive acts by the court.[72] As noted by Snell, equity will not enforce an award for repair of a railway involving continuous supply of engine power, a term in a lease to employ a resident porter and an agreement to publish an article which has not reached its final form. "In such cases, equity's view is that of a wise parent dealing with his children; it is best not to issue orders unless you can be absolutely sure of effecting compliance."[73]

Under this heading fall the cases of agreements to build or repair. *Ryan* v. *Mutual Tontine Westminster Chambers Assn.*[74] is a leading case on the point, wherein the court refused to grant specific performance of an agreement to employ a resident porter who should be in constant attendance and perform certain specified duties. Similarly, an agreement to provide a housekeeper[75], or the obligation of a ship owner under a charter party[76], or a contract to deliver goods by instalments[77], cannot be specifically enforced. Difficulty of supervision is also experienced in building contracts and contracts to keep buildings in repair. Still, however, in suitable cases[78] specific performance would be decreed. Para 3(*c*) of Section 14 deals with building contracts which can be specifically enforced. It is based on the English rule expressed in *Wolverhampton Corpn.* v. *Emmons*[79] which says that the court will order specific performance of an agreement if (*i*) the building work is sufficiently defined by the contract; (*ii*) the plaintiff has a substantial interest in the performance of the contract so that damages would not compensate him, and (*iii*) the defendant is in possession of the land so that the plaintiff cannot employ another person to build without committing a trespass.[80] A writer cannot get specific performance of his contract but he will be entitled to damages for loss of opportunity to enhance his reputation.[81]

---

71. *Dahyalal Bapubhai* v. *Patna Municipality*, ILR 1967 Pat 182: (1967) 8 GLR 167.
72. *C.H. Giles and Co. Ltd.* v. *Morris*, (1972) 1 WLR 307: (1972) 1 All ER 960 (Ch D). See *Her Highness Maharani Shantadevi P. Gaikwad* v. *Savjibhai Haribhai Patel*, (2001) 5 SCC 101: AIR 2001 SC 1462.
73. Hanbury: *Modern Equity*, p. 45. *Her Highness Maharani Shantidevi P. Gaikwad* v. *Savjibhai Haribhai Patel*, (2001) 5 SCC 101. (Continuous duty involved, specific performance inequitable).
74. (1893) 1 Ch 116: 67 LT 820 (CA).
75. *Barnes* v. *City of London Real Property Co. etc.*, (1918) 2 Ch 18: 119 LT 293; *Her Highness Maharani Shantidevi P. Gaikwad* v. *Savjibhai Haribhai Patel*, (2001) 5 SCC 101. (Continuous duty involved, specific performance inequitable).
76. *De Mattos* v. *Gibson*, (1858) 4 De & J 276: 45 ER 108.
77. *Dominion Coal Co. Ltd.* v. *Dominion Iron and Steel Co. Ltd.*, 1909 AC 293: 100 LT 245 (PC).
78. *A.G. (at the relation of Allen)* v. *Colchester Corpn.*, (1955) 2 QB 207: (1955) 2 All ER 124 (QBD). See also *Chitty on Contracts*, 23rd Edn., para 1530.
79. (1901) 1 KB 515: 84 LT 407 (CA).
80. *Snell's Principles of Equity*, p. 581.
81. *Joseph* v. *National Magazine Co. Ltd.*, (1958) 4 All ER 52 (Ch D).

(*c*) *Contracts to transfer goodwill alone.*—"Sale of the goodwill of a business unconnected with the business premises cannot be transferred because of the uncertainty of the subject matter and the consequent incapacity of the court to give specific directions as to what is to be done to transfer it." In *Baxter* v. *Conolly*[82] and *Darbey* v. *Whitaker*[83] this was the law declared, but in *Beswick* v. *Beswick*[84] specific performance for the sale of goodwill without business premises at the suit of the personal representatives of a vendor who had performed his part of the contract, was ordered. This trend must be noted.

(*d*) *Divisible Contracts.*—If a contract is divisible into two or more independent parts or if some of its terms are legal and the rest are illegal and they can be severed, effect can be given to those independent parts, or the terms which are legal can be specifically enforced.

(*e*) *Contracts for arbitration.*—As Snell notes, "equity will not directly enforce an agreement to appoint an arbitrator[85] but the court may indirectly compel performance of the agreement by staying an action which is brought, if the defendant so applies". In India too, the existence of such an agreement bars a suit for specific performance as is provided by sub-section (2) of Section 14. The bar applies equally to the institution as well as the further prosecution of the suit.[86] For such a bar to exist the plaintiff must have refused to refer the controversy to arbitration and this has to be proved, it cannot be simply inferred by mere filing of the plaint.[87] The simple reason behind putting the bar is to prevent people from breaking their promises to refer to arbitration and thus to achieve the result desired. As Pollock and Mulla have expressed,[88] "the procedure for enforcing an award was only under Section 14 of the (Specific Relief) Act" and this view has received statutory force by virtue of an amendment of Section 32 of the Arbitration Act, 1940 contained in Section 43 of the Specific Relief Act, 1963.

(*f*) *Contracts wanting in mutuality.*—As per Cardozo, J., mutuality is important only to secure that the decree will operate without injustice to either party.[89] Where vender has still to complete formalities, specific performance was not possible.[90] A contract, to be specifically enforceable, must at the time when it is made, be mutually binding. In *Forrer* v. *Nash*[91], it was decided that if a vendor has no title to the estate which he has contracted to sell and has no right to compel the real owner to convey it, he cannot force the purchaser to take a conveyance from the true owner, even if he is willing to convey the property,

---

82. (1820) 1 Jac & W 576: 37 ER 487.
83. (1857) 4 Drew 134: 62 ER 52.
84. 1968 AC 58: (1967) 3 WLR 932: (1967) 2 All ER 1197 (HL).
85. *Smith & Service & Nelson & Sons, Re*, (1890) 25 QBD 545: 63 LT 475 (CA).
86. *Shiblal* v. *Hiralal*, (1888) AWN 133.
87. *Koomud Chunder Dass* v. *Chunder Kant Mookerjee*, ILR (1880) 5 Cal 498: 5 Cal LR 284.
88. *Indian Contract Act and Specific Relief Act*, p. 850.
89. Cited in *Snell's Principles of Equity*, p. 582.
90. *Nirmala Anand* v. *Advent Corpn. (P) Ltd.*, (2002) 5 SCC 481.
91. (1865) 35 Beav 167: 55 ER 858.

for the purchaser has no right to compel a conveyance by the true owner. Thus mutuality implies that the specific performance of a contract should be such as can be claimed by or granted to both the parties to the contract. Mutuality does not mean equality and exact arithmetical correspondence. It means that each party must have the freedom to enforce rights under the contract against the other.[92] Where vendor has still to complete formalities, specific performance was not possible. In *Mir Sarwarjan case*[93] the Privy Council decided that no specific performance could be granted in a contract which can be enforced at the option of only one of the parties, but Section 20(4) of the Specific Relief Act provides that it cannot be so refused merely on the ground that the contract is not enforceable at the instance of the other party. The controversy regarding introduction and application of the doctrine of mutuality which existed in India between various High Courts has been put at rest now by introducing Section 20(4) in the Specific Relief Act, 1963.

(*g*) *Contracts to exercise a testamentary power of appointment.*—Courts of equity will not compel a donee of such a power to exercise it, even if it was for value. According to equity, to do so would amount to defeating the donor's intention.

(*h*) *Contracts where compensation is adequate relief.*—This proposition has been discussed in the previous chapter. Stating the gist succinctly, we may say that in case of contracts of ordinary marketable things, since the same are available in the market, money compensation is sufficient here. But in respect of other articles which cannot be so obtained because there is no market for the same, specific performance is a proper remedy.[94]

(*i*) *Agreements to lend money or to mortgage.*—Equity refuses specific performance of such agreements because compensation is adequate relief here. But where it is not so, i.e., in exceptional circumstances, an agreement to execute a mortgage would be specifically enforced. As decided in *Meenakshisundara Mudaliar* v. *Rathnasami Pillai*[95], where a loan has been advanced and the borrower does not execute a mortgage or where a part of the loan is advanced and the lender is willing to perform his part by granting the remaining part of the loan, specific performance of the contract to mortgage would be decreed against the defendant borrower. If the borrower is not willing to repay the loan at once the same result would follow.[96] Section 14(3)(*a*) explains this.

(*j*) *Agreements to form partnership.*—According to Section 14(3)(*b*), where only a formal deed of partnership is to be executed, the parties having commenced to carry on business of partnership, or where the suit is for the

92. *Dasarath Gayen* v. *Satyanarayan Ghosh*, AIR 1963 Cal 325; *Nirmala Anand* v. *Advent Corpn. (P) Ltd.*, (2002) 5 SCC 481.
93. *Mir Sarwarjan* v. *Fakhruddin Mahomed Chowdhuri*, (1912) 39 IA 1: ILR (1912) 39 Cal 232: 13 IC 331.
94. *Bank of India Ltd.* v. *Jamsetji A. H. Chinoy*, AIR 1950 PC 90: 77 IA 76.
95. ILR (1918) 41 Mad 959: 49 IC 291: AIR 1919 Mad 322.
96. *Jewan Lal Daga* v. *Nilmani Chaudhuri*, AIR 1928 PC 80: 55 IA 107.

purchase of the share of a partner in a firm, there would be no objection in decreeing specific performance; otherwise the court does not decree specific performance of an agreement to form and carry on partnership.

(*k*) *Vague contracts.*—Contracts which are so vague in language[1] that their terms cannot be known or fixed definitely, cannot be enforced specifically, *e.g.*, a contract to sell at a fair price or to let out at a fair rent is vague, unclear, indefinite and incomplete for specific enforcement [Section 14(1)(*b*)].

(*l*) *Contracts in their nature determinable.*—Likewise, where *A* and *B* enter into a partnership at will and no duration of the same is specified, such a contract cannot be specifically enforced because *A* and *B* might at once dissolve partnership.[2] It may be otherwise if the partnership is for a definite, or a fixed and defined term.

In a case where the assurance was given by the Food Corporation of India, in writing that it would take the plinths to be constructed by owners of land on lease for a period of three years, the owners invested huge amounts for construction of plinths. The FCI terminated the Contract of lease. The Supreme Court observed that though the contract was not against public policy, or prohibited by any statutory provision of law or ultra vires and the FCI was bound to discharge its obligations on the principle of promissory estoppel (being a statutory corporation), the respondent was entitled to damages as the specific performance of the contract was not possible due to expiry of the period of three years.[3] It is evident that such contracts are in their nature determinable. Section 14(1) (*c*) expresses this idea. The word *volition* used in Section 14(1)(*b*) connotes the volition of the parties to a contract and none else. The remaining types of contracts as enumerated earlier have been discussed before.

A default clause may bar specific performance as the relationship between the parties has to be regulated by the terms of the agreement between them. In *Dada Rao*[4] *case* where agreement for sale of agricultural land itself provided for contingencies of (*i*) Seller refusing to sell and (*ii*) purchaser refusing to buy stipulating the return of earnest money plus another sum in either circumstance, it was held that on facts there was no obligation on the seller to complete the sale transaction and contract could not be specifically enforced.

Specific performance of contract is an equitable relief. It is also a discretionary remedy and courts are not bound to grant it because it is lawful to do so unmindful of equities to be balanced and despite serious in equities that may necessarily result by granting the same.[5] Similarly if the true object of an agreement cannot be fulfilled, it would be inequitable to enforce specific performance of an agreement. Harm to plaintiff's reputation in such a case is

---

1. *Savage* v. *Uwechia*, (1961) 1 WLR 455: (1961) 1 All ER 830 (PC).
2. *Scott* v. *Rayment*, (1868) LR 7 Eq 112: 19 LT 481.
3. *Food Corpn. of India, Bhopal* v. *Babulal Agarwal*, AIR 1998 MP 23.
4. *Dadarao* v. *Ramrao*, (1999) 8 SCC 416.
5. *Nirmala Anand* v. *Advent Corpn. (P) Ltd.*, (2002) 5 SCC 481: AIR 2002 SC 2290.

irrelevant.[6] Where the clauses of a contract are uncertain, specific performance cannot be granted.[7] A contract concluded without complying with the provisions of Article 299 of the Constitution of India, cannot be specifically enforced.[8]

In *Rajasara case* specific performance of a contract, to sell agricultural land with an imperfect title was allowed when the title was perfected.[9] Similarly in one case an old lessee did not exercise option for renewal and during pendency of the eviction proceedings, the old lessee with full knowledge of the new lease continued in possession. Held, the third party is entitled to possession under the new lease.[10]

12. PARTIES TO AN ACTION FOR SPECIFIC PERFORMANCE (SECTIONS 15, 16, 17 AND 19)

Section 15 lays down a list of the kinds of parties besides the actual contractors who are entitled to sue on a contract. Mulla, citing Whitley Stokes,[11] agrees with him that no reason appears why sub-section (*c*) should not have extended to all compromises of doubtful claims. The enforcement of restrictive covenants by way of injunction does not come within this section. Section 19 can be said to be a counterpart of Section 15 as it enumerates the classes of possible defendants who were not original parties to the contract. Stated succinctly, a suit for specific performance of a contract can be maintained by and against—

(*i*) the parties to the contract; and

(*ii*) their representatives in interest.

(*a*) *For whom contracts may be specifically enforced* [*Section 15*].—Section 15 enumerates possible plaintiffs, and consequently specific performance of a contract may be enforced in favour of—

(*i*) a party thereto

(*ii*) representatives in interest or the principal thereto

(*iii*) any person beneficially entitled

(*iv*) the remainderman

(*v*) a reversioner in possession

(*vi*) a reversioner in remainder

(*vii*) the amalgamated company

(*viii*) the company.

---

6. *Her Highness Maharani Shantidevi P. Gaikwad* v. *Savjibhai Haribhai Patel*, (2001) 5 SCC 101: AIR 2001 SC 1462 [Section 14(1)(*d*)].
7. *Shanti Prasad Devi* v. *Shankar Mahto*, (2005) 5 SCC 543: AIR 2005 SC 2905.
8. *Bishan Dayal & Sons* v. *State of Orissa*, (2001) 1 SCC 555: AIR 2001 SC 544.
9. *Rojasara Ramjibhai Dahyabhai* v. *Jani Narottamdas Lallubhai*, (1986) 3 SCC 300: AIR 1986 SC 1912.
10. *H.V. Rajan* v. *C.N. Gopal*, (1975) 4 SCC 302: AIR 1975 SC 261.
11. Pollock & Mulla: *Indian Contract Act and Specific Relief Act*, p. 851.

Representative-in-interest includes assignee of right to repurchase the property.[12] Where the right to reconveyance of property is not a personal right or where there is no express or implied prohibition for its assignment to third party, its specific performance can be obtained by the assignee.[13] As observed in *Shyam Singh case* it includes transferees and assignees from the contracting party in whose favour the contractual right exists except when the contract falls under proviso to Section 15(*b*).[14]

As the general rule goes a contract cannot be enforced except by a party thereto. This rule has however the following exceptions:[15]

Where—

(*i*) a trust is created in favour of a stranger by the contract;

(*ii*) the promisor constitutes himself as agent for the stranger;

(*iii*) it is so provided by a marriage settlement;[16]

(*iv*) the contract itself provides for maintenance;

(*v*) the contract itself provides for marriage expenses;

(*vi*) the aim of the contract itself is to benefit a stranger;

(*vii*) a charge is created in favour of a stranger by the contract;

(*viii*) there is established a privity of contract between the promisor and the stranger;

(*ix*) it would be conducive to justice to allow a stranger to enforce a contract; and

(*x*) the promisor is bound to the stranger on the principle of estoppel.

(*b*) *For whom specific performance cannot be enforced* [*Sections 16 and 17*].—(*i*) One who would not recover compensation for its breach [Section 16(*a*)].

(*ii*) One who becomes incapable of performing or violates any essential term of the contract that on his part remains to be performed, e.g., insolvency [Section 16(*b*)].

(*iii*) One who acts in fraud of the contract, or wilfully acts at variance with or in subversion of relations intended to be established by the contract [Section 16(*b*)]

(*iv*) One who is not ready and willing to perform his part of the contract [Section 16(*c*)].

---

12. *T.M. Balakrishna Mudaliar* v. *M. Satyanarayana Rao*, (1993) 2 SCC 740: AIR 1993 SC 2449.
13. *Habiba Khatoon* v. *Ubaidul Huq*, (1997) 7 SCC 452: AIR 1997 SC 3236.
14. *Shyam Singh* v. *Daryao Singh*, (2003) 12 SCC 160; *Vishweshwar Narasabhatta Gaddala* v. *Durgappa Irappa Bhatkar*, AIR 1940 Bom 339; *Sinnakaruppa Gounder* v. *Karuppuswamy Grunder*, AIR 1965 Mad 506.
15. *Safiur-Rehman* v. *Maherunnissa*, ILR 24 Cal 832.
16. *Nawab Khwaja Mohammed.* v. *Husaini Begum*, 7 LJ 871.

(*v*) One (a vendor or lessor of movable or immovable property) who knowing himself not to have any title to the property, has contracted to sell or let the same[17] [Section 17(*a*)].

(*vi*) One who cannot give the purchaser or lessee a title free from reasonable doubt [Section 17(*b*)].

(*vii*) One who has, previous to such sale or letting, made a settlement of the subject matter of the contract [Section 16-17].

There are two conditions precedent as held in *Bansidhardas* v. *Duryodhan Majhi*[18], to the enforcement of specific performance of a contract and they are that (*i*) one must have either performed or (*ii*) one has been always ready and willing to perform his part of the contract. This requirement is mandatory.[19] Moreover, as the section makes it clear one must assert so or state so in the plaint and must lead evidence to prove his averment.[20]

Readiness means capacity of the plaintiff including his financial ability to pay the purchase price. The continuous readiness and willingness on the part of the plaintiff is a condition precedent to grant relief of specific performance. Right from the date of the execution till date of the decree he must prove that he is ready and has always been willing to perform his part of the contract. This can be proved from the attendant circumstances.[21]

In determining the question as to which party is not ready and willing to perform his part of the contract the court must examine the position of both the parties.[22] Because the bank pass book is not produced, it cannot be presumed that the purchaser has no capacity to pay.[23] Similarly instead of cash payment, presentment of a bank draft would amount to a legal tender.[24]

One must note that readiness and willingness must be continuous. It is a condition precedent. It must exist right from the date of the execution till the

---

17. *Imperial Ice Manufacturing Co.* v. *Munchershaw Barjorji Wadia*, ILR (1889) 13 Bom 415.
18. (1985) 59 Cnt LT 44 (DB).
19. *Anant Prasad* v. *J.S. Sahai*, 1986 BLJ 164; *G. Pillai* v. *P. Nadar*, AIR 1967 SC 868.
20. *Sukhbir Singh* v. *Brijpal Singh*, (1997) 2 SCC 200: AIR 1996 SC 2510.
21. *N.P. Thirugnanam* v. *Dr R. Jagan Mohan Rao*, (1995) 5 SCC 115; *His Holiness Acharya Swami Ganesh Dassji* v. *Sitaram Thapar*, (1996) 4 SCC 526: AIR 1996 SC 2095; *Indira Kaur* v. *Sheo Lal Kapoor*, (1988) 2 SCC 488: AIR 1988 SC 1074; *Pushparani S. Sundaram* v. *Pauline Manomani James*, (2002) 9 SCC 582 (it may be inferred from the totality of circumstances or conduct of plaintiff); *T. Mohan* v. *Kannammal*, (2002) 10 SCC 82; *Manjunath Anandappa* v. *Tammanasa*, (2003) 10 SCC 390 (averment of readiness and willingness to perform); *P.D'Souza* v. *Shondrilo Naidu*, (2004) 6 SCC 649; *Swarnam Ramachandran* v. *Aravacode Chakungal Jayapalan*, (2004) 8 SCC 689 (requirements for fulfilment of this condition); *Pukhraj D. Jain* v. *G. Gopalkrishna*, (2004) 7 SCC 251 (averment in plaint & surrounding circumstances should also indicate the same); *Umabai* v. *Nilkanth Dhondiba Chawan*, (2005) 6 SCC 243 (how to determine the readiness and willingness; inconsistent pleas raised.); *Aniglase Yohannan* v. *Ramlatha*, (2005) 7 SCC 534 (requirement in and manner of complying with readiness and willingness); *Raj Kumar* v. *Dipender Kaur Sethi*, (2005) 9 SCC 304 (averment of readiness & willingness).
22. *Indira Kaur* v. *Shiv Lal Kapoor*, (1988) 2 SCC 488: AIR 1988 SC 1074.
23. *Bibi Jaibunisha* v. *Jagdish Pandit*, (1997) 4 SCC 481.
24. *Sohan Singh* v. *Sarwan Singh*, (1996) 5 SCC 759.

date of the decree.[25] If it is not so, specific performance would not be granted. It is only the vendor-defendant that can raise the plea that the plaintiff was not ready and willing to perform his part of the contract.[26] Moreover the performance of the contract must be within a reasonable time where its terms so require.[27]

There is no bar for decree for specific performance of a contract of a sale under Section 16 and a suit should be filed for the same within the period stipulated under Article 54 of Limitation Act, 1963.[28] Time is always the essence of the contract for reconveyance of the property.[29]

A distinction can be made between "*readiness*" and "*willingness*": the former means the capacity of the plaintiff to perform the contract which includes his financial position to pay the purchase price; while the latter is to be found out from his conduct, which has to be properly scrutinized for the purpose. Readiness and willingness is to be adjudged with reference to the conduct of the party and the attending circumstances.[30]

The plea that the plaintiff was not ready and willing to perform his part of the contract cannot be availed of by the purchasers from the vendor.[31]

It is sufficient for the respondent to establish that they had the capacity to pay the sale consideration. It is not necessary that they should always carry the money with them from the date of the suit till the date of the decree.[32]

The word violates in clause (*b*) incorporates in it the instances where the plaintiff acts in fraud, or in contravention of the contract or at variance with it; however, this clause, as amended, limits the meaning of the word to violation of an essential term of the contract that on his part remains to be performed.

The following are the cases[33] wherein it was held that the plaintiff was proved not to be ready and willing to perform his part of the contract.—

(1) where he had postponing sale from date to date, was short of money and never fulfilled his offer to pay part of sale transaction.[34] But money need not be ready where time is not of essence.[35]

(2) Where in a contract of reconveyance he pleaded that the transaction was a mortgage and he was willing to pay the balance after accounting and the court held it not to be a mortgage. It is obvious

25. *N.P. Thirugnanam* v. *Dr R. Jagan Mohan Rao*, (1995) 5 SCC 115.
26. *Jugraj Singh* v. *Labh Singh*, (1995) 2 SCC 31: AIR 1995 SC 945.
27. *P.R. Deb & Associates* v. *Sunanda Roy*, (1996) 4 SCC 423.
28. *Thakamma Mathew* v. *M. Azamathulla Khan*, 1993 Supp (4) SCC 492: (1993) 21 ALR 170.
29. *Bismillah Begum* v. *Rahmatullah Khan*, (1998) 2 SCC 226: (1998) 2 MLJ 6 (SC).
30. (1996) 4 SCC 526, supra; *see* also (1997) 2 SCC 200 *infra*.
31. *Jugraj Singh* v. *Labh Singh*, (1995) 2 SCC 31: AIR 1995 SC 945.
32. *Sukhbir Singh* v. *Brijpal Singh*, (1997) 2 SCC 200.
33. *See* Banerjee's (Tagore Law Lectures) *Law of Sp. Relief*, Edn. 9, 1992, p. 249.
34. *Chand Rani* v. *Kamal Rani*, (1993) 1 SCC 519: AIR 1993 SC 1742.
35. *Sohan Singh* v. *Sarwan Singh*, (1996) 5 SCC 759.

that the plaintiff was not ready and willing to pay the agreed consideration.[36]

(3) Where in a contract of reconveyance plaintiff sued in *forma pauperis* and pleaded that no sale consideration was payable by them at all and pleaded willingness to pay the sale consideration as a last alternative.[37]

(4) Where the plaintiff falsely pleaded payment of consideration and the court held that no such payment was made. The plaintiff here clearly never intended to make full payment.[38]

(5) Where plaintiff was granted time from the date of passing of the decree of trial court to perform his part of the contract but failed to deposit the required amount within the time allowed or even thereafter.[39]

(6) Where under a compromise it was agreed that in the event contemplating a sale of his share, one co-owner will give first option to the other co-owner, and when that option was given, the other co-owner in his reply questioned the very title of the co-owner-plaintiff giving notice of the option.[40]

(7) Where there was an agreement specifying period of 6 months within which plaintiff had to purchase the stamp papers, tender the balance amount of consideration and require the defendants to execute the sale deed, total inaction for two years after initial payment of a small amount as earnest money by the plaintiff would be a circumstance which would weigh against exercise of discretion for grant of specific performance of the agreement in favour of the plaintiff.[41]

Readiness and willingness cannot be treated as a straight jacket formula. The same is to be found out from facts and circumstances relevant to the intention and contract of the concerned party.[42]

As a general proposition of Law, in the case of sale of immovable property there is no presumption as to time being the essence of the contract. Even if it is not of the essence of the contract the court may infer that it is to be performed in a reasonable time if the conditions are evident (*i*) from the express terms of the contract, (*ii*) from the nature of the property and (*iii*) from the surrounding circumstances, for example: the object of making the contract.[43]

---

36. *Hasan Noorani* v. *Mohan Singh*, AIR 1974 Bom 136.
37. *Harpratap Singh* v. *S.N. Misra*, AIR 1980 All 52.
38. *Biswa Nath* v. *Janki Devi*, AIR 1978 Pat 190.
39. *N.P. Thirugnanam* v. *Dr R. Jagan Mohan Rao* , (1995) 5 SCC 115; see also *P.R. Deb & Associates* v. *Sunanda Roy*, (1996) 4 SCC 423.
40. *Bhagwan Ram* v. *Prabhu Ram*, 1983 ALJ 637.
41. *K. Vidyanadam* v. *Vairavan*, (1997) 3 SCC 1: AIR 1997 SC 1751.
42. *Ramesh Chandra* v. *Chunnilal*, (1970) 3 SCC 140: AIR 1971 SC 1238.
43. *Chand Rani* v. *Kamal Rani*, (1993) 1 SCC 519: AIR 1993 SC 1742.

In this case of sale of immovable property the document of sale contained: "Rs 98,000 only will be paid by the second party to first party within a period of ten days only". The language thus showed that the amount was to be paid before September 6, 1971. The defendant did not pay the amount and thus committed a breach. The word "only" has been used twice over (1) to qualify the amount of Rs 98,000, and (2) to qualify the period of ten days. Having qualified the amount there was no further need to qualify the same unless it be the intention of the parties to make time as the essence of the contract. Despite notices of the vendor to perform vendee's part of the stipulated amount, vendee was not willing to pay the same unless vacant delivery of possession of part of the property was given. In view of the express term of the contract coupled with the conduct of the vendee, held, time was essence of the contract and vendee was not ready and willing to perform the contract. The High Court was therefore justified in setting aside decree for specific performance granted by the trial court.[44]

The ratio of the above case is reiterated by the Supreme Court in *Bibi Jaibunisha case*.[45]

(*c*) *Persons against whom contracts may be enforced* [*Section 19*].—Specific performance of a contract may be enforced against—

(*i*) either party thereto [Section 19(*a*)]

(*ii*) a person claiming under him by a title arising subsequently to the contract, except a transferee for value who paid money in good faith and without notice of the contract [Section 19 (*b*)]

(*iii*) a person claiming under a title, which, though prior to the contract and known to the plaintiff, might have been displaced by the defendant [Section 19(*c*)]

(*iv*) the amalgamated company

(*v*) the company.

In other words as held in *Kasturi* v. *Iyyamperumal case*[46] by the Supreme Court, from a plain reading of S. 19 of the Act it is clear that this section is exhaustive on the question as to who are the parties against whom a contract for specific performance may be enforced. If one examines clauses (*a*) to (*e*) it is clear that persons seeking addition in a suit for specific performance of contract for sale who are not claiming under the vendor but are claiming adverse to the title of the vendor do not fall in any of the categories enumerated in clauses (*a*) to (*e*) of Section 19 of the Specific Relief Act.

---

44. See also *K.S. Vidyanadam* v. *Vairavan*, (1997) 3 SCC 1: AIR 1997 SC 1751.

45. *Bibi Jaibunisha* v. *Jagdish Pandit*, (1997) 4 SCC 481. But see *Kedar Nath Dhingra* v. *Kanwal Bhati*, AIR 1998 P&H 86. (Though time was essence of the contract, the vendor never agitated it. Court grants time on condition. Plaintiff fails to pay. Court dismisses suit and grants compensation of Rs 10,000 to vendor. Court can thus grant consequential order.)

46. (2005) 6 SCC 733: (2005) 3 MPLJ 261: (2005) 3 Mh LJ 1. *See* also *Vasantha Viswanathan* v. *V.K. Elayalwar*, (2001) 8 SCC 133; *Kasturi* v. *Iyyaamperumal*, (2005) 6 SCC 733 (necessary parties thereto).

13. WHEN CONTRACT CANNOT BE ENFORCED EXCEPT WITH A VARIATION (SECTION 18)

When a plaintiff sues for specific performance of a contract and the defendant sets up a defence of variation in the contract under the circumstances mentioned below, the court will not grant specific performance in favour of the plaintiff but with a variation so set up by the defendant in the following cases:

(*a*) When by (*i*) fraud, (*ii*) mistake of fact, or (*iii*) misrepresentation, the contract is in terms or effect different from what the parties agreed to or supposed it to be, or

(*b*) when the contract does not contain all the terms agreed to by the parties on the basis of which the defendant entered into the contract, or

(*c*) where the contract as framed between the parties does not produce the result calculated to produce, which may be as a result of fraud, misrepresentation, mistake or misapprehension and thus the object of the contract is rendered meaningless, or

(*d*) where the parties have, subsequently to the execution of the contract, varied its terms.

Under the circumstances, the plaintiff is put to an election, so to say, between having his suit dismissed or having the judgment with a variation set up. The contract must be in writing and one[47] thing must be noted here that as laid down in *Narain Pattor* v. *Aukhoy Narain*[48], there is a difference between a plaintiff seeking a specific performance and a defendant resisting it. In such a case the plaintiff cannot himself adduce *oral* evidence in order to get specific performance with a variation, but the defendant can resist it and adduce *parol* evidence to show that the contract does not express the real terms of the parties due to fraud, mistake, etc. Thus oral evidence can be in the latter kind of cases and not in the former.[49] However, this general principle is subject to some four exceptions.

It is a basic principle that specific performance must be of a contract in its entirety and in accordance with the exact and actual terms of the same. But where the contract does not express the real terms agreed to between the parties due to some misunderstanding or misdescription, either in respect of the quantity or quality of the subject matter, it cannot be enforced in its entirety except with a variation. Equity desires substantial fulfilment of the contract, not simply a literal one and therefore, where the essence of the contract can be enforced and performed, non-essential circumstances of little importance can be neglected and consequently it justifies a part performance of the contract. On the same principle, specific performance of a contract with a variation is allowed by the English law. It was once believed that such a sort of relief combines in itself

---

47. *Ramsbottom* v. *Gosden*, (1812) 1 Ves & B 165: 35 ER 65; *Narain Pattor* v. *Aukhoy Narain*, ILR (1886) 12 Cal 152.

48. ILR (1886) 12 Cal 152.

49. *Woollam* v. *Hearn*, 2 W & TLC 573.

more than one relief, but on the principle laid down in *Craddock Bros.* v. *Hunt*[50] and under Section 43 of the Judicature Act, 1925, a court can grant all the reliefs to a party in one action and the same principle is incorporated in Section 18 of the Specific Relief Act. In short, we may say that where a contract between the parties does not express its real intention or the object of the contract is frustrated due to not expressing it correctly, and in cases where there is a subsequent variation made to the contract by parties, the court does not treat it as if a new contract has come into existence replacing the old, but the original one exists and it can be specifically enforced with variations alleged therein and proved by the defendant by evidence adduced.

A sues *B* to compel specific performance of a contract in writing to buy a dwelling house. *B* proves that he assumes that the contract included an adjoining yard, and the contract was so framed as to leave it doubtful whether the yard was included or not. The court will refuse to enforce the contract, except with the variation set up by *B*.[51]

14. DISCRETION AND POWERS OF THE COURT (SECTIONS 20 TO 24)

That specific performance is a discretionary remedy[52] and that it will be refused where the enforcement of a contract results in hardship to the defendant or unfair advantage to the plaintiff has been discussed earlier in this chapter. It's difficult to define this field of discretion.[53]

As an important condition one may say that a party desirous of seeking such relief must come with clean hands; or else specific performance would be refused.[54] This relief is discretionary[55] and is not given merely because it is legal but it is governed by sound judicial principles. The circumstances referred to in sub-sections (2) to (4) of Section 20 in regard to exercise of discretion for granting a decree of specific performance are not exhaustive.[56] The discretion of the court has to be exercised in accordance with justice, equity and good conscience and fairness to both the parties.[57] It has to be exercised on sound, reasonable and judicial principles. Specific performance would not be granted where the court thinks that doing so, would generate injustice.[58] Of course the use of discretion

50. (1923) 2 Ch 136: 129 LT 228 (CA).
51. *C.Y. Denny* v. *Hamcock*, (1870) Ch App. 1: 23 LT 686, (where a plan furnished by the seller was misleading).
52. *A.C. Arulappan* v. *Ahalya Naik*, (2001) 6 SCC 133; *Muthusami* v. *Angammal*, (2002) 3 SCC 316; *Manohar Lal* v. *Maya*, (2003) 9 SCC 478.
53. *Satyanarayan* v. *Yellaji Rao*, AIR 1965 SC 1405.
54. *Lourdu Mari David* v. *Louis Chinnaya Arogia Swamy*, (1996) 5 SCC 589.
55. *K.G. Arumugham* v. *K.A. Chinnappan*, (2005) 2 SCC 793; *Devalsab* v. *Ibrahimsab F. Karajagi*, (2005) 3 SCC 342.
56. *Ganesh Shet* v. *Dr C.S. G.K. Setty* , (1998) 5 SCC 381.
57. *Kanshi Ram* v. *Om Prakash Jawal*, (1996) 4 SCC 593; *Surya Narayan Upadhyaya* v. *Ram Roop Pandey*, 1995 Supp (4) SCC 542.
58. *Kallithil Sreedharan* v. *Komath Pandyala Prasanna*, (1996) 6 SCC 218.

depends upon facts and circumstances of each case,[59] where granting of damages is an adequate relief, the specific performance would be refused.[60]

In *Sahadeva Gramani Case*[61] since the agreement was inchoate and vague and since there was no mutuality in agreement specific performance was rightly not granted.

In court has power to refuse this relief. Where specific performance is used as an instrument of oppression to get an unfair advantage over the other party,[62] where damages are adequate relief,[63] where the act of a third party could be regarded akin to champertous[64] and where the property in question is not identifiable,[65] the relief of specific performance would be refused.

In *Jaibunnisha case*[66] the question was about the essence of time. The court held that time is not always the essence of the contract, unless the agreement specifically stipulates and there are special facts and circumstances in support thereof. But this rule that time is not the essence of the contract in case of sale of immovable property was evolved at a time when prices and values were stable and inflation was unknown. This rule is now required to be relaxed, if not modified, particularly in case of urban immovable properties. It is high time, the courts do so.[67]

In one case there was an agreement to sell 100 years old building. The building had six tenants which affected its value. The expert valued the building between sixty to seventy thousand. An agreement for sale price of Rs 65,000 was executed and the court granted the specific performance of the agreement as it was not inequitable. In other words since the transaction had not given unfair advantage to the purchaser, its specific performance was justified.[68]

For refusal to enforce specific performance factors cumulatively or with other factors can form the basis [*see* S. 20(2), Expln. (1) & (2) and sub-sec. (4)].[69] Similarly where there is no concluded contract between the parties, a decree for specific performance could not be granted.[70]

---

59. *S. Rangaraju Naidu* v. *S. Thiruvarakkarasu*, 1995 Supp (2) SCC 680: AIR 1995 SC 1769.
60. *Prakash Chandra* v. *Angadlal*, (1979) 4 SCC 393: AIR 1979 SC 1241.
61. *Sahadeva Gramani* v. *Perumal Gramani*, (2005) 11 SCC 454.
62. *Parakunnan Veetill Joseph's Son Mathew* v. *Nedumbara Kuruvila's Son*, 1987 Supp SCC 340: AIR 1987 SC 2328.
63. *Prakash Chandra* v. *Angadlal*, supra.
64. *S.V.R. Mudaliar* v. *Rajabu F. Buhari*, (1995) 4 SCC 15: AIR 1995 SC 160.
65. *Nahar Singh* v. *Harnak Singh*, (1996) 6 SCC 699.
66. *Bibi Jaibunisha* v. *Jagdish Pandit*, (1997) 4 SCC 481.
67. *K.S. Vidyanadam* v. *Vairavan*, (1997) 3 SCC 1: AIR 1997 SC 1751.
68. *Maria Eduaria A. Gonslaves Mesquita* v. *Shripad Vishnu Kamat Tarkar*, AIR 1998 Bom 41. *See* also *Ram Khilona* v. *Sardar*, (2002) 6 SCC 375: AIR 2002 SC 2548. (Agreement executed. Thereafter 2 more marginal witnesses introduced without knowledge & consent of the vendor. Being not material alteration the validity & enforceability of the agreement is not affected.)
69. *Sen Mukherjee & Co.* v. *Shrimati Chhaya Banerjee*, AIR 1998 Cal 252.
70. *Ganesh Shet* v. *Dr C.S. G.K. Setty*, (1998) 5 SCC 381: AIR 1998 SC 2216.

The fact that considerable amount was spent by respondent on the disputed asset prior to filing the appeal or till the time of hearing of the appeal, would not it was held, render the appeal infructuous. Moreover it raises no unsurmountable equities in favour of the respondent who knew that the appeal was pending.[71] Again in a suit for specific performance of contract of sale of land under Section 20 of the Specific Relief Act, 1963, there was phenomenal increase in value of land during pendency of suit. In this case, the court observed, it would be a sufficient reason to refuse decree because there is no general rule that the plaintiff must necessarily be denied the benefit of increase. While balancing equities the court must bear in mind who is the defaulting party.[72]

In one case a question that was involved was regarding the nature of substantial question of law in case of specific performance of agreement for sale of immovable property.[73]

Normally a suit for specific performance of an agreement for sale of immovable property involves the following questions:

(*i*) Whether the plaintiff was ready and willing to perform his part of the contract in terms of Section 16 of the Specific Relief Act, 1963;

(*ii*) Whether it was a case for exercise of discretion by the court to decree specific performance in terms of Section 20 of the Act;

(*iii*) Whether there were laches on the part of the plaintiff in approaching the court to enforce specific performance of the contract;

(*iv*) Question of limitation may also arise in some cases and in others and

(*v*) Questions like the genuineness of the agreements abandoning of the right to specific performance, a novation and so on, may also arise. No doubt a finding on the above primary aspects would depend upon the appreciation of the pleadings and evidence along with surrounding circumstances. And these questions, by and large may not be questions of law of general importance. But they cannot also be considered to be pure questions of fact based on the appreciation of the evidence in the case. They are questions which have to be adjudicated upon, in the context of the relevant provisions of the Specific Relief Act and the Limitation Act (if the question of limitation is involved). Though an order in exercise of discretion may not involve a substantial question of law, the question whether a court could, in law, exercise a discretion at all for decreeing specific performance, could be a question of law that substantially affects the rights of the parties in that suit. Therefore, in this case the High Court

---

71. *Allahabad Bank* v. *Bengal Paper Mills Co. Ltd.*, (1999) 4 SCC 383: (1999) 96 Comp Cas 804.
72. *Nirmala Anand* v. *Advent Corpn. (P) Ltd.*, (2002) 8 SCC 146. See also *Mahavir Prasad Jain* v. *Ganga Singh*, (1999) 8 SCC 274 (Party abusing the process of court not entitled to equitable relief, *Gobind Ram* v. *Gian Chand*, (2000) 7 SCC 548.
73. *Rajeshwari* v. *Puran Indoria*, (2005) 7 SCC 60.

was not justified in dismissing the second appeal in the manner in which it has done.[74]

We have discussed where the court will grant specific performance or refuse it, and also where it grants the same only with a variation in the contract. It may also grant compensation in suitable cases in addition to specific performance. The section is, however, not exhaustive of all such pleas leading to dismissal of the suit for specific performance.[75] Section 21 speaks about this.

(*a*) *Compensatory Relief (Sections 21 to 24)*.—Under Section 21 the plaintiff may claim and the court may grant a compensatory relief, *i.e.*, the plaintiff may claim here compensation for breach in addition to or in substitution of such performance.[76] There may be cases wherein specific performance is *not advisable to be granted* but still however the plaintiff must be awarded compensation for the breach of the contract made by the defendant. The court will award compensation in such cases.

In *Kalyanpur Lime Works Ltd.* v. *State of Bihar*[77], a substantial part of the lease had already expired and a suit for specific performance was filed. In this case the Supreme Court refused specific performance for the lessee as it had only a few months to run and the lease would have expired by the time the contract could be specifically performed. The court here awarded compensation only to the lessee for the seven years he had been denied possession.[78]

If the court is satisfied that specific performance ought to be granted but that alone is not sufficient to satisfy the justice of the case, the court will award compensation also. Suppose *A* contracts with *B* to sell him a house for Rs 1000, the price to be paid and the possession to be given on January 1, 1877. *A* fails to perform his part and *B* brings a suit for specific performance and compensation, which is decided in his favour on January 1, 1878. The decree may besides ordering specific performance, award to *B* compensation for any loss which he has sustained by *A*'s refusal. This is aptly explained by sub-section (3) of this section.

For deciding compensation principles laid down in Section 73 of the Indian Contract Act will apply, but the plaintiff has to claim it. In suitable cases the court will allow him to amend the plaint for including such a claim. The explanation added to the section points to the situation wherein there is a departure from the English law. English law provided that damages cannot be awarded where specific performance was impossible. But the plain words in the section leave no doubt that compensation can be awarded even where specific

---

74. *Rajeshwari* v. *Puran Indoria*, (2005) 7 SCC 60. (paras 5 & 6).
75. *Faujmal* v. *Nathumal*, AIR 1965 Raj 115.
76. *Jagdish Singh* v. *Natthu Singh*, (1992) 1 SCC 647: AIR 1992 SC 1604.
77. AIR 1954 SC 165.
78. See also *Food Corporation of India* v. *Babulal Agarwal*, AIR 1998 MP 23 wherein court awarded damages as the specific performance was not possible due to expiry of stipulated period. For facts *see* Para 11 (*l*), *supra*. *See* also *State Bank of Saurashtra* v. *Punjab National Bank*, (2001) 5 SCC 751: (2001) 105 Comp Cas 852 (Return of money with interest and award of reasonable damages.)

performance is impossible and in several cases such compensation has been awarded. But a plaintiff cannot by his own act make the specific performance impossible and proceed to claim damages.[79]

(*b*) *Other reliefs*.—The object of Section 21 is to prevent multiplicity of proceedings. Reading this section with Section 24 it follows that a dismissal of the suit for specific performance of a contract or its part thereof shall be a bar for the plaintiff's right to sue for compensation for the breach of such contract or its part. But it does not close the doors for any other relief to which a plaintiff may be entitled by reason of the breach.

Section 22 which is a new section introduced by the Act is also there to avoid multiplicity of proceedings.[80] The section incorporates a rule settled by judicial decisions that the plaintiff in a suit for specific performance may claim a decree for possession even though the right to possession strictly speaking accrues only when specific performance is decreed. Under the section, in suitable cases, the court may direct a refund for earnest money while refusing specific performance. Sub-section (2) gives effect to this rule. Sub-section (3) provides that the court's power under clause (*b*) is without prejudice to its power to award compensation under Section 21.

(*c*) *Liquidation of damages not a bar to specific performance*.—What is agreed by the parties to be done must be done even if a penalty for its non-performance is attached thereto, because liquidation of damages is not an option granted to the other party to perform a contract or not to perform it. This is the principle of equity incorporated in the section. In *Long* v. *Bowrin*[81], *A* contracts with *B* to grant him an underlease of property held by *A* under *C* and that he will apply to *C* for the necessary licence to validate the underlease. If licence is not procured, *A* is to pay *B* Rs 10,000. Now *A* refuses to apply for licence and offers to pay *B* the amount of Rs 10,000. *B* is nevertheless entitled to have the contract specifically enforced if *C* consents to give the licence. Contracts are made to be performed, not to be broken and evade their liabilities. Naming a particular sum, even if it is *in terrorem*, is to secure its performance and therefore the courts will enforce its specific performance.

Section 25 read with Section 43 of the Act provides that the provisions of this chapter apply to enforcement of awards also.

---

79. *A.V.V. Co-op. Housing Society Ltd.* v. *K.K. A. Deo*, AIR 1991 Bom 129.
80. *Babu Lal* v. *Hazari Lal Kishori Lal*, (1982) 1 SCC 525: (1982) ALJ 345.
81. (1864) 33 Beav 585: 10 LT 683.

Chapter XXV

Rectification, Rescission, Cancellation and Declaration

"The remedy of rectification exists to correct, but not to improve an instrument."

—*Whiteside* v. *Whiteside*, 1950 Ch 65: [1949] 2 All ER 913 (CA)

"Rescission is. . . not strictly a judicial remedy but the act of a party entitled to rescind." . . . It is "a right which a party to a transaction sometimes has to set the transaction aside and restore to its former position."

—*Snell's Principles of Equity*, Part VI

"The relief as to cancellation of an instrument is founded upon the administration of the protective justice for fear that the instrument may be vexatiously or injuriously used by the defendant against the plaintiff when the evidence to impeach it may be lost or that it may throw a cloud of suspicion over his title or interest."

—*Jeka Dula* v. *Bai Jivi*, 39 Bom LR 1072: AIR 1938 Bom 37

"A declaratory decree creates no new rights; it only declares what was plaintiff's right before. It is a non-coercive declaration. In many cases a declaration is inherent in the grant of an injunction."

—T.R. Desai: Principles of Equity 8th edn., 1959, p. 231; Hanbury: Modern Equity, para 2, p. 81; *Indumatiben* v. *Union of India*, AIR 1969 Bom 423, cited in Mulla: Indian Contract and Specific Relief Acts, 9th edn., 1972, p. 911

SYNOPSIS

C. *Cancellation (Sections 31 to 33)*
1. Meaning
2. Object of Cancellation
3. What can be Cancelled
4. Illustrations
5. What a Plaintiff must Prove
6. Rectification, Rescission and Cancellation: A Comparison
7. Minor's position

D. *Declaration (Sections 34 and 35)*
1. Meaning
2. Origin and Object of the Provision
3. Essentials for the Relief
4. Use of Declarations and Injunctions
5. Declaration when Refused
6. Merely Declaratory Decree
7. Illustrations
8. Effect of Declaration (Section 35)

Text of Sections 26 to 35

Rectification of Instruments

26. When instrument may be rectified.—(1) When, through fraud or a mutual mistake of the parties, a contract or other instrument in writing [not being the articles of association of a company to which the Companies Act, 1956 (1 of 1956), applies] does not express their real intention, then—

(*a*) either party or his representative in interest may institute a suit to have the instrument rectified; or

(*b*) the plaintiff may, in any suit in which any right arising under the instrument is in issue, claim in his pleading that the instrument be rectified; or

(*c*) a defendant in any such suit as is referred to in clause (*b*), may, in addition to any other defence open to him, ask for rectification of the instrument.

(2) If, any suit in which a contract or other instrument is sought to be rectified under sub-section (1), the court finds that the instrument, through fraud or mistake, does not express the real intention of the parties, the court may, in its discretion, direct rectification of the instrument so as to express that intention, so far as this can be done without prejudice to rights acquired by third persons in good faith and for value.

(3) A contract in writing may first be rectified, and then if the party claiming rectification has so prayed in his pleading and the court thinks fit, may be specifically enforced.

(4) No relief for the rectification of an instrument shall be granted to any party under this section unless it has been specifically claimed:

Provided that where a party has not claimed any such relief in his pleading, the court shall, at any stage of the proceeding, allow him to amend the pleading on such terms as may be just for including such claim.

Rescission of Contracts

27. When rescission may be adjudged or refused.—(1) Any person interested in a contract may sue to have it rescinded, and such rescission may be adjudged by the court in any of the following cases, namely—

(*a*) where the contract is voidable or terminable by the plaintiff;

(*b*) where the contract is unlawful for causes not apparent on its face and the defendant is more to blame than the plaintiff.

(2) Notwithstanding anything contained in sub-section (1), the court may refuse to rescind the contract—

(*a*) where the plaintiff has expressly or impliedly ratified the contract; or

(*b*) where, owing to the change of circumstances which has taken place since the making of the contract (not being due to any act of the defendant himself), the parties cannot be substantially restored to the position in which they stood when the contract was made; or

(*c*) where third parties have, during the subsistence of the contract, acquired rights in good faith without notice and for value; or

(*d*) where only a part of the contract is sought to be rescinded and such part is not severable from the rest of the contract.

Explanation.—In this section "contract", in relation to the territories to which the Transfer of Property Act, 1882 (4 of 1882), does not extend, means a contract in writing.

28. Rescission in certain circumstances of contracts for the sale or lease of immovable property, the specific performance of which has been decreed.—(1) Where in any suit a decree for specific performance of a contract for the sale or lease of immovable property has been made and purchaser or lessee does not, within the period allowed by the decree or such further period as the court may allow, pay the purchase money or other sum which the court has ordered him to pay, the vendor or lessor may apply in the same suit in which the decree is made, to have the contract rescinded and on such application the court may, by order, rescind the contract either so far as regards the party in default or altogether, as the justice of the case may require.

(2) Where a contract is rescinded under sub-section (1), the court—

(*a*) shall direct the purchaser or lessee, if he has obtained possession of the property under the contract, to restore such possession to the vendor or lessor, and

(*b*) may direct payment to the vendor or lessor of all the rents and profits which have accrued in respect of the property from the date on which possession was so obtained by the purchaser or lessee until restoration of possession to the vendor or lessor, and, if the justice of the case so requires, the refund of any sum paid by the vendee or lessee as earnest money or deposit in connection with the contract.

(3) If the purchaser or lessee pays the purchase money or other sum which he is ordered to pay under the decree within the period referred to in sub-section (1), the court may, on application made in the same suit, award the purchaser or lessee such further relief as he may be entitled to, including in appropriate cases all or any of the following reliefs, namely—

(*a*) the execution of a proper conveyance or lease by the vendor or lessor;

(*b*) the delivery of possession, or partition and separate possession, of the property on the execution of such conveyance or lease.

(4) No separate suit in respect of any relief which may be claimed under this section shall lie at the instance of a vendor, purchaser, lessor or lessee, as the case may be.

(5) The costs of any proceedings under this section shall be in the discretion of the court.

29. Alternative prayer for rescission in suit for specific performance.—A plaintiff instituting a suit for the specific performance of a contract in writing may pray in the alternative that if the contract cannot be specifically enforced, it may be rescinded and delivered up to be cancelled; and the court, if it refuses to enforce the contract specifically, may direct it to be rescinded and delivered up accordingly.

30. Court may require parties rescinding to do equity.—On adjudging the rescission of a contract, the court may require the party to whom such relief is granted to restore, so far as may be, any benefit which he may have received from the other party and to make any compensation to him which justice may require.

Cancellation of Instruments

31. When cancellation may be ordered.—(1) Any person against whom a written instrument is void or voidable, and who has reasonable apprehension that such instrument, if left outstanding may cause him serious injury, may sue to have it, adjudged void or voidable; and the court may, in its discretion, so adjudge it and order it to be delivered up and cancelled.

(2) If the instrument has been registered under the Indian Registration Act, 1908 (16 of 1908), the court shall also send a copy of its decree to the officer in whose office the instrument

has been so registered; and such officer shall note on the copy of the instrument contained in his books the fact of its cancellation.

32. What instruments may be partially cancelled.—Where an instrument is evidence of different rights or different obligations, the court may, in a proper case, cancel it in part and allow it to stand for the residue.

33. Power to require benefit to be restored or compensation to be made when instrument is cancelled or is successfully resisted as being void or voidable.—(1) On adjudging the cancellation of an instrument, the court may require the party to whom such relief is granted, to restore, so far as may be, any benefit which he may have received from the other party and to make any compensation to him which justice may require.

(2) Where a defendant successfully resists any suit on the ground—

(*a*) that the instrument sought to be enforced against him in the suit is voidable, the court may, if the defendant has received any benefit under the instrument from the other party, require him to restore, so far as may be, such benefit to that party or to make compensation for it;

(*b*) that the agreement sought to be enforced against him in the suit is void by reason of his not having been competent to contract under Section 11 of the Indian Contract Act, 1872 (9 of 1872), the court may, if the defendant has received any benefit under the agreement from the other party, require him to restore, so far as may be, such benefit to that party, to the extent to which he or his estate has benefited thereby.

Declaratory Decrees

34. Discretion of court as to declaration of status or right.—Any person entitled to any legal character, or to any right as to any property, may institute a suit against any person denying or interested to deny, his title to such character or right, and the court may in its discretion make therein a declaration that he is so entitled, and the plaintiff need not in such suit ask for any further relief:

Provided that no court shall make any such declaration where the plaintiff, being able to seek further relief than a mere declaration of title, omits to do so.

Explanation.—A trustee of property is a "person interested to deny" a title adverse to the title of someone who is not in existence, and for whom, if in existence, he would be a trustee.

35. Effect of declaration.—A declaration made under this Chapter is binding only on the parties to the suit, persons claiming through them respectively, and where any of the parties are trustees, on the persons for whom, if in existence at the date of the declaration such parties would be trustees.

A. RECTIFICATION (SECTION 26)

1. Nature of Rectification

If by mistake a written instrument does not accord with the true agreement between the parties, equity has power to reform or rectify that instrument so as to make it in accord with the true agreement. What is rectified is not a mistake in the transaction itself, but a mistake in the way in which that transaction has been expressed in writing.[1] "Courts of equity do not rectify contracts; they may and do rectify instruments purporting to have been made in pursuance of the terms of contracts."[2]

1. *Frederick E. Rose (London) Ltd.* v. *William H. Pim Jur. & Co. Ltd.*, (1953) 2 QB 450.
2. *Mackenzie* v. *Coulson*, (1869) LR 8 Eq 368, cited in *Snell's Principles of Equity*, Part VII, Chap. 4, p. 610.

As expressed in *Whiteside case*[3] by Evershed, M.R., rectification is a discretionary remedy "which must be cautiously watched and jealously guarded". But unlike remedies such as specific performance, which are based on the inadequacy of the remedy at law, rectification "gives relief from the inflexibility of the common law, and from the nature of the case involves a contravention of its terms".[4] As laid down in *Fowler* v. *Fowler*[5], oral evidence is admissible to prove the agreement and there is no need to show anything in the nature of error on the face of the instrument; but the evidence of the agreement must be compelling. The crux of the remedy is proof of what the parties had actually decided at the time of reaching their agreement and not what they, or one of them, had thought at a later date, or what they might have thought if they had considered the matter in greater detail or in the light of more information than that available to them. In other words, the remedy exists to correct, but not to improve, an instrument.[6]

2. What is Rectification

As pointed out by Hanbury[7], rectification of an instrument is a distinct equitable remedy, based on the facts of an instrument not according with the intentions of the parties to it. It must be very clearly shown that the parties had come to a final and genuine agreement and that the instrument had failed to record it.

As expressed in *Sudha Singh* v. *Munshi Ram*[8], the principle on which the court acts in correcting instruments, is that the parties, are to be placed in the position as that in which they would have store if no error had been committed.

3. Conditions to be satisfied

Mulla presents the position very lucidly and succinctly, that in a proper case the court will amend the language of an instrument for the purpose of making it accord with the true intention of the parties, having ascertained:—

(*i*) what that intention was, and also

(*ii*) that the words as they stand fail to express it.

Rectification cannot be adjudged unless the court is satisfied on both these points.[9]

According to Snell, (*i*) there must be a mistake sufficient to invoke the doctrine, (*ii*) there must be "strong irrefragable evidence"[10] which means that

---

3. *Whiteside* v. *Whiteside*, 1950 Ch 65: [1949] 2 All ER 913 (CA).
4. *Thompson* v. *Hickman*, 76 LJ Ch 254: (1907) 1 Ch 550, 562 per Neville, J.
5. (1859) 4 De G&J 250: 45 ER 97.
6. *Whiteside* v. *Whiteside*, 1950 Ch 65: (1949) 2 All ER 913 (CA).
7. *Modern Equity*, 9th Edn., 1969, p. 661.
8. AIR 1927 Cal 605.
9. Pollock and Mulla: *Indian Contract Act and Specific Relief Act*, 9th Edn., 1972, p. 888; *Snell's Principles of Equity*, pp. 610-619.
10. *Countess of Shelburne*, (1784) 1 Bro CC 338.

there must be "something more than the highest degree of probability".[11] There must be evidence "of the clearest and the most satisfactory description", that will establish the mistake with a "high degree of conviction" and "leave no fair and reasonable doubt upon the mind that the deed does not embody the final intention of the parties". In short, there must be a "convincing proof"[12] of the mistake on the part of the parties. Lastly, (*iii*) there must be absence of alternative remedy. Rectification will not be decreed if the desired result can conveniently be achieved by other means. Thus the material which is sought to be inserted in the written instrument may itself be enforceable as a collateral contract. Again, if those concerned voluntarily rectify the instrument, the court will not decree rectification, even if such a decree would, by operating retrospectively, have fiscal advantages which the voluntary rectification lacks.[13]

There is no need, as Pollock and Mulla observe,[14] to invoke this jurisdiction in case of verbal slips and omissions as are obvious on the face of the writing and can be corrected by the context alone. The remedy of these minor blunders is within the court's ordinary function of construing the expressions used. Even a missing clause (reference to counterpart) can be supplied in an instrument of a well-known form if the sense clearly requires it.

It must be noted that both the preliminary and the finally executed agreement can be rectified and an unskillfully drafted instrument not expressing the real intention of the parties may also be reformed. The proximate origin of mistake lies in the carelessness or want of skill of the draftsman but when the mistake has crept in due to concealment or non-disclosure which defeats the real intention, the party in default will not be allowed to plead that his intention in concealment or non-disclosure was different.

4. When an Instrument may be Rectified (Section 26)

As the section on rectification goes, to avail of this right one has to establish that there had been cause for not truly expressing the real intention of the parties. This relief is to be specifically claimed. Unilateral mistake is no ground for rectification unless there was fraud. To prove fraud or mistake, oral evidence is admissible. It has been however the usage of the English courts of equity that a written instrument will not be allowed to be rectified on oral evidence alone when the alleged mistake is positively denied by the defendant.[15] The Indian practice is also the same as the court has to be satisfied before an order for rectification can be made. Rectification may take place at the instance of either party or their representatives, or by a plaintiff or defendant in any suit, or by the

11. *Fowler* v. *Fowler*, (1859) 4 De G&J 250: 45 ER 97.
12. *Joscelyne* v. *Nissen*, (1970) 2 QB 86; *Lloyd* v. *Stanbury*, (1971) 1 WLR 535: (1971) 2 All ER 267 (Ch D).
13. See *Whiteside case* cited above, wherein rectification was refused of a convenant that mistakenly used the phrase "free of tax" over which the parties had never come to an actual agreement.— *Whiteside* v. *Whiteside*, 1950 Ch 65: [1949] 2 All ER 913 (CA). See also Hanbury: *Modern Equity*, pp. 661-662.
14. *Indian Contract Act and Specific Relief Act*, p. 888
15. Pollock and Mulla: *Indian Contract Act and Specific Relief Act*, citing *Clark* v. *Barnes*, (1929) 2 Ch 368.

court in its own discretion. The rectified contract will be enforced if so prayed by the plaintiff. The material question in rectification is what the parties intended to express and not what they "always intended".

In *Allarakhia case* a steamer was chartered by the plaintiff to sail from Jeddah on 10th August, 1892 (15 days after the Haj) in order to transport pilgrims returning to Bombay. The plaintiffs believed that 10th August, 1892 corresponded with the fifteenth day after the Haj. The defendants had no belief on the subject. They contracted with respect to the English date. In fact 10th August, 1892 did not, but 19th July, 1892 corresponded with the fifteenth day after the Haj. On finding out his mistake the plaintiffs sued the defendants for rectification of the charter party. The court held that the agreement was one for 10th August, 1892 and that the mistake was not mutual. It was one-sided, i.e. on plaintiff's part alone. The document therefore could not be rectified. Even if both the parties were under the mistake the court would not rectify but only cancel the instrument as the agreement was one for 10-8-1892, and that date was a matter materially inducing the agreement.[16]

A intending to sell his house to *B* and one of the three godowns adjacent to it, executes a conveyance prepared by *B*. Through *B*'s fraud all the three godowns are included in the instrument. Of the two godowns so included fraudulently *B* gives one to *C* and lets the other to *D* for rent. *C* and *D* do not know of the fraud of *B*. The conveyance as against *B* and *C* may be rectified so as to exclude from it the godown given to *C*, but it cannot be rectified so as to affect *D*'s lease.[17]

5. Exceptions

The illustration above explains that an instrument will not be rectified so as to prejudice the rights acquired by third parties in good faith and for value.[18]

6. What Instruments are Rectified

Any instrument can be rectified. Snell[19] has given a long list of such instruments, but as the section lays down, articles of association of a company cannot be rectified because the articles are a contract between the company and its shareholders, and *ex hypothesi* the company cannot have had a different intention before incorporation. Nor is there any power to rectify a will short of fraud. One must note that for a mistake of law rectification is available. So far as Section 26 is concerned, the court will allow rectification of an instrument so as to bring the legal consequences into conformity with those intended by the parties. This is the limit of rectification and the court will not allow it to be abused.

---

16. *Haji Abdul Rehman Allarakhia* v. *Bombay & Persia Steam Navigation Co.*, (1892) 16 Bom 56.
17. Illustration to Section 31 of the former Act of 1877; *Ladha Singh* v. *Munshiram*, 13 CWN 717: AIR 1927 Cal 605.
18. Cf. *Mahadeva Aiyar* v. *Gopala Aiyar*, (1911) 34 Mad 51: 8 IC 390.
19. *Snell's Principles of Equity*, p. 617

The words in Section 26(1) "other instrument", as observed in *CIT* v. *Kamla Town Trust*[20] include a trust deed and therefore a civil court has jurisdiction to entertain suit for rectification of a trust deed.

7. Time limit

As decided in *Geerda Kahta* v. *Dharmeswar Saikia*[21], a party can file a suit for rectification at any time when fraud is discovered or a mistake has come to light.

8. Defences

Laches and acquiesence will bar a suit for rectification. Besides, where the remedy sought is found to be inequitable and where it is too late to claim it, as when a rectified contract is no longer capable of performance, the court will not order rectification.

The decree of rectification will have retrospective force. The document has to be read as if it had been originally drawn in its rectified form.[22]

B. RESCISSION (SECTIONS 27 TO 30)

1. General

It is but common sense that a voidable contract cannot be avoided or challenged at the suit of the guilty party, but the innocent party who has become the victim of the transaction and therefore does not affirm the contract but challenges it in order to avoid it, can plead defences that vitiate and render the contract voidable. Under the circumstances, and at the instance of such a party, a court may grant him a remedy of rescission which relieves him of all the obligations of the contract. *Rescission is thus the converse of specific performance*. A right of rescission is not assignable.

2. Nature and Meaning

To rescind, therefore, is "to make of no effect". Rescission is an equitable remedy which is converse to that of specific performance. It is "a right which a party to a transaction sometimes has to set the transaction aside and restored to his former position".[23]

Rescission is thus not strictly a judicial remedy but the act of a party entitled to rescind. In affecting rescission assistance of the court is necessary to decide whether a party is entitled to rescind and to obtain restitution of property handed over pursuant to the transaction. This being an equitable remedy only, a court of equity could do what was necessary to make restitution, *e.g.*, take accounts and make allowances for deterioration in the property dealt with by the contract.[24] Equity therefore intervenes to rescind a contract only on substantial grounds.

---

20. (1996) 7 SCC 349: (1996) 217 ITR 699.
21. AIR 1961 Ass 14.
22. *Craddock Bros.* v. *Hunt*, (1923) 2 Ch 136: 129 LT 228 (CA).
23. *Snell's Principles of Equity*, 27th Edn., 1973, Part VII, Chap. 2, p. 601.
24. *Ibid.*

While adjudging rescission of contract the court is concerned with the question whether the person rescinding the contract was justified in doing so. The court does not create any right which parties did not possess when it makes a declaration that contract has been validly rescinded. The court, one must note, does not rescind the contract. The court is only passing upon the validity of the rescission already made by the party.[25]

3. Grounds for Rescission

Rescission can be adjudged on the grounds of voidability of the contract which includes the following: mistake, misrepresentation, constructive fraud and fraudulent misrepresentation. In case of a contract *Uberrimae fidei* and where there is a term in a contract for its rescission, it can be rescinded. But the right to rescission is lost on account of acquiescence of the plaintiff, on account of impossibility of *restitutio integram*, and due to intervention of third parties in the contract.

The Specific Relief Act, Sections 27 to 30, deals with rescission.

4. Rescission when Adjudged (Sections 27, 28 and 29)

Any person interested in a contract may sue to have it rescinded and the court may adjudge it in the following cases:

(*a*) *Where the contract is voidable or terminable by the plaintiff [Section 27(1)(a)*].—A contract, as we have seen, becomes voidable on account of mistake, misrepresentation, fraud, coercion and undue influence and the party who becomes its victim can avoid it.

Moreover, a contract may contain within itself a term whereby it becomes terminable as when (*i*) a vendor fails to show a good title to the property in question, or (*ii*) when the purchaser fails to pay consideration within a stipulated period. Such contracts are terminable and therefore may be put to an end by the plaintiff and are therefore rescindable.

(*b*) *Where the contract is unlawful for causes not apparent on its face and the defendant is more to blame than the plaintiff [Section 27(1)(b)*].—Where such unlawfulness arises, the maxims *in pari delicto potier est conditio defendantis* and *ex turpi causa non oritur actio* may operate. Moreover, necessity of clean hands will be insisted upon by the court. But even in such cases it is possible that the defendant is more to blame than the plaintiff as when the plaintiff has been the victim of the defendant's oppression, imposition, undue influence and great inequality and hardship due to his age or particular mental condition.

Where *A*, an attorney, induces his client *B*, a Hindu widow, to transfer property to him for the purpose of defrauding *B*'s creditors, the contract can be rescinded at the instance of *B* and here *A*, the attorney and *B*, his client are not on equal level; not only so, *A* is more to be blamed as his fault is greater and

25. *Hungerford Investment Trust Ltd.* v. *Haridas Mundhra*, (1972) 3 SCC 684: (1972) 3 SCR 690.

more serious than that of his client. As decided in *Hari Balkrishna Joglekar* v. *Naro Moreshwar Joglekar*[26] the provisions of this clause do not apply if the parties are in *pari delicto*.

(*c*) *Where in a contract for the sale or lease of immovable property a decree for specific performance is made* and the decree made grants a time to the purchaser or lessee[27] to pay the purchase money or other sum to which he does not comply, the vendor or lessor may apply to have the contract rescinded, and the court may rescind the contract. [Section 28(1)]

(*d*) *Where there is an alternative prayer for rescission (Section 29).*—Where, a suit for specific performance is instituted, a plaintiff may pray in the alternative to rescind the contract and deliver it up for cancellation if it cannot be specifically performed, and the court may order accordingly.

The words in Section 28(1) "in the same suit" mean in the suit itself, i.e. on the original side and not in the execution proceedings. An appeal is a continuation of the suit. After passing the decree for specific performance, the court does not cease to have any jurisdiction. It retains control over the decree even after the decree has been passed. It is open to court to exercise the power under Section 28(1) of the Act either for extension of time or for rescinding the contract as claimed.[28]

5. Refusal for Rescission [Section 27(2)]

In the following cases the court will refuse rescission—

(*i*) where the plaintiff has expressly or impliedly ratified the contract; or

(*ii*) where parties cannot be restored to their original position in which they were at the time the contract was made; or

(*iii*) where third parties have, during the subsistence of the contract, acquired rights in good faith, without notice and for value; or

(*iv*) where only a part of the contract is sought to be rescinded and it is not severable from the rest of the contract.

As noted by Mulla, the sub-clauses of sub-section (2) are a statutory recognition of the case law on the subject.[29]

6. Important Aspects and Effects of Rescission[30]

(*a*) *Damages cannot be recovered.*—A party to a contract may commit such a breach as goes to the root of the contract and releases the other party from his obligation to perform his part. The party so discharged from his obligation may

---

26. ILR (1894) 18 Bom 342.
27. See *Yeshoda* v. *K. Nagarajan*, (1996) 11 SCC 228; *Sardar Mohar Singh* v. *Mangilal*, (1997) 9 SCC 217; *Mohd. Alimuddin* v. *Waizuddin*, (1998) 9 SCC 108: AIR 1997 SC 1995 (Court may extend time for payment.)
28. *Ramankutty Guptan* v. *Avara*, (1994) 2 SCC 642: (1994) 2 MLJ 52 (SC): (1994) 1 GLH 416.
29. *B. Ganapati* v. *S. Rajaram*, AIR 1974 Bom 104; Pollock and Mulla: *Indian Contract Act and Specific Relief Act*, 9th Edn., 1952, p. 895
30. Based on *Snell's Principles of Equity*, pp. 601-607.

yet recover damages for the breach[31], but a party who has rescinded a contract cannot recover damages.

In *Kumar Dhirendra Mullick* v. *Tivoli Park Apartments* (*P*) *Ltd.*[32] the question was regarding the reason for rescission of contract for sale of immovable property. There was increase in value of the property after contract. The court ruled that it has to consider the circumstances prevalent when parties entered into agreements concerned and increase in value of property was not a relevant point to be considered.

(*b*) *Intervention of third parties a bar to rescission.*—A contract void for mistake is void *ab initio.*[33] A contract which a party may rescind is valid unless and until it is rescinded. This is important when third parties have acquired rights under the contract, for this will bar the right to rescission and restitution of property. [Section 27(2)(*c*)]

(*c*) *Restitution in Integrum is possible.*—In illegal contracts, the two maxims *in pari delicto potior est conditio defendantis* and *ex turpi causa non oritur actio* may operate to prevent any restitution of property. On the other hand, a party rescinding a contract is entitled to recover and is bound to restore property which has passed pursuant to the contract. Thus no restitution is possible where restoration and restitution of property passed under the contract is impossible. [Section 28(2)(*b*)]

A enters into a contract with *B* for purchase of goods under a misrepresentation practised by *B*. *A* sells away the goods or consumes them. He cannot get rescission of the contract as restoration of the property to *B* is now impossible.

(*d*) Relief of rescission may be prayed for in the alternative in a suit for specific performance of contract (Section 29), but a person suing for rescission cannot in the alternative sue for specific performance.[34] But if third parties have acquired rights in good faith, for value and without notice, during the subsistence of the contract before its rescission, the same cannot be allowed. [Section 27(2)(*c*)].

(*e*) While granting this relief the court may require the party to whom such relief is granted to do equity, by restoring so far as may be any benefit which he may have received from the other party and to make any compensation to him which justice may require (Section 30). This is on the principle that he who seeks equity must do equity. Thus in case of sale of property, if the vendor has obtained earnest money and the contract is rescinded at his instance, he will be ordered to refund the earnest money received by him. But where a contract is rescinded on account of the purchaser's default, the vendor may forfeit[35] and retain the deposit already received. Here one must note that the vendor cannot

31. *Harold Wood Brick Co. Ltd.* v. *Ferris*, (1935) 2 KB 198: 153 LT 241.
32. (2005) 9 SCC 262.
33. *Cundy* v. *Lindsay*, (1878) 3 App Cas 459: 38 LT 573.
34. *Prem Raj* v. *D.L.F. Housing and Construction* (*P*) *Ltd.*, AIR 1968 SC 1355.
35. *Anandilal Poddar* v. *Gunendra Kr. Roy*, AIR 1966 Cal 107.

recover any unpaid part of the deposit, for it is one thing to forfeit money paid as a pledge and another to seek to enforce an obligation under a contract that has been rescinded.[36]

(*f*) The effect of rescission is restoration of the plaintiff to his original position as if the contract *had not been made*. Consequently, property must be returned, possession given up, and accounts taken of profits or deterioration. But no damages are recoverable because the purpose of damages is to put the party recovering them in the same position (so far as money can do it) as he would have been, *had the contract not been carried out*.[37]

C. CANCELLATION (SECTIONS 31 TO 33)

1. Meaning

The equitable relief of cancellation of an instrument is based on the maxim "he who seeks equity must be prepared to do equity". To cancel has as its first meaning the "removal of written character or other form of record". It literally means to cross out.[38] We may say that a document by cancellation is made inoperative and invalid. It is different from rescission wherein operation of a document is put to an end.

2. Object of Cancellation

The relief as to cancellation of an instrument is founded upon the administration of protective justice, for fear that the instrument may be vexatiously or injuriously used by the defendant against the plaintiff when the evidence to impeach it may be lost or that it may throw a cloud of suspicion over his title or interest.[39] In words of Snell,[40] "its mere existence may nevertheless be embarrassing, e.g., lest some claim be founded upon it, or some third party be deceived by it. This would be done even if the document was wholly void at law, unless the defect appeared on the face of the document, so that it carried its own refutation and there was no need for equity to intervene".[41] In other words, if the instrument is left outstanding it will cause injury to the plaintiff.[42] Sections 31 to 33 make provisions for cancellation.

3. What can be Cancelled

For these reasons, a conveyance made for immoral consideration, a guarantee procured by misrepresentation, a loan made on unconscionable terms, a lease granted at a low rent mistakenly by the lessor which the lessee knew, or where there is a forged document or a conveyance which may endanger a title, or where a document initially valid becomes subsequently ineffective, e.g., by

36. *Lowe* v. *Hope*, 1970 Ch 94: (1969) 3 All ER 605 (Ch D).
37. *Snell's Principles of Equity*, p. 607.
38. Funk and Wagnall: *Standard Handbook of Synonyms, Antonyms and Prepositions*, p. 107.
39. *Jeka Dula* v. *Bai Jivi*, AIR 1938 Bom 37: 39 Bom LR 1072.
40. *Snell's Principles of Equity*, p. 608.
41. *Simpson* v. *Howden (Lord)*, (1837) 3 My & Cr 97: 6 LJ Ch 315.
42. AIR 1923 Mad 109.

release or breaking off the engagement for marriage in contemplation of which it was executed, may be cancelled at the instance of the party to whom it will cause injury.

But it must be noted that mere speculation as to unknown and vague complications arising in the future is hardly any ground for cancellation.[43]

Section 31 of the Specific Relief Act is not limited to a suit for cancellation of a written contract only. It covers a case where a person against whom a written instrument, be it a contract or deed of sale or a deed of trust or any other kind of written instrument, is void or voidable which is sought to be adjudged void or voidable and cancelled.[44]

In other words relief of cancellation would be available when (1) an instrument is void or voidable against the plaintiff; (2) where the plaintiff may apprehend serious injury if the instrument is left outstanding and (3) where it is proper under the circumstances to grant the relief.

As decided in *Cooper* v. *Phibbs*[45], a document vitiated by mutual mistake being a mistake of private rights of the parties, and a document executed under undue influence as was the case in *Huguenin* v. *Baseley*[46] (wherein a widow plaintiff made a voluntary settlement in favour of a clergy), were likewise ordered to be cancelled. But in *Stapilton case*[47], a family arrangement made by a document was not disturbed because equity looks upon such arrangements with favour.

4. Illustrations

(*a*) *A*, the owner of a ship, by fraudulently representing her to be seaworthy, induces *B*, an underwriter, to insure her. *B* may obtain the cancellation of the policy. (Section 31)

(*b*) *A* draws a bill on *B*, *B* endorses it to *C* by whom it appears to be endorsed to *D*, who endorses it to *E*. *C*'s endorsement is forged. *C* is entitled to have such endorsement cancelled, leaving the bill to stand in other respects. (Section 32)

Sections 31 and 32 state that a document can be cancelled *in toto* or in totality, or in suitable cases where it is evidence of different rights or different obligations, it may be cancelled in part and be allowed to stand for the residue. But in case of its cancellation, the party who obtains such relief has to restore so far as may be any benefit which he may have received from the other party and to make any compensation to him which the justice of the case may require. (Section 33)

---

43. *Jeka Dula* v. *Bai Jivi*, AIR 1938 Bom 37: 174 IC 24 (DB): 39 Bom LR 1072.
44. *Manick Lal* v. *Shiva Jute Bailing*, (1948) 52 Cal WN 389.
45. (1867) LR 2 HL 149: 16 LT 678.
46. (1807) 14 Ves 237.
47. *Stapilton* v. *Stapilton*, (1739) 1 Atk 2.

5. What a Plaintiff must Prove

To be entitled for the decree of cancellation a plaintiff may have to show—

(*a*) that it is void or voidable against him under one or the other sections of the Contract Act. One has to note that the person seeking such a cancellation need not be a party to it[48], i.e., the relief may be obtained not only by a party to the instrument but by any person against whom the instrument is void or voidable. Thus if the creditors of a party are defrauded, defeated or delayed, any creditor may sue on behalf of himself and all others.[49] When a person seeking cancellation is not a party to it, the provisions of the Contract Act do not come into play.[50]

(*b*) that the plaintiff has reasonable apprehension that the instrument if left outstanding may cause him serious injury.

Whether "*reasonable apprehension* of serious injury" exists or not can be decided from the circumstances of the particular case with which the court is to deal[51], and the apprehension of a party being sued on convenants in a conveyance apparently binding is "*reasonable apprehension* of serious injury" within the meaning of this section.[52]

(*c*) that the court ought under the circumstances of the case and in exercise of its discretion order the instrument to be delivered up and cancelled. The court has full discretion to order cancellation whether the plaintiff expressly asks for it or not, and therefore the suit is in no case merely declaratory.[53]

6. Rectification, Rescission and Cancellation: A Comparison

It will be fruitful to note here the points of similarities and differences.

(*a*) In so far as rescission and cancellation are concerned, the question at issue in both is whether or not the contract or the instrument is void or voidable.

(*b*) While rescission is "to make of no effect", cancellation is the removal of written character or other form of record. In other words, by rescission the operation of a document is put to an end while in cancellation the document is made inoperative. Thus in rescission, a document remains operative, in cancellation it is rendered inoperative.

(*c*) Relief afforded by rescission is consequently limited in scope while that in cancellation is wider. Rescission is available in regard to contract only, while cancellation is obtainable with regard to any instrument.

---

48. *Manick Lal* v. *Shiva Jute Bailing*, (1948) 52 Cal WN 389.
49. *Ishvar Timapp Hegde* v. *Dewar Venkappa Shaubog*, ILR (1903) 27 Bom 146: 5 Bom LR 19.
50. *Manick Lal* v. *Shiva Jute Bailing*, (1948) 52 Cal WN 389.
51. *Kotrabassappaya* v. *Chenvirappaya*, ILR (1899) 23 Bom 375.
52. Pollock and Mulla: *Indian Contract Act and Specific Relief Act*, p. 900, where they differ from a decision (on the above italicised expression) in *Iyyappa* v. *Ramalakshmamma*, ILR (1890) 13 Mad 549.
53. *Kattaiya Pillai* v. *Ramaswamia Pillai*, AIR 1929 Mad 396: 56 Mad LJ 394.

(*d*) Relief granted in case of rescission is where contract is merely voidable or where its unlawfulness or nullity is apparent on the face of it. In so far as cancellation is concerned, the relief is given in case of void as well as voidable instruments whether nullity is apparent on the face of it or not.

In so far as rectification on one side and rescission and cancellation on the other is concerned, the difference can be laid down as follows:

(*a*) In rectification, the contract that is sought to be rectified though complete and legal and unobjectionable, does not express the real intention of the parties, i.e., the writing therein does not correspond with the intention of the parties. In rescission and cancellation, the contract or the instrument is void or voidable.

(*b*) In the former (rectification), the plaintiff does not want to avoid it altogether. He wants to avoid only a part of it so far as it is on account of error. In the latter, the contract or the instrument as a whole is sought to be avoided.

(*c*) In the former, the relief is in addition to specific performance while in the latter, specific performance can be alternated with rescission, but it cannot be so alternated in cancellation.

(*d*) Thus on the whole the grounds for relief in the former are limited in scope, those in the latter are wider. Besides, in rectification, what is rectified is an error not the instrument[54], in cancellation what is cancelled is the instrument itself.

7. Minor's position

Sub-section (2) of Section 33 makes a clear provision that a defendant who is a minor or a lunatic at the time of making the contract may have to restore, as far as may be, any benefit received by him whether it is proprietary or monetary. But there is no liability for making compensation in such cases. This provision therefore brings an end to a conflict of opinion as to restoration of benefit by a minor. One view was that "restoration stopped where repayment began"; the other view was that a minor should restore the benefit when he has made misrepresentations as to his age.[55] In cases where a minor has not expressly asked for cancellation of an instrument, relying on its being a nullity, the court may make him restore the benefit under this section.

Still, however, the Orissa High Court in *Daneyi case*[56] and the Mysore High Court in *Dyaviah case*[57] are not of one opinion; the former treating a contract by

---

54. *Sabhaji* v. *Nawalsingh*, AIR 1928 Nag 4: 104 IC 736.

55. *Limbaji* v. *Rahi*, ILR (1925) 49 Bom 576: 88 IC 643: AIR 1925 Bom 499 (attempted sale by minor's stepmother, minor required to refund benefit to estate and himself); *Rang Ilahi* v. *Mahbub Ilahi*, ILR (1926) 7 Lah 35: 94 IC 25: AIR 1926 Lah 170 (similar case in Mahomedan law); *Milkhiram* v. *Jivan Singh*, AIR 1953 Pepsu 45.

56. *Daneyi Gurumurty* v. *Raghu Podhan*, AIR 1967 Ori 68; *Mohori Bibee* v. *Dharmodas Ghose*, ILR (1903) 30 Cal 539: 30 IA 114, *followed.*

57. *Dyaviah* v. *Shivamma*, AIR 1959 Mys 188. But see *Mohori Bibee case* and Sections 64 and 65 of Indian Contract Act.

the guardian of the minor as void *ab initio* and holding that neither Section 38 nor Section 41 of the Specific Relief Act, 1877 (Sections 30 and 33 of the Specific Relief Act, 1963 respectively) can apply; and the latter holding that restitution in case of void contracts is also applicable in case of minors who cannot be allowed to have a double advantage.[58]

D. DECLARATION (SECTIONS 34 AND 35)

1. Meaning

Sections 34 and 35 of the Specific Relief Act, 1963 provide for grant by the court of a declaration of status or right of the plaintiff and its effect.

"To *allege* is formally to state as true or capable of proof, but without proving. To *adduce*, literally to lead to, is to bring the evidence up to what has been alleged. Adduce is a secondary word; nothing can be adduced in evidence till something has been stated or alleged, which the evidence is to sustain. To speak of an *alleged* document, an alleged will or an alleged crime, is either to question, or at least very carefully to refrain from admitting, that the document exists, that the will is genuine or that the crime is committed; alleged simply concedes nothing and leaves the question open. But to *aver* is to declare confidently. Declare has often an authoritative force."[59]

We may consequently say that declaration is an authoritative pronouncement by the court in respect of a person's right to property or his status. Section 34 thus makes a provision for a particular type of relief where there is no specific performance, no award of compensation, but merely a declaration of the rights of the parties.

2. Origin and Object of the Provision

In England, before 1873-75, the courts of law and equity had for long made declarations in claims brought against the Crown and the courts of equity had made declarations in other cases where consequential relief was also claimed. But in 1850 an innovation of a very important kind was made (by the Court of Chancery Act, 1850, Section 14 and Chancery Procedure Act, 1852, Section 50) which empowered the Court of Chancery to make a declaration without granting any consequential relief. In 1873-75 the Judicature Act empowered the Supreme Court to make declarations whether or not any consequential relief was or even could be claimed. This led some to form an impression and to assert that declarations are a form of equitable relief.[60] However, the Court of Appeal[61] has held that they are not; they are "neither land nor equity", but primarily statutory.[62]

58. See also *Emperor* v. *Brij Lal*, AIR 1937 Oudh 130: 160 IC 489.
59. Funk and Wagnall: *Standard Handbook of Synonyms, Antonyms and Prepositions*, pp. 38, 50.
60. *Barnard* v. *National Dock Labour Board*, (1953) 2 QB 18: (1953) 1 All ER 1113.
61. *Gray* v. *Spyer*, (1921) 2 Ch 549: 126 LT 238.
62. *Snell's Principles of Equity*, p. 571; Hanbury: *Modern Equity*, p. 81

This provision was incorporated in Section 15 of the Civil Procedure Code, 1859 in India whereby it was lawful for the civil courts to make binding declarations of right without granting consequential relief.[63]

The Code of 1859 was replaced by the Code of 1877 and the provision as to declaration was transferred to Section 42 of the Specific Relief Act, 1877 which now stands before us as Section 34 of the Specific Relief Act, 1963.

The object of the legislature was to grant to the plaintiff a relief granted by the Court of Chancery in cases where no relief at Common Law was available.

Sir Lawrence Jenkins in *Deokali Koer* v. *Kedar Nath*[64] said: "The section does not sanction every form of declaration, but only a declaration that the plaintiff is 'entitled to any legal character or to any right as to any property'; it is the disregard of this that accounts for the multiform and at times, eccentric declarations which find a place in Indian plaints. If the courts were astute, as I think they should be, to see that the plaint presented conformed to the terms of Section 42 (now Section 34) the difficulties that are to be found in such class of cases would no longer arise." Moreover, "it is a common fashion to attempt an evasion of court fees by casting the prayers of the plaint into a declaratory shape. Where the evasion is successful it cannot be touched, but the device does not merit encouragement or favour". The section is thus intended to avoid multiplicity of suits and the courts will not merely make a declaration of a hypothetical or an abstract right without any reference to its practical utility.[65] If the plaintiff being able to obtain any further consequential relief omits to do so, the court shall not grant him a declaratory decree.[66]

In *Abdul Hakim* v. *Habib Khan*[67], the plaintiff, a tenant of a shop, was on basis of an undertaking filed under Section 151 C.P.C. by the parties, was dispossessed of his shop. As he was dispossessed during the pendency of the suit he was entitled to the possession of the shop. The plaintiff wanted to amend the plaint to incorporate the subsequent events. It was his duty to do so. However, his request was objected to by the defendant-petitioner (in H.C.). The court held that if the plaintiff is dispossessed during the pendency of the suit for declaration, amendment of the plaint should not be insisted upon and the plaintiff should be put back in possession so that status quo ante be restored. The act of the defendants in this case amounts to overreaching the process of law and it is the duty of the trial court to protect the rights of the parties as they existed on the date of filing the suit.

But one must note that the section is not exhaustive of the categories of declaratory suits maintainable under the law.[68]

---

63. *Rooke* v. *Lord Kensington*, (1856) 2 K&J 753: 25 LJ Ch 795; *Strimathoo Moothoo Tijia Ragoonadah Ranee Kalandapuree Natchiar* v. *Dorasinga Tever*, (1875) 2 IA 169; *Sadut Ali Khan* v. *Khajeh Abdool Gunnee*, 1873 Supp IA 165.
64. ILR (1912) 39 Cal 704: 15 IC 427.
65. *Sabitri Thakurain* v. *F.A. Savi*, AIR 1933 Pat 306: ILR (1933) 12 Pat 359.
66. *Kumud Ranjan* v. *Manabendra*, AIR 1974 Cal 342.
67. AIR 1998 Raj 107. The court relied on *Azim Khan* v. *State*, 1958 Raj LW 90.
68. *Lakshminarasimha Samayajiyarr* v. *Ramalingam Pillai*, AIR 1920 Mad 573.

3. Essentials for the Relief[69]

To file a suit under this section,

(*a*) The plaintiff must be a person entitled to any legal character at the time of the suit.

(*b*) He must be a person entitled to a right to property.[70] This explains that the interest of the plaintiff must be existing, present interest; it may be a distant possibility of its coming into possession and enjoyment. But a mere contingency howsoever proximate will not suffice if there is no present state of interest.[71]

(*c*) Defendant should have denied these, or be interested to deny this, character or right. That is to say, there must be some present danger or obstacle to the interest which the plaintiff seeks to avoid by the decree. Mere hypothetical, abstract and speculative grounds would not suffice.[72]

(*d*) The plaintiff should not be in a position to ask for relief consequential upon declaration sought. In other words, a cloud must be cast on his title before he can ask for its removal. He must allege and prove hostility on the part of the defendant for no court will move on merely speculative grounds.[73] In other words, if the plaintiff is able to seek further relief he must do so; if he omits to seek it, the decree will be refused to him.

We have to make a note that (*i*) if any of the first three conditions is not fulfilled, the suit should be dismissed. If they are fulfilled but the fourth is not, the court shall not make the declaration requested. (*ii*) The decree creates no new rights. It only declares the plaintiff's right he had. (*iii*) The decree cannot be claimed as a matter of right because it is discretionary. (*iv*) If all the parties are not joined the declaration is not available.[74] (*v*) The court at the most can refuse to make a declaration in case the plaintiff does not pray for consequential relief; it cannot dismiss a suit.[75] (*vi*) The proviso to the section does not stop a plaintiff from seeking a relief he wants unless he asks for the consequential relief. It contemplates only a further relief which could be claimed against the defendant only and not one which could be claimed against anybody else.[76] (*vii*) Such a decree apart from the provisions of Section 11 of CPC, is conclusive between parties to it and persons litigating through them.

---

69. *Jeka Dula* v. *Bai Jivi*, 39 Bom LR 1072: AIR 1938 Bom 37.
70. *Sowrashtra Vipra Sabha* v. *Namakkal Municipality*, (1996) 11 SCC 584.
71. *Wajid Ali Shah* v. *Dianat-ul-lah-Beg*, ILR (1886) 8 All 31.
72. *Sabitri Thakurain* v. *F.A. Savi*, ILR (1933) 12 Pat 359: AIR 1933 Pat 306.
73. *Jeka Dula* v. *Bai Jivi*, 39 Bom LR 1072: AIR 1938 Bom 37: AIR 1930 Lah 803.
74. *Maharaja of Benares* v. *Ramji Khan*, ILR (1905) 27 All 138.
75. *Kunj Bihari* v. *Keshavlal*, ILR (1904) 28 Bom 567.
76. *Humayun Begam* v. *Shah Mahammad Khan*, AIR 1943 PC 94: 207 IC 188.

4. Use of Declarations and Injunctions

The action for a declaration is today commonly used as a remedy in public law either in addition or as an alternative to the injunction.[77] A declaratory decree declares the legal position as to a matter in dispute. In other words it merely declares the right of the decree holder vis-a-vis the judgement debtor, but it does not direct him to do or to refrain from doing any particular act or thing.[78] Such a decree when granted is not in itself an order of the court which has to be obeyed. It can be said to be a non-coercive declaration. It is for this reason that applicants frequently apply for an injunction as well as a declaration so that the relief obtained is, so far as the injunction is concerned, enforceable.[79] Looking from a different angle, in declaration, a court cannot grant the declaratory relief where further relief could be obtained. In case of injunction, there is no such restriction; it can be granted without requesting for a declaration, though one cannot fail to note that in many cases a declaration is inherent in the grant of an injunction.[80]

Section 34 is not exhaustive of cases in which a declaratory decree can be made. Consequently as held in Ratnamala Dassi court has power to grant such a decree independently of the requirements of the section. For example in the instant case a suit by a tenant for declaration relating to his interest in the tenanted property was held as maintainable, as such an interest is property.[81]

5. Declaration when Refused

(*a*) *In case of vexatious litigation.*—In *Deokali Koer case*[82], it was expressed that the section does not sanction every form of declaration, but only a declaration that the plaintiff is "entitled to any legal character or to any right as to any property". If this is disregarded it will give rise to multiplicity of proceedings. Before that, in *Narain Mitter's* case[83], this proposition was expressed by the Privy Council thus: "In every case the court must exercise a sound judgment as to whether it is reasonable or not under all circumstances of the case to grant the relief prayed for. There is so much danger in India of harassing and vexatious litigation that the courts in India ought to be

---

77. Hanbury: *Modern Equity*, Chap. 3, p. 81.

78. *State of M.P.* v. *Mangilal Sharma*, (1998) 2 SCC 510: 1998 SCC (L&S) 599: (1998) 1 LLJ 995.

79. *Hiles* v. *Amalgamated Society of Woodworkers*, 1968 Ch 440: (1967) 3 All ER 70 (Ch D); *Indumatiben Chimanlal Desai* v. *Union of India*, AIR 1969 Bom 423.

80. *Ibid.* See also *Vicco Laboratories* v. *Art Commercia Advertising (P) Ltd.*, (2001) 7 SCC 81 (Art. 136) (Suit for declaration that suit serial exclusively belonged to plaintiffs); *Padikal Madapa* v. *C.B. Kariapa*, (2001) 10 SCC 742 (suit for right of way, air, light and privacy); *Karnataka Board of Wakf* v. *Govt. of India*, (2004) 10 SCC 779; (for declaration of ownership of and title over immovable property); *Prabhakar Adsule* v. *State of M.P.*, (2004) 11 SCC 249 (for declaration of title; failure to produce proper proof; relief rightly denied); *N.V. Srinivasa Murthy* v. *Mariyamma*, (2005) 5 SCC 548 (for declaration of absolute ownership).

81. *Ratnamala Dassi* v. *Ratan Singh Bawa*, AIR 1990 Cal 26.

82. *Deokali Koer* v. *Kedar Nath*, ILR (1912) 39 Cal 704: 15 IC 427.

83. *Narain Mitter* v. *Kishen Soondori Dassee*, 1873 Supp IA 149.

most careful that mere declaratory suits be not converted into a new and mischievous source of litigation".

(*b*) *In case of evasion of court fee.*—When prayer casted in the form of declaratory suit is an attempt at an evasion of court fee[84], such relief would be refused.

(*c*) *In case of multiplicity of suits.*—When it amounts or leads to multiplicity of suits for the same cause of action, relief of declaration may be refused.[85]

In *Ashok Kumar Srivastava case*[86], the appellant was appointed on certain terms and conditions. He was initially put on probation for twelve months. Conditions of his appointment stated that unless a letter appointing him as a probationary Inspector is issued before expiry of his probation period, his services shall stand terminated. No such letter was issued before expiry of probation period. His initial period of probation was also not extended. He therefore sued for declaratory relief that he continues in service. It was held that no such declaration can be given.

Similarly in *Navalram case*[87], it has been held by the Gujarat High Court very recently that a casual unnoticed user of open piece of land cannot be considered as exclusive possession of the land conferring right over the land in the person using it. Here the plaintiff was in exclusive possession of the land. The presumption, therefore, that possession follows the title comes into play and construction of water tank or shed over a small piece of land by the defendant which was convenient in many ways to him and was made use of by him, without notice of plaintiff would not be construed as an act of dispossession of plaintiff necessitating the claim for possession by the plaintiff as contemplated by S. 34 of the Act. Other efficacious remedies are available to the plaintiff.

6. Merely Declaratory Decree

A question was posed in *Kathama Natchiar case*[88], whether the courts in India had power to make a merely declaratory decree otherwise than under Section 15 of the Civil Procedure Code, 1859 (*see* "origin and object" in para 2 above in this section) and it was answered in the negative. The correct view, as expressed by Pollock and Mulla[89], is that Section 34 is exhaustive of the cases in which a decree merely declaratory can be made and that the courts have no power *to make such a decree independently of that section*. This view of the text is approved in *Kishorilal* v. *Begraj*[90] by the Punjab High Court. At all

84. *Deokali Koer* v. *Kedar Nath*, (1912) 39 Cal 704: 15 IC 427.

85. See *Indian Iron & Steel Co. Ltd.* v. *Chhaganlal Marwari*, 1994 Supp (3) SCC 719.

86. *Ashok Kumar Srivastava* v. *National Insurance Co. Ltd.*, (1998) 4 SCC 361: 1998 SCC (L&S) 1137.

87. *Navalram Laxmidas Devmurari* v. *Vijayaben Jayavant Bhai Chavda*, AIR 1998 Guj 17.

88. *Strimathoo Moothoo Tijia Ragoonadah Ranee Kolandapuree Natchiar* v. *Dorasinga Tever*, (1875) 2 IA 169.

89. *Indian Contract Act and Specific Relief Act*, 9th Edn., 1972, p. 910.

90. *Kishori Lal* v. *Beg Raj*, AIR 1952 Punj 387.

events one must note that the proviso to Section 34 is paramount and its effect cannot be avoided. After referring to the observations of the Privy Council in *Sheoparasan Singh case*[1] and *Fischer case*[2], the Calcutta High Court in *Manjur Al Haque case*[3] has upheld this view. This means that a declaratory decree could not be made unless there was a right to consequential relief capable of being had in the same court or in some cases in some other court, i.e., a revenue court. Under the present section a suit would lie for a merely declaratory decree though no consequential relief could be claimed, e.g., a suit by an owner of land against any member of the public who formally claims to use such land as a public road and who thereby endangers the title of the owner.[4] Similarly, a suit lies for a mere declaration that a new valuation by a municipality is not void.[5] Where a defendant is not in possession or not in a position to deliver possession of the suit properties, no "further relief" than a declaration of the right to possession is available to the plaintiff and the proviso to Section 34 is no bar to granting such a relief of declaration.[6] It is however to be noted that a contract of personal service cannot normally be enforced. A court in such circumstances would not grant a declaration that the contract subsists and that the employee, even after having been removed from service can be deemed to be in service against the employer's will and consent.[7] The rule has however the following three exceptions as declared in *Vaish Degree College case* by the Supreme Court.[8]

(*a*) In cases where a statutory body acts in contravention of the mandatory provisions of the statutes;

(*b*) In cases where a public servant is sought to be removed from service in contravention of Article 311 of the Constitution of India[9]; and

(*c*) In cases where a worker is sought to be reinstated on his being dismissed under the Industrial Law.

7. Illustrations

(*a*) *A* is lawfully in possession of certain land. The inhabitants of a neighbouring village claim a right of way across the land. *A* may sue for a declaration that they are not entitled to the right so claimed.

---

1. *Sheoparsan Singh* v. *Ramnandan Singh*, (1916) 43 IA 91: ILR (1916) 43 Cal 694: 33 IC 914: AIR 1916 PC 78.
2. *Fischer* v. *Secy. of State for India in Council*, (1899) 26 IA 16: ILR (1899) 22 Mad (270).
3. *Chowdhury Mohd. Manjural Haque* v. *Shebait of Sri Sri Iswar Lakshmi Narayan Jew Thakur*, AIR 1943 Cal 361.
4. *Chunilalanath* v. *Ram Kishen Sahu*, ILR (1888) 15 Cal 460.
5. *Surendranath* v. *Chairman of the Municipal Commrs. of Mymen Singh*, (1934) 61 Cal 276: AIR 1934 Cal 673: 152 IC 694.
6. *Sunder Singh Mallah Singh Sanatan Dharam High School Trust* v. *Managing Committee*, (1938) 65 IA 106.
7. *J. Tiwari* v. *Jwala Devi Vidya Mandir*, (1979) 4 SCC 160: 1979 SCC (L&S) 356.
8. *Vaish Degree College* v. *Laxmi Narayan*, (1976) 2 SCC 58: 1976 SCC (L&S) 176.
9. *Mysore SRTC* v. *Mirza Khasim Ali Beg*, (1977) 2 SCC 457: AIR 1977 SC 747.

(*b*) *A* alienates to *B* property in which *A* has merely a life interest. The alienation in invalid as against *C*, who is entitled as a reversioner. In a suit by *C*, against *A* and *B* the court may declare that *C* is so entitled.

(*c*) A Hindu widow in possession of property adopts a son to her husband. The person presumably entitled to possession of the property on her death without a son may, in a suit against the adopted son, obtain a declaration that the adoption was invalid. (For contra see *Gummalapura Taggina Matada Kotturuswami* v. *Setra Veeravva*[10]).

8. Effect of Declaration (Section 35)

As the section lays down, a decree under this section is binding on the actual litigating parties, the persons litigating through them, and also to the beneficiaries under the trust. The declaration of status obtained under this section though should generally be operative *in rem* but it has been made clear in *Munyraj case* by the Hyderabad High Court that a declaration made in respect of the adoption of a certain person is not a judgement *in rem*.[11]

---

10. AIR 1959 SC 577: 1959 Supp (1) SCR 968.
11. *Munyaraj* v. *Venkatapati*, 1955 Hyd 172.

Chapter XXVI
Injunctions

"By means of its decrees for specific performance the Court of Chancery obtained command of one great province of law, namely, of contracts for the sale of land. It fashioned another weapon, namely, the injunction, which was far more flexible, far more generally applicable and thereby it obtained not merely certain particular fields of justice, but a power of making its own doctrines prevail at the expense of the common law."

—Maitland: *Lectures on Equity*, p. 318

Injunction is "a judicial process by which one who has invaded or is threatening to invade the rights, legal or equitable, of another, is restrained from continuing or commencing such wrongful Act".

—A.W. Renton: *Encyclopaedia of the Laws of England*, Vol. 6, p. 464

No one can be allowed to use his own property in such a manner that it creates a nuisance for his neighbours.

—*Darshan Ram* v. *Nazar Ram*, AIR 1989 P&H 253.

SYNOPSIS

1. TEXT OF SECTIONS 36 TO 42

Injunction Generally

36. Preventive relief how granted.—Preventive relief is granted at the discretion of the court by injunction, temporary or perpetual.

37. Temporary and perpetual injunctions.—(1) Temporary injunctions are such as are to continue until a specified time, or until the further order of the court, and they may be granted at any stage of a suit, and are regulated by the Code of Civil Procedure, 1908 (5 of 1908).

(2) A perpetual injunction can only be granted by the decree made at the hearing and upon the merits of the suit; the defendant is thereby perpetually enjoined from the assertion of a right, or from the commission of an act, which would be contrary to the rights of the plaintiff.

Perpetual Injunctions

38. Perpetual injunctions when granted.—(1) Subject to the other provisions contained in or referred to by this Chapter a perpetual injunction may be granted to the plaintiff to prevent the breach of an obligation existing in his favour, whether expressly or by implication.

(2) When any such obligation arises from contract, the court shall be guided by the rules and provisions contained in Chapter II.

(3) When the defendant invades or threatens to invade the plaintiff's right to, or enjoyment of, property the court may grant a perpetual injunction in the following cases, namely:—

(*a*) where the defendant is trustee of the property for the plaintiff;

(*b*) where there exists no standard for ascertaining the actual damage caused, or likely to be caused, by the invasion;

(*c*) where the invasion is such that compensation in money would not afford adequate relief;

(*d*) where the injunction is necessary to prevent a multiplicity of judicial proceedings.

39. Mandatory injunctions.—When, to prevent the breach of an obligation, it is necessary to compel the performance of certain acts which the court is capable of enforcing, the court may in its discretion grant an injunction to prevent the breach complained of, and also to compel performance of the requisite acts.

40. Damages in lieu of, or in addition to, injunction.—(1) The plaintiff in a suit for perpetual injunction under Section 38, or mandatory injunction under Section 39, may claim damages either in addition to, or in substitution for, such injunction and the court may, if it thinks fit, award such damages.

(2) No relief for damages shall be granted under this section unless the plaintiff has claimed such relief in his plaint:

Provided that where no such damages have been claimed in the plaint, the court shall, at any stage of the proceedings, allow the plaintiff to amend the plaint on such terms as may be just for including such claim.

(3) The dismissal of a suit to prevent the breach of an obligation existing in favour of the plaintiff shall bar his right to sue for damages for such breach.

41. Injunction when refused.—An injunction cannot be granted—

(*a*) to restrain any person from prosecuting a judicial proceeding pending at the institution of the suit in which the injunction is sought, unless such restraint is necessary to prevent a multiplicity of proceedings;

(*b*) to restrain any person from instituting or prosecuting any proceeding in a court not subordinate to that from which the injunction is sought;

(*c*) to restrain any person from applying to any legislative body;

(*d*) to restrain any person from instituting or prosecuting any proceeding in criminal matter;

(*e*) to prevent the breach of a contract the performance of which would not be specifically enforced;

(*f*) to prevent, on the ground of nuisance, an act of which it is not reasonably clear that it will be a nuisance;

(*g*) to prevent a continuing breach in which the plaintiff has acquiesced;

(*h*) when equally efficacious relief can certainly be obtained by any other usual mode of proceeding except in case of breach of trust;

(*i*) when the conduct of the plaintiff or his agents has been such as to disentitle him to the assistance of the court;

(*j*) when the plaintiff has no personal interest in the matter.

42. Injunction to perform negative agreement.—Notwithstanding anything contained in clause (*e*) of Section 41, where a contract comprises an affirmative agreement to do a certain act, coupled with a negative agreement, express or implied, not to do a certain act, the circumstance that the court is unable to compel specific performance of the affirmative agreement shall not preclude it from granting an injunction to perform the negative agreement:

Provided that the plaintiff has not failed to perform the contract so far as it is binding on him.

2. PREVENTIVE RELIEF

The principles of Chancery Courts postulated that a man will be punished if he does what his conscience tells him not to do. Consequently, the best and the surest way was to prevent him from doing that act by means of an injunction. These principles arose out of the inadequacy of the Common Law and the general tendency of the contemners of law. For example, when a person had by contractual obligations undertaken not to set up a rival business, or not to engage himself in another's service for a particular period, or not to encroach upon another's land, equity would restrict or prevent him from doing that act. Injunction is thus a mode of enforcing specific performance of negative agreements. Since the general purpose of injunction is to restrain the commission, continuance or repetition of some wrongful act which one is under an obligation not to do, the relief provided by the Chancery Court at its discretion to the plaintiff is called preventive relief. But at the same time, one cannot fail to note that the preventive relief protects rights arising otherwise than from contracts as is evidenced by the *Swindon Company case*.[1] In this case Swindon Company, a proprietor of a tenement on a river bank collected and diverted the river water for supplying it to a nearby town, to the detriment of the benefit of the lower riparian owners who filed a suit for injunction and the same was granted as the owner of the lands higher up the stream cannot divert water for the benefit of persons unconnected with any part of the stream.

In a recent case[2] an injunction against proposed location of a cemetery was granted on the same principle. Cemetery in this case was proposed in a crowded residential area and the distance up to the house of the plaintiff was only 78 feet. Consequently there was possibility of noxious gas escaping concrete vaults and obnoxious overflows from underneath cells and pollution of drinking water of the well in the plaintiff's residential compound was not ruled out. It was held that the plaintiff was entitled to injunction as proximity of cemetery to his residence could be a strong and continuous cause for annoyance.[3]

---

1. *Swindon Waterworks Co.* v. *Wilts Berks Canal Navigation Co.*, (1875) 7 HL 697: 33 LT 513 (HL).
2. *St. Joseph Church, Punkumnan* v. *Velu*, AIR 1989 NOC 124 (Ker).
3. *Ibid.*

The Indian Specific Relief Act, 1963, Sections 36 to 42 make provision for this relief by selecting certain leading English principles and incorporating them in the topic.

3. INJUNCTION: ORIGIN, NATURE AND DEFINITION

Before the Judicature Act, 1873, the cases wherein equity interfered and granted preventive relief fell into two classes: (*i*) cases to prevent the iniquitous institution or continuation of judicial proceedings, and (*ii*) cases of wrongful acts unconnected with judicial proceedings. Originally the court of chancery alone had this jurisdiction which resulted in duplication of work as where the plaintiff required an injunction to enforce a legal cause of action but now by the Judicature Act, 1925, Section 45, the High Court grants injunction by an interlocutory order in all cases in which it appears to the court to be just and convenient to do so.[4] The jurisdiction of the court is exercised not on the individual preference of the judge, but "according to sufficient legal reasons or on settled legal principles. It must be 'just' as well as 'convenient' ".

Injunction is an order of the court to a party to the proceedings to do or to refrain from doing a specified act. It is granted in cases in which monetary compensation affords an inadequate remedy to the injured party.[5]

As Maitland puts it, injunction "is an order made by the court forbidding a person or class of persons from doing a certain act, or acts of a certain class, upon pain of going to prison as contemners of the court. The penalty, is not mentioned in the injunction, but if knowing of an injunction you break it, then the court has a large discretionary power of sending you to prison and keeping you there".[6]

The object of an injunction, it should be noted, is usually preventive rather than prohibitive.

4. TYPES OF INJUNCTION (SECTION 36)

An injunction is either (*i*) temporary (Section 37) (*ii*) perpetual or permanent (Sections 37 and 38), or (*iii*) mandatory (Section 39).

Temporary or interlocutory injunction is granted before the trial of an action. Its object is to keep matters *status quo* until the question at issue between the parties is determined. As the section explains, temporary injunctions are such as are to continue until a specified time, or until the further order of the court, and they may be granted at any stage of a suit and are regulated by the Code of Civil Procedure, 1908. They are also called interim injunctions.

Permanent or *perpetual* injunction is granted only after the plaintiff has established his right and the actual or threatened infringement of it by the defendant. As the section goes, a perpetual injunction can only be granted by the

4. Hanbury: *Modern Equity*, pp. 59, 60.
5. *Snell's Principles of Equity*, p. 624; Hanbury: *Modern Equity*, p. 59, *See* Encyclopaedia of the Laws of England, p. 464.
6. Maitland: *Lectures on Equity*, p. 318.

decree made at the hearing and upon the merits of the suit. The defendant is thereby perpetually enjoined from the assertion of a right, or from the commission of an act which would be contrary to the rights of the plaintiff.

As observed in the case of *State of Haryana* v. *State of Punjab*[7] a permanent injunction is final and conclusive of the facts in the context of which it is granted. A temporary by contrast is granted on a prima facie view of the facts and as the word temporary itself indicates it is an interim order pending a final adjudication of the rights of the parties. This distinction is not to be confused with the distinction between a prohibitive or preventive injunction on the one hand and a mandatory injunction on the other. In the first case the party is prevented from doing a particular thing or continuing with a particular action. A mandatory injunction on the other hand commands an action to be done.

From the point of view of time, the injunctions are interlocutory or permanent but from the viewpoint of nature, injunctions may be divided into prohibitory or mandatory.

An injunction restraining the doing or continuance of some wrongful act is called *prohibitory* or *restrictive*. An injunction to restrain the continuance of some wrongful omission is called *mandatory*. Section 39 explains a mandatory injunction thus: "When to prevent the breach of an obligation, it is necessary to compel the performance of certain acts which the court is capable of enforcing, the court may at its discretion, grant an injunction to prevent the breach complained of, and also to compel performance of the requisite acts".

An injunction is an order of the court. An order is more authoritative than a direction. A mandate stresses heavily the idea of the highest authority. Prohibition is wholly negative; it is a command not to do; injunction is generally so used, especially as the requirement by legal authority that certain action be suspended or refrained from, pending final legal decision.[8]

Injunction, thus restrains a person's action in future, it is not a remedy for breaches already made or wrongful acts already done before. It may be that assistance of the court is obtained and such actions restrained before the same are committed. But this is rare, generally the court's assistance is sought only after the act is committed. Consequently, an injunction is given for restraining future actions. In such cases, for the acts done in the past compensation is an adequate relief and a proper remedy. But as a measure of precaution in order to stop those acts (e.g., nuisance) so that they may not assume a permanent and a tangible form, a prohibitive injunction from the court is necessary. For example, where *A* uses *B*'s premises as a shortcut to reach his office, *A* can be restrained by an injunction to repeat such acts and for the acts already committed by him *B* may obtain compensation. When an injunction is granted in order to prevent a threatened wrong it is termed as a *quia timet injunction*. Here a person takes a preventive measure before an event takes place.

7. (2004) 12 SCC 673.
8. Funk and Wagnall: *Standard Handbook of Synonyms Antonyms and Prepositions*, p. 304.

5. DIFFERENCE BETWEEN TEMPORARY AND PERPETUAL INJUNCTION

(*a*) The nature of a temporary injunction is provisional, continuing until a specified time or until the further order of the court. A permanent injunction can only be granted by decree made at the hearing and *holds good without any time limit.*

(*b*) While the former is granted to preserve the *status quo*, the latter is granted to preserve and protect the right established by the plaintiff.

(*c*) While the former can be granted *at any period of the suit*, even *ex parte*, without notice to the other party to show cause why it should not be granted, the latter can only be granted after the trial when the plaintiff has established his case and on the merits of the case.

(*d*) A temporary injunction is an outcome of emergency and therefore it is provisional; *it does not conclude any right.* A perpetual injunction on the other hand *concludes a right*; it is in effect a decree.

(*e*) Consequently, a temporary injunction restrains the defendant for a *particular time only* (till the date of hearing at the most) while a perpetual injunction restrains him for ever.[9]

(*f*) Grant of the former is regulated by the Code of Civil Procedure, Order 39, Rules 1 and 2, while the latter is regulated by Sections 38 to 42 of the Specific Relief Act.[10]

(*g*) A temporary injunction can be dissolved under Order 39, Rule 4 of the CPC, or else it terminates automatically when the suit is decided. A permanent injunction cannot be dissolved as it holds good for ever restraining the defendant perpetually from the assertion of a right or from the commission of an act which would be contrary to the right of the plaintiff.

6. PRINCIPLES GOVERNING INJUNCTION

The general principles underlying the grant of an injunction are similar to those involved in granting specific performance of contracts or of enforcement of other positive obligations. The following are the general points which require particular attention:

(*a*) Whenever a right exists or is created by contract, by ownership of property or otherwise, cognizable by law, an injunction will be issued to protect a violation of that right and the restraining power of the court extends through the whole range of rights and duties recognised by law and would be applied to every case of intended violation unless there are other reasons of policy or expediency which control and limit its exercise.[11]

---

9. *Apaji Patil* v. *Apa*, 4 Bom LR 534: ILR (1902) 26 Bom 735; *Lawndes* v. *Bettle*, (1864) 33 LJ Ch 451: 10 LT 55.
10. *Indu Shekhar* v. *Fule Devi*, 1968 BLR 268.
11. *Bhawarilal* v. *S. Jaichand*, (1975) 1 Kant LJ 1: ILR 1975 Kant 127: AIR 1975 Kant 122, 123; *Pritam Kumar* v. *Nagar Palika (Municipal Committee)*, (1986) 1 CLJ (C&Cr.) 213 P&H.

(*b*) Granting of an injunction is a matter of judicial discretion for the court. Though the grant of injunction is discretionary the same must be exercised on settled principles of law to advance the cause of justice.[12]

(*c*) The court granting an injunction must rightly appreciate the facts and apply to those facts the true principles. Then and only then it becomes a sound exercise of judicial discretion.[13] The exercise of discretion is thus not arbitrary or capricious but is based on sound common sense and is regulated by well settled principles.[14]

(*d*) The court must see that there is a *bona fide* case between the parties.

(*e*) And in that case it must also see on which side, in the event of success, will lie the balance of convenience if the injunction does not issue.[15]

(*f*) If the effect of not granting an injunction will be to deprive the plaintiff for ever of the right claimed by him in the suit, the court should grant a temporary injunction.[16]

(*g*) If the act complained of can be relieved by compensation, the court will exercise its discretion and will not grant injunction. In other words, when an efficacious relief can be obtained by any other usual mode of proceeding, injunction cannot be granted.[17]

(*h*) Injunction is granted to maintain the *status quo ante*.[18]

(*i*) Where a plaintiff establishes his right and also a threatened violation thereof by the defendant, injunction follows more or less as a matter of course. But here also if granting of the same is under the circumstances found to be unjust, inexpedient and oppressive, the court in its discretion will refuse it.

The relief of injunction being equitable and discretionary it cannot be issued in favour of a trespasser or a person who gained unlawful possession as against the true owner.[19]

---

12. *Surya Nath Singh* v. *Khedu Singh*, 1994 Supp (1) SCC 561; see also *T. N. Housing Board* v. *A. Viswam*, (1996) 8 SCC 259.
13. *Subba Naidu* v. *Haji Badsha*, ILR (1903) 26 Mad 168: 13 Mad LJ 13.
14. *Ganpatlal* v. *Nandlal Haswani*, AIR 1989 MP 209.
15. Ibid.; *Doherty* v. *Allman*, (1878) 3 AC 709: 39 LT 129; *S.S.V. Krishnan Pillai* v. *Kilasathammal*, AIR 1928 Mad 810.
16. *Secy., Civil Station Sub-Committee, Nagpur* v. *Govindrao Kashinath Somalwar*, ILR 1937 Nag 313: 170 IC 239: AIR 1937 Nag 137.
17. *Morumal* v. *Gobindram Bikhchand*, AIR 1933 Sind 176; *Holland-Bombay Trading Co.* v. *Essardas Dharamchand*, AIR 1925 Sind 175.
18. *L.D. Meston School Society* v. *Kashi Nath Misra*, AIR 1951 All 558; *E.M. Gopalakrishna Konar* v. *A. Vilanga Konar*, AIR 1926 Mad 132: 90 IC 819.
19. *Premji Ratansey Shah* v. *Union of India*, (1994) 5 SCC 547, 550; see also *T.N. Housing Board* v. *A. Viswam*, (1996) 8 SCC 259.

(*j*) Courts are very slow in granting an injunction against an isolated or occasional breach but in case of a continuous breach or wrong, injunction would be more readily issued.

(*k*) When a suit is for a permanent injunction of one kind, interim injunction of a different kind cannot be granted.[20]

(*l*) No interim injunction can be granted when the suit is for declaration only.[21]

(*m*) A mandatory injunction requires more stronger grounds than those required for obtaining a restrictive injunction.[22]

(*n*) While granting an injunction the court may in its discretion impose equitable conditions according to the circumstances of each case.

(*o*) Injunction rests on the equitable principle that *he who seeks equity must do equity*, and that the plaintiff requesting it must *come with clean hands*. If the plaintiff has acted in an unfair and inequitable manner he cannot have relief.[23]

(*p*) The court is not bound to grant injunction in every case and an injunction to enforce negative convenant would be refused if it would indirectly compel the employee either to idleness or to serve the employer.[24]

(*q*) Once a perpetual and mandatory injunction is given and it becomes final, any attempt to circumvent the same cannot be permitted. Its non-compliance would be continuing disobedience entailing penal consequences.[25]

(*r*) Where a plaintiff apprehends encroachment on his land and proves so, he is entitled to permanent injunction restraining the defendant from encroaching or interfering with peaceful possession of his property.[26]

(*s*) Court should not issue an injunction which in operation is contradictory and ineffective.[27] Relief under Section 41(*h*) being a discretionary equitable relief it should not be granted where other equally efficacious relief is obtainable in any other usual mode or proceeding except in cases of breach of trust.[28] Similarly court should

---

20. *Zandaram Joitaram* v. *Prahladrao Vithalrao*, AIR 1963 Guj 160.
21. *Mohd. Ibrahim Khan* v. *Pateshwari Prasad Singh*, AIR 1960 All 252.
22. *Deutsche Dampschif-fahrts Gesselchaft Hansa of Bermen* v. *Firm of Pestonji Bikhaji*, AIR 1925 Sind 347: 21 Sind LR 170: 89 IC 321.
23. *Basheshar Nath* v. *Municipal Committee*, AIR 1940 Lah 69: 188 IC 264; *Ganesh Panigrahi* v. *Jura Sahu*, AIR 1973 Ori 232, 234.
24. *Gujarat Bottling Co. Ltd.* v. *Coca Cola Co.*, (1995) 5 SCC 545: (1995) 84 Comp Cas 618.
25. *Jai Dayal* v. *Krishna Lal Garg*, (1996) 11 SCC 588.
26. *Kaliappan* v. *Durai*, AIR 1998 Mad 65.
27. *H.M. Kamaluddin Ansari & Co.* v. *Union of India*, (1983) 4 SCC 417: 1983 ALJ 1104.
28. *Municipal. Corpn. of Delhi* v. *Suresh Chandra Jaipuria*, (1976) 4 SCC 719.

not easily interfere in the affairs of autonomous bodies, such as educational institutions or clubs.[29]

(*t*) A plaintiff on the strength of his possession can resist interference from persons who have no better title than himself to the suit property.[30] Once a suit has been filed by the respondent claiming to be the owner of the land and being in possession of it the suit cannot be treated as a suit based on possession without reference to title.[31]

Lastly, an injunction cannot be granted against a person to restrain him from discharging his public duties, for, law will not permit anyone to restrain a person from doing what the public welfare and his own interest requires that he should do.[32] Ordinarily proceedings are not to be stayed by injunction unless the court where they are to be stayed is subordinate to the court wherefrom injunction is sought. As held by the Supreme Court injunction is passed for the purpose of being carried out, not for the fun of passing it.[33] It cannot be demanded as a matter of right.

7. TEMPORARY INJUNCTIONS (SECTION 37)

Section 37 of the Specific Relief Act speaks of temporary injunctions. The granting of this type of injunction is governed by Order 39, Rules 1 and 2. As the rules go, temporary injunction may be granted in the following cases:

1. Where in every suit it is proved by affidavit or otherwise—

(*a*) that any property in dispute in a suit is in danger of being wasted, damaged or alienated by any party to the suit, or wrongfully sold in execution of a decree, or

(*b*) that the defendant threatens or intends, to remove or dispose of his property with a view to defraud his creditors, the court may by order grant a temporary injunction to restrain such act, or make such other order for the purpose of staying and preventing the waste, damage, alienation, sale, removal or disposition of the property as the court thinks fit, until the disposal of the suit or until further orders.

Since we have discussed before the difference between temporary and perpetual injunction and also the general principles governing the grant of injunction it is unnecessary to repeat them, but it would suffice to note here that a temporary injunction is granted until the disposal of the suit or until further orders. In such a case it comes to an end when the suit is disposed of. The effect of a temporary injunction is explained in Rule 2(3).

(2) (1) In any suit for restraining the defendant from committing a breach of contract or other injury of *any kind*, whether compensation is claimed in the suit or not, the plaintiff may, at any time *after the commencement of the suit*, and

---

29. *Shyam Lal Yadav* v. *Kusum Dhawan*, (1979) 4 SCC 143: AIR 1979 SC 1247.
30. *M. Kallappa Setty* v. *M.V. Lakshminarayana Rao*, (1973) 2 SCC 358: AIR 1972 SC 2299.
31. *Nagar Palika* v. *Jagat Singh*, (1995) 3 SCC 426: (1995) 3 Punj LR 224.
32. *Palapatti Raghudu* v. *Nallagadda Erraiya*, AIR 1938 Mad 881: 1938 Mad WN 806.
33. *H.M. Kamaluddin Ansari & Co.* v. *Union of India*, (1983) 4 SCC 417, 428, 429, 432.

either *before or after judgment*, apply to the court for a temporary injunction to restrain the defendant from committing the breach of the contract or injury complained of, or any breach of a contract or injury of a like kind arising out of the same contract or relating to the same property or right.

(2) The court may by order grant such injunction, on such terms as to the duration of the injunction, keeping an account, giving security, or otherwise as the court thinks fit.

(3) In case of disobedience or breach of any such terms, the court granting an injunction may order the property of the person guilty of such disobedience or breach to be attached and may also order such person to be detained in the civil prison for a term not exceeding six months, unless in the meantime the court directs his release.

(4) No attachment under this rule shall remain in force for more than one year, at the end of which time, if the disobedience or breach continues, the property attached may be sold, and out of the proceeds the court may award such compensation as it thinks fit, and shall pay the balance, if any, to the party entitled thereto.

It will be seen that the effect of disobedience of an injunction is attachment of the property of the defendant and six months' civil detention. At this juncture one has to note that the transaction of sale or mortgage of property transferred in breach of a temporary injunction is *not void*. But the alienator incurs the penalty prescribed under Rule 2(3) above. The penalty of "attachment" of property under the rule has a different effect from a "void" contract. In view of Section 64 of the CPC, any private transfer contrary to the attachment is void against all claims enforceable under the attachment.[34] Moreover, the court has inherent powers under Section 151 of the CPC to issue injunction in cases not falling within Order 39, Rule 1 and Rule 2, as decided by the Supreme Court of India in *Manohar Lal's* case.[35] If the breach continues within the period of attachment which will not remain in force for more than one year, the property attached may be sold under Rule 4 and the court may award compensation out of the proceeds thereof to the plaintiff. The State also may be proceeded against under this rule as the State is a person within this rule.[36]

Principles governing temporary injunctions[37]

It must be made clear again that temporary injunctions to restrain a breach of contract are regulated by the present Rule 2, Order 39 of the CPC, while perpetual injunctions to restrain the breach of a contract are regulated by Sections 38 to 42 of the Specific Relief Act. The main consideration as provided by Section 38(2) is that a perpetual injunction cannot be granted to prevent the breach of a contract the performance of which would not be specifically

34. *Beli Ram and Bros.* v. *Ram Lal*, ILR (1925) 6 Lah 380: AIR 1925 Lah 644 (2); *Delhi and London Bank Ltd.* v. *Ram Narain*, ILR (1887) 9 All 497: 7 All WN 107.
35. *Manohar Lal Chopra* v. *Seth Hiralal*, 1962 Supp (1) SCR 450: AIR 1962 SC 527.
36. *State of Bihar* v. *Rani Sonabati Kumari*, (1961) 1 SCR 728: AIR 1961 SC 221.
37. Mulla: *Civil Procedure Code*, Order 39, Rule 2, pp. 802-803.

enforced. Now the performance of a contract is not specifically enforced where damages would afford adequate relief. However that may be, the following rules seem to govern all cases on the subject.

(*a*) *The case to be one for a perpetual injunction or for specific performance.*—As decided in *Chand Sultana* v. *Khurshid Begum*[38], if a suit is brought for a specific performance of a contract and for an injunction to restrain the defendant from committing a breach of the contract, and the plaintiff applies for a temporary injunction to prevent the breach of the contract until the suit is disposed of, the court will decline to grant a temporary injunction if the plaint and the affidavits filed by the parties show on *the face of them* that the case is not one for a perpetual injunction or for specific performance.

(*b*) *Irreparable injury or inconvenience.*—Consequently, to justify a case for temporary injunction not only must the case be such that an injunction is the appropriate relief but there must be a further ingredient that unless the defendant is restrained forthwith by a temporary injunction, irreparable injury or inconvenience may result to the plaintiff before the suit is decided upon its merits.[39] But if a case is a proper one for specific performance, and irreparable injury is likely to be caused unless the breach of the contract is forthwith restrained, the court will grant a temporary injunction to restrain the breach of contract. However, the converse of rule (*a*) above is not always true.

Rule 3.—As per Rule 3 of Order 39, the court shall in all cases, except where it appears that the object of granting the injunction would be defeated by the delay, before granting an injunction, direct notice of the application for the same to be given to the opposite party.

(*c*) *Balance of convenience.*—The applicant must therefore show a *prima facie case* for entitling him to the prayer which if not granted would cause him *irreparable injury*.[40] However, the court always looks to the *balance of convenience*[41] which must be in favour of granting the injunction in favour of the plaintiff.

In urgent cases or cases of great emergency where irreparable damage would ensue if the act complained of is not restrained, injunction *ex parte* may be issued. Such an injunction is also called an *ad interim* injunction because it is issued without issuing a motion to the opposite party and continues in force only up to the time the motion is heard. When an injunction is issued after hearing the motion, it is called an *interlocutory* injunction. Thus, *prima facie* case, irreparable injury and balance of convenience are the three important conditions for obtaining an injunction.[42]

---

38. AIR 1963 AP 365.
39. *Nanabhai Ganpatrao Dhairygvan* v. *Janardhan Vasudev*, (1888) 12 Bom 110; Mulla: *Indian Contract Act and Specific Relief Act*, pp. 263-264, citing Collette on Specific Relief Act.
40. *Mogul Steamship Co.* v. *M' Gregor Gow & Co.*, (1885) 15 QBD 476: 53 LT 268.
41. *Doherty* v. *Allman*, (1878) 3 AC 709: 39 LT 129.
42. *U.P. Avas Vikas* v. *N.N. Rajgopala*, (1989) All WC 494.

8. PERPETUAL INJUNCTIONS (SECTION 38)

When the plaintiff has established his right, a perpetual injunction is issued after the trial. It holds good for ever, restrains the defendant for ever, and since it concludes a right it is in effect a decree. It is granted where there is a question of substantial damage which cannot be compensated by money and where a legal duty is broken. In granting it, the court will look to the plaintiff's conduct and the balance of convenience and consider the question from the viewpoint of preventing multiplicity of judicial proceedings.

When granted

A perpetual injunction will be granted in the following cases:

(*i*) to prevent the breach of an obligation,

(*ii*) in cases of preventing the breach of obligations arising from contract,

(*iii*) to prevent the invasion or threat of invasion to plaintiff's right to property or to its enjoyment.

Though in case of waste or ouster an injunction may be granted against the manager of a joint Hindu Family at the instance of the Coparcener, but nonetheless a blanket injunction restraining permanently from alienating the property of the Joint Hindu Family, even in case of a legal necessity, cannot be granted.[43]

For permanent injunction one has to prove that he is the owner of the property in question, it remained in his possession and the defendant had no right, title or interest therein.[44] Permanent injunction is a discretionary relief and is equitable in nature. It must be granted inter alia on considerations of equity and justice and the appellant who is himself guilty of inequitable conduct cannot claim such relief.[45]

Once a perpetual injunction is granted and becomes final, any attempt to circumvent the same cannot be permitted. Its non-compliance would be a continuing disobedience, entailing penal consequences.[46]

While granting the same, the court will consider the following and satisfy itself as to the conditions laid down in Section 38(3). Where there exists no standard for ascertaining the actual damage caused or likely to be caused by the invasion, where the invasion is such that compensation in money would not afford adequate relief, and where injunction is necessary to prevent multiplicity of judicial proceedings, a perpetual injunction will be granted.

9. MANDATORY INJUNCTIONS (SECTIONS 39 AND 40)

These injunctions are granted to prevent the breach of an obligation and also for the purpose of compelling specific performance of certain acts which

---

43. *Sunil Kumar* v. *Ram Prakash*, (1988) 2 SCC 77: (1988) 1 HLR 573.
44. *Kanchusthabam Satyanarayana* v. *Namuduri Atchutaramayya*, (2005) 11 SCC 109: AIR 2005 SC 2010.
45. *Yamuna Nagar Improvement Trust* v. *Khairati Lal*, (2005) 10 SCC 30: AIR 2005 SC 2245.
46. *Jai Dayal* v. *Krishan Lal Garg*, (1996) 11 SCC 588.

the court is capable of enforcing. The principles underlying these injunctions are the same as those underlying perpetual injunctions.[47]

Two things have to be considered by the court before it proceeds to grant a mandatory injunction, (*i*) what acts are necessary to be done in order to prevent the breach of an obligation, and (*ii*) the requisite acts must be such as the court is capable of enforcing. Such acts may be of various kinds. It must be noted that a mandatory injunction can be granted even after the injury has been completed provided the plaintiff has not lost his right to relief by delay or by acquiescence.

Where *A*, by the construction of new buildings obstructs light to the access and use of which *B* has acquired a right under the Indian Limitation Act, *B* may obtain an injunction not only to restrain *A* from going on with the buildings, but also to pull down so much of them as obstructs *B*'s light.

Section 40 provides that in a suit for perpetual injunction (Section 38) or mandatory injunction (Section 39) the plaintiff may claim damages either in addition to or in substitution for such injunction but the plaintiff must demand it. It rests within the discretion of the court to allow the plaintiff to amend his plaint for this purpose at any stage of the proceedings, but in so allowing it may impose just and equitable terms on the plaintiff. Once his suit to prevent the breach abovesaid has been dismissed, that will bar his right to sue for damages for such breach, as provided by the section.

10. IN WHAT CASES GRANTED[48]

Looking to the list of twenty-six [(*a*) to (*z*)] examples as appended to the unamended Specific Relief Act, 1877, Section 54, it will be clear that in a variety of cases injunctions are available, as (*i*) when there is a breach of an obligation, either arising from contract or (*ii*) arising from a tort, (*iii*) in case of a breach of trust, or (*iv*) in case of a breach of other obligations. In this connection the observations and revelations of the Karnataka High Court[49] are very valuable in that whenever a right exists or is created by contract, by ownership of property or otherwise, cognizable by law, an injunction will be issued to protect a violation of that right and the restraining power of the court extend through the whole range of rights and duties recognised by law and would be applied to every case of intended violation unless there are other reasons of policy or expediency which control and limit its exercise.

(*a*) *To maintain status quo.*—Mainly, the object of an injunction is *to maintain status quo ante.* This is achieved by interlocutory or temporary and mandatory injunction. This we saw before while discussing the difference between temporary and perpetual injunction.

47. *Smith* v. *Smith*, 1875 LR 20 Eq 500: 32 LT 487.

48. *Kanchusthabam Satyanarayana* v. *Namuduri Atchutramayya*, (2005) 11 SCC 109. (equitable considerations.); *Joseph Severance* v. *Benny Mathew*, (2005) 7 SCC 667 (mandatory & prohibitory injunctions; if could be challenged for the first time in second appeal; impermissibility).

49. *Bhawarilal* v. *S. Jaichand*, AIR 1975 Kant 122, 123: ILR 1975 Kant 127.

(*b*) *To restrain judicial proceedings.*—The English law, before 1873, granted "common injunctions" to restrain proceedings opposed to principles of equity, started in Common Law courts. This it did on the extension of the principle contained in the maxim "equity acts *in personam*". Equity had thus a longer arm than that of the Common Law and it used this device to restrain unconscientious proceedings even if it were started in a foreign court when an action on the same matter was pending in an English court. The rest of the injunctions granted by courts of equity were termed as "Special injunctions". The Judicature Act, 1925, Section 41 enacts to this purpose and in result the High Court has still power to restrain the proceedings in a court inferior to it. In India, we have no separate courts and the question of ''common'' injunction therefore does not arise.[50] However, *to restrain the multiplicity of judicial proceedings*, Section 10 of the Civil Procedure Code and Section 38 of the Specific Relief Act make provisions. The object of Section 10 of the CPC is to prevent courts of concurrent jurisdiction from *simultaneously* trying two *parallel* suits in respect of the same matter in issue. For example, *B* residing at Calcutta has an agent *A* at Calicut employed to sell his goods there. *A* sues *B* in Calicut claiming a balance due upon an account in respect of dealings between him and *B*. During the pendency of the suit in the Calicut court, *B* institutes a suit against *A* in Calcutta for an account and for damages caused by *A*'s alleged negligence. Here both the suits are between the same parties and the matter in issue in *B*'s suit is directly and substantially in issue in *A*'s suit. The Calicut court being a court wherein a suit for the purpose is instituted prior in point of time, that suit alone must be proceeded with. Proceedings with the Calcutta court must therefore be stayed. The section applies to courts in India and a suit in a foreign court does not provide a ground for staying a subsequent suit in a court in India.[51]

(*c*) *To prevent breach of a duty or an obligation.*—(*i*) *Contractual Obligations.*—Many cases of injunction fall under this category. In this class of cases, obligations arise by express or implied agreement, i.e., by a contract between the parties. While granting an injunction under Section 38 and Section 42 the court will look to the provision under Section 41(e) also wherein it is expressly stated again as under Section 38(2), that in such cases the court is guided by the rules in Chapter II regarding specific performance of contracts. That is to say, (1) no injunction can be granted in case of contracts, the specific performance of which cannot be granted. However, Section 42 allows it in certain cases. Accordingly, those contracts could be ordered to be specifically performed wherein money compensation is not an adequate relief; and such cases are those where the defendant invades or threatens to invade the plaintiff's right to, or enjoyment of property. Perpetual injunctions will be granted in such cases. Conversely, where the breach is such as can be compensated by money,

---

50. *Modi Entertainment Network* v. *W.S.G. Cricket Pte. Ltd.*, (2003) 4 SCC 341 (Injunction anti-injunction; action in personam; anti-suit injunction to restrain proceedings in foreign court).
51. See Mulla: *Civil Procedure Code*, p. 20 and also O. 41, R. 5 for stay of execution proceedings.

injunction will be refused. Similarly, contracts involving personal skill, violation, etc., and those contracts the specific performance whereof gain for the plaintiff an unfair advantage over the defendant and indefinite contracts will not be specifically enforced and consequently no injunction would be granted. (2) But an injunction can be granted against a person who aids a breach of contract.[52] (3) Injunction, as follows from Section 38(2) and (3), will be granted in almost all cases falling under clause 3(*a*) to 3(*d*) where the plaintiff proves his right to or enjoyment of the property and its breach, actual or threatened, by the defendant. Consequently, against the breach of a patent right, copyright and trade mark[53], it is granted as it is a breach of property right. Against libel, wrongful expulsion from a club-membership[54], for invasion of airspace and continuing trespass[55], for causing injury to plaintiff[56], for causing him annoyance[57], for breach of easementary rights[58] and for wrongful exclusion from the affairs of partnership, injunction will be granted. For breach of trust and waste of property and against prevention of crime, where the act involves injury to property injunction, can be granted.

Injunction to Perform Negative Agreements (*Section 42*).—A contract may contain positive as well as negative terms. When the question of specific performance is raised it becomes important to discuss whether all the terms of a contract will be specifically enforced or only the positive or negative terms. Section 42 solves this problem. For example, *A* contracts with *B* to sing for twelve months at *B*'s theatre and not to sing in public elsewhere without his written permission. Thereafter, *A* makes a breach of the contract. *B* cannot obtain specific performance of the contract to sing, but he is entitled to an injunction restraining *A* from singing at any other place of public entertainment.[59]

Against this judgment there has been much criticism and the English authorities have distinctly refused to go so far, saying that an affirmative agreement does not of itself imply for this purpose a negative agreement to do nothing inconsistent with it[60]; and whether an express agreement is affirmative or negative is a matter of substance and not of verbal form.[61]

In India, in the case of negative convenants, even in cases where the service is not of special or specialised character, injunctions are granted in suitable

---

52. *Rookes* v. *Barnard*, 1964 AC 1129: (1964) 1 All ER 367 (HL).
53. *Exite Laboratories* v. *A.A. Products* (*Ind.*), AIR 1989 NOC 218 (Del).
54. *Lawlor* v. *Union of Post Office Workers*, 1965 Ch 712: (1965) 1 All ER 353 (Ch D).
55. *Moolchand* v. *Chhoga*, AIR 1963 Raj 25.
56. *Darshan Ram* v. *Nazar Ram*, AIR 1989 P&H 253.
57. *St. Joseph Church* v. *Velu*, AIR 1989 NOC 124 (Ker).
58. *Prem Devi* v. *Sohanlal*, AIR 1989 NOC 176 (Raj).
59. *Lumley* v. *Wagner*, (1852) 1 De GM&G 604: 21 LJ Ch 898; *Muddanna* v. *Panthanagere Group Panchayat*, (2003)10 SCC 349. (for permanent injunction).
60. *Whitewood Chemical Co.* v. *Hardman*, (1891) 2 Ch 416: 64 LT 716.
61. *Metropolitan Electric Supply Co. Ltd.* v. *Ginder*, (1901) 2 Ch 799: 84 LT 818.

cases.[62] In *Vinod Chandra Hiralal Gandhi* v. *Vivekanand Mills Ltd.*[63], the Gujarat High Court has held that a negative convenant must be distinct and a mere affirmative stipulation is insufficient to comply with such a negative term. Consequently, a term in a contract of employment to serve for a particular number of years does not imply not serving anyone else during that period. But the Madras High Court has differed from this view.[64] But one thing has to be noted here that the remedy of injunction is discretionary and cannot be claimed as a matter of right. Where the plaintiff has entered into a contract under circumstances which give him an unfair advantage over the defendant within the meaning of Section 20(2)(*a*), injunction will not be granted.[65] Moreover, no injunction will be granted in case of an express negative convenant relating to contracts for personal service if its effect is to compel the performance of the service or to remain idle.[66]

It must be said therefore that in India provisions of Section 42 are far more ahead of the English principle as expressed in *Lumley* v. *Wagner*. It does not require a negative agreement to be express as in *Lumley* v. *Wagner*. Such an agreement may be implied as in *Burn & Co.* v. *McDonald*[67], wherein the defendant agreed diligently and to the best of his ability to devote himself to the duties incumbent on him as a draftsman etc. for a period of five years. It was held that though there was no negative condition in terms in the contract, a negative convenant could properly be implied under this section and an injunction to restrain the defendant from serving any other person during the period was granted.

Even in cases not arising out of contracts of personal service negative stipulations have been implied and injunctions granted. But it all depends upon the Court's discretion and considerations of fairness, as expressed in a value-judgment by Bhagwati, J. in *Lalbhai Dalpatbhai & Co.* v. *Chittaranjan Chandulal Pandya.*[68]

Summing up the topic we may say that (*i*) where a contract comprises an affirmative agreement to do a certain act coupled with a negative agreement, express or implied, not to do a certain act, the court may be unable to enforce the positive or affirmative part of it by specific performance because of personal service or qualifications etc. required for its performance. (*ii*) But the court will enforce the negative agreement not to do a certain act. (*iii*) As per English law, the negative part could be enforced only if it is clear and distinct as was the case

62. *Sunilchand C. Mazumdar* v. *Aryodaya Spg. & Wvg. Mills Co. Ltd.*, AIR 1964 Guj 115: ILR 1963 Guj 891.
63. AIR 1967 Guj 255.
64. *Mac Laboratories (P) Ltd.* v. *V.R. Nathan*, (1967) 1 Mad LJ 353 cf. *V.N. Deshpande* v. *Arvind Mills Co. Ltd.*, ILR 1946 Bom 89: AIR 1946 Bom 423.
65. *Callianji Harjivan* v. *Narsi Tricum*, ILR (1895) 19 Bom 764.
66. Pollock and Mulla: *Indian Contract Act and Specific Relief Act*, pp. 963-964. See also *Lalbhai Dalpatbhai & Co.* v. *Chittaranjan Chandulal Pandya*, AIR 1966 Guj 189; *Niranjan Shankar Golikari* v. *Century Spinning and Manufacturing Co. Ltd.*, AIR 1967 SC 1098, 1104.
67. ILR (1909) 36 Cal 354: 1 IC 829.
68. AIR 1966 Guj 189. See also *Niranjan Shankar Golikari* v. *Century Spinning and Manufacturing Co. Ltd.*, AIR 1967 SC 1098.

in *Lumley* v. *Wagner*, but (*iv*) if the terms are implied injunction cannot be granted. That is to say, in England if the negative terms are implied in the positive terms of a contract, injunction for the breach of a negative term cannot be given. This is the limit of the English law and the courts there, are not prepared to go further. (*v*) But in India Section 42 of the Specific Relief Act goes further than this and provides that "the circumstance that the court is unable to compel the specific performance of the affirmative agreement shall not preclude the court from granting an injunction to perform negative agreement", and the negative terms may be express (as insisted upon by English law) or it may be implied (as provided by our law).[69] This is the present situation and the solution finally rests within the court's discretion.

(*ii*) *Obligations arising under General Law*.—In this class one comes across (1) cases regarding obligations arising under a trust, (2) obligations arising out of a breach which amounts to a tort which in turn includes a number of civil wrongs[70], and (3) any other obligation legal or equitable.

(1) *Trust obligations*: As we have seen in previous chapters a trust is a matter of obligation and the duty lies heavily on a trustee who undertakes the responsibilities that he should not make a breach of trust. A trustee may consequently be restrained by an injunction from selling trust property where it is not necessary to do or where he is not authorised by law or by an instrument of trust. In such cases the question of adequate compensation for the breach complained of may not arise. A breach of confidence can well be restrained as was ruled in a number of English and Indian cases. As expressed by Hanbury[71], there are examples of the issue of an injunction to restrain a breach of an equitable obligation. Trustees have been restrained from distributing an estate inconsistently with the terms of the instrument[72] or from selling for a price below that offered firmly by a prospective purchaser[73] and an injunction was granted to restrain a bankrupt executor from acting[74] and to restrain the publication by students of the unpublished lectures of a university professor[75], and at the instance of a shareholder to restrain a company from disposing of an exceptionally large sum for the benefit of employees.[76] Old Section 54 of the Specific Relief Act, 1877, illustrations (*b*) to (*h*) supply enough like examples as where an injunction can be issued for a threatened breach of trust against the trustees, and against the directors of a company paying dividend out of capital or borrowed money or when they undertake a new adventure in a different line

69. *Burn & Co.* v. *McDonald*, ILR (1909) 36 Cal 354: 1 IC 829.
70. Torts affect a person, his reputation and his property. There are also torts affecting both a person and his property.
71. *Modern Equity*, 9th Edn., 1969, pp. 74-75.
72. *Fox* v. *Fox*, (1870) IR 11 Eq 142: 23 LT 584.
73. *Buttle* v. *Saunders*, (1950) 2 All ER 193 (Ch D).
74. *Bowen* v. *Phillips*, (1897) 1 Ch 174: 75 LT 628.
75. *Caird* v. *Sime*, (1887) 12 AC 326: 57 LT 634 (HL).
76. *Parke* v. *Daily News Ltd.*, (1961) 1 WLR 493: (1961) 1 All ER 695 (Ch. D).

of business, against an executor's misconduct and against an advocate threatening to reveal his client's[77] secret.

(2) *Civil wrongs or Torts*: As Maitland remarks, "a very large part of the whole province of tort is a proper field for injunction. I should say that the only torts which lie outside the field of injunctions are assault and battery, false imprisonment and malicious prosecution. I do not think that an injunction has been used or could be used to prevent these torts, which if they be torts will also at least in most cases be crimes. Here there are other remedies. If you go in fear of a man you can have him bound over to keep the peace, while if you are wrongfully imprisoned the writ of habeas corpus with its rapid procedure should serve your turn. A civil court again must not prohibit a man from instituting criminal proceedings, the Attorney General's *nolle prosequi* should be sufficient preventive check on criminal of an obviously vexatious kind".[78] Nuisance[79], trespass, waste of property and defamation in this connection are the fields wherein this remedy is often resorted to. Generally damages are recovered but where necessary, in suitable cases, injunctions can be availed of as a safeguard against future wrongs i.e., *quia timet action.*

(3) *Any other obligation Legal or Equitable*: Under this class may be included the obligations arising by virtue of membership of an association. Thus injunctions have been granted to professional men who have been dismissed contrary to the rules of their profession, though usually only where improper motive or bad faith can be shown[80] and to members expelled by social clubs. In the latter case, however, the courts seem prepared to interfere not only where rules have been broken, but also where a club has acted in breach of natural justice. In *Labouchere case*[81] the general meeting of a club, summoned without proper notice, expelled the plaintiff without full inquiry, without giving him notice of any definite charge and by a resolution carried by an insufficient majority. The court granted an injunction against such purported expulsion.[82] In such cases important considerations that weigh with the court granting injunction are those incorporated in clause (3)(*b*), (*c*) and (*d*) of Section 38.

11. INJUNCTION WHEN REFUSED (SECTION 41)

The provisions of S. 41 in this regard are clear. As observed in *Cotton Corpn. of India Ltd. case*[83], the equitable principle underlying Section

77. *Fraser* v. *Evans*, (1969) 1 All ER 8: (1969) 1 QB 349 (CA); *District Board* v. *Kailash Nath Kapoor*, ILR 1946 All 21: AIR 1946 All 234; *National Broach & Machine Co.* v. *Churchill, Gear Machines Ltd.*, (1965) 2 All ER 961 (CA).
78. Maitland: *Lectures on Equity*, 1969, p. 325.
79. *Darshan Ram* v. *Nazar Ram*, AIR 1989 P&H 253; *St. Joseph Church* v. *Velu*, AIR 1989 NOC 124 (Ker).
80. *Weinberger* v. *Inglis*, 1919 AC 606: 121 LT 65 (HL).
81. *Labouchere* v. *Wharncliffe (Earl)*, (1879) 13 Ch D 346: 41 LT 638; cf. *Dawkins* v. *Antrobus*, (1881) 17 Ch D 615: 44 LT 557 and see *Young* v. *Ladies' Imperial Club*, (1920) 2 KB 523: 123 LT 191 (CA) and *Lawlor* v. *Union of Post Office Workers*, 1965 Ch 712: (1965) 1 All ER 353 (Ch D).
82. Hanbury: *Modern Equity*, pp. 80-81.
83. *Cotton Corpn. of India Ltd.* v. *United Industrial Bank Ltd.*, (1983) 4 SCC 625: AIR 1983 SC 1272.

41(*b*) is that access to the Court in search of justice according to law is the right of a person who complains of infringement of his legally protected interest and a fortiori therefore, no other court by its action impede access to justice, except the Superior Court, which can injunct a person by restraining him from instituting or prosecuting a proceeding before a Subordinate Court. Section 41(*b*) was enacted in order to avoid multiplicity of proceedings. It must therefore receive such interpretation as would advance the intendment and thwart the mischief it was intended to suppress and keep the path of access to justice through court unobstructed. S. 41(*b*) covers perpetual as well as temporary injunctions.[84]

In the following cases injunctions are refused:

(*i*) to restrain judicial proceedings,

(*ii*) to stay proceeding in a court not subordinate to the one issuing injunction,

(*iii*) to stay proceedings in a criminal court by civil court,

(*iv*) to restrain persons from applying to any legislative body,

(*v*) to prevent breach of a contract not specifically enforceable,

(*vi*) to restrain on act which is not clearly a nuisance,

(*vii*) to prevent a continuing breach wherein plaintiff has acquiesced,

(*viii*) where plaintiff has equally efficacious remedy,

(*ix*) where plaintiff's conduct disentitles him, and

(*x*) where the plaintiff has no personal interest in the matter.

Section 43 is an amendment to the Arbitration Act and Section 44 repeals the Specific Relief Act, 1877.

Grant of injunction may be refused where the defendant's act cannot be construed as an act of dispossession.[85]

A civil court has no jurisdiction to try and adjudicate upon an industrial dispute, if it concerned enforcement of certain rights or liability created only under the Industrial Disputes Act. It therefore cannot grant an injunction.[86]

---

84. *Cotton Corpn. of India Ltd.* v. *United Industrial Bank Ltd.*, (1983) 4 SCC 625: AIR 1983 SC 1272; *Yamuna Nagar Improvement Trust* v. *Khariati Lal*, (2005) 10 SCC 30.
85. *M.S. Baliga* v. *Mangalore City Corpn.*, AIR 1998 Kant 76.
86. *Premier Automobiles Ltd.* v. *Kamlekar Shantaram Wadke*, (1976) 1 SCC 496: 1976 SCC (L&S) 70.

BIBLIOGRAPHY

A.S. Diamond: Primitive Law

Allen: Law in the Making

Anson: Law of Contracts

Ashburner: Principles of Equity

Bogert: Trusts and Trustees

Brunyate: Limitation of Actions in Equity

Buckland: Equity in Roman Law

C.H.S. Fifoot: History and Sources of the Common Law: Tort and Contract

Chafee & Re: Cases and Materials on Equity

Chitty: On Contracts

Coote: Mortgages

Copunger & Skone James: Copyright

Cruise: Digest

D.P. Mittal: Law Dictionary

David & Briarly: Major Legal Systems in the World Today

Dicey: Conflict of Laws

Dymond: Death Duties

Elphinstone: Introduction to Conveyancing

Evershed, M.R.: The Court of Appeal in England

Farwell: Powers

Finlay: Contracts for the Benefit of Third persons

Foa: Landlord and Tenant

Fry: Specific Performance

Goff & Jones: The Law of Restitution

Gower: Principles of Modern Company Law

Gray: Perpetuities

Griswold: Spendthrift Trusts

Halsbury: Laws of England

Hanbury: Modern Equity

Hart: Digest of the Law of Trusts

Hayes: Introduction to Conveyancing

Hohfeld: Fundamental Legal Conceptions

Holdsworth: History of English Law

J.F. Garner: Local Land Charges
Jarman: Wills
Jenks: English Civil Law
Keeton: The Law of Trusts
Kerly: History of Equity
Kerly: Law of Trade Marks
Lawton: Guide to the Law of Trustee Savings Banks
Lee: Elements of Roman Law
Levy-Ullman: English Legal Tradition
Maitland, F.W.: Lectures on Equity
Marshall: Assignment of Choses in Action
Megarry: Miscellany-at-Law
Megarry & Wade: Law of Real Property
Meston: Law of Relating to Money lenders
Palmer: Company Law
Paton: Textbook of Jurisprudence
Pollock: Contracts
Pollock: Leading Cases Done into English
Pollock (Ed): Table Talk of John Selden
Pollock & Maitland: History of English Law
Potter: Historical Introduction to English Law
Powell: Law of Agency
Preston: Estates
R.W. Turner: Equity of Redemption
Roper: Legacies
Roscoe Pound: Cambridge Legal Essays
Rowlatt: Law of Principal and Surety
Ruoff & Roper: Registered Conveyancing
Ryde: Rating
S.F.C. Milson: Historical Foundations of the Common Law
Scott: Trusts
Sheridan & Delany: The Cy-Pres Doctrine
Simpson: Infants
Snell: Principles of Equity
Spence: Equitable Jurisdiction

Spencer Bower & Turner: Estoppel by Representation
Story: Equity
Sugden: Law of Property
Sugden: Powers
Terrell: Law of Patents
Tudor: Charities
Underhill: Law of Trusts and Trustees
Waldock: Mortgages
Waters: The Constructive Trust
Watt: Law of Savings Banks
Williams: Assents
Williams: Vendor and Purchaser
Winfield: Province of the Law of Tort
Wurtzburg & Mills: Building Society Law
Zamir: The Declaratory Judgment

SUBJECT INDEX

Author	Title	ISBN	Price	Qty.
Patel, Bimal N. Jabbal, Dolly & Motiyani, Prachi V.	Eazy Cases: Banking Law, 2014 Edn. (P/B)	9789351451181	325	
Patel, Bimal N. Jabbal, Dolly & Motiyani, Prachi V.	MCQ on Banking Law, R/P 2015 (P/B)	9789351452485	245	
Singh, Avtar	Banking & Negotiable Instruments, 4th Edn., R/P 2022 W/S (P/B)	9789394364264	675	
	Bar Exam			
EBC	All India Bar Examination Guide, 2nd Edn., 2021 (P/B)	9788194800484	1095	
	Business Law			
Singh, Avtar	Business Law, 11th Edn., 2018, R/P 2022 (P/B)	9789351452812	995	
Singh, Avtar	Competition Law, 2012 Edn., R/P 2023 (P/B)	9789394364738	495	
Singh, Avtar	Law of Sale of Goods (Sale of Goods Act 1930; Hire Purchase Act, 1972), 9th Edn., R/P 2022, Revised by Deepa Paturkar (P/B)	9789390715794	465	
	Child and Law			
Pinho, Emidio A. Desouza & Pinho, Andryusha D'costa	Child Abuse: Law Practice and Prevention, 1st Edn., 2021 (P/B)	9789390715657	495	
Rao, Mamta	Law Relating to Women & Children, 4th Edn., R/P 2022 (P/B)	9789351453499	795	
	Civil Procedure			
Takwani, C.K.	Civil Procedure with Limitation Act, 1963, 9th Edn., R/P 2022 (P/B)	9789351452256	995	
	Company Law			
Das, Rinita	Company Law, 1st Edn., 2022 (P/B)	9789390715671	495	
Singh, Avtar	Company Law, 17th Edn., R/P 2023 with Supplement 2021 (P/B)	9789394364707	995	
Singh, Avtar	Company Law: An Introduction, 13th Edn., 2022, Revised by Rinita Das (P/B)	9789394364882	495	
	Constitutional Law and Constitution			
Chandrachud, A.	Due Process of Law, 1st Edn., R/P 2012 (H/B)	9789350286753	800	
Kartikeya, K.	Article 12 – Meaning, Scope and Emerging Judicial Trends, 1st Edn., 2020 (H/B)	9789389656749	995	
Kulshreshtha, V.D.	Landmarks in Indian Legal and Constitutional History, 12th Edn., 2019, R/P 2022 Revised by Sumeet Malik (P/B)	9789351453611	745	
Rai, Udai Raj	Constitutional Law: Governance Structure, 2nd Edn., 2022 (P/B)	9789394364561	825	
Rao, Mamta	Constitutional Law, 2nd Edn., 2021(P/B)	9789389656985	875	
Rao, Mamta	Public Interest Litigation – Legal Aid & Lok Adalats, 5th Edn., 2018, (P/B)	9789388206228	495	
Singh, M.P.	Comparative Constitutional Law, 2nd Edn., 2011 (H/B)	9789350281383	1500	
Shukla, V.N.	Constitution of India, 14th Edn., 2022, Revised by Mahendra Pal Singh (P/B)	9789394364639	1245	
	Contract			
Aston, Joshua	MCQ on Contract Law (in 2 volumes), 2018 Edn.	9788193547229	550 per set	
Rab, Ajar	Drafting Contracts: Basic Principles, 1st Edn., 2022 (H/B)	9789390715329	395	
Singh, Avtar	Contract Law (Easy Law Series), 1st Edn., 2012 (P/B)	9789350287194	195	
Singh, Avtar	Law of Contract & Specific Relief, 13th Edn., 2022, R/P 2023 Revised by Rajesh Kapoor (P/B)	9789394364745	995	
Singh, Avtar	Textbook on Contract & Specific Relief, 8th Edn., 2022 Revised by Varun Malik (P/B)	9789390715862	545	
Vishwanathan, S.	Simply, Legal! – Contracts, 1st Edn., 2021 (P/B)	9788194800422	345	
	Conveyancing, Precedents, Pleadings & Drafting			
Murli Manohar	Art of Conveyancing and Pleading, 2nd Edn., 2004, Revised by R. Prakash (P/B)	8170128080	675 POD*	
	Criminal Law and Procedure			
EBC	Criminal Manual (Three Major Acts, CrPC, IPC & Evidence), Large: 31st Edn., 2020 (H/B)	BB/2458	695	

Author	Title	ISBN	Price	Qty.
Gandhi, B.M.	Indian Penal Code, 4th Edn., W/S 2021, R/P 2022 Revised by K.A. Pandey (P/B)	9789390715367	795	
Kelkar, R.V.	Criminal Procedure, 7th Edn., R/P 2022 Revised by K.N.C. Pillai (P/B)	9789351452102	995	
Kelkar, R.V.	Lectures on Criminal Procedure-Including Probation & Juvenile Justice, 6th Edn., R/P 2022, Revised by K.N.C. Pillai (P/B)	9789394364370	495	
Pillai, K.N.C.	General Principles of Criminal Law, 2nd Edn., R/P 2022 (P/B)	9789351452416	745	
Srivastava, O.P.	Principles of Criminal Law, 7th Edn., 2018, Revised by Kumar Askand Pandey (P/B)	9789351454755	375	
Takwani, C.K.	Indian Penal Code, 2nd Edn., 2022 (P/B)	9789351452324	495	
	Criminology and Penology			
Siddique, Ahmad	Criminology, Penology & Victimology, 7th Edn., W/S 2022 Revised by S.M.A. Qadri (P/B)	9789394364110	745	
	Cybercrimes			
Fatima, Talat	Cyber Crimes, 3rd Edn., 2021 (H/B)	9789390715732	1495	
	Dictionaries			
Chopra, K.	Law Dictionary English to Hindi (Pocket), 4th Edn., R/P 2017, Revised by SCC Editorial Staff (P/B)	9789351454540	245	
Chopra, K.	Law Dictionary English-Hindi (Large) , 4th Edn., 2014, Revised by SCC Editorial Staff (H/B)	9789351451204	450	
	Economics and Law			
Nagar, Ranita	Law and Economics: Breaking New Grounds, 2017 Edn. (H/B)	9789351454625	995	
	Environment and Pollution			
GNLU	Environmental Law: Contemporary Issues, 2019 (H/B)	9789388822527	895	
GNLU	Environmental Law: Decentralised Environmental Governance, 2019 (H/B)	9789388822114	895	
Patel, Bimal N. Motiyani, Prachi V.	Eazy Cases on Environmental Law, 2017 Edn. (P/B)	9789351455066	295	
Patel, Bimal N. Motiyani, Prachi V.	MCQ on Environmental Law, 2015 Edn. (P/B)	9789351452454	195	
Shastri, S.C.	Environmental Law, 7th Edn., 2022 (P/B)	9789394364899	795	
Singh, Gurdip	Environmental Law, 2nd Edn., 2016, R/P W/S 2021 (P/B)	9789389656329	545	
Tandon, Usha	Climate Change: Law, Policy and Governance, 1st Edn., 2016 (H/B)	9789351453376	895	
	Equity			
Gandhi, B.M.	Equity, Trusts and Specific Relief, alongwith a chapter on Fiduciary Relationships, 4th Edn., 2007, R/P 2023 (P/B)	9789394364714	695	
	Entrance Examination			
Bhattacharya, Aniruddha & Jaiswal, Utkrisht	Legal Aptitude for CLAT and Other LLB Entrance Examinations, Foreword by Justice Imtiyaz Murtaza, 3rd Edn., 2018 (P/B)	9789387487260	650	
CLAT Possible	Clat Solved Papers, 2nd Edn., 2017 (P/B)	9789351454724	395	
EBC	All India Bar Examination Guide, 2nd Edn., 2021 (P/B)	9788194800484	1095	
EBC	EBC's Master Guide to Judicial Services Examination, 2nd Edn., 2020 (P/B)	9789389656091	1395	
Sahai, Surabhi Modi	Guide for LLB, CLAT, AILET, SET, DU and Other Law Entrance Exams, 5th Edn., with Solved Paper of CLAT 2022 (P/B)	9789394364509	1045	
	Evidence			
Sarathi, V.P.	Law of Evidence, 8th Edn., 2021, R/P 2022 Revised by K.A. Pandey (P/B)	9789351452829	645	
	Family Law			
Gandhi, B.M.	Family Law (in 2 vol.) (P/B) 2nd Edn., 2019, R/P 2023 Vol. 1	9789394364813	545	
	2nd Edn., 2023, Vol. 2	9789390715596	395	
Gandhi, B.M.	Hindu Law, 4th Edn., 2016, R/P 2022 Revised by Sumeet Malik (P/B)	9789394364462	595	
Rashid, Syed Khalid	Muslim Law, 6th Edn., 2020, R/P 2022 (P/B)	9789394364479	475	

Author	Title	ISBN	Price	Qty.
	Food Security			
Nagar, Ranita	Food Security Law – Interdisciplinary Perspectives, 2014 Edn. (H/B)	9789351450269	485	
	Hindu Law			
Gandhi, B.M.	Hindu Law, 4th Edn., 2016, R/P 2022 Revised by Sumeet Malik (P/B)	9789394364462	595	
	Human Rights			
Joshi, K.C.	International Law & Human Rights, 4th Edn., 2019, R/P 2020 (P/B)	9788194284826	725	
Pathak, Puneet	International Humanitarian & Refugee Law, 1st Edn., R/P 2022 (P/B)	9789394364219	545	
Rao, Mamta	Law Relating to Women & Children, 4th Edn., R/P 2022 (P/B)	9789351453499	795	
	Insolvency			
Singh, Avtar	Law of Insolvency, 5th Edn., 2014 (P/B)	9789350288481	295	
	Insurance			
Singh, Avtar	Law of Insurance, 3rd Edn., 2017, R/P 2022 (P/B)	9789394364653	675	
	Intellectual Property			
Bandyopadhyay, T.K & Bindal, Saurabh	Intellectual Property Law: An Introduction, 2015 Edn. (P/B)	9789351453048	395	
Bindal, Saurabh	MCQ on Intellectual Property Law, 2016 Edn. (P/B)	9789351453277	215	
Gopalakrishnan, N.S. & Agitha, T.G.	Principles of Intellectual Property, 2nd Edn., 2014 (P/B)	9789351450191	535	
Rao, R. Anita & Rao, V. Bhanoji	Intellectual Property Rights - A Primer, R/P 2013 (P/B)	9789350289204	260	
Thomas, Mathew	Understanding Intellectual Property, 2016 Edn. (P/B)	9789351454212	595	
Verkey, Elizabeth	Intellectual Property, 2nd Edn., 2021 (P/B)	9789389656336	645	
	Internship			
Aston, Joshua	Acing Internships-A Practical Guide, 2018 Edn. (P/B)	9789387487826	375	
	International Law			
Jain, Shilpa	An Introduction to Public International Law, 1st Edn., 2016 R/P 2021 (P/B)	9789390715343	360	
Joshi, K.C.	International Law & Human Rights, 4th Edn., R/P 2020 (P/B)	9788194284826	725	
Mujawar, Fatima	Crisp Introduction to International Law, 2016 Edn. (P/B)	9789351453659	125	
Mujawar, Fatima	MCQ on International Law, 2017 Edn. (P/B)	9789351455080	275	
Murthy, B.S.	International Relations and Organisation, 2nd Edn., 2021 Revised by V. Rajyalakshmi (P/B)	9789387487017	325	
Pathak, Puneet	International Humanitarian & Refugee Law, 1st Edn., R/P 2022 (P/B)	9789394364219	545	
Rajyalakshmi, V.	International Organisations, 2018 Edn. (P/B)	9789388206143	495	
Singh, Gurdip	International Law, 3rd Edn., 2015, R/P W/S 2021 (P/B)	9789389656374	645	
	Interpretation of Statutes			
Gandhi, B.M.	Interpretation of Statutes, 2nd Edn., R/P 2022 (P/B)	9789394364363	395	
Sarathi, V.P.	Interpretation of Statutes, 5th Edn., R/P 2022 (P/B)	9789390715381	695	
	Judicial Entrance Exam			
EBC	EBC's Master Guide to Judicial Services Examination, 2nd Edn., 2020 (P/B)	9789389656091	1395	
	Jurisprudence and Legal Theory			
Mahajan, V.D.	Jurisprudence and Legal Theory, 6th Edn., R/P 2022 Revised by VB Coutinho (P/B)	9789394364660	725	
Pillai, P.S.A.	Jurisprudence and Legal Theory, 3rd Edn., R/P 2022 (P/B)	9789351452478	345	
Subbarao, G.C.V.	Jurisprudence and Legal Theory, 9th Edn., R/P 2022 (P/B)	9789394364615	445	
	Labour and Industrial Law			
Coutinho, V.B.	Lectures on Labour Law, 2019 Edn. (P/B)	9789388206532	295	
Malik, PL	Handbook of Labour and Industrial Law, 18th Edn., 2018, Revised by Editorial Staff of SCC (H/B)	9789388206150	1195	

Author	Title	ISBN	Price	Qty.
	Legal Aptitude			
Bhattacharya, Aniruddha & Jaiswal, Utkrisht	Legal Aptitude for CLAT and Other LLB Entrance Examinations, Foreword by Justice Imtiyaz Murtaza, 3rd Edn., 2018 (P/B)	9789387487260	650	
	Legal Education			
Menon, N.R.M.	An Idea of a Law School Ideas from The Law School, 2019 Edn. (H/B)	9789388822794	995	
Menon, N.R.M.	Clinical Legal Education, Reprinted 2019 (P/B)	9789388822374	345	
	Legal Fictions			
Varadachari, V.K.	Legal Fictions, 2nd Edn., 2012, Revised by V.P. Sarathi (H/B)	9789350285190	350	
	Legal History			
Chauhan, S.P.S.	Britishers' Rule in India, 2020 Edn., R/P 2022 (H/B)	9789390715459	1295	
Jatar, Nilakshi & Paranjape, Laxmi	Legal History - Evolution of The Indian Legal System, 2012 Edn. (P/B)	9789350286852	395	
Kulshreshtha, V.D.	A Textbook of English Legal History, 3rd Edn., R/P 2007 (P/B)	8170129950	90	
Kulshreshtha, V.D.	Landmarks in Indian Legal and Constitutional History, 12th Edn., 2019, R/P 2022 Revised by Sumeet Malik (P/B)	9789351453611	745	
Mulchandani, R.R.	Cities of India: A Legal History, 2018 Edn. (H/B)	9789387487994	895	
	Legal Language			
Gandhi, B.M.	Legal Language, Legal Writing & General English, R/P 2022 (P/B)	9789351453451	495	
	Legal Studies			
Kaushik, Shyam Krishan	Legal Studies: Class XI - CBSE, 2nd Edn., 2021 (P/B)	9789390715251	295	
Patnaik, Vaneeta	Legal Studies: Class XII, 2019 Edn., R/P 2020 (P/B)	9789389656992	175	
Singh, Vijay Kumar	Learn the Law, 1st Edn., 2022 (P/B)	9789394364271	425	
Singh, Vijay Kumar	Legal Studies: Class XI - ISC, 1st Edn., 2022 (P/B)	9789394364431	495	
Singh, Vijay Kumar	Legal Studies: Class XII - ISC, 1st Edn., 2022 (P/B)	9789394364974	325	
	Life and Law			
Aston, Joshua	Higher Studies in Law: How and Where to Apply, 2020 Edn. (P/B)	9788194284833	395	
Bansal, Avani	Life at Law School, 2020 Edn. (P/B)	9789389656169	425	
Menon, N.R.M.	An Idea of a Law School Ideas from The Law School, 2019 Edn. (H/B)	9789388822794	995	
	Moot Court			
Malik, Abhinandan	Moot Courts and Mooting, 1st Edn., 2015, R/P 2022 (P/B)	9789390715374	595	
	Media			
Divan, Madhavi	Facets of Media Law, 3rd Edn., 2022 (H/B)	9789351452003	1495	
	Muslim Law			
Rashid, Syed K.	Muslim Law, 6th Edn., 2020, R/P 2022 (P/B)	9789394364479	475	
	Negotiable Instruments			
Patel, Bimal N., Jabbal, Dolly and Motiyani, Prachi V.	Banking Law and Negotiable Instruments Act, 2015 Edn. (P/B)	9789351452683	395	
Singh, Avtar	Banking & Negotiable Instruments, 4th Edn., R/P 2022 W/S (P/B)	9789394364264	675	
Singh, Avtar	Negotiable Instruments: An Introduction, 9th Edn., 2022, Revised by Deepa Paturkar (P/B)	9789390715664	325	
	Partnership			
Singh, Avtar	Law of Partnership: An Introduction, 11th Edn., R/P 2022 (P/B)	9789351453253	395	
	Property			
Sarathi, V.P.	Law of Transfer of Property, Revised by Mallika Taly, 6th Edn., Reprinted 2022 (P/B)	9789394364646	675	
	Public Interest Litigation			
Rao, Mamta	Public Interest Litigation – Legal Aid and Lok Adalats, 5th Edn., R/P 2021 (P/B)	9789390715503	515	

Author	Title	ISBN	Price	Qty.
	Refugee Law			
Pathak, Puneet	International Humanitarian & Refugee Law, 1st Edn., R/P 2022 (P/B)	9789394364219	545	
	Social Justice			
Bhat, P. Ishwara	Law and Social Transformation, 2nd Edn., 2022 (H/B)	9789390715909	1495	
	Social Sciences for Law Student Series			
Agarwal, D.	Sociology, 1st Edn., 2022 (P/B)	9789390715930	495	
Gopalakrishnan, K.C. & Ramdass	Economics (for Law Students) Reprinted, 2012 (P/B)	9789350282397	245	
Gopalakrishnan, K.C.	Legal Economics (Interactional Dimensions of Economics and Law) Reprinted, 2021 (P/B)	9789394364035	395	
Murthy, B.S.	International Relations and Organisation, 2nd Edn., 2021 Revised by V. Rajyalakshmi (P/B)	9789387487017	325	
Murthy, H.V. Sreenivasa	History of India (Part I), Reprinted 2022 (P/B)	9789351453468	345	
Murthy, H.V.S. Elizabeth, V.S.	History of India (Part II), Reprinted 2021 (P/B)	9789389656305	275	
Oommen, T.K. Venugopal, C.N.	Sociology for Law Students, Reprinted 2019 (P/B)	9789388822947	315	
Rathore, L.S. Haqqi, S.A.H.	Principles of Political Theory and Organisation, Reprinted 2021 (P/B)	9789389656480	325	
	Taxation			
Suseela Vasudevan, Jaya	Indirect Taxes: GST and other Indirect Taxes, 2019 Edn. (P/B)	9789388822381	525	
	Torts			
Gandhi, B.M.	Law of Torts with Law of Statutory Compensation & Consumer Protection, 4th Edn., Reprinted 2022 (P/B)	9789351452362	545	
Pillai, P.S.A.	Law of Tort, 9th Edn., R/P 2022, Revised by Abhinandan Malik (P/B)	9789394364349	625	
Vishwanathan, S.	Simply, Legal! – Torts, 1st Edn., 2021 (P/B)	9788194800415	245	
	Women and Law			
Dhanda, A. & Parashar, A	Engendering Law, 1999 Edn., W/S 2007 (H/B)	8170126665	400	
Parihar, Lalita Dhar	Women and Law: From Impoverishment to Empowerment–A Critique, 2011 Edn., R/P 2016 (P/B)	9789351453529	495	
Rao, Mamta	Law Relating to Women & Children, 4th Edn., R/P 2022 (P/B)	9789351453499	795	
Sagade, J.; Jivan, V. & Forster, CC	Feminism in The Subcontinent and Beyond, 2014 Edn. (H/B)	9789351451259	990	

Law Books in Hindi

Author	Title	ISBN	Price	Qty.
Babel, B.L.	A Guide to Civil Practice, 2013 Edn. (P/B)	9789350289006	525	
Babel, B.L.	Apkritya Vidhi (Law of Torts in Hindi), 2nd Edn., 2009 (P/B)	9788170121855	235	
Babel, B.L.	Apradh Shastra evam Dand Shastra (Criminology & Penology in Hindi), 4th Edn., 2013 (P/B)	9789350285251	275	
Babel, B.L.	Chikitsa Nyayashastra (Medical Jurisprudence in Hindi),6th Edn,2014(P/B)	9789351450801	875 POD*	
Babel, B.L.	Hasthlekh evam Anguli Chhap Vigyan (Handwriting & Fingerprints Science in Hindi), 5th Edn., 2013 (P/B)	9789350287262	210	
Babel, B.L.	Nyayik Vigyan (Forensic Science in Hindi), 5th Edn., 2017 (P/B)	9789351454526	295	
Babel, B.L.	Police Anveshan (Police Investigation in Hindi), 5th Edn., 2017(P/B)	9789351454762	365	
Babel, B.L.	Sampatti Antaran Adhiniyam, 1882 (Transfer of Property Act, 1882 in Hindi), 2nd Edn., 2006 (P/B)	9788170129110	450 POD*	
Babel, B.L.	Van Evam Vanya Jeev Sanrakshan Vidhi, (Law Relating to Forest & Wild Life Protection in Hindi), 4th Edn. 2011 (P/B)	9789350281666	385	
Babel, B.L.	Vivah Evam Talak Vidhi (Law of Marriage and Divorce in Hindi), 2nd Edn., 2017 (P/B)	9789351455509	550	

Author	Title	ISBN	Price	Qty.
Chaturvedi, M.D.	Apkrityon ki Vidhi (Law of Torts in Hindi), 2nd Edn., 2008 (P/B)	9788170121510	275	
Chaturvedi, M.D.	Bhartiya Dand Sanhita, 1860 (Indian Penal Code, 1860 in Hindi), 9th Edn., Reprinted 2020 (P/B)	9789388822510	495	
Chaturvedi, M.D.	Prachin Bhartiya Vidhi Vyavastha (Manusmriti ke Vishesh Sandarbh Mein) [Ancient Indian Legal System (with special reference to Manusmriti) in Hindi], 1995 Edn. (H/B)	8170125731	600 POD*	
Chaturvedi, M.D.	Sampatti Antaran Adhiniyam, 1882 aur Bharatiya Sukhachar Adhiniyam, 1882 (Transfer of Property Act, 1882 alongwith Indian Easement Act, 1882 in Hindi) 2nd Edn., 2011 (P/B)	9789350280553	295	
Chaturvedi, M.D.	Sakshya Vidhi (Law of Evidence in Hindi), 3rd Edn., 2011 (P/B)	9789350280614	265	
Chaudhary, R.N.	Kanoonon Ke Nirvachan Ke Siddhant (Principles of Interpretation of Statutes in Hindi), 2010 Edn. (P/B)	9788170128762	295	
Chaudhary, R.N.	Paryabaran Vidhi (Environmental Law in Hindi), 2021 Edn. (P/B)	In Press		
Chopra, K.	Law Dictionary (English to Hindi) 4th Edn., 2014 (H/B)	9789351451204	450	
Chopra, K.	Law Dictionary (English to Hindi) 4th Edn., R/P 2017 (Pocket) (P/B)	9789351454540	245	
Fatima, Talat	Internet Vidhi Evam Cyber Apradh (Internet Law and Cyber Crime in Hindi), 2018 Edn. (P/B)	9789388206273	545	
Joshi, K.C.	Antarrashtriya Vidhi Aur Manvadhikar (International Law and Human Rights in Hindi), 3rd Edn., 2017 (P/B)	9789351455257	395	
Kulshreshtha, V.D.	Bharat ka Vaidhanik Evam Samvaidhanik Itihas (Indian Legal & Constitu-tional History in Hindi), 2nd Edn.,2004, Revised by M.D. Chaturvedi(P/B)	8170128064	195	
Malhotra, I.J.	Hindu Vivah Adhiniyam (Hindu Marriage Act in Hindi), 3rd Edn., 2006 (P/B)	8170129028	295	
Malhotra, I.J.	Madhyastham aur Sulah Adhiniyam (Arbitration & Conciliation Act in Hindi), 2nd Edn. W/S, 2005 (P/B)	8170126703	160	
Murli, Manohar	Abhivachano Ke Prarupan Aur Abhihastantaran Lekhan Ki Kala (Art of Conveyancing & Pleading in Hindi), 4th Edn., 2005, Revised by M.D. Chaturvedi (P/B)	8170127807	850 POD*	
Prasad, Aniruddh	Vidhishastra ke Mool Siddhant (Principles of Jurisprudence in Hindi), 5th Edn., 2016 (H/B)	9789351453314	1000 POD*	
	Vidhishastra ke Mool Sidhant (Principles of Jurisprudence in Hindi), (Shorter Edn.), 2016 Edn. (P/B)	9789351454236	1000 POD*	
Rashid, Khalid	Muslim Vidhi (Muslim Law in Hindi), 2nd Edn., Reprinted 2018, Revised by Prof. V.P. Bhartiya (P/B)	9789388206068	375	
Sharma, Y.S.	Dand Shastra (Penology in Hindi), 1999 Edn. (P/B)	8170126525	95	
Sharma, Y.S.	Kanoonon Ka Nirvachan(Interpretation of Statutes in Hindi),2010 Edn(P/B)	817012980X	250	
Shiva Gopal	Hastantaran Lekhan ke Drishtant aur Prapatra, (Conveyancing, Precedents and Forms in Hindi) 3rd Edn., 2005 (with CD ROM containing Precedents & Forms), Revised by J.V.N. Jaiswal(H/B)	8170128528	325	
Singh, Avtar	Bank-kari Vidhi Evam Parkramya Likhat Adhiniyam (Law of Banking and Negotiable Instruments in Hindi), 6th Edn., 2011 (P/B)	9789350281796	350	
Singh, Avtar	Bhagidari Vidhi evam Seemit Dayitva Adhiniyam(Law of Partnership & Limited Liability Partnership in Hindi), 8th Edn., 2018 (P/B)	9789387487314	295	
Singh, Avtar	Company Vidhi (Company Law in Hindi), 10th Edn., W/S 2021, Reprinted 2022(P/B)	9789390715466	575	
Singh, Avtar	Company Vidhi - Ek Parichay (An Introduction to Company Law in Hindi), 6th Edn., 2019 (P/B)	9789388222206	295	
Singh, Avtar	Mal Vikraya Evam Avkraya Vidhi (Sale of Goods & Hire Purchase in Hindi), 7th Edn., 2018 (P/B)	9789387487253	395	
Singh, Avtar	Madhyastham, Sulah Evam Anukalpi Vivad Niptan Vidhi (Law relating to Arbitration, Conciliation & Alternative Disputes Resolution in Hindi), 4th Edn., Reprinted 2018 (P/B)	9789388206136	345	
Singh, Avtar	Parkramya Likhat (Negotiable Instruments in Hindi), 6th Edn,2012 (P/B)	9789350286999	195	
Singh, Avtar	Samvida Vidhi evam Vinirdist Anutosh Adhiniyam – Ek Parichay [Law of Contract & Specific Relief Act(An Introduction)in Hindi],2nd Edn., 2013 (P/B)	9789350289839	325	

Author	Title	ISBN	Price	Qty.
Singh, Avtar	Samvida Vidhi Ke Siddhant Tatha Vinirdisht Anutosh Adhiniyam, 1963 (Law of Contract & Specific Relief Act,1963 in Hindi), 11th Edn.-R/P 2021(P/B)	9789388206112	645	
Chaudhary, R.N.	Suchna Ka Adhikar Adhiniyam, 2005 (Right to Information Act, 2005 in Hindi), 2013 Edn. (P/B)	9789350289914	225	
Singh, Avtar	Vanijyik Vidhi ke Sidhant (Principles of Mercantile Law in Hindi), 5th Edn., 1996 (P/B)	9788170126300	250	
Singh, R.P.	Uttar Pradesh Bhoomi Vidhi (U.P. Land Laws in Hindi), 2nd Edn., 1995	8170125677	75	
Som, Adheer	Gumnami Baba (in Hindi), 2019 Edn. (P/B)	9789388822138	195	
Subbarao, G.C.V.	Vidhi Shastra evam Vidhi Ke Sidhant (Jurisprudence & Legal Theory in Hindi) Reprinted, 1997 (P/B)	8170121086	125 POD*	
Srivastava, O.P.	Apradhik Vidhi Ke Sidhant (Principles of Criminal Law in Hindi), 5th Edn., 2012, Revised by R.N. Chaudhary (P/B)	9789350287187	675 POD*	
Takwani, C.K.	Prashasanik Vidhi (Administrative Law in Hindi) Translated & Updated, 3rd Edn. 2019 Revised by K.C. Joshi (P/B)	9789388206389	395	

All disputes and complaints are exclusively subject to the jurisdiction of the courts/tribunals/forums at Lucknow only.
Prices quoted herein is/are subject to change without prior notice.

EBC Reader

EBC Explorer